COMPETITION POLICY AND INTELLECTUAL PROPERTY

COMPETITION POLICY AND INTELLECTUAL PROPERTY

EDITED BY

MARCEL BOYER

MICHAEL TREBILCOCK

AND

DAVID VAVER

IRWIN LAW

Competition Policy and Intellectual Property

Published in 2009 by

Irwin Law Inc.
14 Duncan Street
Suite 206
Toronto, ON
M5H 3G8

www.irwinlaw.com

ISBN: 978-1-55221-165-6

Cataloguing in Publication available from Library and Archives Canada

The publisher acknowledges the financial support of the Government of Canada through the Book Publishing Industry Development Program (BPIDP) for its publishing activities.

We acknowledge the assistance of the OMDC Book Fund, an initiative of Ontario Media Development Corporation.

Printed and bound by CPI Group (UK) Ltd, Croydon, CR0 4YY

1 2 3 4 5   13 12 11 10 09

Table of Contents

Introduction

Marcel Boyer,[1] Michael Trebilcock,[2] and David Vaver[3]

The Competition Bureau, in co-operation with the Canadian Intellectual Property Office (CIPO) and the Micro-economic Policy Analysis and Marketplace Framework Policy Branches of Industry Canada, organized a March 2007 symposium as a platform for discussions on the role of competition policy and intellectual property (IP) rights in promoting an efficient and innovative economy. One of the main preoccupations of these institutions is to find the right balance between creating incentives for innovation and the encouragement of vigorous competition in the marketplace.

Given developments such as the prevalence of authorized generic pharmaceuticals, the apparent extension of IP rights, and rapid advancements in communications technology such as digitization, many concerns have emerged over whether the customary methods of licensing IP rights remain the most efficient mechanisms for disseminating IP and encouraging its creation. The institutions mentioned above,

---

1 Professor and Bell Canada Chair in Industrial Economics, Université de Montréal.

2 Professor and Chair in Law and Economics, University of Toronto.

3 Formerly Professor of Intellectual Property and Information Technology Law and Director of the Intellectual Property Research Centre, University of Oxford. He is an Emeritus Fellow at St. Peter's College, University of Oxford.

therefore, decided in 2005 to commission a review paper of the major issues and subsequently identified those they considered the most important for further research. The five papers that were presented and discussed at the symposium are the culmination of that research.

A discussion of the efficiency of customary methods of licensing and distributing IP first requires us to examine the extent to which the current types of IP rights are providing the sort of protection that policy-makers presumably originally contemplated. It has indeed been observed in recent years that IP rights holders have, by various means, attempted to extend their rights beyond that original contemplation. These actions affect the balance not only between innovators and society, but also between competitors in the same market. They also raise issues about consequential impacts on competition and innovation.

Extension of Intellectual Property Rights

Teresa Scassa, Faculty of Law, University of Ottawa

The first paper in this symposium examines how different strategies can be and have been adopted effectively to extend IP rights. The author, Professor Teresa Scassa, identifies two broad categories.

The first is the expansion of IP rights through increasing overlap between areas of protection. Two issues are considered in detail: the overlap between patents and trade-marks, where trade-mark protection is sought over functional features of articles; and the overlap between copyrights and trade-marks. This latter overlap is examined in the context of the use of copyright law to prevent the parallel importation of non-copyright goods, based on copyrights asserted over trade-mark logos or product-wrapper designs.

The second category involves the assertion of weak or uncertain IP rights. Professor Scassa examines the exercise of weak or uncertain IP rights in pharmaceutical patent disputes, particularly in the context of reverse payment settlements in disputes between brand name and generic drug companies.

After providing a detailed exploration of the issues, Professor Scassa examines how the extension of IP rights can affect innovation and competition. The impact on competition can arise from the fact that IP rights create monopolies. These monopolies are normally considered legitimate, and their simple exercise does not attract scrutiny under competition laws. But if an IP right has expanded into something that conveys a monopoly right beyond what Parliament may have intended, how should the resultant monopoly claims be addressed?

The exercise of weak or uncertain rights can result in complex dynamics that lead to potential competition problems. The ability to evaluate the legitimacy of settlement agreements in this context is hindered by the uniquely altered dynamic between the parties, and by the difficulty of assessing the strength of the underlying IP rights.

The impact of such practices on innovation is still unclear and difficult to establish. In the case of the extension of IP rights, parties seek to claim more protection in the duration (*Kirkbi*[4]) or scope of protection (*Kraft Canada*[5]) than might otherwise have been thought available or justifiable by the nature of the right asserted. In both cases, the goal of fostering innovation is not attained. Although some argue that a longer term of patent protection may better serve innovation in the pharmaceutical sector, this is clearly not the legislative policy choice reflected in existing legislation or international treaties. Even if a longer, more secure term of patent protection would arguably foster more innovation, most IP regimes clearly trade this prospect off against other competing public policy considerations.

This paper also proposes various approaches to combat what it considers to be the abusive extension of IP rights. The author offers three possible solutions to the problem of overlapping protection. Legislative amendment is one option, but this is often a slow process. Courts may address overlaps by deliberately drawing the attention of Parliament to specific problems and proposing changes. However, this approach develops piecemeal and tends to serve only those with the resources to engage in litigation in the first place. Finally, competition law may challenge practices aimed at extending IP rights.

Professor Scassa believes that the choice of solution depends on the context in which the issue arises. In general, in the case of overlapping IP rights, judge-made solutions can bring the application of the law more into line with the perceived underlying public policy. Solutions for cases involving the exercise of weak or uncertain rights are more

4 *Kirkbi A.G. v. Ritvik Holdings Inc.*, [2005] 3 S.C.R. 302, 2005 SCC 65 [*Kirkbi*].

5 *Kraft Canada, Inc. v. Euro Excellence* (2004), 33 C.P.R. (4th) 246 (F.C.) [*Kraft Canada*].

diverse and more difficult, turning as they do on the uncertainties inherent in litigation.

The paper also considers how the similarities or differences among IP regimes in the developed world may affect strategies of attempting to extend IP rights across multiple jurisdictions. Indeed, cases where companies try to extend protection are often not limited to one country and can take place simultaneously in several jurisdictions. Growing pressure to harmonize IP regimes is likely to encourage multi-jurisdictional protectionism.

Finally, the author points out the difficulty in measuring the actual prevalence of IP extension strategies. Activities such as overclaiming in relation to weak or uncertain rights rarely generate any kind of public record. One way to tackle this problem is to require the filing of settlement agreements with a public organization (e.g., in the US, the Department of Justice or the Federal Trade Commission). Furthermore, observed cases may only represent the tip of the iceberg and may open the way for other companies to try to use copyright or trademark law to bolster exclusive distribution agreements.

In his commentary, Professor Ejan Mackaay also argues that IP law is out of balance. He reminds us that IP rights are the best institutions we know of to provide incentives for good husbanding of scarce resources and for inventiveness in their use. IP schemes also have the advantage of being decentralized: the decision to provide the right does not depend on someone's assessment of its present or future value. On the other hand, legislators must also make sure that society gets the maximum amount of creation over the longer term.

Professor Mackaay also agrees with Professor Scassa that, over the past quarter-century, IP rights have been continually extended. This phenomenon may have come about because of technological developments that lead to new types of subject matter, the protection of which may suggest extending existing rights on the same basis as was afforded to the older technology. But this argument cannot justify the extension of copyright to the author's life plus fifty or even seventy years throughout most of the developed world, or to every activity on the Internet. He concludes that continual extension of IP rights has indeed upset the underlying equilibrium but points out the difficulty in assessing how much damage is being done since we do not see what creations are prevented from being produced.

Professor Mackaay then asks the question: if IP law is out of balance, how might it be corrected and who should do it? He believes that while Parliament is ostensibly better equipped to handle the policy questions involved, it is, unlike the courts, subject to rent-seeking activities, which offset that advantage. An important first step in seeking to maintain the equilibrium is to articulate clearly where it lies, which would certainly help courts to counter undue IP extension. Professor Mackaay, however, concedes that procedural improvements may require legislative action. Overall, he believes that it would be preferable to seek structural corrections (i.e., in IP law) first and leave behavioural corrections (in particular, through competition law) for fine-tuning at the margin.

In his commentary, Professor Michael Meurer augments Professor Scassa's policy analysis by fitting it into the private-attorney-general framework. This framework views IP as a regulatory regime where appropriate incentives can encourage private parties to bring suits that advance the public interest. Of course, when private incentives are not closely aligned with the public interest, there is the potential for private enforcement cases causing social harm. Professor Meurer draws a parallel between the frivolous suits involving IP rights identified by Professor Scassa and similar litigation activities involving plaintiffs in tort, competition, and other areas of law. However, he argues that the problem may be greater in the realm of IP since the complexity of IP law and the variable scope of IP due to technical issues could perhaps convince defendants that a suit is credible and therefore more likely to elicit a settlement payment.

Professor Meurer agrees with Professor Scassa's view that there seems to be little merit in allowing patent protection to be extended by way of trade dress protection (a form of trade-mark that is sometimes called a "distinguishing guise" in Canada) as there is little prospect that extension increases *ex ante* incentives to invent and its exclusionary effects are readily apparent. Citing developments in the US, Professor Meurer claims that the incentives to expand trade dress have been tempered by making it easier for defendants to recover attorney's fees and requiring plaintiffs to establish secondary meaning by showing that consumers perceive the product design as an indicator of the origin of the product. Increasing the plaintiff's burden makes it possible for defendants to win at summary judgment and avoid trial costs.

By contrast, Professor Meurer advocates caution before condemning as socially wasteful activity litigation to enforce copyrights that facilitate price discrimination. Although it is hard to believe that a pro-plaintiff decision in this type of matter would significantly improve *ex ante* incentives to innovate, it could still increase social welfare if price discrimination results in increased output and total surplus.

Professor Meurer sees cases involving settlements and reverse payments as potentially short-circuiting the regulatory role of the law. Normally, settlements are beneficial to society since they save on litigation costs. However, settlements involving reverse payments could prematurely terminate private litigation that might invalidate a patent and hence remove a barrier to market entry. In these situations settlements do not promote the public interest. However, since such settlements are very difficult to distinguish from settlements that do promote it, Professor Meurer argues that public antitrust enforcement agencies and competition law tribunals are probably the best means for addressing the problem.

Tying and Intellectual Property

Edward M. Iacobucci, Faculty of Law, University of Toronto and Ralph A. Winter, Sauder School of Business, University of British Columbia

Professors Edward M. Iacobucci and Ralph A. Winter prepared the next paper presented at the symposium. In it they provide a survey of the economics of tying in the area of IP. Their objective is to assess how economic theory can assist in developing optimal competition policy for that field. They start by refining the concept of tying and presenting a number of empirical examples.

They first tackle the broad policy issues of whether or not tying in general should be considered anti-competitive and should be absolutely prohibited. They find that affirming that tying is anti-competitive is only one step, albeit an important first step, towards the design of a feasible and appropriate remedy. They believe that this finding is necessary but not sufficient to justify policy intervention in the market. After presenting and reviewing several case studies, they demonstrate that, in some instances, tying is not intended to, and does not in fact, lessen competition. Competition authorities should therefore not intervene in such cases. In other cases, some tying strategies are intended to and can exclude rivals. Such instances invite intervention by the authorities.

The authors then try to identify a set of general evidentiary conditions that would allow the categorization of tying cases into those that increase and those that decrease efficiency. They conclude that antitrust authorities cannot rely on general rules of thumb in reaching conclusions that tying in a given case violates antitrust laws and must instead rely on case-by-case analysis.

They do, however, identify the conditions that are necessary for tying to be found anti-competitive and that would allow the law to approach tying allegations systematically. They argue that, for tying to be potentially harmful, it must cause exclusionary effects in either the tying good or tied good markets. If markets are robustly, even if not perfectly, competitive, such exclusionary effects are unlikely and antitrust authorities should not intervene. Therefore, there necessarily must be market power in the tying good in order for tying to be found anti-competitive.

When particularly considering tying and IP, Professors Iacobucci and Winter suggest that market power is an appropriate requirement for intervention against tying. But if the seller enjoys protection from competition because of IP rights it holds, should it be presumed to have market power? They say no: IP rights may affect the inquiry into whether or not market power exists but they do not obviate the need for the inquiry. They further argue that price discrimination through tying is also not an appropriate basis for intervention.

Professors Iacobucci and Winter identify another important relationship between tying and IP. Particularly given the increasing importance of high-technology industries in the economy, IP rights systematically arise in markets subject to rapid change. Concerns about exclusion and foreclosure may therefore arise more often here than with ties in other areas.

The authors believe that it is too simplistic to take the view that, since IP and dynamic markets are related and since tying is more likely to be problematic in dynamic than in static contexts, antitrust authorities should therefore intervene more against ties in markets involving IP rights. Regulators should be wary of interventions that are not only costly but that, if incorrect, could also undermine valuable gains from innovation in dynamic industries. The authors consider that antitrust authorities must undertake case-by-case analyses that are sensitive to these conflicting concerns. They conclude that the relationship between IP and tying is already complex and is very likely to become even more so in the future.

Professor Tim Brennan begins his commentary on the Iacobucci/Winter paper by commending their excellent contribution to the understanding of tying in both IP and non-IP contexts. He believes that some fairly bright-line rules can be extracted from the study. First, if a tie serves simply to increase a firm's ability to exploit its pre-existing market power over a product, intervention is unlikely to produce benefits unless there is reason to believe that it will not raise the price of that product following termination of the tie. Regulation of that product's price is the best support for such a belief, but intervention based on that belief might be ruled out by the regulated conduct doctrine. Second, if the tie gives the seller of a durable good the ability to exploit locked-in buyers, the resulting harm flows from a contracting failure between buyer and seller. Depending on the nature of the failure, the remedy lies in breach of contract, fraud, or consumer protection law, rather than competition law. Professor Brennan further notes some general considerations about competition law enforcement when IP ties are involved. He believes that regulators should be more concerned with abuses creating dominance, not abuse of dominance. Also, when one considers issues of intent or motivation, an interpretation of "anti-competitive practice" should be confined to intent to exclude competitors. Another, perhaps better choice would be to interpret an anti-competitive practice by reference to anti-competitive effects that are "reasonably foreseeable." Finally, Professor Brennan claims that the goal of competition law should be to maximize total surplus. He however admits that the question of "which welfare counts" is not easy to answer. A competition agency should not be made responsible for assessing all the effects of a practice on total surplus. Some narrowing beyond the community of economists may be necessary and how exactly to achieve that remains to be determined. The author concludes by arguing that using competition law enforcement to fine-tune IP rights is probably not appropriate. This remains a job for Parliament, informed by continuing public debate.

In their comments on the paper written by Professors Iacobucci and Winter, Richard Corley and Navin Joneja agree with much of the authors' analysis and recommendations. In particular, given the limited situations where tying is likely to be anti-competitive as well as the many situations where the effects of tying are unclear, competition authorities should exercise caution before intervening in such matters. Furthermore, the evidentiary hurdle required for intervention should be high, and it should be higher for product-design ties than for contractual ties because of the difficulty of separating circumstances in which tying has a material anti-competitive effect from those in which it provides net economic benefits.

Corley and Joneja recognize that there are economic theories that outline circumstances where competitive harm could arise from tying. They nevertheless argue that these theories should not detract from the consensus view that tying is a constant feature of economic life, and that the primary motivation for this form of strategic behaviour is the achievement of substantial efficiencies that lead to both higher profits and increased consumer welfare. In particular, theories of competitive harm arising from tying should be given less weight in industries characterized by technological innovation and IP rights. In their view, industries with a prevalence of IP rights are generally consistent with low barriers to entry, making it less likely for firms to be able to examine significant market power.

Corley and Joneja discuss the treatment of tying under current Canadian law and note that, under section 77 of the *Competition Act,* no order prohibiting tying should be made where the "tied selling that is engaged in is reasonable having regard to the technological relationship between or among the products to which it applies."[6] They also note that to date, the term "reasonable" has not been interpreted in the jurisprudence but could very well involve a consideration of the types of tying and integration efficiencies described by Professors Iacobucci and Winter.

---

6 R.S.C. 1985, c. C-34.

Effects of "Authorized Generics" on Canadian Drug Prices

Paul Grootendorst, Leslie Dan Faculty of Pharmacy, University of Toronto

In this paper, Professor Paul Grootendorst analyzes the impact of "authorized generics" (AGs — i.e., those selected by the rights holder) on prices and competition in the Canadian prescription drug market, especially their impact on the entry of "independent generics" (IGs).

He finds that the effect of AGs on drug prices is ambiguous. On the one hand, AGs compete against IGs and increase the number of generic competitors, which should lower prices. On the other hand, the threat of AGs' entry into a therapeutic market might deter entry by IGs and thus may lessen competition.

The study concludes that the presence of AGs produces costs and benefits in the Canadian prescription drug market. When AGs are first to enter a drug market, average drug prices drop by about 12 percent; average prices drop by smaller amounts, the larger the AGs' share of the generic market. The author also finds that, irrespective of the impact of AGs' market share on brand prices, AGs are mildly pro-competitive in drug markets that face some generic competition. At the same time, after inquiries made of IG executives, the author found evidence that the threat of AGs' entry decreased their incentive to challenge marginal drug markets. In particular, the threat of AGs' entry increased the threshold market size from $5m to $10m. This range represents the value of brand drug sales in the tenth year after the drug entered the market; an IG will not attempt to enter a market that falls below this threshold. IG executives also stated that AGs have seriously reduced IG retained earnings. Finally, IG executives claimed that brand firms had attempted to use the threat of AG entry to negotiate agreements with the IG to delay entry or not enter at all.

Professor Grootendorst ultimately concludes that a comprehensive evaluation of the competitive effects of AGs would need to verify and quantify these costs and compare these to the benefits of AG competition.

In his commentary, Professor Hollis contends that Professor Grootendorst's study clearly presents the effects of AGs in the Canadian pharmaceutical market. He underlines the important insights offered by the paper: (i) AGs reduce the average price paid for a drug when they enter before an IG; and (ii) AGs have no significant impact on prices once IGs have entered.

He therefore considers that one need only consider the balance between the benefits of early AG entry and the effect on the timing of IG entry in assessing the net impact on prices. If AGs sufficiently delay IG entry, then the overall impact of AGs must be negative.

This leads Professor Hollis to review the various reasons why AGs might delay the entry of IGs. The first step is to understand how IGs enter the market. He explains that IGs can access the market by challenging the patents of the established brand name firm. An IG is therefore likely to face very substantial litigation costs. The ensuing problem is that, if the challenge is successful, other IGs can enter the market without incurring these costs. So for the IG to be willing to incur such costs, there must be an incentive to be the first on the market. Indeed, the order of generic entry has been observed to be an important driver of long-term sales.

Professor Hollis then addresses the question of how AGs affect this process. He finds that when a brand name authorizes a generic to enter first, it eliminates the IGs' advantage from having invested in litigation. In markets with AGs, we should therefore expect an absence of patent challenges. But empirically, the presence of AGs has not stopped firms from challenging patents in large markets. So, in large markets, the author argues that AGs reduce the gain from litigation and therefore lead to delays in litigation and IG entry.

The author underlines two further AG effects on the timing of IG entry. Often the AG is the first to enter the market. Thus, in the long term, AGs reduce the competitiveness of the generic industry by removing firms that could otherwise compete by challenging patents. Also, the author finds that if AGs cause even small delays (i.e., of more than two weeks) in the average entry date of the first IG, their effect on consumer welfare will be negative.

In conclusion, Professor Hollis underlines the fact that the first generic challenger not only offers competition but also reduces the barriers to entry for other generic competitors. This feature is quite unlike that of other markets. Thus, AGs, by reducing the profits that flow from challenging patents, ultimately harm competition.

Compulsory Licensing

Abraham Hollander, Department of Economics, Université de Montréal

The paper prepared by Professor Abraham Hollander addresses a large number of questions in regard to compulsory licensing of patents. These questions range from those seeking to identify the circumstances under which compulsory licences should be granted, to those concerning who should be responsible for granting these licences.

Compulsory licensing appeared as a policy tool early in the twentieth century. Governments used it as an alternative to the drastic sanctions of forfeiture that threatened patentees who abused their rights. However, the emergence of compulsory licensing as a remedy for the non-working of patents had two unintended consequences: (i) it expanded the range of conduct regarded as abusive; and (ii) it gave governments an additional tool to restrict patentees' rights in situations where there was no abuse.

Professor Hollander finds that more recently compulsory licensing has come to be viewed as a possible remedy for the blocking of exploitation of dependent patents.

After surveying the conditions under which compulsory licensing is imposed and enforced in different countries, the author finds that the adoption of the "essential facilities" doctrine (under which licences are readily granted to remedy the withholding of facilities deemed essential to public welfare) would not clarify the situations when compulsory licensing should be granted. Nor would it resolve the issue of what conduct and areas of activity should or should not be immune from competition law.

The study then examines the potential effect of compulsory licensing on innovation. Both theoretical considerations and empirical findings suggest that compulsory licensing, if applied sparingly in an industry, cannot be expected to lower its research and development or affect innovation by firms that rely on the industry's technologies or products.

Finally, the author identifies the drawbacks of having a special board or court grant compulsory licences and concludes that they are more evident than the advantages. Indeed, it appears preferable to leave the responsibility for granting compulsory licences to the commissioner of patents acting under the *Patent Act*.[7] However, because of the difficulty of setting royalties, and because orders to license may be ineffective in the absence of complementary orders, it seems useful to explore ways to expand the range of remedies available to the commissioner of patents and to have applications initially filed under the *Patent Act* also reviewed under the *Competition Act*.

In his commentary, Professor Donald McFetridge finds that the major conclusion of Professor Hollander's paper is that compulsory licensing should be confined to a restricted set of circumstances, making it a relatively rare occurrence. These circumstances are either making use of an exclusive right to foreclose access in Canada to products or processes, or using a patent to foreclose exploitation in Canada of another patent where exploitation would have substantial economic significance.

Professor McFetridge agrees that in competition matters the Competition Tribunal has compulsory licensing available as a possible weapon for conduct that substantially prevents or lessens competition. The other instances in which Professor Hollander sees compulsory licences being issued, especially technology foreclosure, appear to involve commercial disputes. One side alleges infringement while the other alleges unfair conduct. Similarly, allegations by one patentee that the holder of a complementary patent is a holdout are also commercial in nature. Professor McFetridge believes that adjudicating competing claims of this character is the job of courts and that perhaps they, rather than the commissioner of patents, should have responsibility for resolving them.

Professor Richard Gold, in his comments on Professor Hollander's paper, chooses to focus on the role that compulsory licences play in managing the uncertainties inherent in IP rights.

He argues that compulsory licensing constitutes one of the inherent limits on IP rights. It makes enforcement of IP rights subject to a liability rule rather than a property rule. He believes that it is hard to conceive of an IP system that did not contain some sort of liability rule.

In his view, it is important to recognize that compulsory licences are designed *not* to be used. They work best when an actor has a rea-

---

7 R.S.C. 1985, c. P-4.

sonable expectation that the state will issue a compulsory licence if the actor does not change its behaviour. The actor will then prefer to change behaviour rather than suffer the consequence of a (usually) more confining compulsory licence.

A main driver for invoking a compulsory licence is the threat that IP rights are blocking further development. Professor Gold regrets that the *Intellectual Property Enforcement Guidelines*[8] promulgated by the Competition Bureau do not take seriously the need to monitor the anti-competitive use of IP rights in innovation markets.

He concludes by arguing that it is unreasonable for competition law to wait for IP law to sort out these issues and define "clear" rights, since IP law provides rights that are inherently incomplete given uncertainties as to scope and use. Competition law offers an opportunity for picking up where IP law leaves off.

An Evaluation of Collective Copyright Management in Canada

Jacques Robert, HEC Université de Montréal, Fellow CIRANO

Professor Jacques Robert prepared the fifth paper of the symposium. His general objective was to evaluate the Canadian copyright management system based on microeconomic rationales. He tries to answer a number of important questions such as the following: Does the current Canadian system of copyright collectives achieve its general goals? Should alternative designs and mechanism be proposed? What might be a more appropriate model and what challenges would Canada face in moving to another system? What is the logic of the current system and is it consistent with the general interest?

In order to address these questions, Professor Robert begins by identifying the market failures that justify the need for regulation of original works. The first argument is that collectives save transaction costs; the second is that bundling copyrights can improve welfare.

He then reviews the Canadian copyright management system. He considers whether different copyright regimes should be developed for different copyright markets and surveys what is done in other countries.

---

8 Competition Bureau Canada, *Intellectual Property Enforcement Guidelines* (Ottawa: Queen's Printer, 2000), online: www.competitionbureau.gc.ca/epic/site/cb-bc.nsf/en/01286e.

Finally, the author studies the impact and role of technology and tries to identify the new challenges faced by the regulator and how the scope of copyright collective management can be extended to face these new challenges.

In light of his study, Professor Robert offers a number of recommendations and observations. First, pure competition among creators appears not to be the best way to manage copyrights. He argues that pure competition cannot simultaneously achieve the two general objectives of the copyright system, namely (i) efficient dissemination of the creative work and (ii) revenue generation for creators. He concludes that a system of collective management, in order to market blanket licences for extended repertoires, provides a better way to fulfill both of these objectives.

His second observation is that Canadian management of copyright collectives is much like that of other similar countries, other than the United States. Further, recent evolution in the copyright collective system has led to the incorporation of two main types of collective management organizations (CMOs): professional association collectives and collecting collectives. These collectives are helpful for both creators and users alike. Empirically, these collectives seem to be organized efficiently; hence the creation of "super-collectives" is not necessary. Although the author argues that the collectives are still not exploiting information technologies to their full potential, there is little that regulators can do to encourage adoption of these technologies.

Finally, in order to address the threat posed by file sharing and digital copying, the author argues that the role of copyright collectives must be extended to account for these new challenges. He considers that "private copy" rights (the right of individuals to make their own private copy of a protected work) should be clarified to deal with activities that cannot be criminalized and legal rules that cannot be enforced. The levies for private copying should be extended to cover these new activities and generate more revenues for creators.

Paul Audley, in his comments, agrees with Professor Robert that creators should be able to derive the benefits from their creative activity through exercising control over their IP exploitation. This result is, in his opinion, not just desirable, but in fact, socially, culturally, and economically both necessary and productive.

Mr. Audley takes up the issue of enforceability. He shares Professor Robert's view that, because of increasing access to protected works without permission or payment, innovation is necessary in order to sustain, or perhaps more accurately, to revitalize the incentive to create. Otherwise, creators will be forced to limit access to their works by imposing large access fees and complex clearance systems. He then comments on the usefulness of the Canadian Copyright Board in addressing two important problems that copyright collectives typically face: (i) the asymmetry of negotiating power and (ii) the asymmetry of information. He argues that the presence of the Board allows fairer determinations that better reflect the actual value of the rights delivered.

Finally, the author endorses Professor Robert's proposal to expand the existing private copying regime to apply, for example, to MP3 players such as the iPod, although he believes that certain issues must be resolved before implementing such an initiative.

In his comment, Professor Ariel Katz's main criticism of Professor Robert's paper focuses on his bundling justification for collective administration. While Professor Katz does not dispute that bundling of information goods can be efficient, he doubts that the economic literature on bundling of information goods can adequately explain, let alone justify, collective administration. In his view, the bundling argument shares the same flaws with many other efficiency-based justifications for collective administration: it observes diseconomies of scale that likely exist when works are administered individually and concludes too rapidly that the most efficient response is bundling all works into the hands of a copyright collective. In reaching that conclusion, Professor Katz ignores the possibility that the efficiencies of bundling may be achieved when bundles compete with one another, with the likely result of greater quantity and variety of bundles, offered in different sizes and shapes and sold at lower prices.

CHAPTER 1

Extension of Intellectual Property Rights

Teresa Scassa[1]

A. INTRODUCTION

The Supreme Court of Canada has recently stated that patent and copyright laws reflect a balance of interests between creators or innovators and society more generally.[2] More specifically, the interests of society in innovation or creative endeavor are served by providing incentives, in the form of limited monopolies, to innovators. In trade-mark law, the balance is somewhat different. Potentially perpetual rights in trade-marks are given in part to protect the reputation and goodwill developed by businesses as the source of particular goods or services, and in part to protect consumers who should not be confused or misled as to the source of the wares or services they consume.

---

1 Canada Research Chair in Information Law, University of Ottawa. I would like to thank Marcel Boyer, France Chevalier, Marc Duhamel, Alan Gunderson, Randall Hofley, Michael Trebilcock, David Vaver, and Denis Wong for their thoughtful comments on an earlier draft. Thanks also to David Mollica for his research assistance. A portion of this paper in a revised form was published as "The Doctrine of Functionality in Trade-mark Law Post-*Kirkbi*" (2007) 21 I.P.J. 87.

2 *Théberge v. Galerie d'Art du Petit Champlain inc.*, [2002] 2 S.C.R. 336, 2002 SCC 34 [*Théberge*]; *Kirkbi A.G. v. Ritvik Holdings Inc.*, [2005] 3 S.C.R. 302, 2005 SCC 65 [*Kirkbi*]; *Apotex Inc. v. Wellcome Foundation Ltd.*, [2002] 4 S.C.R. 153, 2002 SCC 77 [*Apotex*].

In recent years, concerns have been expressed that the traditional balances struck in intellectual property law have been undermined through a range of practices, rules, and phenomena that contribute to an extension of intellectual property rights beyond what was originally contemplated in the "bargain" with society.[3] Others argue that the shifts are consistent with preserving the public policy objectives of intellectual property legislation, particularly in the context of digitization and globalization.[4] This paper will explore some of the strategies used to extend intellectual property rights and will consider the actual or potential impact of such strategies on innovation and competition.

In this paper, the theme of extension of intellectual property rights is explored within two broad categories. The first is the expansion of intellectual property rights through increasing overlap between areas of protection. Over time, overlaps have arisen between copyright and trade-mark law, trade-mark and patent law, and patent and copyright law. It has also been argued that the additional protection for Digital Rights Management systems anticipated in upcoming copyright law reform will also significantly expand the traditional scope of copyright protection. The extension of intellectual property rights through overlapping protection is largely a function of the way in which the law has been interpreted and applied over time. Although there are many possible examples of overlapping rights, two overlaps are considered in detail in this paper. One is the overlap between patents and trade-marks, where trade-mark protection is sought over functional features of articles. The other is the overlap between copyright and trade-mark. The example considered here is the use of copyright law to prevent the parallel importation of non-copyright goods, based on rights asserted in trade-mark logos or product wrapper designs.

In the case of the overlap between patent and trade-mark rights, the courts have developed a doctrine of functionality that seeks to pre-

---

3 See for example, Teresa Scassa, "Originality and Utilitarian Works: The Uneasy Relationship between Copyright Law and Unfair Competition" (2003–04) 1 University of Ottawa Law & Technology Journal 51; Wendy J. Gordon, "On Owning Information: Intellectual Property and the Restitutionary Impulse" (1992) 78 Va. L. Rev. 149 at 150–59; J.H. Reichman and Pamela Samuelson, "Intellectual Property Rights in Data?" (1997) 50 Vand. L. Rev. 49.

4 See for example, Barry Sookman, "'TPMs' a Perfect Storm for Consumers: Replies to Professor Geist" (2005) 4 C.J.L.T. 23.

vent, as a matter of public policy, the overextension of patent rights through trade-mark law. One issue, therefore, is whether this doctrine is sufficiently effective and flexible to satisfactorily address the issues that might arise. With the copyright/trade-mark overlap, the courts have, over time, developed two parallel regimes under which design trade-marks can be protected. Here, judicial interpretation has created the problem and may be less able to offer a solution if indeed a solution is required.

A second main area for consideration is the expansion of intellectual property protection by means of the deliberate exercise of weak, uncertain, or unfounded intellectual property claims. This activity can occur in a broad range of contexts and has become a matter of increasing concern. In such cases, the extension of intellectual property rights arises through deliberate action of parties, yet there are also deficiencies in the legal regimes that contribute to the ability of parties to extend their rights in this manner. Some of these deficiencies include uncertainty as to the scope of protection or the scope of legal defences, and systemic shortcomings in the granting of rights.

The problem of the exploitation of weak or uncertain intellectual property rights is of very significant dimensions and is much too wide-ranging to properly address in this paper. While a number of circumstances where such issues arise are identified and briefly discussed, the focus of consideration in this paper is on the issue of reverse payment settlements in patent disputes between brand name and generic drug companies. These cases, which have proven problematic in the United States, highlight complex issues arising from a combination of factors. One such factor is a generic drug approval policy that favours the earliest possible entry of generic drugs into the marketplace and which, as a result, alters the traditional dynamics between patent holders and potential patent infringers. Underlying this altered dynamic is the complicating factor that the patents at issue might well be invalid. The uncertain strength of the underlying patent rights contributes to the difficulty in assessing the legality of reverse payment settlements.

Within both broad categories of the extension of intellectual property rights (overlapping protection and the assertion of weak or uncertain rights), competition law concerns may arise. Intellectual property rights create monopolies. These monopolies are, as a matter of public policy, considered legitimate and the simple exercise of those monopoly rights does not attract scrutiny under competition laws. Yet where the rights "form the basis of arrangements between independent entities"[5] and the arrangements give rise to competition harm, competition law concerns may arise.

The extension of intellectual property rights raises concerns about monopolies and competition in a different framework. If an intellectual property right has grown, through judicial interpretation, into something that conveys a monopoly right in a context that goes beyond what Parliament might have intended, how should the resultant monopoly claims be addressed? In the case of the doctrine of functionality, the issue is whether judicial interpretation can correct the balance. In the case of overlapping trade-mark and copyright protection, legislative amendment may be the only solution. In both cases, the underlying public policy concerns must be addressed to determine what rights can legitimately be asserted, and what limits need be placed on those rights. In the case of weak or uncertain intellectual property rights, the issues are enormously complex. Some of the problems may be systemic. For example, if bad patents are routinely granted, it might be necessary to improve the patent system so as to reduce the impact of uncertain patent rights. In some cases, rights are weak or uncertain because there is insufficient caselaw (either qualitatively or quantitatively) to address the interpretive questions that arise. Where parties seek to exploit these uncertainties, disparities in economic resources will result in those with deep pockets prevailing over those with limited resources.

While in some cases, the solution will be to effect a change in the intellectual property regime to eliminate the potential for the over-extension of rights, in other instances the solution may be to address the problem as one of case-specific behaviour that falls afoul of competition law. In the United States, a third option has emerged in which judicially created equitable doctrines of patent misuse and copyright misuse are called upon to redress some of the problems raised by the deliberate assertion of weak or invalid claims to intellectual property.[6]

---

5 Competition Bureau Canada, *Intellectual Property Enforcement Guidelines* (Ottawa: Queen's Printer, 2000) at 7, online: www.competitionbureau.gc.ca/epic/site/cb-bc.nsf/en/01286e.html [IPEGs].

6 For an articulation of the doctrine of patent misuse, see *Morton Salt Co. v. G.S. Suppiger Co.*, 314 U.S. 488 at 493 (1942). For a court decision in the US that applies the doctrine of copyright misuse, see *Lasercomb Am. Inc. v. Reynolds*, 911

The difficulty lies in distinguishing between those cases where the unwarranted monopoly or market dominance arises due to a defect in intellectual property legislation or jurisprudence, where the conduct may be remedied by the application of equitable defences, and where the unwarranted monopoly or market dominance is caused by behaviour that should be subject to sanction under competition law.

Section B of this paper explores the extension of intellectual property rights through overlapping rights. This section begins with a general consideration of the features of overlapping rights. It then moves on to a more specific consideration of the overlap between trade-mark and patent law. This is achieved through a consideration of the recent Supreme Court of Canada decision in *Kirkbi*.[7] In *Kirkbi*, an attempt was made to extend the company's monopoly over the shape of the LEGO brick through the use of the common law of trade-marks. This section of the paper will look at the strategy adopted by Kirkbi, and the state of the doctrine of functionality in Canadian trade-mark law following the decision in *Kirkbi*. The Court's decision will be critically analyzed and compared with the US caselaw around trade dress protection in similar contexts. The analysis will consider whether the approach taken by the Supreme Court of Canada has effectively addressed the potential for trade-mark/patent overlap, and whether any points of concern remain.

The second issue considered in Section B is the overlap between copyright and trade-mark law. It has long been accepted in Canada, as in other jurisdictions, that there are legitimate areas of overlap between trade-mark and copyright law. The most significant area of overlap is where designs receive protection both as trade-marks and as artistic works. Although the *Industrial Design Act*[8] was developed to limit the reach of copyright law to ornamental designs applied to utilitarian articles, trade-marks and product labels are specifically excluded from the industrial design regime. This section focuses on the Supreme Court of Canada's decision in *Euro Excellence v. Kraft Canada, Inc.*[9] In this case, copyrights in the design of chocolate bar

---

F.2d 970 at 979 (4th Cir. 1990). See also *Alcatel USA, Inc. v. DGI Technologies, Inc.*, 166 F.3d 772 at 793 (5th Cir. 1999).

7 Above note 2.

8 *Industrial Design Act*, R.S.C. 1985, c. I-9.

9 2007 SCC 37 [*Euro Excellence*]. The decisions of the courts below are *Kraft Canada Inc. v. Euro Excellence* (2004), 33 C.P.R. (4th) 246, 2004 FC 652 [*Kraft*

labels were invoked to prevent the importation of chocolate bars for sale in Canada outside of the exclusive distribution network. Although the Supreme Court of Canada has rejected the use of trade-mark law to prevent parallel importation, explicitly acknowledging the benefits of competition in the marketplace,[10] the plaintiffs in *Euro Excellence* cases were successful at the Federal Court and the Federal Court of Appeal in using copyright law to stop the importation of legitimately trade-marked, non-counterfeit goods. Although ultimately unsuccessful at the Supreme Court of Canada, for reasons having more to do with the way the Court split than with the merits of their position, the decision of the Court does not entirely close the door on this type of litigation strategy. This paper will examine the issues raised in *Euro Excellence,* with a view to the law in other jurisdictions. It will consider any particular features of Canada's copyright law that may contribute to the dual protection and will discuss potential solutions.

Section C of the paper considers the exercise of weak or uncertain intellectual property rights. The section begins with a review of some of the factors that have contributed to a problem of increasingly uncertain intellectual property rights. These factors include a number of circumstances where the scope of available intellectual property protection or the basic validity of rights claimed is simply unclear. The lack of clarity can flow in part from ambiguous judicial decisions, a paucity of judicial decisions, systemic problems in the granting of patents, or uncertainty in dealing with new technologies. The problems may also arise because of the cost of litigation and the unwillingness or inability of defendants to contest infringement actions. This section will briefly provide a number of examples and illustrations.

The main focus of Section C is a consideration of reverse payments in the settlement of patent litigation. The discussion begins with consideration of a US case in which a payment made by way of settlement of litigation by Schering-Plough to the defendant in an infringement action brought by Schering-Plough. The payment by Schering-Plough to the defendant was in return for its commitment to stay out of the market. The

---

Canada (FC)], aff'd (2005), 47 C.P.R. (4th) 113, 2005 FCA 427 [*Kraft Canada* (FCA)], leave to appeal to S.C.C. granted, 2006 CanLII 16464 (S.C.C.).

10 *Seiko Time Canada v. Consumers Distributing,* [1984] 1 S.C.R. 583 [*Seiko Time*]. In this case, the Court was dealing with a claim of passing off, so the provisions of the *Trade-marks Act* were not at issue.

FTC took issue with this payment and made an order against Schering-Plough, which was later overturned by the Court of Appeals for the Eleventh Circuit[11] In contrast, in another "reverse payment" case, the Court of Appeals for the Sixth Circuit found that the reverse payment settlement entered into by the parties violated antitrust legislation.[12]

Reverse payment settlements effectively result in one party agreeing not to compete with the other. They arise in cases where the validity of the underlying patent is at issue, yet they result in an agreement by the party with the most interest in challenging the patent's validity not to pursue any such challenges. As a result, competition may be reduced both by the agreement not to compete and by the insulation from challenge of a potentially invalid patent monopoly. Yet while they may appear inherently anti-competitive, the law does encourage the settlement of disputes. If the underlying patent is valid, then the plaintiff's monopoly is nothing more than it would have been entitled to under patent law.

In the Canadian context, any such reverse payment settlement would most likely be carried out in the context of litigation under the *Patented Medicines (Notice of Compliance) Regulations* (*PM(NOC) Regulations*).[13] These complex regulations are designed to reconcile the application of patent legislation to pharmaceutical innovation with the necessary drug approval process under the *Food and Drugs Act*.[14] The paper will consider whether and how the *PM(NOC) Regulations* may contribute to reverse payment strategies.

B. THE EXPANSION OF INTELLECTUAL PROPERTY RIGHTS THROUGH OVERLAPPING RIGHTS

1) General Features of Overlapping Rights

The core areas of intellectual property protection are generally considered to be patent, copyright, and trade-mark law. Each of these is

---

11 *Schering-Plough Corp. v. Federal Trade Commission*, 402 F.3d 1056 (11th Cir. 2005) [*Schering-Plough*].

12 *In Re Cardizem CD Antitrust Litigation*, 332 F.3d 896 (6th Cir. 2003), cert. denied 125 S. Ct. 307 (2004) [*Cardizem*].

13 Canada, S.O.R./93-133.

14 R.S.C. 1985, c. F-27.

conceived of as a separate and distinct area; indeed, jurisdiction over patents and copyrights is specifically provided for in separate provisions under Canada's constitution,[15] each is governed by a distinct statute,[16] and each area has its own administrative bodies. Patents are available for inventions, copyrights for original literary, artistic, dramatic, and musical works, and trade-mark protection is available for marks that are distinctive of a particular trade source. From time to time, new legislation has been enacted creating distinct regimes for other subject matter considered to fall outside of these three main areas. Thus, we also have legislation to protect semi-conductor chip design,[17] industrial design,[18] and plant varieties.[19]

These separate regimes indicate a conceptual distinctiveness within each subject area, but also a distinction, at a policy level, between the different types of intellectual property. Indeed, while the areas share some of the same public policy goals, the rationale behind the nature and level of protection for each distinct area varies. The patent monopoly, for example, is seen to be much stronger, though shorter in duration, than copyright protection. As compared to copyright, industrial design protection is substantially shorter in duration. The different legislative regimes reflect different policy choices about the nature and strength of intellectual property monopoly necessary to achieve particular social and economic objectives.

The different regimes, each with their own specific term of protection, subject matter, "users' rights," and so on, suggest, at a policy level, a need to distinguish between the nature and type of protection available depending on subject matter. Nevertheless, over time, areas of overlap have developed between the different regimes, sometimes resulting in multiple layers of protection for the same subject matter. It is the purpose of this section to explore some of these areas of overlap.

This section will focus specifically on the overlap between trademarks and patents, as exemplified by the doctrine of functionality

---

15 *Constitution Act, 1867* (UK), 30 & 31 Vict., c. 3, reprinted in R.S.C. 1985, App. II, No. 5, ss. 91(22) (Patents) and 91(23) (Copyrights).

16 *Copyright Act*, R.S.C. 1985, c. C-42; *Patent Act*, R.S.C. 1985, c. P-4; *Trade-marks Act*, R.S.C. 1985, c. T-13.

17 *Integrated Circuit Topography Act*, S.C. 1990, c. 37.

18 *Industrial Design Act*, above note 8.

19 *Plant Breeders' Rights Act*, S.C. 1990, c. 20.

explored by the Supreme Court of Canada in *Kirkbi*.[20] It will also consider an example of the overlap between trade-marks and copyright; specifically, the use of copyright law to augment the protection available to design trade-marks in the context of parallel importation. Although these areas are the focus of consideration, it is important to note that there are many other areas of overlap that, for reasons of time and space, cannot be considered here. Thus, for example, there is significant (and potentially growing) overlap between copyright and patent law regimes for the protection of computer software. The problems in this area are particularly acute in the US, where the overlap is currently considerably greater than in Canada.[21] There is also potentially significant overlap between patent law and copyright, owing to caselaw that suggests that design drawings of three-dimensional objects may be infringed by the making of the three-dimensional object depicted in the design.[22] Critics of anticipated amendments to the *Copyright Act* that would add a layer of protection for Digital Rights Management (DRM) and Technical Protection Measures (TPMs) have also suggested that such measures will radically alter the nature of protection for works such as computer software.[23]

---

20 *Kirkbi*, above note 2.

21 In the United States it is now accepted that computer software, standing on its own, is eligible for patent protection. See *State Street Bank & Trust Co. v. Signature Financial Group, Inc.*, 149 F.3d 1368 (Fed. Cir. 1998) [*State Street Bank*]. Computer code can also be protected as a literary work in US copyright law. As a result, the overlap in protection is substantial. In Canada, computer code can be protected under the *Copyright Act*. However, to be patentable, the software must still be integrated with a "practical system." See for example, Canadian Intellectual Property Office, *Manual of Patent Office Practice* (1998), online: http://strategis.ic.gc.ca/sc_mrksv/cipo/patents/mopop/mopop-e.pdf at 16.06.

22 *King Features Syndicate, Inc. v. O. & M. Kleeman*, [1941] A.C. 417 (H.L.); *Bayliner Marine Corp. v. Doral Boats Ltd.* (1985), 5 C.P.R. (3d) 289 (F.C.T.D.), rev'd on other grounds (1986), 10 C.P.R. (3d) 289 (F.C.A.), leave to appeal to S.C.C. denied (1986), 14 C.P.R. (3d) 446; *L.B. (Plastics) Ltd. v. Swish Products Ltd.*, [1979] R.P.C. 551 (Ch.D.); *British Leyland Motor Corp. Ltd. v. Armstrong Patents Co. Ltd.*, [1986] A.C. 577 (H.L.); *Spiro-Flex Industries Ltd. v. Progressive Sealing Inc.* (1986), 13 C.P.R. (3d) 311 (B.C.S.C.).

23 See for example, Michael Geist, "Anti-circumvention Legislation and Competition Policy" in M. Geist, ed., *In the Public Interest: The Future of Canadian Copyright Law* (Toronto: Irwin Law, 2005) at 211.

With the exception of DRM and TPM, most instances of overlapping intellectual property rights have arisen as a matter of judicial interpretation. In some cases, the overlap may emerge as an unforeseen and unanticipated result of a particular interpretation initially confined to a limited set of facts. In many cases, the interpretation may seem perfectly appropriate on the facts before the court, only becoming problematic when followed in subsequent cases on other sets of facts. It is also possible that courts are forced to interpret statutes that were not drafted in contemplation of particular forms of technology. As Justice LeBel has noted, "The vast and expanding domain of the law of intellectual property is going through a period of major and rapid changes. The pressures of globalization and technological change challenge its institutions, its classifications and sometimes settled doctrines."[24] Thus, it is difficult to fault courts that have interpreted computer software to fall in the category of "literary works";[25] it is also hard to fault courts that reach the conclusion that some software can also be patentable.[26] In other cases, the interpretation leading to overlapping protection may reveal a flaw in the legislation unintended by Parliament, but present nonetheless.[27] It is important to note as well that, in spite of often being the source of overlapping protection, courts can also limit overlaps, as they have done with the doctrine of functionality to be discussed below.

Overlapping rights are particularly problematic when they create unintended monopolies or extend intellectual property monopolies well beyond their original boundaries. In a sense, a company that is

---

24 *Kirkbi*, above note 2 at para. 37.

25 These early interpretations were later confirmed by treaty. See for example, art. 4 of the World Intellectual Property Organization (WIPO) *Copyright Treaty*, 20 December 1996, online: www.wipo.int/treaties/en/ip/wct/pdf/trtdocs-wo033.pdf; see also art. 10, *Agreement on Trade-related Aspects of Intellectual Property Rights, Including Trade in Counterfeit Goods*, (1994) 25 I.I.C. 209. Canada's *Copyright Act* was amended in 1988 to provide that "'literary work' includes tables, computer programs, and compilations of literary works" (s. 2, definition of "literary work").

26 See the argument to this effect in Teresa Scassa and Michael Deturbide, *Electronic Commerce and Internet Law in Canada* (Toronto: CCH Canadian, 2004) at c. 7 [Scassa and Deturbide].

27 Arguably, the trade-mark/copyright overlap, which will be discussed in Section B(3) below, is an example of this.

able to exploit overlapping intellectual property protection is receiving a windfall, potentially at the expense of competition in the marketplace, further innovation, or consumer choice. As LeBel J. notes,

> The economic value of intellectual property rights arouses the imagination and litigiousness of rights holders in their search for continuing protection of what they view as their rightful property. Such a search carries with it the risk of discarding basic and necessary distinctions between different forms of intellectual property and their legal and economic functions.[28]

Nevertheless, to the extent that such overlaps are the result of statutory provisions and their interpretation by the courts, they result in intellectual property rights, the exercise of which is not inherently anti-competitive.

Indeed, the policy of the Competition Bureau and the wording of the *Competition Act*[29] make it clear that the mere exercise of an intellectual property right cannot be considered anti-competitive.[30] In the words of Justice Harrington of the Federal Court in *Kraft Canada* (FC),[31] those who exploit overlapping protection can be seen as merely "taking care of business."[32] In many circumstances the onus will be on the legislature to amend legislation to correct any unintended consequences. It may be that the unintended consequences are considered relatively trivial; in some cases, they may be considered ultimately desirable. This section of the paper will explore two different sets of circumstances: (i) where judicial interpretation to limit overlaps may suffice, and (ii) where legislative amendment may be necessary.

2) Trade-mark/Patent Overlap

One strategy to extend intellectual property rights has been to seek to use trade-mark law to protect, as trade-marks, features of the product that were part of the since-expired patent monopoly. It is certainly the case that, during a period of patent protection, certain features

---

28 *Kirkbi*, above note 2 at para. 37.

29 R.S.C. 1985, c. C-34.

30 IPEGs, above note 5 at 7.

31 *Kraft Canada* (FC), above note 9.

32 *Ibid.* at para. 46.

of items can become associated with a particular trade source in a way that could be argued to make them perform the functions of a trade-mark. However, the *quid pro quo* of the patent monopoly is the dedication to the public of the patented invention after the expiry of the patent. If competitors are prevented, following the expiry of the patent, from making and marketing the subject matter of the patent, the objectives of the patent system are frustrated.

The doctrine of functionality, which emerged in caselaw and is now reflected, in relation to registered trade-marks, in section 13 of the *Trade-marks Act*[33] has long served the role of excluding from trade-mark protection the functional features of articles. The doctrine of functionality thus assists in preventing the extension of expired patents. However, it also goes further by preventing the use of the *Trade-marks Act* to obtain patent-type monopolies over functional features of unpatented articles.

While the principles underlying the doctrine of functionality are fairly well-established, they are often difficult to apply on a case-by-case basis, and disputes over the validity of "distinguishing guise" trade-marks are relatively common.[34] Distinguishing-guise protection has been sought in the pharmaceutical industry, as attempts are made to protect the distinctive appearance of pills or tablets.[35] Beyond the pharmaceutical industry it is difficult to pinpoint any one area of tech-

---

33 Section 13(1)(b) of the *Trade-marks Act*, above note 16, provides that a distinguishing guise is registrable only if "the exclusive use by the applicant of the distinguishing guise in association with the wares or services with which it has been used is not likely unreasonably to limit the development of any art or industry." Section 13(2) also states: "No registration of a distinguishing guise interferes with the use of any utilitarian feature embodied in the distinguishing guise."

34 In Canada, where there is a significantly smaller amount of litigation than in other jurisdictions, such disputes have been fewer in number. In the US there is a significant volume of caselaw addressing issues of functionality in trade-mark law. This caselaw will be discussed below, in Section B(2). The issue continues to be strenuously litigated in Europe, resulting in numerous ECJ and national court decisions.

35 *Parke, Davis & Co. v. Empire Laboratories Ltd.*, [1964] S.C.R. 351 involved coloured bands that were used to seal capsules [*Parke, Davis*]. *Eli Lilly & Co. v. Novopharm Ltd.* (1997), 73 C.P.R. (3d) 371 (F.C.T.D.) involved a passing-off argument made in relation to the size, shape, and colour of capsules [*Eli Lilly*].

nology or industry that is particularly affected. As will be discussed below, disputes have arisen over trade-marks in relation to razor heads,[36] air fresheners,[37] pizza delivery services,[38] children's toys,[39] door keys,[40] cable ties,[41] hockey helmets,[42] and so forth. The range of contexts in which issues may arise contributes to the complexity of the subject area.

While an attempt to extend patent protection through trade-mark law may occur within a largely national market, such attempts may also be part of a more global strategy. In *Kirkbi*, which will be discussed in greater detail, Kirkbi had sought to extend its monopoly over the LEGO building block in a number of jurisdictions other than Canada. In the US an unsuccessful attempt was made to assert trade dress protection for the shape of the blocks following the expiration of the LEGO patents.[43] A similar strategy of invoking trade-mark protection after patent protection was also unsuccessfully attempted in the United Kingdom.[44] In Hong Kong, copyright protection in design drawings of the LEGO bricks was invoked, also without success, following an expired period of patent protection.[45] In Australia, patent protection was followed by industrial design protection, then an attempt to use copyright.[46] In each of these jurisdictions, the courts

---

36 *Remington Rand Corp. v. Philips Electronics N.V.* (1995), 64 C.P.R. (3d) 467 (F.C.A.), leave to appeal to S.C.C. refused (1996), 67 C.P.R. (3d) vi [*Remington Rand*].

37 *Samaan v. Canada's Royal Gold Pinetree Mfg. Co.* (1986), 9 C.P.R. (3d) 223 (F.C.A.) [*Samaan*].

38 *Pizza Pizza Ltd. v. Canada (Registrar of Trade-marks)* (1989), 26 C.P.R. (3d) 355 (F.C.A.) [*Pizza Pizza*].

39 *Kirkbi*, above note 2.

40 *Dominion Lock Co. Ltd. & Independent Lock Co. v. Schlage Lock Co.* (1961), 38 C.P.R. 88 (Registrar of Trade-marks).

41 *Thomas & Betts, Ltd. v. Panduit Corp.*, (1997), 74 C.P.R. (3d) 185 (F.C.T.D.) [*Panduit* (FC)], rev'd (2000), 4 C.P.R. (4th) 498 (F.C.A.) [*Panduit* (FCA)].

42 *Sport Maska Inc. v. Canstar Sports Group, Inc.* (1994), 57 C.P.R. (3d) 323 (Qc. S.C.) [*Sport Maska*].

43 *Tyco Industries Inc. v. LEGO Systems Inc.*, 5 U.S.P.Q. 2d 1023 (D.N.J. 1987), aff'd 853 F.2d 921 (3d Cir. 1988), cert. denied, 488 U.S. 955 (1988).

44 *Interlego A.G.'s Trade Mark Applications*, [1998] R.P.C. 69 (Ch.D.).

45 *Interlego A.G. v. Tyco Industries Inc.*, [1989] A.C. 217 (P.C.).

46 *Interlego A.G. v. A. Foley (Vic.) Pty. Ltd.*, [1987] F.S.R. 283 (Ch.D.).

sought to limit the ability of the plaintiff company to extend the monopoly over the LEGO blocks first acquired under patent law by invoking other areas of intellectual property protection for essentially the same subject matter. This strategy of monopoly extension was noted by the Federal Court of Canada, where Justice Sexton wrote for the majority: "It appears to me that the appellants are attempting to extend the monopoly they once held over these construction bricks and their knobs through the guise of a trade-mark. Other decisions from cases involving LEGO indicate that this attempt is not their first."[47]

Unlike some other areas of overlapping intellectual property rights, the problems associated with the doctrine of functionality are well-recognized both in the caselaw and in the legislation. There exists a clear recourse for competitors who feel they are being excluded from competition by virtue of a trade-mark over a functional feature of an item. The recent *Kirkbi* decision is seen by many as an important case that clarifies the principles underlying the doctrine of functionality, and which confirms the doctrine's application to both registered and unregistered trade-marks. Nevertheless, *Kirkbi* does not respond to all of the issues and uncertainties surrounding the doctrine of functionality and its application. In the discussion that follows, the *Kirkbi* decision will be described and analyzed, and the outstanding issues will be identified.

a) The Doctrine of Functionality

The common law of passing off, its civil law equivalent,[48] and the *Trade-marks Act* offer protection for what is known in Canada as a "distinguishing guise."[49] A distinguishing guise is defined in the *Trade-marks Act* as

> (a) a shaping of wares or their containers, or
> (b) a mode of wrapping or packaging wares the appearance of which is used by a person for the purpose of distinguishing or so as to

47 *Kirkbi A.G. v. Ritvik Holdings Inc.*, [2004] 2 F.C.R. 241, 2003 FCA 297 [*Kirkbi* (FCA)] at para. 90.

48 Passing off, in civil law, is a form of unfair competition or *concurrence déloyale*. In Quebec, it has been litigated under art. 1053 of the *Civil Code of Lower Canada*, now art. 1457 of the *Civil Code of Quebec*. See for example, *Sport Maska*, above note 42.

49 In the US, the equivalent concept to "distinguishing guise" is "trade dress."

> distinguish wares or services manufactured, sold, leased, hired or performed by others.[50]

In essence, therefore, a distinguishing guise is a three-dimensional trade-mark. Because it is contemplated that the distinguishing guise may be the shape of the wares, there is a risk that trade-mark protection might extend to protecting the actual wares, where the shape is essential to the utility of the wares. Indeed, this is an inherent problem with distinguishing-guise protection to the extent that it reaches beyond protection of distinctive packaging to the appearance of the product itself. As one author notes,

> The problem with protecting product design is that competitors have a right to slavishly copy a competitor's product without fear of liability. As a policy matter, unless the design is protected by a form of intellectual property, such as patent or copyright, competitors are encouraged to copy because it is perceived that consumers benefit from this form of competition.[51]

Open competition between products in the marketplace should mean that, absent intellectual property protection, companies should be free to copy the products of competitors. Trade-mark law has generally not prevented the copying of products but has placed limits on the use of marks in such a way as to cause confusion or deception among consumers. However, where the actual product shape is protected as a distinguishing guise, there is a risk that the trade-mark protection will protect the product itself.

The doctrine of functionality has emerged from caselaw, and has been incorporated into the *Trade-marks Act*, to limit the scope of trade-mark protection for distinguishing guises to only those features of wares that are not a functional element of the wares.[52] In the recent

50 *Trade-marks Act*, above note 16, s. 2: definition of "distinguishing guise."

51 Lars Smith, "Trade Distinctiveness: Solving Scalia's *Tertium Quid* Trade Dress Conundrum" (2005) Mich. St. L. Rev. 243 at 256.

52 Section 13(1)(b) provides that a distinguishing guise is only registrable as a trade-mark if its exclusive use by the applicant in association with the wares or services for which it is registered "is not likely unreasonably to limit the development of any art or industry." Section 13(2) makes it clear that the registration of a distinguishing guise should not interfere "with the use of any utilitarian feature embodied in the distinguishing guise." Finally, s. 13(3)

Supreme Court of Canada decision in *Kirkbi*,[53] LeBel J. emphasized the different functions of patent and trade-mark law, and stated: "despite its connection with a product, a mark must not be confused with the product — it is something else, a symbol of a connection between a source of a product and the product itself."[54] He went on to explain the role of the doctrine of functionality in this regard: "The doctrine of functionality appears to be a logical principle of trade-marks law. It reflects the purpose of a trade-mark, which is the protection of the distinctiveness of the product, not of a monopoly on the product."[55]

In the US, distinguishing guises are known as "trade dress" and are protected both as unregistered and registered marks. The doctrine of functionality is clearly a part of US law. Section 2(e)(5) of the *Lanham Act* states:

> No trade-mark by which the goods of the applicant may be distinguished from the goods of others shall be refused registration on the principal register on account of its nature unless it
>
> . . .
>
> (e) Consists of a mark which
>
> (5) comprises any matter that, as a whole, is functional.[56]

Thus, as in Canada, trade dress cannot be registered as a trade-mark if it is wholly functional. Unregistered trade dress can also be protected under section 43(a) of the *Lanham Act*, which provides for an action similar to passing off. However, 43(a)(3) places limits with respect to trade dress, noting that the person asserting trade dress protection "has the burden of proving that the matter sought to be protected is not functional."[57]

In the United Kingdom, the *Trade Marks Act 1994*[58] provides that "A trade mark may, in particular, consist of . . . the shape of goods or

---

permits the Federal Court to expunge the registration of a distinguishing guise if the registration "has become likely unreasonably to limit the development of any art or industry."

53 Above note 2.

54 *Ibid.* at para. 39.

55 *Ibid.* at para. 42.

56 15 U.S.C.A. § 1052(e)(5) (West 2004).

57 15 U.S.C.A. § 1125(a)(3) (West 2004) [*Lanham Act*, s. 43].

58 (UK), 1994, c. 26.

their packaging."[59] Yet the doctrine of functionality also operates in the UK. A mark is not registrable if it consists exclusively of

(a) the shape which results from the nature of the goods themselves,
(b) the shape of goods which is necessary to obtain a technical result, or
(c) the shape which gives substantial value to the goods.[60]

These provisions are consistent with the wording of the EU directive harmonizing trade-mark law in the EU,[61] and with the *Community Trade Mark Regulation*.[62]

b) *Kirkbi v. Ritvik Holdings*

Kirkbi provides a useful case study of the attempt to extend intellectual property protection through overlapping rights, and of the application of the doctrine of functionality. This section of the paper will explore the strategy adopted by Kirkbi leading up to the litigation. It will then analyze the decision of the Supreme Court of Canada with a view to determining the current status of the doctrine of functionality in Canada and its effectiveness in maintaining a clear boundary between trade-mark and patent law.

Kirkbi is the manufacturer of the LEGO building blocks for children. The blocks come in a variety of shapes and sizes but essentially work through a series of interconnecting studs and holes. The blocks, with their interlocking system, have been protected by a series of patents (which covered various improvements). The first such Canadian patent expired in July 1964; the second, for an improvement, expired in October 1978, and a third expired in September 1988. The blocks have been protected by similar patents around the world. However, since patent protection for the blocks expired, Kirkbi has faced competition

---

59 *Ibid.*, s. 1.

60 *Ibid.*, s. 3.

61 EC *Directive 89/104/EEC of 21 December 1988 to approximate the laws of the Member States relating to trade marks*, [1989] O.J. L. 40/1 at 1-7 [*Directive 89/104/EEC*]. Prior to the changes to UK law to implement this directive, distinguishing guises were not registrable. See *Re Coca-Cola Co.'s Applications*, [1986] 2 All E.R. 274 (H.L.) [*Coca-Cola Co.'s Applications*].

62 EC, *Council Regulation No. 40/94 of 20 December 1993 on the Community trade mark*, [1994] O.J. L. 11/1 [*Community Trade Mark Regulation*].

from others, including most notably in Canada, the defendant Mega Bloks Inc., formerly known as Ritvik Holdings. In order to limit this competition in Canada, it sought protection for the shape of the LEGO block, arguing that the "shaping of the knob configuration of LEGO products constitutes a 'distinguishing guise.'"[63] The knob configuration is, of course, the part of the LEGO block that gives it its "clutch power," and it featured in the patent claims for the blocks.

Section 13(1)(b) of the *Trade-marks Act* renders a distinguishing guise unregistrable if giving the applicant exclusive rights to use it in association with the specified wares or services would be likely "[to] unreasonably . . . limit the development of any art or industry." Kirkbi accepted that functionality would be a bar to the registration of the block's distinguishing guise as a trade-mark. Nevertheless, it argued that since the Act did not include any limitations based on functionality in the definition of a distinguishing guise, and since the Act covered both registered and unregistered trade-marks, there was no such bar or limitation for unregistered marks. Thus section 7(b) of the *Trade-marks Act*, which codifies in part the common law of passing off, could be used to protect the shape of wares as an unregistered trade-mark where that shape had become distinctive of source.

Kirkbi thus accepted that the doctrine of functionality existed and operated to limit the registration of functional elements of trade-marks,[64] but it argued that no such limitations operated for unregistered marks. The Supreme Court of Canada ultimately decided that the doctrine of functionality applied to prevent functional features from becoming protected elements of both registered and unregistered trade-marks, whether in civil or common law.[65] The parameters they set for the doctrine of functionality are thus key to understanding the limits of registered and unregistered trade-marks alike.

---

63 *Kirkbi* (FCA), above note 47 at para. 13.

64 This followed on an earlier attempt by Kirkbi to register the shape of the blocks as a distinguishing guise. This attempt was rejected by the Registrar of Trade-marks. See *Kirkbi*, above note 2 at para. 6.

65 LeBel J. made a point of noting that an equivalent of the doctrine of functionality applied under French civil law in another instance of litigation involving Kirkbi and a French competitor. *Kirkbi*, above note 2 at para. 55 (Paris, 18 October 2000, D.2001.Jur.850 (Annot. J. Passa) at 851).

There have been a number of lower court decisions in Canada that have explored the boundaries of the doctrine of functionality. Although these are quite extensively canvassed at the Federal Court of Appeal, the Supreme Court of Canada did not review or discuss them in any detail. Rather, the Court focused on first principles, stating that the doctrine of functionality in Canadian trade-mark law was well-established and uncontroversial. LeBel J., who wrote for the Court, noted that the Canadian position is consistent with that in other comparable jurisdictions. After a review of foreign caselaw, he stated:

> At the root of the functionality principle in European law, as in Canadian intellectual property law, lies a concern to avoid overextending monopoly rights on the products themselves and impeding competition, in respect of wares sharing the same technical characteristics.[66]

He took note of the fact that Kirkbi had been litigious the world over in various attempts to extend its expired patents through other forms of intellectual property law. He commented that "in a free market, trade-marks should not be used to prolong monopolies on technical characteristics of products . . . . It is simply the way the economy and the market are supposed to work in modern liberal societies."[67]

The Court made short work of the argument that the doctrine of functionality was only meant to apply with respect to *registered* trade-marks. LeBel J. affirmed the view expressed by Sexton J.A. at the Federal Court of Appeal that the doctrine of functionality applies to all marks whether registered or unregistered, "as the legal nature of the marks remains the same."[68] LeBel J. referred to the doctrine of functionality as "a logical principle of trade-marks law. It reflects the purpose of a trade-mark, which is the protection of the distinctiveness of the product, not of a monopoly on the product."[69] He went on to state that "trade-marks law is not intended to prevent the competitive use of utilitarian features of products . . . it fulfills a source-distinguishing function."[70] Thus, the function of trade-marks is to serve as a means

66 *Kirkbi*, above note 2 at para. 52.

67 *Ibid.* at para. 54.

68 *Ibid.* at para. 58.

69 *Ibid.* at para. 42.

70 *Ibid.* at para. 43.

of distinguishing the source of wares or services. Trade-marks are not intended to be used to prevent legitimate competition. To emphasize this point, LeBel J. noted that the doctrine of functionality "prevents abuses of monopoly positions in respect of products and processes. Once, for example, patents have expired, it discourages attempts to bring them back in another guise."[71]

Although the Supreme Court of Canada is clear about the role played by the doctrine of functionality, its position on the scope and application of the doctrine is not well articulated. This is in part because of the nature of Kirkbi's argument. Because of the wording of section 13 of the *Trade-marks Act*, Kirkbi was forced to argue that the doctrine of functionality did not apply to unregistered marks. The essence of the Court's decision, therefore, was to emphasize the policy role played by the doctrine and to affirm that it did apply to both registered and unregistered marks. In other words, *Kirkbi* was a "policy case" decided on a very simple set of facts.

Kirkbi leaves us with a broadly stated doctrine of functionality, but with little guidance as to its application to more challenging fact situations. In *Kirkbi* the Court states that "no mark could consist of utilitarian features."[72] Going beyond this, the Court declares: "A combination of elements primarily designed to perform a function may not be the subject matter of a trade-mark."[73] LeBel J. also cites with approval the following statement of principle from an earlier decision of the Supreme Court of Canada: "The law appears to be well settled that if what is sought to be registered as a trade mark has a functional use or characteristic, it cannot be the subject of a trade mark."[74] Yet each

---

71 *Ibid.* at para. 44.

72 *Ibid.* at para. 46.

73 *Ibid.* at para. 46. On this point, LeBel J. cites *Elgin Handles v. Welland Vale Mfg. Co.* (1964), 43 C.P.R. 20 (Ex. Ct.) [*Elgin Handles*], and *Imperial Tobacco Co. of Canada v. Registrar of Trade Marks*, [1939] Ex.C.R. 141 [*Imperial Tobacco*].

74 *Kirkbi, ibid.* at para. 45, citing from *Parke, Davis*, above note 35 at 354. This latter statement is difficult, at first glance, to reconcile with the decision in *Pizza Pizza*, above note 38, where the court found that, although the telephone number for which registration was sought was functional, it was not a function that related to the wares themselves. Thus, these statements by the Court on functionality must be read with a view to the definition of distinguishing guise, which grounds such a guise in the wares, referring either to the shape of the wares or their containers, or their mode of wrapping or packaging.

of these statements means something slightly different, and the last, the quote from *Parke, Davis,* sets a very wide ambit for the doctrine of functionality.

c) Unresolved Issues

Kirkbi offers little guidance as to how the doctrine of functionality should be interpreted and applied. Part of the problem lies in the limited scope the facts provided for exploring the doctrine of functionality. *Kirkbi* dealt with a product shape covered by a prior patent, and this influenced the Court's approach to the issue. However, it is possible for functionality issues to arise in relation to product shapes where there is no prior patent, or where there is a prior patent but the element of shape is not claimed. In this section, this paper considers some of the lacunae left following the *Kirkbi* decision. These include the reconciliation of the "broad" and the "narrow" rule of functionality, the consideration to be given to prior patents, the relationship of the doctrine of functionality to trade-marks more generally, the definition of "functionality," differences between registered and unregistered trade-marks, and issues of utility compared to ornamentation.

i) The "Broad Rule" and the "Narrow Rule"

In many ways, *Kirkbi* was an easy case. If there is a spectrum of functionality in distinguishing guises, the shape of LEGO blocks would be far towards one end. The distinguishing guise claimed by LEGO was virtually identical to the configuration claimed in the LEGO patents. The distinguishing guise was as close to being the product itself as one can get.[75] On a set of facts such as those in *Kirkbi,* it is easy to state a simple and straightforward rule.

If one views functionality cases as falling along a spectrum, it is certainly the case that the bulk of Canadian caselaw on the subject tends to fall on one end or the other. Cases like *Kirkbi, Imperial Tobacco,*[76] *Parke,*

---

75 Sexton J.A. in the Federal Court of Appeal wrote: "All the features of the LEGO Indicia Mark are dictated by function, and the shape of the top surface of the LEGO basic brick is purely utilitarian," *Kirkbi* (FCA), above note 47 at para. 15.

76 Above note 73: Claiming the cellophane wrapper for cigarette packages with a coloured tear strip as a trade-mark.

Davis,[77] and *Elgin Handles*[78] are on one end of the spectrum. On the other end of the spectrum lie cases such as *Pizza Pizza*,[79] *Samann*,[80] and *IVG Rubber Canada Ltd. v. Goodall Rubber Co.*[81] In the former category of cases, it is almost impossible to separate the distinguishing guise from a functional aspect of the product; in the latter category, the two are easy to distinguish. Both sets of cases are relatively straightforward as a result.

Easy cases tend not to allow for a great deal of nuance in the development of doctrines. Nevertheless, it is clear that the caselaw does not present an entirely consistent articulation of the doctrine of functionality. Indeed, it has been argued that distinct "rules" emerge.[82] One, referred to as the "narrow-rule approach"[83] permits some functionality as long as the matter for which trade-mark protection is sought is not "*primarily* designed to perform a function."[84] The so-called "broad rule" is articulated by the Supreme Court of Canada in *Parke, Davis*, where Hall J. stated: "The law appears to be well settled that if what is sought to be registered as a trade mark *has a functional use or characteristic*, it cannot be the subject of a trade mark."[85] This view would exclude from trade-mark status features that have "a functional use or characteristic" regardless of whether it is *primarily* functional. It is this statement from *Parke, Davis* that is adopted by the Supreme

77 Above note 35: Claiming coloured gelatin bands around two halves of a capsule that serve to seal the two halves and can indicate when the seal is broken.

78 Above note 73: Claiming the colour and consistency of wooden tool handles that are enhanced by a fire-hardening process as a trade-mark.

79 Above note 38: Claim for a pizza delivery telephone number as a trade-mark was allowed.

80 Above note 37: Claim for a pine tree configuration for a pine-scented air freshener was allowed.

81 (1980), 48 C.P.R. (2d) 268 (F.C.T.D.): Claim for a coloured line that spiraled around the length of a rubber hose was allowed.

82 Richard Levy, "The *LEGO* Case: The Supreme Court of Canada Makes It Harder to Protect Product Shapes as Trade-marks" (2006) 96 Trade-mark Rep. 596 [Levy].

83 From *Remington Rand*, above note 36 at 474, cited in *Panduit* (FCA), above note 41 at para. 24.

84 From *Imperial Tobacco*, above note 73 at 145, also cited in *Panduit* (FCA), *ibid.* at para. 24 [emphasis added].

85 *Parke Davis*, above note 35 at 354 [emphasis added].

Court of Canada in *Kirkbi,* although the Court also indicates that the doctrine has been consistently applied through a range of cases, including *Remington Rand,* which may have actually applied the narrow-rule approach doctrine.[86]

To illustrate the differences between the application of the broad rule and the narrow rule, two cases provide useful facts. *Panduit* involved a dispute over a claim that the oval shape of a cable tie head was a distinguishing guise. The shape was not claimed in a since-expired patent for the head but was featured in a drawing that was part of the patent specification. The case illustrates circumstances where a feature is functional (a cable tie head) but its precise appearance may not be (the oval shape). A similar, though much easier, case is *Samann,* where a pine-tree-shaped cardboard substrate for air freshener was considered not to be barred from protection as a distinguishing guise. The substrate was functional; indeed, the air freshener had to be soaked into a suitable substrate. However, the particular shape of the substrate was not "primarily functional." *Panduit* is a more difficult case first, because the head of the cable tie was a feature depicted in the patent specification, and second, because the oval shape of the cable tie head was not so clearly ornamental or fanciful as the shape

86 Justice MacGuigan, in *Remington Rand,* above note 36 at 474, articulated the following test: "If functionality goes either to the trade mark itself (*Imperial Tobacco,* and *Parke, Davis*) or to the wares (*Elgin Handles*), then it is essentially or primarily inconsistent with registration. However, if it is merely secondary or peripheral, like a telephone number with no essential connection with the wares, then it does not act as a bar to registration." Of course, one can question whether the narrow rule, framed in this way, is much different from the broad rule, as it excludes from protection things that do not really qualify as distinguishing guises in the first place. The telephone number in *Pizza Pizza,* above note 38, would not fit the statutory definition of a distinguishing guise, as it is neither the shape of the wares or their container, nor a mode of wrapping or packaging the wares. As well, it is difficult to accept the characterization in *Remington Rand,* above note 36, of the *Imperial Tobacco,* above note 73, and *Parke, Davis, ibid.,* cases as involving issues of functionality in relation to "the trade mark itself," since, in both cases, what was sought to be protected were distinguishing guises in the form of a mode of wrapping or packaging the wares (*Imperial Tobacco*) or a combination of a mode of packaging and the wares themselves (*Parke, Davis* at 414). The more one looks at the cases below, the more difficult it is to say that the law is either clear or well-settled.

of the cardboard substrate in *Samann*. It is clear that the shape of the substrate was relatively immaterial to its function. In *Panduit*, it is less clear that the oval shape of the cable tie head is entirely non-functional. Indeed, the matter was never resolved at trial. It is conceivable that, while not essential to the invention, an oval-shaped cable tie head has advantages over, for example, a rectangular lozenge shape, an elongated triangle shape, an hourglass shape, or any other such configuration. In such circumstances it may well make a difference whether the broad or narrow rule is applied. If the narrow rule of functionality is applied to a shape that is not essential but offers some benefits, the issue would be whether the shape was primarily functional. On an application of the broad rule, a shape that has some advantages over other configurations might be excluded, as it has some degree of functionality. The difference is one of degree, but it is nonetheless important.[87]

In a comment on the Supreme Court's decision in *Kirkbi*, Richard Levy raises challenging questions about the application of the doctrine of functionality following *Kirkbi*. He is critical of the Court for effectively over-simplifying the rule and for stating it without nuance.[88] He argues that the Court's decision "created too high a hurdle for functional product shapes to act as trade-marks."[89] Further, he argues that the Court's conclusion that the doctrine is both well-settled and shared by all comparable jurisdictions is misleading because the focus of the comparison was other LEGO litigation, all of which fell on the easy end of the spectrum. Indeed, he argues that there is considerably more diversity in the law across jurisdictions than the Supreme Court decision would allow.[90] Levy criticizes the Court for "conceptualizing

87 There is a second issue in *Panduit*, above note 41 — one of public policy. Like *Kirkbi*, above note 2, *Panduit* involves a distinguishing-guise claim based on material in a prior patent. A third rule, independent of the broad and narrow rules, might be the general exclusion of matter featured in a patent specification. This issue is discussed in more detail below.

88 Levy, above note 82, argues that there are at least two Canadian cases not considered by the Court in *Kirkbi, ibid.*, which raise more complex issues: *Stiga Aktiebolag v. S.L.M. Canada, Inc.* (1990), 34 C.P.R. (3d) 216 (F.C.T.D.); and *Sport Maska*, above note 42.

89 Levy, *ibid.* at 598.

90 *Ibid.*

trade-marks and patents as mutually exclusive 'watertight' domains"[91] and argues for a more nuanced approach to issues of functionality.

It is not entirely clear whether there really is a broad and narrow rule, or whether the two formulations merely reflect the nuances in the language chosen by judges as they apply the rule to a diversity of fact situations. As will be argued below, the differences in fact and context between the cases may account for the appearance that there are two rules. The broad and narrow rules may simply reflect the different contexts in which disputes may arise and the different ways in which similar principles are articulated. If this is the case, the Supreme Court of Canada may be perfectly correct in reducing the earlier caselaw to a single broad rule. Nevertheless, this does nothing to resolve the difficulties in applying the rule to any given set of facts.

ii) The Role of Prior Patents

The distinguishing guise asserted in *Kirkbi* mapped almost perfectly on to the claims in the expired patent. This made a finding of functionality easy in the case. The issues will not always be as straightforward. In this respect, *Panduit*[92] is important because, although it involves a prior patent, the feature argued to be a distinguishing guise is not expressly claimed in the patent. As noted earlier, *Panduit* involved a dispute between two competitors in the market for cable ties. Cable ties are simple devices used to bundle together groups of cables. The plaintiff, Thomas & Betts, had developed an improved cable tie, which it patented in 1967. This tie involved two pieces: "the first piece being a plastic, integrally formed head and body, and the second piece being a metal tongue or 'barb.'"[93] The strap of the tie would be inserted through the head, and the tongue would act as a locking mechanism. It was the barbed tongue that was the real innovation in the invention. For the duration of the patent, Thomas & Betts was the only manufacturer of these cable ties. The ties it manufactured had an oval-shaped head. The oval-shaped head of the tie was not essential to the invention, and it did not feature in any of the patent claims. However, it was featured in the drawing that was part of the patent specification.

---

91 *Ibid.*

92 *Panduit* (FCA), above note 41.

93 *Ibid.* at para. 5.

When the patent expired, Panduit began manufacturing and selling a cable tie that was virtually identical to that manufactured by Thomas & Betts. Thomas & Betts sued, arguing that the oval-shaped head was an unregistered, distinguishing guise, and that Panduit was infringing on this trade-mark. Panduit filed a motion for summary judgment seeking dismissal of the action. Panduit argued, *inter alia*, that the oval-shaped head was functional and therefore not entitled to trade-mark protection, and that, as the preferred embodiment of the expired patent, it was not entitled to trade-mark protection. Panduit later dropped the functionality argument and focused on the one relating to the preferred embodiment. The motions judge granted the motion for summary judgment, accepting that there could be no trade-mark protection for a feature depicted in the preferred embodiment.[94] That decision was appealed to the Federal Court of Appeal.

The basis for the decision of the motions judge was not strictly a functionality argument. Indeed, there were other shapes of cable tie heads that could conceivably have been used without significantly altering the functionality of the product. Instead, the motions judge accepted that when something is described or depicted in a patent specification it cannot be the subject of a later trade-mark monopoly. The *quid pro quo* of the grant of a patent monopoly is full disclosure of the invention so that others can learn how to make it. The Federal Court of Appeal summarized the position of the motions judge as follows:

> the duty of disclosure imposed by the *Patent Act* requires the inventor to teach the public, having only the specification, how to make the same successful use of the invention as the inventor could and that, as a result, the patentee could not, after the expiration of the patent, assert any trade-mark rights to prevent the public from making the very same preferred embodiment as that described and depicted by the inventor in the patent.[95]

The Federal Court of Appeal rejected this approach as incorrect. Justice Décary stated:

> I have found no authority for such a proposition which, reduced to its simplest or extended to its extreme, would mean that any ele-

94 *Panduit* (FC), above note 41.

95 *Panduit* (FCA), above note 41 at para. 15.

> ment described or depicted in the preferred embodiment — regardless of whether it is claimed or of its importance to the claimed invention — is automatically as a matter of law and without further inquiry disqualified from trade-mark protection.[96]

The Federal Court of Appeal dismissed the argument that non-essential features of the description of an invention — in other words, features not actually claimed in a patent — were automatically excluded from being potential trade-marks. The patent/trade-mark overlap only becomes significant where trade-mark law is invoked to extend protection past the patent term to functional aspects of the patented invention. Thus, the Federal Court of Appeal redefined the question as one of the application of the doctrine of functionality. It reframed the specific issue to whether the oval-shaped head was a distinguishing guise — in other words, that it was both distinctive of source and non-functional. With respect to functionality, the court indicated that a shape would run afoul of the rule if "that shape is so closely related to the invention as to be for all practical purposes an element essential to making full use of the invention."[97] This is a different formulation of the rule than that adopted by the Supreme Court of Canada in *Kirkbi*.[98] The matter was referred back for a decision after trial of the issues but settled before trial.

The same dispute that arose in *Panduit* in Canada also arose in the United States. The US Court of Appeals for the Seventh Circuit reversed a lower court's finding that the oval-shaped cable tie head could not be protected as a trade-mark because it featured in the patent specification and remanded the case for consideration of a number of factual issues.[99] Justice Bauer, for the unanimous appellate court, placed his ruling in the context of the proper relationship between patent and trade-mark law. He emphasized the "right to copy" that

96 *Ibid.* at para. 20.

97 *Ibid.* at para. 23.

98 The Court in *Kirkbi*, above note 2, appears to adopt the rule from *Parke, Davis*: "if what is sought to be registered as a trade-mark has a functional use or characteristic, it cannot be the subject of the mark." See *Parke, Davis*, above note 35 at 354.

99 *Thomas & Betts, Corp. v. Panduit Corp.*, 138 F.3d 277 (7th Cir. 1998) [*Panduit* (US)].

follows on the expiration of a patent and stated that trade-mark law was not meant to extend the patent monopoly by preventing the copying of functional features of patented articles. However, the court here noted, as did the Federal Court of Appeal in Canada, that the oval-shaped cable tie head was not explicitly claimed in the patent, and that therefore the case was distinguishable from other decisions where claimed features were barred from protection under trade-mark law,[100] or where trade-mark protection was denied for features dictated by the patents covering various components.[101]

Justice Bauer rejected a *per se* prohibition "against features disclosed in a patent receiving trade-mark protection after the patent has expired."[102] Instead, it is the doctrine of functionality that must be relied upon to determine whether there is an impermissible attempt to extend the patent monopoly. He described the functionality doctrine as follows: "a configuration of an article cannot receive trade-mark registration if its purpose is to contribute functional advantages to the article or if the configuration results from functional considerations."[103]

The challenge, of course, is being able to draw the line between functional and non-functional features. Bauer J. suggests that where the element claimed as a trade-mark is expressly claimed in the patent it is likely to be functional and not protectable under trade-mark law. However, where the feature is merely described in the patent specification, as was the case with the cable tie head, further inquiry is warranted. That inquiry involves a consideration of distinctiveness (i.e., whether secondary meaning has been acquired by the feature) followed by an analysis of likelihood of confusion. The inquiry into secondary meaning treads to some extent on the territory of functionality. In *Panduit* (US) it was necessary to determine whether the configuration of the cable tie head had become associated with Thomas & Betts as a source of the goods, or whether it had become associated with a desirable or essential feature of the product.[104] This is not a pure

100 *Vornado Air Circulation Systems, Inc. v. Duracraft Corp.*, 58 F.3d 1498 (10th Cir. 1995), cert. denied, 516 U.S. 1067 (1996).

101 *Singer Mfg. Co. v. June Mfg. Co.*, 163 U.S. 169 (1896).

102 *Panduit* (US), above note 99 at 288.

103 *Ibid.*

104 *Ibid.* at 294.

functionality inquiry; rather, it asks whether consumers have associated the feature with the product itself or with the producer, as the source of the product.

Yet even a finding of secondary meaning and likelihood of confusion is not determinative, as the doctrine of functionality can operate as a defense to trade-mark infringement in such cases.[105] In *Panduit* (US), Bauer J. offered several formulations of the functionality test, stating that "a feature is functional if it is one that is costly to design around or to do without, rather than one that is costly to have."[106] A functional feature must also be "necessary to afford a competitor the means to compete effectively."[107] Put another way, "a functional feature is one which competitors would have to spend money not to copy but to design around."[108] Bauer J. indicated that, if it were possible to show that the design at issue was one of only a few usable designs, then trade dress protection could be denied.[109] Evidence of other possible shapes or configurations that could be affordable and effectively used could serve to rebut an argument of functionality.

The leading case in the US on the issue of trade dress protection for material previously covered by a patent is *TrafFix Devices, Inc. v. Marketing Displays, Inc.*[110] In that case, two patents were obtained for a spring mechanism designed to allow roadside traffic signs to withstand strong gusts of winds. The patent holder had established a thriving traffic sign business during the term of the patents, but faced competition on their expiry. TrafFix Devices Inc. began to sell signs that used the same mechanism and that were therefore identical to the products sold by the plaintiff, Marketing Displays, Inc. (MDI). MDI sued, *inter alia*, for trade dress infringement, and TrafFix counterclaimed using antitrust arguments. The focus of the appeal to the US Supreme Court was on the trade dress issues.

---

105 *Ibid.* at 297.

106 *Ibid.*, citing *Schwinn Bicycle Co. v. Ross Bicycles, Inc.*, 870 F.2d 1176 (7th Cir. 1989) [*Schwinn*].

107 *Panduit* (US), *ibid.* at 297, citing from *Schwinn*, *ibid.* at 1188.

108 *Panduit* (US), *ibid.* at 298, citing *W.T. Rogers, Co. v. Keene*, 778 F.2d 334 at 339 (7th Cir. 1985).

109 *Panduit* (US), *ibid.* at 298.

110 532 U.S. 23; 121 S. Ct. 1255 (2001) [*TrafFix* cited to S. Ct.].

The US Supreme Court in *TrafFix* began by affirming that trade dress could be protected under US law, and that, in fact, "protection for trade dress exists to promote competition."[111] The Court also noted that the law requires the person asserting trade dress protection to bear the burden of establishing that the "matter sought to be protected is not functional."[112]

The Court in *TrafFix* expressed similar concerns to the Court in *Kirkbi* over undue extension of monopolies granted under other statutes: "In general, unless an intellectual property right such as a patent or copyright protects an item, it will be subject to copying."[113] In *TrafFix*, the Court identified the key question as "the effect of an expired patent on a claim of trade dress infringement."[114] It stated:

> A utility patent is strong evidence that the features therein claimed are functional. If trade dress protection is sought for those features the strong evidence of functionality based on the previous patent adds great weight to the statutory presumption that features are deemed functional until proved otherwise by the party seeking trade dress protection.[115]

The US Court does not adopt a hard rule to the effect that a prior patent is a bar to protection as a distinguishing guise. Instead, a prior patent is considered strong evidence of functionality, and it is combined with a statutory presumption of functionality, but there is still room to argue otherwise. The presumption can be rebutted by "showing that the feature is not functional, for instance by showing that it is merely an ornamental, incidental, or arbitrary aspect of the device."[116]

The Court in *TrafFix* went on to find that MDI could not rebut the strong presumption of functionality with respect to the dual-spring device. In particular it noted that the dual spring features were clearly superior to a single-spring design, and that this was set out in the patent specification. The Court also noted that the dual-spring design affected the cost of the signs: it was possible to achieve the same effect

111 *Ibid.* at 1259. It does so by helping to eliminate confusion.

112 *Lanham Act*, above note 57, s. 43(a)(3), cited in *TrafFix*, *ibid.* at 1259.

113 *TrafFix*, *ibid.* at 1260.

114 *Ibid.*

115 *Ibid.*

116 *Ibid.*

using three springs, but two springs were as effective and less costly. Thus, to require competitors to use only one spring would force them to make an inferior product; to require them to distinguish their product by using three springs would needlessly increase their costs.

The approach of Canada's Federal Court of Appeal in *Panduit* (FCA) is not inconsistent with that of the US Supreme Court in *TrafFix*. The Court in *TrafFix* accepts that some features of a product that are found in patent claims may not be functional. It states:

> The inquiry into whether such features, asserted to be trade dress, are functional by reason of their inclusion in the claims of an expired utility patent could be aided by going beyond the claims and examining the patent and its prosecution history to see if the feature in question is shown as a useful part of the invention.[117]

Of course, in *Panduit* (FCA), the court was dealing with a feature that was not actually claimed. Thus it is not clear what the *Panduit* court's approach would have been had the shape of the cable tie head actually been referred to in a patent claim. The *TrafFix* Court is of the view that it is possible to rebut functionality even if the feature is claimed. This does seem different from *Kirkbi*; at the very least it is a more nuanced statement.

A more flexible approach to subject matter referenced in patent claims may also leave room to consider features that may have had an element of functionality at the time they were claimed in the patent, but which are no longer purely functional either because they are now an obsolete feature of the invention or because there are now more economical alternatives to the use of those features. A hard and fast rule might state that, once claimed, a feature can never acquire trade-mark status, with the public policy rationale being a desire not to grant one monopoly right on top of another. Yet this is not the rationale behind the doctrine of functionality, which seeks to prevent the use of trade-mark monopolies to claim product features that are actually functional. If a once-functional feature of a patented device becomes peripheral to the device a few years into the term of the patent monopoly, but later serves in some way to make the product distinctive, should protection as a distinguishing guise be precluded?

117 *Ibid.* at 1262.

The US Supreme Court in *TrafFix* ruled that a prior patent in which the trade-mark elements are claimed is "strong evidence"[118] of functionality. Nevertheless, it made it clear that this evidence of functionality could be rebutted in appropriate cases. In the US, where economic functionality is specifically contemplated, it may also be the case that the features claimed in the patent no longer represent the most economical way of achieving the desired end, but they continue to have some impact in the marketplace as an identifier of source that makes it worth continuing to use the particular feature as a trade-mark. It is unclear from *Kirkbi* whether this opportunity to rebut an argument of functionality based on a prior patent exists, or whether the prior patent is conclusive evidence of functionality that rules out trade-mark protection.

Interpreting the UK *Trade Marks Act 1994*,[119] which reproduces the same language as that quoted above, has not resulted in a hard and fast rule with respect to prior patents. Rather, Justice Neuberger of the Chancery Division has stated: "the fact that an applicant has, or has had, the benefit of the protection of a registered patent in respect of the very thing which (or part of which) he seeks to register as a trade mark is a factor which, at least in some cases, ought to be taken into account."[120] The EU's *Community Trade Mark Regulation* expressly bars from registration marks that consist exclusively of

> 1. (e) . . .
> (i) the shape of goods which results from the nature of the goods themselves; or
> (ii) the shape of goods which is necessary to obtain a technical result; or
> (iii) the shape which gives substantial value to the goods.[121]

While this would seem to bar registration of a mark that embraces subject matter claimed in a prior patent, it may not bar such subject matter if it has since become only one of many means to obtain the

118 *Ibid.* at 1260.

119 Above note 58.

120 *Interlego A.G., Re,* [1997] E.W.J. No. 1572 at para. 69 (Ch. D.).

121 Above note 62, art. 1(e). This language is identical to that in the UK *Trade Marks Act 1994*, above note 58.

same technical result, for example, or less commercially valuable to the goods. Prior patents are thus relevant, but not determinative.

To summarize, then, on the role of prior patents, the *Kirkbi* decision would appear to leave a number of questions unanswered. The Court in *Kirkbi* seems to take the position that a prior patent in which the features argued to be a trade-mark are expressly claimed is convincing evidence of functionality. The *Parke, Davis* Court also made it clear that the existence of a US patent was relevant evidence of functionality, even if no Canadian patent existed. *Panduit* raises the interesting question of whether features in the patent specification, even though not expressly claimed in the patent, are evidence of functionality. This issue is not yet conclusively resolved. Similarly, interesting questions about whether claimed features that have lost their practical or economic functionality can later serve as distinguishing guises have not been considered or resolved.

iii) The Scope of the Doctrine of Functionality

Because *Kirkbi* involves utilitarian features claimed in an expired patent, the Supreme Court did not discuss functionality beyond the basic concept of performing a physical function. Yet functionality may require a more nuanced approach. This is certainly the case in the US. Unlike the Supreme Court of Canada in *Kirkbi*, the US Supreme Court in *TrafFix* articulated a series of rules regarding the application of their functionality test. They noted that in an earlier case, *Qualitex*, the Court had summarized the basic principle as follows: "'In general terms, a product feature is functional,' and cannot serve as a trade-mark, 'if it is essential to the use or purpose of the article or if it affects the cost or quality of the article.'"[122] In *TrafFix*, the Court went further, stating: "a functional feature is one the 'exclusive use of [which] would put competitors at a significant non-reputation-related disadvantage.'"[123] The Court held that "a feature is also functional when

---

122 *Qualitex Co. v. Jacobson Products Co.*, 514 U.S. 159 at 165, 115 S. Ct. 1300 (1995) [*Qualitex* cited to U.S.].

123 *TrafFix*, above note 110 at 1261. The Court continued: "It is proper to inquire into a significant non-reputation-related disadvantage in cases of esthetic functionality."

it is essential to the use or purpose of the device or when it affects the cost or quality of the device."[124]

In the UK, the *Trade Marks Act 1994* also contains a broader statement of functionality. Section 3 of the Act, which sets out absolute grounds for refusal of registration, refers to shapes that result from the nature of the wares themselves, shapes necessary to obtain a technical result, and a shape "which gives substantial value to the goods."[125] This reference to value as a utilitarian feature is present in the US caselaw but is absent from both Canadian caselaw and legislation.

iv) Utility and Ornamentation

In *Kirkbi*, the Supreme Court of Canada approached the doctrine of functionality from a public policy point of view, noting that trade-mark law should not be used to extend the life of patents (or, by implication, to provide patent-like protection). In the US, the same principles apply, but to a much broader category of patents. In the US, subject matter that would be covered by Canada's *Industrial Design Act* is chiefly protected through "design patents." Design patents are a distinct category from "utility patents."[126] This latter category maps on to what would be protected under Canada's *Patent Act*.

The *Industrial Design Act* confers a monopoly on the registrant of an industrial design, and it remains an open question whether a protected industrial design can acquire trade-mark status that can effectively extend protection beyond the period of *Industrial Design Act* protection. A "design" under the *Industrial Design Act* can include "features of shape, configuration, pattern or ornament and any combination of those features that, in a finished article, appeal to and are judged solely by the eye."[127] There is clear potential for overlap here

---

124 *Ibid.* at 1261.

125 *Trade Marks Act 1994*, above note 58, s. 3. These provisions in the UK law are consistent with the EU directive harmonizing trade-mark law among member states. See *Directive 89/104/EEC*, above note 61, and the Community Trade Mark Regulation, above note 62.

126 A utility patent is a patent for a useful invention and is essentially equivalent to what is covered by the concept of "patent" in Canada. In the US, a utility patent is contrasted with a "design patent," which offers protection for subject matter closer in nature to what is covered by Canadian industrial design legislation.

127 *Industrial Design Act*, above note 8, s. 2, definition of "design."

between industrial design protection and trade-mark protection. One question that emerged after *Kirkbi* is whether the policy-oriented approach to the issue of functionality will spill over into a bar on extending *Industrial Design Act* protection through trade-mark law. Canadian law recognizes that a design that is intended for mere ornamentation purposes cannot be protected as a trade-mark.[128] Indeed, the Canadian Intellectual Property Office (CIPO) has issued a practice notice stating, *inter alia*, that

> Where an application is filed for the registration of a three-dimensional mark, whether as a distinguishing guise or as an ordinary trade-mark, the Office will assess whether the mark is primarily functional from either an ornamental or a utilitarian point of view. If it is, and if such functionality relates primarily or essentially to the wares or services covered by the application, the mark will not be registrable.[129]

The caselaw in this area is sometimes difficult, as the line between ornamentation and trade-marks becomes particularly problematic; this is especially so with some distinguishing guises.

The issue arose squarely in 2003 in *WCC Containers Sales Ltd. v. Haul-All Equipment Ltd.*[130] The case involved an application to expunge the respondent's distinguishing-guise trade-mark registrations on the basis that, *inter alia*, the marks were not distinctive, the features of the mark were primarily functional, and "[t]he respondent breached the implied promise it made under the *Industrial Design Act*, R.S.C. 1985, c. I-9 to dedicate the design to the public when it obtained the trade-mark after the expiry of its Canadian Industrial Design Registration."[131] The original industrial design registration related to the design of a refuse container that was animal-proof and therefore proved useful in park settings. Justice Kelen accepted evidence of the functionality of the design and ordered the expungement of the mark on this basis. He also

---

128 To be considered a trade-mark, a design must be distinctive of source. A design that is merely ornamental does not serve as a trade-mark.

129 Canadian Intellectual Property Office, Practice Notice, "Three-dimensional Marks" (6 December 2000), online: http://strategis.ic.gc.ca/sc_mrksv/cipo/tm/tm_notice/tmn2000-12-06-e.html.

130 (2003), 28 C.P.R. (4th) 175, 238 F.T.R. 45 (T.D.) [*WCC Containers*].

131 *Ibid.* at para. 2.

found that the respondents used the mark "to limit the development of the art or industry," contrary to section 13(1)(b) of the Act.

The applicant also argued that there should be a bar on seeking distinguishing-guise trade-mark protection where the same design was previously the subject of an industrial design registration. The applicant's argument was that

> implicit in the grant of the 10-year monopoly under the *Industrial Design Act* is a promise to dedicate the design to the public following the expiry of the design registration. The application to register a design as a distinguishing guise after it has been dedicated to the public is contrary to the legislative intent for the grant of a limited monopoly.[132]

The court noted that the argument was supported by a recent article on the topic where the author argued:

> The owner's reputation in association with the design may grow free of competition during the term of the design registration; to allow unlimited trade-mark protection following expiry of the design registration may well unreasonably limit development of the relevant art or industry. Unreasonableness may flow from reneging on the promise to dedicate the design to the public following expiry of the design registration.[133]

Kelen J. noted that there was no statutory provision that excluded trade-mark protection for previously registered industrial designs. He also noted that "registration of the same design as an industrial design and a distinguishing guise is a long-standing practice in Canada."[134]

Kelen J. ultimately rejected the applicant's argument, stating that "legislative responsibility rests with Parliament and it has not chosen to make industrial design protection and trade-mark protection mutually exclusive."[135] While this is true, it is also true that the Supreme

---

132 *Ibid.* at para. 59.

133 Gordon J. Zimmerman, "Extending the Monopoly? The Risks and Benefits of Multiple Forms of Intellectual Property Protection" (2001) 17 C.I.P.R. 345 at 347 [Zimmerman].

134 *WCC Containers,* above note 130 at para. 63. The examples provided included the Coca-Cola bottle and the J-Cloth box.

135 *Ibid.* at para. 63.

Court of Canada did not need any such Parliamentary direction to rule that the subject matter claimed in a patent could not be protected as a trade-mark. Kelen J. relied as well on the "long-held position of the courts not to prohibit the registration of a design as a trade-mark even if it has already enjoyed the protection of an industrial design registration."[136] Finally, he ruled that "it is not within the competency of this Court to read-in the restriction sought by the applicants."[137]

Nevertheless, the policy issues remain alive. In *T-Rex Véhicules inc. c. 615523 Canada inc.*,[138] the Quebec Superior Court considered a claim to protection of the allegedly distinctive appearance of a vehicle as a distinguishing guise. The design had been the subject of a registration, since expired, under the *Industrial Designs Act*. The court noted that, upon the expiration of industrial design protection, the subject matter of the design falls into the public domain. It concluded that the design of the vehicle could not therefore also be a trade-mark.

In the end result, the functional nature of the mark in *WCC Containers* resulted in its expungement, and it is possible to argue that the doctrine of functionality will be effective in preventing any inappropriate registrations of distinguishing-guise trade-marks, whatever their origin. Certainly, considerations of functionality were also present in the *T-Rex* case. Nevertheless, following *Kirkbi*, it is certainly an open question whether there is a public policy issue here that needs to be reconsidered. In the US, where the same subject matter protected by the *Industrial Designs Act* in Canada is protected under design *patents*, the impact of such patent monopolies has been considered at a broader public policy level.[139] Following the decision of the US Supreme Court

136 *Ibid.* at para. 64.

137 *Ibid.*

138 [2006] J.Q. no 15039 (Q.S.C.) [*T-Rex*].

139 One author argues that because the US Supreme Court in *TrafFix* focused solely on functionality and utility patents, it did not resolve the public policy issues in relation to design patents. Further, he argues that by distinguishing between functional features and those that are "ornamental," the Court opened the possibility to argue that subject matter protected by design patents was inherently ornamental and thus non-functional. See Clifford W. Browning, "*TrafFix* Revisited: Exposing the Design Flaw in the Functionality Doctrine" (2004) 94 Trade-mark Rep. 1059 at 1061.

in *Wal-Mart Stores Inc. v. Samara Bros., Inc.*,[140] product configuration trade dress cannot be considered inherently distinctive, and distinctiveness must be proven. Where there has been a design patent registration, the registrant has received a fourteen-year period of exclusivity in which to establish such secondary meaning. The issue is whether this advantage, which flows from a statutory monopoly, should be permitted to be extended in perpetuity under trade-marks legislation. In *WCC Containers*, Kelen J. had found that the shape of the respondent's container was distinctive in a trade-mark sense. Yet his finding of distinctiveness was, in part, based on the fact that there were no other similarly shaped containers in the marketplace. This was a function of the monopoly protection flowing from the industrial design registration. In his discussion of distinctiveness, he cited the following statement from one of the respondent's witnesses: "the sloped bin's 'apparent refusal to topple over draws the eye and is readily remembered.'"[141] The statement neatly conflates functionality with distinctiveness and reveals the policy problems in relying upon distinctiveness that may owe its origin to a prior period of monopoly protection.

In writing about this policy dilemma, one US author argues that different analyses should be applied for design patents than for utility patents. He writes:

> When a court is presented with a trade dress infringement for an existing or expired design patent, it faces a perplexing obstacle. If the court grants an injunction for that which was claimed in a design patent, i.e. the design, it would effectively be extending the term of the patent beyond its statutory life, a result that should not occur. An alternative for the court is to require the infringer to properly label the design, thereby decreasing the likelihood of confusion to the original source of the goods and satisfying the intentions of patent law that, upon expiration of the statutory term, what was claimed is free for the public to use and copy.[142]

---

140 120 S. Ct. 1339 (2000) [*Wal-Mart*].

141 *WCC Containers*, above note 130 at para. 35.

142 Moshe H. Bonder, "*Patent* and *Lanham Acts*: Serving Two Legitimate Purposes or Providing an Indefinite Monopoly?" (2004) 15 Alb. L.J. Sci. & Tech. 1 at 26–27.

The issue of the relationship between industrial design registrations and trade-mark distinguishing guises remains unresolved in Canada. Zimmerman argues that there is "a very good argument for disallowing trade-mark protection in aesthetic features previously protected by a now-expired industrial design."[143] He asserts three main arguments that are similar to the policy considerations underlying the functionality doctrine. He notes that, with industrial design protection, goodwill associated with the design can grow absent of any competition during the period of registration. In addition, it is possible that a perpetual trade-mark monopoly over a particular design may hamper the development of the industry. In such contexts, the *quid pro quo* of monopoly protection — the dedication to the public of the subject matter of the monopoly following its expiration — disappears.[144] Given the Supreme Court's strong policy-based approach in *Kirkbi*, arguments of the kind raised in *WCC Containers* may well deserve revisiting.

In the UK, *Coca-Cola Co.'s Applications*[145] raised a similar issue in the context of an application for registration of the distinctive shape of the Coca-Cola bottle as a trade-mark. The bottle had previously enjoyed a fifteen-year period of protection under the *Registered Designs Act, 1949*.[146] The Court rejected the application, stating that it was "not sufficient for the Coca-Cola bottle to be distinctive."[147] The case is not particularly helpful in that the UK trade-marks legislation at that time did not contemplate the registration of distinguishing guises, and the Court was clearly opposed to this practice. However, it is worth noting that the House of Lords characterized this case as "another attempt to expand on the boundaries of intellectual property and to convert a protective law into a source of monopoly."[148]

v) Registered and Unregistered Trade-Marks

Kirkbi involved an action for passing off under section 7(b) of the *Trade-marks Act*. The plaintiffs accepted that the doctrine of functionality applied in the registration of trade-marks but argued that it

143 Zimmerman, above note 133 at 347.

144 *Ibid.*

145 Above note 61.

146 (UK), 12, 13 &14 Geo. VI., c. 88.

147 *Coca-Cola Co.'s Applications*, above note 61 at 276.

148 *Ibid.* at 275.

did not apply to unregistered marks. The majority of the Federal Court of Appeal had ruled that an action under section 7(b) to protect an unregistered trade-mark could only be brought with respect to those marks that qualified as "trade-marks" under the Act, and that, as the doctrine of functionality applied to "distinguishing guises" under the *Trade-marks Act*, it would apply to unregistered trade-marks in section 7(b) actions as well. The Supreme Court of Canada made no such express distinction, stating simply that "registered or not, marks share common legal attributes."[149] It remains unclear whether the Court's reasoning in *Kirkbi* applies only to section 7(b) actions, because of their link to the statute, or whether it applies as well to the common law tort of passing off. Most commentators are of the view that the two actions are equivalent.[150] Stratton and Lue conclude that *Kirkbi* renders the doctrine of functionality "equally applicable to registered and unregistered marks as there is no fundamental difference between these types of marks."[151] Because the Court seems to make no real distinction between the two, it is likely that the same doctrine would apply at common law. However, as will be discussed below, the approach taken to functionality has varied in common law passing-off actions.

Most of the cases on functionality discussed by the Supreme Court of Canada involved issues of the registrability or validity of allegedly functional marks under the *Trade-marks Act*. *Parke, Davis* is a partial exception, in that the plaintiffs had alleged both trade-mark infringement (to which the defence of invalidity because of functionality was raised) and passing off (to which lack of distinctiveness was the response). In most of the cases, therefore, the litigation followed this general structure: trade-mark infringement was alleged by the plaintiff, and the defendant argued that the marks in question were not registrable because they consisted of functional features.[152] In such cases, functionality is the central focus of inquiry because functional

---

149 *Kirkbi*, above note 2 at para. 58.

150 See for example, A.K. Gill, R.S. Jolliffe, and H.G. Fox, *Fox on Canadian Law of Trade-marks and Unfair Competition*, 4th ed., looseleaf (Toronto: Thompson Carswell, 2004) at §4.2(e).

151 Bruce W. Stratton and Henry Lue, "*LEGO v. Mega Bloks* in the Supreme Court of Canada: Ephemeral Rights in Toy Bricks" (2006) 96 Trade-mark Rep. 587 at 594.

152 Of course, other arguments might be made as well, but this is our focus here.

features of a product may not be registered as trade-marks under the Act.

Distinctiveness is an explicit statutory requirement for registration of a distinguishing guise. It is also a requirement of common law trade-marks, as a mark is not protected at common law unless it has acquired distinctiveness. Yet the role of distinctiveness in the analysis of distinguishing guises is not addressed in *Kirkbi.* Arguably it is not necessary to consider distinctiveness, as once a feature is found to be functional it cannot serve as a trade-mark. Nevertheless, as will be seen in the discussion below, distinctiveness plays a role in comparable US caselaw, and its role in relation to distinguishing guises should not be ignored, particularly in common law passing-off actions.

In passing-off cases, the issues are often framed in a somewhat different manner. Thus, for example, in *Eli Lilly,* a brand name drug manufacturer sued the defendant generic company for passing off, arguing that, by using tablet shapes and colours that were very close to those of the brand name product, it was passing off its product as that of the brand name company. The shape and colour of the tablets could easily be characterized as a distinguishing guise, yet the focus of inquiry in the case was whether the appearance of the brand name tablets was distinctive of Eli Lilly as a source of the product, or whether it was relied upon as indicative of other things such as the kind of medication and the dosage. Justice Reed concluded that the plaintiffs had not succeeded in proving "that the *capsule appearance* has acquired the requisite reputation in the market place as a distinguishing feature of the plaintiffs' product."[153] She also found that there was no likelihood of confusion as to trade source as a result.[154]

The issue of pharmaceutical tablets is an interesting one. In *Ciba-Geigy v. Apotex Inc.,*[155] the Supreme Court of Canada noted in passing that some features of tablets or capsules were dictated by functional considerations and gave the examples that they must be of a size and shape capable of being easily ingested. However, the Court treated other aspects of the appearance (such as colour) as being an issue of

153 *Eli Lilly,* above note 35 at 422 [emphasis in original].

154 *Ibid.* at 423 and 425.

155 [1992] 3 S.C.R. 120.

distinctiveness. In *Eli Lilly*,[156] Reed J.'s conclusion is essentially that the colour of medical tablets can be distinctive of things other than source. This gives a *function* to the colour and shape of the tablets — that of indicating the type and dosage of medication. Indeed, Reed J. makes reference to the US Supreme Court's decision in *Qualitex*,[157] which discussed whether colour alone could constitute a trade-mark. The Court in that case noted that the functionality doctrine might apply in some cases where colour gave a marketplace advantage and gave the example of the colour of a medical pill serving as an indicator of the type of medicine.

Essentially, then, in passing-off cases (whether under section 7(b) or at common law) functionality is often considered in an assessment of distinctiveness. In other words, the question is as follows: is the feature distinctive of source, or does it lack distinctiveness because it is a functional characteristic of the product? A finding of functionality is therefore a finding of lack of distinctiveness, and the feature is disqualified from serving as a trade-mark.[158] However, this approach may lead to results different from an absolute bar to a finding that a functional feature has acquired distinctiveness. Arguably, a passing-off approach leaves somewhat more room for a feature with some degree of functionality to serve as a trade-mark.

In the United States the caselaw seems to suggest that in the case of unregistered trade-marks, and where what is at issue is product-design trade dress, an inquiry into distinctiveness is a first step in the analysis. US caselaw suggests a difference in approach between cases involving unregistered trade-marks and those involving registered marks. In *Wal-Mart* the US Supreme Court indicated that an unregistered trade dress must be distinctive of source and non-functional.[159] The Court in *Wal-Mart* identified distinctiveness as a key first issue. It developed a specific approach to distinctiveness in trade dress cases depending on the kind of trade dress at issue. It distinguished between product-design trade dress (which cannot be inherently distinctive) and product-packaging trade dress (which can be). Trade-mark subject matter that

156 Above note 35.

157 Above note 122.

158 *Parke, Davis*, above note 35 at 354–55.

159 Above note 140 at 1343.

is inherently distinctive does not require proof of secondary meaning in the United States. However, product-design trade dress can never be inherently distinctive. As a result, "in an action for infringement of unregistered trade dress under § 43(a) of the *Lanham Act*, a product's design is distinctive and therefore protectable, only upon a showing of secondary meaning."[160] Thus the Court in *Wal-Mart* established two streams of inquiry for trade dress cases involving unregistered marks. Where the trade dress is product packaging, it is necessary to determine if the packaging is inherently distinctive. If it is, there is no need to show secondary meaning. If it is not, then secondary meaning must be established. Trade dress that is product *design* is never inherently distinctive; secondary meaning must always be established. Of course, it is not always clear whether what is at issue is product or packaging. For example, in the case of the shape or colour of pills or tablets, it is debatable whether one is dealing with packaging or the wares themselves.[161]

The distinctiveness component of the two-part inquiry into the protectability of trade dress in the US is of great importance when dealing with issues of product design. With an allegedly distinctive product-design trade dress, the inquiry would first be into whether the appearance of the product was distinctive of source, or merely of the product itself. Once distinctiveness is established, the doctrine of functionality can be invoked as a defence to infringement. The existence of a prior patent becomes "strong evidence" of functionality where the

---

160 *Ibid.* at 1346. There are elements of this approach in some Canadian cases, but it does not feature in *Kirkbi*, above note 2, which focuses instead on a bald principle of functionality flowing from a distinction between the territory covered by patents and that covered by trade-marks.

161 In the US, another layer of complexity is added in that trade dress can also exist in relation to service marks. In *Two Pesos Inc. v. Taco Cabana Inc.*, 505 U.S. 763 (1992), the US Supreme Court found that the interior décor of a chain of Mexican restaurants was trade dress in relation to restaurant services. As this was neither packaging nor wares, the Court placed it in a category of its own, a *tertium quid*. In Canada, a trade-mark that is a distinguishing guise under the *Trade-marks Act* must be in relation to the shape or packaging of *wares* (see definition of "distinguishing guise" in s. 2, *Trade-marks Act*, above note 16). Nevertheless, it is possible to seek protection for the "get-up" of a restaurant. See for example, *Mr. Submarine Ltd. v. Bikas* (1975), 24 C.P.R. (2d) 135 (Ont. H.C.); *Mr. Submarine Ltd. v. Emma Foods Ltd.* (1976), 34 C.P.R. (2d) 177 (Ont. H.C.); *Mr. Submarine Ltd. v. Voultsos* (1977), 36 C.P.R. (2d) 270 (Ont. H.C.).

features alleged to be trade dress are claimed in the prior patent. While the doctrine of functionality continues to play a role, it is clear that it comes into play only after an inquiry into the issue of distinctiveness.

vi) The Trade-mark

Kirkbi involved an issue of whether a particular product shape could be considered a trade-mark under section 7(b), notwithstanding the fact that it was functional in nature. A product shape clearly fits the definition of a distinguishing guise, which includes the shape of wares or their containers, or a mode of wrapping or packaging wares. It is clear from *Kirkbi* that the doctrine of functionality applies to those things that are encompassed by this definition. The caselaw prior to *Kirkbi* suggests that the doctrine of functionality applied also to features that do not fit the definition of "distinguishing guise." For example, in *Imperial Tobacco,* Justice Maclean found that the cellophane wrapper with the tear strip that was at issue did not fit the statutory definition, which was, at the time "a mode of shaping, moulding, wrapping or packing wares."[162] He found that the box in which the cigarettes were sold was the mode of wrapping or packing the wares, and the cellophane wrapper was something different. He ruled that it was not a distinguishing guise, but also held, more generally, that something that is functional in nature was not the proper subject matter of a trade-mark.[163] In *Parke, Davis,* the Supreme Court of Canada did not apparently limit its holding to distinguishing guises when it ruled that "the coloured bands have a functional use or characteristic and cannot, therefore, be the subject of a trade-mark."[164] In *Elgin Handles,* the appearance of the tool handles after the fire-hardening process was not a mode of shaping of the wares, nor was it a mode of wrapping or packaging the wares. The Court cited *Parke, Davis* for the proposition that an item that has a functional use or characteristic cannot serve as a trade-mark.[165] The decision of the Court in *Elgin Handles* was not about distinguishing guises and functionality, but about the principle

162 *Imperial Tobacco,* above note 73 at 146, citing s. 2(d) of the *Unfair Competition Act,* R.S.C. 1952, c. 274: definition of "distinguishing guise".

163 *Ibid.* at 145. Cited with approval by the Supreme Court of Canada in *Kirkbi,* above note 2 at para. 45.

164 *Parke, Davis,* above note 35 at 354.

165 *Elgin Handles,* above note 73 at para. 10.

of functionality more generally. In other words, "the thing registered cannot be a trade mark if it has a functional use or characteristic."[166] In *Pizza Pizza*[167] as well, the Court examined the telephone number trade-mark from the point of view of functionality, notwithstanding the fact that it was clearly not a distinguishing guise.

Although the Supreme Court of Canada in *Kirkbi* does nothing to change the broader functionality doctrine (i.e., that which extends beyond distinguishing guises), its discussion of the functionality doctrine in relation to unregistered trade-marks focuses exclusively on distinguishing guises. Essentially, the argument before the Court was that the change of the definition of distinguishing guise to remove any reference to functionality meant that a distinguishing guise could have a functional dimension in an unregistered trade-mark; functionality operated merely as a bar to registration under section 13(2) of the *Trade-marks Act*. The Court ruled that this interpretation was not legitimate, and that the doctrine of functionality applied.[168] It would have been helpful to note that the doctrine of functionality has not, in any event, been limited to those things that fall under the definition of a distinguishing guise.

d) Summary

Kirkbi has clarified some aspects of the application of the doctrine of functionality and its role in limiting the extension of patent rights through trade-mark law. The Court made a very clear statement of the public policy underlying the doctrine and emphasized that it was contrary to this public policy to extend patent monopolies over the functional features of products by using trade-mark law. It also made it clear that the doctrine of functionality applied both to registered and unregistered trade-marks. In the context of a prior patent, the Court also indicated that where a feature is specifically claimed in a patent, there is strong evidence of functionality.

Yet the decision did not resolve all of the issues that arise in relation to issues of functionality and trade-mark law. This is due in part to the fairly limited set of facts with which the Court was presented,

166 *Ibid.* at para. 19.

167 Above note 38.

168 *Kirkbi*, above note 2.

and in part to the fact that the issues before it were relatively easy as far as functionality inquiries go. Yet it is also in part due to the Court's insistence that the principle was well-established in prior caselaw, and that this caselaw led to a single and undisputed principle. In fact, earlier caselaw suggests that two possible rules emerge, a broad rule and a narrow rule, and it is not entirely clear which of these rules the Court ultimately embraces.

Kirkbi also does not answer all of the questions that might arise where a product feature is referenced in a prior patent. While the Court makes it clear that the actual claiming of a feature in the patent claims is strong evidence of functionality, it does not address more difficult issues. For example, it does not resolve the issues raised in *Panduit*, where the feature appeared in a drawing in the patent specification, but was not specifically claimed. Nor does it address whether a feature claimed in the patent claims, but which later becomes non-essential to the essence of the invention, can ever become a trade-mark.

US caselaw addresses functionality in a fairly nuanced way, referencing not only the use or purpose of the article, but also its cost or quality. *Kirkbi* focuses on use or purpose and does not address the economic dimensions of functionality. Thus it remains unclear the extent to which features affecting the cost or quality of a product can be considered functional in Canadian law.

Kirkbi also does not resolve the issue of whether the same public policy values articulated in the case apply to instances where a product appearance, protected under the *Industrial Design Act*, can later be claimed as a trade-mark under the *Trade-marks Act*. Indeed, prior to *Kirkbi*, such a design might well be eligible to become a trade-mark. However, because of the Court's policy-based approach to the issues in *Kirkbi*, there may now be a new basis for arguments that this position should be changed.

The decision of the Court in *Kirkbi* does not sit entirely well with caselaw that has evolved in passing off or under the equivalent delict in Quebec. While functionality may be an issue where an unregistered trade-mark is claimed, the Court seems to suggest that the inquiry into functionality is the departure point in considering the existence of an unregistered trade-mark. Yet passing off caselaw in Canada seems to begin with an inquiry into distinctiveness. Functionality may be relevant to the issue of distinctiveness. It may also arise as a defense after it has been established that the features at issue have become distinctive of source. This is consistent as well with caselaw in the US dealing with unregistered trade-marks and passing off.

Finally, *Kirkbi* dealt with product features that clearly fit the definition of "distinguishing guise" in the *Trade-marks Act.* However, the doctrine of functionality has also been applied more broadly in Canada to a range of features that would not meet this definition in the *Trade-marks Act.* While nothing in *Kirkbi* undermines this broader application of the doctrine of functionality, the decision is focused exclusively on the relationship of the doctrine of functionality to distinguishing guises under the *Trade-marks Act.*

The decision in *Kirkbi* is solid on its facts. It also presents a strong policy statement regarding overlapping intellectual property protection, particularly in the context of patents and trade-marks. The lacunae identified in the decision are in part due to issues not raised on the facts. These issues, which include the property policy to guide situations of overlap in trade-mark and industrial design protection and the appropriate approach to issues of functionality involving something more nuanced than features claimed in a prior patent, will likely remain to be decided on a case-by-case basis.

3) Copyright/Trade-mark Overlap

There has long been an overlap between trade-mark and copyright law protection, and this overlap has been accepted by judges in a number of cases.[169] The overlap occurs primarily in the protection given to design trade-marks as "artistic works" under the *Copyright Act.* Essentially, an original design is considered an artistic work under the *Copyright Act* and is thus entitled to a term of protection equivalent to the life of the artist plus fifty years. Where the design also serves as a trade-mark (such as a product logo), there is a dual layer of protection.

---

169 See for example, *Compagnie Générale des Etablissements Michelin – Michelin & Cie v. National Automobile, Aerospace, Transportation and General Workers Union of Canada (CAW-Canada),* [1997] 2 F.C.R. 306 (T.D.) [*Michelin*]; *Rotisseries St-Hubert Ltée v. Syndicat des Travailleurs de la Rotisserie St. Hubert de Drummondville (C.S.N.)* (1986), 17 C.P.R. (3d) 461 (Que. S.C.) [*Rotisseries St-Hubert*]; *British Columbia Automobile Assn v. Office and Professional Employees' International Union, Local 378* (2001), 10 C.P.R. (4th) 423 (B.C.S.C.).

This becomes particularly important where the protection afforded to a design trade-mark under trade-mark law is more limited than that available to the design under copyright law.

The protection available to trade-marks is limited in a number of respects. Trade-mark law does not generally apply to prevent non-commercial uses of logos or design marks.[170] By contrast, copyright law can be used to prohibit virtually all unauthorized reproductions of such designs. Thus in *Compagnie Générale des Etablissements Michelin – Michelin & Cie v. National Automobile, Aerospace, Transportation and General Workers Union of Canada (CAW-Canada)*,[171] a union was enjoined from using a parodic depiction of Michelin's Bibendum (or, commonly, the Michelin Man) on informational pamphlets because the depiction violated Michelin's copyright; the same use did not infringe the Bibendum trade-mark. It is interesting to note that in another line of cases, courts have ruled that single words or even short phrases are not entitled to be protected as literary works under the *Copyright Act*, in part because of the impact this would have on the public's ability to criticize or comment on businesses holding word trade-marks.[172]

The discussion in the section below will consider this copyright/trade-mark overlap in the context of the parallel importation of goods. Parallel importation, also known as grey-marketing, involves the importation of legal goods outside of an authorized distribution network. In 1980 the Supreme Court of Canada considered the legality of grey-marketing in the context of passing off litigation. In *Seiko Time Canada v. Consumers Distributing*[173] the Court made it clear there was nothing inherently illegal about grey-marketing. In a unanimous judgment, the Court ruled that consumers were entitled to benefit from the lower prices and increased choices that open competition in the marketplace would bring. Since *Seiko Time*, a few attempts have been made to use trade-mark law to prevent parallel importation. Yet, except in cases where deliberate attempts at deception were involved, they have been

---

170 *Trade-marks Act*, above note 16, s. 4 articulates what constitutes "use" of a trade-mark. See also *Clairol International Corp. v. Thomas Supply & Equipment Co. Ltd.* (1968), 55 C.P.R. 176 (Ex. Ct.).

171 *Michelin*, above note 169.

172 See for example, *Exxon Corporation v. Exxon Insurance Consultants International Ltd.*, [1982] R.P.C. 69, [1981] 3 All E.R. 241 (C.A.).

173 Above note 10.

largely unsuccessful.[174] This section will examine the extent to which copyright law can be used to limit or prevent parallel importation of legally branded goods, notwithstanding the policy choices reflected in the *Trade-marks Act* and articulated by the courts.

The issue has arisen squarely in the Canadian context in the recent case *Euro Excellence v. Kraft Canada Inc.*[175] This case involved an attempt to use copyright law to prevent the parallel importation of non-copyright goods. The copyright issues in this case deal solely with trade-mark design features of the product labels. The case squarely raised public policy issues that relate to the overlap between copyright and trade-mark law. Although the Supreme Court of Canada ultimately ruled against Kraft Canada in its attempt to block the parallel importation of certain chocolate bars, this result seems to be only because of a combination of the split on the court and the manner in which Kraft Canada formulated its strategy and not because of any underlying principle against using copyright law to prevent parallel importation. The Court was deeply divided, however, on the issues of statutory interpretation as well as on the underlying policy questions raised by the case.

a) The Case[176]

Euro Excellence involved a lawsuit by Kraft Canada Inc. (Kraft Canada) against Euro Excellence, Inc. (Euro Excellence) in relation to the im-

---

174 See for example, *Sony du Canada Ltée v. Impact Electronique* (1991), 39 C.P.R. (3d) 414 (Que. S.C.) [*Sony v. Impact Electronique*]; *Sony du Canada Ltée v. Multitronic* (1991), 42 C.P.R. (3d) 53 (Que. C.A.) [*Sony v. Multitronic*] (selling refurbished goods as new goods); *Sharp Electronics of Canada Ltd. v. Continental Electronic Info, Inc.* (1988), 23 C.P.R. (3d) 330 (B.C.S.C.) [*Sharp Electronics*] (injunction granted against the sale of machines that had not been approved according to relevant safety standards). Where differences in quality are at issue, appropriate labeling may be sufficient. See *Nestle Enterprises Ltd. v. Edan Food Sales, Inc.* (1991), 37 C.P.R. (3d) 480 (F.C.T.D.).

175 Above note 9.

176 For a discussion of the decisions of the courts below, see: Teresa Scassa, "Using Copyright Law to Prevent Parallel Importation: A Comment on *Kraft Canada, Inc. v. Euro Excellence, Inc.*" (2006) 85 Can. Bar Rev. 409. For a thoughtful comment on the decision of the Supreme Court of Canada, see: Mistrale Goudreau, "Commentaire d'arrêt : l'affaire *Euro-Excellence Inc. c. Kraft Canada Inc.* en Cour supreme" (2007) 37 Rev. Gen. de Droit 409.

portation and sale of Côte d'Or and Toblerone chocolate bars in Canada. These bars are manufactured in Europe by Kraft Foods Belgium S.A. and Kraft Foods Schweiz AG respectively. In 1993, Kraft Foods Belgium authorized Euro Excellence to act as the Canadian distributor of its Côte d'Or bars in Canada. This contract later became an exclusive Canadian distribution agreement, which came to an end in 2000. In 2001, Kraft Canada took up distribution of the Côte d'Or bars in Canada. Euro Excellence managed to obtain Côte d'Or bars from an undisclosed European source and continued to distribute them in Quebec. At the same time, it began to import Toblerone bars, which had been exclusively distributed in Canada by Kraft Canada since 1993.

Euro Excellence argued that Kraft Canada "was acting in a predatory manner, wanted to take advantage of its contacts and goodwill and is trying to sacrifice it on the altar of multinational integration."[177] Kraft Canada accused Euro Excellence of free-riding on Kraft Canada's marketing campaigns. Since the goods were not counterfeit goods, and the trade-marks correctly identified the source of the goods, it was clear that trade-mark law or the law of passing off would not be much help to Kraft Canada. Instead, Kraft Canada proceeded against Euro Excellence using arguments based in copyright law.

The doctrine of exhaustion in copyright law means that once a legitimate copy of a work is sold, the owner of the copyright has exhausted its rights with respect to the further sale of that copy. However, if a copy is infringing, exhaustion does not apply. The secondary infringement provisions of the *Copyright Act* apply to dealings with infringing copies of works, including the importation of these infringing works. In order to bring the activities of Euro Excellence within the secondary infringement provisions, Kraft Foods Belgium registered copyrights in the Côte d'Or elephant logo, the Côte d'Or script, and the red shield used on the labels. Kraft Foods Schweiz registered the copyright in its distinctive Toblerone bear and mountain design. Each of the European companies then entered into licensing agreements with Kraft Canada, giving Kraft Canada

> the sole and exclusive right and license in the Territory to produce, reproduce and adapt the Works or any substantial part thereof, in any

177 *Kraft Canada* (FC), above note 9 at para. 13.

> material form whatever, and to use and publicly present the Works in association with the manufacture, distribution or sale in Canada of confectionary products, including, but not limited to, chocolate.[178]

Kraft Canada demanded that Euro Excellence cease and desist from importing and distributing the bars bearing the copyrighted works. It argued that the wording of section 27(2) of the *Copyright Act* supported its demand. When Euro Excellence refused to cease importing the bars, Kraft Canada sued for copyright infringement. Although a range of arguments were made by Euro Excellence in its defence, including challenges to the validity of the copyrights, the case essentially turned on the interpretation of the infringement by importation provisions of the *Copyright Act*.

b) Secondary Infringement

Infringement by importation is a form of secondary infringement of copyright. Primary infringement occurs where one or more of the exclusive rights of the copyright holder are exercised by another without the copyright holder's consent. Secondary infringement involves certain dealings with infringing copies of works, such as their sale, distribution, or importation. The persons who deal in such a manner with an infringing work must know or be imputed to know that the copies they are dealing with infringe copyright. The activities that constitute secondary infringement are set out in section 27(2) of the *Copyright Act*:

> 27(2) It is an infringement of copyright for any person to
> (a) sell or rent out,
> (b) distribute to such an extent as to affect prejudicially the owner of the copyright,
> (c) by way of trade distribute, expose or offer for sale or rental, or exhibit in public,
> (d) possess for the purpose of doing anything referred to in paragraphs (a) to (c), or
> (e) import into Canada for the purpose of doing anything referred to in paragraphs (a) to (c),

---

178 *Ibid.* at para. 18.

> a copy of a work, sound recording or fixation of a performer's performance or of a communication signal that the person knows or should have known infringes copyright or would infringe copyright if it had been made in Canada by the person who made it.

In *Euro Excellence*, Kraft Canada argued that the artistic works on the wrappers were imported and distributed by Euro Excellence in violation of section 27(2). Kraft Canada argued that the works would have infringed upon its exclusive licence to reproduce the works in Canada had they been made in Canada by the European-based companies who printed the European labels. As such, the works were imported in violation of section 27(2)(e). Kraft Canada also argued that Euro Excellence's possession and distribution of the infringing works also violated sub-paragraphs 27(2)(b) and (d). It was argued that this interpretation of the law was supported by section 2.7 of the *Copyright Act*, which reads:

> 2.7 For the purposes of this Act, an exclusive licence is an authorization to do any act that is subject to copyright to *the exclusion of all others including the copyright owner*, whether the authorization is granted by the owner or an exclusive licensee claiming under the owner.[179]

Section 13(7) is also relevant to the issue of the scope of exclusive licences. It provides:

> 13(7) For greater certainty, it is deemed always to have been the law that a grant of an exclusive licence in a copyright *constitutes the grant of an interest* in the copyright by licence.[180]

According to Kraft Canada, therefore, their exclusive licence amounted to a grant of an interest and not a mere authorization to reproduce the copyrighted works. As an exclusive licensee, they were also empowered to sue for infringement of their exclusive rights.[181]

---

179 [Emphasis added].

180 [Emphasis added].

181 *Copyright Act*, above note 16, s. 36. Under s. 36(2) they would be required to join the copyright owner as a party, which they did in this case. See also David Vaver, *Copyright Law* (Toronto: Irwin Law, 2000) at 240–41 [Vaver].

Both the Federal Court and the Court of Appeal ruled in favour of Kraft Canada. Both courts were of the opinion that a proper interpretation of the provisions of the *Copyright Act* required them to find secondary infringement on the facts. While both courts acknowledged the public policy issues raised by Euro Excellence, neither court felt that it would be appropriate to deviate from what they considered to be the plain meaning of the Act. For example, Justice Harrington concluded: "I have found in Kraft's favour because I think the *Copyright Act* compels me to."[182]

The remedy crafted by Harrington J. was an injunction that prohibited the importation of the bars in their copyright-protected wrappers for sale or distribution. However, he noted: "[t]here is nothing to prevent Euro Excellence from replacing the wrappers or otherwise covering over the copyright material."[183] In a subsequent ruling,[184] he approved of a plastic film placed over the logos on the bars by Euro Excellence and permitted the distribution of the bars so long as the copyright-protected logos were covered.

The case was appealed to the Federal Court of Appeal. In a unanimous opinion, the Federal Court of Appeal upheld the decision of Harrington J. Justice Desjardins was clearly of the view that the plain meaning of the legislation dictated the outcome of the case.

It was not until the case reached the Supreme Court of Canada that the public policy issues raised by Euro Excellence found a receptive audience in the form of the dissenting opinion of Justices Bastarache, LeBel, and Charron. The Court was badly split, making it difficult to extract majority and dissenting views. The following brief summary of positions can be offered, followed by a more detailed examination of the public policy considerations addressed by the Court.

Justice Rothstein wrote for himself and Binnie and Deschamps JJ. He found in favour of Euro Excellence on the relatively narrow point that the assignment of an exclusive licence to Kraft Canada by the European-based Kraft companies could not achieve the desired effect under section 27(2). In the view of Rothstein J., an exclusive licensee of

---

182 *Kraft Canada* (FC), above note 9 at para. 61.

183 *Ibid.* at para. 60.

184 *Kraft Canada Inc. v. Euro Excellence* (2004), 33 C.P.R. (4th) 242, 2004 FC 832 [*Kraft Canada* (injunction)].

copyright could not sue the owner of copyright for copyright infringement. The interest they held fell short of ownership. In order to succeed under section 27(2)(e), Kraft Canada had to establish that the imported works would have infringed copyright in Canada had they been made by the parties who made them in Europe. As Kraft Canada could not pursue Kraft Schweiz or Kraft Belgium for copyright infringement, they could not make out this essential element of secondary infringement by importation. In a separate set of reasons, Justice Fish agreed with this outcome. However, the remaining five judges all expressed the view that nothing would limit the rights of an exclusive licensee in this regard. Thus an exclusive licensee of the right to reproduce a work could sue the copyright owner for copyright infringement and is therefore entitled to rely upon section 27(2)(*e*) of the *Copyright Act* with respect to parallel importations of works bearing copyright designs legitimately placed on the goods by the foreign copyright owner but imported into Canada in contravention of the rights of a Canadian exclusive licensee.

Justice Abella and Chief Justice McLachlin took an approach to the issues that echoed that of the courts below. Essentially, they found that the law permitted Kraft Canada to sue for secondary infringement in the circumstances of the case, and that, where the law was clear, it was not appropriate for judges to create limitations based on public policy issues. Abella J. wrote: "To inject an exception for logos on the basis that they are 'incidental' would be to introduce unnecessary uncertainty, inviting case-by-case judicial explorations into the uncharted area of what is 'merely' incidental, 'somewhat' incidental or not incidental at all."[185] She also refused to countenance an approach (put forth by Bastarache J. in dissent) that would interpret the Act so as to protect only the "legitimate economic interests" of copyright holders.[186] Although differing on the issue of the scope of the rights of an exclusive licensee, Rothstein, Binnie, and Deschamps JJ. were in firm agreement about the role of the courts with respect to clearly worded legislation. Justice Rothstein cautioned against interpretations that would have the effect of amending the law: "If Parliament decides that this result is problematic, it can amend the *Copyright Act*. In the meantime, this Court must apply the Act that Parliament has given us."[187]

185 *Euro Excellence*, above note 9 at para. 111.
186 *Ibid.*, Bastarache J. at paras. 85–86, cited by Abella J. at para. 112.
187 *Ibid.*, Rothstein J. at para. 50.

As to the policy-based arguments of Bastarache J., Rothstein J. was blunt. He wrote:

> I accept, of course, that the *Copyright Act* is to be given a purposive interpretation. However, I distinguish between an approach that is rooted in the words of the Act and the approach taken by my colleague Bastarache J. that involves reading words into the legislation that are at odds with Parliament's intent.[188]

It is therefore clear that a majority of the judges of the Court rejected a policy-based interpretation that would effectively limit the scope of the secondary infringement provisions of the *Copyright Act* when dealing with so-called "incidental" works.

By contrast, Bastarache J., who was supported in his reasons by LeBel and Charron JJ., was clearly influenced by arguments based on public policy. He would have interpreted the *Copyright Act* so as to preclude a finding of infringement on facts such as these. He wrote:

> Thus s. 27(2)(e) is meant to protect copyright holders from the unauthorized importation of works which are the result of their skill and judgment. It is not meant to protect manufacturers from the unauthorized importation of consumer goods on the basis of their having a copyrighted work affixed to their wrapper, this work being merely incidental to their value as consumer goods.[189]

In order to achieve this result, Bastarache J. was forced to distinguish between "legitimate" and "illegitimate" economic interests — a point on which he was soundly criticized by both Rothstein and Abella JJ. He wrote:

> This interpretation of s. 27(2) respects copyright's insistence that only *legitimate* economic interests receive copyright protection. To allow s. 27(2) to protect all interests of manufacturers and distributors of consumer goods would upset the copyright balance.[190]

---

188 *Ibid.* at para. 9.

189 *Ibid.* at para. 86, Bastarache J.

190 *Ibid.* at para. 88 [emphasis in original]. The concept of "legitimate interests" also appears in this passage: "The *CCH* decision thus confirms that in order to protect the essential balance which lies at the heart of copyright law, care must be taken to ensure that copyright protection is not allowed to extend beyond the legitimate interests of a copyright holder" (see para. 80).

Justice Rothstein criticized this approach, noting that a decision by courts to protect only "legitimate" economic interests would introduce a "new equitable doctrine of 'legitimate economic interest' to read down the legislation."[191]

Bastarache J. also ventured upon a discussion of the proper scope of trade-mark law and the issue of overlapping intellectual property protection. He wrote:

> This focus on the fundamental natures and purposes of different sorts of intellectual property protections and the necessary divisions between them suggests that each form of protection relies on some core normative notion which must ground the economic interests claimed. Thus, a trade-mark, which protects distinctiveness of marketing and goodwill, cannot be leveraged to extend protection to products themselves, which is usually granted by patent.
>
> . . . Trade-mark law protects market share in commercial goods; copyright protects the economic gains resulting from an exercise of skill and judgment. If trade-mark law does not protect market share in a particular situation, the law of copyright should not be used to provide that protection, if that requires contorting copyright outside its normal sphere of operation. The protection offered by copyright cannot be leveraged to include protection of economic interests that are only tangentially related to the copyrighted work.[192]

On this point, Bastarache J. received some support from Fish J. In separate reasons, Fish J. had subscribed to the reasons of Rothstein J., opting to decide the case on the basis of an interpretation of the scope of the rights of an exclusive licensee. However, he did also indicate some sympathy for the policy-based arguments of Bastarache J. He wrote: "I express grave doubt whether the law governing the protection of intellectual property rights in Canada can be transformed in this way into an instrument of trade control not contemplated by the *Copyright Act*."[193]

---

191 *Ibid.* at para. 8.

192 *Ibid.* at para. 82–83.

193 *Ibid.* at para. 56 (Fish J.).

c) The Australian Experience

Before considering in any detail the public policy issues that are at play in this case, it is worth looking at the Australian experience. A similar issue arose in Australia in the 1980s, and the Australian example was considered by the courts in *Euro Excellence*. It was taken to support the position that the secondary infringement provisions applied in the circumstances.

In *R & A Bailey & Co. v. Boccaccio Pty. Ltd.*[194] the makers of Bailey's Original Irish Cream raised both trade-mark and copyright issues against an importer of the product who acquired his stock from outside the authorized distribution network. Justice Young swiftly rejected the trade-mark infringement arguments. As the marks on the bottles were placed there by the trade-mark owner, to find infringement would "change the nature of the mark from a badge of origin to a badge of control."[195] He stated that the set of exclusive rights granted to the owner under the *Trade Marks Act 1955*[196] "only operates to prevent the sale in Australia of goods which are not the proprietor's but which are marked with the proprietor's mark."[197] A similar outcome would have resulted under Canadian law.

With the trade-mark arguments dismissed, the case turned on whether the importation of the bottles bearing copyright-protected labels was a form of secondary copyright infringement. Three general public policy arguments were raised to counter what appeared to be a matter of straightforward statutory interpretation. The first was that, where an artistic work is created to be a trade-mark, there is a general exception to the principle that an implied licence "cannot be inferred from the mere fact that the owner of the copyright has sold the goods without any express restriction on their subsequent disposal."[198] For artworks that are trade-marks, licence is implied as a matter of commercial necessity. Justice Young rejected this argument, noting that the general rule is that an implied copyright licence is not automatically inferred

---

194 (1986), 4 N.S.W.L.R. 701 (E.D.) [*Bailey's*].

195 *Ibid.* at 707.

196 (Cth.), s. 58.

197 Bailey's, above note 194 at 709–10.

198 From *Interstate Parcel Express Co. Pty. Ltd. v. Time-Life International (Netherlands) BV* (1977), 138 C.L.R. 534 at 545 (H.C.A.), cited *ibid.* at 712.

from the sale of the goods; there must be some basis in the contract of sale for a licence of intellectual property rights to be implied.

The second public policy argument was that a copyright owner who creates a work to serve as a trade-mark automatically surrenders any copyright protection that is inconsistent with the protection afforded under trade-mark law. This argument is based on the proposition that there should be, as a matter of policy, no overlap between trade-mark and copyright protection. This argument was rejected as lacking any foundation in law. According to Young J., there was a "wide proposition that a person who has both a trade mark and a copyright is generally entitled to protection against both."[199]

The third public policy argument was that "as every subsequent commercial dealing in the bottles involves a use of the trade mark, it is necessary that the owner of the copyright in the label be taken to have licensed or consented to any activity which is permitted by the trade mark legislation."[200] This appears to be a reformulation of the "no overlap" argument. Instead of framing "no overlap" as a basis for finding no copyright protection, this version of the argument maintains that the use of an artistic work as a trade-mark carries with it an implied licence to deal with the work in all ways consistent with trade-mark law. This argument was rejected on a number of grounds. Justice Young observed that it did not automatically follow that no further dealings could be made with the goods. The objection was to the labels and not to the underlying goods themselves. He also rejected the argument that copyright law should be subordinate to trade-mark law in this area. He concluded:

> Apart from the *British Leyland* case there has not been as far as I know any judicial indication of any policy of the law that where a person has more than one industrial property right, it can only avail it of the protection afforded to one of those rights and where there is a conflict it is copyright which is disregarded.[201]

---

199 Bailey's, above note 194 at 713.

200 *Ibid.* at 712.

201 *Ibid.* at 714.

Justice Young's conclusion was that the defendants had infringed copyright by "selling or by way of trade, offering or exposing for sale bottles with labels" protected by copyright law.[202]

d) Legislative Amendment in Australia

The decision in *Bailey's* touched off concerns that ultimately led to an amendment of the Australian *Copyright Act 1968*,[203] although reform was slow in coming. Ten years after a 1988 report by the Copyright Law Review Committee of Australia stated that the restriction on parallel importation of goods bearing design trade-marks was "an inappropriate use of copyright,"[204] amendments to the statute were introduced and passed into law. A government press release stated that the amendments were designed to "stop the practice of using copyright in artistic works on packages and labels to prevent businesses and individuals from importing and reselling legitimate products."[205]

The amendments of the Australian *Copyright Act* include product labels in the definition of an "accessory" to an article.[206] Accessories such as labels bearing artistic works would only be captured by the secondary infringement provisions of the Australian law if they are accessories to articles that themselves are protected by copyright, such as, for example, the artistic work or photograph on the cover of a compact disc containing songs. Section 44C of the Act explicitly states:

> 44C (1) The copyright in a work a copy of which is, or is on, or embodied in, a *non-infringing accessory* to an article is not infringed by importing the accessory with the article.
>
> (2) Section 38 does not apply to a copy of a work, being a copy that is, or is on, or embodied in, a *non-infringing accessory* to an

---

202 *Ibid.* at 704.

203 *Bill for Copyright Amendment Act (No. 1) 1998* (Cth.) and *Bill for Copyright Amendment Act (No. 2) 1998* (Cth.), enacted 15 July 1998.

204 Australian Copyright Council, "Recent Amendments to the Australian Copyright Act," by Libby Baulch (18 October 1998), online: www.copyright.org.au/pdf/acc/articles_pdf/A98n18.pdf [Baulch].

205 *Ibid.* at 6.

206 *Copyright Act 1968* (Cth.) Act No. 63 of 1968 as am., s. 10(1), definition of "accessory." Note that the definition also includes written instructions and warranty or other product information in the definition of accessory.

> article, if the importation of the accessory is not an infringement of copyright in the work.[207]

A "non-infringing accessory"[208] is defined as one made in a *Berne Convention*[209] country or in a country that is a member of the World Trade Organization. The making of the copy of the work embodied in the accessory must also be "authorised by the owner of the copyright in that country."[210]

The Australian solution prevents the use of copyright law to inhibit the parallel importation of goods solely on the basis that the label design or other accessories to the goods are copyright-protected works. The legislated solution reflects a policy choice that focuses on the value of open competition, with resulting price reductions and increased consumer choice.[211] It diminishes the monopolistic force of exclusive distribution arrangements since "[b]usinesses that presently don't have the rights to sell certain brands will now be able to source these brands from overseas and sell them."[212]

e) Public Policy

Before considering the public policy issues in detail, it is worth reflecting for a moment on the strategy adopted by Kraft Canada in conjunction with its European counterparts. Kraft maintained an exclusive distribution network for its Belgian and Swiss manufactured chocolate bars. The network relied on a series of contracts, and those within the distribution network were under obligations not to sell the bars outside of the network. By operating an exclusive distribution network, Kraft was in a position to control all aspects of the distribution and sale of the bars, including the kind of product available, the sales points for the products, and their price.

In terms of the Canadian market, it was clear that trade-mark law would be ineffective in stopping any sale or distribution of the bars out-

207 *Copyright Act 1968, ibid.*, s. 44C [emaphasis added].

208 *Ibid.*, s. 10(1), definition of "non-infringing accessory."

209 *Berne Convention for the Protection of Literary and Artistic Works* of 9 September 1886, 828 U.N.T.S. 221, as last revised 24 July 1971 [*Berne Convention*].

210 *Copyright Act 1968*, above note 206 at s. 10(1).

211 Baulch, above note 204 at 6.

212 *Ibid.*

side the exclusive distribution network. Trade-marks are meant to be distinctive of source, and Canadian courts have previously held that where products bear trade-marks that properly indicate the source of the goods, the trade-mark owner is not in a position to object to their sale on the basis that any trade-mark rights have been infringed.[213] For example, Justice Hugessen has stated: "Goods which originate in the stream of commerce with the owner of a trade mark are not counterfeit or infringing goods simply because they may have arrived in a particular geographical market where the trade mark owner does not wish them to be distributed."[214] There can be no consumer confusion as to the source of the goods if the trade-mark accurately identifies that source, even if the product enters the market through non-approved channels. Similarly, the law of passing off would not be available.[215] It would be very difficult to argue that the bars were being passed off as the wares of another trader, when they were so clearly marked as being the wares of Kraft.

By relying on copyright arguments based on artistic works printed on the product labels, Kraft Canada sought to prevent the importation of the bars in their original wrappers. In the Federal Court and Federal Court of Appeal it was able to obtain a remedy in relation to the use of trade-marks that was not available under trade-mark law. The decision of the Supreme Court of Canada does not ultimately preclude the strategy adopted. The fact that the trade-marks at issue were also copyrighted "works" allowed Kraft to protect its exclusive distribution network for the underlying product — the chocolate bars — which themselves were not copyright-protected works. In other words, Kraft Canada has a complete lock on who can import into Canada for sale Toblerone and Côte d'Or chocolate bars in their original, unadulterated wrappers, and bearing their distinctive trade-mark designs. The result eliminates the possibility that other importers/distributors could distribute legal bars in their original packaging, alongside the products imported by Kraft Canada.

The *Seiko Time* decision in Canada and the legislative policy underlying the Australian amendments both suggest that, absent de-

---

213 *Smith & Nephew Inc. v. Glen Oak, Inc.* (1986), 68 C.P.R. (3d) 153 (F.C.A.), leave to appeal to S.C.C. refused (1996), 68 C.P.R. (3d) vi.

214 *Ibid.* at para. 11.

215 *Seiko Time,* above note 10.

ception, allowing parallel importation serves the public policy goal of free and open competition in the marketplace, with resultant benefits to consumers. It is worth noting, however, that there are also policy arguments that favour restrictions on parallel importation. The Australian amendments were not without controversy. Authorized distributors lobbied against the amendments and argued that the status quo would "protect consumers from imported items which may be of inferior quality and may be unsafe, and that removing the parallel importation provisions allows importers to free-ride on the marketing paid for [*sic*] the authorized distributor."[216] The comments reflect two arguments.

The first is that parallel importation protects consumers from inferior or unsafe goods. Yet other laws or regulations can serve these public policy goals. In Canada, for example, trade-mark and passing-off laws have been effective in preventing the importation or sale of goods of an inferior, or at least different, quality from what would be expected.[217] In *Seiko Time*, where the goods were of the same quality, but there were issues around service and warranty recognition, Consumers Distributing was required by the Court to post a clearly visible notice to customers to inform them that Consumers Distributing was not an authorized distributor of the Seiko watches sold on its premises. In *Euro Excellence*, the plaintiff at one point argued that the labels on the chocolate bars distributed by Euro Excellence did

216 *Ibid.* Webster states: "Frequently, the gray marketer will be selling outdated products or products having components which are not readily serviceable or replaceable in Canada. In some cases, the gray marketed products may not comply with packaging, labeling, language or safety requirements." See W. Lee Webster, "Restraining the Gray Marketer: Policy and Practice" (1988) 4 C.I.P.R. 211 at 211 [Webster].

217 See for example, *Sony v. Impact Electronique*, above note 174, *Sony v. Multitronic*, above note 174, and *Sharp Electronics*, above note 174 for examples of circumstances when the sale of goods of different quality were successfully enjoined. In *H.J. Heinz Co. of Canada Ltd. v. Edan Foods Sales Inc.* (1991), 35 C.P.R. (3d) 213 (F.C.T.D.), Heinz Canada was successful in using trade-mark law to prevent the importation of ketchup made in the US, according to a slightly different recipe and bearing the Heinz marks registered in the US, by Heinz US. Heinz Canada was the registered owner of the Canadian Heinz trade-marks. Of course, it is certainly not always the case that the Canadian subsidiary will own the Canadian trade-marks. See Webster, *ibid.* at 215.

not meet federal product labeling requirements and thus might prove unsafe for consumers with allergies. This was purely speculative, however. Harrington J. dismissed this argument as being irrelevant to the issue before him, noting that such matters could be dealt with under legislation governing product labeling.[218]

The second argument put forward by opponents of parallel importation is that parallel importation permits unauthorized distributors to derive the benefits of the advertising and marketing efforts of the authorized distributor without incurring the costs. In this sense, it is a form of unfair competition. This argument, which was raised by those who opposed the Australian copyright amendments, was also put forth by the plaintiff in *Euro Excellence*.[219] It is based on the view that exclusive distributors of goods make a significant investment of resources in marketing and selling the goods. They may also incur other costs, such as fees to acquire the exclusive distribution rights, and they may be subject to minimum purchase requirements.[220] Webster has argued:

> In most cases the gray marketed products will be priced lower than the domestic products typically as a result of the gray marketer having little capital investment and no responsibility for development of the product name and reputation or as a result of fluctuations in the value of the currency. Accordingly, authorized distributors have an interest in ensuring that their distribution rights are protected . . . .[221]

Along the same lines, Duncan Card notes:

---

218 Harrington J. stated: "Any complaint Kraft has concerning a competitor's alleged failure to respect labeling laws should be directed elsewhere." *Kraft Canada* (FC), above note 9 at para. 43. For a discussion of other possible recourses, including recourses by the exclusive distributor against manufacturers who allow products to enter into the grey-market, see Webster, *ibid.* at 225–27.

219 *Kraft Canada* (FC), *ibid.* at para. 16.

220 Duncan C. Card, "Parallel Importation of Copyright Property: A Proposal to Amend the Canadian *Copyright Act*" (1990) 6 I.P.J. 97 at 98 [Card].

221 Webster, above note 216 at 211. See also Robert D. Anderson *et al.*, "Intellectual Property Rights and International Market Segmentation in the North American Free Trade Area" in Robert D. Anderson and Nancy T. Gallini, eds., *Competition Policy and Intellectual Property Rights in the Knowledge-based Economy* (Calgary: University of Calgary Press, 1998) at 401–2 [Anderson *et al.*].

> Having made a considerable financial and administrative investment to secure the exclusive right to buy and sell a product in the specified territory, the distributor finds it commercially vital to maximize its sales and promote its goodwill. Any loss of economic reward or harm to its goodwill because of sales in the territory by any other party who trades on the benefits of the authorized distributor's marketing and advertising expenditures would be extremely unfair.[222]

According to this view, the ability of parallel importers to offer lower cost options to consumers is a direct result of the fact that they are able to avoid the costs that give rise to the exclusive distribution arrangement as well as the costs of advertising and promotion. The lower costs thus flow from a form of unfair competition in the marketplace.[223]

However, the Supreme Court of Canada in *Seiko Time* was aware of these concerns when it emphasized the importance of free and open competition, with its resulting benefits to consumers.[224] Anderson *et al.* note that, where the product imported through parallel channels is a product on which the trade-mark owner has placed its mark, "the exhaustion principle would likely apply since there is no possibility for deception — the owner who markets these goods gives with them an implied licence to resell."[225] The Supreme Court accepted that exclusive distribution arrangements can have the effect of limiting consumer choice and keeping prices high. Without competition, there is no incentive to offer better prices. Further, the Court accepted that

---

222 Card, above note 220 at 98–99. For a nuanced discussion of the policy issues relating to intellectual property and parallel importation, see W.L. Hayhurst, Q.C., "Intellectual Property as a Non-tariff Barrier in Canada, with Particular Reference to 'Grey Goods' and 'Parallel Imports'" (1990) 31 C.P.R. (3d) 289 [Hayhurst].

223 Anderson *et al.*, above note 221 at 402, argue that exclusive domestic distributors can offer benefits to consumers. They state: "Without market segmentation, there would be little or no investment in location-specific assets by domestic distributors. As a result, the domestic consumer would not receive the same level of product quality and variety, service, and information that would prevail under market segmentation. Since both consumers and producers are better off under market segmentation, total welfare is higher."

224 Above note 10 at para. 24, citing John G. Fleming, *The Law of Torts*, 6th ed. (Sydney: Law Book, 1983) at 674 and 676.

225 Anderson *et al.*, above note 221 at 412.

consumers should also have the ability to choose between a "premium version" of the product (i.e., the watch with the warranty and point of sale service) and a cheaper, less enhanced version (the bare watch), as long as they were clear as to what they were purchasing. The *Seiko Time* Court also noted that a manufacturer had remedies available to it that arise from its network of exclusive distribution agreements. If a rogue distributor is selling a product outside the terms of its distribution agreement, thus enabling parallel importation, the manufacturer's remedy may lie in better internal policing and in contractual remedies.[226] In 2002 the Supreme Court of Canada articulated a kind of "first sale" doctrine and emphasized the importance of balancing the rights of the copyright holder with the rights of the party who purchases a legal, authorized reproduction to deal freely with that work.[227] By the same token, the parallel importer who has purchased legal, authorized product is entitled to resell notwithstanding the fact that this might frustrate another distributor's expectations of exclusivity.

In its defence, Euro Excellence argued that the *Copyright Act* should not be used to prevent parallel importation in situations where the copyright works at issue are only ancillary to the product being imported. This was a public policy argument that drew upon the Australian example. They argued that the Supreme Court of Canada's approach to parallel importation and passing off in *Seiko Time* could be extended to the circumstances in their dispute. In *Seiko Time*, it had been argued that the law of passing off should apply to the importation and sale of Seiko watches outside the authorized distribution network. Justice Estey wrote:

> The problem facing the respondent [Seiko Time Canada] is that the logical extension of this proposal grants to a vendor, in the position of the respondent, a monopoly on the sale in Canada of a product to the same extent as it would enjoy if the product were subject to a patent of invention issued to the respondent under the *Patent Act* of Canada. A second cul-de-sac into which such a submission necessarily leads is that the common law, in its personal property sector, would thereby be recognizing a right to entail and control the sale of personal property, however legitimately acquired, where another

226 Above note 10 at paras. 43–44.

227 *Théberge*, above note 2 at paras. 31 and 33.

> person in the position of the vendor, was also marketing the identical item of personal property. Such a principle is foreign to our law.[228]

Euro Excellence argued that the copyright arguments put forward by Kraft Canada would have a substantially similar effect to that described by Estey J. The result would be that the importation of products outside the authorized distribution network could be enjoined if the packaging or labels of those products featured a copyright-protected design. The exclusive distributor/exclusive licensee of the copyright would acquire a *de facto* monopoly over the sale of the goods in their original packaging. This would enable them to control the disposition of personal property legitimately acquired by third parties. Yet these policy arguments did not sway either the Federal Court or the Federal Court of Appeal, both of which ruled that the wording of the *Copyright Act* tied their hands in the matter. Similarly, a majority of judges of the Supreme Court of Canada appears to have adopted an interpretation of the Act that would have the same practical effect. It is not that the courts were opposed to the public policy arguments that favoured an approach tolerant of parallel importation; a majority of judges simply felt that the wording of the Act did not permit them to adopt an approach inconsistent with the wording of the statute.

From a public policy perspective, it does seem problematic that copyright law can be used to extend broader protection to trade-marks than what is available under trade-mark law. Further, this extended protection is available only for trade-marks that qualify for copyright protection, creating an uneven impact depending on the mark at issue. It seems clear that the overlap is unintended as a matter of legislative policy. Yet, as noted earlier, this is not the first time, or the only set of circumstances, where copyright law has been invoked in relation to design trade-marks in order to prevent uses of the marks that would have been permitted under trade-mark law. In both *Michelin*[229] and *Rotisseries St-Hubert Ltée v. Syndicat des Travailleurs de la Rotisserie*

---

228 Above note 10 at para. 26. A similar resistance to the extension of trade-mark law so as to afford patent-like monopolies outside the patent system was expressed by the Supreme Court in *Kirkbi,* above note 2; discussed in Section B(2).

229 *Michelin,* above note 169.

St. Hubert de Drummondville (C.S.N.),[230] for example, the courts ruled that while trade-mark law could not be used to stop unions from using parodied corporate logos on picket signs or informational brochures, copyright law could be used to enjoin these uses of the logos.

Public policy considerations were not entirely absent from the decision of Harrington J. The injunction he granted was tailored so that the chocolate bars could continue to be imported and sold so long as the logos were covered by film that could not be removed without destroying the underlying copyright-protected design.[231] The remedy attempts to protect the copyright in the design logos without giving a monopoly over the importation and sale of the underlying non-copyright-protected goods.

The remedy attempts to protect the copyright works without having the protection of the copyright design giving a monopoly over the importation and sale of the underlying goods. Nevertheless, such a remedy is not entirely successful in resolving the public policy concerns. The *Euro Excellence* injunction can be compared with that which was granted by the court of first instance in *Seiko Time*. In that case, Consumers Distributing was required to post a notice in its showroom indicating that it was not an authorized distributor of Seiko watches, and that the watches were not internationally guaranteed by Seiko Time Canada.[232] Thus, in both *Seiko Time* and *Euro Excellence*, the terms of the injunction are designed to send a message to consumers, indicating that there is something out of the ordinary in the provenance of the goods. However, this is where the similarities end. In *Seiko Time* the required notice provided clear information to the consumer at the point of purchase. It indicated that there was no difference in the nature or quality of the goods, but only in how they were distributed. The remedy in *Euro Excellence* leads to quite a different result. Consumers are faced with a chocolate bar that has an opaque sticker covering its distinctive logo. It is difficult to speculate what message this communicates to consumers. However, it would seem likely that some might have concerns about the authenticity or provenance of the product they purchase. Trade-marks are by definition

230 *Rotisseries St-Hubert*, above note 169.

231 *Kraft Canada* (injunction), above note 184.

232 *Seiko Time*, above note 10 at para. 7.

indicative of trade source,[233] and the obscuring of a trade-mark design must necessarily call the source of the goods into question. Such a remedy undermines the function of the trade-mark in a context where the goods are genuine goods, and the trade-marks indicate the true source of the goods.

The remedy fashioned by the trial court in *Euro Excellence*, unlike that in *Seiko Time*, interfered with the resale of legitimately acquired personal property. Quality chocolate is not sold in bulk. The wrapper and its trade-marks communicate a crucial message of source and quality. In this sense, a product wrapper is not truly "ancillary" to the product in all circumstances. If a consumer is able to distinguish a premium quality product from a more run-of-the-mill product based on its wrapper, a requirement to modify the wrapper will change the consumer view of the underlying product.

f) Competition Dimensions

The preceding pages have explored the issues raised in *Euro Excellence* and have considered whether the problems of overlapping rights are best addressed by the legislature or by the courts. I have suggested that changes to the status quo, which has tolerated significant copyright/trade-mark overlap, are best left to Parliament. Parliament must first consider whether, from a public policy point of view, there is an issue that needs to be addressed, and second, what kind of amendment would be required to fully address the issues. As noted above, the issues can be construed narrowly as a problem with secondary infringement, parallel importation, and the trade-mark/copyright overlap, or the issues of trade-mark/copyright overlap might be considered more broadly.[234] In the next section, I consider whether the problems

---

233 This point was recently strongly affirmed by the Supreme Court of Canada. See *Mattel, Inc. v. 3894207 Canada Inc.*, [2006] 1 S.C.R. 772, 2006 SCC 22 at paras. 21 and 23–24. See also *Kirkbi*, above note 2 at para. 39.

234 For example, the cases of *Michelin*, above note 169, and *Rotisseries St-Hubert*, above note 169, raise issues of overlap outside the context of parallel importation. Trade-mark/copyright overlap issues also arise with fictional characters. Copyright law will extend protection to fictional characters in some circumstances, while those same characters can also be protected as trade-marks. For a discussion of these issues of overlap, see Daniel Gervais and Elizabeth Judge,

that arise in *Euro Excellence* might also be addressed as competition law issues.

Certainly, in *Seiko Time*, the public policy issues considered by the Court relate directly to open competition with its corresponding benefits to consumers. Parallel importation around an exclusive distribution network gives consumers additional choices, particularly when it comes to issues of price. As long as there are no other consumer protection concerns (such as, for example, the quality or authenticity of the goods) the public generally benefits from competition between different sellers of the same goods.

It is worth noting that Australia's copyright legislation was recently amended to remove restrictions on the parallel importation of software.[235] The Australian Copyright Council released a paper that noted that the government amended the legislation due to a long-held view that "parallel importation restrictions have been used by copyright owners to restrict competition, and to charge Australian consumers more than overseas consumers for software and other copyright material."[236]

European law has developed a distinction, similar to that in Canadian competition law, between the existence of intellectual property monopoly rights (which do not, in and of themselves, present any competition law problems) and the exercise of those rights, which may attract scrutiny. Where parties enter into agreements relating to intellectual property rights that have the effect of limiting competition in a marketplace, the exercise of those rights may be actionable. Hays writes:

> There are two parts to the restrictive practice of blocking parallel importation within the market. The first part is the agreement between undertakings evidencing an intention to distort competition. The second is the anti-competitive act itself: the use of intellectual

---

Intellectual Property: The Law in Canada (Toronto: Thomson Carswell, 2005) at 576–80.

235 See Australia's *Copyright Amendment (Parallel Importation) Act 2003* (Cth.).

236 Australian Copyright Council, "Restrictions Lifted on Parallel Importation of Software; Enforcement Provisions Strengthened," by Virginia Morrison (7 April 2003), online: www.copyright.org.au/pdf/acc/articles)pdf/A03n04.pdf.

property rights to enforce what may be an otherwise legally-permissible agreement.[237]

These elements may be present in *Euro Excellence*. In *Euro Excellence*, the first part would be the exclusive distribution agreement, which essentially sets up Kraft Canada as the sole distributor in Canada of the chocolate bars. This agreement on its own is not anti-competitive, as there are no real barriers to parallel importation so long as the goods imported are genuine and of an appropriate quality. It is the second part of the arrangement that signals problems. The assignments by Kraft Belgium and Kraft Schweiz to Kraft Canada of the exclusive rights to reproduce the trade-mark designs in Canada could be characterized as "a use of intellectual property rights to enforce what may be an otherwise legally-permissible agreement."[238] It is thus arguable that the situation in *Kraft Canada* is not so much a problem of the nature and scope of the intellectual property rights than it is a problem of the manner in which those rights have been exercised.

On one level, *Euro Excellence* is a case about the interpretation of the *Copyright Act*. A majority of judges across three levels of court took the position that, absent any ambiguity in the wording of the Act, there was no room for inserting other public policy considerations. Justice Rothstein noted, for example, that in his view "this case turns on a straightforward application of s. 27(2)(e) of the *Copyright Act*."[239] This attitude echoes the approach of the Supreme Court of Canada in *Bishop v. Stevens*,[240] where Justice McLachlin, as she then was, stated: "copyright law is purely statutory law, which 'simply creates rights and obligations upon the terms and in the circumstances set out in the statute' .... First and foremost, then, this case is a matter of statutory interpretation."[241] Recent intellectual property decisions of the Supreme Court of Canada have embraced a more policy-driven ap-

---

237 Thomas Hays, "Anti-competitive Agreements and Extra-market Parallel Importation" (2001) 26 Eur. L. Rev. 468 at 470.

238 *Ibid.*

239 *Euro Excellence*, above note 9 at para. 14.

240 *Bishop v. Stevens*, [1990] 2 S.C.R. 467.

241 McLachlin J. was quoting from an earlier Supreme Court of Canada decision: *Compo Co. v. Blue Crest Music Inc.*, [1980] 1 S.C.R. 357 at 373, Estey J.

proach to its interpretation of the *Copyright Act*.[242] In *Kirkbi*, LeBel J. for the unanimous Court warned of the risks involved in extending the boundaries of intellectual property rights through litigation:

> The economic value of intellectual property rights arouses the imagination and litigiousness of rights holders in their search for continuing protection of what they view as their rightful property. Such a search carries with it the risk of discarding basic and necessary distinctions between different forms of intellectual property and their legal and economic functions.[243]

Justice LeBel is critical of litigation strategies that attempt to exploit overlapping protection. He warns that such tactics can undermine the public policy objectives that underlie the different areas of intellectual property law. These policy objectives balance different interests and economic realities within each regime. Using copyright to protect trade-marks involves a different set of public policy concerns from those mediated by trade-mark law. In *Kirkbi*, the Court set a clear boundary between patent and trade-mark law. However, in *Euro Excellence*, a majority of judges opted for a statute-based approach instead of one driven by public policy concerns. Indeed, Rothstein J. expressly rejected arguments that *Kirkbi* embraced a theory of intellectual property misuse. He wrote: "the decision in that case was anchored in the language of the *Trade-Marks Act* itself and not in a vague notion of trade-mark misuse."[244] He also stated:

> I accept, of course, that the *Copyright Act* is to be given a purposive interpretation. However, I distinguish between an approach that is rooted in the words of the Act and the approach taken by my colleague Bastarache J. that involves reading words into the legislation that are at odds with Parliament's intent.[245]

242 See for example, *Théberge*, above note 2 at paras. 30–33, where Binnie J. sets out the policy balance that informs the purpose of copyright legislation in Canada. See also *CCH Canadian Ltd. v. Law Society of Upper Canada*, [2004] 1 S.C.R. 339, 2004 SCC 13 [*CCH Canadian*]; and *Society of Composers, Authors and Music Publishers of Canada v. Canadian Assn. of Internet Providers*, [2004] 2 S.C.R. 427, 2004 SCC 45 .

243 *Kirkbi*, above note 2 at para. 37. This case is discussed in greater detail in Section B(2).

244 *Euro Excellence*, above note 9 at para. 12.

245 *Ibid*. at para. 9.

While the result may threaten the more open competition resulting from parallel importation, the approach of the majority of judges in *Euro Excellence* seems wise. There are strong arguments against judicial activism in this area. The Australian experience clearly demonstrates that the reform of the law to address the concerns raised by the facts of this case has a certain level of complexity to it.[246] Any change to the law would have to anticipate the range of situations that might arise. Broad consultation would be desirable both to explore the full range of situations that would be affected, but also to consider the significantly divergent views on the issues. The courts are not well positioned to speculate as to possible future scenarios, or to engage in broad consultations. In Australia, the amendments required study and consultation, and, in their drafting, were fairly intricate. A more systematic policy review than could be offered by a court may be appropriate.

From a policy point of view it might also be the case that the scope of the issues goes beyond parallel importation and reaches more generally to the proper relationship between copyright and trade-mark law when one is dealing with design trade-marks eligible for protection under both regimes. In the *Bailey's* case, Justice Walsh rejected arguments that trade-mark designs should not also be eligible for copyright protection largely on the basis that there was no authority to support this position. In Canada, as noted earlier, there is actually authority to support the opposite view. The courts in *Michelin* and *Rotisseries St-Hubert* accepted that trade-mark designs are eligible for both copyright and trade-mark protection. Further, section 64(3) of the *Copyright Act* clearly indicates that design trade-marks are protected by copyright law. That section deals with the relationship between copyright and industrial design protection. The general rule under the statute is that copyright in designs applied to useful articles is not infringed when the article is reproduced in a quantity of more than fifty.[247] Section 64(3)(b) creates an exception for, *inter alia*, a work used as or for "a trade-mark or a reproduction thereof or a label." Thus

246 In his careful review of intellectual property rights and parallel importation, Hayhurst, above note 222 at 294, identifies a wide range of policy considerations he describes as "some of the considerations that legislatures may face in striking the right balance between territorial intellectual property rights and freedom of trade."

247 *Copyright Act*, above note 16, s. 64(2).

the legislation clearly contemplates that both trade-mark designs and product labels can be works in which copyright subsists.

Where parallel importation is the issue, it is also not sufficient to consider only the trade-mark/copyright overlap in the context of trade-mark design logos or product labels. Similar copyright infringement arguments could be raised with respect to instruction booklets, warranty information, or other literature included with a product that is imported into Canada. Such works may also be eligible for copyright protection. This supports the view that the issue is best remedied by legislative intervention. A properly tailored legislative exception would not stop at logos or labels and would address all relevant "non-infringing accessories," as is the case in Australia.

In *Euro Excellence*, certain of the justices of the Supreme Court of Canada expressed openness to the concept of a doctrine of copyright misuse, although none of the judges would have decided the case on that basis. Justice Fish indicated that had he not sided with Rothstein J. on the issue of the scope of an exclusive licence, he might have been inclined to decide the case on grounds "relating to the integrity of Canadian law regarding intellectual property rights."[248] For his part, Justice Bastarache found it unnecessary to decide the matter on the basis of the doctrine of copyright misuse. However, he left open the possibility that such a doctrine might be successfully invoked in another case.[249]

The doctrine of copyright misuse, developed in the United States, permits the defendant to argue that, as a matter of equity, the court should grant no remedy to the plaintiff on the basis that the plaintiff has exercised their rights in an abusive manner.[250] While it is clear that the introduction of such a doctrine is gaining support in some circles in Canada,[251] it was less evident that *Euro Excellence* was an appropri-

---

248 *Euro Excellence*, above note 9 at para. 53.

249 *Ibid.* at para. 98.

250 For an exploration of the doctrine of copyright misuse, see G. Gervaise Davis III, "The Affirmative Defence of Copyright Misuse and Efforts to Establish Trade-mark Misuse, and Fraud on the Copyright Office: Establishing Limitations on the Scope of Copyright Owners Rights Based on Several Theories," *Patent, Copyright, Trade-marks and Literary Property Course Handbook Series*, Practicing Law Institute, Order No. 8816 (June 2006) [Davis].

251 See, for example, Robert J. Tomkowicz and Elizabeth F. Judge, "The Right of Exclusive Access: Misusing Copyright to Expand the Patent Monopoly" (2006) 19 I.P.J. 351 [Tomkowicz and Judge].

ate case for its application. To begin with, the doctrine has uncertain boundaries. Tomkowicz and Judge argue that it should apply where a party uses copyright "in a way which is contrary to public policy."[252] In *Euro Excellence*, although the exercise of Kraft Canada's copyrights seems to go beyond what may have been the intended reach of the *Copyright Act*, a majority of judges found that Kraft Canada's claim was legitimate. If that result is problematic or undesirable from a public policy point of view, the appropriate solution is legislative amendment rather than the imposition of a penalty on a party that has exercised a right that the Act apparently confers. A more appropriate case for the articulation of such a doctrine might be in a case where a party has asserted rights that it could not reasonably have believed that it held.

4) Summary of Overlapping Rights

In the examples of *Kirkbi* and *Euro Excellence*, I have explored two specific instances where there is an actual or potential overlap between different kinds of intellectual property protection. The potential for overlapping protection is often unanticipated by the legislature or is at least not fully anticipated. The result may create circumstances that may be exploited by parties seeking either to extend or enhance their intellectual property monopolies.

In some circumstances, the overlap in protection is addressed by the courts. Thus, in *Kirkbi*, the Supreme Court of Canada develops a strong, policy-based argument against allowing features claimed in prior patents to be protected as distinguishing guises under the law of passing off. In *Kirkbi*, there was no new innovation to be protected — LEGO was attempting to extend a monopoly that it had already enjoyed for years under its prior patents. The Court was of the view that this was contrary to public policy, and should be discouraged. It would seem that this is an instance where legislative amendment or intervention is not warranted. Nevertheless, as noted in the discussion of this case, the adversarial process is not always the best forum for wide-ranging policy-making. A number of situations were identified that are not fully resolved by the *Kirkbi* decision.

In some cases, the policy issue may be much broader than it appears on the surface. *Euro Excellence* is an example of such a situation.

252 *Ibid.* at 390.

Although the case dealt specifically with parallel importation and copyright law, the trade-mark/copyright overlap issues go significantly beyond this context. Courts must be wary of sweeping policy-based approaches where there are a host of related issues that may not be raised on the facts before the court, yet may be affected by an overly broad decision. In such cases, legislative intervention may be the preferred approach. This is particularly apposite in cases, like *Euro Excellence*, where there is much less consensus about the proper approach to the public policy issues than there was in a case like *Kirkbi*.

C. THE EXERCISE OF WEAK OR UNCERTAIN INTELLECTUAL PROPERTY RIGHTS

1) The Growth of Weak/Uncertain Intellectual Property Rights

Uncertain intellectual property rights can contribute to the problem of the extension of intellectual property rights, largely because the uncertainties can generally only be resolved by litigation. Litigation is costly and often risky.[253] Some parties cannot afford to litigate, while others will be highly motivated to resolve disputes prior to a final court decision. The tendency to resolve disputes extra-judicially may serve some public policy objectives, but it may also leave a range of unresolved interpretive issues that contribute to uncertainties regarding the scope or even existence of intellectual property rights.

The cost of litigation, combined with uncertainties as to the existence or scope of rights means that parties can assert intellectual property claims, even if those claims are of dubious validity, against a wide range of organizations or individuals who may be wary of challenging the claims because of the large costs involved in doing so. The practice has been referred to as "overclaiming,"[254] and it can arise in any area

---

253 For example, it is frequently the case in patent infringement litigation that the invalidity of the patent will be alleged in defence. If the patent is declared invalid, the loss to the patent holder could be substantial, as it opens up competition not just to the defendant, but to any other would-be maker or user of the patented invention.

254 See for example, Teresa Scassa, "Table Scraps or a Full Course Meal? The Public Domain in Canadian Copyright Law" in Faculty of Law, McGill University, ed., *Intellectual Property at the Edge: New Approaches to IP in a Transsystemic World* (Montreal: Centre for Intellectual Property Policy, 2006); and Teresa

of intellectual property protection. To provide an illustration from the field of copyright law, the fair dealing exception has traditionally been very narrowly construed by courts in Canada.[255] Yet a recent Supreme Court of Canada decision[256] suggests that the scope of the fair dealing defence may be broader than anticipated. The Court's interpretation of the fair dealing defence in the *Copyright Act* represents such a dramatic break from both past caselaw and the wording of the statute itself that one academic has called for an amendment to the *Copyright Act* to adjust it to fit the Court's interpretation.[257] This gulf between the legislation and the Court's interpretation is likely to create a great deal of uncertainty about the scope of the defence in any given case, and the low volume and slow pace of litigation in Canada will likely increase the speculative nature of any fair dealing defence that is raised. As fair dealing can only be raised as a defence to a claim of copyright infringement, a party hoping to test the boundaries of the recent Supreme Court of Canada position on fair dealing must be prepared to absorb the costs and the risks of litigation. Until there is a more stable body of caselaw, the scope of the fair dealing exception will be very unpredictable; the unpredictability of the defense, in turn, acts as a brake on matters ever reaching the courts. For many defendants, the uncertainty will not be worth the substantial litigation costs.

In some circumstances, the rights asserted may be largely fabricated, but a lack of awareness of copyright law, combined with a fear of being sued, may lead individuals or organizations to respect the unsubstantiated claims.[258] In the United States, a doctrine of "copyright misuse"[259] is emerging as an equitable defence that can be raised in

---

Scassa, "Nickled and Dimed: The Dispute over Intellectual Property Rights in the Bluenose II" (2004) 27 Dal. L.J. 293 ["Nickled and Dimed"].

255 Vaver, above note 181 at 190.

256 *CCH Canadian*, above note 242.

257 Carys Craig, "The Changing Face of Fair Dealing in Canadian Copyright Law: A Proposal for Legislative Reform" in M. Geist, ed., above note 23 at 461.

258 For example, some reprints of books that have fallen into the public domain contain notices that assert that no reproduction of any kind, other than uses for fair dealing purposes, is permitted. For those who are unaware that copyright no longer subsists in the works, this may place limits on the uses they make of the works.

259 Davis, above note 250.

copyright litigation where the defendant successfully asserts that the plaintiff has exercised its copyrights in an abusive manner. However, at present it remains a defence and so relies upon a willing defendant to assert it.[260] Where individuals or organizations cannot afford litigation, they are likely to submit to the bogus or overstated claims to copyright.

In the US, Michael Meurer has argued that courts must be more open to using their powers to limit what he terms "opportunistic" and "anti-competitive intellectual property litigation."[261] He posits that courts have at their disposal a number of tools that they must become more willing to use in intellectual property litigation. For example, he argues that courts must be more cautious about granting preliminary injunctions and more open to declaratory judgment suits and should encourage summary judgment for defendants. He argues that these tools, already at the disposal of the courts, can help to mitigate the effects of oppressive litigation strategies.

It is also possible in trade-mark law to either assert trade-mark rights that are highly vulnerable to challenge,[262] or overstate the scope or reach of registered trade-marks. The consequences are similar to those that arise in the context of copyright law: parties who are risk-averse, or who can ill-afford to defend themselves in litigation will acquiesce to the asserted rights. While this is a dynamic present in other areas of law, the degree of change and uncertainty in intellectual property law may make the problems in that area more acute.

Finally, as intellectual property rights take on increasing importance in the knowledge-based economy and in an Internet age, the range of parties against whom these rights are asserted has diversified significantly. Intellectual property rights are increasingly asserted against public institutions, such as schools, libraries, or universities,

---

260 In a recent article, Tomkowicz and Judge argue that the Canadian *Copyright Act* should be amended to include either a cause of action or a defence of copyright misuse. See Tomkowicz and Judge, above note 251.

261 Michael J. Meurer, "Controlling Opportunistic and Anti-Competitive Intellectual Property Litigation" (2002–03) 44 B.C.L. Rev. 509.

262 For a detailed discussion of a case where such claims were asserted on a wide scale, see "Nickled and Dimed," above note 254.

or against individuals for their largely private conduct.[263] These defendants are either largely risk-averse or unable to afford to mount a defence, leaving the field wide open for overclaiming.

It is perhaps, in patent law, that the stakes in relation to the extension of intellectual property rights are highest, and where the consequences of such activity are most deeply felt by a broader segment of the public. The patent system itself contributes to the problem: the US patent system in particular has been widely criticized for systemic problems that have led to the granting of large numbers of allegedly "bad" patents.[264] Some of the problems that have been identified include a high turnover in patent examiners, leading to an overall lack of experience;[265] incentives for examiners to grant, rather than reject patent applications;[266] the rapid expansion of the patent system to embrace software, business method, and gene patents without a concomitant increase in expertise or resources to examine patents in these areas;[267] and the lack of an appropriate means to search prior art in newly emerging technological fields.[268] The result has been a proliferation of patents that have been referred to by some as "probabilistic patents."[269] These are patents where the property entitlement must be assessed as a matter of probability, as the patent may be highly vulnerable to challenge. The impact on innovation of the proliferation of probabilistic patents has been the subject of some debate. Most seem

---

263 For a discussion of these issues, see Daniel Gervais, "Use of Copyright Content on the Internet: Considerations on Excludability and Collective Licensing" in M. Geist, ed., above note 23 at 517.

264 For a thorough critique of the US patent system, see Adam Jaffe and Josh Lerner, *Innovation and Its Discontents: How Our Broken Patent System Is Endangering Innovation and Progress, and What to Do about It* (Princeton, NJ: Princeton University Press, 2004) [Jaffe and Lerner]. See also Ben Klemens, *Math You Can't Use: Patents, Copyright, and Software* (Washington, DC: Brookings Institution Press, 2006).

265 Jaffe and Lerner, *ibid.* at 12–13.

266 *Ibid.* at 133–38.

267 *Ibid.* at 138–42.

268 *Ibid.*

269 Centre interuniversitaire de recherche sur la science et la technologie, "Reappraising the Efficiency of Probabilistic Patents and Prescriptions for Patent Policy Reform," by Marc Banik (2006), online: https://depot.erudit.org/retrieve/1373/2006_02.pdf.

to suggest that such patents hinder innovation,[270] while a few suggest that the impact may be less dire.[271]

The above-described concerns are all evident in the Canadian context as well. Although the Canadian patent system is generally considered less problematic than that in the US, this is in part because Canada is a less important patent jurisdiction. Canadian innovators with products with any market scope must inevitably contend with the US patent system. Yet there are features that are particular to Canada that increase either the likelihood of uncertain intellectual property rights or exacerbate the problems that may flow from the assertion of such rights. For example, compared to the US, Canada is a jurisdiction with a relatively small volume of intellectual property litigation. Given that most cases settle, or are prompted to settlement at the injunctive stage, the lower volume of litigation produces a proportionately much lower volume of judicial decisions on substantive issues in the legislation. As a result, there is relatively little articulation or interpretation of many key issues in Canadian intellectual property law. For example, while the US Supreme Court in *Diamond v. Chakrabarty*[272] settled the issue in the US that lower life forms were patentable in the 1980s, Canada had nothing more than a Patent Appeal Board (PAB) decision on the subject from 1982,[273] until the Supreme Court of Canada in *Harvard College v. Commissioner of Patents*[274] decided, almost grudgingly, that since people had been relying on the PAB decision for so long, it would accept that lower life forms are patentable, but that higher life forms would not be considered patentable.[275] Although there are few

---

270 This is the position taken in a leading article on the topic. See Herbert Hovenkamp, Mark Janis, and Mark A. Lemley, "Anticompetitive Settlement of Intellectual Property Disputes" (2003) 87 Minn. L. Rev. 1719 [Hovenkamp, Janis, and Lemley].

271 See for example, Thomas F. Cotter, "Refining the 'Presumptive Illegality' Approach to Settlements of Patent Disputes Involving Reverse Payments: A Commentary on Hovenkamp, Janis and Lemley" (2003) 87 Minn. L. Rev. 1789 [Cotter]; Ian Ayre and Paul Klemperer, "Limiting Patentees Market Power without Reducing Innovation Incentives: The Perverse Benefits of Uncertainty and Non-injunction Remedies" (1999) 97 Mich. L. Rev. 985.

272 447 U.S. 303; 100 S. Ct. 2204 (1980).

273 *Re Application of Abitibi Co.* (1982), 62 C.P.R. (2d) 81 (P.A.B.).

274 [2002] 4 S.C.R. 45.

275 *Ibid.* at para. 201.

significant differences between the US and Canadian patent legislation with respect to patentable subject matter, Canada is still operating on the basis of decisions from the 1980s on the patentability of computer software and business methods,[276] while the US, in much more recent court interpretations, has opened the door to the patentability of inventions in both categories.[277]

In the section below, I will consider one particular issue that has arisen in the American context, which raises issues about probabilistic patents. The practice, which involves reverse payments as a form of patent litigation settlement, typically arises between large corporate players: brand name and generic pharmaceutical companies. Yet the impact is felt widely, both on individuals without drug plans, and on governments who subsidize drug costs for hospitals, the elderly, and those on social assistance.

2) Reverse Payments in Patent Litigation Settlement

In the early 2000s the US Federal Trade Commission took issue with a payment made by way of settlement of litigation by Schering-Plough to the defendant in an infringement action brought by Schering-Plough.[278] Essentially, as part of the settlement agreement, Schering-Plough paid the defendant a sum of money to stay out of the market. The settlement left the underlying patent validity issues unresolved. Although the FTC ultimately made an order against Schering-Plough,[279] this order was overturned by the Court of Appeals for the Eleventh Circuit.[280] In another "reverse payment" case, the Court of Appeals for the Sixth Circuit found that the "reverse payment" settlement agreement

---

276 See the discussion of this caselaw in Scassa and Deturbide, above note 26 at c. 7.

277 See above note 21. See also Scassa and Deturbide, *ibid.*

278 On 30 March 2001, the FTC filed a complaint against Schering-Plough, Upsher, and American Home Products Corporation.

279 The FTC complaint was heard before an administrative law judge in 2002. The decision, which was in Schering-Plough's favour, was appealed to the full Commission, which ruled, on 8 December 2003, that the settlements violated the *Federal Trade Commission Act*, 15 U.S.C. §§ 41–58 [*FTC Act*] and the *Sherman Act*, 15 U.S.C.A. §§ 1–7 (West 1997).

280 Judicial review of the Commission's Order was sought, and it was subsequently overturned by the US Court of Appeals for the Eleventh Circuit. See *Schering-Plough*, above note 11.

was a *per se* violation of antitrust legislation.[281] The *Schering-Plough* and *Cardizem* cases are but two examples of a growing trend in pharmaceutical patent cases.

There is some significant concern about the practice of reverse payment settlements. Such settlements effectively result in one party agreeing not to compete in exchange for a significant payment. Some have suggested that reverse payments are only likely to be made where there is a real question about the validity of the underlying patent, yet the settlements result in the party with the most interest in challenging the patent agreeing not to pursue any such challenges. As a result, competition may be reduced both by the agreement not to compete, and by the removal of potential challenges to illegitimate patent monopolies. On the other hand, assuming a valid patent, the settlement may simply be an effective means of resolving a legal dispute, and the monopoly achieved by the plaintiff is nothing more than would have been available under patent law. Cases such as *Schering-Plough* raise interesting issues regarding the exercise of intellectual property rights, and these issues will be explored below.

a) Frequency of the Problem

Reverse payment settlements have become increasingly common in the United States. In a recent statement to the Special Committee on Aging of the United States Senate, Commissioner Jon Leibowitz of the FTC described these practices as abuses of the Hatch-Waxman amendments to the *Food, Drug and Cosmetic Act* (the *Hatch-Waxman Act*).[282] Leibowitz identified numerous instances of antitrust enforcement actions brought by the Commission against brand name and generic drug companies.[283] The problem was significant enough that the *Hatch-Waxman Act* was amended by the *Medicare Modernization*

---

281 *Cardizem,* above note 12.

282 *Drug Price Competition and Patent Term Restoration Act of 1984,* Pub. L. No. 98-417, 98 Stat. 1585 (codified as amended at 21 U.S.C. § 355 (1994) [*Hatch-Waxman Act*].

283 United States Federal Trade Commission, "Prepared Statement of the Federal Trade Commission before the Special Committee on Aging of the United States Senate on Barriers to Generic Entry" (20 July 2006) at 3, notes 8 and 9, online: www.ftc.gov/os/2006/07/P052103BarrierstoGenericEntryTestimony Senate07202006.pdf [*Barriers to Generic Entry*].

Act in 2003[284] to require that a notice of settlement between brand name and generic companies must be provided to both the FTC and the Department of Justice. Since the amendments to the *Hatch-Waxman Act*, the FTC reports annually on the patent settlements entered into by drug companies. In 2005, for example, the FTC reported that twenty settlement agreements were received, eleven of which were final settlements of patent litigation between brand name and generic companies.[285] Of these, three of the eleven agreements included a payment by the brand name company to the generic company, combined with an agreement by the generic company not to compete in the relevant market.[286] A previous study, carried out between 1992 and 1999 reported that eight settlement agreements involving reverse payments had been entered into between brand name and generic companies.[287] This represented over half of all settlement agreements during that period.[288]

The FTC notes that since it began scrutinizing patent settlements, and since the *Medicare Modernization Act* amendments implemented the requirement to file settlement agreements, the incidence of reverse payment patent settlements dropped notably. In fact, in 2005, the FTC stated that it was:

> not aware of any pharmaceutical settlement between a brand-name manufacturer and a generic filer that included both a payment to the generic company and an agreement by the generic company not to market its product between 2000 and the end of fiscal year 2004.[289]

---

284 *Medicare Prescription Drug Improvement and Modernization Act of 2003*, Pub. L. 108-173, 117 Stat. 2066 [*Medicare Modernization Act*].

285 United States Federal Trade Commission, "Agreements Filed with the Federal Trade Commission under the *Medicare Prescription Drug Improvement and Modernization Act of 2003*, Summary of Agreements Filed in FY 2005: A Report by the Bureau of Competition," online: www.ftc.gov/os/2006/04/fy2005drugsettlementsrpt.pdf [FTC 2005 Report].

286 *Ibid.* at 3.

287 United States Federal Trade Commission, "Generic Drug Entry Prior to Patent Expiration: An FTC Study" Federal Trade Commission (July 2002), online: www.ftc.gov/os/2002/07/genericdrugstudy.pdf.

288 *Ibid.*

289 *Barriers to Generic Entry*, above note 283 at 13–14.

Nevertheless, the FTC notes that two recent court decisions[290] have threatened to reverse the impact of its efforts. The decisions in these cases, which will be discussed in some detail below, reopened the door to reverse payment settlements. The three reverse payment settlements in the FTC 2005 Report were made following these court decisions. The FTC also notes that in the first half of 2006, reverse payments, combined with an agreement by the generic company not to enter the market, have formed a part of "seven of ten agreements between brand-name and generic companies."[291]

b) Linked to Regulatory Scheme

Reverse payment settlements are rooted in the particular regulatory framework established under what is known in the US as the *Hatch-Waxman Act*. This Act was enacted in 1984 in conjunction with patent term restoration provisions[292] as part of a package of measures designed to ensure the speedy entry of generic drugs into the marketplace following either the expiration of a patent or a successful challenge to the patent's validity. It is necessary to understand how the *Hatch-Waxman Act* operates in order to understand the context in which reverse payment settlements arise.

The *Hatch-Waxman Act* harmonizes the drug approval process under US food and drugs legislation with the patent regime. A party who files a drug approval application is typically required to submit detailed documentation setting out the results of extensive clinical research into the safety and efficacy of the drug in question. This is the process typically followed by innovators — those who have developed

290 *Schering-Plough*, above note 11; *In Re Tamoxifen Citrate Antitrust Litigation*, 429 F.3d 370 (2d Cir. 2005) [*Tamoxifen*].

291 *Barriers to Generic Entry*, above note 283 at 16–17.

292 Patent term restoration provisions attempt to balance the length of time needed for regulatory approval before a new drug can be marketed with the objective of providing a twenty-year term of patent protection. Thus, if it takes five years from the date of patenting to get regulatory approval for a drug so as to bring it to market, patent restoration provisions could add five years to the term of protection. For a critique of the assumptions underlying the current patent restoration terms in the US, see Gerald J. Mossinghoff, "Overview of the *Hatch-Waxman Act* and Its Impact on the Drug Development Process" (1999) 54 Food & Drug L. J. 187.

a new drug or medication — and it is called a New Drug Submission, or NDS. It is also possible to submit an application for approval of a pharmaceutical product that is based on, and refers to, the research done by an innovator who has already filed and received approval for a bioequivalent drug. This is called an Abbreviated New Drug Application, or ANDA. ANDAs are governed by § 355(j)(2), which requires that the applicant address any potential patent concerns that might arise if approval were given. The applicant must certify one of the following: that no patent has been filed for the drug; that the patent has expired; or that, if the patent has not expired, the patent is either "invalid or will not be infringed by the manufacture, use, or sale of the new drug for which the application is submitted."[293] If the applicant claims that the patent is either invalid or will not be infringed, it must give notice to the patentee and the holder of the approved application. The legislation then allows for approval to be granted to the drug subject to the resolution of any patent issues. However, this approval is subject to a thirty-month litigation period provided for in the Act. If an applicant for an ANDA notifies the patent owner that in its view the patents are either invalid or not infringed, the patent owner has forty-five days in which to launch a patent infringement suit. Once that suit is commenced, the ANDA cannot be approved within a thirty-month period.[294]

The *Hatch-Waxman Act* also provides for a 180-day exclusivity period for the first party to submit an ANDA in relation to a particular drug. A subsequent applicant for an ANDA for the same drug will be given an approval date that is "180 days after the date of the first commercial marketing of the drug . . . by any first applicant."[295] This period of exclusivity was of key importance in early reverse payment settlements, as a first applicant who, as part of a settlement agreement, agrees not to market the drug, could effectively prevent other applicants from entering the market with their generic versions.[296]

---

293 *Hatch-Waxman Act*, above note 282, § 355(j)(2)(A)(vii)(IV).

294 An exception to this is where a final appellate decision has been rendered. However, this is not an event that is likely to occur within thirty days of filing a patent infringement suit.

295 *Hatch-Waxman Act*, above note 282, § 355(j)(5)(BB)(iv).

296 The 180-day exclusivity period could also be triggered by a district court decision on the patent issues. However, if, as part of the settlement agreement,

Although the *Hatch-Waxman Act* may have had the desired effect of facilitating early entry of generic products onto the market, and of consequently lowering the cost to consumers as well as to governments providing prescription drug coverage, the Act also altered the dynamics between generic and brand name drug manufacturers.[297] As the chairman of the Federal Trade Commission recently noted,

> The *Hatch-Waxman* legislation altered the competitive landscape in a manner that has a significant impact on antitrust analysis. By increasing the potential economic value of generic entry, the statute also increased the incentive for brand and generic manufacturers to conspire to share rather than compete for the expected profits generated by sales of both brand and generic drugs.[298]

In 2003 *Hatch-Waxman*[299] was amended by the *Medicare Prescription Drug Improvement and Modernization Act*,[300] which implemented key changes designed to address some of the flaws in *Hatch-Waxman* that had been exploited by drug companies. Most relevant to the issue of reverse payment settlements were amendments that provided that the 180-day exclusivity period can be forfeited if certain conditions are not met.[301] For example, if the first applicant fails to market the drug

---

litigation was brought to an end, then this triggering event could no longer occur.

297 See for example, United States Federal Trade Commission, "Prepared Statement of the Federal Trade Commission Regarding Competition in the Pharmaceutical Industry, before the Committee on Energy and Commerce Subcommittee on Health," United States House of Representatives, Washington, DC, 9 October 2002, online: www.ftc.gov/os/2002/10/generictestimony021009.pdf [*Prepared Statement*].

298 Deborah Platt Majoras, "A Government Perspective on IP and Antitrust Law" (delivered at the IP Grab: The Struggle between Intellectual Property Rights and Antitrust, American Antitrust Institute, Washington, DC, 21 June 2006), online: www.ftc.gov/speeches/majoras/060621aai-ip.pdf.

299 The *Medicare Modernization Act*, above note 284, implemented key amendments that were designed to address some of the flaws in the *Hatch-Waxman Act*, which had been exploited by drug companies.

300 *Ibid.*

301 For example, if the first applicant fails to market the drug within seventy-five days of the date on which approval of the first applicant's application is made effective, or thirty months after the date of submission of the application by the first applicant.

within seventy-five days of the date on which approval of the first applicant's application is made effective, or thirty months after the date of submission of the application by the first applicant, the 180-day period is forfeited. If the patents expire, the exclusivity period is also lost. The 180-day period of exclusivity can also be forfeited if the first applicant has entered into an agreement with the patent owner, and the FTC or the attorney general has filed a complaint that gives rise to a final decision that the agreement has violated antitrust laws. The *Medicare Modernization Act* also requires that all settlement agreements relating to the manufacturing, marketing, or sale of the drug at issue, or to the exclusivity period, be filed with the FTC and the Department of Justice.[302]

c) Litigation and FTC Action

There are three key periods to consider in analyzing reverse payment settlements in the United States. The first period, following the enactment of the *Hatch-Waxman Act*, sees the emergence of the reverse payment settlement as a strategy relied upon by brand name and generic drug companies. The second period, in which there are virtually no reverse payment settlements, follows on the enactment of the amendments in the *Medicare Modernization Act*. The third period follows on important judicial decisions in the *Schering-Plough* and *Tamoxifen* antitrust actions, which appear to have opened the door once more for reverse payment settlements and to have significantly hampered the antitrust enforcement activities of the FTC in this area.

i) Period I

In the first period of activity by the FTC, the FTC focused on patent settlement agreements reached between brand name and generic companies in disputes arising under the *Hatch-Waxman Act*. In the first of these actions, the FTC brought a complaint against Abbott Laboratories and Geneva Pharmaceuticals, Inc. over a settlement agreement by which the brand name company, Abbott, paid roughly $4.5 million per month in order to delay entry onto the market of Geneva's generic product. The settlement allegedly included an agreement by Geneva

302 *Medicare Modernization Act*, above note 284, § 1112.

not to transfer its rights to the 180-day market exclusivity period.[303] In a second case from that time period, the FTC brought a complaint against Hoechst Marion Rouseel, Inc. and Andrx Corp. relating to a settlement agreement that involved Hoechst's brand name product Cardizem CD.[304] The settlement in this case involved a reverse payment combined with an agreement not to transfer rights to the 180-day exclusivity period.[305]

Both the Abbott and Hoechst cases were resolved by the FTC through consent orders.[306] In general terms, the orders prohibited agreements in which the generic company would agree not to enter the market with a non-infringing product or not to transfer its 180-day exclusivity period. The orders also required court approval of any reverse payment settlement agreements, with adequate notice to be provided to the FTC so that it could make submissions to the court.

Notwithstanding the consent order in the Hoechst case, which brought to an end the FTC proceedings against Hoechst and Andrx, a class action suit was brought against Hoechst and Andrx in relation to the allegedly anti-competitive agreement entered into in relation to Hoechst's drug Cardizem CD. The suit was brought under the *Sherman Act*,[307] as well as state antitrust and consumer protection legislation. It alleged that the reverse payment settlement entered into by the parties was a *per se* illegal restraint of trade that gave rise to antitrust injuries.[308]

---

303 United States Federal Trade Commission, Abbott Laboratories, Dkt. No. C-3945 (22 May 2000) (consent order), online: www.ftc.gov/os/2000/05/c3945complaint.htm; Geneva Pharmaceuticals, Inc., Dkt. No. C-3946 (22 May 2000) (consent order), online: www.ftc.gov/os/2000/05/c3946complaint.htm.

304 United States Federal Trade Commission, Hoechst Marion Roussel, Inc., Dkt. No. 9293 (8 May 2001) (consent order), online: www.ftc.gov/os/2001/05/hoechstdo.htm.

305 *Ibid.*

306 See United States Federal Trade Commission online: www.ftc.gov/os/2000/03/abbot.do.htm (Abbott consent order); www.ftc.gov/os/2000/03/genevad&o.htm (Geneva consent order); www.ftc.gov/os/2001/05/hoechstdo.htm (Hoechst/Andrx consent order).

307 Above note 279.

308 At the district court level, a motion was brought by the defendants for summary judgment dismissing the action. The motion was denied by the district court

The facts giving rise to this dispute are as follows. Andrx, a generic pharmaceutical company, had filed an ANDA with the Food and Drug Administration (FDA) for approval of a generic version of Hoechst's Cardizem CD on 22 September 1995. It also filed a certification that its product did not infringe on any of the Hoechst patents. Andrx was the first to file, and, under the *Hatch-Waxman Act* as it stood at the time, it was entitled to the 180-day period of exclusivity. Hoechst subsequently filed a patent infringement suit against Andrx, triggering the thirty-month waiting period under the Act, during which the FDA could not grant approval to the generic version. Andrx then filed antitrust and unfair competition counterclaims against Hoechst. On 15 September 1997, the FDA gave temporary approval for Andrx's generic version. Final approval would only be given once the thirty-month stay on approval had come to an end in July 1998. The agreement between Andrx and Hoechst, which became the focus of the subsequent antitrust proceedings, was entered into nine days after the tentative approval of the generic version by the FDA. Under the agreement, Andrx undertook not to market a generic version of Cardizem CD until the earliest of three possible events occurred: (i) Andrx obtained a final and unappealable determination that the generic product did not infringe on Hoechst's patents; (ii) Hoechst and Andrx entered into a licence agreement; or (iii) Hoechst entered into a license agreement with a third party. Andrx agreed to discontinue its antitrust and unfair competition claims. It also agreed to pursue its ANDA and it undertook not to transfer its rights to the 180-day exclusivity period. For its part, Hoechst agreed to pay Andrx $40 million per year on a quarterly basis from the date when Andrx received final FDA approval.

Final approval of the Andrx generic version was given on 9 July 1998, one month after the expiry of the thirty-month waiting period. Hoechst began its quarterly payments to Andrx, and Andrx refrained from bringing its product to market. Andrx did not begin to market its product until 23 June 1999, triggering the start of the 180-day exclusivity period. By this time, Andrx had received over $89 million in payments from Hoechst.

---

judge, and the issues were appealed to the US Court of Appeals for the Sixth Circuit.

In the end, Andrx began to market its product over a year after receiving FDA approval. By virtue of the 180-day exclusivity period, it was also able to keep other generic manufacturers from entering the market for a further 180 days. It was this delay that the plaintiffs in the antitrust litigation argued caused them antitrust injury. They claimed that, but for the reverse payment settlement, the generic product would have entered the marketplace much sooner and given them a significantly lower-priced generic option.

In considering the defendants' motions to dismiss, Justice Oberdorfer for the Sixth Circuit Court upheld the district court judge's ruling, which denied the motions. Oberdorfer J. reviewed US antitrust principles and noted that while some restraints on trade require a detailed fact-finding exercise to evaluate, others will be considered unlawful *per se*, "because they 'have such predictable and pernicious anti-competitive effect, and such limited potential for procompetitive benefit.'"[309] An agreement should be treated as unlawful *per se* when the court is able "to predict with confidence that the rule of reason will condemn it."[310] The *per se* rule thus functions as a "'conclusive' presumption of illegality."[311] It is applied in cases where the facts fit into a certain type of restraint on trade that is considered by the courts to be almost certainly unlawful. Oberdorfer J. noted: "The classic examples are naked, horizontal restraints pertaining to prices or territories."[312]

Oberdorfer J. did not hesitate to characterize the agreement between Andrx and Hoechst as *per se* illegal. He noted:

> There is simply no escaping the conclusion that the Agreement, all of its other conditions and provisions notwithstanding, was, at its core, a horizontal agreement to eliminate competition in the market for Cardizem CD throughout the entire United States, a classic example of a *per se* illegal restraint of trade.[313]

---

309 *Cardizem*, above note 12 at 906, citing *State Oil Co. v. Khan*, 522 U.S. 3 (1997).

310 *Ibid.*

311 *Ibid.*, citing *Arizona v. Maricopa Cty. Medical Soc.*, 457 U.S. 332 (1982).

312 *Ibid.* at 907. A horizontal restraint involves an agreement entered into by "competitors at the same level of the market structure" and is used in contrast to a vertical restraint, which involves anti-competitive agreements between players along a supply chain.

313 *Ibid.* at 908.

Oberdorfer J. did not accept the characterization of the agreement as a settlement of a patent dispute. He stated:

> it is one thing to take advantage of a monopoly that naturally arises from a patent, but another thing altogether to bolster the patent's effectiveness in inhibiting competitors by paying the only potential competitor $40 million per year to stay out of the market.[314]

The finding that the agreement was *per se* unlawful did not end the matter. The court noted that in order to succeed with their damages claims the plaintiffs, as private parties, would have to establish that they had suffered injury as a result of the anti-competitive agreement. The defendants' motion to dismiss the suit on the basis that no antitrust injury had been alleged by the plaintiffs had been rejected by the district court, and this decision was confirmed by Oberdorfer J.

An antitrust injury is one that the antitrust laws were intended to prevent, and there must be a causal link between the injury and the unlawful conduct.[315] The alleged injury in this case was the fact that the plaintiffs were forced to pay a higher price for Cardizem CD than they would have paid had the generic product gone to market as soon as it was approved by the FDA. Oberdorfer J. noted that the essence of the complaint by the plaintiffs was that "but for the Agreement, specifically the payment of $40 million per year, the plaintiffs would not have suffered their injury."[316] Oberdorfer J. acknowledged that the defendants were prepared to contest this point but found that the issue could not be resolved on a motion to dismiss.

It was argued by the defendants that the plaintiffs' action failed the "necessary predicate" test. This test, which arose in earlier Sixth Circuit caselaw, requires that the "illegal antitrust conduct was a necessary predicate to their injury or that defendants could exclude plaintiffs only by engaging in the antitrust violation."[317] The defendants argued that in order to meet this test, "a plaintiff must allege that the only way the defendants *could* have caused the plaintiff's injury was

314 *Ibid.*
315 *Ibid.* at 909.
316 *Ibid.* at 911.
317 *Ibid.* at 912, citing *Hodges v. WSM, Inc.*, 26 F.3d 36 at 39 (6th Cir. 1994).

by engaging in the antitrust violation."[318] Here, the defendants were prepared to argue that Andrx was perfectly entitled to decide not to enter the market with its generic product, and thus there was another possible cause of the same injury. Justice Oberdorfer rejected this approach. The kind of alternate cause that would be acceptable under this test would have to be a "physical or 'impenetrable' legal impediment to Andrx's production and sale of its FDA-approved generic product."[319] Alternatively, it would have to demonstrate some legal right exercised by the defendants "that indisputably caused plaintiff's injury."[320]

Oberdorfer J. was similarly dismissive of the argument that the plaintiff's action should be dismissed because it was fear of patent-infringement damages that kept Andrx from entering the market. He noted that a trier of fact might well find that the substantial reverse payments were an indication that Hoechst had little confidence in the strength of its patents, or that the patent infringement litigation was a "paper tiger." These issues would have to be resolved at trial.

Another case in this period involved brand name drug manufacturer *Schering-Plough* and three respondents. While one respondent, American Home Products (AHP), accepted the issuance of a final consent order,[321] the complaint against Schering-Plough and the other respondent companies, Upsher-Smith and ESI Lederle (ESI), proceeded to court. The outcome of this litigation will be dealt with in a consideration of Period III.

Period I thus reflects a period in which reverse payment settlements emerged as a means of resolving disputes arising under the *Hatch-Waxman* regime. These settlements exploited certain features of the regime and attracted the attention of the FTC. The FTC treated settlements in which payments were made to generic companies in return for an agreement to stay out of the marketplace as inherently anti-competitive in nature. In addition to its enforcement efforts with respect to the cases outlined above, the FTC also lobbied for changes

---

318 *Ibid.* at 912 [emphasis in original].

319 *Ibid.* at 914.

320 *Ibid.*

321 United States Federal Trade Commission, Schering-Plough Corp., Dkt. No. 9297 (consent order as to AHP issued 2 April 2002), online: www.ftc.gov/os/2002/04/Schering plough_do.htm.

to the *Hatch-Waxman Act* to address some of the features of this regime that the FTC considered to contribute to the problem.[322]

ii) Period II

The *Medicare Modernization Act*, referred to earlier, was introduced in response to the FTC's concerns over the exploitation of certain features of the *Hatch-Waxman Act*. The changes wrought to *Hatch-Waxman Act* have been outlined above. Key features included a provision setting out circumstances in which the 180-day exclusivity period would be forfeited (removing the ability of the first applicant to delay all others from entering the marketplace) and a requirement that all settlement agreements relating to patent disputes triggered by the regime be filed with the FTC and the Department of Justice. Following these amendments, and prior to the Court of Appeal decisions that will be discussed below, the FTC indicated that none of the fourteen settlements reported under the *Medicare Modernization Act* requirements for the fiscal year of 2004 involved reverse payments combined with an agreement by the generic limiting its entry into the marketplace.[323]

The changes effected by the *Medicare Modernization Act* and the position and actions taken by the FTC in Period I seem to have acted as an effective deterrent to reverse payment settlements. However, this period of abatement proved to be relatively short-lived. Litigation relating to settlement agreements made before the *Medicare Modernization Act* amendments was still ongoing, and the decisions in these cases were to have a significant impact on the work of the FTC in this area. In the FTC's Summary of Agreements Filed in FY 2005, it noted that three out of eleven settlement agreements filed with the FTC contained reverse payment clauses combined with a restriction on the

322 See for example, US Federal Trade Commission, Prepared Statement of the Federal Trade Commission on "Competition in the Pharmaceutical Marketplace: Antitrust Implications of Patent Settlements," before the Committee on the Judiciary, United States Senate, 24 May 2001, online: www.ftc.gov/os/2001/05/pharmtstmy.htm; *Prepared Statement*, above note 297.

323 US Federal Trade Commission, Agreements Filed with the Federal Trade Commission under the *Medicare Prescription Drug, Improvement and Modernization Act 2003*: Summary of Agreements Filed in FY 2004, online: www.ftc.gov/os/2005/01/050107medicareactrpt.pdf.

generic company's market entry with a competing generic product.[324] The FTC noted that two of these three settlement agreements occurred after the *Schering-Plough* decision. This decision, which undermines the ability of the FTC to challenge reverse payment settlements, is part of Period III, as outlined below.

iii) Period III

The third period in reverse payment settlement cases in the US flows from court decisions arising from challenges to FTC complaints made in Period I. In particular, Schering-Plough and two of the three generic companies involved in the dispute over Schering's K-Dur 20 took issue with the FTC's position on their settlement agreement.

In this case, Upsher-Smith was the first applicant for an ANDA for a generic version of Schering's brand name K-Dur 20 product. Upsher-Smith certified that, in its view, its product would not infringe any valid patent held by Schering. This triggered a patent infringement suit by Schering. The suit was later settled, and it was the terms of this settlement agreement that prompted the FTC complaint. The settlement involved a reverse payment and a delay of the commencement of Upsher-Smith's 180-day exclusivity period, such that no other generic company could enter the market until March 2002, seven years from the start of Schering's patent infringement suit against Upsher-Smith. ESI filed an ANDA after Upsher-Smith. It also certified that its product would not infringe on any patent held by Schering. Patent infringement litigation against ESI was commenced in 1996. This suit was settled by an agreement in which ESI agreed to refrain from marketing a generic version of K-Dur 20 until January 2004 and agreed to market only one generic version of the drug after this date, until the patent for K-Dur 20 expired in the fall of 2006. Schering also agreed to pay substantial sums of money to ESI. These settlements were challenged by the FTC. The FTC complaint was adjudicated by an administrative law judge, who ruled that both settlements were lawful settlements of litigation. This decision was appealed to the full Commission, which

---

324 US Federal Trade Commission, Agreements Filed with the Federal Trade Commission under the *Medicare Prescription Drug, Improvement and Modernization Act 2003*: Summary of Agreements Filed in FY 2004, online: www.ftc.gov/os/2006/04/fy2005drugsettlementsrpt.pdf.

reversed the initial decision, finding a violation of the *FTC Act*[325] and the *Sherman Act*.[326] This decision was further appealed by Schering-Plough and Upsher-Smith to the US Court of Appeals for the Eleventh Circuit. That court overturned the FTC ruling.[327]

In reaching its decision, Justice Fay of the Court of Appeals noted that the US *Patent Act*[328] provides for a presumption of patent validity. The K-Dur 20 patent was not due to expire until September 2006, and, if valid, it would prohibit market entry by generic drug manufacturers until after the patent expired. This was characterized by the court as giving Schering "the legal right to exclude Upsher and ESI from the market until they proved either that the '743 patent was invalid or that their products, Klor-Con and Micro-K 20, respectively, did not infringe Schering's patent."[329] The court noted that while a patent monopoly may appear at first glance to be anti-competitive, "a patent holder does not incur antitrust liability when it chooses to exclude others from producing its patented work."[330]

The court noted that a patent owner has the right to grant licences, or to choose not to grant such licences. The patent owner is free to exercise these rights; however, the owner must not exercise the rights in an anti-competitive manner. The issue, therefore, was whether the appellant's actions reflected a legitimate exercise of patent rights, or anti-competitive agreements. The court noted that Schering's agreements with Upsher-Smith and ESI actually gave both companies a licence to sell a form of the drug before the expiry of the patent. The FTC had been unable to establish that the validity of Schering's patent could be successfully challenged. Thus, the settlements allowed the generic companies to enter the market prior to the expiration of the patent term in a context where the FTC was unable to prove that, had the litigation proceeded, the patent would have been struck down and an earlier market entry would have been possible. The Court of Appeals framed the issue as "whether there is substantial evidence to support

---

325 Above note 279, § 45.

326 *Ibid.*

327 *Schering-Plough*, above note 11.

328 35 U.S.C.A. § 282 (West 1997).

329 *Schering-Plough*, above note 11 at 1066–67.

330 *Ibid.* at 1067.

the Commission's conclusion that the challenged agreements restrict competition beyond the exclusionary effects of the '743 patent."[331]

As part of the settlement agreement with Upsher-Smith, Schering had paid a substantial sum of money, ostensibly for licences for an Upsher-Smith product, that Schering never subsequently marketed. The FTC had alleged that this was a sham transaction: the real goal was to pay Upsher-Smith not to compete in the market with K-Dur 20. The Court of Appeals rejected this argument, noting that the fact that the Commission had found the licences to ultimately be worthless to Schering "overlooks the very nature of the pharmaceutical industry where licenses are very often granted on drugs that never see the market."[332] Fay J. went on to note that:

> There is nothing to refute that these payments are a fair price for Niacor and the other Upsher products. Schering-Plough made a stand-alone determination that it was getting as much in return from these products as it was paying, and just because the agreement also includes Upsher's entry date into the potassium chloride supplement market, one cannot infer that the payments were solely for the delay rather than the licenses.[333]

The court ruled that the settlement agreement between Schering and Upsher-Smith was legal.

Similarly, the court found nothing illegal in the settlement between Schering and ESI. The court was even more skeptical of the Commission's ruling on this settlement agreement. Fay J. noted: "It seems the sole indiscretion committed in the context of the ESI settlement is the inclusion of monetary payments."[334] However, the court was not convinced that the amounts paid were unreasonable in the context of the settlement of patent litigation. Fay J. observed that the litigation was certain to be "a bitter and prolonged process"[335] and pointed out that at the time of settlement there had already been fifteen months of mediation. The court cited prior authority to the effect that "parties to a

331 *Ibid.* at 1068.

332 *Ibid.* at 1071.

333 *Ibid.*

334 *Ibid.*

335 *Ibid.* at 1072.

patent dispute may exchange consideration to settle their litigation."[336] Further, the court observed that "[p]atent owners should not be in a worse position, by virtue of the patent right, to negotiate and settle surrounding lawsuits."[337] The court ruled that this particular settlement was reasonable in all the circumstances.

Finally, the court had to consider whether the settlement agreements were anti-competitive. It noted that the law required a demonstration that such agreements be anti-competitive in *effect*. Mere speculation is not sufficient. Fay J. stated that settlement of disputes without litigation was a preferred public policy outcome. The court noted that the Commission's position "requires the conclusion that but for the payments, the parties would have fashioned different settlements with different entry dates."[338] This, in turn, was premised on the view that it would have been possible for the parties to enter the market sooner, but for the agreements (and payments). The court observed that the balance between parties in the pharmaceutical context had been altered by the *Hatch-Waxman Act*. Prior to the Act, the generic companies would have had to bear the cost of clinical trials in order to obtain approval and would have also incurred other costs before bringing a product to market prior to the expiration of the patent. They then risked being sued for patent infringement. While the brand name company would lose sales in the short term, a successful patent infringement suit would have allowed them to recover lost profits, and bar their competitors from the marketplace. Thus, early entry was highly risky for generic companies. After the *Hatch-Waxman Act*, generics could provoke litigation leading to a challenge to the patent's validity prior to incurring significant costs for product development and market entry. They might face significant legal costs, but if they were successful, they would be able to enter the market early.[339] Thus the Act placed generic companies in a better position to challenge patent validity, while brand name manufacturers were more vulnerable to the invalidation of their patents. The court accepted this shift as

336 *Ibid.*

337 *Ibid.*

338 *Ibid.* at 1073.

339 See generally, *ibid.* at 1073–74.

being relevant to the kinds of settlements that could be expected post-*Hatch-Waxman*. Fay J. wrote:

> By entering into the settlement generics, Schering realized the full potential of its infringement suit — a determination that the '743 patent was valid and that ESI and Upsher would not infringe the patent in the future. Furthermore, although ESI and Upsher obtained less than what they would have received from successfully defending the lawsuits (the ability to immediately market their generics), they gained more than if they had lost. A conceivable compromise, then, directs the consideration from the patent owner to the challengers. Ultimately, the consideration paid to Upsher and ESI was arguably less than if Schering's patent had been invalidated, which would have resulted in the generic entry of potassium chloride supplements.[340]

Thus, the Court of Appeals considered the reverse payment settlements to be appropriate in the circumstances. In fact, the court referred to reverse payment settlements as "a natural by-product of the *Hatch-Waxman* process."[341] Apart from the *Hatch-Waxman* dynamics, the court also noted that the costs of litigation were significant and wide-ranging. It cited the "caustic environment of patent litigation" as a drag on innovation,[342] stating that "[t]he intensified guesswork involved with lengthy litigation cuts against the benefits proposed by a rule that forecloses a patentee's ability to settle its infringement claim."[343] The court expressed concern that the Commission's position, which was based on its own allowance for litigation costs that the court characterized as "naïve," would render almost any patent litigation settlement illegal.[344]

An application for *certiorari* to the US Supreme Court in *Schering-Plough* was denied.[345] It is worth noting that the US Department of Justice filed an *amicus curiae* brief in relation to the petition for the writ of *certiorari*. The Department of Justice argued against granting *certiorari*, stating that it was not an appropriate case in which to

---

340 *Ibid.* at 1074.
341 *Ibid.*
342 *Ibid.* at 1075.
343 *Ibid.*
344 *Ibid.*
345 *Certiorari* denied, 26 June 2006.

"determine the proper standards for distinguishing legitimate patent settlements."[346] The position of the Department of Justice was that, in the patent context, "a settlement involving restrictions on the sale of the products in question is not necessarily impermissible."[347] It noted as well that, while some competition-related concerns may be relevant, it must be kept in mind that the *Hatch-Waxman Act* "may also create unique justifications for reverse payments."[348] More specifically, the Department of Justice submitted:

> the ability of prospective generic competitors in effect to force patent holders to initiate infringement litigation upon the filing of ANDAs, before any actual infringement has occurred, reduces the litigation risk for the generic manufacturers. In combination with the inherent difficulties in predicting litigation outcomes and the potentially devastating consequences for the patent holder if it were to lose the litigation, the resulting gross disparities in the litigants' respective risks may tend to increase the cost of settlement for patentees in the *Hatch-Waxman* context and make reverse payments more likely, even when the patentee's legal claims are strong.[349]

The Department of Justice thus identified a complex regime with conflicting public policy considerations. It emphasized as well that the settlement of legal disputes was also a public policy goal. The Department of Justice took the position that there was nothing inherently anti-competitive in reverse payment settlements, and that something more must be required before finding such settlements unlawful. In particular, the it urged that the likelihood of the success of the parties' claims be assessed. The Department of Justice was critical of the FTC's approach, both because it considered such settlements to be inherently suspect and because it assessed the strength of the parties' claims based on its interpretation of their subjective assessments, as reflected in the terms of their settlement agreements. The Department of Jus-

---

346 US Department of Justice, Brief for the United States as *Amicus Curiae, Federal Trade Commission v. Schering-Plough Corp.*, No. 05-273 (May 2006), online: www.usdoj.gov/atr/cases/f216300/216358.pdf [*Amicus Curiae Brief*].

347 *Ibid.* at 8.

348 *Ibid.* at 10.

349 *Ibid.*

tice argued for a more objective assessment of the relative strengths of the claims.

In a case that followed on the heels of *Schering-Plough, In Re Tamoxifen Citrate Antitrust Litigation*,[350] the Court of Appeals for the Second Circuit also turned its attention to the legitimacy of a reverse payment settlement. In December 1985, Barr Laboratories, Inc. (Barr), a generic drug manufacturer, filed an ANDA with the FDA for approval of a generic version of Imperial Chemical Inc.'s (ICI) drug for breast cancer treatment called Tamoxifen. In 1987, Barr amended its ANDA to include a certification that its product would not infringe on the newly granted ICI patent. ICI responded by commencing a patent infringement lawsuit against Barr. In 1992, a judge declared the Tamoxifen patent invalid, on the grounds that ICI had withheld material information from the PTO.[351] The decision was appealed. However, in 1993, while the appeal was still pending, the parties entered into the settlement agreement that was to become the focus of the later antitrust action. Under the terms of this agreement with Zeneca, which was now the owner of the patent, Barr agreed not to market its own generic version of Tamoxifen until the Zeneca patent expired in 2002. In return, Zeneca would pay Barr $22 million. Barr also received a non-exclusive licence to market Tamoxifen manufactured by Zeneca, but to be sold under Barr's own label. In the antitrust proceedings, the plaintiffs alleged that the agreement was based on an unwritten understanding between the parties that should another generic company attempt to enter the market, Barr would invoke its 180-day exclusivity right. It was noted that five years later, and with other generic drug manufacturers poised to enter the market, Barr did in fact successfully invoke this exclusivity period. As a part of the settlement agreement, Barr and Zeneca agreed to file a joint motion to dismiss the pending appeal in the patent litigation, and to have the judgment below vacated. They did so, and the ruling of patent invalidity was vacated.

Subsequent to the settlement agreement, three other generic drug manufacturers filed ANDAs for generic versions of Tamoxifen. Zeneca filed patent infringement suits in each case. In each case, the courts declined to rely on the vacated judgment. In all three cases, the

---

350 Above note 290.

351 *Imperial Chem. Indus. PLC v. Barr Labs., Inc.*, 795 F. Supp. 619 (S.D.N.Y. 1992).

patent was held to be valid.[352] Prior to June 1998, the FDA applied a "successful defence" rule in relation to the 180-day period of exclusivity. In other words, the period was available to a generic manufacturer who had successfully defended itself against a patent infringement suit. While the litigation with other generic companies was pending, the FDA removed this requirement, and Barr applied for its 180-day exclusivity period. It was successful, thus delaying the entry into the market of the other generic versions until 180 days after Barr would trigger the running of the period. As Barr was already selling Zeneca-manufactured Tamoxifen under its own label, it had little incentive to begin marketing its own generic version. In the end, the other generic companies did not enter the market until after Zeneca's Tamoxifen patent expired in 2002.

The antitrust litigation in this case arose out of a series of lawsuits filed throughout the United States, which took issue with the 1993 settlement agreement. The various suits eventually merged into a consolidated class action, which alleged that the agreement

> (1) enabled Zeneca and Barr to resuscitate a patent that the district court had already held to be invalid and unenforceable;
> (2) facilitated Zeneca's continuing monopolization of the market for Tamoxifen;
> (3) provided for the sharing of unlawful monopoly profits between Zeneca and Barr;
> (4) maintained an artificially high price for Tamoxifen; and
> (5) prevented competition from other generic manufacturers of Tamoxifen.[353]

The defendants brought a motion to dismiss, which was granted by the district court.[354] The decision was appealed to the Court of Appeals for the Second Circuit.

Justice Sack for the majority of the Court of Appeals began by noting that the essence of a patent is "the right to exclude others from

---

352 *Zeneca Ltd. v. Novopharm Ltd.*, 111 F.3d 144 (Fed. Cir. 1997); *Zeneca Ltd. v. Pharmachemie B.V.*, 2000 WL 34335805 (D. Mass. 2000); *AstraZeneca UK Ltd. v. Mylan Pharms., Inc.*, No. 00-2239, slip op. at 2–3 (W.D. Pa. Nov. 30, 2000).

353 *Tamoxifen*, above note 290 at 380.

354 *In Re Tamoxifen Citrate Antitrust Litig.*, 196 F. Supp. 2d 1371 (2001); *In Re Tamoxifen Citrate Antitrust Litigation*, 277 F. Supp. 2d 121 (E.D.N.Y. 2003).

making, using, offering for sale, or selling the invention throughout the United States."[355] He also noted that the tensions between antitrust laws and patent monopolies were complicated in the case of pharmaceuticals by the *Hatch-Waxman Act*. Further, he noted that the courts are under an obligation to encourage the settlement of litigation, and that the public interest is generally best served by the settlement of lengthy and complex litigation.[356] He noted that the settlement of conflicting patent claims is not precluded by the *Sherman Act*, even where such a settlement might have an adverse effect on competition:[357]

> Rules severely restricting patent settlements might also be contrary to the goals of the patent laws because the increased number of continuing lawsuits that would result would heighten the uncertainty surrounding patents and might delay innovation.[358]

In this regard, Sack J. also noted that the outcomes of patent litigation were uncertain, and it was not appropriate to speculate what the results of any particular instance of litigation would be. He was unwilling to accept that, simply because a lower court had invalidated the patent in the litigation between Barr and ICI, this decision would have been upheld on appeal. He observed that subsequent courts, in litigation between Zeneca and other generic manufacturers, had upheld the Zeneca patent.[359] Essentially, Sack J. refused to accept the premise that there was something inherently problematic about the timing of the settlement agreement between Barr and Zeneca.

Sack J. next considered the issue of the legality of reverse payments. He noted that while it was typical of most patent settlements that the payment will flow from the alleged infringer to the patent holder, the balance in pharmaceutical cases is significantly altered by the *Hatch-Waxman Act*. He rejected the view that reverse payments were *per se* a violation of antitrust law. He noted that "reverse payments are particularly to be expected in the drug-patent context be-

---

355 *Tamoxifen*, above note 290 at 385, citing *Patent Act*, above note 328 at §§ 154(a)(1)–(2).

356 The decision in *Schering-Plough*, above note 11, was also cited as authority for this point. See *Tamoxifen*, *ibid*. at 386.

357 *Tamoxifen*, *ibid*. at 386.

358 *Ibid*. at 387.

359 *Ibid*. at 388.

cause the *Hatch-Waxman Act* created an environment that encourages them."[360] Echoing the reasoning from *Schering-Plough*, he noted that an alleged patent infringer under the *Hatch-Waxman Act* has much less at stake, as it is still at the approval-seeking stage, has not actually entered the market, has not incurred marketing and distribution costs, and has no exposure to large awards of damages that would wipe out any profits it might have made. By contrast, its main risk under the *Hatch-Waxman Act* is incurring legal fees, although, if it is successful in defending against the patent infringement action, it will be able to enter into highly profitable competition with the brand name drug manufacturer. Sack J. noted that as a result, "a generic marketer has few disincentives to file an ANDA with a paragraph IV certification. The incentive, by contrast, may be immense . . . ."[361] On the other side, the patent holder faces substantial risks. If the challenge to its patent is successful, it faces the loss of its monopoly. If it is successful with its patent-infringement suit, it will preserve its monopoly but is otherwise not entitled to damages or other compensation because the suit takes place before the generic manufacturer has entered the market.[362] Sack J. concluded by stating: "Under these circumstances, we see no sound basis for categorically condemning reverse payments employed to lift the uncertainty surrounding the validity and scope of the holder's patent."[363]

The next issue considered by the court was whether, if reverse payments themselves are not *per se* unlawful, their magnitude might be an indicator of illegality. The plaintiffs in the case had alleged that the amounts in the settlement agreement at issue were excessive. Sack J. agreed that, superficially at least, the amounts raised some questions:

> There is something on the face of it that does seem "suspicious" about a patent holder settling patent litigation against a potential

---

360 *Ibid.* at 390.

361 *Ibid.* at 391.

362 Normally, in an infringement action, the successful plaintiff will be entitled to damages for losses suffered due to the presence in the marketplace of a competing product that has diminished its sales. It may also be entitled to an accounting of the defendant's profits. Under the *Hatch-Waxman* regime, the infringement suit is brought before the defendant has entered the marketplace.

363 *Ibid.* at 391.

> generic manufacturer by paying that manufacturer more than either party anticipates the manufacturer would earn by winning the lawsuit and entering the newly competitive market in competition with the patent holder.[364]

Nevertheless, he was of the view that this apparent windfall could be explained:

> so long as the patent litigation is neither a sham nor otherwise baseless, the patent holder is seeking to arrive at a settlement in order to protect that to which it is presumably entitled: a lawful monopoly over the manufacture and distribution of the patented product.[365]

He noted that where a patent holder loses its monopoly, it will lose a substantial portion of its market to competition. It will also likely have to lower the price it charges for its product. Because of the lower prices being charged for the drug, in the absence of a patent, the total profits of the brand name company and the generic company would be lower than the profits of the brand name company alone with its patent monopoly intact. In the words of Sack J.,

> [i]t might therefore make economic sense for the patent holder to pay some portion of that difference to the generic manufacturer to maintain the patent-monopoly market for itself. And, if that amount exceeds what the generic manufacturer sees as its likely profit from victory, it seems to make obvious economic sense for the generic manufacturer to accept such a payment if it is offered.[366]

Thus, the size of the payment alone is not an indicator of unlawfulness. Nor would it be appropriate to speculate as to the strength of the challenged patent. Sack J. noted that one could not assume that, because a patent holder offered a generic manufacturer a large sum of money in settlement of litigation, it did so because it knew its patent to be of dubious validity. He noted: "Whatever the degree of the patent holder's certainty, there is always some risk of loss that the patent holder might wish to insure against by settling."[367] The court was unwilling to de-

---

364 *Ibid.* at 392.
365 *Ibid.*
366 *Ibid.* at 393.
367 *Ibid.* at 394.

clare presumptively illegal settlements involving payments to generics of sums in excess of what they would earn in the market if they were successful in challenging the patent holder's patent.

Sack J. noted that there were issues that arose around the protection of weak patents. However, he did not consider the issue as one that could be resolved easily. He stated: "So long as the law encourages settlement, weak patent cases will likely be settled even though such settlements will inevitably protect patent monopolies that are, perhaps, undeserved."[368] A requirement that all patent disputes arising under the *Hatch-Waxman Act* be resolved by litigation rather than settlement would be "contrary to well-established principles of law."[369] He opined that "[w]hatever damage is done to competition by settlement is done pursuant to the monopoly extended to the patent holder by patent law unless the terms of the settlement enlarge the scope of that monopoly."[370]

Sack J. also considered whether other terms in the settlement agreement were unlawful. He framed the question as one of determining "whether the 'exclusionary effects of the agreement' exceed the 'scope of the patent's protection.'"[371] He concluded that they did not. He noted that, unlike the *Cardizem* case, the agreement did not extend patent monopolies by placing restraints on the introduction or marketing of other non-infringing products.[372] In *Cardizem*, the patent at issue covered only specific formulations of a compound; it was possible for there to be formulations other than those covered by the patent. In *Tamoxifen*, by contrast, the patent was for the compound itself; assuming the patent is valid, there could be no non-infringing equivalents. Thus in *Tamoxifen*, unlike in *Cardizem*, a restriction on marketing other generic versions did not unlawfully extend the scope of the patent monopoly by preventing the marketing of non-infringing products.

Sack J. also noted that in *Tamoxifen*, the agreement ended the patent litigation between the parties but left the field open for other gen-

368 *Ibid.* at 395.
369 *Ibid.* at 396.
370 *Ibid.*
371 *Ibid.* at 397, citing *Schering-Plough*, above note 11 at 1076.
372 In *Cardizem*, above note 12, Andrx agreed not to market bioequivalent and/or generic versions of Cardizem that were not at issue in the patent litigation.

eric companies to challenge the validity of Zeneca's patents. Further, under the FDA's rules at the time, Barr, by ending its litigation, was not eligible for the 180-day exclusivity period, leaving the field open for another generic company to seek approval and challenge Zeneca's patent. Sack J. distinguished this from *Cardizem*, arguing that in *Cardizem* the generic company had agreed not to enter the market with its FDA-approved generic, creating a bottleneck as other generic companies would have to wait until its 180-day exclusivity period was triggered and then ran its course. The generic company in *Cardizem* had also agreed not to relinquish or transfer its exclusivity period.[373]

Sack J. noted that the harm allegedly suffered by the plaintiffs (i.e., that they could not purchase cheaper generic versions of Tamoxifen) did not flow from the terms of the settlement agreement, but rather flowed from the fact that subsequent generic challengers to Zeneca's patent failed to have the patent declared invalid. Sack J. sidestepped the issue of the finding of invalidity that was vacated by joint application of Barr and Zeneca by commenting that "there is no legal requirement that parties litigate an issue fully for the benefit of others."[374]

Far from precluding competition entirely, Sack J. found that the settlement agreement actually permitted a limited form of competition, as Barr was given a licence to market Zeneca's version of Tamoxifen. Under this part of the agreement, money flowed from Barr to Zeneca "decreasing the value of the reverse payment."[375] Sack J. admitted that the competition was limited, and that the price differential between Zeneca's and Barr's products was slight compared to the normal differential between brand name and generic drugs. Nevertheless, it was more competition than might otherwise have occurred had Zeneca declined to license the drug as it was entitled to do under its patent. As Sack J. remarked, "The Agreement is no doubt 'anticompetitive' . . . . It limited competition between generic tamoxifen and Zeneca's branded product. But, as we have seen, because it did not exceed the scope of the tamoxifen patent, it was not an *unlawful* anticompetitive agreement."[376]

---

373 *Tamoxifen*, above note 290 at 398–99.

374 *Ibid.* at 399.

375 *Ibid.*

376 *Ibid.* at 402.

Justice Pooler dissented in the case. He was critical of the majority's decision on a number of grounds and noted that its general approach to the antitrust issues "is insufficiently protective of the consumer interests safeguarded by the *Hatch-Waxman Act* and the antitrust laws."[377] Pooler J. rejected the majority's view that an antitrust plaintiff must show that patent litigation initiated under the *Hatch-Waxman Act*, and later settled in a reverse payment settlement, was a sham. He wrote:

> Thus, commentators, precedent, and policy suggest the majority's requirement that an antitrust plaintiff show that a *Hatch-Waxman* lawsuit settled by agreement was a sham — assuming that the agreement did not convey benefits beyond the scope of the patent — is unjustified. A more searching inquiry and a less stringent standard are required to properly protect all interests.[378]

Pooler J.'s preferred approach in such cases is to evaluate "the strength of the patent as it appeared at the time at which the parties settled."[379] He would then also consider the amount of the reverse payment, the amount the generic manufacturer would have earned during its period of exclusivity, and "any ancillary anti-competitive effects of the agreement including the presence or absence of a provision allowing the parties to manipulate the generic's exclusivity period."[380]

d) Analysis

It is clear from the caselaw that there is no consensus either on the legality of reverse payment settlements or on the proper analytical approach to bring to bear on assessing them. It is fair to say that such settlements, at least in the context of disputes arising under the *Hatch-Waxman Act*, are not *per se* illegal. Their legality will depend on a range of factors, some of which will be very difficult to assess. Further, it is important to note that some changes have been made to the *Hatch-Waxman Act* in order to limit potential anti-competitive effects. The most notable of these is the amendment, under the *Medicare Modern-*

---

377 *Ibid.* at 408.

378 *Ibid.* at 411.

379 *Ibid.* at 412.

380 *Ibid.*

ization Act, which provides for the forfeiture of the 180-day exclusivity period in certain circumstances.

There has been some academic consideration of the issues raised in reverse payment settlements. In an oft-cited[381] article by Hovenkamp, Janis, and Lemley, the authors identify the tensions between intellectual property law and antitrust law and propose an analytical framework for reconciling them. They note that this reconciliation will only be required in a small number of cases. At one end of the spectrum, they posit, are cases where the settlement agreements do not have anti-competitive effects, and the existence of intellectual property rights is not relevant to the analysis. At the other end of the spectrum lie disputes where the settlement agreement would be anti-competitive whether or not intellectual property rights were involved. It is only the middle set where, in their words, "the agreement itself looks like an antitrust violation but the presence of IP rights might absolve it,"[382] that requires a balancing of the tensions between intellectual property rights and antitrust law.

For Hovenkamp, Janis, and Lumley the presence of intellectual property rights in this middle category of cases renders traditional antitrust analysis ineffective. They note that in this narrow set of cases, the agreement would be considered anti-competitive but for the presence of the underlying intellectual property monopoly right. If the underlying patent is invalid, the agreement is most certainly anti-competitive. However, if the underlying patent is valid, the agreement might actually be pro-competitive. This was certainly the majority's view of the agreement in *Tamoxifen*.[383] The problem then becomes how to deal with the issue of the validity of the underlying patent in antitrust proceedings. Indeed, it is this issue that attracts the most attention in academic writing.

In the section below I will consider some of the problematic features of settlement agreements between brand name and generic drug companies under the *Hatch-Waxman Act* and their treatment in the caselaw and literature.

---

381 For example, the article was cited by the majority in *Tamoxifen, ibid.*

382 Hovenkamp, Janis, and Lemley, above note 270 at 1724.

383 Above note 290.

i) Timing

The timing of a settlement may raise competition law issues. As noted earlier, the validity of the underlying patent is key to the legitimacy of the reverse payment agreement. If the litigation is settled after a finding at first instance of patent invalidity, there may be more serious competition law concerns than if the litigation is settled before such a decision is reached. *Tamoxifen* provides a good illustration. There, the settlement came after a decision by a lower court, which found Zeneca's patent to be invalid. It was argued that, at this point, an agreement to have that decision vacated and to settle the matter, rather than to proceed with an appeal, made the agreement anti-competitive. In other words, once the innovator had a decision that its patent was invalid, a settlement agreement that had the innovator paying the generic not to compete was inherently problematic. The majority of the Court of Appeal took a different view. It noted that the finding of invalidity could well have been overturned on appeal, and that it was not appropriate to draw conclusions about the patent's ultimate validity or invalidity.[384] Pooler J. was of a different opinion. For him, the relevant point in time for assessing the legitimacy of the settlement agreement was at the time of the settlement. At that point in time, there was a lower court decision finding the patent invalid. In Pooler J.'s view, "the patent could no longer be considered presumptively valid."[385] He was of the view that, given the findings of fact by the judge at first instance and the fact that the Court of Appeal could have only overturned the decision on the basis of clear error, it was reasonable to conclude that, at the time of the settlement, it was "fairly likely, if not certain, that Barr would prevail."[386]

The relevance of the timing of a settlement thus depends on other factors in the courts' general approach to the issue of reverse payment settlements. One key consideration is whether the presumption of patent validity survives an initial finding of invalidity by a court at first instance. Another issue may be the weight that is given to the standard of review by the appellate court. If the appeal is not a hearing *de novo*, and deference is due to the findings of fact of the court below, this may

---

384 *Ibid.* at 388.

385 *Ibid.* at 413.

386 *Ibid.* at 414.

also suggest that it is more likely than not that the lower court decision will be upheld. This position is much easier to take if one assumes that the presumption of validity has been displaced. Nevertheless, the outcome on appeal remains speculative, particularly if the appellate-level court has a record of overturning findings of invalidity at first instance.

ii) The Fact of a Settlement Itself

There is a general consensus that the mere fact of a settlement of a patent dispute cannot be considered *per se* unlawful. The courts are quite clear that the settlement of disputes is something to be encouraged,[387] and the mere fact that there is a settlement is not a trigger for antitrust scrutiny. Yet many settlements of patent disputes result in agreements that appear, superficially at least, to raise antitrust issues. Hovenkamp, Janis, and Lumley acknowledge this when they state: "some of those agreements would be illegal per se if created in the absence of a genuine IP dispute."[388] Once again, the key issue becomes the validity of the underlying patent. If there is not much likelihood that the patent is valid, then a reverse payment settlement becomes highly questionable. Thus, while the mere fact of settlement is not, in and of itself, a trigger for greater scrutiny, the *bona fides* of the settlement may depend on the merits of the underlying dispute. This has proven to be one of the thorniest issues with which the courts have had to grapple. Indeed, part of the tension between the majority and the dissent in *Tamoxifen* was over whether it was appropriate to dismiss the plaintiff's action without a fuller record on which to assess the merits of the underlying intellectual property dispute.

Notwithstanding the fact that the settlement of disputes is something that the courts must encourage, antitrust scrutiny is appropriate where there is risk of harm to the public interest. As Hovenkamp, Janis, and Lumley note, "the parties to an IP dispute have a strong incentive to enter into agreements that maximize their own interests but disserve

---

387 For example, this point is strongly made by the court in *Tamoxifen*, above note 290 at 386. See also David Vaver, "Without Prejudice Communications — Their Admissibility and Effect" (1974) 9 U.B.C.L. Rev. 85, where he discusses the public policy goals of the "without prejudice" rule as applied to settlement negotiations.

388 Hovenkamp, Janis, and Lumley, above note 270 at 1721.

the public's interest with respect to either competition or innovation."[389] For this reason Hovenkamp, Janis, and Lumley favour judicial scrutiny of settlement agreements having an anti-competitive effect. They also state that "harsher scrutiny is appropriate when it appears clear that alternative, less harmful settlement arrangements were available."[390]

iii) The Existence and Size of a Reverse Payment

In the context of disputes arising under the *Hatch-Waxman Act*, the courts in the US have generally been reluctant to find that the existence of a reverse payment makes a settlement *per se* illegal. This is largely because the *Hatch-Waxman Act* significantly alters the dynamics between the parties. As noted above, the generic drug company will be sued for infringement before it enters the market and thus its exposure is much less than if it had already incurred costs for manufacturing, marketing, and selling the product. The brand name company, by contrast, risks losing its patent monopoly and may have strong incentives to reach a settlement with the generic company rather than risk a finding of patent invalidity.[391] In its *Amicus Curiae Brief* in *FTC v. Schering-Plough*, the Department of Justice took the position that "the mere presence of a reverse payment in the *Hatch-Waxman* context is not sufficient to establish that the settlement is unlawful."[392]

Nevertheless, there are some who are of the view that the size of a reverse payment may be an indicator of the legitimacy of the agreement. Hovenkamp, Janis, and Lumley write: "[t]he very fact that the pioneer finds it worthwhile to pay a large exclusion payment tends to establish market power."[393] They also suggest that the payment indicates some uncertainty about the validity of the patent,[394] although the courts have generally been reluctant to draw such inferences about the underlying patent. Hovenkamp, Janis, and Lumley accept the premise that an exclusion payment indicates uncertainty about the validity of the patent and they are prepared to conclude that such payments are

389 *Ibid.* at 1722.

390 *Ibid.*

391 See discussion of the features of the *Hatch-Waxman Act* in Hovenkamp, Janis, and Lumley, *ibid.* at 1751–54.

392 *Amicus Curiae Brief*, above note 346 at 11.

393 Hovenkamp, Janis, and Lumley, above note 270 at 1758.

394 *Ibid.* at 1757–58.

therefore, on average, anti-competitive.[395] Yet this view is not unanimously shared. As noted earlier, courts tend to be unwilling to draw the inference that a reverse payment indicates a weak patent. Another academic, Thomas Cotter, is also critical of this perspective. In a comment on the Hovenkamp piece, he writes:

> The fact that plaintiffs sometimes prefer reverse payments to licenses suggests that reverse payments sometimes promise a higher payoff to the plaintiff than would granting a license. The analysis above further demonstrates that a preference for reverse payments is not necessarily proof of an anticompetitive scheme.[396]

Cotter is of the view that there are risks involved in restricting the ability of parties to use reverse payment settlements. He indicates that this approach might "decrease the value of at least some valid and infringed pharmaceutical patents,"[397] although he is reluctant to draw conclusions about the actual significance of any such effect. In any event, he concludes that

> For better or worse, patents exist, and they reflect a legislative judgment that their benefits exceed their costs. For antitrust law to undermine the value of valid and infringed patents, which a rule discouraging reverse payments would in some instances do, is troubling.[398]

He likens such a result to a form of compulsory licensing and notes that US law has tended away from compulsory licensing schemes for patents. The exception is where such licensing is required to remedy antitrust violations, but he notes that in those cases the remedy is applied on specific facts and not as a catch-all rule.[399]

---

395 *Ibid.* at 1758.

396 Cotter, above note 271 at 1809.

397 *Ibid.*

398 *Ibid.* at 1810.

399 *Ibid.* Hovenkamp, Janis, and Lumley, above note 270 at 1761, disagree on this point. They note that there is no compulsory licensing taking place: if the patent owner is confident of the strength of the patent, it retains the option of litigating the patent infringement suit and enforcing its monopoly through that means.

iv) Strength of Patent

The validity of the underlying patent, which is at issue in reverse payment cases, is clearly at the heart of the antitrust issues. If the underlying patent is invalid, or likely invalid, then the agreement may well be anti-competitive. Patents, once granted, are entitled to be presumed valid. However, a variety of systemic and institutional flaws in the US patent system,[400] combined with the complexity of many patent claims in the pharmaceutical and biotechnology areas,[401] and further combined with patent office practices that may lead to flawed patents,[402] mean that many granted patents may well be found invalid if challenged. The situation is further complicated by tensions between courts of first instance and the Court of Appeals for the Federal Circuit.[403] The result is that while patents must legally be presumed valid, in practical terms, many granted patents may actually be highly susceptible to challenge. This dimension can prove problematic in the context of patent dispute settlements. It is certainly the case that the underlying validity of the patent at issue in reverse payment settlements has been a key issue in antitrust complaints and in FTC challenges to these settlements. As Hovenkamp, Janis, and Lumley note, "the uncertain scope and validity of IP rights may encourage a collusive settlement, serving both to remove the uncertainty and to permit the two firms to share monopoly profits."[404] One of the goals of the *Hatch-Waxman Act* was to facilitate challenges to patents that were acting as barriers to the entry of generic products into the marketplace. A finding of invalidity certainly opens the field to greater competition and significantly lower drug prices.

It is difficult to know how best to factor into the analysis the foibles of the patent system. Hovenkamp, Janis, and Lumley are prepared to assume that the presence of a reverse payment indicates that the patent holder believes its patent is weak or of uncertain validity. Cotter

---

400 See generally Jaffe and Lerner, above note 264.

401 Lerner and Jaffe document the difficulties posed by the problems faced by the Patent Office in retaining patent examiners skilled in emerging areas such as biotechnology, *ibid.* at 135–37. They also identify problems around the ability to identify prior art in emerging and rapidly evolving areas, *ibid.* at 145–49.

402 *Ibid.* at c. 5.

403 *Ibid.* at c. 4.

404 Hovenkamp, Janis, and Lumley, above note 270 at 1722.

is less quick to reach this conclusion. Instead, he proposes that courts faced with antitrust claims engage in some sort of exercise to assess the strength of the contested patent.[405] The problem is in determining what kind of inquiry is appropriate, and on what standard the patent should be judged. For example, if a court concludes that the challenge to a patent's validity has a 75 percent chance of success, does this mean that the settlement is anti-competitive? Hovenkamp, Janis, and Lumley advocate a standard of a "significant" probability that the patent would be invalidated.[406] Cotter notes that a somewhat more searching inquiry into patent validity might be warranted and suggests that an abbreviated hearing on the merits of the patent claim might be appropriate.[407] O'Rourke and Brodley agree that a reverse payment is an indicator of potentially weak patent rights, however, they stop short of advocating an assessment of patent validity in the antitrust proceedings.[408] They raise concerns that such an approach would unduly complicate the proceedings,[409] and they prefer instead an approach that could consolidate the antitrust proceedings with the patent infringement litigation.[410] In *Schering-Plough*, the FTC was reluctant to adopt an approach that would directly assess the strength of the patent, preferring instead to measure the size of the settlement against the "expected value" of the lawsuit,[411] although the expected value of the litigation must surely be related to the validity of the underlying patent claims.

Hovenkamp, Janis, and Lumley and Cotter consider that the size of the reverse payment might be one factor in assessing the underlying strength of the patent. A reverse payment sum that is close to what the plaintiff might have incurred in legal costs had the suit proceeded suggests that the patent was likely valid and infringed, and that, therefore,

---

405 Cotter, above note 271 at 1811.

406 Others question what "significant" would mean in practical terms. See Maureen A. O'Rourke and Joseph F. Brodley, "An Incentives Approach to Patent Settlements: A Commentary on Hovenkamp, Janis & Lemley" (2003) 87 Minn. L. Rev. 1767 at 1783 [O'Rourke and Brodley].

407 Cotter, above note 271 at 1812.

408 O'Rourke and Brodley, above note 406 at 1782.

409 *Ibid.* at 1783.

410 *Ibid.*

411 *Amicus Curiae Brief*, above note 346.

there is nothing anti-competitive in the fact of the reverse payment.[412] But Cotter is unwilling to assume that a higher settlement amount is necessarily problematic. He writes:

> When the amount of the reverse payment is higher than the saved litigation expenses but less than the defendant's potential loss at trial, it is still likely that the patent was valid and infringed, although one can devise cases in which higher payments are consistent with a high probability of success, and low payments are consistent with a low probability of success.[413]

At some point, Cotter concedes, the size of the reverse payment may be a strong indicator of an anti-competitive agreement. Yet he notes that it is difficult to formulate a rule that would apply in all cases.[414] He suggests:

> In cases in which the amount of the payment substantially exceeds the parties' avoided litigation costs, the sensible solution may be to give them a choice of proving either that the payment is consistent with a high probability of success on the merits, in light of the parties' expected gains and losses, or that the patent is valid and infringed.[415]

Of course, other terms of the agreement, aside from the reverse payment, may also be indicators, one way or another, of the legitimacy of the settlement agreement.[416]

Hovenkamp, Janis, and Lumley differ with Cotter on the issue of size of reverse payments. They argue that they "do not think it follows that because it is rational for the patentee to agree to an exclu-

---

412 Cotter, above note 271 at 1812; Hovenkamp, Janis, and Lumley, above note 270 at 1800–1. O'Rourke and Brodley, above note 406 at 1782, generally agree that a reverse payment that is equivalent to anticipated legal costs is usually legitimate. They note that collateral costs to litigation can be inflated to produce an amount that is inappropriate.

413 Cotter, *ibid.* at 1814.

414 *Ibid.* at 1815.

415 *Ibid.*

416 These might include an agreement by the defendant to maintain its rights under the 180-day exclusivity period or an agreement not to go to market with non-infringing equivalents to the patented product. See Cotter, *ibid.*

sion payment, that payment cannot be anticompetitive."[417] For these authors, the relationship is straightforward: "the less likely the patentee is to win, the more it is willing to pay a generic to stay out of the market."[418] Hovenkamp, Janis, and Lumley propose an approach whereby a reverse payment automatically triggers a presumption that the settlement is unlawful. The onus would then shift to the infringement plaintiff to show that it is likely to win its infringement lawsuit, and that the amount of the reverse payment is no more than its anticipated litigation costs, should the lawsuit proceed.[419]

v) *Delayed Entry*

Instead of (or in addition to) a reverse payment, an agreement may contain a provision whereby the generic company agrees to delay its entry into the market. The period of delayed entry may be less than the remaining term of the patent monopoly. Hovenkamp, Janis, and Lumley describe such terms as an effective split of "the uncertainty costs of the litigation."[420] They find this type of clause, standing on its own, as legitimate because it "allows the parties to capture the economic significance of uncertainty as to patent outcome."[421] However, when an exclusion clause is also present, they caution that scrutiny is warranted. Further, they note that there is a risk that an exclusion payment will be hidden by the parties "agreeing under the table that the parties will cartelize the industry after entry."[422] For these reasons, they suggest some caution in scrutinizing delayed entry provisions.

O'Rourke and Brodley advocate the use of delayed entry provisions as a means of resolving the problems posed by reverse payment settlements. They argue that "settlement agreements in *Hatch-Waxman Act* cases should be limited to delayed entry by the generic producer (and of course may also provide for payment of royalties by the generic manufacturer)."[423] In their view this would eliminate the need to prove patent validity, as the term of the delayed entry would be a good indi-

---

417 Hovenkamp, Janis, and Lumley, above note 270 at 1758.
418 *Ibid.*
419 *Ibid.* at 1759.
420 *Ibid.* at 1762.
421 *Ibid.*
422 *Ibid.* at 1763.
423 *Ibid.* at 1786.

cator of the parties' assessment of the strength of the patent. A weak patent would lead to a shorter delay in market entry, while a strong patent would mean a longer delay. Yet another economist argues that such settlements can still harm consumer interests. Schrag argues that this "split-the-difference" analysis ignores the fact that there might be other parties who would enter the market if a finding of patent invalidity was made. He also posits that such settlements decrease the incentive for innovation in the form of inventing around existing patents.[424]

vi) Canadian Law

It is clear that the *Hatch-Waxman Act* has been a factor in the use of reverse payment settlements in the pharmaceutical context in the United States. The *Hatch-Waxman Act*, by altering the traditional dynamics between parties in patent disputes, has given rise to both reverse payment settlements and uncertainty as to the legitimacy of such payments. Any assessment of the likelihood of reverse payment settlements in Canada and their potential anti-competitive effects must necessarily first involve an assessment of Canada's equivalent to the *Hatch-Waxman Act*: the *Patented Medicines (Notice of Compliance) Regulations*.[425] The discussion below will take into account the October 2006 amendments to these regulations.[426]

Similar to *Hatch-Waxman*, the *PM(NOC) Regulations* were introduced as part of a complex scheme designed to allow the quickest possible entrance into the market of generic pharmaceutical products while still respecting the term of patent protection of the innovator products.[427] In the words of the Supreme Court of Canada, "The *NOC*

---

424 See Joel Schrag, "The Value of a Second Bite at the Apple: The Effect of Patent Dispute Settlements on Entry and Consumer Welfare," Bureau of Economics, Washington, DC, Working Paper No. 281, January 2006, online: www.ftc.gov/be/workpapers/wp281.pdf.

425 *PM(NOC) Regulations*, above note 13.

426 *Regulations Amending the Patented Medicines (Notice of Compliance) Regulations*, S.O.R./2006-242, 5 October 2006, *Canada Gazette*, Vol. 140, No. 21 (18 October 2006), online: http://canadagazette.gc.ca/partII/2006/20061018/html/sor242-e.html [*PM(NOC) Amendments*].

427 Regulatory Impact Analysis Statement Regarding Regulations Amending the *Patented Medicines (Notice of Compliance) Regulations*, S.O.R./2006-242, 5 October 2006, *Canada Gazette*, Vol. 140, No. 21 (18 October 2006), online: http://canadagazette.gc.ca/partII/2006/20061018/html/sor242-e.html at 9 of 22 [RIAS].

Regulations lie at the intersection of two regulatory systems with sometimes conflicting objectives."[428] These systems are, as is the case in the United States, the patent system and the drug approval process.

The *Patent Act*[429] provides that a party can work a patent prior to the expiration of the patent term if it is for the purpose of gaining regulatory approval so that the product can be brought swiftly to market on the expiration of the patent.[430] Since regulatory approval is often a lengthy process and can take two or more years from the expiry of a patent to obtain,[431] this provision allows for a crucial head start so that entry into the market can occur virtually at the moment the patent expires.[432]

The head start provided under the "early-working exception" is counterbalanced by the *PM(NOC) Regulations*. The *PM(NOC) Regulations* tie the regulatory approval process to the patent regime. Regulatory approval for pharmaceutical products must be obtained under the *Food and Drugs Act* (*FDA*).[433] An application for regulatory approval can be made either in the form of a New Drug Submission (NDS), or an Abbreviated New Drug Submission (ANDS). An NDS would have to be accompanied by detailed documentation, including research results sufficiently detailed to allow the minster to determine that the proposed drug is safe and effective. However, as is the case under the *Hatch-Waxman Act*, where a generic drug manufacturer seeks approval for a generic version of an already approved drug, it is allowed to submit an ANDS. In an ANDS, the generic manufacturer maintains that the proposed drug is the "pharmaceutical equivalent" of an

---

428 *AstraZeneca Canada Inc. v. Canada (Minister of Health)*, 2006 SCC 49 at para. 12 [*AstraZeneca*].

429 Above note 16.

430 *Ibid.*, s. 55.2(1). In *AstraZeneca*, above note 428 at para. 13, the Supreme Court noted that without the early working exception, "the *FDA* approval process will likely add at least two years to the effective monopoly of the patent owner, which is two years of monopoly longer than the *Patent Act* contemplates."

431 *Bristol Myers Squibb v. Canada (Attorney General)*, [2005] 1 S.C.R. 533, 2005 SCC 26 at para. 11 [*Bristol Myers*].

432 The RIAS, above note 427 at 9, refers to this as the "early-working" exception. It notes that "The generic pharmaceutical industry estimates that early-working can accelerate the market entry of its products in Canada by some three to five years."

433 R.S.C. 1985, c. F-27.

already approved drug, and the documentation submitted for that previously approved drug is relied upon for approval. Again, similar to the situation under the *Hatch-Waxman Act*, a much less rigorous research and screening process is required for approval of a generic drug that is the bioequivalent of an already approved drug. Approval is given in the form of a Notice of Compliance (NOC).

As with the *Hatch-Waxman Act*, the *PM(NOC) Regulations* integrate this drug approval process with patent considerations. Where a person has filed for an NDS or a Supplementary New Drug Submission (SNDS),[434] that party may submit a patent list to the minister, setting out specified information including any Canadian patent owned by the person that contains a claim for the medicinal ingredient, the formulation that contains that ingredient, and the dosage form or use of the medicinal ingredient "that has been approved through the issuance of a notice of compliance in respect of the submission."[435] Where a generic drug company applies for regulatory approval using an ANDS, and it "directly or indirectly compares that drug with, or makes reference to, another drug marketed in Canada under a notice of compliance issued to a first person and in respect of which a patent list has been submitted,"[436] the second manufacturer is given certain options. It can either explicitly state that it accepts that the NOC will not issue until the relevant patent or patents expire, or it may make an allegation that challenges the validity or the continued subsistence of the patent(s).[437] It may also allege that none of the relevant patent claims would be infringed by the making, constructing, using, or selling by that person of the drug for which the submission for the notice of compliance is filed.[438] The allegations are made in a Notice of Allegation (NOA). The person being served with the NOA, the patent holder, has forty-five days to apply to a court for an order of prohibition to prohibit the minister from issuing the NOC until the expiration of the patent that is the subject of the allegation.[439]

434 *PM(NOC) Regulations*, above note 13, s. 4(1), as amended by *PM(NOC) Amendments*, above note 426.

435 *Ibid.*, s. 4(2)(a)–(d), as amended by *PM(NOC) Amendments, ibid.*

436 *Ibid.*, s. 5(1), as amended by *PM(NOC) Amendments, ibid.*

437 *Ibid.*, s. 5(1)(b), as amended by *PM(NOC) Amendments, ibid.*

438 *Ibid.*, s. 5(1)(b)(iv), as amended by *PM(NOC) Amendments, ibid.*

439 *Ibid.*, s. 6(1).

The *Regulatory Impact Analysis Statement* for the recent amendments to the *PM(NOC) Regulations* refers to the scheme as "a very potent patent enforcement mechanism."[440] A patent holder who applies for an order of prohibition is entitled to benefit from a twenty-four-month automatic stay on the issuance of a NOC.[441] The Supreme Court has noted that "the court hearing the prohibition application has no discretion to lift the stay even if it thinks the innovator's case for interim relief is weak."[442] The Court has also observed that the twenty-four-month stay is "'in addition to' whatever remedies a patent owner has under the ordinary law of patents."[443] The recent amendments attempt to moderate the effects of this stay so as not to "defeat the overall purpose of the policy,"[444] which is to facilitate the earliest possible entry of generic products onto the market while still respecting patent rights.

The *PM(NOC) Regulations* have been much litigated in Canada, and problems in interpreting the scope of their application have most recently given rise to amendments seeking to clarify certain key points, and to maintain the overall objectives of the scheme. While these regulations raise a variety of issues in the Canadian context, it is worth noting that they remain significantly different from the *Hatch-Waxman Act* regime and in this respect may not lend themselves as easily to reverse payment settlements.

The RIAS published with the regulations notes that many stakeholders, during the consultation process, pressed the government to consider a regime that more closely mapped onto the US regime. It was noted that there was less consensus as to which features of *Hatch-Waxman Act* should be adopted in Canada, and that opinions tended to break down along innovator/generic lines.[445] The RIAS noted that in the late summer of 2005 a draft framework for a US-style regime

---

440 RIAS, above note 427 at 9 of 22.

441 The statutory freeze may come to an end if certain conditions are met (for example, the expiry of the patent at issue). Otherwise it remains in effect. See *PM(NOC) Regulations*, above note 13, s. 6.

442 *Bristol Myers*, above note 431 at para. 24.

443 *AstraZeneca*, above note 428 at para. 2.

444 RIAS, above note 427 at 10 of 22. The central modification is to amend the regulations so as to prevent the listing of multiple new patents over time so as to give rise to a succession of twenty-four-month stays in relation to a single ANDS.

445 RIAS, *ibid*. at 19 of 22.

was circulated for comment. The feedback received led to the current amendments, which are described as providing an "increased convergence with US law."[446] Nevertheless, key differences remain.

One of the most significant differences is the absence of the 180-day exclusivity period. As noted in the discussion above, this period has been a prominent factor in a number of reverse payment settlement agreements in the US, although its impact was significantly moderated by the *Medicare Modernization Act*[447] amendments in 2003. In the US, reverse payment settlement agreements played on the ability of the party entitled to the exclusivity period to prevent other generic companies from entering the market until it has chosen to trigger the period, and the 180 days have passed.

If reverse payment settlements do occur in the Canadian context, the preliminary consideration of the validity of the patent or the likelihood of infringement in the prohibition proceedings may make it easier to determine whether the settlement was anti-competitive. Under the *PM(NOC) Regulations*, the NOA triggers a process by which a brand name company can apply for an Order of Prohibition to stop the issuance of an NOC in relation to a generic product. During the prohibition proceedings, the court will make a preliminary assessment of the validity of the underlying patents if they are challenged. If the court is of the view that the patents are likely valid and likely to be infringed by the making of the generic version, it will grant the order. With this outcome, the generic company is forced to wait until the patents expire before it can proceed to market. On the other hand, if the court is of the view that the patents at issue are either likely not valid or not to be infringed, it may decline to issue the Order of Prohibition. Although the generic company will have suffered up to twenty-four-months' delay, it can then receive its NOC and proceed to market.

The twenty-four-month bar on the granting of an NOC also comes to an early end if the patent expires or is found invalid before the end of the twenty-four-month period.[448] There are other circumstances

446 *Ibid.* at 20 of 22.

447 Above note 284.

448 *PM(NOC) Regulations*, above note 13, s. 7(2). It also comes to an end if there is a court decision finding that no claim for the medicine or use of the medicine at issue is infringed.

that may cause the period to come to an end or be shortened.[449] Further, the *PM(NOC) Regulations* scheme contains a provision allowing a court to make an order for relief by way of damages where an application for an order of prohibition is withdrawn or discontinued by the applicant, or dismissed by the court hearing the application.[450] A loophole in the *PM(NOC) Regulations* regime that allowed patent holders to manipulate the patent list so as to obtain successive twenty-four-month stays against competitors has been closed by amendments to the regulations.[451] A recent decision of the Supreme Court of Canada has also achieved the same effect as a matter of interpretation for cases arising before the amendments.[452]

Even if an NOC is granted, the patent holder can choose to sue the generic company for patent infringement, as the prohibition proceedings do not preclude the exercise of other recourses. It is not clear that, even at this point, a reverse payment settlement would be made. The situation is different from that under *Hatch-Waxman*, where it is actual patent infringement litigation that is commenced and that is being settled at the outset. Under the *PM(NOC) Regulations*, the prohibition proceedings result in a preliminary view of the patent's validity and of the likelihood of infringement. This may give the parties a much clearer sense of their relative positions, thus decreasing the likelihood of a reverse payment settlement. Nevertheless, it is worth noting that the *PM(NOC) Regulations* do not contain a requirement that all settlement agreements be filed with the Competition Bureau, making oversight more difficult than it currently is in the US.

The courts have been very clear in the US that the mere exercise of the rights that flow from the patent monopoly does not, in and of itself, amount to anti-competitive activity. The situation is the same in Canada. The point is made clear in the *Intellectual Property Enforcement*

---

449 *Ibid.*, s. 7(3) (where the patent owner has consented to the "making, constructing, using or selling of the drug in Canada by the second person"); s. 7(4) (where an application has been withdrawn, discontinued or dismissed); and s. 7(5)(a) (where the court exercises discretion conferred under the regulations to shorten the period based on the conduct of the first person).

450 *Ibid.*, s. 8(1) and (4), as amended by *PM(NOC) Amendments*, above note 426.

451 *PM(NOC) Regulations*, *ibid.*, s. 4.1.

452 *AstraZeneca*, above note 428.

Guidelines (IPEGs) issued by the Competition Bureau.[453] The IPEGs state that the mere exercise of an intellectual property right does not raise competition concerns and define such an exercise as "the exercise of the owner's right to unilaterally exclude others from using the IP."[454] The IPEGs go on to indicate that the choice by an owner to use or not use its IP rights is also part of the "mere exercise" of IP rights. Nevertheless, the IPEGs make it clear that some dealings with IP rights may attract scrutiny. In particular,

> [w]hen joint conduct of two or more firms lessens or prevents competition, the competitive harm clearly flows from something more than the mere exercise of the IP right to refuse. To the extent that conduct such as conspiracy, bid-rigging, joint abuse of dominance, market allocation agreements and mergers restricts competition among firms actually or potentially producing substitute products or services, the presence of IP should not be a mitigating factor.[455]

Nevertheless, were they to occur in the Canadian context, reverse payment settlements would raise some of the same difficult problems that have arisen in the US. It would likely be difficult to determine precisely when a reverse payment settlement crosses the line from a legitimate means of settling complex and uncertain litigation over an underlying legitimate monopoly right, and when it amounts to an anti-competitive agreement. In Canada, as in the US, the issue might well turn on the strength or weakness of the underlying patent. This is a difficult matter to determine in the absence of conclusive litigation of the issues. Further, unlike the current situation in the US, there is

---

453 IPEGs, above note 5 at 7.

454 *Ibid.* See also *Competition Act*, R.S.C. 1985, c. C-34, s. 79(5).

455 IPEGs, above note 5 at 8. A recent decision by the Federal Court of Appeal confirms that some dealings with IP rights may run afoul of the *Competition Act*, *ibid.* See also *Competition Act*, s. 32. In *Eli Lilly & Co. v. Apotex, Inc.*, 2005 FCA 361 [*Eli Lilly*(2)], the court noted that s. 32 of the *Competition Act* would apply when intellectual property rights were used in such a way as to lessen competition. While the right to assign a patent is provided for in s. 50 of the *Patent Act*, above note 16, the court observed that "an interpretation of section 50 which does not immunize the assignment of patents from section 45 [of the *Competition Act*] is consistent with the purpose of the *Competition Act* . . ." *Eli Lilly* (2) at para. 32.

no requirement in Canada for settlement agreements to be filed with the Competition Bureau, raising challenges for oversight.

The Order of Prohibition provided for under the *PM(NOC) Regulations* does not result in the same level of consideration that a patent infringement suit or a challenge to patent validity would provide. Such an action is governed by the Rules of the Federal Court,[456] and the decision is made on a summary basis. The main issue before the court is whether the allegations made by the generic drug company in its NOA are sufficient to warrant the minister granting an NOC.[457] The proceedings do not preclude the parties independently pursuing patent infringement litigation.

In Canada, as in the United States, a patent is presumed valid.[458] This presumption of validity does not seem to be raised to the same plane as it is in the US;[459] nevertheless, it is likely to be the starting point in any consideration of the legitimacy of a settlement agreement. In such cases, the existence of a very weak patent would bolster the view that the reverse payment was unlawful. It is worth noting that when a brand name drug company brings a motion for an Order of Prohibition under the *PM(NOC) Regulations*, that company bears the burden of rebutting the allegations in the Notice of Allegation filed by the generic company. In other words, if the generic company has alleged that the patents are invalid, the party applying for the Order of Prohibition must establish that the allegations of invalidity are unfounded.[460] However, the Federal Court of Appeal has also made it clear that "a finding of invalidity or infringement, for the purposes of this kind of proceeding is not determinative of that issue in any subsequent action."[461]

---

456 *Federal Courts Rules*, S.O.R./98-106, ss. 300*ff.*

457 Francois M. Grenier et Catherine Lemay, "Le Règlement sur les mèdicaments brevetés (Avis de conformité)" (2003) 20 C.I.P.R. 51 at 59–60.

458 *Patent Act*, above note 16, s. 45.

459 In *Apotex*, above note 2 at para. 45, the Court referred to the statutory presumption of patent validity as being "rather weakly worded."

460 *Pfizer Canada Inc. v. Canada (Minister of Health)* (2005), 43 C.P.R. (4th) 241 at para. 58 (F.C.T.D.) [*Pfizer*]. The rebuttable presumption of validity is not entirely irrelevant to the applicant. See *Axcan Pharma Inc. v. Pharmascience Inc.* (2006), 50 C.P.R. (4th) 321 at para. 10 (F.C.T.D.).

461 *Pfizer*, *ibid.* at para. 57.

Unlike the scheme under the *Hatch-Waxman Act*, therefore, the Canadian *PM(NOC) Regulations* provide for a summary basis on which issues of patent validity can be litigated. The outcome of the summary proceedings is directly related to whether an NOC will be issued by the minister of health. Once a generic company receives an NOC, it may proceed to market with its product. However, the summary proceedings do not preclude separate patent infringement proceedings or other proceedings alleging patent invalidity.[462]

It is not clear whether the same incentives to enter into reverse payment settlements exist under the *PM(NOC) Regulations* as they do under the *Hatch-Waxman Act*. Both regimes alter the balance between innovators and generic companies, although there are also key differences in the two regimes. The lack of an exclusivity period, a process for the summary consideration of patent validity and infringement issues, and the separation of the *PM(NOC) Regulations* scheme from the full litigation of patent validity and infringement issues may diminish the likelihood of reverse payment settlements arising in the Canadian context. Indeed, the greater concern in the Canadian context would appear to be the proliferation of authorized generics.[463] Nevertheless, the potential for settlement of disputes with anti-competitive effects is still present, and the lack of a requirement to file such settlements with the Competition Bureau lessens the ability to scrutinize and evaluate the terms of such settlements.

Even if such settlements were to be scrutinized, the same issues that arise in the US context would prove problematic in Canada. As in the US, the settlement of litigation is considered to be in the public interest. Where the normal balance between the parties has been altered by a regime such as *Hatch-Waxman* or the *PM(NOC) Regulations*, the terms of settlement may be altered to reflect the change in

---

462 See, for example, *Apotex Inc. v. Syntex Pharmaceuticals International Ltd.* (1999), 1 C.P.R. (4th) 22 (F.C.T.D.), where a declaration of patent invalidity was granted notwithstanding the fact that an Order of Prohibition had earlier been granted under PM(NOC) proceedings.

463 RIAS, above note 427 at 21 of 22. Authorized generics are generic versions of brand name drugs that are marketed under a generic name by the brand name drug company. Competition law issues surrounding authorized generics are discussed in another paper from the symposium. See P. Grootendorst, "Effects of "Authorized Generics" on Canadian Drug Prices," found in this book.

balance. Reverse payments may not be inherently inappropriate. The challenge is to distinguish between concessions legitimately made as part of the compromise required to settle litigation where the validity or infringement of uncertain intellectual property rights are in dispute, and those that are made so as to unduly limit competition.

D. CONCLUSIONS

This paper has explored in detail three contexts in which strategies can be adopted to effectively extend intellectual property protection. These strategies have fallen into two general categories. The first involves the exploitation of overlapping intellectual property rights. The facts that gave rise to the *Kirkbi*[464] litigation provide an illustration of an attempt to exploit a potential overlap in protection between patent law and trade-mark law. The dispute in *Euro Excellence*[465] similarly illustrates an exploitation of the overlap between copyright and trade-mark protection. The second general category involves the exercise of weak or uncertain intellectual property rights so as to effectively extend the protection that might otherwise be available to the rights holder. This phenomenon was considered chiefly in relation to pharmaceutical patent disputes, where reverse payment settlements may be used to shore up and insulate potentially invalid patents from challenge.

The contexts in which intellectual property rights may be extended are as diverse as the possible solutions. This paper has also considered various approaches to combating the extension of intellectual property rights. Legislative amendment is one option, but it is often slow in coming. In Australia the legislative changes that responded to the *Bailey's*[466] decision were implemented more than ten years after that case was decided. As seen in *Kirkbi*, courts may remedy problems of overlap through their interpretation of the legislation or their development of the common law. Yet, judicially imposed limits also occur slowly and may develop in a piecemeal fashion depending upon the fact situations presented to the courts. Courts have the option to address problems of overlap by deliberately drawing the attention of

---

464 Above note 2.

465 Above note 9.

466 Above note 194.

Parliament to specific problems and recommending changes. Furthermore, they may refuse to grant equitable remedies on specific facts or may even develop equitable doctrines such as copyright or patent misuse. However, these latter approaches also develop in a piecemeal fashion, and they tend only to serve defendants who have the resources to engage in litigation in the first place.

In some cases, competition law provides a further means of challenging practices aimed at extending intellectual property rights. However, as seen in the reverse payment settlement cases, transgressions of competition rules may be difficult to prove, particularly where a finding of a violation requires speculation as to the likely validity of underlying intellectual property rights.

The proper approach to take to the range of issues that fall under the general umbrella of extension of intellectual property rights may depend on the context in which the issues arise. With overlapping rights, the overlaps are often unintended and evolve as a matter of interpretation over time. Where this is the case, the overlap likely does not reflect the policy underlying the legislation. Such situations lend themselves more easily to judge-made solutions, as a purposive judicial interpretation can be used to bring the application of the law more into line with the underlying public policy.

With the exercise of weak or uncertain rights, the circumstances are different. The case of reverse payment settlements offers an interesting example of a complex dynamic leading to potential competition problems. There, competing public policy concerns for the promotion of innovation through the patent system on the one hand, and for affordable health care on the other, have resulted in a scheme for approval of generic drugs that alters the traditional litigation dynamics between parties in intellectual property disputes. The underlying intellectual property rights may be weak or uncertain, but the altered litigation dynamics provide incentives for patent holders to share their monopoly profits with a generic challenger rather than to risk a finding of patent infringement. The ability to evaluate the legitimacy of settlement agreements in this context is hindered by the uniquely altered dynamic between the parties, and by the difficulty of assessing the strength of the underlying intellectual property rights. Added to the difficult dynamics imposed by the regulatory scheme are the uncertainties created by systemic flaws in the examination and grant of patents.

In many ways, it is the role of litigation to explore the relative strength of claims. However, the exploitation of weak or uncertain rights may likewise be a function of an economic or power imbalance that insulates the intellectual property claims from challenge. In other cases, systemic defects may be a contributing factor. This is the case, for example, where a patent system produces a significant volume of questionable patents. Additionally, it is possible that better oversight (such as the requirement to file settlement agreements with the Competition Bureau) may resolve some, if not all, of the concerns. The solutions in cases of the exercise of weak or uncertain rights are more diverse; they are also more difficult as they turn on the inherent uncertainties that arise in the context of litigation.

There are sufficient similarities in intellectual property regimes among many Western jurisdictions that strategies for extending intellectual property rights may be pursued in multiple jurisdictions. This is certainly the case with the strategy pursued in *Euro Excellence*; it was successfully used in a previous case in Australia. It is also the case that Kirkbi's attempt to extend its protection for its LEGO blocks was not limited to Canada. Similar attempts, followed by litigation, took place in a range of other countries. The growing pressure to harmonize intellectual property regimes is likely to contribute to similar strategies being pursued in multiple jurisdictions.

It is difficult to assess the actual prevalence of the kinds of activities considered in this paper. This is so for a number of reasons. First, as noted in the discussion of overclaiming in relation to weak or uncertain rights, much of the activity occurs in a manner that is difficult to detect, and where it does not appear on any kind of public record. In the US, when reverse payment settlements became problematic, the *Hatch-Waxman Act* was amended to require the filing of settlement agreements with the Department of Justice and the FTC. Without such a filing requirement, it is extremely difficult to oversee conduct that arises in the settlement of disputes.

Second, cases like *Euro Excellence* present what might be the tip of an iceberg. As a result of the decision of the Supreme Court of Canada[467] it may be expected that the number of instances in which copyright law is used to bolster an exclusive distribution agreement will

467 *Euro Excellence*, above note 9.

increase. Actual numbers may be difficult to assess, as few parties will be willing or able to withstand an aggressive litigation strategy. Certainly, anecdotally there has been a great deal of interest in this case. An approach similar to that used by Kraft Canada in *Euro Excellence* could be pursued in relation to the importation of any product bearing copyright-protected labels or designs or, for that matter, instruction booklets or other literary works contained in the product packaging.

Beyond the particular examples considered in detail in this paper, it is clear that the practice of overclaiming is widespread and, while not limited to disputes over intellectual property rights, is complicated in the context of IP by a number of factors. There is often a significant resource gap between IP rights holders and IP users. Overclaiming tends to be successful when those against whom claims are made have limited resources to challenge those claims. Further, there is a significant knowledge gap as well. IP has traditionally been a highly specialized area of law, practised chiefly in large firms, and in firms located in central Canada. These factors contribute to the inability of IP users with more limited resources and in less central regions of the country to garner accurate or affordable information or advice about their rights.

Another dynamic at play in the area of IP rights relates to the relatively slow evolution of caselaw in this area. For example, although there are many significant unresolved issues to explore in relation to copyright in computer software or on the Internet in Canada, there are very few cases addressing issues in this area. In the US, where the volume of litigation is much higher, a larger number of court decisions leads to a much quicker articulation of legal principles. In Canada, the contexts change rapidly, yet the small volume of cases making it to the courts results in an increase in uncertainty surrounding the scope or strength of intellectual property rights.

It is difficult to see how the strategies for extension of intellectual property rights considered in this paper contribute to further innovation. In the context of the extension of intellectual property rights, parties seek to claim more protection, either in terms of duration of protection (*Kirkbi*) or scope of protection (*Euro Excellence*) than would otherwise have been available. The exploitation of overlaps in this manner cannot reflect the public policy balance struck in the existing legislation. In neither *Kirkbi* nor *Euro Excellence* is the goal of fostering innovation served. In *Euro Excellence*, the strategy adopted is aimed at preserving an exclusive distribution network, and while it might be arguable that exclusive distribution networks protect consumers, it is difficult to see how they contribute to innovation. In *Kirkbi*, the objective of the strategy adopted was to extend a monopoly over a product that had been in existence for a very considerable period of time. It is again difficult to see how this contributes to innovation.

The case of reverse payment settlements is more complex. The *Hatch-Waxman Act* specifically sought to balance the protection of IP rights with the speedy entry of generic products into the marketplace as soon as patent protection expired. While it might be arguable that a longer term of patent protection would better serve innovation in the pharmaceutical sector, this is clearly not the legislative policy choice reflected in either the *Patent Act* or the *Hatch-Waxman Act*. Even if it is arguable that a longer, more secure term of patent protection will foster more innovation, the *Hatch-Waxman Act* (and the *PM(NOC) Regulations*) regime clearly places in the balance other competing public policy considerations. It must also be remembered that reverse payment settlements may be entered into in part to shield a bad patent from a successful challenge to its validity. As bad patents may serve as a brake on innovation, and as an imposition of unwarranted costs on the general public, it is difficult to see how the goals of fostering innovation are furthered by settlements that deliberately extend the life of bad patents by insulating them from attack. The challenge is, of course, to separate out those settlements that work against public policy from those that are consistent with a legitimate exercise of intellectual property rights.

Commentary on "Extension of Intellectual Property Rights"

Ejan Mackaay[1]

A. INTRODUCTION

Teresa Scassa's core thesis is that the balance at the root of intellectual property rights has been gradually displaced towards an extension of those rights well beyond what was contemplated in their original design, and that the displacement is detrimental to innovation and competition. The law is out of kilter. This observation will be the first tier of this brief comment.

This thesis is illustrated in two extensions, the first where one intellectual property right is used to overcome the limits of another — such as the attempt to rely on trade-mark law to shore up an expired patent right — and the other where payments are made to a competitor to stay out of one's field, even where one has no intellectual property right to stand on. The paper is interesting in its detailed presentation of cases and practices in this particular stretch of the intellectual property-competition law interface. It shows how actors react rationally to the overtures provided by legal structures and puts institutional flesh on the rather bony structures economists usually offer to tackle the issues of that interface.

1 Professor in the Faculty of Law and Director of the Centre for Business Law and International Trade (CDACI), Université de Montréal.

If the law is out of kilter, how might it be corrected and who should do it? Some formulas are more promising than others. Our hands may be tied by what happens elsewhere, if diversity of law is taken here to be undesirable. Moreover, the cost of the corrective process must be a consideration: patent litigation, even on meritorious claims, is so costly as to exert a stifling effect on innovation. Teresa Scassa's view of where to look (and where not to look) for remedial action warrants discussion. This will be the second tier of the comment.

B. INTELLECTUAL PROPERTY LAW OUT OF KILTER?

Intellectual property rights borrow the logic of traditional property rights in that these are the best institutions we know to provide incentives for good husbanding of scarce resources and for inventiveness in their use.[2] The borrowing is only partial because the object of intellectual property rights, that is forms of information, is not naturally scarce and, indeed, advancement of knowledge is facilitated by easy sharing of knowledge.[3] Knowledge is cumulative. Information works best when it freely circulates.

Yet talent for creating innovation is scarce and it looks like we need special incentives to draw it into innovative activity. Intellectual property is only one of the techniques we use for providing such incentives. It has the advantage of being decentralized: if your creation qualifies, you are entitled to your right; the decision does not depend on someone's assessment of its value.

The right restricts the free circulation of information in order to give you the opportunity of cashing in on your creation: a limited

---

2 The following considerations draw on the chapters on "La propriété et les droits reels" and "La propriété intellectuelle" in E. Mackaay and S. Rousseau, *Analyse économique du droit* 2e éd. (Montreal: Paris/Éditions Thémis, 2008).

3 See R.R. Nelson, "The Simple Economics of Basic Scientific Research" (1959) 67 Journal of Political Economy 297; R.R. Nelson, "The Market Economy, and the Scientific Commons" in M.-A. Frison-Roche and A. Abello, eds., *Droit et économie de la propriété intellectuelle* (Paris: Librairie générale de droit et de jurisprudence, 2005) at 27–50; J. Boyle, "Fencing Off Ideas" (2002) 131 Daedalus 13 at 23, online: http://james-boyle.com/daedalus.pdf; D.L. Burk, *Intellectual Property in the Context of E-science*, Minnesota Legal Studies Research Paper No. 06-47 (2006), online: http://ssrn.com/abstract=929479.

monopoly, if you will. This entails that you can stop others from using your creation without your permission (that is, without paying the price you set). Intellectual property rights open the door to rewarding the creation we see; the drawback is that they simultaneously close the door (at least somewhat) on creations to come, which we do not yet see. The reason is that later creations build on earlier ones; rarely does a creation arise *ex nihilo*. Knowledge cumulates. What one should like to ensure is that society gets the maximal amount of creation over the longer term.

What you earn with your right is determined in an equally decentralized way: it depends ultimately on what numerous consumers are willing to pay for products incorporating your creation. The intellectual property rights therefore entail a gamble on the success of the creation. Taken over all creators, the institution may be likened to a lottery, the "innovation lottery" as Scherer has termed it.[4] Scherer shows that the spoils of that lottery are extremely skewed: a few innovators earn mega-bucks, some fetch a decent return, and most should be happy not to lose their shirt. That holds for pharmaceuticals (patent field) as well as for cultural products (copyright).

It is intriguing to ask what draws people to partake in such an extremely unfair lottery. Surely it must be the belief, in most cases mistaken as it will turn out, that one's creation will hit the jackpot (the "pot-of-gold logic").

How large does the pot of gold have to be to draw people into the lottery? It is tempting to reason that it would be sufficient if it provided a decent return on the creator's investment. But this would be to put the cart before the horse, because you decide whether to invest in your creation on the prospects of being rewarded. The size of the reward you foresee determines the range of creative endeavour you would be willing to devote your time and talent to. Of course, you hope to earn back your investment, but you will find out if you can only after you have made your decision to invest. If you do not earn back your investment, you draw lessons from that for future ventures. Highly innovative but

---

4 F.M. Scherer, "The Innovation Lottery" in R. Cooper Dreyfuss, D. Leenheer, and H. First, eds., *Expanding the Boundaries of Intellectual Property: Innovation Policy for the Knowledge Society* (Oxford: Oxford University Press, 2001) at 3–21.

also risky ventures may be undertaken in the hope of unusually large returns on investment. The information-technology world offers several examples such as Amazon, eBay, PayPal, and Google.

The point of the very novelty in creative endeavour is that we cannot fully rely on past endeavours to guide us in determining how large the pot of gold has to be for future ones. The larger it is, the greater the lengths people may be expected to go to in order to win it. Sag has argued that there are initially increasing, but then decreasing returns to scale in extending the monopoly granted by way of intellectual property rights.[5] For the moment, however, this is a mere hypothesis and, at all events, we do not know anything about the actual shape of those curves and hence about the optimal size of the pot of gold.

Perhaps we do have a handle on a different aspect of the intellectual property rights puzzle. I argued earlier that as one extends intellectual property rights to reward creations that are visible now, one closes it to the same extent for creations to come, which are not yet visible. The problem with the latter is that it is hard to have an accurate picture of the importance of creations that are prevented from arising by too stringent intellectual property rights. A hint of this may be gleaned from the wave of innovation that followed the initial deregulation of the telephone interconnect market, and later of other aspects of the North American telephone system in the 1970s. Until deregulation, everything seemed to indicate that we had the best of all worlds. The monopoly provided by regulation seemed to give us as much innovation as we could afford. Yet upon deregulation, competition, here as elsewhere, revealed itself as a discovery procedure or, to be put it more bluntly, an eye-opener:[6] the wave of innovation showed what we had been depriving ourselves of all those years.

The Supreme Court of Canada has recalled the implicit equilibrium underlying intellectual property rights in *Théberge*:

---

5 M.J. Sag, "Beyond Abstraction: The Law and Economics of Copyright Scope and Doctrinal Efficiency" (2006) 81 Tul. L. Rev. 187–250, online: http://papers.ssrn.com/sol3/papers.cfm?abstract_id=916603, Figs. 1 and 3.

6 F.A. Hayek, "Competition as a Discovery Procedure" in F.A. Hayek, ed., *New Studies in Philosophy, Politics, Economics and the History of Ideas* (Chicago: University of Chicago Press, 1978) 179–90; I.M. Kirzner, *How Markets Work—Disequilibrium, Entrepreneurship and Discovery* (London: Institute of Economic Affairs, 1997).

> The *Copyright Act* is usually presented as a balance between promoting the public interest in the encouragement and dissemination of works of the arts and intellect and obtaining a just reward for the creator (or, more accurately, to prevent someone other than the creator from appropriating whatever benefits may be generated).[7]
>
> . . .
>
> Excessive control by holders of copyrights and other forms of intellectual property may unduly limit the ability of the public domain to incorporate and embellish creative innovation in the long-term interests of society as a whole, or create practical obstacles to proper utilization.[8]

The reach of an intellectual property right can conveniently be analysed along four dimensions: the objects it will protect; the conditions to be met for the right to be available (lowering these thresholds will in fact make more objects subject to protection); the remedies it affords the title holder; and the duration of the right. Summary inspection of the main intellectual property rights of patent and copyright shows that over the past quarter-century, these rights have been extended on all or nearly all of those dimensions. We protect intangible objects such as software and business methods as well as elements of the human genome, even though, traditionally, ideas and elements of nature were excluded from protection, presumably because of the monopolistic effects that would entail. As the law has developed, the tests of originality for copyright and of novelty and non-obviousness for patents have been progressively watered down, interlocutory injunctions to stop alleged infringements of intellectual property rights are routinely granted, and the duration of copyright has been continually extended — in the US, it has roughly doubled every half-century since the first *Copyright Act*.

To be sure, new technological developments throw up new objects, whose protection may require an extension of existing rights on the same grounds as protection that was afforded for products of older technology. But in no way could this argument justify, for instance, the

---

7 *Théberge v. Galerie d'Art du Petit Champlain inc.*, 2002 SCC 34 at para. 30, 210 D.L.R. (4th) 385, 17 C.P.R. (4th) 161, 23 B.L.R. (3d) 1 [*Théberge*].

8 *Ibid.* at para. 32.

extension of copyright to life plus seventy years throughout most of the developed world and to any activity on the Internet. Indeed, a very recent paper by Boldrin and Levine, relying on a range of empirical data, puts forth the daring argument that for patents, ten years of protection would do, and for copyright, two years.[9] Unbridled extension of intellectual property rights has thrown the underlying equilibrium out of kilter. How much damage is being done is difficult to assess: we do not see the creations that are prevented from arising.

C. ON REMEDIAL ACTION

Teresa Scassa expresses doubts regarding the courts' ability to tackle the problems thrown up by the unbridled extension of intellectual property rights: "The Courts are not well positioned to speculate as to possible future scenarios, or to engage in broad consultations." Fair enough, but an economist would reply: "what is the alternative?" And I feel distinctly less sanguine than does Teresa Scassa about Parliament's ability to do better.

As a guiding principle, it is helpful to recall a distinction often made in Europe between structural and behavioural corrections. Where possible, one should aim for corrections built into the structures (here intellectual property law) and only in the last resort correct deficiencies by latching on to behaviour (competition law). Clear structures allow actors in the field to plan their activities confidently; this fosters legal certainty. Fine-tuning sanctions of behaviour in particular cases is a more delicate business and fraught with uncertainties for those subject to it.

Where patents are considered misused to block advances by others—as James Watt is thought to have done with his patent on

---

9 M. Boldrin and D.K. Levine, "Growth and Intellectual Property," NBER Working Paper no. 12769 (2007) at 22. See also M. Boldrin and D.K. Levine, *Against Intellectual Monopoly* (Cambridge: Cambridge University Press, 2008). Earlier *The Economist* magazine had already made a pitch for a drastically reduced term for copyright: "The 14-year term of the original 18th-century British and American copyright laws, renewable once, might be a good starting point," "Copyrights—A Radical Rethink" *The Economist* (25 January 2003) at 15; repeated in "Media Companies Are Jubilant at a Supreme Court Judgment, but Congress Should Take Them On" *The Economist* (2 July 2005) at 14.

steam engines, and Alexander Graham Bell, with patents on aspects of the telephone process—pointing to the cross-licensing one is engaged in or to a patent pool one belongs to is a structural answer.[10] Successful patent pools have operated in the heavy manufacturing industries (aircraft, trains, cars). Whether patent pools continue to be an appropriate answer to the charge of patent misuse is a moot point. Where patents cover complementary inventions, patent pools work for the general good by avoiding blocking patents; where they cover substitutes, they may lead to cartelization, to the detriment of the general welfare.[11] In the case of patent pools encompassing thousands of patents, as they do in the present information technology industry, this last risk is a distinct possibility.

So let us focus on intellectual property laws and have them strike the right balance between reward for the creations we see and openness to the creations we do not yet see, a balance that seems to have been contemplated when these laws were originally enacted. Do the legislators get it right? David Nimmer's analysis of how American legislators have recently mangled the *Copyright Act*[12] gives cold comfort to the idea of putting faith in our parliamentarians.[13] Fifty amendments were introduced in the US *Copyright Act*[14] over twenty-five years. Nimmer analyses the changes in detail and feels justified to conclude that there is a straightforward correlation between the length and complexity of the amendments and the extent to which they ostensibly pander to interest groups (rent-seeking, in other words). The US *Copyright Act* is less readable now than it was a quarter-century ago, and this is probably equally true of the copyright acts (and intellectual property codes) of most other developed nations, Canada included.

---

10 S.C. Carlson, "Patent Pools and the Antitrust Dilemma"(1999) 16 Yale J. on Reg. 359 at 363.

11 C. Shapiro, "Navigating the Patent Thicket: Cross Licenses, Patent Pools, and Standard-setting," in A.B. Jaffe, ed., *Innovation Policy and the Economy*, vol. 1 (Cambridge, MA: MIT Press, 2001) at 119–50, online: http://faculty.haas.berkeley.edu/shapiro/thicket.pdf.

12 17 U.S.C. §§ 101–810.

13 D. Nimmer, "Codifying Copyright Comprehensibly" (2004) 51 UCLA L. Rev. 1233.

14 Above note 12.

The problem in Canada is that while Parliament has the means to "speculate as to possible future scenarios, or to engage in broad consultations," to use Teresa Scassa's terms, in a representative democracy it may also disproportionately lend an ear to organized pressure groups, as the public choice literature has reminded us.[15] Where there are opposing pressure groups on either side of a policy issue, as in the patent field, the danger is not too great, but where an organized industrial lobby faces dispersed consumer interests, as is the case with respect to copyright, one must fear the worst. It is a small wonder that the duration of patents is essentially unchanged, whereas that of copyright has been continually extended.

Doubts about the legislative process do not entail the conclusion that all is well with the judicial process, as indeed Teresa Scassa points out. The enforcement cost of relying on the courts is such that the mere threat of legal action on the part of a large player is sufficient to scare off the smaller upstarts. This cannot be a good thing for the collective welfare because most dramatic creations are the work of upstarts.[16] The validity of patents is unlikely to be settled by the courts in those circumstances.

Many players will be reluctant to enforce their patent claims in court, not only because of the cost, but also, more perniciously, because they risk losing their patent altogether should the lawsuit go against them. Settling under those circumstances would usually seem to be the more sensible business decision. Once more, the validity of the underlying patent is not examined in court.

Yet relative certainty surrounding the validity of patents and about the areas they cover is essential for the most highly creative ventures to go forward. Uncertainty slows innovation. We cannot gauge the full extent of the damage we are doing to ourselves, but we can at least state the general direction of the nefarious effects, as Jaffe and Lerner have done.[17] One of their proposals for reform is to alleviate the procedure for

---

15 See for instance I. Shughart, F. William, and L. Razzolini, eds., *The Elgar Companion to Public Choice* (Cheltenham: Edward Elgar, 2001); W.C. Mitchell, and R.T. Simmons, *Beyond Politics—Markets, Welfare, and the Failure of Bureaucracy* (Boulder, CO: Westview Press, 1994).

16 W.J. Baumol, online: www.nber.org/papers/w10578.

17 A.B. Jaffe and J. Lerner, *Innovation and Its Discontents: How Our Broken Patent System Is Endangering Innovation and Progress, and What to Do about It*

contesting patents early on. The decision to post patent applications on the Internet for public consultation and to allow for opposition to be expressed at that stage looks like a promising step forward. The decision, by the United States Supreme Court,[18] to curtail recourse to interlocutory injunctions for stopping alleged patent infringements is another welcome step, considering the travails that the Canadian firm Research in Motion has had to go through at the hands of American courts to keep its Blackberry on the market. It would go some way to taking the sting out of the "patent ambush" or the "patent troll."

To express yet another doubt about the appropriate role for the courts: should the courts be in the business of dictating that Côte-d'Or chocolate can be marketed if its copyrighted elephant is covered by a sticker?[19] The Supreme Court of Canada has recently considered this.

D. CONCLUSION

In summary, Teresa Scassa is right in underscoring that the equilibrium implicit in our intellectual property rights law is being surreptitiously displaced towards more extensive intellectual property rights and that this is likely to have deleterious, but hard to gauge effects on competition and innovation. What corrective steps would be apposite and upon which institutions would it be incumbent to undertake them is a more delicate question. While Parliament is ostensibly better equipped to handle the policy questions involved, it is, unlike the courts, subject to rent-seeking activities that would offset that advantage. An important step in seeking to maintain the equilibrium is to articulate where it lies, as indeed our Supreme Court has started to do. That should certainly help the courts in countering undue extensions of intellectual property rights. Some procedural improvements may require legislative action. Overall, it would seem preferable to seek structural corrections (intellectual property rights law) first and

---

(Princeton: Princeton University Press, 2004).

18 *eBay Inc. v. MercExchange*, 126 S. Ct. 1837,164 L. Ed. 2d 641, 2006 U.S. LEXIS 3872, 74 U.S.L.W. 4248 (2006).

19 *Kraft Canada, Inc.* v. *Euro Excellence* (2004), 33 C.P.R. (4th) 246, 2004 FC 652, aff'd (2005), 47 C.P.R. (4th) 113, 2005 FCA 427, rev'd 2007 SCC 37.

leave behavioural corrections, in particular through competition law, for fine tuning at the margin.

Commentary: The Social Costs of Rent-seeking by Intellectual Property Owners

Michael J. Meurer[1]

In her interesting paper, Teresa Scassa analyzes some of the methods that intellectual property (IP) owners have used to expand their rights "beyond what was originally contemplated" by policy-makers. She puts these methods in two categories: (i) exploitation of overlapping rights, and (ii) assertion of weak or uncertain rights. I agree with most of the doctrinal analysis in her paper and I share her concern about unwarranted expansion of IP rights. In this comment, I augment her policy analysis by fitting it into a familiar and more general framework—the "private-attorney-general framework."

The private-attorney-general framework applies to situations in which a private party is encouraged to bring suit to advance the public interest. People often think of IP as a property regime, but it also makes sense to think of IP as a regulatory regime. In particular, IP laws are regulatory laws designed to encourage the private production of information. IP owners are given standing to sue parties who engage in "unfair competition." If the IP owner is rational, then these suits are profitable. If the law is well designed, then these suits are also socially desirable, and the threat of suit achieves the regulatory object-

1 Professor and Michaels Faculty Scholar, Boston University School of Law.

ive of deterring unfair competition and encouraging the production of information.

Indirect regulation via private attorneys general has social value because private parties often have stronger incentives and better information than public officials. Strong private incentives are created by awarding profitable remedies to successful private plaintiffs. Ideally, these plaintiffs have good information about the behaviour subject to regulation — often because they are harmed by inappropriate behaviour. Product safety is regulated in part through tort law because injured parties have important information about harm caused by some product. Anti-competitive conduct is regulated in part through competition law because certain parties have important information about the performance of their markets.

In this comment I will draw parallels between the behaviour criticized by Scassa and similar behaviour by plaintiffs in tort law, competition law, and other areas of law that rely on private enforcement. In a nutshell, Scassa identifies examples of socially costly rent-seeking that we should expect to see when the legal system generously gives out "tickets" to bring lawsuits against successful businesses.

A. INCENTIVE MISALIGNMENT

Private enforcement causes social harm when the private incentives of the IP owner are not closely aligned with socially optimal incentives. Private enforcement works well when an IP owner sues to enjoin a pirate who copies information in a way that undermines the incentive to create the information. Private enforcement works badly when an IP owner sues an innovative party to avert legitimate competition or gain some other private advantage.

Walker Process v. Food Machinery provides an example of an anti-competitive patent lawsuit.[2] Food Machinery fraudulently obtained a patent on a sewage treatment process and used the patent in a failed attempt to exclude Walker from its market. Food Machinery sued Walker for patent infringement, and Walker counterclaimed with the allegation that Food Machinery illegally monopolized the relevant

---

2 *Walker Process Equipment, Inc. v. Food Machinery & Chemical Corp.*, 382 U.S. 172 (1965).

market. The US Supreme Court reversed the lower courts and held that section 2 of the *Sherman Act*[3] permits this sort of claim.[4]

Opportunistic IP lawsuits probably are a more common rent-seeking problem. By definition, opportunistic suits are weak on the merits, but they often succeed in drawing a nuisance settlement payment from a defendant, especially when the defendant has made investments that would make it costly to stop using the IP in question. A company named S Industries filed at least thirty-three trade-mark suits between 1995 and 1997. "The plaintiff used the mark Sentra with over-the-counter, discount computer mouse pads. In one case, it sued a company named Centra, which used the mark in association with expensive data management software bought by petrochemical, aerospace, and other manufacturing industries. The US Court of Appeals for the Seventh Circuit found that the lawsuit lacked merit and was oppressive . . . ."[5]

Incentive alignment problems also appear in the arena of competition law. More than twenty years ago, an influential article by Baumol and Ordover warned that competition law can be used to subvert competition.[6] Good competition policy probably requires that private enforcement protects competition rather than competitors. Ideally, a competitor should be allowed to bring a private action only against a defendant who has harmed competition (usually the interests of consumers). A competitor should not be allowed to bring a private action that advances its own interests in a way that harms consumers (and competition generally).

The assertion of weak IP rights parallels practices that have been criticized in other areas of the law. Many commentators assert that tort and securities plaintiffs often bring frivolous lawsuits in American courts. The incentive problem is often linked to the assertion that a plaintiff's case is weak on the facts. Despite factual weakness, a

---

3 15 U.S.C.A. §§ 1–7 (West 1997).

4 This sort of antitrust claim rarely succeeds. It is not clear whether this kind of anti-competitive threat has been effectively deterred, or if instead, it is just hard for victims to detect the fraud and prove their case.

5 M.J. Meurer, "Controlling Opportunistic and Anti-competitive Intellectual Property Litigation" (2003) 44 B.C.L. Rev.. 509 at 518 [Meurer].

6 W.J. Baumol and J.A. Ordover, "Use of Antitrust to Subvert Competition" (1985) 28 J.L. & Econ. 247.

plaintiff's attorney may press a case in the hope of winning a nuisance settlement payment.

Rent-seeking costs from weak or frivolous suits may be a bigger problem in IP than in most areas of the law. The main difficulty faced by plaintiffs in these suits is convincing defendants that the suit is credible. The credibility of socially harmful IP suits is aided by the complexity of IP law. The scope of IP rights is variable and courts are prone to error when dealing with difficult technical issues related to scope. In addition, complexity and strong remedies can impose significant costs on defendants even at an early stage of litigation.[7]

How can we identify problems with incentive alignment that cause socially harmful suits by a private attorney general? This is a difficult task. In the IP context, we need to assess whether an IP suit is weak on the facts, or whether the plaintiff's harm is outside the set of harms that the law was intended to regulate. Many IP suits are costly and fact-intensive and it may be difficult to assess whether a suit is frivolous. Furthermore, the traditional approach to IP law identifies unfair competition that undermines the incentive to create intellectual property as the harm subject to regulation. When I frame the problem this way, competition lawyers are apt to immediately sense why IP law has rent-seeking problems. It may be difficult for courts to properly distinguish fair competition that hurts an IP owner from unfair competition that undermines creative incentives.

Because it is difficult to identify socially harmful IP lawsuits it is also difficult and costly to deter them. Nevertheless, IP rent-seeking costs in the American patent system are so large that judges and policy-makers must take steps to address them.[8] The social costs have not been quantified in copyright or trade-mark law, but anecdotal evidence suggests these costs may be large too.[9] Economists Boldrin and

---

7 See Meurer, above note 5 at 512–16 for more details.

8 If rent-seeking costs are broadly defined to include costs to inadvertent infringement, then patent owners impose enormous rent-seeking costs on defendant-innovators. See generally, J. Bessen and M.J. Meurer, *Patent Failure: How Judges, Bureaucrats and Lawyers Put Innovators at Risk* (Princeton: Princeton University Press, 2008), which finds that the costs of the patent system exceed the benefits for the average publicly traded American firm.

9 See generally, Meurer, above note 5, which lists examples of opportunistic and anti-competitive patent, copyright, and trade-mark litigation.

Levine believe the social costs of patent and copyright are so large that they should be abolished.[10] In this comment, I take a more moderate approach and suggest reforms that mitigate rent-seeking costs.

B. REFORMS TO MITIGATE IP RENT-SEEKING COSTS

Scassa illustrates the problem of overlapping rights with the case *Kirkbi*.[11] The case concerns an attempt to "replace" expired patent protection on the design of LEGO blocks with trade dress protection (a form of trade-mark that is denoted as "distinguishing guise" in Canada). The argument in favour of trade dress protection here is that consumers associate the design of the blocks with a particular manufacturer, and therefore the design functions as a trade-mark. This assertion is plausible, but problematic, because the very same design is functional and was patented.

I think she is right to worry about socially wasteful rent-seeking in this sort of case. She notes that the expansion of rights in a case like this is unlikely to provide much of an investment incentive for future toy designers. The extra rents are earned after the patent expires (the distant future at the time of the block design). And the odds that a product design would eventually serve as an indicator of product origin are rather small.

If an expansive approach to trade dress protection in a case like this provides little *ex ante* investment incentive, then the law should be evaluated based on *ex post* effects. The exclusionary effect of trade dress protection was apparent in *Kirkbi* and I do not see potential offsetting benefits.

Kirkbi is not unique. *Yankee Candle v. Bridgewater Candle*[12] is an American case that vividly depicts an established firm using a trade dress lawsuit to exclude a competitor. An established candle-maker brought a trade dress lawsuit against an entrant candle-maker. The trade dress was the method of selling candles, specifically the meth-

---

10 M. Boldrin and D.K. Levine, *Against Intellectual Monopoly* (New York: Cambridge University Press, 2008), online: http://dklevine.com/general/intellectual/againstnew.htm.

11 *Kirkbi A.G. v. Ritvik Holdings Inc.*, [2005] 3 S.C.R. 302, 2005 SCC 65 [*Kirkbi*].

12 *Yankee Candle Co. v. Bridgewater Candle Co.*, 142 F. Supp. 2d 111 (D. Mass. 2001) [*Yankee Candle*].

od of displaying red and green candles on shelving in the shape of a Christmas tree. The plaintiff offered no evidence indicating that this method of selling candles functioned as a trade-mark.[13] The district court rejected these claims and chastised the plaintiff for bringing a suit "to intimidate, discourage and financially damage an upstart competitor."[14]

Trade dress protection is also troubling because of its role in promoting opportunistic lawsuits. In 1992, easy-to-obtain trade dress protection was lauded by the US Supreme Court in *Two Pesos v. Taco Cabana* as an aid to small business.[15] Eight years later in *Wal-Mart v. Samara Bros.*,[16] Justice Scalia backtracked from that sentiment and expressed concern that trade dress protection can too easily be used to harm competition and promote opportunism, because even weak trade-mark lawsuits can impose significant costs on defendants. Scalia observed: "Competition is deterred, however, not merely by successful suit but by the plausible threat of successful suit, and given the unlikelihood of inherently source-identifying design, the game of allowing suit based upon alleged inherent distinctiveness seems to us not worth the candle."[17]

Besides illustrating rent-seeking costs from trade dress lawsuits, *Yankee Candle* and *Wal-Mart* also illustrate steps that American courts have taken to control the problem. In *Yankee Candle* and in other cases, courts have shifted attorney's fees to defendants when trade-mark, copyright, and patent plaintiffs have asserted weak IP cases. In *Wal-Mart* the US Supreme Court made it harder to win a product-design trade dress case, and easier for a defendant to win on summary judgment.

The *Wal-Mart* Court rejected a rule that recognized certain product designs are inherently distinctive. The US now requires that a plaintiff must establish secondary meaning (i.e., the plaintiff must show that consumers perceive the product design is an indicator of

13 *Ibid.*, the plaintiff also presented a specious copyright claim in the suit.

14 *Ibid.* at 113–14.

15 *Two Pesos, Inc. v. Taco Cabana, Inc.*, 505 U.S. 763 (1992).

16 *Walmart Stores, Inc. v. Samara Bros., Inc.*, 529 U.S. 205 (2000) [*Wal-Mart*].

17 *Ibid.* at 214.

the origin of the product). This rule helps defendants deal with weak or frivolous trade dress claims.

The new rule makes it possible for defendants like those in *Wal-Mart* and *Yankee Candle* to win at summary judgment and avoid trial costs. Under the old rule, the defendant would need to win an argument of non-infringement at trial. A summary judgment victory significantly reduces legal fees, puts potential defendants in a stronger bargaining position, and makes it harder for rent-seekers to make credible threats to enforce weak trade dress lawsuits. Fee-shifting has a similar laudatory effect.

Scassa takes a second look at the problem of overlapping rights by turning her attention to *Kraft Canada.*[18] The dispute in this case raises a very different kind of rent-seeking problem from *Kirkbi*—it raises the question of when and whether IP law should facilitate price discrimination. In this context, we must be careful before condemning the rent-seeking as socially wasteful.

The plaintiff in this case owns the copyright in the labels of Swiss and Belgian chocolate bars. The plaintiff tried to use copyright law to segregate the Canadian market from European markets. Specifically, the plaintiff argued that copyright law allowed it to stop unauthorized importation of chocolate bars featuring the copyrighted labels.

Like the *Kirkbi* case, it is hard to believe that a pro-plaintiff decision in this case would significantly affect the *ex ante* incentive to invest in designing higher quality labels for chocolate bars. In contrast to *Kirkbi,* it is quite possible that a pro-plaintiff decision could have a positive social welfare effect *ex post.* The difference is attributable to the ambiguous effect of price discrimination on social welfare.

I have argued elsewhere that a major concern when evaluating copyright policy is the effect of copyright law on price discrimination.[19] For example, the public performance right facilitates fine-grained price discrimination by music licensing organizations. This practice raises output and total surplus. If copyright law lacked a public performance right, price discrimination would still be practiced, but it would take

18 *Euro Excellence Inc. v. Kraft Canada Inc.*, [2007] S.C.J. No. 37, 2007 SCC 37 [*Kraft Canada*].

19 M.J. Meurer, "Copyright Law and Price Discrimination" (2001) 23 Cardozo L. Rev. 55.

some less efficient form — like temporal price discrimination. Whether copyright law should promote geographic price discrimination for chocolate bars (or even software) is a much harder problem that may have different answers in different markets. Further, market segregation in cases like *Kraft Canada* has implications for efficient marketing and distribution. Since welfare analysis in this area is tricky, I will avoid making any reform suggestions.

The last section of Scassa's paper turns the table on my private-attorney-general analysis. The section addresses pharmaceutical patent litigation. But the private attorney general is not necessarily the patent owner seeking to block infringement. Scassa focuses on reverse payments used to settle patent litigation between brand name and generic pharmaceutical companies. Several of these cases have been subject to competition law scrutiny in the US Competition law has been called on to guard against failure by *defendants* as private attorneys general.

These cases illustrate a well-known threat to private-attorney-general regulation — socially harmful settlement. Normally, settlement is praised and encouraged because it avoids litigation costs. But settlement by a private attorney general raises the concern that the regulatory goal of the law will be short-circuited. Generic drug companies in the US frequently initiate challenges to the scope or validity of pharmaceutical patents. When they succeed they deliver a public benefit by tearing down an entry barrier. Settlement can undo that public benefit if the parties to the litigation settle and share the rents that flow by maintaining the entry barrier.

Cases with socially harmful settlement are hard to distinguish from cases with normal settlement that preserves the patent-based rents of a legitimate drug innovator, and reform will be difficult. Reforms internal to patent law probably cannot make much headway reducing rent-seeking from harmful settlements. The natural reform to consider is to improve the quality of pharmaceutical patent examination. In theory, better examination could weed out invalid patents and thereby reduce the need for generic companies to act as private attorneys general. This might be too expensive given that most pharmaceutical patents are not commercially exploited. But perhaps costs could be reduced to a manageable level by targeting only those patents that follow on an earlier pharmaceutical invention that has already been commercialized (or is far along in the drug approval process). Reform of the *Hatch-Waxman*

Act,[20] the relevant drug law, also can affect the frequency of harmful settlements, but it is a blunt instrument.

In my earlier discussion of problems from overlapping IP rights I optimistically asserted that the IP rent-seeking problems could be addressed within IP law.[21] That is fortunate, because competition law is cumbersome and creates its own hazard of unleashing unproductive rent-seeking. But competition law is probably the best tool for addressing reverse payment settlements. Sophisticated oversight requires public enforcement agencies and competition law courts to delve into patent law questions. Thus, these cases are difficult, but the stakes are high enough to warrant the effort.

20 21 U.S.C. § 355 (1994).

21 For a general discussion of the role of IP law in regulating vertical restraints see M.J. Meurer, "Vertical Restraints and Intellectual Property Law: Beyond Antitrust" (2003) 87 Minn. L. Rev. 1871.

CHAPTER 2

Tying and Intellectual Property

Edward M. Iacobucci and Ralph A. Winter[1]

A. INTRODUCTION: SETTING THE STAGE

1) What Is Tying?

Tying, or tied selling, is a restriction placed by a multi-product seller whereby the terms of the purchase of one product are conditioned on the purchase of another. In perhaps no other area of competition policy is there greater dispute over the appropriate legal rule as to when a practice should be prohibited. The analysis and development of optimal competition policy towards tying is especially challenging in the area of intellectual property where the complexities of innovation incentives and rapidly evolving technology are at play.

This chapter surveys the economics of tying in the area of intellectual property, with the aim of contributing to optimal competition policy. We begin in this introduction by delineating more precisely the types of practices that competition law and analysts describe by the terms "tying" or "tied sales" and then providing an overview of

---

1 Edward Iacobucci is a Professor at the Faculty of Law, University of Toronto, and Ralph Winter is a Professor at the Sauder School of Business, University of British Columbia. The authors would like to thank Marcel Boyer, Tim Brennan, France Chevalier, Richard Corley, Alan Gunderson, Randall Hofley, David Vaver, Michael Trebilcock, and Denis Wong for helpful comments on prior drafts.

the market contexts and cases in which tying is observed. We focus in this chapter on the role of intellectual property in relation to tying, although the general theory of tying incentives is essential to an understanding of the issues when intellectual property (IP) is involved. In this introduction, we also set out the criteria that we use to discuss an optimal competition policy towards tying.

The concept of tying can be refined along three dimensions. The first important distinction is *requirements tying* versus *bundling*. Requirements tying is the restriction imposed by a seller that to buy one of its products, A, a buyer must purchase all of its requirements of another product, B, from the seller. In other words, the right to purchase product A carries with it an obligation *not* to purchase the product B (or close substitutes) from any other seller. This restriction is one of exclusivity. Examples of requirements contracting include the restriction that a franchisee purchase its inputs only from the franchisor;[2] the classic example of the restriction imposed by IBM that buyers of IBM adding machines buy all of their requirements of punch cards from IBM; and the restriction that buyers of photocopiers purchase all toner or service from the same company.[3]

A bundling restriction, on the other hand, requires a buyer to purchase two goods, A and B, in fixed proportions (for example, one unit of B must be purchased with each unit of A). Along with this strategy of "pure bundling" is the strategy of "mixed bundling" in which buyers can purchase individual products separately but also have an option to purchase them together. Pure bundling is observed when left and right shoes are sold together, when cars are sold only with tires, or (an obviously more contentious example) when purchasers of Microsoft's operating system obtain the Microsoft's Windows Media Player in the operating system package. Mixed bundling is practised by McDonald's restaurants in offering the option of meal packages that are priced lower than the sum of individual components of the packages.

In requirements contracting, the primary good is often referred to as the "tying good," and the good whose purchase from other firms

2 See for example, *Siegel v. Chicken Delight*, 448 F.2d 43 (9th Cir. 1971) [*Chicken Delight*].

3 See for example, *Director of Investigation and Research v. Xerox (Canada) Inc.*, CT-1989-004.

is restricted as the "tied good." In mixed bundling strategies where a good B is offered alone as an option, but must be purchased by all buyers of good A, good A is called the tying product and good B the tied product.

The second important dimension in defining tying strategies is in technological tying versus contractual tying. Technological tying occurs in the bundling context when two products that could feasibly be offered as separate products are bundled together in a way that makes it technologically impossible for consumers to purchase one component but not the other. Software is again a source of examples of this type of tying. In the requirements tying context, as opposed to bundling, technological tying refers to the design of a primary good (e.g., an inkjet printer) for which the only compatible variable inputs (the toners) are those produced by the seller. Contractual tying occurs when a firm bundles two distinct products together in the package sold to consumers, or where a firm prohibits the purchase of a variable input from another seller as a condition of the purchase of a piece of equipment.

The distinction between technological tying and contractual tying is important in two respects. First, as a policy matter contractual tying may be easy to prohibit, whereas the prohibition of technological tying in any particular case may require the feasibility of disassembling an integrated product. Second, technological tying may in some circumstances be invoked by a dominant seller as a *commitment* against "undoing" the strategy, whereas such a commitment is more difficult with contractual tying. This commitment may be needed when tying is used as a strategy to deter entry. A well-established principle in economics is that the credibility of entry-deterrence strategies depends on commitment of the incumbent. And the commitment may be important not just in affecting a potential entrant's actions but also *vis-à-vis* the policy-maker, who may be able to undo a contractual tie but not a technological tie.

The third dimension along which tying strategies may vary is the size of the price discount offered to the buyer accepting tying. A strategy of offering buyers a 25 percent discount on the primary product if they agree to the exclusive purchase of the complementary product, or a (mixed bundling) strategy of offering a discount of 25 percent on a bundle if it is purchased as a bundle, is a weaker form of tying than absolute insistence on the tying restraint. Our analysis of tying will apply to this form of tying as well.

2) The Policy Issue

When is tying anti-competitive? When should tying be prohibited? These two questions may appear to be the same, they are not. Consider a dominant firm in a market with rapidly changing technology (the kind of market in which intellectual property is likely to be prominent). It may be true as a matter of theory that the market would be more competitive if the dominant firm could be forced to maintain the separate development of some individual products, being allowed to integrate products into bundles only when such bundling is efficient. But this policy of prohibiting inefficient bundling might well be impossible to enforce in that it would require nearly as much information and continual involvement in the market by the policy-maker as by the firm itself. Another policy, imposing fines or other penalties when a dominant firm is found to have tied inefficiently may be feasible, but may impose too much uncertainty in the market. A finding that tying is anti-competitive is only one step, albeit an important first step, towards the design of a feasible and appropriate remedy. This finding is necessary but not sufficient to justify policy intervention in the market.

3) The Policy Criterion

In our search for policy conclusions grounded in the economic analysis of tying, we adopt the criterion of economic efficiency: the maximization of total gains from a market, whether these gains are achieved by consumers (in the form of consumer surplus) or by shareholders of firms in the market. A remedy is preferred when it increases total efficiency. This objective incorporates the feasibility and cost of policy alternatives. In adopting this goal, we reject the notion that the competitiveness of a market is an appropriate policy objective but accept market competitiveness as a means of achieving greater efficiency where appropriate.

4) Positive versus Normative Analysis of Tying

The heart of our survey is the delineation of the incentives to adopt tying strategies. Why would a firm adopt tying in a particular set of circumstances? This positive question must be answered before any normative or policy analysis can be offered. The necessity of a positive theory may seem obvious, but it describes a difference between an economic approach to competition policy in this area and some legal decisions. In *Chicken Delight*,[4] for example, the court rejected a quality-assurance defence of tying franchise inputs on the basis that less restrictive means of achieving this assurance were available to the franchisor. This approach fails to ask specifically why a franchisor would adopt tying and then to spell out the welfare consequences of the most persuasive explanation, adopting instead a dubious theory that policy should redirect franchisors' strategies towards those that appear less restrictive of competition.

Traditionally, exclusivity restrictions such as tying were viewed by courts as anti-competitive on their face.[5] When a monopoly in the tying good uses tying the effect can be a second monopoly in the tied-good market, and the impact of the practice — it is argued — is therefore to reduce competition. The Chicago School responded to this argument by noting that a monopolist can extract monopoly profit only once: if tying were a restriction that served to extract additional profits, the monopolist would do better by instead raising the price of the principal product. Post-Chicago economists, especially Michael Whinston, showed that tying can in some circumstances be used profitably to extend market power from one market to another. Many prominent competition economists, however, have come to the conclusion that post-Chicago economics provides relatively weak guidance for policy-makers. Michael Whinston concluded that, with respect to the appropriate competition policy in the Microsoft case, the most striking aspect of the state of economic knowledge about tying is how little we know.[6] Ken Hylton and Michael Salinger (the current Director of the

---

4 See above note 2.

5 Some legislatures held the same view. Until recently, the UK patent regime, for example, established that tying an unpatented product to a patented product was not only an unenforceable requirement, but such tying would also bar any patent infringement claim by the patent-holder against any third party, not just the buyer. See for example, *Patents Act 1977* (UK), 1977, c. 37, s. 44; and repeal in *Competition Act 1998* (UK), 1998, c. 41, s. 70.

6 M. Whinston, "Exclusivity and Tying in *U.S. v. Microsoft*: What We Know and Don't Know" (2001) 15:2 Journal of Economic Perspectives 63 at 70 [Whinston].

Bureau of Economics at the Federal Trade Commission in the US) concluded that the post-Chicago literature had established the theoretical possibility of abuse through tying by a dominant firm, but that using this literature to justify antitrust hostility towards tying is problematic.[7] Our review supports a conservative approach towards government intervention in the area of tying. The complexity of tying cases in circumstances where the practice is potentially anti-competitive presents a severe challenge to the design of appropriate intervention. Economic theory can offer, at best, a guide towards case facts that tend to favour a hands-off approach versus a more interventionist approach, but it is an inescapable conclusion that simple policy prescriptions or rules are unavailable.

The remainder of our paper proceeds as follows. Section B reviews a variety of prominent theories of tying, showing that tying can be efficient in some cases and inefficient in others. Throughout Section B we describe how intellectual property rights relate to the different theories of tying. We stress the relationship between IP and tying further in Section C, which describes and analyzes three tying cases that centrally involved IP rights. Section D sets out our views on optimal policy towards tying generally, and towards IP and tying in particular.

B. GENERAL THEORIES OF TYING

1) Cost-efficient Tying

Tying is ubiquitous. Gloves are sold in pairs, cars are sold with wheels, and hamburgers are sold as a beef patty and a bun. These examples of course raise no competition policy objections. Tying is used in these transactions because it minimizes the sum of production and transactions costs. It would be more costly for a consumer to buy tires and a car separately than for a car manufacturer to install the tires (due to the economies of scale and production efficiencies) and the market provides the obvious solution. Where cost efficiencies dictate, prod-

---

See also, L. Kaplow, "Extension of Monopoly Power through Leverage" (1985) 85 Colum. L. Rev. 515 [Kaplow].

7 K. Hylton and M. Salinger, "Tying Law and Policy: A Decision-theoretic Approach" (2001) 69 Antitrust L.J. 469 at 470–71.

ucts will be tied (sold in packages) whether the market is competitive, monopolistic, or anything in between.

Because the cost efficiency explanation of tying is so dominant empirically it is worth elaborating upon. Evans and Salinger offer an extensive analysis of cost efficiencies in tying.[8] These authors point out that in the last case in which the US Supreme Court considered tying, *Jefferson Parish*,[9] an efficiency explanation was offered by the defendants and the district court was persuaded of the efficiencies of the practice in this case.[10] But the US law provides no scope for an efficiency defence of tying. The Supreme Court, while finding the practice legal in this case, did not in its majority opinion rely on efficiencies and in fact stated that the two products in this case were efficiently provided as separate products.[11] The Court's decision relied on the absence of market power on the part of the hospital, one of the requirements for tying to be illegal under the *per se* ruling.

Jefferson Parish is a decision not based on economics or even solid logic. If the hospital operated in a competitive market (having no market power) then cost efficiency *was* the likely reason for the adoption of the tie since competitive markets generally yield efficient outcomes. The only consistent interpretation of the decision is that the Court believed that the hospital was mistaken in its adoption of the strategy. Our perspective is that courts should never second-guess the deci-

8 D. Evans and M. Salinger, "Why Do Firms Bundle and Tie? Evidence from Competitive Markets and Implications for Tying Law" (2005) Yale J. on Reg. 22 at 37–89 [Evans and Salinger].

9 *Jefferson Parish Hosp. v. Hyde*, 466 U.S. 2 (1984) [*Jefferson Parish*].

10 See *ibid.* at 17:

> The evidence presented was that defendants instituted a closed system anesthesiology department because they believed the system resulted in the best quality of patient care. Specifically the system insures twenty-four hour anesthesiology coverage, aids in the control and standardization of . . . operations because it is not necessary to accommodate physicians with outside commitments; it permits the physicians, nurses, and other technicians in the department to develop a work routine and a proficiency with the equipment they use in patient treatment; and it increases the Board's ability to monitor the medical standards exercised because there are fewer individuals involved, maintenance of equipment is simplified and equipment breakdowns are minimized by limiting use to one group of physicians.

11 *Ibid.* at 21–23.

sions of sellers as not being in their own interests. The Court is in a much weaker informational position than sellers. The first step towards an assessment of tying in any particular case must be a positive economic theory of why sellers, acting correctly in their own interest, would adopt the practice.

Evans and Salinger note that pure bundling can arise in a competitive or monopolistically competitive market because of costs.[12] Where there are substantial costs (on the part of either the producer or the consumer) to the production and sale of separate components, or moderate costs but little demand for one or more of the components, then the market might offer only the pure bundle. With sufficient heterogeneity in consumer tastes in addition to the costs of offering separate products, the market will yield mixed bundling, with the bundle at a discount relative to the costs of separate products. Evans and Salinger illustrate the cost-based theory of tying with a number of markets, including the market for cold remedies.[13] In this market, both bundles (pills with a variety of medicinal ingredients) and separate products (individual drug remedies) are offered. The discount for the bundle is so large that Evans and Salinger suggest that it reflects not differences in demand elasticities (as in the price discrimination theory of bundling, discussed below) but simply the fact that the cost of offering a bundle is only slightly more than the cost of offering individual components.[14] Most costs for cold remedies are in the packaging, distribution, and marketing.

While the competitive market cases that Evans and Salinger discuss do not involve contentious legal cases, the demonstration that cost efficiencies can explain bundling clearly extends to situations with market power. It must be considered as an alternative hypothesis to any monopoly-power based theory of tying.

2) Bundling as Price Discrimination

If there were no cost advantage to bundling over the offer of separate products, then a competitive market would yield separate products,

---

12 Evans and Salinger, above note 8 at 52, adopt a model of monopolistic competition in which positive profits are ruled out by a contestability assumption.

13 *Ibid.* at 66–70.

14 *Ibid.* at 70.

not bundling. A firm with market power, however, may be induced to implement bundling as a means of extracting more surplus from consumers. Consider, for example, a monopolist producing at zero cost two products, A and B, and facing two types of consumers (ten consumers of each type). Half of the consumers value product A highly and product B less highly: these consumers would be willing to pay $10 for one unit of product A and $4 for one unit of product B. The other half of the consumers have the opposite preferences, with a higher value for product B.

Consider the three possible strategies: sell each good separately at $4; sell each good separately at $10 dollars; or, sell a bundle of the goods at $14.[15] The profits generated by these three strategies are $160; $200; and $280. Pure bundling dominates the other two strategies (or any other strategy) because it extracts the full surplus from consumers. Under our criterion of economic efficiency (total surplus maximization), pure bundling is not only the privately efficient strategy among these three strategies, it is also the unique, socially efficient strategy. Prohibiting bundling would decrease total surplus because those individuals valuing a good at $4 are allocated the good in the tying optimum, but not without tying. Indeed, in this example bundling is Pareto improving in that it increases the welfare of some agents (the shareholders) while harming none (since in no scenario is there positive consumer surplus).

The classic references on bundling as price discrimination are Stigler[16] and Adams and Yellin.[17] Adams and Yellin develop the intuition suggested by our example that bundling can extract greater surplus when the valuations for two different products are negatively correlated across products.[18] Mixed bundling may be profitable as well

---

15 It is easily argued that no other strategy can be profitable.

16 G.J. Stigler, "*United States v. Loew's, Inc.*: A Note on Block-booking" in P. Kurkland, ed., *Supreme Court Review* (Chicago: University of Chicago Press, 1963) 152–57.

17 W.J. Adams and J.L. Yellen, "Commodity Bundling and the Burden of Monopoly" (1976) 90 Quarterly Journal of Economics 475.

18 Negative correlation is, in general, a sufficient but not necessary condition for profitable bundling; see R.P. McAfee, J. McMillan, and M.D. Whinston, "Multiproduct Monopoly, Commodity Bundling, and Correlation of Values" (1989) 114 Quarterly Journal of Economics 371.

when there are a sufficient number of consumers with extreme preferences (a very high value for a particular product and a very low value for the other product).

Bundling, like price discrimination generally, may increase welfare (as in the above example) or decrease welfare, depending on the circumstances in the market. A policy that would ban tying where it facilitates price discrimination has no economic foundation.

3) Tying in Aftermarkets

A variety of tying theories arise in the context of a durable good and complementary goods used in conjunction with the durable good. Sellers often tie the complementary goods, sometimes referred to as "aftermarket products," to the tying good. Examples of such tying, including antitrust cases on the matter, abound. As mentioned above, IBM tied sales of punch cards to the purchase of an IBM computer.[19] International Salt tied sales of salt to its patented salt injecting machines.[20] Franchisors may tie the sales of inputs necessary for a franchisee's business to the initial sale of a franchise; franchisees are contractually committed to buying the franchisor's inputs.[21] Printer manufacturers may tie the sale of ink to printers.[22] Sellers of a durable piece of machinery may effectively tie the purchase of service on the machine to the machine by refusing to sell replacement parts to independent service operators.[23]

In this section, we review a number of explanations associated with tying in aftermarkets, including discussion of the welfare effects of each theory. We highlight the importance of intellectual property to these theories. IP is important in two ways. First, IP laws may be instrumental in enforcing the tying arrangement. For example, a ma-

---

19 See *IBM Corp. v. United States*, 298 U.S. 131 (1936) [*IBM*].

20 See *International Salt Co. v. United States*, 332 U.S. 392 (1947) [*International Salt*].

21 See for example, *Chicken Delight*, above note 2, where a chicken restaurant franchisor ties sales of paper buckets to sale of franchise.

22 See *Illinois Tool Works Inc. v. Independent Ink, Inc.*, 547 U.S. 28 (2006) [*Independent Ink*].

23 See for example, *Eastman Kodak Co. v. Image Technical Services Inc.*, 504 U.S. 451 (1992) [*Kodak*]; *Canada (Director of Investigation and Research) v. Xerox Canada Inc.* (1990), 33 C.P.R. (3d) 83 (Comp. Trib.) [*Xerox*].

chine manufacturer may rely on IP laws to prevent rivals from producing replacement parts that would facilitate the provision of service by independents. Second, protecting the value of intellectual property may provide a motivation for tying. For example, franchisors may want to protect the value of their brand by requiring franchisees only to use high-quality inputs in operating their franchises. IP and tying are thus closely linked in the aftermarket context.

a) Price Discrimination: Tying as Metering

Tying may be a useful tool for a seller to meter a buyer's demand for the tied-good package, and to charge higher-demand buyers a higher overall price than lower-demand buyers. To understand the conditions that support the price discrimination motivation for tying, consider first the no-price-discrimination benchmark in which a monopolist sells a durable good (call it a "machine") to homogeneous customers. Suppose that each buyer gets a value of ten for the machine, and once the machine is purchased, has a downward sloping demand curve for the aftermarket product (call it "service"). In this setting, the monopolist can maximize the total surplus from each relationship by setting the aftermarket price at marginal cost — and the monopolist can then extract this maximum surplus via a price for the machine. Alternatively, the monopolist can let buyers purchase the aftermarket product in a competitive market. Where buyers are homogeneous, in short, the manufacturer can realize all of this surplus with or without tying. This example illustrates the Chicago School point that relying on tying merely to extend market power into the tied-good market does not in itself raise profits for the seller. Rather, if the seller has market power, the price it charges in the tied-good market to homogeneous customers extracts all surplus. Maximum profits are achieved without tying.

The situation changes, however, if customers are heterogeneous since then the possibility of price discrimination arises.[24] The quantity demanded of aftermarket products is likely to be correlated across consumers with the demand for the entire durable-aftermarket package. Charging a super-competitive price for the aftermarket product allows the seller effectively to charge a higher price to high-value demanders,

---

24 For an early exposition of tying as metering, see W. Bowman, "Tying Arrangements and the Leverage Problem" (1957) 67 Yale L.J. 19.

since these demanders purchase more aftermarket products. The amount of aftermarket purchases acts as a signal, or meter, for the buyer's value of the product and is "taxed" accordingly with a price in excess of marginal cost. Tying is necessary for the metering strategy because in its absence buyers could source aftermarket products in a competitive market, and the seller would be unable to charge a super-competitive price.

A numerical example illustrates the metering properties of tying in aftermarkets. Suppose that there are two kinds of customers, one that values the machine at 10 and 2 units of service at 10 per unit, and another that values the machine at 10 and 3 units of service at 10 per unit. Suppose that a unit of service costs 5 to provide, while a machine costs 10. A non-tying, single-price seller of the machine cannot fully extract surplus from the high demander without alienating low demanders. That is, if the seller allowed competition in service and charged 25 for the machine, it would realize profits of 15 each from high demanders but would not sell to low demanders who would, if they purchased, realize negative surplus at a price of 25. In contrast, if the seller ties, charges 10 for the machine and 10 per unit of service, it sells both to high and low demanders and extracts all surplus from each. Variation in demand across customers for a variable input into the operation of the durable thus gives rise to the potential for profitable price discrimination.

Like other kinds of price discrimination, the practice of metering reflects some degree of market power, since a seller in a purely competitive market has no leeway to charge super-competitive prices. But this does not imply that tying in this context is or should be treated as suspect. The fact that price discrimination *reflects* market power does not imply that price discrimination *enhances* market power to the detriment of society.[25] Rather, price discrimination is often efficient in that it increases the quantity sold of a product. In the preceding example, tying as price discrimination ensures that both low and high demanders buy the machine-service package, while the inability to tie could result in prices that exclude low demanders from market.[26] The correct

---

25 See M. Trebilcock, R. Winter, P. Collins, and E. Iacobucci, *The Law and Economics of Canadian Competition Policy* (Toronto: University of Toronto Press, 2002) c. 5 [Trebilcock *et al.*].

26 Whether the seller would set machine prices that exclude low demanders depends on the relative numbers of high and low demanders.

comparison when evaluating the effects of price discrimination is not between the discriminatory pricing strategy and competitive pricing, but rather between discriminatory pricing and a single-price strategy that reflects the seller's market power and would be adopted if price discrimination were restricted. On balance, economists tend to view price discrimination, and thus tying as metering, as often market-expanding and therefore efficient.

The metering theory is probably the most important explanation of tying in aftermarkets. Metering is a plausible explanation in each of the cases discussed above. Tying ink to printers, salt to canning machines, punch cards to computers, service to machines, and toner fluid or paper to photocopier machines could all result from a metering incentive. Franchisors tying inputs to franchise sales could also result from price discrimination, since more profitable franchises will purchase more inputs than less profitable franchises.[27]

Intellectual property is often essential in establishing tying. First, tying for price discrimination requires some degree of market power. Such market power in the tying-good market may be protected in part by intellectual property. The machine sellers in *International Salt* and *Independent Ink*, for example, had IP rights in their machines, which may have conferred the requisite market power to impose price discrimination.[28] Similarly, the franchise brand in franchising cases can confer some market power on franchisors.[29]

In addition, sellers rely on intellectual property rights to enforce the tying arrangement. For example, printer manufacturers rely on

---

27 See B. Klein and L. Saft, "The Law and Economics of Franchise Tying Contracts" (1985) 28:2 J.L. & Econ. 345. Not that price discrimination is most plausible where the buyer knows its valuation better than the seller and metering is required to induce the buyer to reveal its valuation. In the franchise setting, however, it is often plausible that franchisors know the value of a franchise better than franchisees: see E. Iacobucci, "Revisiting the Law and Economics of Franchise Tying Contracts" (2007) [unpublished]. In such a setting, signalling, discussed below at Section B(3)(b), may be a more plausible explanation of tying than metering.

28 The question of how much market power was conferred on sellers by a patent was the subject of the recent appeal in *Independent Ink*, above note 22, in which the US Supreme Court held unanimously that a patent does not *necessarily* confer market power for the purposes of antitrust law.

29 See *Chicken Delight*, above note 2.

patented cartridges to exclude independent toner suppliers from supplying printer owners.[30] A machine seller may rely on patented replacement parts to prevent third parties from supplying independent service organizations.[31]

A modern example of a tying arrangement that may serve as a meter and relies on IP rights for enforcement can be found in a set of allegations by an American plaintiff concerning Apple's marketing of its iPod music and video players.[32] Apple sells iPods and also sells online music and videos at its iTunes website. A US plaintiff recently accused Apple of tying in that, through proprietary Digital Rights Management (DRM) technologies and other factors, the songs at iTunes can be played only on iPods, and iPod users cannot easily purchase from Apple's rival online music and video sellers.[33] The United States District Court for the Northern District of California refused to dismiss on summary judgment the plaintiff's complaint about unlawful tying. We will return to this example at different points in our analysis, but we note here that the arrangement could well reflect metering. According to the plaintiff's allegations, iPod buyers who seek to download online music or video are induced to buy from Apple. High-*value* demanders of the iPod–iTune bundle are high-*quantity* demanders, or intensive demanders, of iTunes. Apple can thus extract greater surplus from high demanders for the package by raising the price of iTune songs and videos above marginal cost. The quantity of iTunes demanded by a consumer meters (or signals) the buyer's value of the package.

Tying in the metering context does not enhance the *social* value of intellectual property itself, though it does result in a greater share of the social value being realized by the seller. Thus, to the extent that metering enhances the private profits of the tying-good producer, metering will have an effect on innovation. For example, some commentators have suggested that franchise tying arrangements will induce greater creativity in franchise-system innovation.[34] Even outside the

---

30 See *Independent Ink*, above note 22.

31 See *Kodak*, above note 23.

32 See *Tucker v. Apple Computer, Inc.*, 493 F. Supp. 2d 1090 (Northern Dist. California 2006) [*Tucker*].

33 *Ibid.*

34 B. Klein, "Market Power in Franchise Cases in the Wake of *Kodak*: Applying Post-Contract Hold-up Analysis to Vertical Relationships" (1999) 67 Antitrust L.J. 283.

intellectual property context, there is no compelling basis for prohibiting tying when the role of the strategy is to allow metering. In the intellectual property context, the additional value of higher profits in stimulating innovation creates a further argument against government intervention in prohibiting the practice.

b) Tying as a Response to Asymmetric Information about Quality: *Ex Post* Informational Asymmetry

For a variety of reasons, tying in aftermarkets may respond to asymmetric information about the tying good's quality. Tying may address concerns about preserving the tying good's reputation for quality *after* the products have been used. Tying may also signal the good's quality *before* the products have been purchased. We analyze the use of tying as a means of conveying information about quality below, dividing the theories into *ex ante* and *ex post* asymmetric information problems.

By definition, aftermarket products are used in conjunction with the durable good. The quality of the aftermarket product can affect the operation of the durable good, but buyers may not be able to discern the cause of poor performance between an inferior tying or aftermarket good. Several defendants, from IBM[35] to International Salt[36] to Kodak,[37] have argued that they have required customers to buy their high-quality aftermarket products in order to preserve or enhance the tying good's reputation for quality. Courts have on occasion accepted the argument that tying is a response to such quality control concerns.[38] In *Jerrold Electronics,* the court accepted that a seller of novel television antennae required buyers to use its service in order to ensure that high-quality service was performed, and that buyers would not blame Jerrold's equipment for poor performance resulting from poor service.[39] Rather than engaging in the costly and possibly fruitless exercise of attempting to specify minimum levels of service quality in contracts with its customers, Jerrold simply tied to preserve its reputation.

---

35 See *IBM*, above note 19.

36 See *International Salt*, above note 20.

37 See *Kodak*, above note 23.

38 See for example, *United States v. Jerrold Electronics*, 187 F. Supp. 545 (U.S. Dist. Ct., E. Penn. 1960) [*Jerrold Electronics*].

39 *Ibid.*

The lack of information on the part of buyers about quality is not a sufficient condition for tying, however. Buyers who cannot discern responsibility for poor performance *ex post* may nevertheless be capable of realizing that independent aftermarket providers do not have the same stake in the reputation of the durable as the durable manufacturer, and that therefore independent providers do not have the same incentives to provide high-quality aftermarket products.[40] Buyers concerned with quality will tend to avoid purchasing from independent providers, and if they do purchase from independents will attribute, with high probability, the lack of quality to the service provider.

If a buyer, however, is willing to accept greater risk of inferior aftermarket products, then there is a potential externality between buyer and seller that tying might address: the buyer does not internalize any potential reputational harms to the seller from the buyer's use of inferior aftermarket products that flow from observation by other buyers of quality problems (or word-of-mouth). But even where this externality is significant, tying may not be necessary. The use of predictably inferior third-party aftermarket products could conceivably *enhance* the reputation of the durable. This would arise where third-party aftermarket products are used, but the durable nevertheless performs well. In such circumstances, outside observers would upgrade their view of the product even more than they would where the durable supplier's aftermarket products were used.[41] Only where there are buyers that are relatively indifferent to aftermarket quality, and where the use of predictably poor-quality aftermarkets is likely on net to hurt the seller's reputation, is it plausible that tying remedies the buyer-seller quality control externality. In these circumstances, tying can play a quality control role.

Tying as quality control is socially beneficial. Innovators who have developed a high-quality product are able to protect consumers from confusion about the product's quality. This enhances the private and social value of the seller's trade-mark and other intellectual property that it has in the tying good. Jerrold's antennae, for example, proved to

40 See E. Iacobucci, "Tying as Quality Control: A Legal and Economic Analysis" (2003) 32 J. Leg. Stud. 435 [Iacobucci, "Tying as Quality Control"].

41 Iacobucci, *ibid.*, shows that the technological interaction between the tied and tying goods is essential to determining whether inferior tied goods will predictably enhance or hurt the tying good's reputation.

be successful, resulting in profits for Jerrold, but also in gains for buyers. Protecting the investment in a brand, patent, or other intellectual property typically provides the motivation for tying in the quality control context. In addition, just as in the price discrimination setting, tying for quality control may in part rely on IP rights for enforcement, as where a seller of a durable good would refuse to supply third parties with proprietary parts in order to prevent them from providing inferior service.

The theory of *ex post* quality control just reviewed depends upon confusion on the part of the buyer about the effect of inferior aftermarket products on the performance of the durable aftermarket package. There is another kind of *ex post* quality control explanation that does not rely on the buyer's confusion. The explanation is particularly plausible in the franchise context.[42] Franchisees may knowingly purchase inferior inputs, and may explicitly recognize the effects of inferior inputs, but may do so because of a free-rider problem among franchisees: franchisees realize the full benefits of cheaper inputs, while sharing the reputational costs to the franchise brand from low-quality inputs with the franchisor and other franchisees. In this setting, and in other settings where the buyer shares the direct cost of performance with the seller (as where there is a warranty, for example), the seller has an interest in committing the buyer to purchasing high-quality aftermarket products. The franchisor internalizes more of the franchise brand's value than the franchisee and may impose tying as a means of protecting the brand. Anticipating the free-rider problem, franchisees would be willing *ex ante* to accept the tying arrangement as value-maximizing the contractual term, though *ex post* franchisees may prefer to void the tying arrangements.

As in the distinct, but similar, case where tying addresses potential confusion over attribution of blame for poor performance, tying to preserve the franchise's reputation for quality is socially desirable. Tying in this manner allows franchise systems to maintain their reputations for quality, which in turn helps preserve franchisors' incentives to innovate in developing high-quality franchise systems. Tying enhances the franchise trade-mark's private and social value. IP concerns help explain why tying is adopted in the franchise setting.

---

42 See B. Klein and L. Saft, "The Law and Economics of Franchise Tying Contracts" (1985) 28 J.L. & Econ. 345 [Klein and Saft].

c) Tying as a Response to Asymmetric Information about Quality: *Ex Ante* Information Asymmetry

Tying in aftermarkets may also remedy difficulties for buyers in determining the quality of the durable good prior to purchase. Tying can signal quality. For example, suppose that the quality of a durable is given by its longevity: it may last for one, two, or three periods. It costs more to produce a durable that lasts longer. Without a means of signalling that the durable is high quality, there may be attenuated incentives for the seller to sell a durable that lasts three periods, given that buyers cannot determine quality *ex ante* and therefore will be reluctant to pay for the additional costs associated with a high-quality durable.

Aftermarket tying could help the seller signal quality.[43] Suppose that the buyer requires one unit of an aftermarket product in each period of the durable's use, from one to three periods. The high-quality seller could charge a relatively low price for the durable but could tie aftermarket products and charge super-competitive prices for the tied goods in each of the three periods. Such a pricing strategy could allow the high-quality seller to recoup the opportunity costs of a low durable price since it sells three tied goods, but might not allow a low-quality seller to recoup, given that the latter would sell only one tied good.

This explanation may be applicable where there is a correlation between the demand for aftermarket goods and the quality of the durable. This may not always be plausible. Expenditures on service, for example, may be greater the *lower* the quality of the durable. But there are settings where this correlation is plausible. The franchise setting provides a good example of where the signalling theory might apply.[44] Franchisors seeking to signal to prospective franchisees that a particular franchise opportunity will be profitable may rely in part on tying arrangements. The more successful the franchise is, the more inputs it will require. By tying and charging a super-competitive price for inputs, the franchisor signals quality.

Again, there is a clear relationship between IP and tying. The seller's reputation for quality affects the value of either its trade-mark or whatever intellectual property, such as a patent, that it relies on in

43 See for example, M. Schwartz and G. Werden, "A Quality-signaling Rationale for Aftermarket Tying" (1996) 64 Antitrust L.J. 387.

44 See Iacobucci, "Revisiting the Law and Economics of Franchise Tying Contracts," above note 27.

producing the durable. By allowing high-quality sellers to signal the quality of their brand or durable, tying can enhance the value of IP, which in turn enhances the incentives to invest in high-quality IP. IP helps explain the motivation for tying. And, again, IP may be useful in enforcing the tie, such as where the aftermarket tying is enforced in part by relying on IP rights to exclude independent suppliers of the aftermarket product from the market.

d) *Ex Ante* Uncertainty and Risk-sharing

Suppose that neither the buyer nor the seller has a perfect prediction of the value of a particular durable good over time. The value is inherently uncertain and both parties may share the same expectational distribution as to the future value. Tying can then address risk-aversion on the part of the buyer.[45] Suppose that the durable can last one, two, or three periods, and suppose now that the buyer and seller accurately believe each outcome to be equally probable. And, suppose that one unit of an aftermarket product is required per period.

In the case where the seller simply sells the durable good and the aftermarket product is supplied competitively, the buyer bears all the risk of the durable's longevity. It may be mutually beneficial for the buyer and seller to agree to share the risk by selling the durable at a lower price and tying the aftermarket product to the durable. The seller can charge a supra-competitive price that results in greater profits for it the better the machine performs, which shifts some of the risk of the durable's performance from the buyer to the seller.

Again, the franchise setting is suitable for this tying motivation. Franchisees are often small business-people who may be risk-averse, while franchisors may have diversified investors and also can diversify across a portfolio of franchises. It is therefore often efficient for franchisors to bear some of the risk of the franchise's performance. Selling the franchise opportunity at a lower price but charging super-competitive prices for tied inputs shifts risk efficiently.

A related theory, which we also group under risk-sharing recognizes that franchisees are of limited wealth and, therefore, that — simply because of this wealth constraint — even a risk-neutral franchisee can-

45 See S. Liebowitz, "Tie-in Sales, Risk Reduction and Price Discrimination" (1983) 21 Economic Inquiry 387–99.

not purchase the franchise for the expected present value of the flow of profits. The optimal contract then allocates some future rents to the franchisor, through tying and a positive markup on the input, balancing at the margin (for the franchisor) the cost of the inefficiency induced by the positive markup with the rents left with the franchisee.[46]

Unlike the other information-based explanations of tying, risk-sharing tying does not enhance the perception of the durable's IP, such as its brand or patents. Rather, risk-sharing simply represents an efficient method of selling the durable. IP may, however, be relevant in enforcing the tie, such as where proprietary parts are sold as aftermarket products.

e) Aftermarket Tying as a Lack of Commitment

This theory of tying in aftermarkets is quite unlike the others in that tying is inefficient, reflecting a lack of commitment on the part of the seller. To this point, our surveyed explanations of tying have been based on efficiency or price discrimination.

At any point in time after they have begun selling the durable good, sellers have an "installed base" of past customers that must purchase aftermarket products specific to the durable, including parts and service, or buy a new durable at whatever the durable costs. Once this installed base exists, there is a temptation for sellers, regardless of past policies in aftermarkets, to impose a tie in the aftermarket and charge super-competitive prices that exploit the installed base's switching costs.[47] Even in competitive markets, there is a risk that the seller will change aftermarket policies once the durable has been sold; durable markets are competitive at the time of the sale, but the installed base is to some extent dependent on brand-specific aftermarket products.

While the seller realizes profits *ex post* from exploiting the installed base, buyers will anticipate such exploitation when purchasing the machine. Indeed, in competitive markets sellers would be com-

---

46 The classic reference for this type of model is D. Sappington, "Limited Liability Contracts between Principal and Agent" (1983) 29 Journal of Economic Theory 1–21.

47 See Severin Borenstein, Jeffrey MacKie-Mason, and Janet Netz, "Antitrust Policy in Aftermarkets" (1995) 63 Antitrust L.J. 455–82. See also, Borenstein *et al.*, "Exercising Market Power in Proprietary Aftermarkets" (2000) 9 J. Econ. & Management Strategy 157–88 [Borenstein *et al.*].

pelled to lower their durable prices below cost to the point where they make zero profits overall. Social inefficiencies nevertheless result because durable prices fall below cost and aftermarket prices are above cost.

Under this lack of commitment theory, the seller and buyer would jointly be better off if the seller could credibly commit not to impose a tie on aftermarket products in the future. But such a commitment may be difficult or impossible to achieve. Buyers and sellers cannot enter into complete, fully contingent contracts over the life of the durable that specify aftermarket prices in all future states of the world. And committing to competitive markets in aftermarkets may not be easy to achieve because of intellectual property matters. In *Kodak*[48] in the US, and *Xerox*[49] in Canada, for example, sellers of photocopiers decided to stop supplying independent service providers with their proprietary parts, which effectively required their installed base to purchase service from Kodak and Xerox. Kodak and Xerox could have avoided this risk only by relinquishing IP rights over components for their photocopiers, otherwise they would retain the right in the future to exclude third-party suppliers and raise prices in aftermarkets. Abandoning IP rights, however, would likely undermine their incentives to have invested in the IP in the first place.

While extra-contractual mechanisms, like a reputation for not exploiting the installed base, may limit the dangers from inefficient commitment, it is reasonable to conclude that sellers often will have leeway *ex post* to impose a tie in aftermarkets.[50]

---

48 Above note 23.

49 *Ibid.*

50 In a rational-expectations world, it may be that a seller will initially sell the durable at a loss while tying in aftermarkets. Anticipating opportunistic tying *ex post*, Iacobucci shows that the seller may also tie in the first period when selling the durable in order to limit inefficiencies from discounted prices: by bundling a good valued more by inelastic demanders with the durable, the seller can sell at an effective discount while screening out inefficient sales to elastic demanders who do not value the durable at cost. See E. Iacobucci, "A Switching Costs Explanation of Tying and Warranties" (2008) 37 J. Legal Stud. 431 [Iacobucci, "Switching Costs"].

4) Tying as Leverage of Monopoly Power

a) The Traditional View and the Chicago Response

A traditional view of tying is that it is profitable because it allows a monopolist in one market to achieve a monopoly position in another. Two monopolies are better than one. Suppose that a firm has a monopoly position for product A: product A is only used in conjunction with a second product, B, and the market for product B is competitive. If the monopolist imposes tied sales, requiring consumers to purchase all of their requirements of B as a condition of purchasing A, then — the theory goes — the firm will have achieved monopolies in two markets instead of just in market one. Two monopolies are more profitable than one and tying is thus a means of leveraging one monopoly into two.

The Chicago School showed this argument to be wrong. Suppose, to take a very simple example, that a firm had a monopoly on jars but that the lids for the jars were competitively supplied. Suppose that the cost of producing either product is $10 and that each consumer values a jar and lid together at $40. (To set aside price discrimination arguments for tying, we assume that all consumers are identical.) In the absence of tying, the lids are available at the competitive price (equal to the cost of production) of $10, leaving the monopolist free to charge $30 for the jars. The monopolist earns a profit of $20 per jar. If the monopolist required consumers to purchase only pairs of lids and jars together (i.e., engaged in bundling), then the monopolist would produce the bundle for $20, sell it for $40, and again make $20 profit. The monopolist, in other words, can "collect its monopoly profit only once." A monopoly over two perfectly complementary goods is no more profitable than a monopoly over one of the goods.[51]

The prediction, that tying is not always profitable as a means of leveraging market power from one market into two, is strengthened with examples in which the strategy would achieve two monopolies but strictly reduce expected profit. Suppose, for example, that the cost of production of right-footed shoes by competitors is random, and the monopolist commits to tying before knowing this cost. If the cost

---

51 The argument is easily extended to the case where a variable amount of the complementary good is used. In this case, the optimal price for the monopolist to charge for the complementary good *is* the competitive price, in the absence of any incentive for price discrimination.

turns out to be lower than the monopolist's cost of production, then the monopolist would have lost profits from the commitment to tie. In spite of the gain in the extent of monopoly from one market to two, the monopoly's profits fall with tying. This is because the buyer-monopoly pair is not procuring right-footed shoes at the lowest cost; and the monopolist bears the entire cost of this inefficiency because, whatever the realization of costs, it is extracting all surplus in the transaction.

To take a second example in which tying can reduce profits, suppose that all users of product A need one unit of product B, but there is some variation in tastes across consumers as to the brand of product B. The monopolist and one rival compete in the market for product B. Some consumers prefer the monopolist's brand; some prefer the rival's brand. Whinston shows in this case that the monopolist loses if it adopts the strategy of tying.[52] The total surplus in the market suffers from the failure of consumers to all purchase their preferred product, and the monopolist, being forced to extract a share of a smaller "pie," may lose as a result. The two examples in which tying reduces profit are similar in that the tying strategy leads the monopolist to produce and sell a product for which it is not the most efficient producer.

The Chicago School was, in short, correct in its critique of the traditional position that tying is profitable and anti-competitive whenever it allows a firm to extend a monopoly from one market into a monopoly in two markets.

b) The Whinston Theory

The Chicago School was incorrect, however, in arguing that leverage of market power from one market to two is *never* profitable. Whinston showed that tying can be a profitable means of leveraging market power.[53] There are three key assumptions in Whinston's theory: (i) the entrant incurs a fixed cost in the market for the tied good; (ii) some buyers of the tied good do not purchase the tying good; and (iii) a monopolist selling the tying good can commit to tying (e.g., the tie is technological).

We start with a numerical example. Consider a pair of markets for the two goods in question (A and B) that departs from the previi-

---

52 Whinston, above note 6.

53 M. Whinston, "Tying, Foreclosure and Exclusion" (1990) 80 American Economic Review 837.

ous theory in three ways. First, purchasers of good B are of two types. "Joint" consumers always purchase A and B together. (If these were the only consumers, the previous analysis would continue to apply and tying would not be profitable.) "Separate" consumers purchase B only. Suppose that there are 100 consumers of each type.

Second, the market for B is not perfectly competitive but instead is served by two firms: (i) the monopolist from market A and (ii) a rival firm that produces only product B. In the absence of tying, the two firms split market B equally, each selling to fifty consumers of each type, or 100 consumers each in total.

Finally, suppose that the rival firm faces some fixed costs (e.g., costs of developing its version of product B) in order to sell in the market. And suppose that to cover the fixed costs in this market, the rival firm *needs* to sell to at least seventy-five consumers. In the absence of tying, the rival firm is able to cover the fixed cost because it services 100 consumers and therefore profitably competes in the market.[54]

The purpose of tying into market B by the monopolist in A will be to garner profits, not by monopolizing sales to joint consumers (the maximum profit from the joint consumers could be obtained by setting the price of the complementary good A appropriately) but from the monopolization of separate consumers. When the monopolist ties goods A and B together, it captures all joint consumers in market B. It splits the separate consumers with its rival (if the rival chooses to enter the market), thus leaving the rival with only fifty consumers. This is not enough to cover the fixed costs, and the rival will not enter the market when the monopolist commits to tying—or, if it has entered the market, it will not renew the fixed-cost investment to remain in the market.

In short, the monopolist in A is able to gain the monopoly over separate consumers in B by *depriving* the rival firm of a share of the joint consumers. Monopolizing the joint consumers is profitable not because of the returns earned from these consumers directly, but because of the entry-deterrence (or exit-inducing) effect the monopolization has on the rival firm, and the monopolization of the separ-

54 The presence of network effects is an assumption that can substitute for the assumption of fixed costs in this theory and in applications of the theory may well be more important. To keep the exposition simple, however, we set aside network effects until the discussion below of a case example.

ate consumers that this entry deterrence allows. Without its share of the joint consumers, the rival firm cannot compete for the separate consumers. The incumbent monopolist garners full monopoly profits from the separate consumers, which it could not do without the strategy of tying.

The following illustration of Whinston's theory is offered by Carlton and Heyer (and attributed to Rob Gertner);

> Consider the case of a hypothetical island on which there is a monopoly hotel serving many tourists. Natives live on the island. The hotel operates a restaurant, which competes for diners, both tourists and natives, in competition with local restaurants. By tying meals to lodging, the hotel can so diminish the number of tourists dining at local restaurants that, in the extreme, lack of scale prevents any local restaurants from surviving. The hotel thus acquires a monopoly over natives in the provision of restaurant services.[55]

Whinston's theory shows that market power in one market can be profitably extended to market power in two markets provided that (i) not all consumers in the second market use the product in the two markets jointly; (ii) in the absence of tying, there is some market power, for example a duopoly, in the second market; and (iii) a rival or rivals incur some fixed costs, such as costs of product development or continual product updating, in the second market.

The theory is potentially applicable to the various charges of anti-competitive tying against Microsoft in the US[56] and European cases.[57] One can describe these cases generally (and very crudely) as based on allegations that Microsoft ties its operating system for personal computers, Windows, to applications such as its Internet browser, the Windows Media Player, and (in earlier cases and allegations) word-processing and spreadsheet programs. This is done not so much through contractual tying as through the integration of code into the operating system that replicates the functions of some applications

55 D. Carlton and K. Heyer, "Appropriate Antitrust Policy towards Single-firm Conduct," Economic Analysis Group Working Paper 08-2, Antitrust Division, U.S. Department of Justice, March 2008.

56 *U.S. v. Microsoft*, Civil Action No. 98–1232 (CKK), 6 November 2001 [*Microsoft*].

57 European Commission Case No. COMP/C-3/37.792/Microsoft, March 2004 [European Microsoft Case].

and facilitates the Microsoft version of other applications — or even hampers the functionality of rivals' applications.

In terms of our explanation of the Whinston theory, market A is the operating system market, in which Microsoft is dominant, and market B is any applications market. The three conditions of the Whinston theory are met. In every applications market there is market power: software is produced with very low marginal cost and substantial markup of price over marginal cost. Fixed costs arise in the development and continual upgrading of software. Network effects, which can substitute for fixed costs in supporting the predictions of the Whinston model, are also present in that the value of an application to any consumer is increasing in the number of consumers adopting the application. And because Microsoft does not have a *complete* monopoly in the operating system market with the development of substitute operating systems such as Linux and the more prominent MacIntosh operating system, there are consumers in the applications market who demand the applications but not the Windows operating system. By tying its operating system to applications, Microsoft is able to collect monopoly profits not only from consumers who use its own operating system, but also from consumers who use applications such as Microsoft Word or Excel on MacIntosh computers or on Linux operating systems.

The Whinston theory as we have described it captures the basic incentive for a firm to leverage market power from one market into market power in a related market. While it can capture the profitability of tying as deterring entry into the secondary market, it does not capture the full dynamics of tying incentives. We complete this section of the paper with a description of three dynamic extensions of the Whinston theory. Taken together, these extensions strengthen the conclusion that a monopolist in one market can profitably use tying strategically to exclude rivals in a second market, thus extending or leveraging its monopoly power.

Microsoft's incentive to tie its applications should be stronger the less secure its current monopoly is in the operating system market. Establishing a monopoly in an applications market ensures that even if Microsoft were to lose its monopoly in the operating system market it would be left with at least one monopoly in the set of complementary goods consisting of the operating system and each application. As the jar and lid example demonstrates above, achieving a monopoly in either of a pair of complementary markets is as profitable as ensuring monopoly in both markets.

c) Dynamic Extension: Insuring a Monopoly

The first dynamic extension of the leverage theory, which we label "insuring a monopoly theory," expands on this point.[58] Consider a monopolist in market A, which competes in market B but faces perfect competition in market B. (Unlike the Whinston theory, there is no market power in market B.) The monopolist gains full monopoly profits currently and would gain nothing in terms of current profits from tying. However, we introduce innovation by supposing that production will take place in the future as well, and that with some probability there is an innovation in each market. More specifically, suppose that there are two periods of production. The monopolist operating in either market in the first period has a probability pH of achieving a "drastic" innovation in that market that can be used in the second period (a drastic innovation being one that assures an unconstrained monopoly in a market if no other firm achieves the same innovation). Similarly, there is a probability pH of a successful innovation in market B for use in period two by competitive producers in that market — but if such a competitive innovation occurs it is experienced by all competitors or potential competitors in the market. Finally, if competitors are excluded from market B in the first period, then these firms experience an innovation with probability $pL < pH$ (and, again, for simplicity assume that the innovation is achieved by all firms or by none at all). The probability of innovating while outside the market is naturally lower, because successful innovation benefits from market experience via a learning-by-doing effect. Similarly, the rivals achieve an innovation with probability pL in the primary market from which they are, by assumption, excluded currently.

While the monopolist's current profits are independent of whether it captures a monopoly in one market or in both, it can use the tying strategy to exclude competitive rivals from the second market currently so as to reduce the probability of the rivals successfully innov-

58 This theory is developed fully in J. Choi and C. Stefandis, "Tying, Investment and the Dynamic Leverage Theory" (2001) 32:1 RAND Journal of Economics 52.

ating in market B. The monopolist's expected future profits depend only on the probability that it achieves a monopoly position in at least one of the two markets—and this probability is higher if competitive rivals are forced into an innovation success rate of pL instead of pH in the market in which they compete and innovate. Tying does not protect a future monopoly with certainty, but it increases the chance that a monopoly will be preserved in at least one of the two markets.

In this dynamic theory, market power is not necessary in the second market for tying to be profitable. If one considers as endogenous the resources that competitive rivals put into innovation, the anti-competitive impact of tying is strengthened: with a lower chance of success, competitive rivals will invest less in innovation than they otherwise would and the exclusionary impact of tying, in reducing the probability of the monopolist being bumped out of a monopoly position in at least one of the markets, is magnified.

d) Dynamic Extension: The Barrier to "Browser-based Entry"

The US *Microsoft*[59] case involving the tying of Microsoft's Internet browser to its operating system created what could be called "a barrier to browser-based entry into the operating system market." This theory involves three concepts. The first is the concept of a network barrier to entry into the operating system market. The network barrier to entry (also called the "applications barrier to entry") refers to the fact that any new entrant into the operating system market must attract enough demand that applications programmers will be induced to write to the system—but unless applications programmers are willing to write to the system, the demand for the system will not emerge. The simultaneous emergence of demand for the system and applications writing to the system is necessary for success.

The second concept that is important for this theory is the notion of "middleware." Middleware refers to a program, such as Java, that interfaces between an operating system and an application. Suppose that Java or another middleware program became established in the market. Then applications programmers could write their code to Java. This means that any new entrant into the operating system would no longer need to attract applications to program the interface with its

59 Above note 56.

new operating system. It would simply need an interface with Java or another middleware. The network barrier to entry into the operating system market would disappear.

The final ingredient in this theory is the fact that independent browsers, as an alternative to Internet Explorer, facilitate the development of middleware. Java as a middleware is used for applications on browsers and, at least at times in the past, has been seen as potentially interfacing between all applications and any operating system. Microsoft, by inhibiting the development of Java (and even introducing its own version of Java in an effort to disrupt the universality of the middleware), has, according to this theory, strengthened the network barrier to entry into operating systems.

e) Dynamic Extension: The Carlton-Waldman Theory

The final dynamic extension of the leverage theory of tying has been offered recently by Carlton and Waldman.[60] In the simplest version of the Carlton-Waldman model, a monopolist competes in two periods with a potential rival, in two markets — the market for a primary good and the market for a complementary good. The rival can enter the complementary market in either period but can only enter the primary market in the second period because, as of the first period, the rival has not yet developed a primary product. The rival faces entry costs for entering either market. Finally, the rival's primary product is identical to the monopolist's primary product, if the rival enters this market, but the rival's complementary product is assumed to be superior (so as to emphasize the fact that tying can exclude a superior firm). Note that entry into the primary market by the rival has a payoff in terms of sales of the combined (superior) products in the second period.

The outcome of this model is that the monopolist, by tying in the first period, can prevent the entrant from selling at all in that period. The reduced set of markets in which the entrant can compete restricts the set of sales that the entrant can use to cover its fixed costs of entry into both markets. The failure of the entrant to produce in the comple-

60 D. Carlton and M. Waldman, "The Strategic Use of Tying to Preserve and Create Market Power in Evolving Industries" (2002) 33:2 RAND Journal of Economics 194–220.

mentary market means that the profitability of entering the primary market is reduced, possibly to the point where this entry is not worthwhile. It thus can deter entry of the rival.

The Carlton-Waldman theory is similar to the Whinston theory in that tying deters entry by restricting the set of transactions that a potential entrant can use to cover fixed costs. But the Carlton-Waldman theory points out that entry is deterred into the primary market as well, whereas in the Whinston theory the outcome of tying is the deterrence of entry in the complementary good market.. The theory is similar as well to our second dynamic extension of the leverage theory, in which the entry into the primary market is deterred by preventing browser-facilitated entry (via middleware); but the Carlton-Waldman theory shows that simply limiting the size of the combined markets that the rival can capture is enough to deter entry into both.

5) Tying and Optimal Second-best Pricing: Tying Patented with Non-patented Products

Our final theory of the incentives for and the welfare consequences of tying fits squarely into the intellectual property context. Should a firm with a monopoly on one product, as a result of a patent, be allowed to tie the product to a non-patented product? If a firm has been granted a patent on product A, should it be allowed to condition the sale of A on being the sole supplier of product B that is otherwise available in the marketplace?

This strategy might well appear to the untrained eye to be an unwarranted extension of monopoly power beyond the product on which the patent was granted. Temporary monopoly power is a necessary evil or cost that we tolerate in order to provide incentives for product and process innovation. If a patent holder is able to exclude competitors from a second market as well as the "legitimate" monopoly established by the patent, is it not extending its monopoly beyond the range that patent policy has determined necessary to induce innovation incentives?

We suggest that the normative question of optimal competition policy towards tying patented and non-patented goods must be addressed by considering the optimality of the *package* of patent policy and competition policy together. In other words, suppose that we were designing *de novo* patent policy and competition policy together, with the objective of achieving maximum welfare; what rule would emerge as to the legality of tying an unpatented product, B, to the patented product, A? The key in this approach is to understand how tying affects the well-known trade-off between innovation incentives and static market efficiency that is at the core of optimal patent policy.[61]

To reduce the theory to its starkest form, consider a firm that is investing research dollars to develop a new product, A. The demand for A is already known, but the event of discovering a means of producing A is random. The probability of this event is a function of the amount of investment by the firm, and the optimal amount of investment by the firm depends of course on the intellectual property protection that the firm can expect if it does succeed in discovering the product. We assume that this protection takes the form of a patent that will last for "t" years, after which the market becomes perfectly competitive. This is the classic Nordhaus model.[62]

In the Nordhaus model, the optimal patent length, t, balances at the margin the social benefits from increased incentive to innovate, and increased probability of discovering the product and achieving the gains to trade (or "total surplus") in the market, with the inefficiency from monopolization over the patent period. We introduce into this model a second product, B, which is available in a competitive market. The producer of A is in a position, if it so desires, to tie the sale of A to the condition that it supply all requirements of B as well. An example that comes close to fitting the model is the plaintiff's allegations, discussed above, concerning Apple's strategy of tying iPod and iTunes.[63] Apple could allow other suppliers freely to compete to sell

---

61 One might argue that the *joint* optimality of patent policy and competition policy is the wrong starting point to understand the policy towards tying — one should instead take current patent policy as given and that current patent policy assumes that tying is illegal. We reject the notion that competition policy should be designed to circumvent any inefficiencies or inadequacies in patent policy. Competition authorities are not in a position to fine-tune the incentives provided by patent policy. The implication is that the design of policy towards a practice such as tying patented and non-patented goods together should be understood as an aspect of the joint optimality of patent and competition policy.

62 W. Nordhaus, *Invention, Growth and Welfare: A Theoretical Treatment of Technological Change* (Cambridge: M.I.T. Press, 1969) at 3–7.

63 *Tucker*, above note 32.

songs for iPods. Instead, the plaintiff in *Tucker* alleges that Apple creates technological obstacles that impede rival sellers from attempting to sell to iPod users. That is, Apple allegedly ties songs to its patented digital player.[64]

The proposition that we wish to establish is that any patent policy (patent life, t) combined with a competition policy that prohibits tying is *Pareto dominated* by some patent policy and a competition policy that allows tying. The key is an insight offered by Meyer Burstein.[65] Tying a competitive good to a monopolized good allows a monopolist to achieve a pair of prices across two goods that is preferred by both consumers and itself to the pair of prices consisting of the monopoly price for good A and the competitive price for good B.

In the context of the simple model sketched above, suppose that "Pm" is the monopoly price of good A (and also, for simplicity, the monopoly price of good B) and that both goods can be produced at constant cost "c." For convenience, assume that demand for the two products is generated by identical consumers.[66]

Figure 1 below depicts the price paid (Pm, c) that is available to the consumers of goods A and B, during the patent period, if tying is prohibited. (After the patent period, both goods are available at price c.) Figure 1 also depicts iso-surplus (total surplus) curves and iso-profit lines. (These indifference curves are unusual in that this is a space of prices. The total surplus corresponding to a given pair of prices, for example, is defined as the surplus that the pair would generate in the two markets.)

Two points should be noted. First, the efficient set of prices is the set on the envelope curve between the surplus-maximizing pair of prices (c, c) and the profit-maximizing pair of prices (Pm, Pm). These

---

64 The Apple/iPod example may appear similar to the aftermarket cases, with the tunes being the variable input. This analogy is incorrect, however. The two products are complementary, of course, but a household purchases variable amounts of each product.

65 M. Burstein, "A Theory of Full-line Forcing" (1960) 55 Nw. U.L. Rev. 62; and F. Mathewson and R.A. Winter, "Tying as a Response to Demand Uncertainty" (1997) 28:3 RAND Journal of Economics 566.

66 This assumption is not necessary but simplifies the exposition. With heterogenous consumers, the techniques of Mathewson and Winter, *ibid.*, could be applied to extend the results.

Figure 1: Ramsey Prices

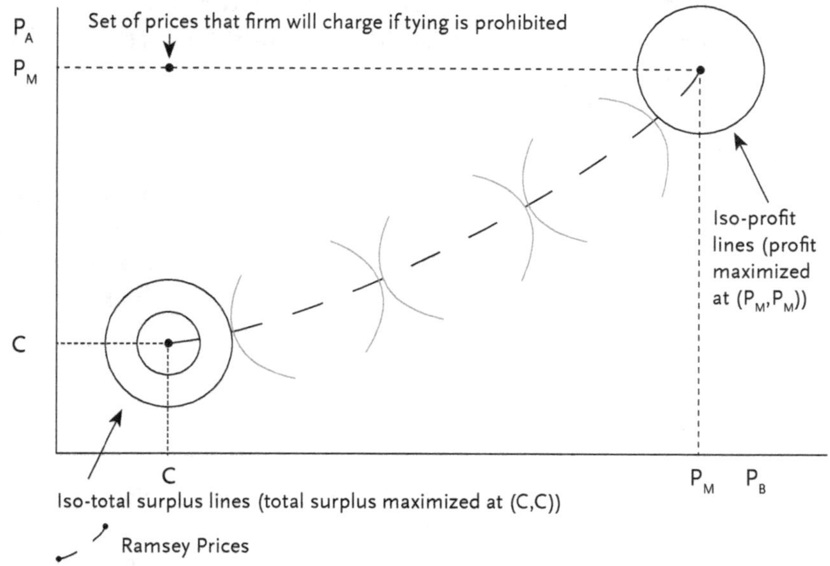

are referred to as "Ramsey Prices."[67] Second, the non-tying price pair (Pm, c) is not on the efficient price, or Ramsey Price, envelope. The implication is that starting from the non-tying pair of prices, a monopolist could move to a price pair that is better for consumers and therefore would not deter consumers from purchasing and is also more profitable. Both sides of the innovation incentive/static efficiency trade-off can be improved when tying is allowed. And if the monopolist moves to an efficient price pair that yields only higher profit (but not higher surplus), the policy-maker is free to reduce the patent length slightly, with the result that both profits and consumer surplus increase.[68] In short, tying allows a move to efficient Ramsey Prices, with the result

67 Where goods A and B are independent in demand (not the case for the real-world examples tht we discuss), the Ramsey Prices satisfy $(P_A - c) \div P_A = k \div E_{dA}$ and $(P_B - c) \div P_B = k \div E_{dB}$ as k varies between 0 and 1. That is, Ramsey Prices are prices that are marked up across the two markets in proportion to the inverse elasticity of demand.

68 This theory is simplified and incomplete, in that no explanation is offered for why all surplus is not extracted from the homogenous consumers by the monopolist via a fixed fee. The full analysis requires heterogeneity in consumers.

that innovation incentives and static efficiency improve, and both consumers and the monopolist's shareholders are better off.[69]

The following table summarizes the various theories that we have outlined in this paper.

Table 1: Description of Theories

	Theory	**Summary or Example**	**Potential Basis for Intervention to Prohibit Tying?**
1	Cost-efficient Tying	Left shoes and right shoes; *Jefferson Parish*	No
2	Bundling as price discrimination	Movie distribution; McDonald's meal specials	No
	Aftermarkets		
3a	Tying as metering	Photocopiers and toner; IBM adding machines and cards	No
3b	Response to asymmetric info on quality: *Ex post* info problems	1. Tying protects supplier reputation by avoiding reputational spillovers 2. Tying protects franchise system against free-riding by franchisees through purchase of cheap inputs	No
	Ex ante info problems	Tying signals durability; tying is more advantageous for longer-lasting machine	No
3c	Inefficient lack of commitment	Tying exploits the installed base of demand	Yes

69 An alternative explanation for Apple's DRM is that Apple was pressured into it by music suppliers. As Apple's CEO Steve Jobs explains,

> Since Apple does not own or control any music itself, it must license the rights to distribute music from others, primarily the "big four" music companies: Universal, Sony BMG, Warner and EMI. These four companies control the distribution of over 70% of the world's music. When Apple approached these companies to license their music to distribute legally over the Internet, they were extremely cautious and required Apple to protect their music from being illegally copied. The solution was to create a DRM system, which envelopes each song purchased from the iTunes store in special and secret software so that it cannot be played on unauthorized devices.

Steve Jobs, 6 February 2007, online: www.apple.com/hotnews/thoughtsonmusic.

	Theory	Summary or Example	Potential Basis for Intervention to Prohibit Tying?
4a	Whinston (1990)	Tying can extend monopoly, to consumers of the tied good alone, by preventing a rival from achieving scale in the tied-good market	Yes
4b	Dynamic extension: ensuring a monopoly	Preventing entry in both markets today increases chance of monopoly in future	Yes
4c	Tying to erect a barrier to "browser-based" entry into primary good	*US v. Microsoft*	Yes
4d	Carlton-Waldman	Tying limits size of combined markets, limiting entry into both	Yes
5	Tying as implementing efficient Ramsey pricing	Tying a non-patented good to a patented good; Apple's DRM-facilitated tying of iPod to iTunes	No

Under many of the theories outlined, the impact of tying is either pro-competitive or ambiguous. Under other theories, the impact of tying is anti-competitive. The key for policy, of course, is to determine how to distinguish the theories. If the distinction is difficult as an evidentiary matter, what is the optimal competition policy? We discuss this general issue in the context of cases in the next section and summarize the discussion in the conclusion to the chapter.

C. CASE STUDIES

1) *US v. Microsoft*[70] and the European Microsoft Case[71]

US v. Microsoft involved charges that Microsoft engaged in exclusionary behaviour in violation of US antitrust laws. Among other practices, Microsoft offered its Internet browser, Internet Explorer, as a bundle with its Windows operating system. Microsoft also entered into various exclusionary contracts with computer manufacturers, In-

70 Above note 56.

71 Above note 57.

ternet service providers, online services, such as America Online, and software vendors. In each of these contracts, Microsoft tied access to Windows to the obligation of preferential treatment for Internet Explorer. These methods included[72]

i) requiring computer manufacturers who licensed Windows 95 for installation on new machines to also install Internet Explorer;
ii) selling the products bundled together at retailers;
iii) requiring that computer manufacturers not remove the Internet Explorer icon from the desktop and not place any icons on the desktop larger than the Microsoft icons;
iv) prohibiting programs that launch during the boot sequence that give users an easy way to choose Navigator, the main competing product, over Internet Explorer;
v) physically integrating Internet Explorer into Windows so that, after 1998, it could not even be removed with the "software uninstall" feature;
vi) rewarding or pressuring some computer manufacturers for promoting Internet Explorer over Navigator;
vii) instituting exclusionary contracts with each of fourteen of the largest Internet service providers whereby the providers would be placed in the Windows Internet Connection Wizard (easing connection with the provider) in return for accepting restrictions, including a promise not to offer other browsers or web links to other browsers to customers;
viii) instituting exclusionary contracts with four online services, tying access to inclusion in the Windows Online Services Folder, which listed services whose access software was included in Windows, and to limits on promoting and distributing browsers other than Internet Explorer;
ix) instituting exclusionary contracts with Internet content providers that tied placement in the Windows Channel Bar, which facilitated access to a content provider's website, to the choice of Internet Explorer as the provider's default or preferred browser; and
x) instituting exclusionary contracts with software vendors, conditioning access to beta releases of Windows and technical infor-

72 Whinston, above note 6.

mation on the software's use of Internet Explorer as its default browser for any hypertext-based user interface as well as the adoption of Microsoft's "HTML Help" system, accessible only through Internet Explorer, to implement the software's help system.

Some of these strategies are tying in the narrow sense that one product (Windows) is tied to the *exclusive* use of a complementary product. Others are financial inducements to tie. Broadly speaking, these are all attempts to tie the use or re-sale of Windows to the obligation to use or favour Internet Explorer. If there is a distinction to be drawn among Microsoft's practices, it is between the physical tie between the operating system and the browser and the contractual restrictions.

A number of theories that we have reviewed fit various aspects of the Microsoft case. The theory that Microsoft tied its Internet browser to its operating system so as to prevent browser-based entry is of course a possible fit. The theory that Microsoft tied applications to its operating system, so as to increase the probability of retaining a future monopoly in at least one of the two classes of products (the "ensuring a monopoly") is also plausible. These are variations on the Whinston-based theory of leveraging monopoly. On the other side of the ledger, the argument is that Microsoft's integration of the browser and various applications into its operating system is cost-efficient both technically and in saving consumers' time spent shopping and integrating new applications into their personal computers.

We do not take a position here on whether the myriad collection of incentives and potential consequences of tying in the various Microsoft cases justify a remedy such as that imposed by the European Commission.[73] It is reasonable to conclude that Microsoft intended to exclude its rivals from the operating system market or the applications market, or at least that it benefited from the increased likelihood of such exclusion. Even a superficial assessment of this case, however, would

---

73 The European Commission ordered Microsoft to disclose to competitors the interfaces required for its products to be able to communicate with the Windows OS. Microsoft was also required to offer a version of its Windows OS without Windows Media Player to PC manufacturers (or when selling directly to end-users). In addition, Microsoft was fined €497 million for abusing its market power in the EU. See European Microsoft Case, above note 57.

require a study longer than this entire survey. We again note the conclusion reached by Michael Whinston in his survey of the Microsoft tying matters. In reviewing what economic theory tells us about the net effects of tying in the case, Whinston concludes, "What is striking about the area of exclusive contracts and tying . . . is how little the current literature tells us about what these effects are likely to be."[74]

2) *Canada (Director of Investigation and Research) v. Xerox Canada*[75]

a) Facts

The facts in *Xerox*, a case that turns on IP rights in tying and tied products, are as follows. Xerox Canada (Xerox) manufactured and sold and leased photocopy machines in Canada. It received a number of older photocopiers back from customers after the relevant leases were complete. Xerox either scrapped them, or refurbished them for resale. In 1982, however, it concluded that it had a surplus of used machines. Xerox and an employee, Terry Reid, decided that it would be mutually advantageous if Xerox sold some of the used machines to a company that Reid established and controlled, Exdos, and it would refurbish and resell the machines. Xerox also adopted a policy of supplying proprietary parts to Exdos. Exdos used the parts both to refurbish the second-hand machines and to provide post-sale service to its photocopier customers. Along with Exdos, other Independent Service Organizations (ISOs) grew in prominence in servicing Xerox photocopiers.

In 1987 Xerox US, the parent of Xerox Canada, adopted a policy of refusing to sell proprietary parts to ISOs. Instead it announced that it would only sell parts to end-users. Because of delays that would result from an end-user ordering parts in the event of a photocopier needing service, the decision not to sell parts to ISOs effectively barred ISOs from competing in the aftermarket service business. Exdos launched a complaint under the refusal to deal section of the *Competition Act*'s section 75,[76] which the director of investigation and research took to the tribunal. The tribunal held that Xerox had substantially affected

74 Whinston, above note 6 at 79.

75 *Xerox*, above note 23.

76 *Competition Act*, R.S.C. 1985, c. C-34.

Exdos' business, and that Exdos' complaint met the other requirements of section 75 such that a remedy was appropriate.[77] It ordered Xerox to supply Exdos on usual trade terms.[78]

b) Analysis

Xerox is a classic aftermarket tying case, analogous to the well-known *Kodak* case in the United States.[79] The supplier of a durable changed its parts supply policy and by doing so effectively imposed a tie, supported by intellectual property rights, on its customers: all buyers of Xerox photocopiers were effectively compelled to buy service only from Xerox itself. Intellectual property, patent in particular, is key in such circumstances since it prevents rival suppliers from manufacturing the relevant parts.

In order to evaluate the appropriate antitrust response to such a tying arrangement, it is helpful to consider two distinct situations. First, suppose that Xerox had market power in selling photocopiers. Second, suppose that Xerox did not have market power when initially selling the machines but realized situational market power in the supply of parts and service to past customers. Past customers, the "installed base," faced significant switching costs in acquiring parts and service: if they wished to acquire something other than Xerox parts in response to a price increase, they would have to acquire a photocopier from a different manufacturer.

i) Xerox Has Market Power Ex Ante

Suppose that there was limited competition for photocopiers at the relevant time. The record in *Xerox* is not complete on this question, since market power was not, as the tribunal noted, a requirement under section 75 of the *Competition Act. Ex ante* market power (that is, market power when initially selling the machines) was not implausible: the tribunal observed that Xerox had a 90 percent share of the

---

77 The provision at the time did not require a showing of an adverse effect on competition.

78 *Xerox*, above note 23.

79 Indeed, the tribunal cited the Ninth Circuit's *Kodak* opinion extensively, see *Xerox*, *ibid*.

high-volume photocopier market; almost 50 percent of the medium-volume market; and 33 percent of the low-volume market.

The existence of market power in the tying good does not imply that a tying arrangement is anti-competitive. The question, now directly asked by the revised section 75 in the *Competition Act*, is whether the tie lessens competition. Tying can theoretically foreclose competition and leverage monopoly profitably. The foreclosure explanations, however, are not applicable in a case like *Xerox*. Xerox was not concerned about service from ISOs eventually displacing original equipment, in contrast to Microsoft, for example, which may reasonably have had concerns that tied goods, like Internet browsers, would eventually displace the tying good (i.e., the operating system). Moreover, it is also implausible that Xerox was attempting to raise entry barriers in either the service or original equipment market. ISOs did not take long to make significant inroads in Xerox aftermarkets, which is consistent with the conclusion that there was little in the way of structural entry barriers, or economies of scale, that might have presented obstacles to new service providers. A prospective entrant to the photocopier industry would not suffer from the absence of an existing, developed ISO market.

Having said that, there is a possible connection between Xerox's (possible) market power and its tying strategy. Rather than *expanding* or *preserving* its market power, if it had market power, it is reasonable to surmise that Xerox adopted tying to better *exploit* its market power. In particular, the tying strategy allowed it to price discriminate: users of copiers with greater demand would require more in the way of parts and service. Tying permitted Xerox to charge a supra-competitive price on both parts and service, which in turn allowed Xerox to extract a greater surplus from high demanders than low demanders.

There is a subtlety to the basic metering argument in this context. Since Xerox had intellectual property rights in its parts, which allowed it to exclude ISOs by refusing to supply parts, it could have metered demand to a significant extent simply by charging ISOs high prices for parts. There was, however, reason for Xerox to have opted to exclude ISOs. Parts and service are to some extent substitutes. If service is supplied at competitive prices and parts are supplied at supra-competitive prices, there is an inefficient bias for copier customers in favour of acquiring service over parts. The price discrimination mechanism is more efficient without this bias. By tying both parts and service, Xerox could charge supra-competitive prices but could also charge efficient relative prices and avoid inefficient substitution by customers between parts and service.

The price discrimination explanation of Xerox's behaviour does not invite antitrust intervention. Price discrimination can be inefficient, such as when policing the tying arrangement costs almost as much as the private profit realized by the seller: the profit represents a socially neutral transfer, while the costs of enforcement are real social costs. But price discrimination is frequently efficient. In this context, tying service as well as parts to the machine avoids inefficient relative prices between service and parts. Tying as price discrimination allows Xerox to exploit its market power in aftermarkets more efficiently.

ii) Ex Post *Market Power*

Suppose now that Xerox did not have market power when it initially began selling photocopiers, but realized situational market power after having a sufficient number of past customers. This installed base would not purchase parts from another copier manufacturer in response to a significant price increase because it would also need to acquire a different brand of photocopier. While there is commentary and caselaw suggesting otherwise, imposing restrictions on tying in order to limit exploitation of situational market power is not sensible policy, as we explain.

The *Kodak*[80] courts imposed restrictions on *ex post* exploitation of market power in part because of a lack of faith in the ability of customers *ex ante* to anticipate the effects of high prices. That is, the Supreme Court did not accept the theory that robust competition *ex ante* would necessarily discipline high prices *ex post.* Because of informational imperfections, customers might not fully anticipate high prices in the future, which in turn leaves them vulnerable to exploitation through tying of a kind observed in *Kodak* and *Xerox.*

Such an emphasis on market imperfections in ordering an antitrust remedy is misplaced. Setting aside the empirically contestable question of whether buyers are capable of accounting for aftermarket prices when making acquisitions, considerations that one would think

---

80 Above note 23.

obvious to sophisticated purchasers of expensive photocopy equipment, tying law does not address these circumstances. Tying law is concerned about the preservation or enhancement of market power. If a legal response to informational imperfections were justified, it would make more sense for the law to address the problem (information imperfections) and not to deal instead with the alleged symptom of the problem, tying. Mandatory warranties, for example, or mandatory disclosure of maintenance costs, would be more appropriate than preventing tying, a practice that in this context does not appear to create or preserve market power, but rather may simply result in the more efficient exploitation of market power.

Another line of argument in support of orders like those in *Xerox* is that *ex ante* competition is not a perfect solution to *ex post* situational market power. As Borenstein, MacKie-Mason, and Netz suggest,[81] *ex ante* competition may lead to discounted copier prices in order to compensate for *ex post* high prices from situational market power. Such an outcome in some sense protects customers from their own possible ignorance about future exploitation, in that anticipation of *ex post* exploitation by *sellers* results in lower copier prices *ex ante*. But a price pattern of low copier prices and high aftermarket prices creates its own inefficiencies. Low-demand buyers are priced into the machine market because of potentially below-cost pricing in the initial sale, while buyers purchase too little aftermarket service from a social perspective because of supra-competitive prices.

In our view, concern about a "bargain-rip-off" pricing pattern, a concern that arises generally in markets with switching costs,[82] does not invite antitrust intervention.[83] The social costs of such an outcome are not likely to be significant.[84] Moreover, sellers have the incentive and a variety of means, including reputational bonds, to resist the temptation to indulge in bargain-rip-off pricing. Antitrust remedies

---

81 Above note 47.

82 See J. Farrell and P. Klemperer, "Coordination and Lock-in: Competition with Switching Costs and Network Effects" in M. Armstrong and J. Porter, eds., *Handbook of Industrial Organization* (New York: North-Holland, 2007) at 1967–2072.

83 See Iacobucci, "Switching Costs," above note 50.

84 C. Shapiro, "Aftermarkets and Consumer Welfare: Making Sense of *Kodak*" (1995) 63 Antitrust L.J. 483.

against tying are a blunt and inappropriate instrument for dealing with an inefficient price path. This is particularly so when one considers the difficulties antitrust enforcement agencies would have in determining the reasons for a particular outcome in a particular case. Banning tying of the kind observed in *Xerox* could lead to inefficient deterrence of socially valuable price discrimination, since antitrust enforcers would have little basis for determining whether a tie was designed to price discriminate or to exploit past customers.

c) Conclusion

If Xerox had market power when it imposed the aftermarket tie, it is probable that it was engaging in price discrimination by refusing to sell proprietary parts to ISOs. Competition policy should not intervene in such a case. If, on the other hand, Xerox only had *ex post* situational market power, there are potential inefficiencies from the practice, but competition policy intervention is inappropriate: the potential social costs are small and the seller itself, unlike in most competition policy contexts, has itself an incentive to commit to not exploiting its customers.

3) *Siegel v. Chicken Delight*[85]

a) Facts

Chicken Delight was a business system franchisor that sold franchise opportunities. The franchises were fast food restaurants that used the "Chicken Delight" name. Chicken Delight did not charge franchises a fee or royalties, but rather, in exchange for the licence to use the Chicken Delight name and system, the franchisee would commit to purchasing certain inputs only from the franchisor. Franchisees were required to buy "a specified number of cookers and fryers and to purchase certain packaging supplies and mixes exclusively from Chicken Delight."[86] The prices Chicken Delight charged for the tied goods exceeded market prices.

Several franchisees launched a class action against Chicken Delight seeking treble damages under US tying law. The argument was that Chicken Delight required buyers of the licence to use the Chicken

85 See *Chicken Delight*, above note 2.

86 *Ibid.* at 47.

Delight name, the tying good, also to buy tied goods in the form of the branded ingredients and packaging. Given that Chicken Delight had market power in the tying good, the argument continued, the tie was *per se* illegal. Market power arose because of Chicken Delight's IP rights, specifically, its ownership of the valuable trade-marks associated with the franchise system. The trial court agreed, and the Ninth Circuit affirmed this conclusion.

b) Analysis

The difficulty in analyzing *Chicken Delight* is not in deciding whether the tying was anti-competitive, it was not, but rather in assessing what precisely explained the arrangement. First, we set out our reasons for concluding that the tying arrangement was not anti-competitive, and second, we turn to the more difficult question of explaining the arrangement.

i) The Absence of an Anti-competitive Explanation

There are two fundamental reasons why it is reasonable to conclude that the tying arrangement was not anti-competitive. First, Chicken Delight did not have market power. Second, there is no reasonable theory of how tying in this case could have foreclosed competition.

On the matter of requisite market power, the Ninth Circuit Court agreed with the trial court that the possession of a valuable trade-mark conferred market power on Chicken Delight. There were several problems with the Ninth Circuit's analysis. First, it never precisely defined the market over which Chicken Delight was alleged to have power. Indeed, it is not unreasonable to argue that franchises are simply investment opportunities that must compete with millions of other investment opportunities. Even if the key input of the franchisee is labour, not capital, an entrepreneur presumably has a vast range of potential investments, including starting her own franchise system. But even if the market is defined more narrowly to include only franchises, there was no suggestion of a lack of competition in this market. Selling franchises is a competitive business.

It appears that the Ninth Circuit Court concluded that Chicken Delight had market power in selling fast food franchises. While no analysis of this market is in fact offered, in explaining its conclusion that a registered trade-mark conferred market power, the court observed that "It can hardly be denied that the Chicken Delight trade-mark is distinctive; that it possesses goodwill and public acceptance unique to it and not enjoyed by other fast food chains."[87] Rather than closely examining the fast food franchise market, the court rested its analysis on a presumption of market power: "Just as the patent or copyright forecloses competitors from offering the distinctive product on the market, so the registered trade-mark presents a legal barrier against competition . . . . Accordingly we see no reason why the presumption that exists in the case of the patent and copyright does not equally apply to the trade-mark."[88]

This analysis is unconvincing. Any business could adopt a registered trade-mark. This does not confer market power that gives rise to concern about the exclusionary nature of tying. Similarly, the possession of a patent for a product that nobody wants (which represents the vast majority of patents), or the possession of copyright in a work that nobody wants to read, does not confer market power. Recognizing these considerations in *Independent Ink*,[89] the US Supreme Court recently rejected earlier doctrine that held that patents confer market power on their holders *per se*.

This is not to say that IP is irrelevant to an analysis of market power. To be sure, if there were indicia of actual market power, like a high market share for Chicken Delight in a thoughtfully identified market, then the existence of its trade-mark would contribute to an analysis of barriers to entry. Any entrant cannot free ride on Chicken Delight's past investment in its trade-mark, but rather must invest *de novo* in its own trade-mark. But, on its own, a trade-mark is not indicative of market power.

Even if there were market power, there is no evidence that tying in this case could have foreclosed competition. Imposing the tie could not have had an impact on entrants to the franchise-system market. Chicken Delight had no significance in the chicken ingredients or packaging markets, so requiring its franchisees to purchase supplies exclusively from Chicken Delight would not have created the slightest obstacle for entrants to the franchise-system market: there were plenty of options for rivals' franchisees to source ingredients. Similar-

---

87 *Ibid.* at 50.

88 *Ibid.*

89 Above note 22.

ly, given their competitive structure, it is implausible to think that the tie could have affected competition in the tied-good markets. There was no antitrust reason to intervene in *Chicken Delight.*

ii) Explaining the Tying Arrangement

It is more difficult to identify the motivation for the tie precisely than to rule out an anti-competitive explanation. A common explanation of tying in the franchise setting is quality control.[90] Each franchise bears only a fraction of the benefits of the system's reputation for quality, while it would realize fully the cost-saving benefits of using inferior inputs in providing its services. There is an externality among franchisees. One way of remedying the incentive to chisel on quality is to have the franchisor police quality by compelling franchises to purchase inputs only from the franchisor. Since the franchisor better internalizes the reputation of the franchise system than any given franchisee, tying can address quality control issues in franchises.

This explanation, while plausible in the abstract, fails to completely explain the tying arrangement in *Chicken Delight,* but not for the reasons the court gave in rejecting it. The court in *Chicken Delight* rejected the quality control explanation on the argument that a franchisor concerned about quality could contractually stipulate the quality of inputs that were necessary and allow franchisees to choose where to buy these inputs. The court did not appreciate, however, that contracts over quality may be difficult to write initially and may also be difficult to monitor. Tying contracts limit these contractual difficulties.

Rather, the plausibility of quality control is challenged more convincingly by the lack of evidence about the dangers of inferior inputs in this particular case. For example, it is not clear that the quality of the paper buckets that franchisees used would directly impact the system's reputation for quality. Indeed, as a matter of fact, the paper packaging that the franchisor sold its franchisees was virtually indistinguishable from other packaging that franchisees would acquire. To monitor the tying arrangement, Klein and Saft report that Chicken Delight took to

90 See for example, Klein and Saft, above note 42 at 345; Iacobucci, "Tying as Quality Control," above note 41.

marking its buckets with ink only detectable with ultraviolet light.[91] While the structure of the quality control argument generally fits the franchise context, the facts of *Chicken Delight* did not.

Another argument that is commonly advanced to explain franchise tying arrangements is that they are price discrimination devices: more profitable franchises require more inputs, and thus the tie results in greater surplus extraction from high-value franchises. While the argument is not entirely implausible, for it to apply the buyer must know more about the value of the franchise than the franchisor. If franchisor and franchisee are equally knowledgeable about the value of the franchise, the price of the franchise can be set accordingly. However, if the franchisee knows more about the value of the franchise, then tying as metering makes sense. The empirical question is whether it is reasonable to suppose that franchisees, who often are inexperienced business people, know more than franchisors about the franchise's value. In the majority of instances, we suggest, this informational assumption is not plausible.

There are two related explanations. If both parties are symmetrically informed about the franchise value, but this value is risky, then the tying arrangement could be an efficient risk-sharing device between the relatively risk-neutral franchisor with its portfolio of franchises and the risk-averse individual franchisee. Alternatively, a franchisor that is more confident in the value of the franchise than a franchisee may signal its confidence by lowering the fixed price on the franchise and instead take its returns from the sale on the performance of the franchise. Tying arrangements can signal quality.

To summarize, while the weight on various incentives for the tying arrangement is not crystal clear, it is plain that Chicken Delight was not behaving anti-competitively when it tied certain supplies to its trade-mark.

D. CONCLUSION: OPTIMAL POLICY

In this concluding section we summarize our review of the theories of tying and our case studies that focused on tying and IP rights, and then turn to the question of optimal (efficient) policy towards tying in

91 *Ibid.* at 348.

the presence of IP rights. We review the Canadian law on tying, and then analyze the law based on our survey of the economics of tying and intellectual property. We also draw on US comparative experience in reaching our conclusions.

1) Summary

Without question, tying has exclusionary effects. By requiring or inducing purchasers of a product to buy a second product, the tie-in excludes sales of the second product by rival suppliers. But to conclude that the practice is exclusionary does not answer the efficiency-oriented policy inquiry. Our review of the theories shows that efficiency and exclusion are often related. For example, price discrimination is often efficient, but sometimes can only be implemented by a seller of a durable looking to charge a supra-competitive markup on an aftermarket product through the imposition of a tie that completely excludes competition in the aftermarket product. The relevant policy question is not whether tying excludes rival sellers, nor is it whether tying leads to a less competitive market structure, but whether the strategy has the consequence of reducing efficiency.

Some instances of tying can be exclusionary and inefficient. Anticompetitive effects can result in either the tying-good market or the tied-good market. The seller of the tying good, for example, may wish to hinder entry into the tied-good market by imposing a tie, which prevents entrants into the tied-good market from achieving scale in that market. This can lessen competition in the tied-good market, and can also lessen competition in the tying-good market by compelling entrants to enter both tying- and tied-good markets. Alternatively, tying-good sellers may fear that producers of the tied good could eventually compete with the tying-good seller. Tying can deter future competition in the tying-good market by limiting competition in the tied-good market.

Tying can also be efficient. Indeed, given the prevalence of tying in competitive markets, it is reasonable to conclude that tying is efficient much more often than not. The most basic explanation of tying is that there are direct cost savings from selling two products together rather than apart. Selling two shoes together is a form of tying but is obviously explained by such efficiencies. Tying can facilitate efficient price discrimination, such as where a durable-good seller ties aftermarket products at a markup. Tying can efficiently share risk between a seller and a buyer, such as where a franchisor ties the franchisee's inputs in order to share the profits from the franchise's operation. Tying can protect the seller's reputation for quality. This quality control explanation is most plausible where there is some sharing of costs of poor performance between the tying-good seller and buyer. For example, franchise systems share the reputational costs of a franchise's poor performance, and thus there are incentives for the franchisor to tie quality inputs to the franchise. On a related note, tying can signal quality: where greater use of the tied good correlates with the quality of the tying good, tying and charging a lower price for the tying good and a higher price for the tied good can be efficient.

The theoretical diversity of tying is reflected in the case studies in this survey. Two cases relate to the common setting of a durable-good seller tying aftermarkets to the durable. In *Xerox*,[92] Xerox imposed a service tie on its machine buyers by refusing to sell proprietary parts to ISOs; in *Chicken Delight*,[93] the franchisor required its franchisees to buy supplies from the franchisor alone. *Xerox* is plausibly explained by price discrimination. *Chicken Delight* could be explained by price discrimination, though that explanation depends on the franchisee having better information about the value of the franchise than the franchisor, which may be a dubious premise. Alternatively, it could be explained by risk-sharing, signalling, and/or quality control. Whatever the precise motivation for tying in *Chicken Delight* and *Xerox*, it is implausible that the sellers were seeking to lessen competition in either the aftermarket or the durable-good market itself. Competition authorities should therefore not intervene in such cases.

In contrast, it is reasonable to conclude that Microsoft intended to exclude rivals from producing Windows-compatible applications.[94] This could be to protect Microsoft's market power in applications in the event that its dominance in Windows diminishes, or it could conceivably be to help protect its Windows dominance by requiring operating system producers to innovate with respect to both operat-

---

92 Above note 23.

93 Above note 2.

94 See *Microsoft*, above note 56.

ing systems and applications. The strategy increased the *ex ante* probability of retaining a monopoly in particular applications, such as the browser market or media player market, regardless of whatever happened to the operating system market. Such instances of tying invite antitrust intervention. But the challenge, as we discuss below, is to craft a workable remedy.

2) Existing Canadian Competition Law on Tying

Three provisions in the Canadian *Competition Act*[95] potentially address tying. First, section 77 allows the Competition Tribunal to make an order in response to a "major supplier" in a market that requires or induces its customers to buy other products, when such a requirement has an exclusionary effect that has lessened or is likely to lessen competition substantially. Second, section 79 allows the tribunal to make an order where a dominant firm adopts a practice that substantially lessens competition; tying could be such a practice. Third, section 75 allows the tribunal to make an order against a supplier's refusal to supply a product where the refusal harms its customers because of insufficient competition in the supply of the product, and where such a refusal to supply would have an adverse effect on competition. Section 75 could have, and did have in the *Xerox* case, a direct application to aftermarkets tying: by refusing to supply ISOs with parts, Xerox established a tie in the service market.

Two important prerequisites to a finding that an order is appropriate emerge under these sections. First, the seller must have market power. Certainly, to be subject to an order under the abuse of dominance provision,[96] the seller must be dominant.[97] Similarly, under section 77, the seller must be a "major supplier," which requires a showing of market power.[98]

The requirement of market power is somewhat murky in the case of section 75 of the *Competition Act*, though it is clear that the seller's

95 Above note 76.

96 See *Competition Act, ibid.* at s. 79.

97 See for example, *Canada (Director of Investigation and Research) v. NutraSweet Co.* (1990), 32 C.P.R. (3d) 1 (Comp. Trib.) [*NutraSweet*].

98 See for example, *Canada (Director of Investigation and Research) v. Tele-Direct Publications Inc.* (1997), 73 C.P.R. (3d) 107 (Comp. Trib.) [*Tele-Direct*].

refusal to supply must have an impact that relates to insufficient competition in the product. The confusion arises because of potential debate over the meaning of the "product." If the "product" in section 75 is narrowly understood to be the product sold by a holder of particular IP rights, such as a trade-mark or a patent, then the requirement that there be insufficient competition in the product is easy to meet. In *Xerox*,[99] for example, there were other suppliers of photocopier parts, but not of Xerox photocopier products. When *Xerox* was decided, section 75 did not require an adverse effect on competition generally, which may have led the tribunal to take a narrow view of "product," which in turn lessens the importance of market power. We return to the relationship between IP and market power in discussing optimal policy below.

Beyond market power, it is a requirement for application of a remedy to tying that there must be a lessening of competition. Both sections 77 and 79 of the *Competition Act* require a showing of a "substantial lessening of competition" for an order to be appropriate, while section 75 requires an "adverse effect" on competition. To show a substantial lessening of competition, cases establish that the practice in question must "preserve or add to" the seller's market power.[100] The requirement of a showing of competitive effects lessens the importance of the market power requirement, given that competitive markets produce neither sellers with market power nor sellers that can substantially lessen competition. That is, to show an adverse effect on competition, there must be a showing of market power as well. As we discuss below, however, even though a showing of a substantial lessening of competition is sufficient to show market power, it makes sense as a matter of policy to maintain market power as an independent requirement.

Another key element of the analysis concerns efficiency explanations for the practice. There is no efficiency defence *per se* in any of the tying provisions, though the *Competition Act* provides that the tribunal shall not make an order where tied selling "is reasonable having regard to the technological relationship between or among the products."[101] Efficiencies are relevant to an examination of tying, however, in several ways. Most fundamentally, efficiency inevitably affects the basic ques-

---

99 Above note 23.

100 See *NutraSweet,* above note 97.

101 See *Competition Act,* above note 76 at s. 77(4)(b).

tion of whether a seller is tying two separate products, which is in effect the central concern of section 77(4)(b). In *Tele-Direct*, the tribunal held, following the US Supreme Court in *Jefferson Parish*,[102] that the existence of two products turned on the existence of separate demand for the products.[103] This inquiry in part turns on whether the separate provision of the products is efficient. The tribunal stated: "Assuming demand for separate products, if efficiency is proven to be the reason for bundling, there is one product. If not, there are two products."[104] Thus, when Evans and Salinger argue that the most common explanation for tying is the realization of cost efficiencies,[105] it is open in at least some of these cases in Canada (as in the US) to argue that the arrangements do not involve tying at all — the efficiencies suggest a single product.

Efficiencies are also relevant under section 79, which requires a predatory, exclusionary, or disciplinary motivation for the impugned practice. As Trebilcock *et al.* state, "If circumstances suggest a pro-competitive, or efficiency, motivation, the requisite predatory, exclusionary, or disciplinary intent will not be present and there is no anticompetitive effect."[106] Section 79(4) also appears to contemplate efficiency, stating that the tribunal should consider whether the impugned practice "is a result of superior competitive performance."[107] The wording is a bit odd, given that most efficiency explanations of a contractual practice run the other way around (i.e., superior competitive performance results from the practice). But it is arguable that section 79(4) allows another avenue for efficiency arguments to be introduced into an evaluation of tying. Given the potential for efficiencies associated with tying, we suggest that section 79(4) be interpreted liberally to provide a statutory basis for an efficiency defence.

3) Optimal Law and Policy on Tying

It is abundantly clear that tying can have a wide range of explanations. Tying can increase or decrease efficiency depending on the circum-

---

102 *Jefferson Parish*, above note 9.
103 *Tele-Direct*, above note 98.
104 *Ibid.* at 115.
105 Evans and Salinger, above note 8.
106 M. Trebilcock *et al.*, above note 25 at 527.
107 *Competition Act*, above note 76 at s. 79(4).

stances. Moreover, as the survey of the economic theory of tying suggests, no clear set of general evidentiary conditions has emerged that would allow the categorization of tying cases into those that increase efficiency and those that decrease efficiency. Antitrust authorities, we conclude, cannot rely on general rules of thumb in reaching conclusions that tying in a given case violates antitrust laws. Rather, they must instead rely on a case-by-case analysis.

The requirement of examining each case on its own merits does not, however, suggest that rules of thumb are irrelevant. There are necessary conditions for tying to be anti-competitive that allow the law to approach tying allegations in a systematic way. Most fundamentally, for tying to potentially have anti-competitive effects, there must be market power in the tying good. Of course, some degree of market power is common. In any differentiated goods market, the seller can raise price above marginal cost. The focus should therefore be on the potential for significant market power, not simply market power that reflects imperfect competition. Tying is potentially harmful where it has exclusionary effects in either the tying- or tied-good markets. If markets are robustly, even if not perfectly, competitive, such exclusionary effects are unlikely and antitrust authorities should not intervene.

The law in Canada, as in the US, aptly establishes this requirement. As reviewed, market power is a prerequisite for a finding that tying is anti-competitive. This requirement provides an efficient filter for antitrust authorities.

Market power, however, is not sufficient to conclude that tying is inefficient. Whether or not the seller has market power, tying can allow efficient signalling of quality, efficient risk-sharing, quality control, and so on. Special conditions, particularly dynamic considerations concerning the threat of entry in the tying- and tied-good markets over time, must be present for tying to be anti-competitive. Again, Canadian law is appropriate in this respect. Rather than following the US approach, which holds that tying is *per se* illegal if the seller has market power, tying is not subject to an order under the *Competition Act* unless the practice substantially lessens competition, or, in the case of refusals to supply that effectively result in a tie, has an adverse effect on competition. Given the range of explanations that apply to tying independent of the seller's market power, such an approach is appropriate.

The substantial lessening of competition test begs the question of whether the seller's market power ought to be treated as an independent requirement for the application of a remedy in a tying case. If it can be shown that the practice substantially lessens competition, it must be that the seller has market power. If the second requirement is a sufficient condition for the first, it might be suggested that the first requirement ought not to be separately considered. We disagree. The market-power requirement is useful in its own right because it is a useful initial screen for the authorities in evaluating potentially anticompetitive tying (and because the market-power test is invariably invoked as a prerequisite into any test for the substantial lessening of competition in any case). Rather than moving directly to a potentially complex analysis of the motivations and effects of a particular tying arrangement, the authorities can investigate the presence of market power by relying on relatively straightforward criteria (market shares, barriers to entry). If the analysis reveals the absence of market power, the more complicated step of identifying effects can be avoided.

The core of Canadian law on tying is the criterion of "substantial lessening of competition" under sections 77 or 79, or "adverse effect" on competition under section 75. And it is on the application of this criterion that economics theory must be brought to bear. Substantial lessening of competition cannot be applied to a single market alone, in particular to only the tied-good market, if the law is to be consistent with the economic theory of the efficiency effects of tying. In the tied-good market, there is often an apparent reduction in competition in the case of requirements tying, since firms other than the tying firm are excluded. But optimal tying often involves an increase in the price of the tied good in combination with a decrease in the price of the tying good. In the metering theory of tying, for example, a monopolist raises the price of the tied good while lowering the price of the tying good. The overall welfare effects are ambiguous, but a misguided focus on the tied sales market alone would lead to the conclusion that the strategy had lessened competition.

Another way of considering this point is from the perspective of market definition. It may appear that the tied-good market is always a competition market. Sometimes, as in the "insuring a monopoly theory" this is valid. Under this theory, an operating system is bundled with an application in order to realize market power in at least one market (the application market or the operating system market). Often, however, the relevant market for requirements tying cases should be the market for the overall package of the basic product and the tied goods. This is where competitive discipline is brought to bear on any attempts to exercise market power, regardless of the state of availability of substitutes for the tied product. For example, we have shown in this chapter that a seller of a patented good may wish to tie a non-patented good in order to spread the distortions associated with supra-competitive pricing. In such a case, focusing only on the lessening of competition in the tied-good market would miss the benefits of lower prices in the tying-good market.

The emphasis on the competitive effects of the practice is appropriate in exempting from antitrust remedial orders tying that is motivated by price discrimination. Tying or bundling as a means of practising price discrimination should not be of concern to antitrust authorities. Price discrimination, while conceivably harmful, is often beneficial. It is not a useful expenditure of regulatory resources to attempt to micro-regulate strategies designed for price discrimination. By focusing on the competitive effects of the practice, particularly on the exclusionary, predatory, or disciplinary effects that abuse of dominance requires, the law in Canada appropriately steers clear of orders against tying or bundling based on price discrimination.

Finally, even in the absence of a full-blown efficiency defence, the emphasis on a showing of anti-competitive effects permits inquiry into the efficiency effects of tying in a given case, beyond those efficiency considerations that arise in inquiring into whether there are two products. As discussed in *Tele-Direct*,[108] if the seller shows that there is an efficiency explanation for a practice, the requisite exclusionary, predatory, or disciplinary motivation is absent. Again, given the range of efficiency explanations for tying, allowing scope for these considerations is appropriate.

The structure of the test for anti-competitive tying in Canada makes sense. It sensibly sets out market power and a lessening of competition as independent requirements. As we discuss above, however, the lessening-of-competition test must be applied to the relevant market — in requirements tying cases this is the market for the over-

---

108 Above note 98.

all bundle of the product and tied goods. Our final comment on the structure of Canadian tying law generally concerns the presumptions that the authorities should make when inquiring into the lessening of competition. Antitrust authorities should take a cautious approach to their analysis. Because of the complexity of the issues and factual circumstances, the authorities and courts are unlikely to be able to identify precisely the effects of tying in a given case. Given the relative rarity of anti-competitive tying, the authorities should exercise modesty and require significant evidence of anti-competitive effects before seeking or making an order against tying. This is especially so given the fluctuations over time in the theory of tying. Taking a harsh approach to tying based on the intellectual fashions of the day could lead to inappropriate *per se* rules against tying, as they have in the US. A cautious approach to intervention in markets is more appropriate.

Aside from setting a "high hurdle"[109] to a finding that tying in a particular case is anti-competitive, antitrust authorities ought also to be cautious in ordering remedies. Where tying is accomplished by contract, a remedy to anti-competitive tying is straightforward: the parties must cease relying on tying in their contracts. But tying is often achieved by product integration. The costs of ordering the disintegration of a product exceed the costs of ceasing to rely on a contractual practice. Given the costs of such interventionist remedies, and the almost inevitable residual doubts about the anti-competitive nature of the tie, authorities should be even more cautious than usual in making orders in the face of tying-by-integration. We recognize that excessive *ex post* deference to tying-by-integration leads directly to increasing *ex ante* incentives to rely on such tying. We would thus not recommend that the authorities *never* make an order against an integrated product. But, given that the costs to the seller of unbundling an integrated product exceed the costs of ceasing to rely on contractual tying, exercising relative restraint in making orders in integrated tying cases rather than contractual tying cases does not necessarily change the expected costs of each practice to the seller. Since sellers care about the costs of breaking up an integrated product, restraint in these cases does not necessarily create perverse incentives.

---

109 See D. Carlton and M. Waldman, "Theories of Tying and Implications for Antitrust Policy," Johnson School Research Paper Series #24-06 (July 2005) at 28.

4) Special Issues Concerning Intellectual Property

Several important features of optimal tying law and policy are influenced by intellectual property considerations. Perhaps of greatest significance is the question of how IP rights affect the analysis of market power. Market power is appropriately considered a requirement for an order against tying. If the seller enjoys protection from competition because of intellectual property rights that it holds, should there be a presumption that the seller has market power?

The US caselaw has considered this matter expressly, as discussed in the *Chicken Delight*[110] case study. In *Chicken Delight* itself, a trade-mark was found to confer market power. This is the high water-mark of overestimating the market impact of IP rights. Any seller could have a trade-mark. It is nonsensical to conclude that a trade-mark confers market power. While the court in *Chicken Delight* noted that the trade-mark was valuable given the franchisor's experience and reputation, it is the experience and reputation that is valuable, not the fact of trade-mark *per se*.

The conferral of patent, copyright, or trade-mark protection clearly protects the seller from some kinds of competition, but this, in itself, is no more significant for competition than the fact that a particular restaurant that occupies a physical space prevents rival restaurants from occupying the same space. Differentiation among products is the norm in a market economy. IP protection simply offers another mechanism for differentiation. In short, the presumption of market power because of IP is misplaced. The Canadian Competition Bureau's *Intellectual Property Enforcement Guidelines*,[111] and recently the US Supreme Court case of *Independent Ink*,[112] appropriately rejected such a presumption.

Of course, IP is relevant to the market-power inquiry even though a presumption that market power flows from IP is inappropriate. For example, potential rivals to a seller of a patented product face a barrier to entry that would not exist absent the patent. But there is nothing peculiar about the nature of the inquiry: whenever market power is

110 Above note 2.

111 (Ottawa: Industry Canada, 1991–2008). See online: www.competitionbureau.gc.ca/epic/site/cb-bc.nsf/en/h_00168e.html.

112 Above note 22.

in question, it is appropriate to examine barriers to entry. IP rights may affect this inquiry, but IP rights do not obviate the need for the inquiry.

The link between IP rights and market power is also relevant to aftermarket cases. Aftermarket cases involving apparently opportunistic changes in policy, such as *Xerox*, hinge on the existence of IP rights. The reason that Xerox could be seen as controlling the market for its parts is that the parts were proprietary. Xerox could, of course, commit not to impose a tie *ex post* simply by relinquishing its IP rights in its parts, which in turn would permit competitive entry into the Xerox parts market. Because Xerox would want to protect the investment in developing its machines, however, it would be reluctant to relinquish these rights, and therefore the risk emerges of *ex post* expropriation of buyers' surplus through tying. When Borenstein *et al.*[113] offer the justification for the *Kodak*[114] decision that it helps sellers of durables commit not to exploit their installed base, one can think of their analysis as essentially protecting IP rights: without *Kodak*, the argument runs, sellers must either give up IP rights or face an inefficient incentive to exploit past customers.

Whether IP rights ought to be seen as conferring market power on the seller in opportunistic aftermarket cases depends entirely on whether an *ex ante* or *ex post* view of market power is appropriate. In *Kodak* itself, Kodak argued that it did not have market power because of *ex ante* competition in the photocopier market. *Ex post*, of course, Kodak was the only supplier of its proprietary parts. The US Supreme Court held that market imperfections, including naivety on the part of Kodak's customers, may have allowed Kodak to exploit its *ex post* market power. Borenstein *et al.* further point out that even if there were perfect competition, *ex post* Kodak would have an incentive to exploit its situational market power because of an inability contractually to commit not to do so; any competition *ex ante* would simply drive down the price of the machines.[115] Both Kodak and its customers would, under the Borenstein *et al.* theory, prefer a commitment not to raise prices *ex post* since drafting a fully contingent contract to

---

113 Above note 47.

114 Above note 23.

115 Borenstein *et al.*, above note 47.

address the problem is not feasible. (How, for example, would one perfectly account for fluctuating input costs in aftermarkets over time? How would one contractually specify aftermarket quality perfectly?)

Market and contractual imperfections, particularly in longer term contracts, are omnipresent. But this in itself does not invite antitrust intervention. The correct question is: What is the best legal instrument for addressing any inefficiency that might arise due to these imperfections? In our view, antitrust law is not suited to remedying contractual problems that the parties themselves have incentives to address. The parties can rely on a number of mechanisms[116] to eliminate *ex post* situational market power resulting from IP rights, including reputations and contracts, such as a contractual commitment to "second sourcing" parts and service. While these mechanisms may be imperfect, competition law is not better equipped than the parties themselves to deal with contractual difficulties. Competition law should be invoked only when the parties, because of a lack of competition, do not themselves have the correct incentives to choose efficient contractual terms. The fact that IP rights sometimes confer the power to exploit past customers *ex post* because of contractual infirmities does not raise market-power issues that fall within the purview of antitrust authorities.

Another aftermarket tying motivation relevant to IP rights is price discrimination. Sellers may rely on their IP rights over aftermarket products in order to establish price discrimination. As we have discussed, price discrimination also is not an appropriate basis for intervention. Aftermarket tying, which often depends on IP, is not typically problematic from an antitrust viewpoint.

The most important relationship between tying and IP is indirect. As we have discussed, the anti-competitive explanations of tying arise in dynamic settings. Sellers anticipating change in either the tying- or tied-good market may tie in order to be better positioned in each market in the future. IP rights, particularly given the increasing im-

116 Even bundling itself can be a partial remedy: see Iacobucci, " Switching Costs," above note 50. By bundling products that are more valuable to high demanders when initially selling the durable, rather than simply discounting, a seller in an *ex ante* competitive market with *ex post* situational market power can offer, in effect, a steeper discount to those with high demand, thus avoiding the inefficient sales to low demanders that a straight discount invites.

portance of high-technology industries in the economy, systematically arise in markets subject to rapid change. Concerns about exclusion and foreclosure may therefore arise more often with tying in markets in which IP rights are of prominent importance than with other kinds of tying.

What this implies for the optimal antitrust approach to tying is not immediately apparent. It would be simplistic and wrong to take the view that since IP and dynamic markets are related, and since tying is more likely to be problematic in dynamic contexts than static contexts, antitrust authorities should be more interventionist against tying in markets where IP is prominent. The counter-consideration is that dynamic and innovative markets, all other things being equal, are generally less subject to antitrust concern. If perfection in antitrust enforcement could be achieved without cost, then the authorities should intervene even in the face of ephemeral market power that inevitably will be disrupted by innovation. But of course such conditions do not exist. Instead, antitrust regulators should be wary of imposing intervention that is not only costly, but if incorrect could also undermine valuable gains from innovation in dynamic industries.

IP and tying tend to be more significant in dynamic, innovative industries. This makes tying of more serious concern, given that exclusionary theories of tying are dynamic. But it also makes identification of appropriate intervention more difficult, and erroneous antitrust intervention more costly. Antitrust authorities must undertake case-by-case analyses that are sensitive to these conflicting concerns.

Another aspect of the complex interrelationship among IP, tying, and technology is illustrated by the implications of DRM. DRM will likely have opposing effects on the likelihood of tying in the future. On the one hand, DRM facilitates tying by creating technological incompatibilities between differing companies' technologies. To return to an example discussed above, Apple is alleged to enforce an iPod–iTunes tie by relying in part on DRM. On the one hand, the combination of IP and technology that allows the seller to exert control over the future use of that IP will facilitate tying. On the other hand, DRM may diminish sellers' desire to tie. Suppose, for example, that Apple ties iTunes to the iPod in order to meter demand for the iPod. Rather than relying on online song purchases to meter demand, it may be that music publishing companies will license songs on a per-play basis by relying on DRM. This would result in good data on the use of digital music players like the iPod. In such a world, Apple could, in effect, piggyback on the DRM-facilitated monitoring of iPod use by copyright holders to meter use and therefore demand for the iPod, and music publishers and Apple should be able to arrive at a mutually agreeable arrangement that does not rely on iTunes (as it does at present). For example, Apple could require iPod users to upload their record of use of their players on a monthly basis and could collect royalties for copyright holders, as well as a surcharge.

In short, the relationship between IP and tying is already complex and is very likely to become even more complex in the future. Economic analysis of the type that we have outlined in this survey is invaluable to arrive at the correct outcome in any given case, and a rich set of theories are available to match to the evidence in each case. Often, many theories will be consistent with the evidence; and even where the exclusionary theories that we have outlined are the best fit, crafting a remedy that actually improves market performance presents an additional challenge. No succinct list of rules exists that summarizes optimal antitrust policy. Antitrust policy on tying can either be straightforward or intelligent, but not both.

Commentary: Bright Lines and Cautionary Notes[1]

Timothy J. Brennan[2]

A. INTRODUCTION

Edward Iacobucci and Ralph Winter's contribution to the symposium[3] is a thorough and excellent summary of the economics of tying as they are and should be applied in Canadian law. It should be required reading for all in the competition bar and enforcement community. In many respects, its value to that audience is that it does not restrict

---

1 Thanks go to the Bureau for inviting me to participate in the symposium, to Ralph Winter and Ed Iacobucci for an excellent paper and presentation, and to Gill Allen, Richard Corley, Abraham Hollander, Ariel Katz, Bill Kovacic, David Vaver, and other conference participants for their provocative questions and comments. Special thanks go to Alan Gunderson for organizing the symposium and for many thoughtful and useful discussions on intellectual property and competition law while I was at the Bureau.

2 Professor, Public Policy and Economics, University of Maryland, Baltimore County, and Senior Fellow, Resources for the Future, Washington, DC. Email: brennan@umbc.edu. During 2006, the author held the T.D. MacDonald Chair in Industrial Economics at the Competition Bureau. The opinions expressed here are his alone and do not reflect the views of the Bureau, the commissioner, or her staff.

3 See E. Iacobucci and R. Winter, "Tying and Intellectual Property," chapter 2 in this book.

its analysis to intellectual property (IP); rather, it uses IP to illustrate general principles for the analysis of tying.

That approach has considerable merit, in that to an increasing extent competition authorities are viewing IP as just another form of property.[4] The Competition Bureau of Canada's *Intellectual Property Enforcement Guidelines* (IPEGs) set out the principle that IP law is designed to extend to creative works and innovative product protections akin to those afforded by conventional property, in particular, the right to exclude.[5] Along with that right, IP is not that different from conventional property rights, which may also entail certain time limits and use restrictions roughly akin, if distantly so, to restrictions placed on copyrights or patents.[6]

So, to a first approximation and maybe more, one should look at potentially anti-competitive practices involving IP as we would with conventional property. Collusion is inherently no better or worse if it involves sellers with competing IP as it is with sellers with competing factories or stores. Mergers involving IP raise the same questions as mergers do generally—whether the parties are in the same relevant market, who else is in the market, and what would be the unilateral or coordinated effects.[7] Even with abuse of dominance, while the exclusive rights in IP may convey market power, the Bureau's approach, as stated in its IPEGs, is to investigate in particular contexts whether IP fits a general framework for assessing potential practices.[8]

However, the IPEGs themselves and the symposium indicate a need to appreciate that along some dimensions, IP is not the same as conventional property. Accordingly, I begin by reviewing some of the

---

4 For a US example, see *Illinois Tool Works, Inc. v. Independent Ink, Inc.*, 547 U.S. 28 (2006).

5 Competition Bureau Canada, *Intellectual Property Enforcement Guidelines* (2000), online: http://strategis.ic.gc.ca/pics/ct/ipege.pdf, especially section 3.2 [IPEGs].

6 T. Brennan, "Copyright, Property, and the Right to Deny" (1993) 68 Chicago-Kent L. Rev. 675.

7 Competition Bureau Canada, *Merger Enforcement Guidelines* (Sept. 2004), online: www.competitionbureau.gc.ca/PDFs/2004%20MEGs.Final.pdf. Section 5.6 includes a firm's IP as one of a number of factors influencing the amount of competition that might be lost if that firm is acquired by a competitor.

8 IPEGs, above note 5 at 4.1.

reasons why IP draws particular policy attention and raises suspicions that might not be present in other competition law contexts. After that review, we turn to Iacobucci and Winter's discussion of tying cases. As a matter more of clarification than correction, we classify tying cases into three categories: rent extraction, lock-in exploitation, and dynamic monopolization.[9] Although Iacobucci and Winter state that they offer no "bright line" remedies, one can extract fairly straightforward recommendations against the use of competition law to address concerns raised by the first two of those categories. Dynamic monopolization may be a problem, but a look at the *Microsoft* case,[10] which Iacobucci and Winter describe as a possible good example, shows that establishing harm in those settings may be harder than Iacobucci and Winter suggest.

We conclude with cautionary notes suggested by Iacobucci and Winter's assessments relating to the roles of prior dominance and intent in abuse cases. In particular, we need to be careful in casting "competition" as "net economic welfare" as the objective for competition law enforcement to maximize. This brings us back to the focus of the symposium, as disputes about the meaning of "welfare" in competition law are most pointed when public values at the heart of IP controversies come into play.

B. WHY IP MATTERS

As observed above, the trend in competition law enforcement, certainly in the US and to some extent in Canada, is that IP is just another form of property. As such, it complements markets and competition in the same ways that tangible private property does. In the short run, conventional property law enables exchange. It gives people the clarity of ownership to ensure that when they buy or sell something, they know what they are offering and what they are getting. As Ronald Coase famously pointed out, if property rights are clear and there are no other impediments to exchange ("transaction costs"), trade will

---

9 Here I use the term from US antitrust law, specifically s. 2 of the US *Sherman Act*, 15 U.S.C. § 2.

10 *United States v. Microsoft Corp.*, 87 F. Supp. 2d 30 (D.D.C. 2000), aff'd in part, rev'd in part, and remanded in part, 253 F.3d 34 (D.C. Circ. 2001) [*Microsoft*].

achieve efficient outcomes.[11] Without property, there could be few if any markets, and thus little if any competition. Over the longer run, private property, abetted by clear contract law, allows persons, individually or collectively through firms, to realize the benefits of production. Without clear ownership of what comes out of a factory or office, one has few if any incentives to accumulate the resources necessary to produce goods for sale.

IP rights could be understood as just another form of private property rights, with the only difference being that special laws are necessary to make up for the fact that unlike physical property, there is no natural way to keep others from using IP and thus prevent creators from exploiting its value. But the understanding is not that simple. One reason, perhaps most prominent but conceptually least profound, is that IP rights appear to be a government grant of a monopoly because of the right to exclude. But as noted above, conventional property works because it similarly grants rights to exclude. Moreover, as courts and the Bureau have recognized, exclusion *per se*, through IP or conventional property, does not convey market power. One may have an exclusive right to grant access to X, yet face stiff competition from (equally excludable) Y and Z.

Two other reasons, one directly economic and one less so, are more profound. By their nature, IP rights protect goods that are inherently informational. In the patent context, it is the design of a new product or service or a process for making existing products that is protected. Copyright prevents the unauthorized duplication of creative works that, while sometimes embodied in physical objects (books, CDs, film), are, as the digital age reveals, fundamentally information. Leaving aside the need for physical objects, information inherently can be made available to an additional person at no cost. Hence, the right to exclude, and thus to charge a positive price for access to the information protected by IP rights, creates an inefficiency—the price of the product will exceed its (zero) marginal cost of production.[12] Some

---

11 R.H. Coase, "The Problem of Social Cost," (1960) 3 J.L. & Econ. 1.

12 Trade-marks may be somewhat different in this respect because the relevant information is about the source of the product itself. Giving X the right to use Y's trade-mark not only reduces Y's incentive to invest in developing and marketing its products, but it also may mislead consumers into thinking that X's product was produced by Y and, in some cases, is the same as Y when it is not.

users who would want the information (i.e., put a positive price on it) will be denied use.

This denial provides the basis for some explicit exceptions (e.g., "fair dealing" or, in the US, "fair use" standards) in copyright and public disclosure of designs in patents.[13] However, it also provides a rationale for a perception that IP rights are necessary evils to be eluded. Here, the contrast with physical property is important. Conventional property rights protect both economic virtues of *ex post* allocative efficiency — getting objects to those who value them the most — and *ex ante* productive efficiency — providing incentives to product the objects in the first place. Because IP rights fail the *ex post* test, they can be justified only by the *ex ante* considerations, providing the incentive to innovate or create. At any time, then, the benefits of IP are always in the future and uncertain, while the effects of the denials of access to, say, copyrighted music or patented drugs are immediate. As IP rights enforce the right to deny by preventing *ex post* competition in the sale of a patented product or copyrighted work, tension between those rights and the objective of competition law ought not to be surprising.[14]

The informational aspect of IP creates a second tension absent from most conventional property as well. Informational goods are valued not only because they contribute to economic wealth as measured by consumer willingness to pay. They are associated with non-economic social objectives such as education, citizenship, and culture. Hence, exclusion is about more than the exercise of market power or incentives to innovate; it is about restricting the advancement of collective knowledge or the ability to obtain the information one may need to participate in the political process.[15] Much of the reluctance

---

13 For fair dealing, see *Copyright Act*, R.S.C. 1985, c. C-42, ss. 29, 29.1, and 29.2; the US fair use statute is *Copyrights*, 17 U.S.C. 107. For patent disclosure and availability, see *Patent Act*, R.S.C. 1985, c. P-4, ss. 10(1), 27(3); in the US see *Patents*, 35 U.S.C. 41(i)(1), 111(a).

14 A tension specific to Canada identified during the symposium was that as a net consumer of IP, Canada would be better off with weak IP rights. In the terms here, the gains to it from *ex post* low prices would exceed any losses from reduced *ex ante* incentives to innovate or create.

15 Under any reasonable set of standards for IP protection, society will be in a range where there is a trade-off between *ex ante* incentives to produce works and *ex post* usage of those works once produced. For a discussion of how

to enforce IP rights springs from their perceived inconsistency with these social values.[16]

As Iacobucci and Winter point out, the *ex ante* dynamic rationale for IP interacts with competition law enforcement in a number of ways. While IP rights allow pricing above marginal cost and may create significant market power, they are also inherently important in the same sectors where innovation and creativity are prominent. Any market power in IP-intensive markets may be short-lived,[17] as new products and processes come along that render former monopolies obsolete. That "creative destruction," associated with Joseph Schumpeter,[18] may erase any IP-related market power in less time than it would take to litigate a case. On the other hand, as Iacobucci and Winter also point out, tying in IP-intensive markets could be troublesome to the extent that it changes the strategic interaction between incumbents and potential entrants so as to create or preserve market power beyond that established by the IP right.[19]

---

different policy standards (economic efficiency, number of works produced, aggregate usage) affect the design of fair use rules, see T. Brennan, "Fair Use as Policy Instrument" in W. Gordon, Lisa Takeyama, and Ruth Towse, eds., *Developments in the Economics of Copyright: Research and Analysis* (Northampton, MA: Edward Elgar, 2005) at 80–102.

16 At the conference, I observed that unlike in other areas of the law (competition, torts, contracts), IP law professors tend to disparage the law in which they specialize. David Vaver responded that IP professors view IP as like a pet dog, which can be a wonderful companion, but only after it's trained to behave.

17 An important topic that is not the subject of Iacobucci and Winter's paper or this comment is how one defines market power in IP-related markets. On the one hand, price will inherently be above marginal cost. If marginal cost is zero, any positive price is more than 5–10 percent above marginal cost; it will be infinitely above marginal cost in percentage terms. On the other hand, the relevant price is not marginal cost but the "competitive price." Presumably, in these markets a competitive price would be that just necessary to cover all costs — one might think of it as greater of the minimum average cost of production and marginal cost. However, ascertaining whether a firm has market power by virtue of IP depends upon determining just when a price covers those costs, a task that is difficult, if not impossible.

18 B. Seligman, *Main Currents in Modern Economics, Vol. 3, The Thrust Toward Technique* (Chicago: Quadrangle, 1971) at 702–3.

19 Section 79(5) of the *Competition Act* states, "For the purpose of this section, an act engaged in pursuant only to the exercise of any right or enjoyment of

C. TYING PRACTICES AND POLICIES

Iacobucci and Winter emphasize that tying could be harmful to the extent that it subverts the process of dynamic competition. To reach that conclusion, they comprehensively survey the breadth of economic effects and rationales for tying. In that survey, IP may be relevant as creating one of the goods or services tied to the other, or the means by which a tie between two goods would be enforced. However, in most of those cases, whether or not IP is at issue, the effect of tying is ambiguous at best and in many cases efficiency-enhancing. The most important evidence for the efficiency of tying is its ubiquity. It is widely applied in contexts where significant market power is not an issue, as Iacobucci and Winter point out in describing how a tie can facilitate quality control, preserve a brand's reputation, signal high quality, or simply offer consumers the convenience of being able to buy two things at once.[20] Moreover, where tying could be harmful, remedies under competition law would likely make matters worse or other areas of the law would be better suited. Consequently, for some categories "bright line" rules may well be appropriate. Such rules should err on the side of allowing tying. To see this, we can divide the tying practices surveyed by Iacobucci and Winter into three categories: (i) rent extraction, (ii) lock-in exploitation, and (iii) dynamic monopolization.

1) Rent Extraction

A monopolist or other firm with market power typically is limited in how much profit it can directly extract from buyers. Such a seller typically cannot extract maximum potential profit if it has to charge the same price for all of its products, and such sales are its only source of revenue. If it could, it would attempt to extract more money from buyers in one of two ways. First, it might try to charge buyers a fee in order to buy the product at all — a "two-part tariff." From the seller's per-

---

any interest derived under the *Copyright Act, Industrial Design Act, Integrated Circuit Topography Act, Patent Act, Trade-marks Act* or any other Act of Parliament pertaining to intellectual or industrial property is not an anti-competitive act."

20 See also D.E. Evans and Michael Salinger, "Why Do Firms Bundle and Tie? Evidence from Competitive Markets and Implications for Tying Law" (2005) 22 Yale J. on Reg. 37–89.

spective, the ideal solution would be to sell each unit at marginal cost, and charge each buyer a fixed fee equal to the surplus they get from purchasing at marginal cost. Second, the seller might try to profit by charging each buyer different prices for each unit he or she buys, a form of price discrimination.[21] The seller's profits would be maximized if it could charge the reservation price for each unit sold.

Tying can facilitate either of these practices. For two-part tariffs, a seller (S) can say that a buyer can purchase its good (X) only if it purchases an unrelated good (Y) from it as well, at a price above the competitive price. One effect of the tie would be to say that to get X at all, a buyer has to pay a fixed fee equivalent to the premium it pays S for paying a supra-competitive price for Y.[22] For price discrimination, if the quantity of Y purchased (e.g., printer ink) is correlated with willingness to pay for X (the printer), then the tied sale can allow S to, in effect, charge more for X to those willing to pay more for X.

Ties that allow rent extraction, absent other efficiencies (which are quite likely to be present, as Iacobucci and Winter note), will likely make some consumers worse off, but they also are likely to improve efficiency overall. Two-part tariffs and price discrimination encourage sellers to increase sales, since they can do so without having to cut price and thereby sacrifice profits from pre-existing sales. The increased output generally reflects an increase in overall efficiency. In Canada, where total surplus is the general standard for evaluating competitive effects, these practices are likely to be beneficial under the law.[23] If the total surplus standard is weighted to favour those with less wealth,[24] these practices should be viewed even more favourably. The gainers

---

21 One could think of two-part tariffs as a form of price discrimination, where units above the first purchased by a particular buyer are sold to that buyer at marginal cost, and the first unit purchased by a buyer equals that buyer's surplus from the unit and being able to purchase subsequent units at marginal cost.

22 P. Greenlee, D. Reitman, and D. Sibley, "An Antitrust Analysis of Bundled Loyalty Discounts," Economic Analysis Group Discussion Paper No. 04-13 (Revised) (2006), online: http://ssrn.com/abstract=600799.

23 In jurisdictions that rely on consumer welfare alone, these practices may not be judged as favourably, *ibid.*

24 *Canada (Commissioner of Competition) v. Superior Propane, Inc.* (2002), 18 C.P.R. (4th) 417 (Comp. Trib.), aff'd (2003), 23 C.P.R. (4th) 316 (F.C.A.) [*Superior Propane*].

are going to be those with lower willingness to pay and who would not have been able to purchase the product if the seller would have had to cut prices charged to those with greater willingness to pay.

This also points out a difficulty with remedies. As Iacobucci and Winter point out, prohibiting ties for rent extraction will likely induce sellers to set a high price for all and cut back supplies sold at lower prices. Those who had been paying high prices will gain, but those who had been paying low prices now lose. The net benefits, even leaving out the lost profit to the seller, may be negative. The only remedy for a rent-extraction tie that is sure to increase welfare would be to prevent the seller from charging its single profit-maximizing price for X if tying Y to it is prohibited. As the Bureau and tribunal are not in the business of price regulation, such remedies are likely to be institutionally as well as economically undesirable.

This suggests a "bright line" rule: do not prohibit tying for rent extraction.[25] The only exceptions would be when the bureau and tribunal would be confident that if the tie were broken, the seller would not simply raise the price of its product back to its high profit-maximizing level. One exception, probably rare, is if there is some transactional impediment that prevents the seller from raising the price of the tying product.[26] A more likely scenario would be when the price of the seller's product is regulated, and the tie to unregulated product Y, enforced through discriminatory access to X, serves to extract surplus from X purchasers.[27] Regulation of X not only provides the anti-com-

25 See D. Carlton and K. Heyer, "Extraction vs. Extension: A Basis for Formulating Antitrust Policy Toward Single Firm Conduct" (2008) 4:2 Competition Policy International 285.

26 One example could be that Microsoft might be able to extract additional profits by tying particular software to its operating system by restricting access to its program interfaces. In principle, breaking the tie would lead Microsoft to raise the price of access to those interfaces. But if doing so is precluded by circumstance (for example, that it cannot raise the price of those interfaces because providers of all sorts of complementary software producers use them) then breaking the tie will not raise price. T. Brennan, "Do Easy Cases Make Bad Law? Antitrust Innovation or Missed Opportunities in *U.S. v. Microsoft*" (2001) 69 Geo. Wash. L. Rev. 1042, see especially 1082–84 ["Do Easy Cases Make Bad Law?"].

27 T. Brennan, "Why Regulated Firms Should Be Kept out of Unregulated Markets: Understanding the Divestiture in *U.S. v. AT&T*" (1987) 32 Antitrust Bull. 741.

petitive incentive to tie Y that is absent in unregulated sectors, but it means that breaking the tie would increase welfare.

Whether such a remedy is available in Canada under the "regulated conduct doctrine" is doubtful, as enforcement policy is to defer to the regulator when access to the regulated service is the cause of the anti-competitive effect.[28] As the Bureau has said,

> Accordingly, the Bureau will not pursue a matter under any provision of the Act where Parliament has articulated an intention to displace competition law enforcement by establishing a comprehensive regulatory regime and providing a regulator the authority to itself take, or to authorize another to take, action inconsistent with the Act, provided the regulator has exercised its regulatory authority in respect of the conduct in question.[29]

As long as a regulator continues to regulate the terms and conditions of access granted to competitors in unregulated markets who need the regulated service, the Bureau will defer to the regulator even if ties enforced by discrimination would subvert competition in the unregulated market. The situation may be no different in the US. Although this theory served as the rationale for the US antitrust action against AT&T that led to its breakup in 1984,[30] the recent decision in *Verizon v. Trinko*[31] suggests that antitrust enforcement will similarly defer to regulatory authority even if the action of the regulated firm subverts competition in an otherwise unregulated market.[32]

2) Lock-in Exploitation

A second category of cases that one can identify from Iacobucci and Winter involves the exploitation of purchasers of a product who cannot easily switch to the products of others. The typical example would be a durable good, such as a printer, for which there is no economically

---

28 Competition Bureau Canada, *Technical Bulletin on "Regulated" Conduct* (June 2006), online: www.competitionbureau.gc.ca/eic/site/cb-bc.nsf/eng/02141.html.

29 *Ibid.* at 6.

30 *U.S. v. AT&T*, 552 F. Supp. 131 (D.D.C. 1982).

31 540 U.S. 398 (2004) [*Trinko*].

32 T. Brennan, "*Trinko v. Baxter*: The Demise of *U.S. v. AT&T*" (2006) 50 Antitrust Bull. 635.

relevant market for resale. Another form of lock-in could involve a series of products sold by a particular company (e.g., versions of operating systems) where the costs of learning a new system are substantial. In either case, the key idea is that once buyers choose to purchase a product, they face significant costs of switching to a product from a competitor.

In such situations, after the purchase, the seller of the initial product would want to extract money from those buyers up to the point where they were just indifferent between staying with that product and incurring the costs to switch to another. This extraction could be undertaken through contractual or technological ties of aftermarket products or services — parts, consumables, maintenance, or other complements — to the initial product. From a competition law perspective, the concern is that the aftermarket is monopolized through the tie.

As with the rent-extraction story, there may well be efficiencies associated with ensuring the use of a specific aftermarket good or service (e.g., quality control). Aftermarket monopolization may also serve as a means for price discrimination, also likely to increase output and net economic benefit. The difference between the rent-extraction category discussed above and this case is that here the market power is created only after buyers have committed to the product. Prior to that commitment, the durable good may well have been offered in a competitive market. Although such initial competition may result in the aftermarket profits being competed away, there may still be a residual inefficiency, in that the initial product price is too low — below its marginal production cost — and the aftermarket prices are too high. One gets too many printers, but too few pages printed.[33]

One could even posit that the sellers of the durable goods would want to be prevented from *ex post* exploitation of locked-in customers. A credible commitment to aftermarket competition and low prices would allow them to charge more for the product up front. Buyers

33 In the US, the initial competition for the durable good was not sufficient to justify dismissing antitrust concern with monopolization of aftermarkets, see *Eastman Kodak v. Image Technical Services, Inc.*, 504 U.S. 451 (1992). However, this case has had little effect on subsequent aftermarket cases. D. Goldfine and K. Vorrasi, "The Fall of the *Kodak* Aftermarket Doctrine: Dying a Slow Death in the Lower Courts" (2004) 72 Antitrust L.J. 209.

would be willing to pay more as they could themselves extract the most value from the product after its purchase by being able to obtain complements of competitive products.[34]

As Iacobucci and Winter point out, we cannot reject the possibility that lock-in exploitation will lead to inefficient outcomes. However, that does not mean that competition law is the best solution. That these effects exist only after a specific seller's product has been purchased by a specific buyer suggests that the most appropriate place to begin considering remedies is in contract law. There are three possibilities. First, to the extent that pre-empting aftermarket competition violates an explicit provision of a contract, one should treat this as a breach with appropriate damages. Second, if the pre-emption violates a non-contractual but explicit promise made by the seller of the product, laws against fraud or misleading advertising would be appropriate. Last, if there was no explicit contract or representation, pre-emption might still be a violation of consumer protection laws or commercial codes if a reasonable buyer would have expected the seller to allow aftermarket competition.

In none of these situations is it helpful to interpret this conduct as a violation of laws against competition. It should be left to situations when the harms to consumers are the result of conduct that contracts, actual or ideal, could not prevent.[35] Under US law, the consequences of confusing contract with competition law are exacerbated by the ability of plaintiffs to get three times the damage award for an antitrust violation than for a breach of contract. The resulting incentives to transform breaches into competition violations resulted in the unwarranted application of antitrust law to a wide range of vertical conduct. This effect remains incompletely corrected in US antitrust law. Many international standards take US caselaw as source material and this has resulted in these misapplications of antitrust to contract issues

---

34 Gaibax and Laibson, using behavioural economics methods, suggest that aftermarket tying would allow sellers to exploit myopic consumers. *Ex ante* competition among the durable-good providers would lead to sales to sophisticated consumers below cost. X. Gabaix and D. Laibson, "Shrouded Attributes, Consumer Myopia, and Information Suppression in Competitive Markets" (2006) 121 Quarterly Journal of Economics 505.

35 See T. Brennan, "'Vertical Market Power' as Oxymoron: Horizontal Approaches to Vertical Antitrust" (2004) 12:4 Geo. Mason L. Rev. 895.

becoming part and parcel of competition laws around the world. The bottom line is that lock-in exploitation suggests a second "bright line" test: These cases should be brought as violations of contract, fraud, or consumer protection law rather than competition law.

3) Dynamic Monopolization

Iacobucci and Winter find that the most important category of tying practices that warrant scrutiny under competition law involve dynamic monopolization. In Canadian competition law terms, the issue is not so much abuse *of* dominance as it is abuses that *create* dominance.[36] The question is whether tying limits opportunities for future competition by changing the strategic options competitors may have.[37] For example, in the *Microsoft* case Iacobucci and Winter discuss that the tying of the Internet Explorer browser to the Windows operating system allegedly pre-empted competition in operating system markets. It allegedly did so, limiting the ability of Netscape to get a toehold in the browser market and establish itself as a platform to support applications.

Iacobucci and Winter, however, understate the difficulty of establishing dynamic monopolization in that, if future competition is at stake, one needs to define the future markets and identify the competitive effects of the tie. It is not enough to find that the tie has enabled a present monopolist to extract profits or pre-empt competition in an aftermarket. The *Microsoft* case illustrates these difficulties.[38] To see these, refer to Figure 1, which sets out what it would have taken

---

36 The first two categories, rent extraction and lock-in exploitation, fit the literal definition of "abuse of dominance" more accurately, but in those cases, competition law is either unlikely to be effective (outside regulated sectors, where it may be otherwise inapplicable) or the wrong type of law to apply.

37 Along with Iacobucci and Winter, see also D. Carlton and M. Waldman, "The Strategic Use of Tying to Preserve and Create Market Power in Evolving Industries" (2003) 33 RAND Journal of Economics 194. An application of the principle of dynamic monopolization to the *Microsoft* case, above note 10, is in "Do Easy Cases Make Bad Law?" above note 25 at 1071–77.

38 It may be useful to remember that the highest US court to assess the record in the *Microsoft* case rejected the tying claim. See the decision referenced at *Microsoft, ibid.*

to prove the dynamic monopolization via tying.[39] The time path goes from the top down, but it is easier to describe the evidentiary requirements by going from the bottom up.

Figure 1: Requirements to Prove Dynamic Monopolization in the Microsoft Case[40]

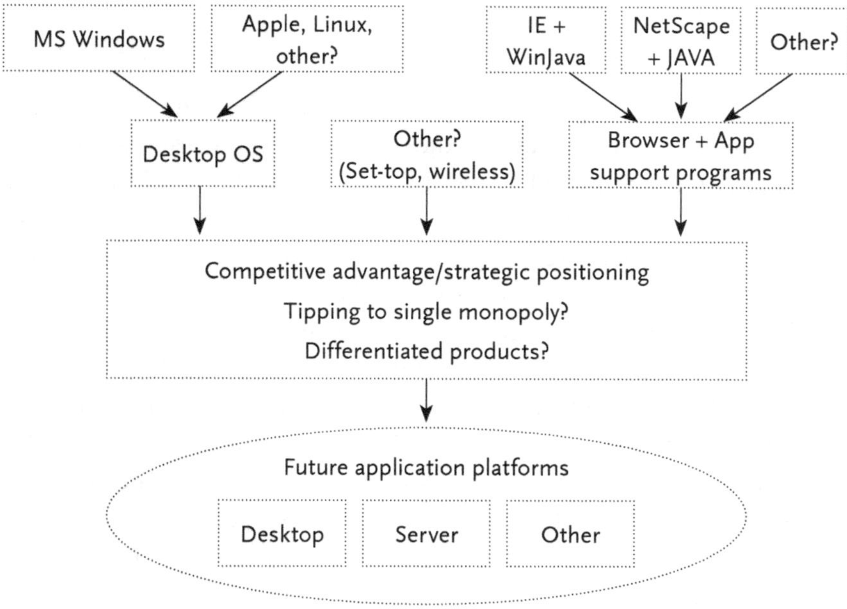

The first necessary step is to delineate the market that is going to be pre-empted by the tie. This will be a future market, perhaps one that does not exist at present. In the *Microsoft* case, the plaintiffs erroneously claimed, and the courts erroneously agreed, that the relevant market was "Intel-based PC operating systems." However, the crux of the dynamic theory was that future applications platforms would be supplied not just by Windows-like PC operating systems, but also perhaps by browsers along with applications, such as Java, that allow web-based use of applications resting on distant servers rather than the user's PC. These potential competitors in the future application

39 This figure and the supporting discussion were originally in T. Brennan, "The Legacy of *U.S. v. Microsoft*" (2004) 26:4 Regulation 22.

40 *Ibid*. at 24.

platform market had not been and would never be in a market for "Intel-based PC operating systems."

Next, in the middle, one needs to describe how competition in that future application market would take place. Would buyers regard PC-resident programs and web-accessed server-based programs as close substitutes, or as differentiated products? Would network externalities imply that this was a "winner-take-all" market, or would two or more platforms survive?

The answers would help establish who was in the market to compete to be a future application platform, and what the competitive effects of Microsoft's conduct would be. The case presupposed that PC operating systems and browser-based platforms would compete, but one would want to know if others would be available. At the time of the litigation, there were suggestions that set-top boxes for broadband cable services would support application platforms. Were the case brought today, one might ask if the systems on hand-held smart phones, such as the BlackBerry, would be in the market.[41] Finally, at the top of the page, Figure 1 is showing that the path to a substantial lessening of competition has a credible starting point. If the plaintiffs were correct about PC operating systems and browsers as the only two routes into the (never defined) future application platform market, one has to examine who else might be in these markets (e.g., Google) and how they might play a role in the dynamic chain.

The major Microsoft cases in the US and European Union[42] generally failed this test. On the US side of the Atlantic, the plaintiffs probably thought they showed a case involving static monopolization, but instead they showed only that Microsoft had engaged in a series of practices that (allegedly) impeded Netscape's ability to distribute its browser. This is a static case with direct effects only on the market for browsers. Although Microsoft's intention may have been to limit browser competition in order to preclude subsequent competition in application platforms, intention does not suffice to prove dynamic monopolization.

---

41 Microsoft participates in that market as well, offering versions of Windows that support Microsoft programs on some models of smart phones.

42 European Commission Case No. COMP/C-3/37.792/Microsoft (2004) [EU case].

From an erroneous market definition on down, the plaintiffs failed to define the appropriate market and trace through the steps necessary to show how Microsoft's practices would lead to its monopolization. That the plaintiffs failed to do so is not difficult to explain, as proving all of those steps would have made for a much more difficult case. The price paid for the easy way out was ineffectual relief. Microsoft was forced only to eliminate contractual provisions that impeded distribution of competing browsers. More substantial relief (e.g., breaking the tie by forcing Microsoft to divest control of Internet Explorer and allow its development as a potential future application platform) was absent.

The EU case also failed to address the future application platform issue, but it perhaps had no aspiration to do so. The heart of those cases is that Microsoft impeded competition from software-for-workgroup servers and rival media players.[43] One might imagine that the first of these could be a route, like browsers, into some future application platform market. However, acknowledging that possibility illustrates that the lifting necessary to show monopolization of future applications was very heavy and not done. Media players seem an unlikely path into the future application platform market. Here, the tying issue is simply one of rent extraction. Other than a case directed at Microsoft's contractual practices with computer manufacturers or online service providers that may have cornered a market in distributing media players, the EU case may be more about protecting competitors than economic efficiency or protecting the interest of consumers.[44]

---

43 Europa, European Union press release, "Commission concludes on Microsoft investigation, imposes conduct remedies and a fine," case IP/04/382 (24 March 2004), online: http://europa.eu/rapid/pressReleasesAction.do?reference=IP/04/382&format=PDF&aged=1&language=EN&guiLanguage=en.

44 At least according to Microsoft's counsel, unbundling seems to fail the market test. Less than .005 percent of sales of the Windows XP operating systems sold in the EU were the XPN version, without Windows Media Player. "Microsoft Criticizes EC's Antitrust Claims" Computer Business Review Online (25 April 2006), online: www.cbronline.com/article_news.asp?guid=871D6E1C-0699-4A01-97F4-AF74A3F47B15.

D. CONCLUSIONS AND CAUTIONS

Iacobucci and Winter have provided an excellent contribution to our understanding of tying, both in and out of IP contexts. Their study lends support to some fairly "bright line" rules:

- If a tie serves simply to increase a firm's ability to exploit its pre-existing market power over a product, a case is unlikely to produce benefits unless there is reason to believe that it will not raise the price of that product following a break in the tie. Regulation of that product's price is the best support for such a belief, as in the US case twenty-five years ago against AT&T, but bringing cases predicated on that belief may be ruled out by the regulated conduct doctrine.
- If the tie gives the seller of a durable good the ability to exploit locked-in buyers, the harm is the result of a contracting failure between those buyers and the seller. Depending on the nature of the failure, cases should be brought under contract, fraud, or consumer protection law, not competition law.

Iacobucci and Winter correctly identify what is called "dynamic monopolization" as the tying effect most deserving of competition law enforcement. However, a look at the most prominent recent cases nominally along these lines, the US and EU *Microsoft* cases, shows that making such a dynamic case is more difficult than Iacobucci and Winter may suggest.[45]

Assessing tying in the context of IP brings to mind a few general considerations about competition law enforcement. First is that the

---

45 The discussion below emphasizes the *Microsoft* case as an example, but Iacobucci and Winter may also have an optimistic interpretation of one of the leading models of the potential strategic effects of tying, in M. Whinston, "Tying, Foreclosure, and Exclusion" (1990) 80 American Economic Review 837. The crux of Whinston's argument is that a monopolist (M) in good A might tie its supplies of B to A. If B is used in fixed proportions to A, then M will reduce its output of B only if it reduces its output of A. Since it has market power in A, reducing sales in A will be costly (as price is above marginal cost). This makes credible an otherwise spurious commitment that M will not accommodate an entrant in B by reducing its output in B, thus potentially discouraging entry. Whether this model has ever been established to apply to an actual instance of tying is doubtful.

strongest cases conceptually for prosecuting tying under competition law involve dynamic monopolization, where dominance is not already present or predetermined. The "Chicago" critique of tying cases, that tying is presumptively efficient, had it right insofar as it was based on whether tying by an established monopolist would increase market power and reduce welfare.[46] The insight of post-Chicago analysis is that practices such as tying could be harmful in that they may change strategic relationships, leading to the creation of new monopolies where none are or would have been present.[47] However, this correction, combined with the insights regarding rent extraction and lock-in exploitations taken from Iacobucci and Winter, suggests that it is counterproductive to require prior dominance before finding a practice anti-competitive. As noted above, we should be more concerned with abuses creating dominance, not abuse of dominance.

A second issue to consider in abuse cases relating to tying is the role of intent or, as Iacobucci and Winter say, motivation. The *Microsoft* case may have been driven by the view that intent would suffice to infer monopolization of a future application platform market from monopolizing of a present market in distribution of browsers, but that turned out to be incorrect, at least as far as establishing a case for appropriate relief to protect that future market. More recently, the Federal Court of Appeal in *Canada Pipe* interpreted in section 79(1)(b) of the *Competition Act*, the definition of "anticompetitive practice," as referring to intent to exclude competitors.[48] Such a standard runs the risk of being too broad, as any competitor who wants to capture share from its rivals runs the risk of intending to exclude. A better choice would

---

46 In addition, the critique relied on the profit sacrifice associated with tying — reduced demand for the monopoly product — to argue that a monopolist would tie other products to its product only if it produced countervailing efficiencies that outweighed the costs from depressing demand. It is ironic that "profit sacrifice" has now come to be regarded in the US as a necessary condition for anti-competitive conduct rather than evidence of unexplained efficiency. See *Trinko*, above note 30.

47 This perspective is reflected in the recent Federal Court of Appeal decision in *Commissioner of Competition v. Canada Pipe*, 2006 FCA 233, which endorsed at para. 38 a test that a practice has a significant effect on competition if "but for" the practice, the market would be significantly more competitive [*Canada Pipe*].

48 *Ibid.* at paras. 66–73.

be to interpret the definition of an anti-competitive practice as one for which the anti-competitive effects are "reasonably foreseeable."[49]

A last point is to note that (we) economists cannot have our cake and eat it too when it comes to the interpretation of the objectives of competition law. One could defend competition law as a means to achieve populist ends, such as preserving rights to ply the trade of one's choice without fear of being driven out business by large enterprises. A second objective could be political, to control the size of firms and, thereby, the clout they may have in influencing legislation and policy. A third could be to protect competition as an activity, focusing on preserving the numbers of competitors and the degree to which they can set prices and locate independently of the wishes of manufacturers. However, the goal of competition policy is stated in fairly narrow economic terms — in Canada it is to maximize total surplus, weighted when necessary by distributional considerations.[50]

This objective may not be as clear as (we) economists believe. The definition of "competitive" is not "welfare maximizing," but instead refers to a market process.[51] Equating competition with welfare maximization is, however laudable, a pragmatic policy abstraction. Iacobucci and Winter find it appropriate that Canadian law's emphasis on "competitive effects" "steers clear of orders against tying or bundling based on price discrimination." But if the only meaning of "substantial lessening of competition" is to "reduce total surplus," the *Competition Act* would seem to oblige the Competition Tribunal to assess price discrimination to see if in fact total surplus went up, or whether the losses to those who pay higher prices exceed gains to those who buy at lower prices plus increased profits to the seller.

It turns out that "which welfare counts" is not an easy question to answer. One can imagine many instances where the output reduction created by collusion, horizontal mergers, or abusive practices increases total welfare by reducing the incidence of a negative side effect or

---

49 *Ibid.* at para. 73.

50 See *Superior Propane*, above note 24. For a critique of the emphasis in the US on consumer surplus, see K. Heyer, "Welfare Standards and Merger Policy: Why Not the Best?" (2006) 2 Competition Policy International 29.

51 A libertarian objection to equating competition with efficiency is that doing so can justify state intervention into private enterprise on the grounds that the latter fails to meet this particular state objective.

"externality." For example, fixing beer prices might reduce the welfare of beer drinkers, but it might also increase welfare overall by reducing the incidence of drunk driving. It is not the job of the Competition Bureau or any competition agency to attempt to assess all of the effects on total surplus relating to a practice. Some narrowing, relating to "competition," as understood outside the community of economists, is necessary; a precise conception of how to do that narrowing may remain to be determined.

This returns us to the topic of the symposium. As discussed above, the special relationship of IP to tying and competition law more generally is driven in part by the view that IP rights are about more than maximizing the present discounted value of the difference between aggregate willingness to pay for innovative goods and creative works and the costs of bringing those goods and works to market. Values relating to culture, citizenship, and the growth of knowledge all play a role. For this reason, using competition law enforcement to fine-tune IP rights is probably not appropriate. The values and expertise for the former, while surely crucial in fostering efficiency, fail to cover the breadth of considerations relevant to making all of the balances necessary in designing patent and copyright law. That remains a job for Parliament, informed by the continuing public debate of which the symposium was an important contribution.

Commentary on "Tying and Intellectual Property"

Richard F.D. Corley and Navin Joneja[1]

A. INTRODUCTION

This paper addresses the issues raised by Iacobucci and Winter in their paper on tying and intellectual property.[2] It outlines their main theses and responds to them. We agree with much of what they say.

At the outset, it should be noted that the policy criterion the authors use in their analysis is that of economic efficiency — the maximization of total gains from a market, whether these gains are achieved by consumers (in the form of consumer surplus) or by shareholders of firms.

Using this standard, the authors conclude that tying is not necessarily harmful since tying may, in many cases, increase efficiency. Furthermore, the authors note that it is difficult to categorize tying

---

1 Richard Corley and Navin Joneja are partners in the Competition Group at Blake, Cassels & Graydon LLP. Richard Corley is also co-Head of Blake's Information Technology Practice Group and assisted the Competition Bureau of Canada in the development of the *Intellectual Property Enforcement Guidelines*. We gratefully acknowledge the assistance of Dela Avle in preparing these comments.

2 Edward Iacobucci and Ralph Winter, "Tying and Intellectual Property," chapter 2 in this book.

cases into specific baskets (e.g., those that increase efficiency versus those that might decrease efficiency). Therefore, competition authorities are cautioned against relying on any particular rule or rules of thumb in reaching a conclusion that a specific form of tying should be prohibited by competition law. Based on a review of economic literature, the paper advocates "a conservative approach towards government intervention in the area of tying. The complexity of tying cases in circumstances where the practice is potentially anti-competitive presents a severe challenge to the design of appropriate intervention." Although a case-by-case analysis is preferred, the authors offer some helpful guidelines, including the following:

- With respect to the requirement for market power in the tying good, the paper suggests that the focus should be on the potential for significant market power, not simply market power that reflects imperfect competition: if markets are robustly, if not perfectly, competitive, exclusionary effects are unlikely and antitrust authorities should not intervene.
- With respect to the economic effects of tying, different theories will yield different results. For instance, tying can result in increases in the price of the tied good and at the same time a decrease in the price of the tying good, and in the appropriate situation these could offset each other (for instance where the relevant market could be defined as one that is for the overall bundle of the tied and tying goods).
- The authors also state that tying, as a means of price discrimination or bundling, should not be of concern to antitrust authorities because price discrimination, while conceivably harmful, is often beneficial.
- The authors conclude that the structure of the test for anti-competitive tying in Canada makes sense because it sets out market power and a lessening of competition as independent requirements. However, they caution that the lessening-of-competition test must be applied appropriately to the relevant market.
- In addition, whether or not the seller has market power, tying can allow efficient signalling of quality, efficient risk-sharing, quality control, etc. Therefore, special conditions — particularly dynamic considerations concerning the threat of entry in the ty-

ing and tied-good market over time — must be present for tying to be anti-competitive.

The authors note the relative rarity of truly anti-competitive tying practices — a point that was discussed at some length by a number of the commentators at the symposium — and would require that authorities adduce clear evidence of the anti-competitive effects of a tying practice before seeking an order against tying. They conclude that taking a strict enforcement approach to tying, given the lack of consensus concerning the potential anti-competitive effects, could lead to inappropriate rules or presumptions, such as those that arose in the past in the United States.

Further, the authors state that a finding that tying is anti-competitive is only one step, albeit an important first step, towards the design of a feasible and appropriate remedy. Where anti-competitive tying is accomplished by contract, the remedy would be straightforward — the parties would be enjoined from relying on tying in their contracts. But, where tying is achieved through product integration or product design, which may be the case in technology-based industries, the costs of ordering the separation of products that are technologically integrated are greater; accordingly, authorities should be even more cautious in making orders in respect of such tying practices.

With regard to IP rights, the authors laud the Competition Bureau of Canada's *Intellectual Property Enforcement Guidelines*,[3] while criticizing a number of US cases such as *Chicken Delight*[4] for over-emphasizing the market impact of IP rights, concluding for instance that "it is nonsensical to conclude that a trade-mark confers market power." They also cite the US case of *Independent Ink*[5] for appropriately repudiating such a presumption. Using various examples, the authors note that the relationship between IP and tying is very complex and is likely to be even more complex in the future. They note that often, a number of differing theories will be consistent with the factual evidence and, even where exclusionary theories may fit best, crafting

---

3 Competition Bureau Canada, *Intellectual Property Enforcement Guidelines* (2000), online: http://strategis.ic.gc.ca/pics/ct/ipege.pdf.

4 *Siegel v. Chicken Delight*, 448 F.2d. 43 (9th Cir. 1971) [*Chicken Delight*].

5 *Illinois Tool Works Inc. v. Independent Ink, Inc.*, 547 U.S. 28 (2006) [*Independent Ink*].

a remedy that improves market performance presents an additional challenge. In short, no succinct list of rules exists that summarizes optimal antitrust policy in this area.

B. COMMENTARY

We are in agreement with much of the analysis proffered by the authors and the recommendations they make. Given that it is, in almost all cases, unclear that tying results in anti-competitive and inefficient outcomes, competition authorities, and reviewing courts and tribunals should take a restrained approach. Current economic thinking supports such a perspective — intervention only makes sense in a very limited set of circumstances, and even in these circumstances, the evidentiary hurdle required for intervention should be high because of the difficulty in separating circumstances in which tying has a material anti-competitive effect from those in which tying provides net economic benefits.

In this regard, there are a number of legitimate reasons why firms engage in tying. These include reasons of efficiency, which may include price discrimination, and other strategic motivations. Efficiency benefits include minimizing transaction costs, a reduction in searching and sorting costs, and "variable proportions" — for instance, where it eliminates inefficient input substitution when one product is characterized by market power. Other reasons for tying include homogenizing preferences, metered sales (where a firm takes advantage of variable proportions to price discriminate), and product differentiation.

However, no economic theory reviewed finds that market power or dominance is a sufficient condition for tying to have anti-competitive effects. At most, the relevant economic literature says that tying may be anti-competitive in certain unclear instances. The main implication of several decades of economic investigation into the competitive effects of tying is that there should be no presumption on the part of competition authorities that tying is anti-competitive, even when undertaken by firms with market power.

With respect to exclusionary tying, the Chicago School and the critics in the post–Chicago School outline the main issues. The Chicago School's theory on tying, which is enjoying a resurgence in economic literature, postulates that tying has nothing to do with trying to achieve a monopoly in the tied product because, for complementary products, whether they are tied or not, the monopolist's profits remain the same (monopoly profits can only be extracted once).

This position does have its critics. For example, one of the post-Chicago theories, advocated by Whinston, is that a firm enjoying monopoly power in the tying good *might* have an anti-competitive incentive to tie when the tied-good market is imperfectly competitive if, *in addition*, tying keeps potential rivals out of the market for the tied product or, alternatively, helps the monopolist to preserve its market power in the tying product. The "foreclosure" theory suggests that, through tied selling, a monopolist deprives its competitors in the tied-good market of adequate scale, thereby lowering their profits below the level that would justify remaining active (or, alternatively, entering) in that market.

Under a related theory, a commitment to tying through a physical tie involving incompatible products is posited to leverage monopoly power. For example, when goods that are not exclusively complementary are tied (i.e., some use of the tied product is discrete from use of the tying product), it could prevent other producers of that good from entering the market, or force them to exit the market. Although this situation could reduce the monopolist's short-term profits (in the tying product) the theory suggests that these reductions would be offset by increased profits in the tied products as prices are raised because of lack of competition in the market for the tied product.

Another similar example posited by the post-Chicago School analyzes tying in a two-stage market. This is the situation where the monopoly component is essential for only a first period of time, but not thereafter. By physically tying its products from the outset, the monopolist commits to depriving its rival of sales in the earlier period, which may force the rival out of the market for the longer term. This, in turn, would reduce the monopolist's profits in the initial period but *may* increase its profits in the second period by more than it lost in the first period.

While it is possible that these theories of anti-competitive tying may have some merit under specific circumstances, they have less application, and should be given less weight, in industries characterized by technological innovation and IP rights. The prevalence of IP rights is generally consistent with low barriers to entry; there is, for instance, no barrier to entry for new ideas, new technologies, etc. Moreover, where network effects are present, there is a constant pressure on an incumbent firm to innovate (regardless of its market share) because a leapfrogging technology could capture a significant market share in a very short period of time. This is recognized by Whinston himself:

> A second reason that long term welfare effects are difficult to gauge is that the software industry is . . . an industry very much in the Schumpeterian mode. A single leader often dominates a category until some significant shift (often due to innovation in hardware) causes a new dominant firm to emerge. The race to become the leader, or to retain that position, induces firms — both leaders and wannabes — to make huge research and development expenditures.[6]

For largely these reasons, in *Microsoft*, the D.C. Court of Appeal held that the *per se* analysis traditionally applied to tied selling was inappropriate in the "software platform" context and instead adopted a "rule of reason" approach.[7] However, the court's conclusion has been interpreted as going beyond "software platforms" and creating a "technology exception" to the use of the *per se* rule in tying cases.

In any event, even though certain economic theories have provided examples of situations where tying may be anti-competitive, they do not detract from the consensus view (with which we agree) that tying is a constant feature of economic life, and that the primary motivation for this form of strategic behaviour is the achievement of substantial efficiencies that lead to both higher profits and increased consumer welfare. Even the post-Chicago School thinking concedes that the welfare effects of tying are, at worst, ambiguous. Those models should not therefore be interpreted as supportive of an interventionist approach to the analysis of tying cases, especially in relation to tying through technology/IP rights.

---

6 M.D. Whinston, "Exclusivity and Tying in *US v. Microsoft:* What We Know, and Don't Know" (2001) 15:2 Journal of Economic Perspectives 63 at 79.

7 *United States v. Microsoft Corp.*, 87 F. Supp. 2d 30 (D.D.C. 2000), aff'd in part, rev'd in part, and remanded in part, 253 F.3d 34 (D.C. Circ. 2001) [*Microsoft*].

C. TYING UNDER CURRENT CANADIAN LAW

Canadian law has established an appropriate approach to tying. Tying is addressed by section 77 of the *Competition Act*, which requires that there must be two products; there must be a *practice* of tying; the tied selling must be engaged in by a "major supplier" or be "widespread in the market"; and it must, or be likely to, result in "substantial lessening of competition."[8] The various theories demonstrate that it may be difficult to conclude if and when there has been such substantial lessening of competition.

Moreover, under the Canadian *Competition Act*, no order prohibiting tying shall be made where the "tied selling that is engaged in is reasonable having regard to the technological relationship between or among the products to which it applies."[9] The term "reasonable" has not been interpreted in this context but could very well involve a consideration of the types of tying and integration efficiencies described throughout the paper and this commentary. As discussed above, making a determination of illegal tying is even more difficult in the IP field. We agree with the authors when they note a distinction between technological tying and contractual tying. While concerns with the latter may be effectively remedied with a targeted restriction, there is a real danger that interference with the technological integration of functionality will harm the very economic interests that the law is seeking to protect.

To date, Canadian law has provided little definitive guidance on tying in the IP context. IP tying cases are further complicated by the fact that IP rights are typically subject to low barriers to entry (indicating that there is limited market power) and the impact of network effects (which creates constant pressure for firms to innovate to remain at the "cutting edge," lest they lose their place as the industry leader and relinquish very significant market share in a very short period of time).

In Canada, as in the United States, the applicable *Intellectual Property Enforcement Guidelines* explicitly address tying arrangements and state that authorities will consider both the anti-competitive effects and the efficiencies attributable to the tying. Viewed in this

---

8 R.S.C. 1985, c. C-34.

9 *Ibid.* at s. 77(4)(b).

economically enlightened manner, it would appear as though very few tied-selling cases have been appropriately brought in the past. (The US cases in which the impugned tying arrangement could reasonably have been expected to have had an anti-competitive effect typically involved the use of tying to subvert price regulation in regulated areas, such as tying other services to price-regulated local exchange telephone services.)

D. FUTURE DIRECTION OF THE LAW

Iacobucci and Winter's paper and the resulting discussion on tying and intellectual property has a number of competition policy implications. Policy makers should recognize that a restrained approach to tied selling, which recognizes the efficiency enhancing characteristics of tying, is clearly appropriate. Moreover, the need to adopt a restrained approach to the enforcement of tying provisions is even more compelling in the context of technology industries — in order to avoid the loss of efficiency benefits (including those associated with vigorous innovation).

In an ideal world, one would be able to define rules that clearly differentiate anti-competitive tying from pro-competitive instances. But such differentiation is practically impossible — even Whinston concludes that "the specification of a practical legal standard [is] extremely difficult."[10] Courts have difficulty in judging motivation and a policy of aggressive intervention may hurt rather than help efficiency by prohibiting or deterring efficient tying. Even in strategic tying situations, welfare effects can be ambiguous and courts are unlikely to be able to distinguish between good and bad strategic tying.

Accordingly, the evidentiary hurdle required for intervention in tying cases should be high, and it should be higher for product-design ties than for contractual ties. Substantial weight should be given to plausible efficiency rationales (meaning that intervention should be rare). As a final note (since we are discussing an ideal world) it is imperative that there be consistency and coordination across jurisdic-

---

10 M.D. Whinston, "Tying, Foreclosure and Exclusion" (1990) 80 American Economic Review 837 at 855–56.

tions. The different results achieved in the Microsoft case in Europe[11] from those in the US case demonstrate the need for greater coordination, and how the lack thereof leaves conflicting legal conclusions and unresolved policies in an area where the underlying economic theories are fairly consistent.

11 European Commission Case No. COMP/C-3/37.792/Microsoft (2004).

CHAPTER 3

Effects of "Authorized Generics" on Canadian Drug Prices[1]

Paul Grootendorst[2]

A. INTRODUCTION

This paper examines how the use of "authorized generics" (AGs) influences Canadian prescription drug prices. An AG[3] is "the actual brand name drug product, manufactured by the brand company, but sold as a generic by a licensee or subsidiary of the brand, competing with independent generics."[4] AGs are to be distinguished from independent generics (IGs), which operate independently from the brand firm.

Theoretically, AGs have offsetting effects on drug prices. On the one hand, AGs compete against IGs and, as I discuss below, increases in the number of generic competitors should lower prices. On the

1 Financial support from Industry Canada and the Competition Bureau is gratefully acknowledged. M.S. Shim, Yuqian Lu, and Ivana Todorovic provided capable research assistance. The author thanks Aidan Hollis and participants at the symposium for helpful comments on an earlier draft.

2 Associate Professor, Leslie Dan Faculty of Pharmacy, University of Toronto.

3 Authorized generics are sometimes referred to as "pseudo-generics."

4 A. Hollis and B.A. Liang, "Assessing the Effects of Authorized Generics on Consumer Prices" (2007) 10:1 J. of Biolaw & Bus. 10.

other hand, as Hollis[5] and Kong and Selden[6] have noted, the threat of AG entry into a therapeutic market might deter entry by IGs and this would lessen competition. Moreover, brand firms might increase prices of their brand drugs to increase demand for their AG if there are no IGs available.

Why might the threat of AG entry deter entry by an IG? According to Hollis,[7] the reason is that the AG, should it be the first generic to enter a market, typically captures a significant and durable market share. This reduces the demand for the IG and may make entry into marginally profitable therapeutic markets unprofitable. One would therefore expect that the threat of AG entry might deter IG entry in markets with only modest revenue potential.

B. GENERIC DRUG COMPETITION IN THE CANADIAN DRUG MARKET

How does generic drug competition lower drug prices? In a conventional market, increases in the number of suppliers reduce the average price paid by consumers — suppliers lower prices in an attempt to gain market share. In the limiting case, known as a perfectly competitive market (one with very many buyers and sellers of a homogenous product), price will decline to the marginal production cost. The Canadian market for generic prescription drugs is different. First, two generic companies, Apotex and Novopharm, control over half of the market.[8] Second, although there are many consumers in this market, including private insurance plans and cash-paying customers, the market is dominated by several large provincial government drug plans, notably the plans operating in Ontario (the Ontario Drug Benefit Program

---

5 A. Hollis, "The Anti-competitive Effects of Brand-controlled 'Pseudo-generics' in the Canadian Pharmaceutical Market" (2003) 29:1 Can. Pub. Pol'y 21.

6 Y. Kong and J. Seldon, "Pseudo-generic Products and Barriers to Entry in Pharmaceutical Markets" (2004) 25 Review of Industrial Organization 71.

7 A. Hollis, "The Importance of Being First: Evidence from Canadian Generic Pharmaceuticals" (2002) 11 Health Economics 723.

8 B. Skinner, "Generic Drugopoly: Why Non-patented Prescription Drugs Cost More in Canada than in the United States and Europe," Fraser Institute Public Policy Sources, No. 82 (Fraser Institute, 2004) online: www.fraserinstitute.ca/admin/books/files/GenericDrugopoly.pdf.

or ODB) and Quebec (RAMQ) that cover the drug costs incurred by seniors, those with high drug costs relative to income, and other groups. The ODB is the single largest drug plan in Canada; it dictates the amount that it is willing to pay for generic drugs, and these prices become the *de facto* prices charged to other customers.

The amount that ODB is willing to pay for generic drugs is a proportion of brand drug prices. During the period from May 1993 to September 1998, the ODB invoked the "75/90" regulations. The 75/90 regulations stipulated that the first generic entrant's price could not exceed 75 percent of the incumbent branded drug price. When the second generic entered the market, the maximum reimbursement price dropped to 67.5 percent of the branded drug price (i.e., 75 percent of the first generic entrant's price: 75 percent of 90 percent = 67.5 percent). During the period from November 1998 to September 2006, the ODB limited the first generic entrant's price to 70 percent of the incumbent branded drug price. When the second generic entered the market, the maximum reimbursement price dropped to 63 percent of the branded drug price (i.e., 70 percent of the first generic entrant's price: 70 percent of 90 percent = 63 percent). Since October 2006, the ODB reimbursement of generic drugs is limited to 50 percent of the brand drug price. The ODB, however, will consider increasing the reimbursement of the first generic entrant by up to 70 percent, on a case-by-case basis.

Anis, Guh, and Woolcott[9] present evidence that generic prices in Ontario are set close to the ODB maximum generic drug reimbursement prices. The prices charged for generic drugs in other provinces tend to match ODB prices. Generic firms that attempted to charge more would soon be undercut by wholesalers who sell drugs at ODB prices.

How then do generic firms compete for market share? Once they become available for sale, generic drugs rapidly replace branded drugs, owing to the reimbursement policies of almost all drug plans, public and private alike. Most plans limit reimbursement of multi-sourced drugs (i.e., drugs for which there are both brand and generic forms

---

9 A. Anis, D.P. Guh, and J. Woolcott, "Lowering Generic Drug Prices: Less Regulation Equals More Competition" (2003) 41 Medical Care 135 [Anis *et al.*].

available for sale) to the price of the generic drug.[10] Drug plan beneficiaries do have the option of paying extra to get the higher priced brand-version of the drug, but relatively few are willing to pay extra. The first generic, therefore, gains a large market share and can charge 70 percent of the branded drug price. Once there are several generics available, generic firms compete for sales to large pharmacy chains, such as the Shoppers Drug Mart chain, and independent pharmacies by lowering prices charged to these pharmacies. Competition occurs through the generosity of cash and in-kind rebates; these rebates drive down the effective price paid by the pharmacy for generic drugs. The difference between the ODB reimbursement price and the pharmacy's actual acquisition cost becomes part of the pharmacy's revenues. Anecdotal evidence suggests that this margin can be as high as 60 percent of the formulary price of generic drugs. Anis[11] reports that when the Nova Scotia public drug plan replaced formulary pricing with a system in which only the actual acquisition costs were reimbursed, generic drug prices fell by about 40 percent.

The rebate system was disrupted by regulations enacted by the ODB in October 2006. In an attempt to manage program costs, the ODB appropriated some of the rebate amounts that were accruing to pharmacy chains. It did so by reducing the maximum that it would reimburse generic drugs to 50 percent of the brand drug price and limiting the rebate amounts generic firms paid to pharmacies for ODB-reimbursed drugs to 20 percent of the ODB reimbursement price.[12] Although ODB did not regulate rebates paid for drugs that it did not reimburse, it applied a code of conduct that required that *all* generic

---

10 The Quebec RAMQ plan is notable for its willingness to pay for the brand version of the drug for fifteen years (from the date of formulary inclusion of the brand drug) even if generic versions are available for sale.

11 A. Anis, "Pharmaceutical Prices with Insurance Coverage and Formularies" (1992) 25:2 Canadian Journal of Economics 420.

12 To offset these revenue losses, the Ontario government increased the dispensing fee (from $6.46 to $7.00 per prescription) and, in recognition of professional services traditionally rendered by community pharmacists without payment, established new funding (cited to be in the area of $50 million for 2006–07) as compensation for these services. Further details on the legislation are available online: www.health.gov.on.ca/english/public/legislation/drugs/hu_drugsact.html.

drug rebates that Ontario pharmacies received (from sales of generic drugs to both the ODB and private payers) be used for patient care. Rebates could no longer be taken as personal income. These regulations appear to be actively enforced: the ODB just recently announced that each Ontario pharmacy is required to submit quarterly reports on the amount of rebate revenue received and how these revenues are used.

It is unclear how these regulations will affect the prices received by generic firms. On the one hand, the maximum rebate that can be paid on ODB prescriptions is limited to 20 percent of the ODB price — limiting the rebates should increase prices received by generics. On the other hand, this limit does not apply to non-ODB prescriptions, so generics might still use rebates to compete for this segment of the Ontario market, as well as the rest of the domestic market. Moreover, the maximum generic price is now 50 percent of the brand price (although, as stated earlier, it is possible that the first generic entrant might be able to negotiate a higher amount). It seems likely that this new, lower generic price will be available to the rest of the domestic market, although pharmacy chains are actively resisting this at present.

C. WHY MIGHT A BRAND FIRM INTRODUCE AN AG?

Under the terms of the "NOC-link" section of the *Patent Act*,[13] IG firms must declare to the brand firm their intention of introducing a generic copy onto the market.[14] This declaration, and any resulting litigation over the validity of brand firm's patents, gives the brand firm some indication of the timing of IG entry to the market. If no IG is expected to enter, then the AG will not. If it appears that IG entry is likely, then the brand firm may launch an AG, for two reasons.

First, launching an AG might be profitable. Relative to IG firms, the brand firm faces low fixed market-entry costs. Because the AG is the brand drug, the brand firm does not face the costs of conducting

13 R.S.C. 1985, c. P–4.

14 IG firms must declare, using a "Notice of Allegation" (NOA), that their generic drug will not infringe any of the brand firm's patents — but this has the effect of signaling their intentions to enter a therapeutic market. A brand firm can delay the regulatory approval of the generic drug (technically the issuance by Health Canada of a "Notice of Compliance," or NOC, indicating that the drug is bioequivalent to the brand drug) by alleging patent infringement.

bioequivalence studies,[15] nor does it face the costs of challenging the validity of any outstanding patents. Also, the costs of establishing manufacturing capacity have already been incurred at the time of the brand drug launch. The brand firm must pay a fee for the licensee to sell the AG drug, but these costs would likely be less than the fixed costs incurred by IG firms.

Should it decide to enter a market, the brand firm is faced with the decision of launching its AG before the IG drug, or not. By launching before the IG, the AG initially captures the entire share of the generics market. Moreover, if it is the only generic available on the market, it need not pay pharmacies any rebate (since the pharmacy has no choice but to carry it) and this will increase net reimbursement. These benefits may be short-lived however — as the number of generic competitors increase, the AG's market share will decrease and the amount of rebate needed to gain access to pharmacy shelves increases.[16] More importantly, by launching before the IG, it will cannibalize its brand drug sales. Specifically, during the period from November 1998 to September 2006, the AG realized only 70 percent of the price paid for the brand version of the drug. Accepting a 30 percent price cut (and after the recent changes to the ODB reimbursement, up to a 50 percent price cut) makes sense only if the AG realizes a compensatory increase in market share relative to the share it would realize if it launched alongside (or after) the IG.

Launching an AG before the IG could increase profits for another reason: if the AG is the only generic on the market, then the brand firm could potentially coordinate the prices charged for the brand and AG forms of the drug in a way that maximizes profits. In particular, as Hollis notes,[17] by pricing the brand version relatively high, it can increase the amount that it charges for the AG version of the drug,

---

15 Health Canada requires evidence that IGs are bioequivalent with the brand drug and also have acceptable potency, purity, and stability. Hollis cites a newspaper article that indicates that these development and clinical testing costs typically range from $0.5 million to $3 million per drug: A. Hollis, "How Do Brands' 'Own Generics' Affect Pharmaceutical Prices?" (2005) 27 Review of Industrial Organization 329 [Hollis (2005)].

16 One way that a major IG firm is reported to have gained AG's market share is to purchase from pharmacies the AG's inventory, replacing it with its own product.

17 Hollis (2005), above note 15.

subject to price regulations imposed by the federal government and provincial drug plans.

The second reason that the brand firm might find it in its interest to launch an AG is to establish a reputation among IGs that it will launch an AG in "marginally profitable" markets — markets in which the presence of the AG can tip the balance between economic profitability and loss. This might deter future IG entry into such markets.

D. EXISTING EVIDENCE

In theory, the impact of AGs on drug prices is ambiguous. What does the evidence indicate? There is no empirical evidence on the effects of AGs on the decision by an IG to attempt to enter a drug market. The evidence on the effect of AGs on drug markets in which IGs do enter is mixed. The one Canadian study found AGs to be mildly anti-competitive. Hollis analyzed sales data for the thirty-one drugs in Canada for which the first generic competitor entered during the years 1994–97. He concludes:

> This paper shows that pseudo-generics appear to increase both brand and generic drug prices, in line with a simple theoretical model .... The econometric analysis shows that a 10% increase in the pseudogeneric share of generic sales leads to brand prices about 1% higher, controlling for the number of generics and the years since the first generic entered. Since the typical pseudo-generic controls about 40% of generic sales in the first few years of generic entry, this implies about a 4% increase in brand prices, compared to the case of no pseudo-generic. The direct impact of pseudo-generics on generic drug prices appears to be similar in scale.[18]

The evidence in the US is mixed. The Pharmaceutical Research and Manufacturers of America (PhRMA), the association of US brand drug firms, commissioned IMS Consulting to assess the effects of AGs on US generic prices. The study[19] found that AGs were pro-competi-

18 *Ibid.* at 348.

19 The study is available at www.phrma.org/files/IMS%20Authorized%20Generics%20Report_6-22-06.pdf [accessed 23 Nov. 2006] See also: www.phrma.org/news_room/press_releases/authorized_generics_can_lead_to_lower_drug_prices.

tive. Specifically, the study compared markets with and without AGs present and found that average generic prices (measured as a fraction of the brand drug price) were lower — on average 15.8 percentage points lower — in markets with AGs present.

In response, the Generic Pharmaceutical Research and Manufacturers of America (GPhRMA), the association of US independent generic firms, commissioned Hollis and Liang to evaluate the PhRMA study methods. The study, which appeared in the Journal of Biolaw & Business,[20] challenged both the measurement of the price variables in the PhRMA study as well as the methods used to identify the impact of AGs on price. For instance, Hollis and Liang suggested that the PhRMA study finding of greater percentage discounts to brand prices in markets with AGs is due in part to higher brand prices in markets with AGs, rather than lower generic prices. In other words, during the period immediately following IG entry, prices of the brand drug increased more in markets with AGs than in markets without AGs. They also question whether the influence of AGs on prices can be captured with a simple comparison of markets with and without AGs present. In particular, they note that these markets likely also differ with respect to sales volume, number of anticipated entrants, potential for licensing, and other factors that could independently affect price discounts. Finally, Hollis and Liang note that the PhRMA study does not address the effects of potential AG entry on the likelihood that an IG will attempt to enter a market.

When they reanalyzed the data used in the PhRMA study, Hollis and Liang found some evidence of a very modest anti-competitive effect. Specifically, in markets with AGs present, the average discount of generics off of branded prices was less than in markets without an AG (17.7 percent versus 17.1 percent).

E. RESEARCH OBJECTIVES

Industry Canada and the Competition Bureau asked me to investigate the following questions about the prevalence and effects of AGs in Canadian pharmaceutical drug markets:

---

20 Above note 4.

1) In what proportion of drug markets are authorized generics present?
2) How important is the invocation of the automatic twenty-four-month stay under the *PM(NOC) Regulations* in determining the entry of authorized generics?
3) What are the characteristics of the drug markets that authorized generics enter? In particular, how important is market size in explaining authorized generic entry?
4) What is the impact of authorized generics on drug prices and the entry of independent generics?
5) How important are market opportunities in the US at explaining the decisions of independent generic firms to enter a particular market?

F. METHODS

Questions 2 and 5 were addressed using qualitative methods — I interviewed executives of major brand and generic firms as well as representatives of the IG trade association (the Canadian Generic Pharmaceutical Association (CGPA)).

The remaining questions were addressed by analyzing IMS Health Canada data on the national, monthly sales of the generic and brand versions of all dosage forms and strengths of the molecules in which the first generic drug (authorized or independent) launched over the period 1998–2004. I identified the AG drugs using the NOC database produced by Health Canada.[21] Specifically AG drugs were identified as those generic drugs that have received New Drug Submission (NDS) status; independent generics have Abbreviated New Drug Submission (ANDS) status.[22] Not all NDS-status generic drugs are AGs, however. I consulted with IMS Health Canada, Jack Kay of Apotex, and Brogan Inc. to help identify the NDS drugs that were not AGs.

Using these data, I determined the proportion of drug markets in which an AG has entered (question 1); estimated regression models of

---

21 See online: www.nocdatabase.ca.

22 According to Jack Kay, COO of Apotex, an AG drug would not cite any bioequivalence data on its product monograph, whereas an IG would. Unfortunately, I could not locate the product monographs of the generic drugs in this study.

the probability of AG entry in the molecule market (question 3); and, finally, estimated regression models of the average price for the molecule as a function of the presence of an AG (question 4).

The probability of AG entry was modelled to be a function of, *inter alia*, an estimate of the expected total sales revenue for all dosage forms and strengths of the molecule in the year before the launch of the first generic; indicators of year of first generic launch; and finally indicators of the company producing the brand drug.

I describe the methods to estimate the influence of AGs on drug prices below.

G. RESULTS

1) In What Proportion of Drug Markets Are Authorized Generics Present?

I defined a drug market as a unique combination of molecule and dosage form; hence I distinguished, for instance, the oral solid version of cyclosporine from its oral liquid and injectable forms. I distinguished between the different dosage forms of the same molecule because in some cases the pattern of generic drug entry varied by dosage form. In the case of cyclosporine, for instance, an AG (but not an IG) launched an oral solid, while an IG (but not an AG) launched an oral liquid. Neither an AG nor an IG launched an injectable form. Of the eighty-three drugs in the sample, however, most were oral solids (tablets and capsules) that were not available in other dosage forms.

Table 1 provides a cross-tabulation of IG and AG entry into the eighty-three drug markets. An AG entered thirty-two (39 percent) of the eighty-three drug markets in the sample, while an IG entered seventy-four (89 percent) of the eighty-three markets. Both an IG and an AG entered in thirty-one (37 percent) markets. The 39 percent AG entry rate over this time period is consistent with Hollis' (2005) finding: "In 1999, the total pharmacy sales of these generics drugs totaled approximately $500 million, of which the pseudo-generic share was 34.6 percent."[23]

23 Hollis (2005), above note 15 at 332.

Table 1: Cross-tabulation of AG and IG Entry in Eighty-three Drug Markets

=1 if authorized generic launched	=1 if independent generic launched		Total
	0	1	
0	8.00	43.00	51.00
	15.67	84.31	100.00
	88.89	58.11	61.45
1	1.00	31.00	32.00
	3.13	96.88	100.00
	11.11	41.89	38.55
Total	9.00	74.00	83.00
	10.84	89.16	100.00
	100.00	100.00	100.00

Note: first number in each cell is the frequency, the second number is the row percentage and the third number is the column percentage.
** Due to rounding-off of the data, numbers may not add up precisely.*

Table 2 provides information on the timing of the AG and first IG in the same market. Of the thirty-one markets in which both an AG and an IG entered, the IG entered first in sixteen, the AG entered first in ten, and they both entered in the same month in five markets.

Table 2: Timing of AG and First IG Market Entry

Number of Months by Which AG Precedes IG	Frequency	Percent	Cumulation
–39	1	3.23	3.23
–27	1	3.23	6.45
–25	1	3.23	9.68
–21	1	3.23	12.9
–18	1	3.23	16.13
–12	1	3.23	19.35
–6	1	3.23	22.58
–5	1	3.23	25.81
–4	1	3.23	29.03
–3	1	3.23	32.26
–2	2	6.45	38.71
–1	4	12.9	51.61
0	5	16.13	67.74
1	3	9.68	77.42

Number of Months by Which AG Precedes IG	Frequency	Percent	Cumulation
2	3	9.68	87.1
3	1	3.23	90.32
8	3	9.68	100.00
Total	31	100.00	

Note: a positive number means that the AG entered before the IG.
** Due to rounding-off of the data, numbers may not add up precisely.*

There is some evidence that in small to medium markets (markets with sales of $50 million or less), the AG is no more likely than the IG to enter first. In the four largest markets, however, the AG comes in no later than the IG.

Table 3 presents summary data on the fraction of markets with AGs and IGs present, by the total sales of the drug in 1998. The fraction of markets with an AG or IG tends to increase with the value of 1998 sales of the drug.

Table 3: Fraction of Drug Markets with Authorized Generics and Independent Generics Present, by Quintiles of Total Sales of the Drug in 1998 ($ Millions)

Quintile	Mean	Median	Min.	Max.	% with AGs	% with IGs
1	0.00	0.00	0.00	0.00	19	77
2	0.91	0.84	0.33	1.74	13	63
3	4.55	4.52	2.58	7.26	31	100
4	12.80	13.63	7.33	20.39	59	100
5	83.69	45.84	23.07	308.62	69	100

Appendix 1 presents detailed information on IG and AG entry into the eighty-three markets, as well as year-specific sales in these markets.

2) How Important Is the Invocation of the Automatic Twenty-Four-Generics?

My sense from the literature and discussions with industry representatives is that the *PM(NOC)* (*NOC-link*) *Regulations* facilitate the entry of AGs, although they are not absolutely necessary. A brand firm will normally not launch an AG unless it is confident that an IG will indeed enter. Under the *NOC-link Regulations*, the brand firm can more accurately ascertain the date of expected entry of an IG into a therapeutic market than it could without the *NOC-link Regulations*. The reason is that under the *NOC-link Regulations*, an IG firm is obliged to notify the brand firm of its intention to enter. The *NOC-link Regulations* also give the brand firm the right to delay the issuance of an NOC by alleging patent infringement. The ensuing litigation provides the brand firm with much more information on the entry date than it would otherwise have. For instance, the brand firm can monitor the progress of the trial and hence forecast its outcome, providing it with information with which it can determine whether and when it should ready an AG. However, without the *NOC-link Regulations*, the only information that the brand firm would have about IG entry is the expiration date of its patents, and Health Canada NOC approval of an IG drug.

It is important, however, not to overstate the importance of the *NOC-link Regulations* in informing the brand firm of the expected market entry date of an IG. First, my data indicate that brand firms do not always attempt to beat IG firms to the market with an AG, especially in markets with only modest revenue potential. In larger markets however, the AG enters at the same time or some months before the IG. Second, my brand firm contacts mentioned that even if they were notified of the imminent entry of an IG by some other means (say the issuance by Health Canada of an NOC) they could still launch an AG at about the same time as an IG. The reason is that an IG will usually achieve significant sales volumes only some time after it receives its NOC. In particular, it takes some time for the provincial drug plans to list the IG on its formulary (which is the point in time at which demand for the drug increases markedly). Moreover, AGs might also be able to launch faster than IGs. According to the CGPA, several provincial government drug plans — including the plans operating in Alberta and Newfoundland — require generics to submit evidence of bioequivalence before they will reimburse the generic drug (the other plans accept Health Canada certification of bioequivalence). Vetting the bioequivalence data for an IG takes longer than that for an AG (since the AG is the brand drug, bioequivalence is a non-issue). Depending on the frequency with which the assessment committees meet and make their recommendations regarding bioequivalence, and the frequency with which these recommendations are acted upon by formulary committees, the AG might get listed on a provincial formulary before an IG.[24]

3) What Are the Characteristics of the Drug Markets that Authorized Generics Enter? In Particular, How Important Is Market Size in Explaining Authorized Generic Entry?

I estimated a probit regression model of the probability of AG entry into the drug markets. The probability was modelled as a function of (i) indicators of the brand drug firm (in the event that different brand firms are more or less likely to use AGs); (ii) indicators of the year of entry of the first generic (authorized or independent); as well as (iii) indicators of the quintiles of market sales in the twelve-month period prior to generic entry. These quintiles divide the drug markets into five evenly sized groups, ranked by sales from smallest to largest. The markets in the bottom quintile had annual sales of between $0.01 and $1.73 million; the markets in the top quintile had annual sales of between $50.84 and $485.20 million (Table 4).

---

24 An IG executive I interviewed recounted how their launch of Ramipril was pre-empted by an AG:

> We got our NOC on December 12, after years of litigation, and sent our submission to Alberta by courier on December 13. It arrived December 14. Sanofi-Aventis arranged for a NOC for authorized-generic to be issued to Ratiopharm on December 13. Because they did not have to file a substantive submission in Alberta but are automatically accepted because same as brand, Alberta considered their submission complete on December 13. Our submission had to include data and was very large, and thus could not be transmitted by fax. It arrived at Alberta Health on December 14 as aforesaid. Alberta fast-tracks the first generic. Hence they proceed to immediately list the ratio product and not ours, and ratio thus took the whole Alberta market . . . .

Interview of IG Executive (8 March 2007), conducted by the author by email [Interview of IG Executive].

Table 4: Mean, Median, Minimum, and Maximum Total Sales ($ Million) in Drug Market in the Year before Generic Entry, by Sales Quintile

Quintile	Mean	Median	Minimum	Maximum
1	0.73	0.73	0.01	1.73
2	4.75	4.94	1.76	7.11
3	14.02	14.78	7.21	18.55
4	25.92	25.46	20.07	35.90
5	161.99	121.27	50.84	485.20

The model estimates indicate that of the three factors considered above, factor (iii), market size, is the strongest predictor of AG entry. Holding constant the influence of factors (i) and (ii), the bigger the market size, the greater the likelihood of AG entry. Compared to markets in the lowest sales quintile, AGs were 33 percentage points more likely to enter markets in the second lowest sales quintile ($p = 0.196$), 45 percentage points more likely to enter markets in the middle sales quintile ($p = 0.059$), 43 percentage points more likely to enter markets in the second highest sales quintile ($p = 0.081$), and 64 percentage points more likely to enter markets in the top sales quintile ($p = 0.004$).

A useful summary statistic is the R-squared; this statistic reflects the amount of variation in the outcome variable that is explained by predictor variables. I note that my AG entry probability model pseudo-R-squared is decent (29 percent) for a cross sectional data set. This likely reflects the strong predictive performance of pre-IG market sales; the remaining explanatory variables had apparently little explanatory power. Specifically, there were no noticeably different probabilities of AG entry among the different brand firms (Novartis Pharma and Pfizer had slightly higher probabilities of issuing AGs than the other brand firms, but it is not clear if this is a chance result). Similarly, there were no discernable trends in the likelihood of AG entry by year.

4) What Is the Impact of Authorized Generics on Drug Prices and the Entry of Independent Generics?

Recall that, theoretically, AGs have offsetting effects on drug prices. On the one hand, AGs compete against IGs, and increases in the number of generic competitors should lower prices. On the other hand, the brand firm might raise prices on its branded drug to increase the sales revenue accruing to its AG drug. Moreover, the threat of AG entry into a therapeutic market might deter entry by IGs and this would lessen competition.

One therefore needs to assess the net effect of AGs on drug prices. One can do so by considering the effects of AGs on drug prices in drug markets with and without generic drugs present. The impact of AGs on markets with a generic drug (AG or IG) present can inform the impact of AG competition on drug prices, after accounting for the fact that brand firms might increase branded drug prices when an AG is present. I develop and estimate a drug price model that addresses this question. This model uses IMS data on the average prices charged for the drug molecules in which a generic drug entered between 1998 and 2004. This model, however, does not inform the question as to how the threat of AG entry deters IG entry in marginally profitable markets and how the attendant reduction in competition translates into higher prices. The impact of AGs on IG entry is the difference between the likelihood of IG entry with the threat of AG entry present, and the likelihood of IG entry without the threat of AG entry. It is difficult to estimate this impact. While data on the drug markets in which IGs have entered are readily available, it is difficult to determine which drug markets IGs would have attempted to enter had it not been for the threat of AG entry. In particular, while we can directly observe the drug markets in which all relevant patents have expired but in which there are no IGs, it is not obvious which patent-protected drug markets would have been successfully challenged by IG firms (perhaps because the patents were sufficiently weak) but were not due to the threat of AG entry. Yet these data are required to address the question.

I explored various approaches to addressing this question. For instance, I investigated whether it was possible to analyze annual data on the threshold market size, above which an IG enters. If the advent of AG competition in the Canadian market occurred recently then it might be possible to examine time series data on these market size thresholds in periods before and after the advent of AG competition. It turns out, however, that AGs have competed in the Canadian market since at least 1987, making it difficult to collect data in the period before AG competition began.

Instead of conducting a quantitative analysis of AGs on the likelihood of IG entry, I used qualitative methods. Specifically I interviewed executives of a major domestic IG firm about the effect of the threat of AG entry on the threshold market size above which the IG will attempt to enter. I describe the results of these interviews below.

H. QUANTITATIVE ANALYSES

I developed a linear regression model of average prices charged to consumers (i.e., drug insurers and patients paying out of pocket) each month, in each of the eighty-three drug markets described in Appendix 1. The average monthly price in each of these markets is simply the total monthly sales revenues across all strengths and manufacturers of the drug (including brand and generic firms) divided by the total number of milligrams (mg) of the drug dispensed. The total mg of the drug dispensed, in turn, is the number of units dispensed times the strength in mg per unit. I deemed expenditure per mg of drug dispensed to be the best measure of average price charged — it automatically standardizes prices charged to consumers for differences in the market shares of the brand and generic products. Importantly, it is sensitive to any increases in brand price that might occur after AG entry. And, unlike a price measure based on expenditure per prescription, my measure is sensitive to the number of units dispensed per prescription and the strength per unit.

The IMS sales data are derived from a sample of total prescription drug sales and volumes at over 2,000 representative retail pharmacies. The sales data include all wholesale and retail markups and dispensing fees, so that some of my consumer price variable represents payments to wholesalers and pharmacies. Below, I explain how my model will account for the influence of variation in such payments.

I modelled the average drug and month-specific price as a function of the following covariates:

- Indicators of various levels of the authorized-generic share of the *generic* prescription volume, measured as the total number of mgs dispensed. As Hollis notes, this variable was thought to better capture the degree of AG market penetration than a simple binary indicator of AG entry.[25] The use of multiple indicators,

25 Hollis (2005), above note 15, presents evidence that the AG share of the generic market is endogenous in the price model; that is, AG share is correlated with

each indicating the degree of AG penetration (0 percent, 1–20 percent, 21–40 percent, 41–60 percent, 61–80 percent, 81–100 percent) allows for non-linear effects of AG entry on price.[26]
- Indicators of various levels of the number of independent generic competitors
- Drug-market-specific indicators (included to pick up time-invariant differences in the price per mg of the different molecules; this will also pick up the influence of market size and other time-invariant factors that might affect entry by IG and AG firms)
- Quarter of year indicators (included to pick up time-period-specific changes in the price common to all the different drug markets, such as changes in pharmacy and wholesaler markups and fees)

I modelled the effects of AG generic market shares and other predictor variables on the *log* average price per mg. Focusing on log price allowed me to assess the effects of changes in the AG market share on relative (percentage) price changes, which is intuitively more appealing than absolute changes in price per mg.[27]

I used all available data, except that I removed observations on Nefazodone after it was pulled from the market due to safety concerns in January 2004. Although there were a few price observations available after this date, the average price was very poorly estimated.

I also estimated the price model using the subset of the data that remained after dropping observations on drug markets in which the

---

an unobserved component of price. He therefore developed an instrumental variables estimator using as an instrument the number of months by which the AG beats the first IG to market. I deal with the possible endogeneity of AG share in my price model by using the one-period lagged values of AG share and number of IGs instead of their contemporaneous values.

26 In some versions of the empirical price models, I distinguished between AGs that are licensed to a subsidiary of the brand firm from the AGs that are licensed to an IG firm in order to assess whether this distinction makes a difference to the estimated impact of AG generic drug share on average price. The data were not sufficiently informative to detect a difference.

27 The log transformed price model is also more consistent with the data than the linear price model: I subjected the average price model to the boxcox transform to determine whether a linear or log specification was more appropriate — the linear specification was handily rejected in favour of the log specification.

price and generic market share data were measured with considerable error.[28] Measurement error can decrease the precision of one's model estimates and I wanted to ensure that my results were robust to measurement error.[29] The reader is invited to inspect drug-market-specific data on monthly average price, average brand drug price, generic drug share of the market, and authorized generic drug share of the market to assess the degree of measurement error in these drug markets.[30]

The price models fit the data quite well — R-squared values all exceed 95 percent (see Appendix 2 for details of the model results). Moreover, the parameter estimates are plausible. The models suggest, for instance, that increases in the number of independent generic drugs reduce average prices.

The models suggest that AGs are mildly pro-competitive. Focusing on the results in model 1.3, when AGs capture 80–100 percent of the generic market, that is, when they are the first or among the first to enter the market, they unambiguously reduce prices by about 11 percent. When the AG generic market share is in the range of 21–80 percent, prices drop by a smaller degree — between 5 and 7 percent. When the AG generic market share is in the range of 1–20 percent, prices drop by an even smaller degree — about 3 percent. This suggests that the average per mg price of the brand drug increases as IGs take market share away from the AG (otherwise the additional competition provided by IGs would lower average price).

---

28 Recall that the IMS sales data are estimates based on a representative sample of pharmacies. For some drugs with low prescribing volumes, the price estimates are highly variable. This could be because of the limitations of survey sampling. It could also reflect a limitation with my data. I had to enter manually into my database sales data for the years 1998–2000 (IMS data older than seventy-two months are available in hardcopy only). The dollar sales and quantities data in these hardcopies are rounded to the nearest 1,000 dollars or units, which can introduce measurement error when the underlying sales volumes are small.

29 Specifically, I removed the following drugs: Amiodarone Inj, Cefuroxime Axetil Liquid, Ciprofloxacin Liquid, Clavulanic Acid Liquid, Clindamycin Inj, Clindamycin Liquid, Cyclosporine Inj, Cyclosporine Liquid, Fenofibrate, Fluconazole Inj, Fluconazole Liquid, Ketorolac Inj, Labetalol Inj, Lamotrigine Chewable, Piperacillin, Propofol, Tizanidine, Vancomycin Inj, and Warfarin Inj.

30 This information is presented online: http://individual.utoronto.ca/grootendorst/pdf/drugpricegraphs.pdf.

To investigate further, I estimated models of the impact on AG generic market share on the average *brand drug* price per mg. These models suggest that average brand prices are slightly higher (between 2 and 8 percent) when AGs control between 1 and 40 percent of the generic market compared to when they are not sold at all (brand prices are essentially unchanged when AGs control 41–100 percent of the market).

I. QUALITATIVE ANALYSES

The generic firm executive indicated that AGs have their primary anti-competitive effect on the decision of IGs to enter a drug market. He indicated that with AGs present, and under the current set of ODB drug reimbursement regulations, he will not bother challenging a drug market with less than $10 million in annual sales. The following two paragraphs paraphrase his reasoning:[31]

Generics can charge at most 50 percent of the brand price so that potential revenues drop to $5 million. Even if his IG firm is the first on the market, he can get at most 75 percent of the entire market (recall that RAMQ and some private plans will continue to cover brand drugs even with generics available). This reduces revenues to 0.75 × $5 million = $3.75 million. Under the new ODB regulations, the cost of rebates to pharmacies is about 40 percent (down from over 50 percent). Hence revenues net of rebates are 0.6 × $3.75 million = $2.25 million. Production costs (raw materials, labour and indirect overheads, including depreciation) are roughly 40 percent of revenues; revenues net of production costs are therefore 0.6 × $2.25 million = $1.35 million. Selling expenses, including administration, distribution, and the legal costs of challenging patents reduce net revenues by a further 15 percent; hence 0.85 × $1.35 million = $1.15 million remains after deducting selling expenses. R&D costs (including the costs of obtaining regulatory approval to sell the generic) represent a further 15 percent of sales, hence 0.85 × $1.15 million = $0.98 million remains.

Hence net revenues are about $980,000 for each year in which they control the generic market. The anticipated flow of net revenues over time, accounting for the usual patterns of IG competition and gradual

---

31 Interview of IG Executive #2 (20 February 2007), conducted by the author over the telephone [IG Executive #2 interview].

obsolescence of the drug market, is sufficiently lucrative for the firm to challenge a drug market. However, if an AG does enter, the IG firm can expect to lose about 50 percent of the market so that net revenues fall to 0.5 × $980,000 = $490,000 annually, which is the point at where the IG firm would not bother challenging. If the IG firm was certain that there would be no AG entry, it would challenge drug markets with $5+ million in annual sales.

Taking the statements of the IG executive at face value, the effect of the threat of AG entry is to increase the minimum market size that justifies a challenge from the IG from $5 to $10 million. Assuming that generic prices would be about 50 percent of brand prices if an IG did enter, and assuming that no other generics enter markets with less than $10 million in annual sales, the threat of AG competition raises consumer costs by about 50 percent for every market not challenged. Assuming that the average size of the markets that go unchallenged on account of the threat of AG entry is $7.5 million, the threat of AG entry increases drug payer costs by $3.75 million annually (over the remaining life of the drug) for every market that goes unchallenged.

The IG executive stated that AG competition discourages them from challenging brand drugs with sales well above $10 million for which developing and producing a generic drug is particularly costly, for two reasons.[32] First, as before, the threat of AG would take away IG market share and therefore revenues. Second, AG competition in markets the IG has entered has reduced their retained earnings. This reduction in retained earnings has hampered their ability to finance development of specialized production capacity and the cost of clinical studies (according to the IG executive, many drugs are not amenable to bioequivalence studies and require comparative clinical trials that

32 The IG executive cited as examples the following brand drugs (with annual sales) that will not likely be challenged: Eprex $200 million, Remicade $170 million, Enbrel $160 million, Herceptin $160 million, Flovent HFA $130 million, Advair $125 million, Duragesic $115 million, Aranesp $115 million, Rituxin $110 million, Rebif $ 85 million, Neupogen $80 million, Prevnar $75 million, Symbiocort $60 million, Spiriva $ 60 million, Advair MDI $60 million, Copaxone $60 million, Zoladex LA $55 million, Betaseron $50 million, Lupron Depot $50 million. A brand firm executive countered that he would be very surprised if at least some of these drugs were not challenged by a generic. See IG Executive #2 interview, *ibid.*

can cost many millions or even tens of millions of dollars per study). The CGPA shared with me a survey of eight participating generic firms conducted by IBM Global Business Services that, at face value, corroborates the claims of the IG executive. (The study was based on firms' responses that were not audited or otherwise validated by IBM.) The IBM study concludes: "Canadian generic pharmaceutical manufacturers continue to experience a financial loss on their sales in Canada. The net loss on Canadian sales was –2.7% in 2002 and the net loss for 2005 remained at –2.7%."[33]

In order to validate these claims, one would need to analyze data on the minimum market size below which no generics will enter. According to the executive at the IG firm, the decision by an IG firm to challenge a brand drug is typically based on the sales of the brand drug in the tenth year that it has been on the market. To verify the claims by the IG executive, one would need to construct a time series of the year ten sales of brand drugs and determine, for each of these drugs, whether an IG was observed to eventually enter.

J. FURTHER DETERRENT EFFECTS OF AGs ON IG ENTRY

Finally, the IG executive claimed that brand firms have attempted to use the threat of AG entry to negotiate agreements with their IG firm to delay entry until entry by another IG firm is imminent, at which time their IG firm will launch an AG. The proposed agreements involve sharing with the IG firm some of the consumers' savings that would have been realized by IG competition.[34]

---

33 IBM Global Business Services, "Supply Chain Costing and Financial Survey—2006 Update," Report prepared for the Canadian Pharmaceutical Association (21 August 2006).

34 In IG Executive #2 interview, above note 31, the executive stated:

> Just as is now happening systematically in the US, brand companies in Canada are also using the threat to launch an authorized generic to extort deals with generic firms; i.e. they say: "if you proceed with an independent generic, we will launch an authorized generic and sell at low prices (subsidized by the continuing high priced sales under the brand label) and you will make nothing. So let's make a deal (at the expense of consumers) to avoid or delay competition and somehow share the benefits." The deals involve one or more features:

1) How Important Are Market Opportunities in the US at Explaining the Decisions of Independent Generic Firms to Enter a Particular Market?

IG firm representatives stated that market opportunities in the US do not affect their decisions to enter domestic drug markets. The reason is that they incur fixed entry costs each time they challenge a brand drug in one of their three primary markets (Canada, the US and the EU). These costs include the legal and related costs of challenging outstanding patents, and the costs of obtaining regulatory approval, the requirements of which typically vary by market. The different jurisdictions do not recognize court decisions made in other jurisdictions so that, for example, if an IG earns the right to sell a generic drug in the US that does not automatically allow it to sell in Canada. Moreover, regulations concerning the size, shape, colour, and chemical properties of both the active ingredients and binding agents vary by jurisdiction so that the costs of obtaining regulatory approval must be incurred separately for each market.

K. DISCUSSION

My analyses suggest that when AGs are among the first to enter a market, prices drop by about 12 percent. This seems plausible: the first generic is regulated to launch at a price no greater than 70 percent of the brand price and this should depress average prices paid for the drug. When AGs control between 1 and 40 percent of the generic market, the average price paid per mg of the brand drug increases slightly. It is unclear why this is the case. A brand firm contact did not believe that actual prices increase because both federal regulators (i.e., the Patented Medicine Prices Review Board) and provincial drug plans limit drug price growth. One possibility is that the brand sales that do accrue after substantial entry by IGs are for rarely used, non-gen-

---

1. Generic agrees not to proceed with its own product and to sell the authorized generic, but not until another independent generic is approved or about to be approved; and/or
2. Generic agrees not to launch its own product, but instead takes over manufacture of the product for the brand, and gets paid more for doing so than it would earn if it competed.

ericized dosage forms and strengths that carry a higher per mg price than the forms/strengths that have been genericized. Irrespective of the impact of AG market share on brand prices, however, I find that AGs are mildly pro-competitive *in drug markets that face some generic competition.*

But IG firm executives state that the threat of AG entry has decreased their incentive to challenge "marginal" drug markets. In particular the threat of AG entry has increased the threshold market size from $5 million to $10 million — the value of brand drug sales in the tenth year that it has been on the market, below which the IG firm will not attempt to enter.

IG executives also stated that AGs reduce IG earnings in markets that IGs do enter. The attendant loss of retained earnings hampers their ability to challenge brand drugs with sales well above $10 million, but which have particularly high entry costs. Finally, the IG executives claimed that brand firms have attempted to use the threat of AG entry to negotiate agreements with their IG firm to delay entry until entry by another IG firm is imminent, at which time their IG firm will launch an AG.

A comprehensive evaluation of the competitive effects of AGs would need to verify and quantify these costs and compare these to the benefits of AG competition.

APPENDIX 1

Characteristics of the Drug Markets in Which a Generic Launched between 1998–2004

Brand Drug Info			Authorized Generic (AG) Info			Independent Generic (IG) Info					Total Sales of the Drug, by Year ($M)							Drug Sales, Prior to IG Entry	
Drug	*Firm*	*Launch Date*	*AG*	*AG Launch Date*	*AG Firm*	*IG*	*First IG Launch Date*	*First IG Firm*	*AG Headstart over IG (Months)*	*No. of IGs*	*1998*	*1999*	*2000*	*2001*	*2002*	*2003*	*2004*	*12 Months Prior*	*13–24 Months Prior*
ALENDRONATE	Merck Frost Canada	1996m1	0			1	2003m5	Novopharm		2	42.021	64.025	79.440	90.891	109.292	143.824	168.461	121.269	93.853
AMCINONIDE	Stiefel	1979m1	1	2004m2	Ratiopharm	1	2003m8	Taropharma	−6	1	3.000	3.229	4.900	6.204	6.642	7.011	6.861	6.961	6.386
AMIODARONE	Wyeth Pharmaceutical	1986m5	1	2000m6	Ratiopharm	1	1999m6	Novopharm	−12	6	23.074	26.225	22.814	27.584	29.402	29.346	27.796	25.460	20.906
AMIODARONE INJ	Wyeth Pharmaceutical	1986m5	0			1	2001m1	Sandoz Canada Inc.		2	0	0	0	0.003	0.008	0.022	0.010		
BETAXOLOL	Alcon Canada	1986m7	0			1	2000m6	Sandoz Canada Inc.		1	10.678	10.378	9.633	9.003	8.159	7.396	6.403	10.050	10.517
BISOPROLOL	Biovail Pharma	2000m7	0			1	2003m8	Sandoz Canada Inc.		2	0	0	0.078	2.651	10.036	18.952	24.291	15.423	6.561
BRIMONIDINE	Allergan	1997m12	1	2002m9	Ratiopharm	1	2002m12	Pharmascience	3	1	4.065	10.669	13.905	14.628	15.356	13.178	12.173	15.323	14.572
BUTORPHANOL	Bristol Myers Squibb	1994m10	0			1	2000m10	Apotex Inc.		2	7.261	8.220	6.797	5.644	5.673	5.218	4.743	7.206	8.088
CALCITONIN (SALMON)	Sanofis Aventis	1976m8	0			1	2000m1	Novartis Pharma		3	0	0	4.295	9.637	14.268	14.781	13.330		
CARVEDILOL	GlaxoSmithKline	1996m10	0			1	2003m9	Apotex Inc.		5	6.573	10.635	13.528	17.008	20.116	22.737	21.818	21.570	19.067
CEFADROXIL	Bristol Myers Squibb	1981m1	1	2000m3	Novopharm	1	2000m4	Apotex Inc.	1	1	1.739	1.728	1.472	1.652	1.776	1.929	1.968	1.670	1.697
CEFUROXIME AXETIL	GlaxoSmithKline	1990m8	1	2001m10	Ratiopharm	1	2001m12	Apotex Inc.	2	1	30.016	32.047	32.359	28.120	19.104	16.215	14.553	28.752	33.483
CEFUROXIME AXETIL LIQUID	GlaxoSmithKline	1990m8	0			0				0	0.997	1.079	1.260	1.260	1.143	1.102	0.951		

Brand Drug Info			Authorized Generic (AG) Info			Independent Generic (IG) Info					Total Sales of the Drug, by Year ($M)							Drug Sales, Prior to IG Entry	
Drug	*Firm*	*Launch Date*	*AG*	*AG Launch Date*	*AG Firm*	*IG*	*First IG Launch Date*	*First IG Firm*	*AG Headstart over IG (Months)*	*No. of IGs*	1998	1999	2000	2001	2002	2003	2004	*12 Months Prior*	*13–24 Months Prior*
CIPROFLOXACIN	Bayer Pharma	1989m1	1	2004m2	Pharma-science	1	2004m2	Apotex Inc.	0	9	76.961	85.165	92.363	87.006	87.132	91.789	81.028	91.781	87.487
CIPROFLOXACIN LIQUID	Bayer Pharma	1989m1	0			0				0	0	0	0.144	0.296	0.298	0.305	0.344		
CITALOPRAM	Lundbeck	1999m3	1	2004m1	Pharma-science	1	2004m1	Apotex Inc.	0	8	0	7.638	50.753	97.748	141.228	191.635	196.280	191.635	141.228
CLAVULANIC ACID	GlaxoSmithKline	1984m4	1	2001m6	Ratiopharm	1	2001m6	Apotex Inc.	0	2	14.363	14.297	15.437	16.904	14.294	14.827	13.990	17.456	13.933
CLAVULANIC ACID LIQUID	GlaxoSmithKline	1984m4	1	2002m8	Ratiopharm	1	2002m4	Apotex Inc.	−4	1	5.949	5.407	5.630	6.034	5.872	5.144	4.627	5.865	6.125
CLINDAMYCIN	Pfizer	1970m3	1	2000m6	Ratiopharm	1	2000m3	Novopharm	−3	4	14.867	19.278	19.754	18.242	19.260	20.017	20.880	20.070	15.426
CLINDAMYCIN INJ	Pfizer	1970m3	0			1	2000m6	Sandoz Canada Inc.		4	0	0	0.160	0.264	0.253	0.428	0.444		
CLINDAMYCIN LIQUID	Pfizer	1970m3	0			0				0	0.473	0.473	0.470	0.484	0.599	0.646	0.622		
CLOBAZAM	Pendopharm	1991m4	1	2000m6	Ratiopharm	1	1998m9	Novopharm	−21	4	4.335	4.095	4.311	4.740	4.948	4.998	5.044	4.229	
CLOZAPINE	Novartis Pharma	1991m4	0			1	2003m5	Genpharm Pharma		2	15.455	18.293	21.558	26.323	30.915	36.175	39.976	32.525	27.858
COLISTIN	Erfa Canada Inc.	1971m4	0			1	2002m10	Sterimax Inc.		1	0	0	1.019	1.677	1.657	2.201	2.837	1.615	1.655
CYCLOSPORINE	Novartis Pharma	1984m4	1	2002m4	Sandoz Canada Inc.	0				0	0	0	0.035	0.031	0.078	0.825	1.306		
CYCLOSPORINE INJ	Novartis Pharma	1984m4	0			0				0	0	0	0.001	0.002	0.002	0.004	0.006		
CYCLOSPORINE LIQUID	Novartis Pharma	1984m4	0			1	2002m8	Apotex Inc.		1	0	0	0	0.001	0.013	0.102	0.257		0.002

Brand Drug Info			Authorized Generic (AG) Info			Independent Generic (IG) Info					Total Sales of the Drug, by Year ($M)							Drug Sales, Prior to IG Entry	
Drug	*Firm*	*Launch Date*	*AG*	*AG Launch Date*	*AG Firm*	*IG*	*First IG Launch Date*	*First IG Firm*	*AG Headstart over IG (Months)*	*No. of IGs*	*1998*	*1999*	*2000*	*2001*	*2002*	*2003*	*2004*	*12 Months Prior*	*13–24 Months Prior*
DEFEROXAMINE	Novartis Pharma	1973m1	1	2000m10	Novartis Pharma	1	2000m12	Mayne Pharma CDA	2	1	0	0	1.022	1.842	2.940	3.164	2.464	1.730	
DIVALPROEX	Abbott	1984m4	1	1999m6	Novopharm	1	1999m5	Nu–Pharm Inc.	−1	4	26.868	33.427	31.477	34.551	36.951	37.521	38.064	29.424	25.494
DOXAZOSIN	Astrazeneca	1992m3	1	2001m6	Ratiopharm	1	1999m12	Apotex Inc.	−18	5	11.655	13.825	12.816	11.673	11.386	11.190	10.807	13.726	11.441
ETIDRONIC ACID	P&G Pharma	1979m7	0			1	2003m12	Genpharm Pharma		1	4.706	2.386	1.929	1.579	1.272	1.068	0.830	1.079	1.298
FENOFIBRATE	Fournier	1991m1	0			1	1998m1	Apotex Inc.		3	0.884	0.945	0.730	0.549	0.393	0.345	0.329		
FENOFIBRATE MICRO	Fournier	1995m3	1	1999m7	Pharma-science	1	1999m6	Apotex Inc.	−1	7	60.761	62.971	59.390	56.639	46.093	40.514	36.132	62.658	58.032
FLAVOXATE	Paladin	1986m11	0			1	2002m7	Apotex Inc.		3	4.895	4.711	4.487	4.235	3.221	2.239	1.665	3.789	4.482
FLOCTAFENINE	Sanofis Aventis	1980m9	0			1	2002m7	Apotex Inc.		1	2.575	2.211	1.684	1.333	1.026	0.627	0.520	1.211	1.501
FLUCONAZOLE	Pfizer	1990m9	1	2002m8	Novopharm	1	1999m5	Apotex Inc.	−39	4	7.328	6.873	7.750	7.930	8.293	7.846	7.663	7.110	6.792
FLUCONAZOLE 150MG	Pfizer	1995m3	1	2002m8	Novopharm	1	2000m5	Apotex Inc.	−27	4	9.502	12.385	14.212	14.706	15.601	16.277	16.830	13.066	10.953
FLUCONAZOLE INJ	Pfizer	1990m9	0			1	2004m5	Omega		2	0	0	0.001	0.002	0.007	0.004	0.026	0.019	0.014
FLUCONAZOLE LIQUID	Pfizer	1990m9	0			0				0	0.358	0.628	0.599	0.435	0.505	0.521	0.532		
FLUNARIZINE	Pharmascience	1990m6	0			1	2000m6	Novopharm		2	3.469	2.935	2.637	2.533	2.363	1.831	1.563	2.590	3.448
FOSINOPRIL	Bristol Myers Squibb	1992m5	1	2004m5	Linson	1	2003m12	Novopharm	−5	1	44.463	53.352	59.049	62.182	62.575	61.748	50.649	61.847	62.368
GABAPENTIN	Pfizer	1994m5	1	2001m3	Pharma-science	1	2001m11	Apotex Inc.	8	6	12.264	22.724	40.600	60.616	66.861	80.575	95.887	58.795	36.907
GLICLAZIDE	Servier Lab	1990m10	1	1998m9	Genpharm Pharma	1	1998m9	Novopharm	0	4	13.631	14.735	15.856	16.483	16.193	16.141	16.665	13.168	

Brand Drug Info			Authorized Generic (AG) Info			Independent Generic (IG) Info					Total Sales of the Drug, by Year ($M)							Drug Sales, Prior to IG Entry	
Drug	*Firm*	*Launch Date*	*AG*	*AG Launch Date*	*AG Firm*	*IG*	*First IG Launch Date*	*First IG Firm*	*AG Headstart over IG (Months)*	*No. of IGs*	*1998*	*1999*	*2000*	*2001*	*2002*	*2003*	*2004*	*12 Months Prior*	*13–24 Months Prior*
HYDROXY-CHLOROQUINE	Sanofis Aventis	1952m1	0			1	2003m1	Apotex Inc.		2	8.474	14.367	15.595	17.110	18.549	19.045	17.718	18.549	17.11
HYDROXYUREA	Bristol Myers Squibb	1981m7	0			1	2001m6	Genpharm Pharma		2	3.946	4.528	4.734	4.872	3.954	3.679	3.549	4.941	4.504
KETOROLAC	Roche	1991m4	0			1	1998m7	Novopharm		3	14.063	13.065	11.612	11.156	11.201	10.930	10.728	14.242	
KETOROLAC INJ	Roche	1991m4	0			1	2000m6	Sandoz Canada Inc.		3	0.332	0.371	0.267	0.313	0.288	0.266	0.315	0.349	0.354
LABETALOL	Shire Canada Inc.	1983m12	0			1	2001m7	Apotex Inc.		1	2.770	3.646	4.079	4.842	5.069	4.886	4.942	4.538	3.836
LABETALOL INJ	Shire Canada Inc.	1983m12	0			1	2000m11	Sandoz Canada Inc.		1	0	0	0.002	0.002	0.003	0.002	0.003	0.005	
LAMOTRIGINE	GlaxoSmithKline	1995m2	1	2002m10	Ratiopharm	1	2002m9	Apotex Inc.	–1	3	5.578	8.115	11.129	13.771	17.239	17.721	19.503	16.029	12.776
LAMOTRIGINE CHEWABLE	GlaxoSmithKline	1995m2	0			0				0	0	0	0.022	0.051	0.074	0.105	0.103		
LEFLUNOMIDE	Sanofis Aventis	2000m4	0			1	2004m10	Apotex Inc.		1	0	0	2.240	9.840	13.982	17.921	21.211	20.814	17.050
LORATADINE	Schering Health Care	1988m6	0			1	2001m10	Apotex Inc.		1	5.423	5.324	5.036	5.368	4.895	4.391	3.921	5.289	5.056
MELOXICAM	Boeringher Ingelheim	2000m10	1	2004m2	Ratiopharm	1	2003m12	Pharma-science	–2	6	0	0	0.239	22.995	43.469	51.451	46.405	50.835	42.324
METHAZOL-AMIDE	Wyeth Pharma-ceutical	1977m1	0			1	2002m9	Apotex Inc.		1	1.722	1.613	1.263	1.135	0.645	0.236	0.247	0.941	1.184
MIDAZOLAM	Roche	1988m2	0			1	2000m6	Sandoz Canada Inc.		4	0	0	0.161	0.337	0.421	0.446	0.528		
MIRTAZAPINE	Organon	2001m5	0			1	2004m1	Pharma-science		4	0	0	0	2.412	13.846	25.024	30.201	25.024	13.846
MISOPROSTOL	Pfizer	1986m4	1	2001m12	Novopharm	1	2002m2	Apotex Inc.	2	2	15.783	13.660	10.221	7.782	5.961	3.977	3.410	7.624	10.040

Brand Drug Info			Authorized Generic (AG) Info			Independent Generic (IG) Info					Total Sales of the Drug, by Year ($M)							Drug Sales, Prior to IG Entry	
Drug	*Firm*	*Launch Date*	*AG*	*AG Launch Date*	*AG Firm*	*IG*	*First IG Launch Date*	*First IG Firm*	*AG Headstart over IG (Months)*	*No. of IGs*	*1998*	*1999*	*2000*	*2001*	*2002*	*2003*	*2004*	*12 Months Prior*	*13–24 Months Prior*
MOMETASONE	Schering Health Care	1991m1	1	2004m1	Pharma-science	1	2004m2	Ratiopharm	1	1	9.902	12.122	18.586	23.089	23.977	22.639	23.967	22.412	23.94
NABUMETONE	GlaxoSmithKline	1994m4	0			1	1999m4	Apotex Inc.		5	17.370	15.537	6.992	4.623	3.733	3.179	2.816	18.292	15.187
NEFAZODONE	Bristol Myers Squibb	1994m5	1	2001m2	Linson	1	2001m1	Apotex inc.	−1	5	28.875	35.044	35.904	30.248	19.989	12.824	0.019	35.904	35.044
NORFLOXACIN	Merck Frosst Canada	1986m7	0			1	1998m12	Apotex Inc.		5	20.386	16.246	13.998	13.602	12.951	11.748	10.745	20.395	
OMEPRAZOLE	Astrazeneca	1989m6	0			1	2004m2	Apotex Inc.		1	308.624	347.441	419.006	485.661	497.623	489.416	449.887	485.196	497.270
OXAPROZIN	Pfizer	1997m1	0			1	2001m11	Sandoz Canada Inc.		2	3.119	2.271	0.888	0.539	0.400	0.317	0.305	0.570	1.017
PAMIDRONIC ACID	Novartis Pharma	1992m5	1	2003m11	Pharma-science	1	2001m10	Mayne Pharma CDA	−25	1	0	0	1.381	1.738	2.036	2.113	2.159	1.764	2.615
PAROXETINE	GlaxoSmithKline	1993m5	1	2003m10	Ratiopharm	1	2003m10	Apotex Inc.	0	7	141.428	187.954	227.924	251.222	270.704	280.91	214.452	281.474	266.212
PIPERACILLIN	Wyeth Pharma-ceutical	1982m6	0			1	2003m5	Mayne Pharma CDA		1	0	0	0.004	0.004	0.003	0.008	0.012	0.007	0.014
PRAVASTATIN	Bristol Myers Squibb	1990m10	1	2000m7	Linson	1	2001m3	Apotex Inc.	8	9	154.869	164.267	167.505	140.784	137.448	134.226	117.134	167.598	164.787
PROPAFENONE	Abbott	1987m11	1	2001m6	Pharma-science	1	2001m4	Apotex Inc.	−2	2	13.627	15.235	15.728	16.908	15.245	11.713	9.930	16.127	15.348
PROPOFOL	Astrazeneca	1990m10	0			1	2000m6	Hospira		3	0	0	0.018	0.068	0.058	0.063	0.070		
SERTRALINE	Pfizer	1992m2	1	1999m9	Novopharm	1	1999m10	Apotex Inc.	1	9	118.018	139.604	124.800	113.005	109.288	104.978	99.962	135.730	113.587
SIMVASTATIN	Merck Frosst Canada	1990m8	0			1	2003m1	Apotex Inc.		11	182.128	200.179	211.731	242.938	335.441	331.731	285.324	335.441	242.938
SUFENTANIL	Janssen-Ortho Inc.	1985m10	0			1	2002m2	Sandoz Canada Inc.		1	0	0	0.009	0.031	0.047	0.132	0.134	0.033	0.016

Brand Drug Info			Authorized Generic (AG) Info			Independent Generic (IG) Info					Total Sales of the Drug, by Year ($M)							Drug Sales, Prior to IG Entry	
Drug	*Firm*	*Launch Date*	*AG*	*AG Launch Date*	*AG Firm*	*IG*	*First IG Launch Date*	*First IG Firm*	*AG Headstart over IG (Months)*	*No. of IGs*	*1998*	*1999*	*2000*	*2001*	*2002*	*2003*	*2004*	*12 Months Prior*	*13–24 Months Prior*
	Novartis Pharma		1	2000m4	Pharma-science	1	2000m12	Apotex Inc.	8	5	26.777	27.439	27.850	24.918	24.002	25.053	25.308	28.099	27.173
TERCONAZOLE	Janssen-Ortho Inc.	1990m12	0			1	2004m11	Taro Pharm		1	8.197	8.037	7.485	7.123	6.579	6.145	5.378	5.487	6.203
TICLOPIDINE	Roche	1991m9	0			1	1998m6	Apotex Inc.		8	26.882	21.034	14.842	11.413	9.093	7.295	5.889	26.551	
TIZANIDINE	Shire Canada Inc.	1999m11	0			1	2004m12	Apotex Inc.		1	0	0	0.635	1.208	1.747	2.234	2.613	2.574	2.206
TRIFLURIDINE	Theramed Ltd.	1984m10	0			1	2004m3	Sandoz Canada Inc.		1	0.788	0.879	0.820	0.821	0.855	0.888	0.909	0.896	0.858
TRIMEBUTINE	Axcan Pharma	1983m12	0			1	2002m12	Apotex Inc.		1	5.119	5.539	6.104	6.346	6.586	5.981	5.333	6.573	6.340
VANCOMYCIN	Lilly	1959m1	0			0				0	0	0	0.866	1.697	1.941	2.410	4.179		
VANCOMYCIN INJ	Lilly	1959m1	0			1	2000m8	Pharma Partners		3	0	0	0.149	0.233	0.336	0.616	0.782	0.134	
WARFARIN	Bristol Myers Squibb	1956m5	0			1	2000m11	Taro Pharm		3	47.216	55.335	61.880	60.847	62.113	65.131	66.736	61.550	53.652
WARFARIN INJ	Bristol Myers Squibb	1956m5	0			0				0	0	0	0.003	0.007	0.005	0.010	0.008		

APPENDIX 2

Models of Log Average Price in Markets with Generic Entry

Model 1.1

Model specification:

- All drug markets used
- Indicators of one period lagged AG generic market share
- Indicators of total number of generic drugs introduced
- Drug-market-specific indicators
- Quarter of year indicator variables dropped
- Robust standard error estimator used

Linear regression

Number of obs	=	6021
F(97, 5922)	=	.
Prob > F	=	.
R-squared	=	0.9913
Root MSE	=	0.24311

	lap	Coef.	Robust Std. Err.	t	P>t	[95% Conf. Interval]
laggshare20	−.0145032	.0134825	−1.08	0.282	−.0409338	.0119274
laggshare40	−.0586768	.0113652	−5.16	0.000	−.0809568	−.0363968
laggshare60	−.0604383	.0123816	−4.88	0.000	−.0847108	−.0361657
laggshare80	−.0479509	.014568	−3.29	0.001	−.0765094	−.0193924
laggshare100	−.1086092	.0119177	−9.11	0.000	−.1319722	−.0852462
ldtotgen1	−.1157372	.0135166	−8.56	0.000	−.14223W	−.0892398
ldtotgen2	−.1955292	. 0128613	−15.20	0.000	−.220742	−.1703164
ldtotgen3	−.2491113	.0159344	−15.63	0.000	−.2803485	−.2178741
ldtotgen4	−.2650327	.0121951	−21.73	0.000	−.2889397	−.2411258
ldtotgen5	−.3045973	.0131185	−23.22	0.000	−.3303143	−.2788804
ldtotgen6	−.2723459	.0191917	−14.19	0.000	−.3099686	−.2347233
ldtotgen7	−.3274495	.0146875	−22.29	0.000	−.3562424	−.2986566
ldtotgen8	−.3444357	.0169227	−20.35	0.000	−.3776103	−.311261
ldtotgen9	−.4054365	.0179062	−22.64	0.000	−.4405392	−.3703339
ldtotgen10	−.5595747	.014723	−38.01	0.000	−.5884372	−.5307122
ldtotgen11	−.5645092	.0149968	−37.64	0.000	−.5939084	−.5351101
drug2	3.428896	.0088876	385.81	0.000	3.411473	3.446319
drug3	−2.8618	.0104877	−272.87	0.000	−2.882359	−2.84124
drug4	1.195959	.0904644	13.22	0.000	1.018616	1.373302
drug5	4.191443	.0106382	394.00	0.000	4.170588	4.212298
drug6	−.6420946	.0084044	−76.40	0.000	−.6585702	−.625619
drug7	4.755167	.0097976	485.34	0.000	4.73596	4.774373
drug8	2.575338	.0230683	111.64	0.000	2.530116	2.620561
drug9	−2.639401	.0288492	−91.49	0.000	−2.695956	−2.582846
drug10	−.475864	.0107014	−44.47	0.000	−.4968427	−.4548853

	lap	Coef.	Robust Std. Err.	t	P>t	[95% Conf. Interval]
drug11	−4.09638	.0116516	−351.57	0.000	−4.119222	−4.073539
drug12	−3.324511	.0101459	−327.67	0.000	−3.3444	−3.304621
drug13	−4.622968	.021668	−213.35	0.000	−4.665445	−4.580491
drug14	−3.289993	.0104862	−313.74	0.000	−3.31055	−3.269437
drug15	−5.053125	.0084384	−598.82	0.000	−5.069667	−5.036582
drug16	−1.00875	.0104285	−96.73	0.000	−1.029194	−.9883065
drug17	−3.977562	.0121738	−326.73	0.000	−4.001427	−3.953697
drug18	−5.18226	.0090506	−572.59	0.000	−5.200002	−5.164517
drug19	−3.392844	.0106829	−317.60	0.000	−3.413787	−3.371902
drug20	−2.768377	.045196	−61.25	0.000	−2.856977	−2.679776
drug21	−4.541323	.0122875	−369.59	0.000	−4.56541	−4.517235
drug22	−1.417252	.0116229	−121.94	0.000	−1.440037	−1.394467
drug23	−1.513434	.010407	−145.42	0.000	−1.533835	−1.493032
drug24	.0904029	.0192183	4.70	0.000	.052728	.1280777
drug25	−1.257087	.0219797	−57.19	0.000	−1.300175	−1.213999
drug26	−1.015056	.0311714	−32.56	0.000	−1.076164	−.9539489
drug27	−1.565534	.0989576	−15.82	0.000	−1.759527	−1.371541
drug28	−1.946037	.0150807	−129.04	0.000	−1.975601	−1.916473
drug29	−4.584397	.0140168	−327.06	0.000	−4.611875	−4.556918
drug30	.5060018	.0094763	53.40	0.000	.4874248	.5245789
drug31	−3.169093	.0096308	−329.06	0.000	−3.187973	−3.150213
drug32	−3.514334	.0207674	−169.22	0.000	−3.555045	−3.473622
drug33	−2.973235	.0105299	−282.36	0.000	−2.993878	−2.952593
drug34	−4.164655	.008904	−467.73	0.000	−4.18211	−4.1472
drug35	−4.587265	.0123362	−371.86	0.000	−4.611449	−4.563082
drug36	−.790091	.0140769	−56.13	0.000	−.8176868	−.7624951
drug37	−.3180133	.0092303	−34.45	0.000	−.336108	−.2999185
drug38	1.876656	.3634283	5.16	0.000	1.164204	2.589108
drug39	−1.949321	.0287602	−67.78	0.000	−2.005702	−1.892941
drug40	−.0539281	.0161459	−3.34	0.001	−.0855798	−.0222763
drug41	−.9879428	.0095992	−102.92	0.000	−1.006761	−.9691248
drug42	−3.983419	.0098794	−403.20	0.000	−4.002786	−3.964051
drug43	−3.374512	.0116816	−288.87	0.000	−3.397412	−3.351612
drug44	−4.066363	.0085229	−477.11	0.000	−4.083071	−4.049655
drug45	−4.063714	.0133109	−305.29	0.000	−4.089808	−4.037619
drug46	−.645858	.0129643	−49.82	0.000	−.6712727	−.6204432
drug47	.2043898	.0173437	11.78	0.000	.1703898	.2383899
drug48	−4.27634	.0108578	−393.85	0.000	−4.297625	−4.255054
drug49	1.067576	.1796458	5.94	0.000	.7154051	1.419748
drug50	−2.562369	.0118583	−216.08	0.000	−2.585616	−2.539123
drug51	−1.551582	.0121523	−127.68	0.000	−1.575404	−1.527759
drug52	1.086123	.0083284	130.41	0.000	1.069796	1.102449

	lap	Coef.	Robust Std. Err.	t	P>t	[95% Conf. Interval]
drug53	−.4997754	.0099135	−50.41	0.000	−.5192095	−.4803414
drug54	−.5312374	.0124582	−42.64	0.000	−.55566	−.5068148
drug55	−2.922354	.0118087	−247.47	0.000	−2.945503	−2.899204
drug56	1.37354	.0214483	64.04	0.000	1.331493	1.415586
drug57	−1.262043	.0103086	−122.43	0.000	−1.282251	−1.241834
drug58	2.67766	.0099918	267.99	0.000	2.658072	2.697247
drug59	3.719948	.0105767	351.71	0.000	3.699214	3.740682
drug60	−4.641267	.0132655	−349.88	0.000	−4.667272	−4.615262
drug61	−3.315048	.0095249	−348.04	0.000	−3.333721	−3.296376
drug62	−3.339985	.0118625	−281.56	0.000	−3.36324	−3.316731
drug63	−.4396876	.0081908	−53.68	0.000	−.4557447	−.4236306
drug64	−4.836603	.0126927	−381.05	0.000	−4.861486	−4.811721
drug65	2.316317	.0862683	26.85	0.000	2.1472	2.485435
drug66	−.7146585	.0137181	−52.10	0.000	−.741551	−.687766
drug67	3.314119	.0727712	45.54	0.000	3.171461	3.456777
drug68	−.7801151	.0111608	−69.90	0.000	−.8019942	−.7582359
drug69	−3.564098	.0143805	−247.84	0.000	−3.592289	−3.535907
drug70	−.4325102	.0687193	−6.29	0.000	−.5672252	−.2977953
drug71	−1.866399	.0097092	−192.23	0.000	−1.885433	−1.847366
drug72	−.5040115	.0163011	−30.92	0.000	−.5359676	−.4720555
drug73	6.605436	.0276082	239.26	0.000	6.551314	6.659558
drug74	−2.419718	.0124577	−194.23	0.000	−2.44414	−2.395297
drug75	−2.084197	.009074	−229.69	0.000	−2.101985	−2.066408
drug76	−3.694298	.0146621	−251.96	0.000	−3.723041	−3.665555
drug77	.1037097	.0152011	6.82	0.000	.07391	.1335093
drug78	3.304044	.018963	174.24	0.000	3.26687	3.341219
drug79	−3.893479	.0096407	−403.86	0.000	−3.912379	−3.87458
drug80	−1.210858	.007939	−152.52	0.000	−1.226421	−1.195295
drug81	−2.370689	.1018381	−23.28	0.000	−2.570329	−2.17105
drug82	−.2474393	.0126145	−19.62	0.000	−.2721684	−.2227103
drug83	2.228096	.1489024	14.96	0.000	1.936193	2.519999
_cons	−1.604222	.0076982	−208.39	0.000	−1.619313	−1.58913

Variable Definitions	
variable name	**description**
lap	log average brand price
dag	=1 if AG on market
ldag	=1 if dag[t−1]=1
aggshare20	=1 if 0% < aggshare ≤ 20%
aggshare40	=1 if 20% < aggshare ≤ 40%
aggshare60	=1 if 40% < aggshare ≤ 60%
aggshare80	=1 if 60% < aggshare ≤ 80%
aggshare100	=1 if 80% < aggshare ≤ 100%

Variable Definitions	
variable name	**description**
laggshare20	=1 if 0% < aggshare[t−1] ≤ 20%
laggshare40	=1 if 20% < aggshare[t−1] ≤ 40%
laggshare60	=1 if 40% < aggshare[t−1] ≤ 60%
laggshare80	=1 if 60% < aggshare[t−1] ≤ 80%
laggshare100	=1 if 80% < aggshare[t−1] ≤ 100%
ldtotgen1	=1 if number of IGs[t−1] = 1
ldtotgen2	=1 if number of IGs[t−1] = 2
ldtotgen3	=1 if number of IGs[t−1] = 3
ldtotgen4	=1 if number of IGs[t−1] = 4
ldtotgen5	=1 if number of IGs[t−1] = 5
ldtotgen6	=1 if number of IGs[t−1] = 6
ldtotgen7	=1 if number of IGs[t−1] = 7
ldtotgen8	=1 if number of IGs[t−1] = 8
ldtotgen9	=1 if number of IGs[t−1] = 9
ldtotgen10	=1 if number of IGs[t−1] = 10
ldtotgen11	=1 if number of IGs[t−1] = 11
drug2	drugid=AMCINONIDE
drug3	drugid=AMIODARONE
drug4	drugid=AMIODARONE INJ
drug5	drugid=BETAXOLOL
drug6	drugid=BISOPROLOL
drug7	drugid=BRIMONIDINE
drug8	drugid=BUTORPHANOL
drug9	drugid=CALCITONIN (SALMON)
drug10	drugid=CARVEDILOL
drug11	drugid=CEFADROXIL
drug12	drugid=CEFUROXIME AXETIL
drug13	drugid=CEFUROXIME AXETIL LIQUID
drug14	drugid=CIPROFLOXACIN
drug15	drugid=CIPROFLOXACIN LIQUID
drug16	drugid=CITALOPRAM
drug17	drugid=CLAVULANIC ACID
drug18	drugid=CLAVULANIC ACID LIQUID
drug19	drugid=CLINDAMYCIN
drug20	drugid=CLINDAMYCIN INJ
drug21	drugid=CLINDAMYCIN LIQUID
drug22	drugid=CLOBAZAM
drug23	drugid=CLOZAPINE
drug24	drugid=COLISTIN
drug25	drugid=CYCLOSPORINE
drug26	drugid=CYCLOSPORINE INJ
drug27	drugid=CYCLOSPORINE LIQUID

Variable Definitions	
variable name	**description**
drug28	drugid = DEFEROXAMINE
drug29	drugid = DIVALPROEX
drug30	drugid = DOXAZOSIN
drug31	drugid = ETIDRONIC ACID
drug32	drugid = FENOFIBRATE
drug33	drugid = FENOFIBRATE MICRO
drug34	drugid = FLAVOXATE
drug35	drugid = FLOCTAFENINE
drug36	drugid = FLUCONAZOLE
drug37	drugid = FLUCONAZOLE 150MG
drug38	drugid = FLUCONAZOLE INJ
drug39	drugid = FLUCONAZOLE LIQUID
drug40	drugid = FLUNARIZINE
drug41	drugid = FOSINOPRIL
drug42	drugid = GABAPENTIN
drug43	drugid = GLICLAZIDE
drug44	drugid = HYDROXYCHLOROQUINE
drug45	drugid = HYDROXYUREA
drug46	drugid = KETOROLAC
drug47	drugid = KETOROLAC INJ
drug48	drugid = LABETALOL
drug49	drugid = LABETALOL INJ
drug50	drugid = LAMOTRIGINE
drug51	drugid = LAMOTRIGINE CHEWABLE
drug52	drugid = LEFLUNOMIDE
drug53	drugid = LORATADINE
drug54	drugid = MELOXICAM
drug55	drugid = METHAZOLAMIDE
drug56	drugid = MIDAZOLAM
drug57	drugid = MIRTAZAPINE
drug58	drugid = MISOPROSTOL
drug59	drugid = MOMETASONE
drug60	drugid = NABUMETONE
drug61	drugid = NEFAZODONE
drug62	drugid = NORFLOXACIN
drug63	drugid = OMEPRAZOLE
drug64	drugid = OXAPROZIN
drug65	drugid = PAMIDRONIC ACID
drug66	drugid = PAROXETINE
drug67	drugid = PIPERACILLIN
drug68	drugid = PRAVASTATIN
drug69	drugid = PROPAFENONE

Variable Definitions	
variable name	**description**
drug70	drugid=PROPOFOL
drug71	drugid=SERTRALINE
drug72	drugid=SIMVASTATIN
drug73	drugid=SUFENTANIL
drug74	drugid=TERBINAFINE
drug75	drugid=TERCONAZOLE
drug76	drugid=TICLOPIDINE
drug77	drugid=TIZANIDINE
drug78	drugid=TRIFLURIDINE
drug79	drugid=TRIMEBUTINE
drug80	drugid=VANCOMYCIN
drug81	drugid=VANCOMYCIN INJ
drug82	drugid=WARFARIN
drug83	drugid=WARFARIN INJ

Model 1.2

Model specification:

All drug markets used
Indicators of contemporaneous AG generic market share
Indicators of total number of generic drugs introduced
Drug-market-specific indicators
Quarter of year indicator variables dropped
Robust standard error estimator used

Linear regression

Number of obs	=	6021
F(97, 5922)	=	.
Prob > F	=	.
R-squared	=	0.9913
Root MSE	=	.24313

	lap	Coef.	Robust Std. Err.	t	P>t	[95% Conf. Interval]
aggshare20	−.0105929	.0136842	−0.77	0.439	−.0374189	.0162331
aggshare40	−.0522137	.0115961	−4.50	0.000	−.0749463	−.0294812
aggshare60	−.0542677	.0126691	−4.28	0.000	−.0791037	−.0294317
aggshare80	−.0358775	.0143117	−2.51	0.012	−.0639335	−.0078214
aggshare100	−.1090576	.0108704	−10.03	0.000	−.1303675	−.0877477
ldtotgen1	−.1177324	.0136421	−8.63	0.000	−.144476	−.0909888
ldtotgen2	−.1989836	.0129264	−15.39	0.000	−.224324	−.1736432
ldtotgen3	−.2536046	.0159592	−15.89	0.000	−.2848905	−.2223188
ldtotgen4	−.2694731	.0122699	−21.96	0.000	−.2935266	−.2454196
ldtotgen5	−.3099103	.0131406	−23.58	0.000	−.3356707	−.28415
ldtotgen6	−.2779776	.0192726	−14.42	0.000	−.315759	−.2401963

	lap	Coef.	Robust Std. Err.	t	P>t	[95% Conf. Interval]
ldtotgen7	−.3318518	.0146718	−22.62	0.000	−.3606138	−.3030898
ldtotgen8	−.3496621	.0171132	−20.43	0.000	−.3832102	−.316114
ldtotgen9	−.4077835	.0177947	−22.92	0.000	−.4426676	−.3728994
ldtotgen10	−.5605023	.0146102	−38.36	0.000	−.5891437	−.5318609
ldtotgen11	−.5654369	.014886	−37.98	0.000	−.5946189	−.5362548
drug2	3.429279	.0089652	382.51	0.000	3.411704	3.446854
drug3	−2.86251	.0104349	−274.32	0.000	−2.882966	−2.842053
drug4	1.197134	.0905085	13.23	0.000	1.019704	1.374563
drug5	4.192197	.0106819	392.46	0.000	4.171256	4.213137
drug6	−.6420058	.0083677	−76.72	0.000	−.6584095	−.625602
drug7	4.756508	.0097239	489.16	0.000	4.737445	4.77557
drug8	2.576453	.0230295	111.88	0.000	2.531307	2.621599
drug9	−2.636428	.028884	−91.28	0.000	−2.693051	−2.579805
drug10	−.4756078	.0106807	−44.53	0.000	−.4965459	−.4546697
drug11	−4.09965	.011384	−360.12	0.000	−4.121967	−4.077334
drug12	−3.326335	.010132	−328.30	0.000	−3.346198	−3.306473
drug13	−4.623513	.0216556	−213.50	0.000	−4.665966	−4.58106
drug14	−3.29026	.0105161	−312.88	0.000	−3.310875	−3.269645
drug15	−5.053669	.0084066	−601.15	0.000	−5.070149	−5.037189
drug16	−1.008959	.0104552	−96.50	0.000	−1.029455	−.988463
drug17	−3.980263	.0121731	−326.97	0.000	−4.004126	−3.956399
drug18	−5.183275	.009052	−572.61	0.000	−5.201021	−5.16553
drug19	−3.394211	.0109229	−310.74	0.000	−3.415624	−3.372799
drug20	−2.766091	.0452021	−61.19	0.000	−2.854703	−2.677478
drug21	−4.541867	.0122656	−370.29	0.000	−4.565912	−4.517822
drug22	−1.418962	.0114887	−123.51	0.000	−1.441484	−1.39644
drug23	−1.513451	.010434	−145.05	0.000	−1.533905	−1.492997
drug24	.0908014	.0192193	4.72	0.000	.0531245	.1284783
drug25	−1.255388	.0218897	−57.35	0.000	−1.2983	−1.212476
drug26	−1.015601	.0311628	−32.59	0.000	−1.076691	−.9545104
drug27	−1.564483	.0989786	−15.81	0.000	−1.758517	−1.370449
drug28	−1.945167	.0151425	−128.46	0.000	−1.974852	−1.915482
drug29	−4.586229	.0141653	−323.76	0.000	−4.613998	−4.55846
drug30	.5071197	.0094278	53.79	0.000	.4886378	.5256017
drug31	−3.169349	.0096148	−329.63	0.000	−3.188198	−3.150501
drug32	−3.512637	.0208007	−168.87	0.000	−3.553414	−3.47186
drug33	−2.974646	.0105846	−281.04	0.000	−2.995395	−2.953896
drug34	−4.16377	.0088913	−468.30	0.000	−4.1812	−4.14634
drug35	−4.587113	.0122424	−374.69	0.000	−4.611112	−4.563113
drug36	−.7892319	.0140721	−56.08	0.000	−.8168183	−.7616454
drug37	−.3177196	.009234	−34.41	0.000	−.3358216	−.2996177
drug38	1.876311	.3634578	5.16	0.000	1.163801	2.588821

	lap	Coef.	Robust Std. Err.	t	P>t	[95% Conf. Interval]
drug39	-1.949866	.0287508	-67.82	0.000	-2.006228	-1.893504
drug40	-.0537035	.0160927	-3.34	0.001	-.0852509	-.022156
drug41	-.9884011	.0096051	-102.90	0.000	-1.007231	-.9695716
drug42	-3.983983	.0099427	-400.69	0.000	-4.003474	-3.964491
drug43	-3.379436	.0115724	-292.03	0.000	-3.402122	-3.356749
drug44	-4.06628	.008486	-479.17	0.000	-4.082915	-4.049644
drug45	-4.063055	.0132263	-307.19	0.000	-4.088984	-4.037127
drug46	-.6430602	.0130039	-49.45	0.000	-.6685525	-.6175679
drug47	.2057248	.017307	11.89	0.000	.1717968	.2396529
drug48	-4.275899	.010812	-395.48	0.000	-4.297094	-4.254703
drug49	1.068229	.1796112	5.95	0.000	.7161254	1.420332
drug50	-2.562973	.0118708	-215.91	0.000	-2.586244	-2.539702
drug51	-1.552126	.0121302	-127.96	0.000	-1.575906	-1.528347
drug52	1.085651	.0083073	130.69	0.000	1.069365	1.101936
drug53	-.4994066	.0099429	-50.23	0.000	-.5188983	-.4799149
drug54	-.5318038	.012967	-41.01	0.000	-.5572239	-.5063837
drug55	-2.922249	.0117665	-248.35	0.000	-2.945316	-2.899182
drug56	1.37662	.0214047	64.31	0.000	1.334659	1.418581
drug57	-1.261782	.0103467	-121.95	0.000	-1.282066	-1.241499
drug58	2.676545	.0100342	266.74	0.000	2.656875	2.696216
drug59	3.719556	.0105187	353.61	0.000	3.698935	3.740176
drug60	-4.638484	.0133447	-347.59	0.000	-4.664645	-4.612324
drug61	-3.317023	.0096558	-343.53	0.000	-3.335951	-3.298094
drug62	-3.336692	.0118492	-281.60	0.000	-3.359921	-3.313464
drug63	-.4399919	.0081819	-53.78	0.000	-.4560314	-.4239524
drug64	-4.835942	.012752	-379.23	0.000	-4.860941	-4.810943
drug65	2.316373	.0864238	26.80	0.000	2.146951	2.485795
drug66	-.7148425	.0137109	-52.14	0.000	-.7417208	-.6879642
drug67	3.314073	.0727775	45.54	0.000	3.171403	3.456744
drug68	-.7814533	.0114489	-68.26	0.000	-.8038973	-.7590094
drug69	-3.566118	.0143731	-248.11	0.000	-3.594294	-3.537941
drug70	-.430422	.0687178	-6.26	0.000	-.565134	-.29571
drug71	-1.868536	.0096466	-193.70	0.000	-1.887446	-1.849625
drug72	-.5036286	.0161735	-31.14	0.000	-.5353345	-.4719226
drug73	6.605944	.0276234	239.14	0.000	6.551792	6.660096
drug74	-2.421016	.0123109	-196.66	0.000	-2.44515	-2.396882
drug75	-2.084717	.009048	-230.41	0.000	-2.102455	-2.06698
drug76	-3.690633	.0145974	-252.83	0.000	-3.719249	-3.662017
drug77	.103165	.0151834	6.79	0.000	.0734	.1329301
drug78	3.303716	.0189645	174.21	0.000	3.266539	3.340893
drug79	-3.893447	.009637	-404.01	0.000	-3.912339	-3.874555
drug80	-1.211402	.0079052	-153.24	0.000	-1.226899	-1.195905

	lap	Coef.	Robust Std. Err.	t	P>t	[95% Conf. Interval]
drug81	−2.367788	.1018102	−23.26	0.000	−2.567373	−2.168203
drug82	−.2457044	.0126145	−19.48	0.000	−.2704334	−.2209753
drug83	2.227551	.1489006	14.96	0.000	1.935652	2.519451
_cons	−1.603677	.0076633	−209.27	0.000	−1.6187	−1.588654

Model 1.3

Model specification:

Drug markets with apparent measurement error removed
Indicators of one period lagged AG generic market share
Indicators of total number of generic drugs introduced
Drug-market-specific indicators
Quarter of year indicator variables dropped
Robust standard error estimator used

Linear regression

Number of obs	=	4931
F(78, 4851)	=	.
Prob > F	=	.
R-squared	=	0.9984
Root MSE	=	.10427

	lap	Coef.	Robust Std. Err.	t	P>t	[95% Conf. Interval]
laggshare20	−.0250899	.012511	−2.01	0.045	−.049617	−.0005628
laggshare40	−.0687131	.0084515	−8.13	0.000	−.0852817	−.0521444
laggshare60	−.066947	.0082947	−8.07	0.000	−.0832084	−.0506856
laggshare80	−.0535387	.0109299	−4.90	0.000	−.0749661	−.0321112
laggshare100	−.1085286	.0104509	−10.38	0.000	−.129017	−.0880401
ldtotgen1	−.1154129	.0062483	−18.47	0.000	−.1276624	−.1031634
ldtotgen2	−.1998336	.007496	−26.66	0.000	−.2145291	−.1851381
ldtotgen3	−.219235	.0077548	−28.27	0.000	−.2344379	−.2040321
ldtotgen4	−.2563404	.0091505	−28.01	0.000	−.2742795	−.2384014
ldtotgen5	−.2951241	.0105049	−28.09	0.000	−.3157185	−.2745298
ldtotgen6	−.2614242	.0175769	−14.87	0.000	−.2958829	−.2269654
ldtotgen7	−.3179284	.0129441	−24.56	0.000	−.3433048	−.292552
ldtotgen8	−.3353393	.0160302	−20.92	0.000	−.3667657	−.3039129
ldtotgen9	−.3976185	.0175061	−22.71	0.000	−.4319384	−.3632986
ldtotgen10	−.5572985	.0148967	−37.41	0.000	−.5865029	−.5280942
ldtotgen11	−.5622331	.0151673	−37.07	0.000	−.5919678	−.5324983
drug2	3.429628	.0088644	386.90	0.000	3.412249	3.447006
drug3	−2.863683	.0104299	−274.56	0.000	−2.88413	−2.843235
drug4	(dropped)					
drug5	4.191028	.0091422	458.43	0.000	4.173105	4.208951
drug6	−.6422252	.0083619	−76.80	0.000	−.6586183	−.6258321

	lap	Coef.	Robust Std. Err.	t	P>t	[95% Conf. Interval]
drug7	4.75491	.0097303	488.67	0.000	4.735834	4.773986
drug8	2.576388	.0228519	112.74	0.000	2.531588	2.621188
drug9	−2.643734	.0271156	−97.50	0.000	−2.696893	−2.590575
drug10	−.4785822	.0106185	−45.07	0.000	−.4993993	−.4577651
drug11	−4.092119	.0112189	−364.75	0.000	−4.114113	−4.070125
drug12	−3.322148	.0097714	−339.99	0.000	−3.341304	−3.302991
drug13	(dropped)					
drug14	−3.290371	.0101746	−323.39	0.000	−3.310318	−3.270425
drug15	(dropped)					
drug16	−1.008902	.0101901	−99.01	0.000	−1.028879	−.9889243
drug17	−3.97426	.0118716	−334.77	0.000	−3.997534	−3.950986
drug18	(dropped)					
drug19	−3.397835	.0104677	−324.60	0.000	−3.418357	−3.377314
drug20	(dropped)					
drug21	(dropped)					
drug22	−1.419217	.0107626	−131.87	0.000	−1.440316	−1.398117
drug23	−1.513489	.0104364	−145.02	0.000	−1.533949	−1.493029
drug24	.090045	.0189407	4.75	0.000	.0529125	.1271774
drug25	−1.257338	.0212384	−59.20	0.000	−1.298975	−1.215701
drug26	(dropped)					
drug27	(dropped)					
drug28	−1.946472	.0137951	−141.10	0.000	−1.973516	−1.919427
drug29	−4.581994	.013702	−334.40	0.000	−4.608856	−4.555132
drug30	.5060398	.0093887	53.90	0.000	.4876337	.524446
drug31	−3.169344	.0095927	−330.39	0.000	−3.18815	−3.150538
drug32	(dropped)					
drug33	−2.974267	.0105455	−282.04	0.000	−2.994941	−2.953593
drug34	−4.172583	.0083274	−501.07	0.000	−4.188908	−4.156257
drug35	−4.587583	.0121986	−376.07	0.000	−4.611498	−4.563668
drug36	−.7965055	.0131938	−60.37	0.000	−.8223713	−.7706397
drug37	−.319436	.0090024	−35.48	0.000	−.3370848	−.3017873
drug38	(dropped)					
drug39	(dropped)					
drug40	−.0542577	.0159906	−3.39	0.001	−.0856065	−.0229088
drug41	−.9873014	.0093753	−105.31	0.000	−1.005681	−.9689216
drug42	−3.983799	.009486	−419.96	0.000	−4.002396	−3.965202
drug43	−3.37712	.0110202	−306.45	0.000	−3.398725	−3.355516
drug44	−4.066488	.0084677	−480.23	0.000	−4.083088	−4.049887
drug45	−4.063469	.0129194	−314.52	0.000	−4.088797	−4.038141
drug46	−.6465993	.0103117	−62.71	0.000	−.666815	−.6263837
drug47	(dropped)					
drug48	−4.276704	.010256	−417.00	0.000	−4.296811	−4.256598

	lap	Coef.	Robust Std. Err.	t	P>t	[95% Conf. Interval]
drug49	(dropped)					
drug50	−2.562644	.0118294	−216.63	0.000	−2.585835	−2.539453
drug51	(dropped)					
drug52	1.085906	.008081	134.38	0.000	1.070064	1.101749
drug53	−.5001285	.0093928	−53.25	0.000	−.5185426	−.4817144
drug54	−.5297909	.01234	−42.93	0.000	−.5539828	−.5055989
drug55	−2.922664	.0117077	−249.64	0.000	−2.945616	−2.899711
drug56	1.362701	.0206438	66.01	0.000	1.322229	1.403172
drug57	−1.261771	.0103118	−122.36	0.000	−1.281987	−1.241555
drug58	2.682531	.0091293	293.84	0.000	2.664633	2.700428
drug59	3.72053	.0104531	355.93	0.000	3.700037	3.741023
drug60	−4.656806	.0104594	−445.23	0.000	−4.677311	−4.636301
drug61	−3.314236	.0093734	−353.58	0.000	−3.332612	−3.29586
drug62	−3.345091	.0106155	−315.12	0.000	−3.365902	−3.32428
drug63	−.4399313	.0081176	−54.19	0.000	−.4558455	−.4240171
drug64	−4.835949	.0125915	−384.07	0.000	−4.860634	−4.811264
drug65	2.318381	.0863028	26.86	0.000	2.149188	2.487573
drug66	−.7155094	.0133825	−53.47	0.000	−.7417452	−.6892737
drug67	(dropped)					
drug68	−.7805302	.0108418	−71.99	0.000	−.8017849	−.7592754
drug69	−3.55916	.0140885	−252.63	0.000	−3.58678	−3.53154
drug70	(dropped)					
drug71	−1.863737	.0095944	−194.25	0.000	−1.882547	−1.844928
drug72	−.5064923	.0165345	−30.63	0.000	−.5389075	−.4740771
drug73	6.605061	.0273482	241.52	0.000	6.551446	6.658676
drug74	−2.42787	.0111934	−216.90	0.000	−2.449814	−2.405925
drug75	−2.084405	.0087793	−237.42	0.000	−2.101617	−2.067194
drug76	−3.703824	.0139771	−264.99	0.000	−3.731225	−3.676422
drug77	(dropped)					
drug78	3.303804	.01892	174.62	0.000	3.266713	3.340896
drug79	−3.893778	.0095614	−407.24	0.000	−3.912522	−3.875033
drug80	−1.211062	.0075566	−160.27	0.000	−1.225877	−1.196248
drug81	(dropped)					
drug82	−.2542743	.0120617	−21.08	0.000	−.2779208	−.2306278
drug83	(dropped)					
_cons	−1.604017	.0073033	−219.63	0.000	−1.618335	−1.589699

Model 1.4

Model specification:
Drug markets with apparent measurement error removed
Indicators of contemporaneous AG generic market share
Indicators of total number of generic drugs introduced
Drug-market-specific indicators
Quarter of year indicator variables dropped
Robust standard error estimator used
Linear regression

Number of obs	=	4931
F(78, 4851)	=	.
Prob > F	=	.
R-squared	=	0.9984
Root MSE	=	.10437

	lap	Coef.	Robust Std. Err.	t	P>t	[95% Conf. Interval]
aggshare20	−.0210724	.0127095	−1.66	0.097	−.0459887	.003844
aggshare40	−.0612468	.0086204	−7.10	0.000	−.0781468	−.0443469
aggshare60	−.0604142	.0084447	−7.15	0.000	−.0769696	−.0438588
aggshare80	−.0409022	.0104166	−3.93	0.000	−.0613234	−.020481
aggshare100	−.1086218	.0096326	−11.28	0.000	−.1275061	−.0897375
ldtotgen1	−.1174343	.0062876	−18.68	0.000	−.1297609	−.1051078
ldtotgen2	−.2039383	.0075801	−26.90	0.000	−.2187988	−.1890779
ldtotgen3	−.2242902	.007813	−28.71	0.000	−.2396071	−.2089732
ldtotgen4	−.2611748	.0092339	−28.28	0.000	−.2792775	−.2430721
ldtotgen5	−.3009351	.0105722	−28.46	0.000	−.3216613	−.2802088
ldtotgen6	−.2674645	.0177035	−15.11	0.000	−.3021714	−.2327576
ldtotgen7	−.3228255	.0129235	−24.98	0.000	−.3481614	−.2974896
ldtotgen8	−.3407293	.0162714	−20.94	0.000	−.3726285	−.30883
ldtotgen9	−.3999904	.0173976	−22.99	0.000	−.4340976	−.3658832
ldtotgen10	−.5583134	.0147698	−37.80	0.000	−.5872689	−.5293579
ldtotgen11	−.5632479	.0150426	−37.44	0.000	−.5927383	−.5337576
drug2	3.429904	.0089333	383.94	0.000	3.412391	3.447417
drug3	−2.864482	.0103778	−276.02	0.000	−2.884828	−2.844137
drug4	(dropped)					
drug5	4.191755	.0091624	457.50	0.000	4.173792	4.209717
drug6	−.6421497	.008326	−77.13	0.000	−.6584724	−.6258269
drug7	4.756092	.0096714	491.77	0.000	4.737132	4.775052
drug8	2.57767	.0228069	113.02	0.000	2.532958	2.622382
drug9	−2.640238	.027155	−97.23	0.000	−2.693474	−2.587002
drug10	−.4782689	.0105897	−45.16	0.000	−.4990296	−.4575081
drug11	−4.095683	.0109711	−373.31	0.000	−4.117191	−4.074175
drug12	−3.324103	.0097517	−340.87	0.000	−3.343221	−3.304985
drug13	(dropped)					
drug14	−3.29052	.0101979	−322.67	0.000	−3.310513	−3.270527

	lap	Coef.	Robust Std. Err.	t	P>t	[95% Conf. Interval]
drug15	(dropped)					
drug16	−1.008953	.010194	−98.98	0.000	−1.028937	−.9889679
drug17	−3.97703	.0118505	−335.60	0.000	−4.000262	−3.953797
drug18	(dropped)					
drug19	−3.399145	.0106675	−318.64	0.000	−3.420058	−3.378231
drug20	(dropped)					
drug21	(dropped)					
drug22	−1.421188	.0106625	−133.29	0.000	−1.442091	−1.400285
drug23	−1.513514	.0104698	−144.56	0.000	−1.53404	−1.492989
drug24	.0904123	.0189364	4.77	0.000	.0532884	.1275362
drug25	−1.255897	.0212387	−59.13	0.000	−1.297535	−1.21426
drug26	(dropped)					
drug27	(dropped)					
drug28	−1.945627	.013837	−140.61	0.000	−1.972753	−1.9185
drug29	−4.583867	.013799	−332.19	0.000	−4.610919	−4.556815
drug30	.5075391	.0093322	54.39	0.000	.4892438	.5258344
drug31	−3.16964	.0095762	−330.99	0.000	−3.188414	−3.150867
drug32	(dropped)					
drug33	−2.975684	.0105736	−281.43	0.000	−2.996413	−2.954956
drug34	−4.17156	.0082909	−503.15	0.000	−4.187814	−4.155307
drug35	−4.587465	.0121004	−379.12	0.000	−4.611187	−4.563743
drug36	−.7953889	.0132043	−60.24	0.000	−.8212753	−.7695025
drug37	−.3188726	.009023	−35.34	0.000	−.3365617	−.3011835
drug38	(dropped)					
drug39	(dropped)					
drug40	−.0540666	.0159335	−3.39	0.001	−.0853034	−.0228298
drug41	−.9876824	.0093619	−105.50	0.000	−1.006036	−.9693287
drug42	−3.984374	.009552	−417.12	0.000	−4.0031	−3.965648
drug43	−3.382046	.0107469	−314.70	0.000	−3.403115	−3.360978
drug44	−4.066417	.0084293	−482.41	0.000	−4.082942	−4.049891
drug45	−4.062758	.0128179	−316.96	0.000	−4.087887	−4.037629
drug46	−.6432536	.0103788	−61.98	0.000	−.6636007	−.6229064
drug47	(dropped)					
drug48	−4.276294	.010195	−419.45	0.000	−4.296281	−4.256307
drug49	(dropped)					
drug50	−2.563089	.0118475	−216.34	0.000	−2.586315	−2.539862
drug51	(dropped)					
drug52	1.085392	.0080543	134.76	0.000	1.069602	1.101182
drug53	−.4997912	.0094145	−53.09	0.000	−.5182479	−.4813346
drug54	−.5302009	.0128379	−41.30	0.000	−.555369	−.5050327
drug55	−2.922594	.0116631	−250.58	0.000	−2.945459	−2.899729
drug56	1.366066	.0205686	66.42	0.000	1.325742	1.40639

	lap	Coef.	Robust Std. Err.	t	P>t	[95% Conf. Interval]
drug57	−1.261438	.010363	−121.73	0.000	−1.281754	−1.241122
drug58	2.681419	.0091142	294.20	0.000	2.663551	2.699287
drug59	3.720116	.0103533	359.32	0.000	3.699819	3.740413
drug60	−4.65371	.0105557	−440.87	0.000	−4.674404	−4.633016
drug61	−3.316207	.0094934	−349.32	0.000	−3.334818	−3.297595
drug62	−3.34142	.0106104	−314.92	0.000	−3.362221	−3.320619
drug63	−.440276	.0081077	−54.30	0.000	−.4561708	−.4243812
drug64	−4.835184	.012664	−381.80	0.000	−4.860011	−4.810357
drug65	2.31856	.086477	26.81	0.000	2.149026	2.488094
drug66	−.7156838	.0133707	−53.53	0.000	−.7418964	−.6894712
drug67	(dropped)					
drug68	−.7819502	.0111049	−70.42	0.000	−.8037207	−.7601796
drug69	−3.561285	.0140689	−253.13	0.000	−3.588866	−3.533703
drug70	(dropped)					
drug71	−1.866035	.0095125	−196.17	0.000	−1.884684	−1.847386
drug72	−.5060657	.0163938	−30.87	0.000	−.5382051	−.4739263
drug73	6.605538	.0273584	241.44	0.000	6.551903	6.659173
drug74	−2.429198	.0110348	−220.14	0.000	−2.450831	−2.407565
drug75	−2.084969	.0087464	−238.38	0.000	−2.102116	−2.067822
drug76	−3.699753	.0139224	−265.74	0.000	−3.727047	−3.672458
drug77	(dropped)					
drug78	3.303435	.0189211	174.59	0.000	3.266341	3.340529
drug79	−3.893781	.0095568	−407.44	0.000	−3.912517	−3.875046
drug80	−1.211651	.0075129	−161.28	0.000	−1.226379	−1.196922
drug81	(dropped)					
drug82	−.2522375	.0120597	−20.92	0.000	−.27588	−.2285949
drug83	(dropped)					
_cons	−1.603429	.0072581	−220.92	0.000	−1.617658	−1.5892

Models of Log Average Brand Drug Price

Model 2.1

Model specification:

All drug markets used
Indicators of one period lagged AG generic market share
Indicators of total number of generic drugs introduced
Drug-market-specific indicators
Quarter of year indicator variables dropped
Robust standard error estimator used

Linear regression

Number of obs	=	5851
F(97, 5752)	=	.
Prob > F	=	.
R-squared	=	0.9908
Root MSE	=	.25123

	lbap	Coef.	Robust Std. Err.	t	P>t	[95% Conf. Interval]
laggshare20	.0559338	.0183238	3.05	0.002	.0200122	.0918553
laggshare40	.0030756	.0128514	0.24	0.811	−.0221179	.0282691
laggshare60	−.0297272	.012212	−2.43	0.015	−.0536674	−.005787
laggshare80	−.0250321	.0129111	−1.94	0.053	−.0503427	.0002785
laggshare100	.010653	.0084845	1.26	0.209	−.0059799	.0272858
ldtotgen1	−.0093424	.0130851	−0.71	0.475	−.0349941	.0163092
ldtotgen2	−.0049055	.0149745	−0.33	0.743	−.0342612	.0244502
ldtotgen3	.0081458	.0190863	0.43	0.670	−.0292705	.0455621
ldtotgen4	.0122816	.0138309	0.89	0.375	−.0148322	.0393954
ldtotgen5	−.0103949	.0141981	−0.73	0.464	−.0382285	.0174387
ldtotgen6	−.0090506	.016817	−0.54	0.590	−.0420183	.0239171
ldtotgen7	.0161695	.0148068	1.09	0.275	−.0128575	.0451964
ldtotgen8	−.0504284	.0183806	−2.74	0.006	−.0864613	−.0143955
ldtotgen9	−.0542209	.0195283	−2.78	0.006	−.0925037	−.0159381
ldtotgen10	−.1444078	.0142261	−10.15	0.000	−.1722964	−.1165193
ldtotgen11	−.1515666	.014272	−10.62	0.000	−.1795451	−.1235881
drug2	3.443023	.0119551	288.00	0.000	3.419587	3.46646
drug3	−2.78537	.0120313	−231.51	0.000	−2.808955	−2.761784
drug4	.8871435	.254309	3.49	0.000	.3886021	1.385685
drug5	4.177795	.0130074	321.19	0.000	4.152295	4.203294
drug6	−.5944186	.0127104	−46.77	0.000	−.6193357	−.5695014
drug7	4.772518	.0124816	382.36	0.000	4.74805	4.796987
drug8	2.787629	.0298291	93.45	0.000	2.729153	2.846105
drug9	−1.033019	.02121	−48.70	0.000	−1.074598	−.991439
drug10	−.4641923	.0135078	−34.36	0.000	−.4906726	−.437712
drug11	−4.157622	.0165985	−250.48	0.000	−4.190161	−4.125082
drug12	−3.249803	.0121041	−268.49	0.000	−3.273532	−3.226075

	lbap	Coef.	Robust Std. Err.	t	P>t	[95% Conf. Interval]
drug13	−4.594584	.0232485	−197.63	0.000	−4.64016	−4.549008
drug14	−3.281638	.0116213	−282.38	0.000	−3.30442	−3.258855
drug15	−5.02474	.0119166	−421.66	0.000	−5.048101	−5.001379
drug16	−1.010392	.0123972	−81.50	0.000	−1.034695	−.9860886
drug17	−3.976778	.0154748	−256.98	0.000	−4.007115	−3.946442
drug18	−5.1956	.0131083	−396.36	0.000	−5.221297	−5.169903
drug19	−3.430759	.0178838	−191.84	0.000	−3.465818	−3.3957
drug20	−3.427962	.0466137	−73.54	0.000	−3.519343	−3.336582
drug21	−4.512938	.0148936	−303.01	0.000	−4.542135	−4.483741
drug22	−1.403388	.0134839	−104.08	0.000	−1.429822	−1.376955
drug23	−1.50797	.0122909	−122.69	0.000	−1.532064	−1.483875
drug24	.1683544	.0203481	8.27	0.000	.1284645	.2082443
drug25	−1.053521	.0173147	−60.85	0.000	−1.087464	−1.019577
drug26	−.9866719	.0322938	−30.55	0.000	−1.04998	−.9233638
drug27	−1.175967	.0275747	−42.65	0.000	−1.230024	−1.12191
drug28	−2.000148	.0160905	−124.31	0.000	−2.031692	−1.968605
drug29	−4.55561	.0160751	−283.40	0.000	−4.587123	−4.524097
drug30	.518353	.0133062	38.96	0.000	.4922678	.5444382
drug31	−3.144337	.0125647	−250.25	0.000	−3.168969	−3.119706
drug32	−2.914179	.0340491	−85.59	0.000	−2.980928	−2.84743
drug33	−2.937712	.0126092	−232.98	0.000	−2.962431	−2.912993
drug34	−4.136542	.0127273	−325.01	0.000	−4.161492	−4.111592
drug35	−4.523372	.0129657	−348.87	0.000	−4.54879	−4.497955
drug36	−.7342836	.0175511	−41.84	0.000	−.7686903	−.6998769
drug37	−.3127318	.0130472	−23.97	0.000	−.3383091	−.2871544
drug38	2.333579	.3960594	5.89	0.000	1.557153	3.110004
drug39	−1.920937	.0299719	−64.09	0.000	−1.979693	−1.862181
drug40	−.0587803	.0199623	−2.94	0.003	−.0979139	−.0196468
drug41	−.9551508	.0121437	−78.65	0.000	−.9789571	−.9313445
drug42	−3.961661	.0125784	−314.96	0.000	−3.98632	−3.937003
drug43	−3.385661	.0133355	−253.88	0.000	−3.411804	−3.359519
drug44	−4.028366	.0115795	−347.89	0.000	−4.051066	−4.005666
drug45	−4.085842	.0186397	−219.20	0.000	−4.122383	−4.049302
drug46	−.6634102	.0175194	−37.87	0.000	−.6977548	−.6290656
drug47	.1901531	.0208251	9.13	0.000	.149328	.2309782
drug48	−4.210754	.0131806	−319.47	0.000	−4.236592	−4.184915
drug49	2.373001	.300763	7.89	0.000	1.783392	2.96261
drug50	−2.533266	.0145783	−173.77	0.000	−2.561845	−2.504687
drug51	−1.523197	.0147822	−103.04	0.000	−1.552176	−1.494219
drug52	1.1125	.0116452	95.53	0.000	1.089671	1.135329
drug53	−.5107356	.0122158	−41.81	0.000	−.5346832	−.486788
drug54	−.5167644	.0149592	−34.55	0.000	−.54609	−.4874388

	lbap	Coef.	Robust Std. Err.	t	P>t	[95% Conf. Interval]
drug55	−2.828496	.0220283	−128.40	0.000	−2.87168	−2.785312
drug56	1.526103	.0366979	41.59	0.000	1.454161	1.598044
drug57	−1.251718	.0118528	−105.61	0.000	−1.274954	−1.228482
drug58	2.71236	.013825	196.19	0.000	2.685258	2.739462
drug59	3.731453	.0126012	296.12	0.000	3.70675	3.756156
drug60	−4.701861	.0156983	−299.51	0.000	−4.732636	−4.671086
drug61	−3.291904	.0121288	−271.41	0.000	−3.315681	−3.268127
drug62	−3.304896	.0154808	−213.48	0.000	−3.335245	−3.274548
drug63	−.4201292	.0112669	−37.29	0.000	−.4422166	−.3980417
drug64	−4.851578	.0141414	−343.08	0.000	−4.879301	−4.823856
drug65	2.729626	.0946773	28.83	0.000	2.544022	2.915229
drug66	−.7026916	.0147765	−47.55	0.000	−.7316591	−.673724
drug67	3.306012	.0748868	44.15	0.000	3.159206	3.452819
drug68	−.7325962	.0125488	−58.38	0.000	−.7571965	−.7079958
drug69	−3.469357	.0156127	−222.21	0.000	−3.499964	−3.438751
drug70	−.1653174	.1174832	−1.41	0.159	−.3956287	.0649938
drug71	−1.839823	.0123729	−148.70	0.000	−1.864079	−1.815568
drug72	−.4708784	.0180187	−26.13	0.000	−.5062018	−.4355551
drug73	6.648509	.0417862	159.11	0.000	6.566592	6.730425
drug74	−2.431776	.0136561	−178.07	0.000	−2.458547	−2.405005
drug75	−2.057044	.0122784	−167.53	0.000	−2.081114	−2.032974
drug76	−3.620665	.0165256	−219.09	0.000	−3.653061	−3.588268
drug77	.1321015	.0173766	7.60	0.000	.0980367	.1661662
drug78	3.321275	.0201994	164.42	0.000	3.281677	3.360874
drug79	−3.862895	.012898	−299.49	0.000	−3.88818	−3.83761
drug80	−1.182473	.0115681	−102.22	0.000	−1.205151	−1.159796
drug81	−2.039128	.1068016	−19.09	0.000	−2.248499	−1.829757
drug82	−.2776742	.0168242	−16.50	0.000	−.3106559	−.2446924
drug83	2.25648	.1491759	15.13	0.000	1.964039	2.548921
_cons	−1.632606	.0114042	−143.16	0.000	−1.654963	−1.61025

Model 2.2

Model specification:

- All drug markets used
- Indicators of contemporaneous AG generic market share
- Indicators of total number of generic drugs introduced
- Drug-market-specific indicators
- Quarter of year indicator variables dropped
- Robust standard error estimator used

Linear regression

Number of obs	=	5851
F(97, 5752)	=	.
Prob > F	=	.
R-squared	=	0.9908
Root MSE	=	.25123

	lbap	Coef.	Robust Std. Err.	t	P>t	[95% Conf. Interval]
aggshare20	.0592315	.0183065	3.24	0.001	.0233438	.0951192
aggshare40	.0062601	.0128695	0.49	0.627	−.0189689	.0314891
aggshare60	−.0282474	.0124288	−2.27	0.023	−.0526126	−.0038822
aggshare80	−.0141399	.0129476	−1.09	0.275	−.039522	.0112422
aggshare100	.0054312	.0076125	0.71	0.476	−.0094921	.0203544
ldtotgen1	−.0100861	.0132183	−0.76	0.445	−.0359991	.0158268
ldtotgen2	−.0067755	.015004	−0.45	0.652	−.0361889	.022638
ldtotgen3	.0057101	.0190748	0.30	0.765	−.0316836	.0431038
ldtotgen4	.0088987	.0138991	0.64	0.522	−.0183487	.0361461
ldtotgen5	−.0141709	.0142154	−1.00	0.319	−.0420384	.0136966
ldtotgen6	−.0130531	.0168377	−0.78	0.438	−.0460614	.0199552
ldtotgen7	.0134816	.014795	0.91	0.362	−.0155221	.0424854
ldtotgen8	−.0550646	.0186456	−2.95	0.003	−.091617	−.0185121
ldtotgen9	−.0561901	.0193611	−2.90	0.004	−.0941452	−.0182351
ldtotgen10	−.1450488	.0141548	−10.25	0.000	−.1727976	−.1173001
ldtotgen11	−.1522076	.0142009	−10.72	0.000	−.1800468	−.1243684
drug2	3.442466	.0119284	288.59	0.000	3.419082	3.46585
drug3	−2.786113	.0119956	−232.26	0.000	−2.809629	−2.762597
drug4	.8879709	.2542008	3.49	0.000	.3896416	1.3863
drug5	4.178041	.0130015	321.35	0.000	4.152553	4.203528
drug6	−.5943994	.0126915	−46.83	0.000	−.6192796	−.5695192
drug7	4.773935	.0124452	383.60	0.000	4.749537	4.798332
drug8	2.788192	.0298577	93.38	0.000	2.72966	2.846724
drug9	−1.031263	.0211926	−48.66	0.000	−1.072809	−.9897177
drug10	−.4639415	.0134462	−34.50	0.000	−.4903011	−.4375818
drug11	−4.158651	.0165107	−251.88	0.000	−4.191018	−4.126284
drug12	−3.250154	.0120758	−269.15	0.000	−3.273827	−3.226481
drug13	−4.594822	.0232318	−197.78	0.000	−4.640365	−4.549279
drug14	−3.282542	.0116076	−282.79	0.000	−3.305298	−3.259787

	lbap	Coef.	Robust Std. Err.	t	P>t	[95% Conf. Interval]
drug15	−5.024979	.0118839	−422.84	0.000	−5.048275	−5.001682
drug16	−1.011457	.0124557	−81.20	0.000	−1.035875	−.987039
drug17	−3.978743	.0155905	−255.20	0.000	−4.009306	−3.948179
drug18	−5.196694	.0131216	−396.04	0.000	−5.222417	−5.170971
drug19	−3.430486	.0179454	−191.16	0.000	−3.465666	−3.395306
drug20	−3.426815	.046619	−73.51	0.000	−3.518205	−3.335424
drug21	−4.513176	.0148674	−303.56	0.000	−4.542322	−4.484031
drug22	−1.405081	.0134423	−104.53	0.000	−1.431433	−1.378729
drug23	−1.507983	.0122557	−123.04	0.000	−1.532009	−1.483957
drug24	.1684679	.0203503	8.28	0.000	.1285737	.2083621
drug25	−1.050998	.0171821	−61.17	0.000	−1.084682	−1.017315
drug26	−.98691	.0322818	−30.57	0.000	−1.050194	−.9236255
drug27	−1.176205	.0275606	−42.68	0.000	−1.230234	−1.122176
drug28	−1.999859	.0160892	−124.30	0.000	−2.0314	−1.968318
drug29	−4.555773	.0161725	−281.70	0.000	−4.587478	−4.524069
drug30	.5181748	.0132948	38.98	0.000	.4921119	.5442376
drug31	−3.144468	.0125315	−250.93	0.000	−3.169034	−3.119901
drug32	−2.913331	.0340726	−85.50	0.000	−2.980126	−2.846536
drug33	−2.939117	.0126288	−232.73	0.000	−2.963874	−2.91436
drug34	−4.136018	.0126961	−325.77	0.000	−4.160907	−4.111128
drug35	−4.52335	.0129248	−349.97	0.000	−4.548688	−4.498013
drug36	−.7350727	.0175793	−41.81	0.000	−.7695347	−.7006107
drug37	−.3138176	.0130839	−23.99	0.000	−.339467	−.2881682
drug38	2.333415	.3960793	5.89	0.000	1.556951	3.10988
drug39	−1.921175	.0299589	−64.13	0.000	−1.979906	−1.862444
drug40	−.0587317	.0199222	−2.95	0.003	−.0977867	−.0196766
drug41	−.9562732	.0121807	−78.51	0.000	−.9801519	−.9323944
drug42	−3.961262	.0125253	−316.26	0.000	−3.985816	−3.936707
drug43	−3.389328	.0134725	−251.57	0.000	−3.415739	−3.362917
drug44	−4.028348	.0115498	−348.78	0.000	−4.05099	−4.005706
drug45	−4.085555	.0185763	−219.93	0.000	−4.121972	−4.049138
drug46	−.6618385	.0174958	−37.83	0.000	−.6961368	−.6275402
drug47	.1908353	.0207812	9.18	0.000	.1500963	.2315742
drug48	−4.210624	.0131619	−319.91	0.000	−4.236426	−4.184822
drug49	2.373011	.3007433	7.89	0.000	1.783441	2.962581
drug50	−2.534737	.0145965	−173.65	0.000	−2.563352	−2.506123
drug51	−1.523435	.0147558	−103.24	0.000	−1.552362	−1.494508
drug52	1.112289	.011611	95.80	0.000	1.089527	1.135051
drug53	−.5106332	.0121877	−41.90	0.000	−.5345257	−.4867407
drug54	−.5183452	.0151536	−34.21	0.000	−.548052	−.4886383
drug55	−2.828498	.0220224	−128.44	0.000	−2.87167	−2.785326
drug56	1.528136	.0367543	41.58	0.000	1.456084	1.600189

	lbap	Coef.	Robust Std. Err.	t	P>t	[95% Conf. Interval]
drug57	−1.251521	.0118013	−106.05	0.000	−1.274656	−1.228386
drug58	2.711862	.0138427	195.91	0.000	2.684725	2.738999
drug59	3.731509	.0125955	296.26	0.000	3.706817	3.756201
drug60	−4.70016	.0156604	−300.13	0.000	−4.73086	−4.66946
drug61	−3.293955	.0120981	−272.27	0.000	−3.317671	−3.270238
drug62	−3.302438	.0154613	−213.59	0.000	−3.332748	−3.272128
drug63	−.4202777	.011229	−37.43	0.000	−.4422908	−.3982645
drug64	−4.851241	.0141103	−343.81	0.000	−4.878902	−4.823579
drug65	2.728047	.0945052	28.87	0.000	2.542781	2.913313
drug66	−.7030711	.014791	−47.53	0.000	−.7320671	−.6740751
drug67	3.305774	.0748816	44.15	0.000	3.158978	3.45257
drug68	−.7331843	.0125502	−58.42	0.000	−.7577875	−.7085812
drug69	−3.470705	.0155486	−223.22	0.000	−3.501186	−3.440224
drug70	−.1642891	.1175132	−1.40	0.162	−.3946592	.066081
drug71	−1.841538	.0124017	−148.49	0.000	−1.86585	−1.817226
drug72	−.4704755	.0179335	−26.23	0.000	−.5056319	−.4353191
drug73	6.648656	.0417843	159.12	0.000	6.566743	6.730569
drug74	−2.43209	.0136364	−178.35	0.000	−2.458823	−2.405358
drug75	−2.057273	.0122463	−167.99	0.000	−2.08128	−2.033266
drug76	−3.618214	.0165023	−219.26	0.000	−3.650564	−3.585863
drug77	.1318634	.0173543	7.60	0.000	.0978425	.1658842
drug78	3.321118	.020179	164.58	0.000	3.281559	3.360676
drug79	−3.862918	.0128729	−300.08	0.000	−3.888153	−3.837682
drug80	−1.182712	.0115345	−102.54	0.000	−1.205323	−1.1601
drug81	−2.037566	.1068212	−19.07	0.000	−2.246976	−1.828156
drug82	−.2766855	.0167567	−16.51	0.000	−.3095348	−.2438361
drug83	2.256242	.1491733	15.12	0.000	1.963806	2.548678
_cons	−1.632368	.01137	−143.57	0.000	−1.654658	−1.610079

Model 2.3

Model specification:

- Drug markets with apparent measurement error removed
- Indicators of one period lagged AG generic market share
- Indicators of total number of generic drugs introduced
- Drug-market-specific indicators
- Quarter of year indicator variables dropped
- Robust standard error estimator used

Linear regression

Number of obs	=	4919
F(78, 4839)	=	.
Prob > F	=	.
R-squared	=	0.9981
Root MSE	=	.11283

	lbap	Coef.	Robust Std. Err.	t	P>t	[95% Conf. Interval]
laggshare20	.0756729	.0178476	4.24	0.000	.0406835	.1106624
laggshare40	.0238561	.0102227	2.33	0.020	.003815	.0438972
laggshare60	−.0166727	.0084813	−1.97	0.049	−.0332999	−.0000456
laggshare80	−.0133237	.0093263	−1.43	0.153	−.0316074	.00496
laggshare100	.0143089	.0067084	2.13	0.033	.0011574	.0274604
ldtotgen1	−.0129131	.0064376	−2.01	0.045	−.0255336	−.0002925
ldtotgen2	−.0235389	.0082889	−2.84	0.005	−.0397889	−.007289
ldtotgen3	−.0164033	.0090347	−1.82	0.069	−.0341155	.0013089
ldtotgen4	−.0042068	.0109803	−0.38	0.702	−.0257332	.0173195
ldtotgen5	−.0295492	.0114328	−2.58	0.010	−.0519626	−.0071358
ldtotgen6	−.0289591	.0148404	−1.95	0.051	−.058053	.0001349
ldtotgen7	−.0019183	.0124794	−0.15	0.878	−.0263837	.0225471
ldtotgen8	−.0679157	.0171667	−3.96	0.000	−.1015702	−.0342611
ldtotgen9	−.0696698	.0185645	−3.75	0.000	−.1060647	−.033275
ldtotgen10	−.1486249	.0135951	−10.93	0.000	−.1752776	−.1219723
ldtotgen11	−.1557837	.0136431	−11.42	0.000	−.1825304	−.129037
drug2	3.43999	.0116159	296.15	0.000	3.417218	3.462762
drug3	−2.785868	.0116506	−239.12	0.000	−2.808709	−2.763028
drug4	(dropped)					
drug5	4.178393	.0116119	359.84	0.000	4.155628	4.201158
drug6	−.5945569	.012515	−47.51	0.000	−.619092	−.5700217
drug7	4.77054	.0121567	392.42	0.000	4.746707	4.794373
drug8	2.792774	.0298692	93.50	0.000	2.734217	2.851331
drug9	−1.014878	.0187297	−54.19	0.000	−1.051597	−.9781592
drug10	−.4621227	.0129461	−35.70	0.000	−.4875029	−.4367425
drug11	−4.166495	.0162408	−256.54	0.000	−4.198334	−4.134655
drug12	−3.255568	.0114845	−283.48	0.000	−3.278082	−3.233053
drug13	(dropped)					
drug14	−3.283397	.0111274	−295.07	0.000	−3.305212	−3.261583
drug15	(dropped)					
drug16	−1.012263	.0119551	−84.67	0.000	−1.035701	−.9888261
drug17	−3.981256	.0152976	−260.25	0.000	−4.011247	−3.951266
drug18	(dropped)					
drug19	−3.428771	.0169723	−202.02	0.000	−3.462045	−3.395498
drug20	(dropped)					
drug21	(dropped)					
drug22	−1.408704	.012745	−110.53	0.000	−1.43369	−1.383718
drug23	−1.508151	.0120366	−125.30	0.000	−1.531748	−1.484554
drug24	.1683176	.0200038	8.41	0.000	.1291012	.2075341
drug25	−1.057252	.0162659	−65.00	0.000	−1.089141	−1.025364
drug26	(dropped)					
drug27	(dropped)					

	lbap	Coef.	Robust Std. Err.	t	P>t	[95% Conf. Interval]
drug28	−1.999341	.0147253	−135.78	0.000	−2.028209	−1.970473
drug29	−4.555908	.0154598	−294.69	0.000	−4.586216	−4.5256
drug30	.5198893	.0130207	39.93	0.000	.4943627	.5454158
drug31	−3.145546	.0122775	−256.20	0.000	−3.169615	−3.121476
drug32	(dropped)					
drug33	−2.94066	.0123224	−238.64	0.000	−2.964817	−2.916502
drug34	−4.130733	.0119245	−346.41	0.000	−4.15411	−4.107356
drug35	−4.523849	.012514	−361.50	0.000	−4.548383	−4.499316
drug36	−.732393	.016593	−44.14	0.000	−.7649228	−.6998632
drug37	−.3123926	.0126404	−24.71	0.000	−.3371736	−.2876116
drug38	(dropped)					
drug39	(dropped)					
drug40	−.0591285	.0195548	−3.02	0.003	−.0974648	−.0207921
drug41	−.9580241	.0118813	−80.63	0.000	−.9813169	−.9347313
drug42	−3.96134	.0119495	−331.51	0.000	−3.984767	−3.937914
drug43	−3.384157	.0126728	−267.04	0.000	−3.409001	−3.359312
drug44	−4.028499	.0113275	−355.64	0.000	−4.050706	−4.006292
drug45	−4.083764	.017866	−228.58	0.000	−4.11879	−4.048739
drug46	−.6470645	.0146014	−44.32	0.000	−.67569	−.618439
drug47	(dropped)					
drug48	−4.210715	.0124587	−337.97	0.000	−4.235139	−4.18629
drug49	(dropped)					
drug50	−2.536578	.0144018	−176.13	0.000	−2.564812	−2.508344
drug51	(dropped)					
drug52	1.110905	.0112006	99.18	0.000	1.088947	1.132864
drug53	−.5108256	.0115239	−44.33	0.000	−.5334178	−.4882334
drug54	−.5185916	.014643	−35.42	0.000	−.5472985	−.4898847
drug55	−2.829089	.0218694	−129.36	0.000	−2.871963	−2.786215
drug56	1.538604	.036154	42.56	0.000	1.467726	1.609483
drug57	−1.249777	.0114334	−109.31	0.000	−1.272192	−1.227363
drug58	2.710737	.013002	208.49	0.000	2.685248	2.736227
drug59	3.728449	.0121478	306.92	0.000	3.704634	3.752264
drug60	−4.688074	.0126809	−369.70	0.000	−4.712934	−4.663214
drug61	−3.295076	.0118356	−278.40	0.000	−3.31828	−3.271873
drug62	−3.291243	.0139743	−235.52	0.000	−3.318639	−3.263847
drug63	−.4214237	.0109231	−38.58	0.000	−.4428379	−.4000096
drug64	−4.848445	.0137098	−353.65	0.000	−4.875322	−4.821567
drug65	2.725683	.0939921	29.00	0.000	2.541416	2.90995
drug66	−.7043099	.014367	−49.02	0.000	−.7324757	−.676144
drug67	(dropped)					
drug68	−.7346175	.0120173	−61.13	0.000	−.7581769	−.7110581
drug69	−3.473583	.0150818	−230.32	0.000	−3.50315	−3.444016

	lbap	Coef.	Robust Std. Err.	t	P>t	[95% Conf. Interval]
drug70	(dropped)					
drug71	−1.845075	.0120302	−153.37	0.000	−1.868659	−1.82149
drug72	−.4683861	.0173672	−26.97	0.000	−.5024337	−.4343384
drug73	6.648635	.0415339	160.08	0.000	6.56721	6.730061
drug74	−2.429491	.0123522	−196.68	0.000	−2.453707	−2.405275
drug75	−2.058726	.0118078	−174.35	0.000	−2.081874	−2.035577
drug76	−3.604807	.0148759	−242.32	0.000	−3.63397	−3.575643
drug77	(dropped)					
drug78	3.319938	.0200022	165.98	0.000	3.280724	3.359151
drug79	−3.863587	.012612	−306.34	0.000	−3.888312	−3.838862
drug80	−1.184198	.0110403	−107.26	0.000	−1.205842	−1.162554
drug81	(dropped)					
drug82	−.2671934	.0153518	−17.40	0.000	−.2972898	−.237097
drug83	(dropped)					
_cons	−1.630881	.0108685	−150.06	0.000	−1.652189	−1.609574

Model 2.4

Model specification:

- Drug markets with apparent measurement error removed
- Indicators of contemporaneous AG generic market share
- Indicators of total number of generic drugs introduced
- Drug-market-specific indicators
- Quarter of year indicator variables dropped
- Robust standard error estimator used

Linear regression

Number of obs	=	4919
F(78, 4839)	=	.
Prob > F	=	.
R-squared	=	0.9981
Root MSE	=	.11278

	lbap	Coef.	Robust Std. Err.	t	P>t	[95% Conf. Interval]
aggshare20	.0786967	.0178285	4.41	0.000	.0437449	.1136486
aggshare40	.0273265	.0101583	2.69	0.007	.0074117	.0472413
aggshare60	−.0151976	.0085613	−1.78	0.076	−.0319817	.0015865
aggshare80	−.0029807	.0092351	−0.32	0.747	−.0210857	.0151244
aggshare100	.0085505	.0060746	1.41	0.159	−.0033584	.0204595
ldtotgen1	−.0137173	.0064977	−2.11	0.035	−.0264558	−.0009788
ldtotgen2	−.0257415	.0083336	−3.09	0.002	−.0420791	−.0094038
ldtotgen3	−.0190002	.0090727	−2.09	0.036	−.0367868	−.0012136
ldtotgen4	−.0078155	.0110741	−0.71	0.480	−.0295258	.0138948
ldtotgen5	−.0332709	.0115262	−2.89	0.004	−.0558676	−.0106742

	lbap	Coef.	Robust Std. Err.	t	P>t	[95% Conf. Interval]
ldtotgen6	−.0326297	.0149438	−2.18	0.029	−.0619264	−.0033331
ldtotgen7	−.0045479	.0124976	−0.36	0.716	−.0290488	.019953
ldtotgen8	−.072115	.0175386	−4.11	0.000	−.1064985	−.0377314
ldtotgen9	−.071189	.0184343	−3.86	0.000	−.1073286	−.0350494
ldtotgen10	−.1492701	.0135273	−11.03	0.000	−.1757897	−.1227505
ldtotgen11	−.1564288	.0135755	−11.52	0.000	−.183043	−.1298147
drug2	3.43938	.0115862	296.85	0.000	3.416665	3.462094
drug3	−2.786948	.0116046	−240.16	0.000	−2.809699	−2.764198
drug4	(dropped)					
drug5	4.178648	.0115802	360.84	0.000	4.155945	4.201351
drug6	−.5945404	.0124973	−47.57	0.000	−.6190409	−.5700399
drug7	4.77208	.012129	393.44	0.000	4.748302	4.795859
drug8	2.793428	.0299033	93.42	0.000	2.734804	2.852052
drug9	−1.012869	.018719	−54.11	0.000	−1.049567	−.9761711
drug10	−.4618743	.0128872	−35.84	0.000	−.4871391	−.4366095
drug11	−4.167593	.016176	−257.64	0.000	−4.199305	−4.13588
drug12	−3.256039	.0114532	−284.29	0.000	−3.278492	−3.233585
drug13	(dropped)					
drug14	−3.284561	.0111003	−295.90	0.000	−3.306322	−3.262799
drug15	(dropped)					
drug16	−1.01364	.0120247	−84.30	0.000	−1.037213	−.9900656
drug17	−3.983351	.0154049	−258.58	0.000	−4.013552	−3.95315
drug18	(dropped)					
drug19	−3.428582	.016972	−202.01	0.000	−3.461855	−3.395309
drug20	(dropped)					
drug21	(dropped)					
drug22	−1.410682	.0127428	−110.70	0.000	−1.435664	−1.3857
drug23	−1.508168	.0120007	−125.67	0.000	−1.531695	−1.484641
drug24	.1684294	.0200017	8.42	0.000	.129217	.2076418
drug25	−1.054527	.0162051	−65.07	0.000	−1.086296	−1.022758
drug26	(dropped)					
drug27	(dropped)					
drug28	−1.999039	.0146987	−136.00	0.000	−2.027855	−1.970223
drug29	−4.556236	.0154942	−294.06	0.000	−4.586612	−4.525861
drug30	.5196418	.0130281	39.89	0.000	.4941008	.5451827
drug31	−3.145698	.0122416	−256.97	0.000	−3.169697	−3.121699
drug32	(dropped)					
drug33	−2.942223	.0123201	−238.81	0.000	−2.966376	−2.91807
drug34	−4.130178	.011909	−346.81	0.000	−4.153525	−4.106831
drug35	−4.523837	.0124671	−362.86	0.000	−4.548278	−4.499396
drug36	−.7332619	.016628	−44.10	0.000	−.7658604	−.7006634
drug37	−.3135471	.0126824	−24.72	0.000	−.3384102	−.2886839

	lbap	Coef.	Robust Std. Err.	t	P>t	[95% Conf. Interval]
drug38	(dropped)					
drug39	(dropped)					
drug40	−.0590867	.019509	−3.03	0.002	−.0973333	−.0208402
drug41	−.9593793	.0119244	−80.46	0.000	−.9827566	−.9360021
drug42	−3.960946	.0118898	−333.14	0.000	−3.984255	−3.937637
drug43	−3.387587	.0127182	−266.36	0.000	−3.41252	−3.362653
drug44	−4.028484	.0112973	−356.59	0.000	−4.050632	−4.006336
drug45	−4.08344	.0177896	−229.54	0.000	−4.118316	−4.048564
drug46	−.6452372	.0145906	−44.22	0.000	−.6738414	−.6166331
drug47	(dropped)					
drug48	−4.210586	.0124284	−338.79	0.000	−4.234951	−4.18622
drug49	(dropped)					
drug50	−2.53818	.0144221	−175.99	0.000	−2.566454	−2.509906
drug51	(dropped)					
drug52	1.110666	.0111598	99.52	0.000	1.088788	1.132544
drug53	−.5107257	.0114848	−44.47	0.000	−.5332412	−.4882103
drug54	−.5205542	.0148523	−35.05	0.000	−.5496713	−.491437
drug55	−2.829102	.0218629	−129.40	0.000	−2.871963	−2.786241
drug56	1.54077	.0362169	42.54	0.000	1.469768	1.611771
drug57	−1.249547	.0113895	−109.71	0.000	−1.271875	−1.227218
drug58	2.710042	.0129813	208.76	0.000	2.684593	2.735492
drug59	3.728328	.0121185	307.66	0.000	3.70457	3.752086
drug60	−4.686283	.0126601	−370.16	0.000	−4.711103	−4.661464
drug61	−3.297348	.0117804	−279.90	0.000	−3.320443	−3.274253
drug62	−3.28866	.0139798	−235.24	0.000	−3.316066	−3.261253
drug63	−.4215952	.0108812	−38.75	0.000	−.4429274	−.400263
drug64	−4.848051	.0136785	−354.43	0.000	−4.874867	−4.821235
drug65	2.723817	.0937909	29.04	0.000	2.539944	2.90769
drug66	−.7050047	.0143435	−49.15	0.000	−.7331246	−.6768849
drug67	(dropped)					
drug68	−.7354118	.0119952	−61.31	0.000	−.7589278	−.7118958
drug69	−3.475145	.0149888	−231.85	0.000	−3.50453	−3.44576
drug70	(dropped)					
drug71	−1.847103	.0120418	−153.39	0.000	−1.87071	−1.823495
drug72	−.4680093	.0172819	−27.08	0.000	−.5018896	−.434129
drug73	6.648784	.041529	160.10	0.000	6.567368	6.7302
drug74	−2.42986	.0122881	−197.74	0.000	−2.45395	−2.405769
drug75	−2.058984	.0117681	−174.96	0.000	−2.082055	−2.035913
drug76	−3.602403	.0148933	−241.88	0.000	−3.631601	−3.573206
drug77	(dropped)					
drug78	3.319756	.0199801	166.15	0.000	3.280586	3.358927
drug79	−3.863623	.0125847	−307.01	0.000	−3.888294	−3.838951

	lbap	Coef.	Robust Std. Err.	t	P>t	[95% Conf. Interval]
drug80	−1.184467	.0109976	−107.70	0.000	−1.206027	−1.162906
drug81	(dropped)					
drug82	−.2660906	.0152957	−17.40	0.000	−.2960771	−.2361041
drug83	(dropped)					
_cons	−1.630613	.0108252	−150.63	0.000	−1.651835	−1.609391

Commentary on "Effects of 'Authorized Generics' on Canadian Drug Prices"

Aidan Hollis[1]

Paul Grootendorst has written an excellent, clear study on the effects of authorized generics (AGs) in the Canadian pharmaceutical market. The study offers a few important insights. First, AGs reduce the average price paid for a drug when they enter the market before an independent generic (IG). Second, AGs have no significant impact on prices once IGs have entered. An implication of these two findings is that one need only consider the balance between the benefits of early entry by AGs and the effect on the timing of generic entry in assessing the net impact on prices. If AGs sufficiently delay generic entry, then their overall impact must be negative.

It is therefore important to understand why AGs might delay generic entry. To do this, we need to understand the process of generic entry. One of the most relevant features of the generic drug industry is the requirement to undertake patent challenges pursuant to the *Patented Medicines (Notice of Compliance) Regulations* (or the *PM(NOC) Regulations*).[2] When a generic firm claims, through a Notice of Allegation, that the remaining patents on a given brand name drug are invalid, it is likely to face very substantial litigation costs. If the generic is suc-

1 Associate Professor, Department of Economics, University of Calgary.

2 Canada, S.O.R./93-133.

cessful in its validity challenge, and there are no other patent hurdles, it can begin to compete in the drug market. Unfortunately for the litigating generic, other generic firms will also be able to enter following the same path, typically without incurring the same litigation costs.[3] Since generic firms that follow incur very low or even zero litigation costs, this appears to be a dominant strategy. So why does any generic firm bother to litigate? The reason, of course, is that the first firm to succeed in its procedures under the *PM(NOC) Regulations* may be able to enter slightly earlier than its rivals.[4] If no such advantage existed, it would not make sense for any generic firm to ever engage in patent litigation: it would always be better to wait for another firm to pay for litigation.[5]

There are, however, a couple of wrinkles. First, under the damages provisions of the *PM(NOC) Regulations*, a generic firm that challenges a patent and is kept out of the market because of a patent that is ultimately found to be invalid may be compensated for the losses created by delay. Until revision of the *PM(NOC) Regulations* in 2006, it was arguable that the potential compensation included the actual profits of the brand firm during its period of unwarranted monopoly. Following recent revisions to the regulations, damages are now limited to the generic's lost profits. The possibility of being compensated may create some incentives to challenge patents that the generic firm believes likely to be found invalid. However, no actual damages were awarded during the many years of this provision, and the first damages hearing was held in late 2007. This is therefore, at best, an extremely uncertain incentive.

Second, a generic might choose to litigate if it believed that no other firm would be willing to do so. Thus, between litigating and ob-

---

3 Following generics may use the same claims in their Notice of Allegation as the successful generic. The patentee need not even oppose later Notices of Allegation, since once one generic has entered it is unlikely to be concerned with multiple generics; in fact, by not opposing later Notices of Allegation, the patentee can "punish" the generic that was successful by enabling more generic competitors.

4 This also means that a very important feature of successful generic companies is the ability to ramp up production very quickly following a successful court decision.

5 In the United States, this advantage is constructed by law: the first generic entrant is granted a six-month exclusivity period during which it is protected from other generics.

taining a share of the generic market with no advantage, or not litigating and obtaining no share of the generic market, a firm might choose to engage in litigation. However, this is a difficult situation: it has to be the case that no other generic firms are willing to litigate, but one firm is — if two firms are willing to litigate, both should wait for the other to litigate. If one firm has a significant advantage in the market, it may be willing to be the one to invest in litigation.

If, for most markets, the costs of litigation can be avoided by follower generics, we would therefore expect little litigation. Of course, we do observe a great deal of litigation, which implies that there must be some benefit to litigating. As discussed above, much of that benefit likely derives from being the first generic to enter.

My own research,[6] as well as that of others, has shown that the order of generic entry is an important driver of long-term sales, with the first generic having a substantial advantage over the second, and the second having a smaller advantage over the third. This may be due to inertia among pharmacies and patients once a generic has established its position in pharmacies.

So how do AGs fit into all this? When a brand name firm authorizes a generic to enter first, it eliminates the IG firm's advantage from having invested in litigation. Now the benefit to the litigating IG firm is the difference between being second and third, instead of the difference between being first and second. Since the benefit of being first instead of second is larger than the benefit of being second instead of third, the benefit from challenging the patent is considerably reduced.

Will this lead to an absence of patent challenges? As we have seen, the presence of AGs has not stopped firms such as Apotex, Novopharm, Pharmascience, Cobalt, and Ranbaxy from challenging patents under the *PM(NOC) Regulations*. What is certain, however, is that the incentives to litigate are reduced because of AGs.

A question that arises is how a reduction in the incentive to challenge all patents will affect consumers. As Professor Grootendorst's study notes, it may stop generic firms from challenging patents in relatively small markets. In larger markets, the effect will be more

6 Aidan Hollis, "The Importance of Being First: Evidence from Canadian Generic Pharmaceuticals" (2002) 11 Health Economics 723.

subtle: generics will require a higher probability of success in patent challenges before deciding to litigate. To understand this point, it is important to recognize that patents are only probabilistically valid. While some patents are very strong, others may be seen to be relatively weak — that is, they are less likely to be upheld in court as valid. Given that most prescription drugs are protected by a variety of patents that expire at different times, generic firms should only make a claim of invalidity when the remaining patents are sufficiently weak. But what is "sufficiently weak"? That depends in part on what the gains from success are — the smaller the gains from a successful patent challenge, the less profitable it is on an expected basis to challenge any given patent. Therefore, if the gain from successfully challenging patents is smaller, generic firms will wait for the expiry of more patents before they challenge.

As discussed above, AGs reduce the gain from litigation and will therefore lead to delays in litigation and generic entry. Thus, for larger markets, generic firms will continue to engage in litigation, but they will do so later in the presence of AGs. Notably, the delays will not be readily observable, since the outside observer cannot identify patent strength reliably.

There are two additional effects of AGs on the timing of IG entry. In many cases, AG agreements are made with firms that would otherwise challenge patents. The AG may be the firm that would have been the first IG. AGs also reduce the equilibrium number of generic firms active in the Canadian marketplace, since they effectively transfer a large portion of the profits from the generic industry to patentees. Thus, in the long term, they have the effect of reducing the competitiveness of the generic industry, in the sense of removing firms that could otherwise compete by challenging patents.

How long are the delays likely caused by AGs? Unfortunately, that cannot be answered. An interesting perspective is given by comparing the effect of gains from early AG entry through price reductions, to the effect of losses if IG entry is delayed. According to Grootendorst's findings, average prices fall by approximately 12 percent when AGs enter in advance of IGs.

Suppose that an AG enters two months before the first IG for 50 percent of drugs. This would yield a reduction in annualized average costs to consumers of approximately 1 percent, assuming no change in the timing of the first IG.[7] Competitive generic entry following a decision of patent invalidity yields average price decreases of approximately 25 percent. Now suppose that the first IG firm is delayed on average by fifteen days because of reduced incentives caused by AGs. This yields an *increase* in annualized average costs to consumers of approximately 1 percent.[8]

Thus, if AGs cause even small delays (i.e., of more than two weeks) in the average entry date of the first IG, their effect on consumer welfare will be negative. Note that the later AGs enter — provided they enter before the first IG — the more negative their impact must be, since the effect on price reduction is less, while the effect on deterring IGs is the same.

An interesting question is whether one should treat AGs as similar to unbranded goods produced by brand manufacturers in other industries. For example, it is well known that certain appliance manufacturers produce similar products for sale under various names. Should we think of AGs in the same way? No, because there is an important difference. As discussed above, generic pharmaceutical competition in drugs is blocked by patents, and in most markets competition is only enabled by the firm that shows that the remaining patents are either invalid or not infringed by the generic equivalent. Unless generic firms are meaningfully rewarded for challenging patents under the *PM(NOC) Regulations*, they will not do so and competition will not occur. The first generic challenger not only offers competition itself, it reduces the barriers to entry for other generic competitors. This is quite unlike other markets. Thus, AGs, which have the effect of reducing the profits of challenging patents, ultimately harm competition.[9]

---

7 This is calculated as 50% × 2/12 × 12% = 1%.

8 Note that if the first IG is delayed, this will delay the entry of the AG, whose entry timing is of course dependent on the expected entry date of the first IG.

9 This argument suggests that there is no reason to object to AGs introduced following the expiry of all relevant patents, rather than after a finding of patent invalidity or non-infringement.

CHAPTER 4

Compulsory Licensing

Abraham Hollander[1]

A. INTRODUCTION

Compulsory licensing is the procedure whereby a government authority gives a public or private person permission to use subject matter covered by a patent or other intellectual property right without the consent of the parties that hold exclusive rights to those uses. The licence spells out the scope of authorized uses and the amount of royalty owed to rights holders.

A compulsory licence may be limited in time and granted on the condition that the licensee undertake a specific action. The issuance of a compulsory licence does not bar exploitation of the intellectual property by the rights holder.

Compulsory or non-voluntary licensing starts with an application by a public or private person. It is followed by a verification to establish whether the conditions that allow compulsory licensing under national patent law are met.

---

1 Professor, Department of Economics, University of Montreal, e-mail: abraham.j.hollander@umontreal.ca. My thanks to Marcel Boyer, France Chevalier, Marc Duhamel, Alan Gunderson, Randall Hofley, Michael Trebilcock, and David Vaver for their comments and suggestions.

A compulsory licence under patent law differs from a right of remuneration under copyright law. The latter entitles rights holders to compensation but gives potential users of the protected material an automatic and unconditional right to specific utilizations of the protected material. The term "statutory licence" denotes a regime that obligates rights holders to license their works to specified classes of users on terms set by governments. "Licence of right" designates a regime whereby any person with an interest in the exploitation of a patent is automatically granted a licence after the lapse of a set time period.

Courts adopt a remedy akin to compulsory licensing when they order infringing parties to compensate rights holders for lost profits as an alternative to the issue of an injunction to cease infringement. They may do so when injunctions impose too large a cost on society, or too much hardship on an infringer whose offence was minor or unintended.[2]

More often than not, compulsory licences are issued as remedies for conduct that violates specific provisions of competition law.

Compulsory licensing appeared as a policy tool early in the twentieth century.[3] At first, governments saw mandatory licensing as an alternative to the drastic sanction of forfeiture that threatened patentees who abused their rights. Because governments considered the grant of

---

2 In *City of Milwaukee v. Activated Sludge Inc.*, 69 F.2d 577 at 593 (7th Cir. 1934) [*Milwaukee*], a US court invoked its discretion to refuse the injunction of an infringing activity because doing so would have closed down a municipal sewage treatment plant: The court opined that "where the health and the lives of more than half a million people are involved, we think no risk should be taken." A recent decision by the US Supreme Court sets out a four point test to be applied when considering whether to issue a permanent injunction for infringement. *E-Bay Inc v. Mercexchange* (2006), L.L.C. (No. 05-130) 401 F.3d 1323.

3 In 1790 the US Congress tried to legislate compulsory licensing as a remedy for failure to provide adequate supply and excessive pricing. The attempt failed. Compulsory licensing became possible under German law in 1877 and entered the *Paris Convention for the Protection of Industrial Property*, 828 U.N.T.S. 305, 28 September 1979 (as amended) in 1925, art. 5(2) and 5(3) [*Paris Convention*]: Penrose cited by M. Halewood, "Regulating Patent Holders: Local Working Requirements and Compulsory Licenses at International Law" (1997) 35:2 Osgoode Hall L.J. 243–87. On the codification of compulsory licensing in German law, see T. Penrose, *The Economics of the International Patent System* (Baltimore: Johns Hopkins Press, 1951) at 76.

a patent as a means to encourage the development of industry, abuse became synonymous with the unjustified failure to work.[4]

The emergence of compulsory licensing as a remedy to non-working of patents had two unintended consequences: (i) it expanded the range of conduct regarded as abusive and therefore subject to compulsory authorizations; and (ii) it gave governments an additional tool to restrict patentees' rights in situations where there was no abuse.

Some countries permitted compulsory licensing when rights holders worked their patents but sold at "unreasonably high" prices. Others made provisions for compulsory licensing on broadly defined public interest grounds. More recently, compulsory licensing came to be viewed as a possible remedy to the blocking of exploitation of dependent patents.[5]

At the beginning of the 1990s, the patent laws of more than one hundred countries made provisions for mandatory licensing.[6] The most common justifications were non-use, emergencies and national security needs, anti-competitive practices, and the impossibility of working major dependent patents. A number of countries targeted specific industries. Some subsumed various justifications in a broad public interest criterion.

In 1923 Canada enacted special provisions for pharmaceuticals and food products. For another ten years it relied on forfeiture to penalize the failure to manufacture or license within two years of patent issue. The 1935 revision of the *Patent Act*[7] converted non-working patent into an abuse that could be remedied by compulsory licensing. Forfeiture became a remedy of last resort. The 1969 amendments of the *Patent*

---

4 Until the 1930s, Canadian law required patentees to work the patent. The latter meant initiating local manufacture, or local licensing within a two-year period of issuance of the patent. The penalty for non-compliance was forfeiture. See J. H. Reichman and C. Hasenzahl, *Non-voluntary Licensing of Patented Inventions: The Canadian Experience* (Geneva: UNCTAD/ICTSD Capacity Building Project on Intellectual Property Rights and Sustainable Development, 2002) [Reichman and Hasenzahl (2002)].

5 A patent is called dependent when it cannot be practised without infringing a pre-existing patent.

6 G. Julian-Arnold, "International Compulsory Licensing: The Rationales and the Reality" (1993) IDEA 349, gives a concise survey of these provisions.

7 1935, S.C. 1935, c. 32.

Act[8] initiated a period of aggressive compulsory licensing. The amended Act made it possible for any person to apply for a licence to *import* medicines produced with patented processes.[9] The commissioner of patents rarely refused such licence. The effect was a rapid growth in the number of licences granted.

Upon joining *NAFTA*,[10] Canada abolished its special regime for patented medicines and removed non-working from the list of conduct deemed abusive under the general regime. In order to conform to *NAFTA* and the TRIPS Agreement[11] it also amended the conditions that authorize the use of patented inventions by governments.

This paper addresses the following questions:

1) Under what circumstances should a compulsory licence be granted, keeping in mind the potential adverse effects this could have on innovation? More specifically, what should be the factors for potential application of the compulsory licence mechanism(s)? Should the list of criteria for determining whether to grant a compulsory licence be exhaustive? What criteria, if any, should be added to the existing list?
2) Should Canada adopt the American concept of the essential facility doctrine and apply it to intellectual property? Would the adoption of this approach make it clearer as to the circumstances when compulsory licensing should be considered?
3) Who should be responsible for granting a compulsory licence? Should the responsibility lie with the commissioner of patents, with competition authorities, with both, or neither? If neither, should the authority be given to specific industry regulators such as the Canadian Radio-television and Telecommunications Com-

---

8 *Patent Act Amendment Act*, 1969, S.C. 1968, c. 49.

9 Under the 1969 reforms only process and product-by-process patents were available for pharmaceutical inventions. See Reichman and Hasenzahl (2002), above note 4 at 33.

10 *North American Free Trade Agreement between the Government of Canada, the Government of Mexico and the Government of the United States*, 17 December 1992, Can. T.S. 1994 No. 2, 32 I.L.M. 289 (entered into force 1 January 1994) [*NAFTA*].

11 *Agreement on Trade-related Aspects of Intellectual Property Rights*, 15 April 1994, *Marrakesh Agreement Establishing the World Trade Organization*, Annex 1C, 1869 U.N.T.S. 299 [TRIPS Agreement].

mission? Alternatively, should this be left entirely up to private litigants and the courts?

4) Who should determine the royalty rate and how should it be done? Should it be done by the same body that determines whether or not to grant a compulsory licence? What factors should be considered when determining a royalty rate?
5) Should there be a more formalized board to assist the commissioner(s) on whether to grant or apply for a compulsory licence? If so, what should be its mandate and how should its composition be determined?
6) Of the various approaches, what are the advantages and disadvantages to each? How do they compare in terms of providing (i) an open and fair process, (ii) a timely process, and (iii) an adjudicator with the requisite expertise, including the ability to determine "fair" and "reasonable" terms for the compulsory licence?

Section B starts by examining the provisions of international treaties that constrain Canada's freedom in regard to compulsory licensing. Then, the section looks at the conditions under which licences that do not serve as remedies under competition law are granted in Canada and in the United States. It also makes a brief reference to provisions on compulsory licensing in the proposed text for a European patent law. Section C examines compulsory licensing under competition law. It looks primarily at the treatment of unilateral refusals to license, focusing on the role played by the "essential facilities" doctrine in proceedings that concern refusals of access to intellectual property. Because of a dearth of cases in Canada, the analysis looks at American and European cases. The section concludes that adoption of the doctrine would not make more clear when compulsory licensing should be considered. Section D looks at the potential effect of compulsory licensing on innovation. It concludes that, as long as orders to license are made sparingly, they will have no perceptible effect on research and development in the economy. Section E discusses the circumstances under which compulsory licences should be considered under the *Patent Act*.[12] It explains that the conditions defining abuse under section 65 of the *Patent Act* are not grounded in economic theory and offers

12 R.S.C. 1985, c. P-4 [*Patent Act*].

two alternative conditions. The determination of licensing terms, more particularly royalties, is the subject of Section F. A final section discusses the pros and cons of alternative institutional arrangements.

B. COMPULSORY LICENSING UNDER PATENT LAW

1) International Treaties

Canada's freedom to determine the conditions under which it grants compulsory licences is limited by its obligations under the *Paris Convention*, the TRIPS Agreement, and the *NAFTA*.

Under the *Paris Convention* signatories may issue compulsory licences when patentees have abused their exclusive rights. Member states are allowed to define the conduct that constitutes abuse, but the convention prohibits the grant of a licence when the patentee justifies an *a priori* abusive action or inaction by "legitimate reasons." It directs that compulsory licences be non-exclusive and non-transferable, except when the unit that exploits the licence changes ownership.[13]

The *NAFTA* and TRIPS Agreement provisions in regard to compulsory licensing are almost identical. Article 31 of the TRIPS Agreement and Article 1709 of *NAFTA* recognize national emergencies, circumstances of extreme urgency, anti-competitive practices, public non-commercial use, and dependent patents as non-limiting grounds for issuing compulsory licences.

Both TRIPS and *NAFTA* focus on the procedures and conditions that must surround the issuance of a compulsory licence. They demand that licences be considered on their individual merits. This requirement rules out the possibility of blanket authorizations for categories of technologies or enterprises. The treaties assert that licences may be issued only if attempts to obtain authorization from rights holders on reasonable terms have been unsuccessful within a reasonable period of time. Exceptions to the latter requirement are situations of national or extreme urgency, and public non-commercial use of the licence.

---

13 It also requires that the issuance of a non-voluntary licence for failure to work or insufficient working be delayed for a period of four years from the date of application for the patent, or three years from the date of the grant, whichever period expires last.

The agreements also stipulate that a compulsory licence must serve primarily to supply the home market of the licensee, except when used as a remedy to anti-competitive conduct.[14]

Under both treaties, compulsory licences must be non-exclusive and have duration and scope limited to the purpose for which they are granted.[15] The licences must be withdrawn subject to adequate protection of the legitimate interest of the licensee if the circumstances that led to their issuance cease to exist and are unlikely to recur. Licensees may not assign their rights to a third party except with the part of the enterprise or goodwill that enjoys the use for which the licence was granted.

NAFTA and the TRIPS Agreement require that adequate remuneration be paid to rights holders, taking into account the economic value of the authorization.[16] The treaties provide for a judicial review of the

---

14 In the *Doha Declaration on the TRIPS Agreement and Public Health*, 14 November 2001, WT/MIN(01)/DEC/2 [*Doha* Declaration], WTO countries acknowledged that this provision meant that countries lacking a pharmaceutical production capacity could not make effective use of the compulsory licensing option. On 30 August 2003, they adopted a decision to waive the restriction of exports for pharmaceuticals on an interim basis. The waiver was subsequently made permanent. In May 2004, Canada adopted legislation to allow generic producers to obtain compulsory licences — valid for two years and renewable once — to manufacture in Canada generic versions of a number of patented drugs, and to export them to a list of eligible countries: see R. Elliott, "Pledges and Pitfalls: Canada's Legislation on Compulsory Licensing of Pharmaceuticals for Export" (1996) 1 International Journal of Intellectual Property Management 94–112. The conditions under which manufacture and export may take place are set out in ss. 21.01 to 21.20 of the *Patent Act*. The regulations can be found in the *Canada Gazette*, online: http://canadagazette.gc.ca/partII/2005/20050601/html/sor143-e.html and http://canadagazette.gc.ca/partII/2005/20050601/html/sor141-e.html.

15 In the case of semi-conductor technology it is limited to non-commercial use or to remedy anti-competitive conduct.

16 Members are free to determine the meaning of reasonable commercial terms and adequate remuneration. UNCTAD-ICTSD Project on IPRs and Sustainable Development, *Resource Book on TRIPS and Development* (New York: Cambridge University Press, 2005) [UNCTAD (2005)] holds, at page 470, that the TRIPS Agreement's rules on compensation embody "substantial flexibility as a consequence of the use of the terms 'in the circumstances of each case', indicating that factors relating to the underlying reasons for the grant of the license may be taken into account in establishing the level of compensation.

authorizations and of all decisions relating to remuneration, by a distinct higher authority in a member country.[17]

The treaties differ from each other in regards to the licensing for reasons of patent dependency. The TRIPS Agreement provides that

> where a license is issued to permit the operation of a second patent that cannot be exploited without infringing a first patent, the invention claimed in the second patent shall involve a major advance of considerable technical significance in relation to the invention claimed in the first patent and the owner of the first patent shall be entitled to a cross-license on reasonable terms to use the invention claimed in the second patents.[18]

The use authorized in respect of the first patent is non-assignable except with the assignment of the second patent.[19]

NAFTA, by contrast, states that a signatory "shall not authorize the use of the subject matter of a patent to permit the exploitation of another patent except as a remedy for an adjudicated violation of domestic laws regarding anti-competitive practices."[20]

Granting authorities are instructed to 'take into account the economic value of the authorization' but are not required to base the royalty payable to the patent holder on that value .... The term 'adequate' generally is used to indicate something that is sufficient, or meets minimum standards, but not more than that."

17 "Although Article 31 does not eliminate the requirement of compensation for compulsory licences to remedy anticompetitive practices, neither does it suggest that this compensation may not be strictly limited to reflect governmental objectives. Article 31(k) explicitly recognizes that '(T)he need to correct anticompetitive practices may be taken into account in determining the amount of remuneration in such cases.' Specifically, royalties may be less than for other compulsory licences and the license need not be granted predominantly to supply the home market." See UNCTAD (2005), *ibid* at 476.

18 A second or dependent patent is a patent that cannot be worked without infringing one or several earlier patents.

19 TRIPS Agreement, above note 11, art. 31(1) i, ii, and iii. UNCTAD (2005) points out that the requirement that the second invention involve an important technical advance involves a subjective judgment and that a similar provision that existed under German patent law was abandoned in European patent law because it is exceedingly difficult to distinguish important from unimportant technical advances.

20 *NAFTA*, above note 10, art. 1709(10).

The TRIPS Agreement also provides for exceptions to patent protection. Article 30 states that WTO members "may provide exceptions to the exclusive rights conferred by a patent, provided that such exceptions do not unreasonably conflict with a normal exploitation of the patent and do not unreasonably prejudice the legitimate interest of the patent owner, taking into account of the legitimate interests of third parties." Article 30 does not, however, enumerate specific acts that may be exempted. In this regard, UNCTAD (2005) stresses that "TRIPS has not attempted to constrain the freedom of Members to determine the *grounds* of the possible exceptions but has established the substantive *conditions* for their admissibility."[21] Useful guidance with respect to the grounds may come from WTO caselaw and comparative and national law negotiating history (included are use of invention for research and training, commercial experimentation to test and improve, testing for seeking regulatory approval, parallel imports, rights based on prior use).[22] Exceptions under Article 30 — unlike non-voluntary licenses under Article 3 — operate automatically; that is, without the need to obtain a specific authorization.[23]

2) Canada

a) Authorizations to Governments

Under Section 19 of the *Patent Act* the commissioner of patents may, on application by the Government of Canada or a province, authorize the use of a patented invention by that government. The commissioner may not authorize the licence unless the applicant has established that efforts to obtain a voluntary licence at reasonable terms have been unsuccessful within a reasonable period.[24] This requirement is waived in

21 UNCTAD (2005), above note 16 at 432 [emphasis in original].

22 *Ibid.* at 432–33. Conditions under which awarding prior user rights is attractive from an efficiency perspective are given in C. Shapiro, "Prior User Rights" (2006) 96:2 The American Economic Review 92–96. In 2000, a WTO Panel found s. 55.2(2) of the Canadian *Patent Act*, which permits competitors to manufacture and stockpile patented medicines before expiration of the patent, was not a "limited exception" within the meaning of art. 30 of the TRIPS Agreement, above note 11.

23 See UNCTAD (2005), above note 16, cc. 22 and 23

24 Section 19.1 of the *Patent Act*, above note 12. However, in the case of semi-conductor technology, no use other than public non-commercial use may be

a situation of national or extreme urgency, or when the use for which authorization is sought is a public, non-commercial use.

Licences issued to the Canadian government have served primarily for purposes of national defence.[25] The issuance of compulsory licences to a government in Canada is not contingent on any abusive conduct by the patentee.

The uses authorized under the compulsory licence may not be exclusive or transferable and must serve primarily to supply the domestic market.[26] Their scope and duration must be limited to the purpose for which authorization is given, and the patentee must be notified of any use of the patented invention. The licence may be terminated upon application of the patentee if the commissioner is satisfied that the circumstances that led to its issuance have ceased to exist and are unlikely to recur. The authorized user must "pay to the patentee such amount as the Commissioner considers to be adequate remuneration in the circumstances, taking into account the economic value of the authorization."[27] Appeals of the commissioner's rulings are decided by the Federal Court Trial Division. They may eventually end up before the Federal Court of Appeal.[28]

The *King* decision established that compensation is to be determined as if the parties were bargaining on equal terms.[29] Specifically, that the patentee should not be allowed to use monopoly power to

---

authorized, see s. 19.1(4).

25 *The King v. Irving Air Chute C. Inc.* (1949), 10 C.P.R. 1 (S.C.C.) (patent for parachute components) [*King*]; *Canada v. Canada (Secretary of State)* (1953), 1 S.C.R. 417 (patent for improved production of aluminium); *Pathfinder Camping Products Ltd.* (1982), 65 C.P.R. (2d) 119 (Commr.) [*Pathfinder*] (patents for anchoring tent pegs); *Formea Chemical Ltd v. Polymer Cop. Ltd.* (1968), 55 C.P.R. 38 (S.C.C.) (patents for synthetic rubber).

26 In Canada, unlike the US, independent contractors who supply the government without agency status cannot obtain a licence under s. 19 of the *Patent Act*, above note 12. See J.H. Reichman and C. Hasenzahl, *Non-voluntary Licensing of Patented Inventions: Historical Perspective, Legal Framework under TRIPS, and Overview of the Practice in Canada and the USA* (Geneva: UNCTAD/ICTSD Capacity Building Project on Intellectual Property Rights and Sustainable Development, 2003) at 460.

27 *Patent Act*, *ibid.*, s. 19(4).

28 Sections 69(3) and 69(4).

29 *King*, above note 25. This decision was handed down before the latest amendment of s. 19 of the *Patent Act*.

exploit a state of public emergency, and that he cannot be expected to contribute to the emergency in a greater, relative way than any other citizen. Subsequent decisions determined that compensation must be "consistent with the maintenance of research incentives and the importance of both the substance and the process"[30] but should not be designed to approximate the licensee's total profits from using the invention.[31]

In *Re Pathfinder Camping Products Ltd.*, the commissioner refused to accept as "reasonable compensation" the terms of a non-compulsory American licence on the same product on the grounds that "the larger and more lucrative American market is not automatically an indicator of what would be normal in Canada."[32] He also determined that the amount paid on a non-exclusive licence should not be higher than on an exclusive licence.[33]

b) Authorizations in Response to Abuses of Exclusive Rights

Section 65(2) of the *Patent Act* declares the following conduct abusive: (i) the failure to meet demand for the patented article in Canada to an adequate extent and on reasonable terms; (ii) the refusal to grant a licence on reasonable terms, which causes a prejudice to a person or industry in Canada, or prejudices the establishment of a new trade in Canada, where it is in the public interest that licence be granted; (iii) the attachment of conditions to a licence by the patentee that causes a prejudice to a trade in Canada or to any person engaged therein; (iv) the utilization of a process patent using materials not protected to unfairly prejudice in Canada the manufacture, use, or sale of any materials.

In *Torpharm* the Federal Court held that section 65(2) was a deeming provision that should be read expansively rather than exhaustively. Specifically, it held that section 65(2) should not be viewed as

30 *Aktiebolaget Astra, Apotekarnes Kemiska Fabriker v. Novocol Chemical Manufacturing Co. of Canada Ltd.* (1964), 44 C.P.R. 15 (Exch. Ct.).

31 *Ibid.*

32 *Pathfinder*, above note 25.

33 A licence is said to be exclusive if the agreement with the licensee contains a commitment by the patentee not to authorize use of the licensed technology to another person. In the absence of such a commitment the licence is said to be non-exclusive.

"an exhaustive listing of the grounds of abuse which can lead to relief, including the grant of a compulsory licence."[34] The apparent implication is that the commissioner could issue a licence in a case of patent dependency although section 65 makes no explicit reference to such a situation.

The characterization of the elements that constitute abuse remains somewhat tentative. Adequate supply would seem to require that the patentee meet at least a "reasonable proportion" of demand,[35] but inadequate supply due to a sudden increase in demand is not deemed abusive.[36] Pricing that puts the patented product beyond the reach of consumers (or the great majority of consumers) may well fall within the definition of abuse.[37] Also, the acknowledgment of inability to supply by the patentee may release the commissioner from the obligation to establish inadequacy of supply.[38]

The term "trade of any person" refers to the existing trade of any person.[39] Public interest is understood to include the concerns of the purchasing public, traders, manufacturers, patentees, licensees, and inventors generally. Specifically, public interest takes account of the importance of stimulating research and innovation under a strong and predictable patent system.[40] Reichman and Hasenzahl claim that discrimination between licensees and arbitrary exclusions of potential licenses could also be abusive.[41]

In *Torpharm* the Federal Court held *in obiter* that (i) it is the ability to meet demand in Canada and not for export that counts; (ii) a demand by a local firm for an input used in the manufacture of a

---

34 *Torpham v. Commissioner of Patents and Attorney General of Canada,* 2004 F.C. 673 [*Torpham*].

35 Reichman and Hasenzahl (2002), above note 4 at 20.

36 *EC Walker & Sons Ltd.* (1953), 13 Fox Pat C. 190.

37 Reichman and Hasenzahl (2002), above note 4 at 22. Unreasonably high royalties have been found to be tantamount to a refusal to license. *International Cone Co. Ltd. v. Consolidated Wafer Co.,* [1926] 2 D.L.R. 1015 (Ex. Ct.), cited in M. Trebilcock *et al., The Law and Economics of Canadian Competition Policy* (Toronto: University of Toronto Press, 2002) at 617.

38 *Puckhandler Inc. v. BADS Industries Inc.* (1998), 81 C.P.R. (3d) 261 (Commr.).

39 *Patent* Act, above note 12 at s. 65(1).

40 *Sarco Co. Inc. v. Sarco Canada Ltd.* (1969), 2 Ex. C.R. 190.

41 See above note 4 at 22.

product destined for export is considered to be a demand in Canada;[42] (iii) to assess the reasonableness of the terms of voluntary licences the commissioner must give consideration to the submissions made by the patentee and the applicant; and (iv) neither the applicant's loss of opportunity, nor the patentee's loss of royalty income if no licence is granted, constitute abuse by themselves.[43]

A recent judgment handed down by the Federal Court elucidates the elements that constitute abuse under sections 65(2)(c) and (d).[44] It also clarifies on which issues the court will accord considerable deference to the commissioner.

This case involved an appeal by Brantford Chemicals Inc. from a decision by the commissioner refusing a compulsory licence that would have allowed the firm to produce and sell sodium enalapril-sodium iodide complex (SESIC). Brantford holds a patent on SESIC and on a method for producing sodium enalapril (SE) from it. SE is a salt used in the treatment of hypertension and congestive heart failure. The pharmaceutical giant Merck holds earlier patents on a family of compounds — including enalapril — that serves the same therapeutic purpose.

The process that led to the application for a compulsory licence was initiated by Torpharm when it sent letters to Brantford and Merck indicating a desire to acquire SESIC. Merck remarked that it did not produce SESIC and pointed out that Brantford could not produce unlicensed SESIC. Brantford responded by requesting a voluntary licence. When that request went unanswered, Brantford filed two consecutive applications for a compulsory licence. And, upon rejection of these applications Brantford appealed to the Federal Court. The court held that "in so far as patent matters are concerned, the Commissioner and his delegates undoubtedly have a high degree of specialized expertise, which is superior to that of the Court. This suggests that, to the extent that this expertise is actually engaged in relation to the specific questions in issue, these decisions should be accorded considerable deference."[45]

---

42 The court held that in regard to the test of whether Canadian demand is met, a demand for a bulk product is different from a demand for a finished product.

43 *Torpharm*, above note 34.

44 *Brantford Chemicals Inc. v. Canada (Commissioner of Patents)* (2006), [2007] 4 F.C.R. 547 (Fed. Ct.).

45 *Ibid.* at 563.

The court rejected the appellant's claim that the commissioner misinterpreted section 65(2)(c) by examining the extent to which the more general demand was met for sodium enalapril tablets rather than the demand for SESIC and SE specifically. It stressed that the appellant had not provided evidence that these products had different therapeutic attributes than Merck's enalapril product, which was available on the Canadian market. The court also held that, under section 65(2)(c), the term "demand" refers to actual demand and not "anticipated" demand. The judge opined that actual demand could not have existed at the time the application was made because SE had not been approved for sale in Canada. More importantly, the court held the demand had to originate from the public at large and not from a single trader such as Torpharm.

The court also called attention to the fact that the existence of abuse under 65(2)(d) requires the fulfillment of all three conditions listed under that section. On the facts, the court accepted the commissioner's conclusion that there had not been a refusal because the two-month period that separated the request for a voluntary licence and the application for a compulsory licence was insufficient for Merck to consider Brantford's demand.[46] Because the absence of a refusal meant that the first requirement under section 65(2)(d) was not met, the court did not have to address the other elements of abuse.[47]

3) United States

The US does not have a general statutory regime authorizing the issue of compulsory licences of patents to private persons. However, the US government enjoys broad powers to seize and use — or have its designated private agent use — patented inventions without incurring liability for infringement other than the obligation to pay "reasonable and entire compensation." Between 1948 and 2002, US courts have ruled on almost 300 cases of compulsory licensing relating to a great

---

46 *Ibid.* The court held that because this matter is a finding of fact, the commissioner is entitled to deference.

47 Specifically, the court did not speak to the commissioner's claim that the onus of suggesting terms for a voluntary licence fell on the prospective licensee, and that prejudice in an export market was irrelevant under that section.

variety of technologies.[48] Reichman (2006) notes that a royalty of 6 percent was commonly applied to such licences until 1992 and it never exceeded 10 percent.[49]

Special provisions for compulsory licensing can be found in the *Atomic Energy Act*,[50] the *Clean Air Act*,[51] and the *Plant Protection Act*.[52] These laws give the executive branch of the American government the power to issue a compulsory licence upon showing that (i) there is a public interest, or need for the patented invention; (ii) there is no substitute for the patented technology; and (iii) it is impossible to obtain a licence in another way.

Compulsory licensing is also allowed under the *Bayh-Dole Act* for technologies developed with federal funding.[53] Before 1980, inventions that sprung from federally funded research were normally not patented. Congress enacted the *Bayh-Dole Act* to address two concerns: (i) to ensure that foreign competitors of US corporations should not benefit from the sale of products based on research funded by the American taxpayer; and (ii) to avoid situations where the costly development of products based on government-funded science — in particular pharmaceuticals — is held back because copying cannot be prevented.

The *Bayh-Dole Act* allows recipients of federal research monies to patent their inventions. It conditions their right to exclude on making "available to the public on reasonable terms" the patented products resulting from that research. *Bayh-Dole* patentees may grant non-exclusive

---

48 C. Chien, "Cheap Drugs at What Price to Innovation: Does the Compulsory Licensing of Pharmaceuticals Hurt Innovation?" (2003) 18:1 Berkeley Tech. L.J. 3–57.

49 J.H. Reichman, "Compulsory Licensing of Patented Inventions: Comparing United States Law and Practice with Options under the TRIPS Agreement" (Paper presented to the AALS Mid-year Workshop on Intellectual Property, Vancouver, Canada, 14–16 June 2006), online: www.aals.org/documents/2006intprop/JeromeReichmanOutline.pdf [Reichman (2006)]. He also reports that the rate has trended upward as a result of application of *Georgia Pacific* factors. See Section E below for the list of these factors.

50 42 U.S.C. § 2011 (1954).

51 42 U.S.C. § 7411 (1990).

52 7 U.S.C. § 7701 (2000).

53 The *Bayh-Dole Act* is codified in 35 U.S.C. §§ 200–12 and implemented by 37 C.F.R. 401 [*Bayh-Dole*].

as well as exclusive licences, but the latter are limited to manufacturing in the United States unless no licensee likely to manufacture there can reasonably be found.[54] The Act allows the federal government, on its own initiative or at the request of a third party, to effectively ignore the exclusivity of a patent and grant additional licences to other "reasonable applicants." This right is referred to as a "march-in" right. It can only be exercised upon a determination that a particular criterion is met. These criteria include (i) failure by the patentees to take reasonable steps towards timely, practical application of the invention; (ii) failure to reasonably meet health and safety needs; and (iii) failure to grant licences that are "reasonable under the circumstances."[55] Reichman argues that although patentees retain the freedom to choose their marketing strategies, they contravene the *Bayh-Dole Act* when their contracts with licensees result in an undersupply of the market or a distortion of competition.[56]

US patent law refers to conduct such as proscribed attempts to extend the duration or scope of protection as "misuse."[57] Patentees guilty of misuse are deprived of the ability to enforce their exclusive rights before the courts until the misuse ended and its effects have vanished. Conceptually, the logic of patent misuse is not the same as antitrust reasoning. While antitrust is interested in effects on competition in specific markets, the patent system concerns regulation, use, and disclosure of inventions, which may occur across a number of markets.

In *Morton Salt*[58] the US Supreme Court held that patent misuse did not require a violation of the antitrust laws. Specifically it held that antitrust may provide an understanding as to why a particular con-

54 A. Miller, "Repairing the *Bayh-Dole Act*: A Proposal for Restoring Non-Profit Access to University Science" (2005), online: www.bc.edu/bc_org/avp/law/st_org/iptf/articles/content/2005093001.html [unpublished].

55 Furthermore, the federal agency that funds the patented research retains a "nonexclusive, non-transferable, irrevocable, paid-up license to practice or have practiced for or on behalf of the Unites States any subject invention," *ibid*.

56 J.H. Reichman, "Testimony before NIH Public Hearing on March-in Rights under the *Bayh-Dole Act*" (Statement of Professor Reichman, Washington, DC, USA, 25 May 2004) [Reichman (2004)].

57 A patentee could extend the scope of the patent by gaining control over products not described in the invention; she could extend the term by imposing restrictive conditions on licensees that extend beyond the life of the patent while the patent is alive.

58 *United States v. Morton Salt*, 338 U.S. 632 (1950) [*Morton Salt*].

duct is questionable, but "the foundation of a patent misuse case must rest on patent principles, not antitrust."[59] However, a subsequent decision determined that "[t]he doctrine of patent misuse is an affirmative defence to a suit for patent infringement, and requires that the alleged infringer show that the patentee has impermissibly broadened the 'physical or temporal scope' of the patent grant with anticompetitive effect . . . ."[60] The *Patent Misuse Reform Act* partly resolves the inconsistency, by stating that, unless the conduct involves tying, possession of market power by the patentee is not required to find misuse.[61]

However, in the opinion of some commentators it fails to achieve that goal. Feldman deplores that the legal opinions "begin with the mantra that patent misuse does not require a violation of the antitrust laws and then essentially proceed to apply the test for antitrust violation."[62] He argues that the analysis of patent holder behaviour to determine the existence of misuse should be determined on the basis of patent policy. One of the objectives of patent policy is to limit the amount of duplication of research that would result from the expansion of the duration and scope of protection by rights holders. This concern is not addressed by antitrust.

In a recent decision, the US Supreme Court held that a patent does not automatically confer market power, and that therefore, in cases involving a tying arrangement, market power in the tying product requires evidence of power. In doing so the Court rejected the approach of *Morton Salt*[63] — that possession of a patent created a strong presumption of market power.[64]

While misuse historically applied only to patents, it has now been espoused by courts for copyright as well. Lasercomb, a developer of a computer-aided design program, made the grant of a licence contingent on the licensees' acceptance not to develop a competing product for a

---

59 R. Feldman, "Should We Breathe Life into Patent Misuse?" (2003), online: www.law.berkeley.edu/institutes/bclt/ipsc/papers/IPSC_2003_Feldman.pdf [unpublished] [Feldman].

60 Chief Judge Markey of the Court of Appeals for the Federal Circuit in *Windsurfing International Inc. v. AMF. Inc.*, 782 F.2d 995 (Fed. Cir. 1986).

61 35 U.S.C. § 271 (2006).

62 Feldman, above note 59 at 32.

63 See above note 58.

64 *Illinois Tool Works Inc. v. Independent Ink, Inc.*, 547 U.S. 28 (2006).

period that extended beyond the period of protection granted under copyright law. This was held to be an attempt to extend the scope as well as term of protection, and for that reason constituted misuse.[65]

4) European Union

The conditions under which compulsory licences are issued are different across jurisdictions, as patent protection remains under the jurisdiction of member states.[66] The laws of Belgium, Denmark, Finland, France, Greece, Italy, the Netherlands, Spain, Sweden, and the United Kingdom make explicit provision for compulsory licensing when necessary to allow the working of a dependent patent. In Germany, a compulsory licence in case of dependency may only be granted if the use of the pre-existing (dominant) patent is necessary in the public interest.

Orders to license under patent law are rare in EU countries. Perkins and Chance[67] refer to a 1999 study that claims that not a single compulsory licences has been granted in Germany since 1950. They also indicate that licences are seldom granted in France. The French case they refer to involves a 1973 order to license given to Hoechst by the Paris Tribunal de Grande Instance. The chemical company had refused to license a patent that it did not exercise in France.[68]

Attempts to create a unitary patent regime for the EU have thus far been unsuccessful, but there exists a draft proposal of such patent law.[69] Article 21(2) of the proposal stipulates that

---

65 *Lasercomb America v. Reynold*, 911 F.2d 970 (4th Cir. 1990) [*Lasercomb*].

66 The *Convention on the Grant of European Patents*, 5 October 1973, EPO, as amended [*Munich Convention*], only sets down the procedure that must be followed to ensure that a single application provides protection in all states. However, the scope of protection in each territory is determined by national law.

67 D. Perkins and C. Chance, "Compulsory Licensing in Europe" (Paper presented to the ICC/AIPLA Joint Conference: The Future of TRIPs: Impact of the Doha Public Health Declaration, Paris, France, 13 September 2002) at 1–10, online: www.aipla.org/Content/ContentGroups/Meetings_and_Events1/International_Symposia1/perkins.pdf [Perkins and Chance (2002)].

68 The Hoechst decision is referred to in Perkins and Chance (2002), *ibid.* at 5.

69 Council of the European Union, *Proposal for a Council Regulation on the Community Patent* (2000), Inter-institutional file 2000/0177 (11 June 2003), online http://register.consilium.eu.int/pdf/en/03/st10/st10404en03.pdf.

> [O]n request, the Community Patent Court may grant a compulsory licence in respect of a first patent to the proprietor of a national or Community patent . . . who cannot use his patent (second patent) . . . without infringing a Community patent (first patent), provided that the invention . . . claimed in the second patent . . . involves an important technical advance of considerable economic significance in relation to the invention claimed in the first patent. The Community Patent Court may take any measure it regards as useful to verify the existence of such a situation. In the case of a compulsory licence in respect of a dependent patent or plant variety right, the owner of the first patent shall be entitled to a cross-licence on reasonable terms to use the patented invention or protected plant variety.[70]

The only other ground for granting compulsory licence under the proposal is lack or insufficiency of *exploitation* of the patent unless the patentee can provide legitimate reasons to justify his inaction.

C. COMPULSORY LICENSING UNDER COMPETITION LAW

Competition authorities have relied on compulsory licensing to remedy anti-competitive effects of mergers, refusals to deal or licence, and other forms of exclusionary conduct. The majority of licences have been issued in the context of consent decrees.[71] Reichman notes that in the United States "about 75 to 80 percent of all civil cases end in consent decrees." He also remarks that "a surprisingly large number of these decrees entail divestitures or compulsory licences . . . especially in cases of mergers and acquisitions."[72]

As a general rule, American and European competition law gives the owner of an asset, even a dominant firm, the freedom to exercise its own good judgment as to the parties with whom it deals.[73] In principle, competition authorities do not intervene unless the refusal

---

70 *Ibid.*

71 A consent decree is a judicial decree expressing a voluntary agreement between parties to a suit, especially an agreement by a defendant to cease activities alleged by the government to be illegal in return for an end to the charges. See definition online: http://en.wikipedia.org/wiki/Consent_decree.

72 Reichman (2006), above note 49 at 4.

73 The situation is not exactly the same in Canada. See Section C(3) below.

has an anti-competitive effect or intent. Nevertheless, American and European courts have occasionally held that a firm with monopoly control over a product or facility must make it available to a competitor when refusal to do so forecloses competition in a market. Under the so-called "essential facilities doctrine," it is primarily the supplier's status as a monopolist that creates that obligation.

The doctrine has been most controversial when invoked to justify compulsory licensing as a remedy to unilateral refusals to deal. Although repeatedly referred to by lower courts, neither the US Supreme Court nor the European Court of Justice has stated that it considers the doctrine to be established law.[74]

1) United States

The origins of the essential facilities doctrine are generally attributed to a Supreme Court decision in *United States v. Terminal Railroad Ass'n of St. Louis*.[75] A group of fourteen railroads had set up an association that took control of all bridges, tunnels, and switching yards in the St. Louis area. The association denied access to these facilities to the remaining ten railroads in the area. This effectively closed off the outside railroads from providing transportation services to St. Louis and across the Mississippi. The US government brought suit to dissolve the association as an illegal restraint of trade and an attempt to monopolize.

The Supreme Court rejected that remedy. It was receptive to the defendants' claim that consolidation of the facilities made for more efficient railroad service. On that basis, it decided not to dissolve the association provided that it agreed to admit any railroad as a member on the same terms and conditions as the initial members.

In the years that followed, US courts have repeatedly invoked the essential facilities doctrine. In some instances, control of the facility had resulted from a merger or concerted action; in others it had been built by a single firm and remained under its ownership. Orders were issued in instances where denial of access would have resulted in the

---

74 In *Verizon Communications Inc. v. Law Offices of Curtis V. Trinko, LLP*, 540 U.S. 398 (2004), the US Supreme Court stressed that its conclusions would be unchanged if the doctrine were considered established law [*Trinko*].

75 *United States v. Terminal Railroad Ass'n of St. Louis*, 224 U.S. 383 (1912).

elimination of existing competition and where it would have prevented the emergence of new competition.

Many cases examined in the literature under the essential facilities heading were decided without any reference to the doctrine. And, higher courts have failed to allude to the doctrine in instances where lower courts had invoked it.

MCI is the key decision under the doctrine. The court in *MCI* set forth four conditions for application of the essential facilities doctrine, which have since been adopted by virtually every US court.[76] They are

i. Control of the essential facility by a monopolist; [77]
ii. a competitor's inability practically or reasonably to duplicate the essential facility;[78]
iii. denial of the use of the facility to the competitor;
iv. feasibility of providing access to the facility.

In regard to the requirement that the refusal be anti-competitive there are nuances in commentators' opinions. Hovenkamp, Janis, and Lemley maintain that "while the (*MCI*) court doesn't discuss it directly, it seems important to add that withholding an essential facility is illegal only if it has the effect of foreclosing competition in the downstream market, and therefore helping the defendant to acquire or maintain a monopoly in that market."[79] Pitovsky holds that "US court opinions suggest that, while not required to establish antitrust liability under the essential facilities doctrine, liability is particularly appropriate when the denial is motivated by an anticompetitive animus — usu-

---

76 *MCI Comm. Corp. v. AT&T,* 708 F.2d 1081 (7th Cir. 1983) [*MCI*].

77 Essential is to be understood as essential for competition, in the sense that its control carries with it the power to eliminate competition. "However, this element does not go so far as to require that the restriction causes the party denied access to go out of business," R. Pitovsky, D. Patterson, and J. Hooks, "The Essential Facilities Doctrine under U.S. Antitrust Law" (2002) 70 Antitrust L.J. 450 [Pitovsky *et al.* (2002)].

78 Or obtain the benefits provided from access from other sources.

79 H. Hovenkamp, M.D. Janis, and M.A. Lemley, "Unilateral Refusals to License in the U.S." (2002) 2:1 Journal of Competition Law and Economics 20 [Hovenkamp *et al.*].

ally demonstrated by a change in existing business practices with the specific intent to harm rivals."[80]

A patentee's refusal to license is a form of refusal to deal that antitrust courts have been reluctant to challenge. The reason is that such refusal represents an exercise of rights granted by intellectual property law. Imposing a duty to deal therefore undermines the very foundation of intellectual property law.[81]

US courts have in fact ordered access to an input protected by intellectual property. However, they have done so where the input would have been essential without the protection conferred by patent or copyright law. Hovenkamp *et al.* claim to be aware of no case in which a US court stated that an intellectual property right *itself* was an essential facility that had to be licensed.[82]

In *Data General v. Grumman*, the First Circuit Court dealt with a refusal to supply copyrighted material.[83] When the defendant ceased to supply diagnostic software needed by independent service organizations and rejected their request for a licence, the organizations claimed violation of the antitrust laws. The court opined that since neither the *Sherman Act*[84] nor the *Copyright Act*[85] works as a partial repeal of the other, it had to reconcile the two. It determined that "while exclusionary conduct can include a monopolist's unilateral refusal to license a copyright, an author's desire to exclude others from use of its copyrighted work is a presumptively valid business justification for any immediate harm to consumers."[86] Specifically, the court held that copyright protection provided a rebuttable presumption of a valid business justification for the refusal to grant access. On the facts, it determined that the presumption had not been rebutted because no competitive market had existed in the period that preceded the refusal to supply.

The Ninth Circuit Court took a different stance in *Image Technical Services v. Eastman Kodak*.[87] The defendant had cut off the supply of

---

80 Pitovsky *et al.* (2002), above note 77 at 450.

81 Hovenkamp *et al.*, above note 79 at 21.

82 *Ibid.*

83 36 F.3d 1147 (1st Cir. 1994) [*Data General*].

84 15 U.S.C.A. §§ 1–7 (West 1997).

85 17 U.S.C.

86 *Data General*, above note 83 at 1187.

87 125 F.3d 1195 (9th Cir. 1997) [*Kodak*].

parts required by independent repairers of photocopiers. On remand from the Supreme Court, the judge upheld a jury finding of antitrust liability.[88] He concurred with the rebuttable presumption approach of *Data General*, while conceding he could not find a case where a court had imposed antitrust liability for a refusal to sell or license a copyright. On the facts he concluded that the presumption had been rebutted because the defendant had refrained from claiming patent and copyright infringement until the late stages of litigation.[89]

Although the facts in the subsequent *Xerox*[90] case parallel those in *Kodak*, the Federal Circuit Court adopted a radically opposed standpoint. It refused to view the defendant's denial of patented parts to independent service organizations as an antitrust violation. The judge reaffirmed a lower court's ruling that a patentee's right to exclude is within the limits of the patent monopoly for the reason that it is specifically authorized by the patent statute. More importantly, he agreed with the lower court that there was nothing in patent law to limit the exclusionary power of a patent to a particular antitrust market. Specifically, the judge claimed that the antitrust laws do not limit a patentee's right to refuse to deal or license in any market within the scope of the patent grant.[91] The judge opined that limiting the right to refuse to deal to specific markets "makes it very difficult to assess up front — when crucial investment decisions are made — how a court

88 The Supreme Court did not make specific reference to refusals to deal but noted that "power gained through some natural and legal advantage such a patent, copyright, or business acumen can give rise to liability if a seller exploits his dominant position in one market to expand his empire into the next." [504 U.S. 451 at 480 n29] cited by R. Myrick and J. Gleklen, "Antitrust Liability for the Exercise of Intellectual Property Rights under U.S. Law," online: http://74.125.95.104/search?q=cache:cd2iIqDoUMAJ:www.aippicanada.org/archives/web_documents/Vortrag_Myrick.pdf+Antitrust+Liability+for+the+Exercise+of+Intellectual+Property+Rights+Under+U.S.+Law&hl=en&ct=clnk&cd=3&gl=ca [Myrick and Gleklen (2002)].

89 He also overturned an order by a lower court that Kodak sell parts at a "reasonable" price because this would entail "utility-like" regulation that was beyond a court's function. The defendant was allowed to set monopoly prices on the patented parts and the copyrighted materials, Myrick and Gleklen (2002), *ibid.* at 19.

90 *SCM v. Xerox Corp.*, 645 F.2d 1195, 1206 (2d Cir. 1981) [*Xerox*].

91 *Ibid.*

ultimately would evaluate key business issues such as whether a firm will be able to capture the full value of the technology it is developing, whether it will be forced to share the technology with others, and what sort of arrangements it can implement in developing and marketing products based on that technology."[92] In the opinion of Hovenkamp *et al.*, this decision nearly establishes a *per se* rule of legality for refusing to license intellectual property.[93] The Federal Circuit Court also concurred with the lower court in rejecting the appropriateness of an inquiry into the subjective intent of the refusal to license, a consideration that had been determinative in *Kodak*.

Two other cases are particularly relevant to compulsory licensing as a remedy against unilateral refusals to license intellectual property. In *US v. Microsoft*, the court established that even though a refusal to sell or license copyrighted material is presumptively legal, the presumption does not extend to uses of the material that the law does not reserve for the exclusive use of the rights holder.[94] Specifically, a rights holder cannot claim immunity by merely showing that the material to which the plaintiff wants access is intellectual property; rather, he must establish that the plaintiff's intended uses of the material are infringing.

The *Trinko*[95] case revolved around the assertion that Verizon Communications had acted in violation of the *Telecommunications Act of 1996*,[96] which obligated Verizon to share its network with competitors and grant competitors access to operations support systems. The US Supreme Court held that regulation by the 1996 Act did not preclude application of the *Sherman Act*, but that such application did not entail that Verizon's obligations under the *Telecommunications Act* were enforceable under the *Sherman Act*.[97] In the Court's opinion the real issue was whether Verizon, by refusing to deal, had violated a duty under the *Sherman Act*.

In this regard the Court noted that as a general rule no such duty existed under the *Sherman Act*. It stressed that forcing a firm to share infrastructure or other source of advantage would diminish the in-

---

92 Myrick and Gleklen (2002), above note 88 at 30.

93 Hovenkamp *et al.*, above note 79.

94 *U.S. v. Microsoft*, 253 F.3d 34 at 63 (D.C. Cir. 2001).

95 Above note 74.

96 Pub. Law No. 104-104, § 652, 110 Stat. 56 (1996).

97 *Trinko*, above note 74.

centive of the monopolist and of its competitors to invest in valuable facilities. The Court further argued that

> [T]he mere possession of monopoly power and the concomitant charging of monopoly prices, is not only not unlawful; it is an important element of the free-market system. The opportunity to charge monopoly prices — at least for the short term — is what attracts "business acumen" in the first place; it induces risk-taking that produces innovations and economic growth. To safeguard the incentive to innovate, the possession of monopoly power will not be found unlawful unless it is accompanied by an element of anticompetitive conduct.[98]

This emphasis on innovation certainly suggests that in the US one's freedom not to share an asset with competitors applies with much greater force to intellectual property than to physical property.[99]

The Supreme Court further expressed its lack of enthusiasm in relation to compulsory licensing, stating that "enforced sharing also requires antitrust courts to act as central planners, identifying the proper price, quantity, and other terms of dealing — a role for which they are ill-suited."[100]

2) European Union

The list of conduct that Article 82 of the *Treaty of Rome* terms abusive does not cover unilateral refusals to deal.[101] Nevertheless, the European Commission (EC) holds that a unilateral refusal to deal can violate Article 82 when it involves the denial of access to an essential facility.

---

98 *Ibid.* at 407.

99 The Supreme Court also remarked that a refusal to continue a profitable existing relationship "may have evidentiary significance" because a firm that forgoes a profitable transaction must be doing so in the expectation of higher profits after eviction of a competitor, *ibid.*

100 *Ibid.* at 408. The Court held that *Trinko* was distinguishable from *Aspen Skiing Co. v. Aspen Highlands Skiing Co.*, 472 U.S. 585, where the defendant was ordered to grant access because in the latter case the defendant had turned down a request to sell at retail prices to a competitor while selling to others. By doing so it gave up short-run profits, which pointed to anti-competitive intent.

101 *Treaty Establishing the European Community*, as amended, 25 March 1957, 298 U.N.T.S. 11, online: www.hri.org/docs/Rome57 [*Treaty of Rome*].

The EC's first reference to an essential facility is the *Commercial Solvents* decision,[102] which was clarified in subsequent decisions. In *B & I Line Plc v. Sealink Harbours Ltd. and Sealink Stena Ltd.* the EC affirmed that

> a dominant undertaking which both owns or controls, and itself uses an essential facility, i.e. a facility or infrastructure without access to which competitors cannot provide services to their customers, and which refuses its competitors access to that facility or grants access to competitors only on terms less favourable than those which it gives its own services, thereby placing the competitors at a competitive disadvantage, infringes Article 86 [now 82], if the other conditions of that Article are met . . . . Specifically, where . . . the competitor is already subject to a certain level of disruption from the dominant undertaking's activities, there is a duty on the dominant undertaking not to take any action which will result in further disruption.[103]

The subsequent *Sea Containers* decision clarifies that a refusal to supply can violate Article 82 only if it lacks an objective justification.[104]

The facilities deemed essential by European competition authorities have almost exclusively been physical structures. The EC has granted a compulsory licence in application of the essential facilities doctrine in only two instances. The second time it did so as an interim measure, which was subsequently squashed by the Court of First Instance (CFI).[105]

Magill[106] is the key application of the essential facility doctrine to intellectual property under EU competition law. Magill — a publish-

---

102 *Commercial Solvents v. Commission*, [1974] E.C.R. 223 [*Commercial Solvents*].

103 [1992] 5 CMLR 255 at paras 41 and 42.

104 *Sea Containers v. Stena Sealink-Interim Measures*, O.J. 1994 L15/8 at para. 66 [*Sea Containers*].

105 Although the EC has alluded to the essential facilities doctrine on many occasions, neither the CFI nor the European Court of Justice (ECJ) has stated that it is part and parcel of European Community competition law.

106 89/205/EEC: *Commission Decision of 21 December 1988 Relating to a Proceeding under Article 86 of the Treaty of Rome* (IV/31.851 — *Magill TV Guide/ITP, BBC and RTE*) [*Magill*].

er — had launched a multi-channel weekly television guide in Ireland. Local viewers did not have access to such a guide before. Broadcasters had been publishing a guide limited to their individual upcoming radio and television programs. Upon launch of the new guide, the broadcasters commenced copyright proceedings to have reproduction of their program lists enjoined. When they won in local courts and rejected an application for a licence to their lists, Magill counterclaimed, alleging abuse under Article 82 of the *Treaty of Rome*.

The EC concurred. It ordered the grant of a licence at a reasonable royalty.[107] The ruling was upheld by the ECJ. The highest court restated the tenet that while a refusal to license intellectual property does not as a matter of principle violate Article 82, the principle does not apply when the refusal pursues an aim that is manifestly contrary to Article 82.[108] The ECJ insisted though that the circumstances justifying a departure from the general rule had to be "exceptional."

On the facts, the ECJ held that the circumstances in *Magill* were exceptional for three reasons: (i) the refusal had rendered impossible the emergence of a *new product* for which there was a demonstrable and unsatisfied consumer demand; (ii) the refusal lacked an objective justification; and (iii) the refusal allowed broadcasters to monopolize the separate market of television guides.[109]

The *Ladbroke* decision confirmed the applicability of the essential facilities doctrine to an asset protected by copyright.[110] It also tightened the new product requirement of *Magill* by emphasizing that there had to be a specific, constant, and regular demand for the product whose production was impeded by the refusal to deal.[111]

---

107 *Ibid.*

108 *RTE & ITP v. Commission* Cases C-241 & 242/91 P (1995), E.C.R. I-743. See also I. Van Bael, *Competition Law of the European Community*, 4th ed. (The Hague: Kluwer Law International, 2004).

109 The Court held that by reserving the market in weekly TV guides to themselves, the broadcasters were monopolizing it even though they did not produce or sell a multi-channel guide, see *Magill*, above note 106.

110 The Court held that a refusal to license could be discriminatory and as such abusive under art. 82. *Tiercé Ladbroke*, Case T-504/93, [1997] E.C.R. II-923 [*Ladbroke*].

111 The judge in *Ladbroke* also affirmed that a refusal to supply did not violate art. 82 of the *Treaty of Rome* "unless it concerned a product or service which was essential for the exercise of the activity in question, in that there was no real

The conditions underwent additional sharpening in *Oscar Bonner*, a case that did not involve intellectual property. In *Oscar Bonner* the European Court of Justice set out a three-point test.[112] A refusal to deal would violate Article 82 of the *Treaty of Rome* if (i) it was likely to eliminate all competition on the part of the person applying for access; (ii) it lacked an objective justification; and (iii) it was indispensable, "inasmuch as there is no actual or potential substitute in existence."[113] The Court in *Oscar Bonner* did not refer to the new product criterion emphasized in *Magill*.

IMS is the second major case in which the EC viewed intellectual property as an essential facility.[114] IMS is a leading firm engaged in the collection of data on pharmaceutical sales. It tracks the sales of pharmaceutical products, processes the data, and sells summary reports to drug manufacturers. The reports are used to monitor the performance of sales representatives and determine their pay. IMS gives an account of sales in Germany on the basis of an aggregation into 1,860 geographical areas, which is referred to as the "brick structure." The aggregation protects the confidentially of sales to individual buyers — a requirement under German privacy laws.

A competitor entered the German market and started off by offering reports based on a different aggregation formula. Customers, however, insisted on the 1,860 format they had become accustomed to. The

---

or *potential substitute, or* was a new product whose introduction might be prevented . . . ." [emphasis added] E. Derclaye, "Abuses of Dominant Position and Intellectual Property Rights: A Suggestion to Reconcile the Community Courts Case Law" (2003) 26:4 World Competition 658 at 689 argues that this provides an alternative to the *Magill* conditions.

112 *Oscar Bonner GmbH & Co. KG. v. Mediapoint* (1998), E.C.R. I-7791 [*Oscar Bonner*].

113 The third condition can only be met if plausible alternatives to the facility, even of an inferior quality are absent. Specifically, the lack of alternatives has to be a consequence of "technical, legal or economic obstacles and not result from the limited capacities of the specific competitor requiring access." The implication is that a facility cannot be essential if the applicant either alone or in combination with others could build an alternative facility that would not expose him to a permanent and "serious handicap by comparison to the existing facility," *ibid.*

114 *IMS Health GmbH & Co. OHG v. NDC Health GmbH & Co. KG* (2004), Case C-418/01 [*IMS*].

entrant conformed and started using the 1,860 brick structure.[115] IMS then sued for copyright infringement and won. When IMS refused a request for a licence for the 1,860 brick structure, the entrant filed a complaint with the EC on grounds of abuse of dominance.

To avoid the elimination of competition that drawn-out litigation would entail, the EC ordered IMS to license the structure as an interim measure.[116] The EC regarded the 1,860 map as an essential input and saw IMS's refusal to license as devoid of objective justification.[117]

The president of the Court of First Instance overruled the EC's measure on the following grounds: (i) the EC had not paid heed to the new product requirement laid down in *Magill*, and (ii) the market in which the plaintiff intended to compete was the very same market in which IMS operated.[118]

The suspension was upheld by the ECJ.[119] The Court confirmed that it was the concurrence of all three conditions that made the circumstances exceptional in *Magill*. However, it also affirmed that these conditions were not necessary to find a refusal to license as abusive of Article 82.

In response to a request for a preliminary ruling by the German court, the ECJ revisited the recurrent question of whether application of the essential facilities doctrine requires the existence of two separate, relevant markets. In this regard, the ECJ affirmed that the mere fact that a good or service to which access is sought is not marketed individually does not preclude a finding of a separate market. The possibility of identifying a potential, or even a hypothetical market, would be sufficient. The determinative factor is to identify two *stages* of production and their interconnectedness, in that the upstream product is indispensable for the supply of the downstream product. This certainly appears to be a lesser requirement than the existence of two separate markets.

---

115 For all intents and purposes, the 1,860 brick structure had become a *de facto* industry standard for reporting sales to pharmacies.

116 At the time, the injunction of the German court was being appealed.

117 *Commission Decision of 3 July 2001 Relating to a Proceeding Pursuant to Article 82 of the EC Treaty* (Case COMP D3/38.044: NDC Health/IMS HEALTH: Interim measures) [*Commission Decision on IMS*].

118 *IMS Health Inc. v. Commission of the European Communities*, Court of First Instance of the European Communities (Case T-184/01 R).

119 *IMS*, above note 114.

Specifically, the ECJ held that

> the refusal by a dominant undertaking to allow access to a copyrighted product indispensable for operating in a secondary market may be abusive only where the undertaking which requests the license does not intend to limit itself essentially to duplicating the goods and services already offered on the secondary market by the owner of the copyright, but intends to produce new goods or services not offered by the owner of the right and for which there is a potential demand.[120]

On the factual question of whether the plaintiff offered a new product, the ECJ deferred to the German court. The ECJ did not provide any guidance as to what constitutes a new product.

Several authors have called attention to the fact that *Magill* and *IMS* share a circumstance that makes them more exceptional than competition authorities have acknowledged. In both cases copyright was granted under national law, but the rewards from protection seemed highly disproportionate to the effort and creativity that went into creation of the protected material. Derclaye has suggested that this imbalance may have been a contributory factor in the decision to mandate licensing. She also remarks that the EC may have been influenced by the fact that IMS and the plaintiffs in *Magill* were supplying their copyrighted material free-of-charge to parties with whom they did not compete.[121]

---

120 *Ibid.* at para. 49. Hatzopoulos argues that the absence of a reference to "newness" in essential facility cases such as *Oscar Bonner*, above note 112, that do not involve intellectual property rights, means that this condition applies only when the essential element is covered by one or more of such rights. See V. Hatzopoulos, "The EU Essential Facilities Doctrine," European Legal Studies, Research Paper in the Law, 2/2006 (2006) at 48, online: www.coleurop.be/file/content/studyprogrammes/law/studyprog/pdf/ResearchPaper_6_2006_Hatzopoulos.pdf.

121 E. Derclaye, "An Economic Approach to What the Conditions of Abuse of Dominant Position of Copyright Should Be," Society for Economic Research Paper (2003) at 10, online: www.serci.org/2003/derclaye.pdf.

The treatment of *Magill* and *IMS* stands in stark contrast to earlier decisions in *Volvo*[122] and *Renault*.[123] The automobile companies had refused to license their design rights to independent firms that sought to manufacture and sell body panels. The ECJ held that the refusal did not violate Article 82 of the *Treaty of Rome* because "the right of the proprietor of a protected design to prevent third parties from manufacturing and selling or importing, without his consent, products incorporating that design constitutes the very subject-matter of his exclusive right."[124] The independents had not claimed an intention to operate in a market that fell outside the scope of the design rights. In *Magill*, by contrast, the Court opined that the broadcasters sought to rely on copyright protection to defend a monopoly in the market of television listings to which they could not claim an exclusive right on the basis of copyright.

In *Microsoft*,[125] the EC faced once again the question of immunity from Article 82 on copyright grounds. The impugned conduct revolved around Microsoft's refusal to provide access to essential code and interface information that would ensure efficient working of competitors' application and server software with the Windows platform.[126] The defendant, who had consistently supplied this information to selected producers of complementary products, and had done so free of charge, halted the supply and rejected their requests for information when it gained a significant foothold in their market.

The EC began by pointing out that in order to determine whether Microsoft had acted abusively, it did not have to confine itself to the question of whether the conditions that made *Magill* exceptional in the view of the ECJ were in fact met. To establish whether *Microsoft*

---

122 *AB Volvo v. Erik Veng (UK) Ltd.* Case 238/87, [1988] E.C.R. 6211 [*Volvo*].

123 *CICRA v. Renault*, Case 53/87, [1988] E.C.R. 6039 [*Renault*].

124 *Volvo*, above note 122 at para. 2. The Court added, however, that in a secondary market that depended on the intellectual property protected panels, Volvo had certain obligations to continue to supply firms that operated alongside Volvo's own maintenance operation. This obligation is apparently not contingent on the intellectual property holder's share of the secondary market.

125 *EC Commission v. Microsoft*, Case COMP/C-3/37.792 [*Microsoft*].

126 The other alleged abuse concerned bundling of the Windows Media Player with the operating system. It does not relate to the subject matter covered in this report.

was exceptional, it could take account of the totality of circumstances surrounding the case.

Upon consideration of these circumstances, the EC determined that disclosure of the interface information — part of which was protected by patents, copyrights, and trade secrets — was necessary to allow competitors' software to work with the Windows platform as efficiently as with Microsoft's own software. Specifically, the EC held that the defendant's refusal to supply would put competitors "at a strong disadvantage in the work group server operating system market, to the extent where there is a *risk* of elimination of competition."[127]

On that basis, it found that Microsoft had been acting abusively by "refusing to supply *Sun* and other undertakings with the specifications for the protocols used by Windows . . . and allow these undertakings to implement [such] specifications for the purpose of developing interoperable work group server operating systems products."[128] By finding abuse on the basis of "strong disadvantage" to competitors, the EC had adopted a weaker standard than the complete foreclosure of a competitor required under the *Oscar Bonner* and *Magill* test.[129]

In regard to the cessation of supply, which had not taken place in *Oscar Bonner* or in *Magill,* the EC opined that while this was not necessary for finding abuse, it was nevertheless a matter of interest in the assessment of "instances of refusal to supply."[130]

The EC did not investigate whether Microsoft's refusal blocked the introduction of a new product. Instead, it examined the effect of disclosure of interface information on innovation by the industry as a whole. It concluded that non-disclosure would prevent Microsoft's rivals from reaping significant rewards from innovation in workgroup operating systems. Because the effect of disclosure on Microsoft's in-

---

127 *Microsoft,* above note 125 at 589. The EC's *Microsoft* decision was handed down a month before the ECJ stated the applicable conditions in *IMS,* above note 114.

128 *Microsoft, ibid.* recital 456.

129 Killick claims that the "Commission's approach requires a near-perfect, 'native' level of interoperability, even though it admits that interoperability is a matter of degree and recognises that a lower level of interoperability exists," See J. Killick, "IMS and Microsoft Judged in the Cold Light of *IMS*" (2004) 1:2 Competition Law Review 23 at 41 [Killick (2004)].

130 *Microsoft,* above note 125 at 556.

centives to innovate would be minor, the EC concluded that it would not offset the positive effect on its rivals' incentives to innovate.[131] If so, incentives to innovate for the industry as a whole would be stronger.

On the basis of these considerations the EC ordered Microsoft to disclose specifications for a limited number of protocols used by Windows workgroup servers, make them available to third parties, and allow their use by *any* interested third party.[132]

It did, however, restrict the scope of disclosure to interface information and stressed that Microsoft was entitled to reasonable remuneration for information protected as intellectual property. "Reasonable" meant that Microsoft was entitled to remuneration that did not reflect the strategic value of its rights. This opaque formulation probably means that the remuneration should not account for the contribution that the intellectual property made to Microsoft's current and future profits by contributing to the effectiveness of the barriers to entry.

The *IMS* and the *Microsoft* cases raise interesting issues with regard to the interaction of intellectual property and industry standards. Anderman has argued that *Microsoft* had a special obligation to *continue* to supply. Specifically, he maintains that "by initially opting for an 'open' system as a strategy to grow and achieve dominance, the owner of an IP protected industrial standard creates expectations."[133] This makes it difficult to refuse to continue to supply downstream contractors under EC competition law. Similarly, Killick maintains that the real issue in *IMS* was not a conventional refusal to supply, but an appropriation by means of copyright of what was, until then, thought to be an open standard, agreed between *IMS* and the industry.[134]

---

131 Microsoft argued that its refusal had objective justification because relinquishing its intellectual property would eliminate its incentives to innovate. Killick (2004), above note 129 at 41 stresses that the EC's balancing test is not based on any ECJ precedent and that its use "will dramatically reduce legal certainty."

132 To that extent it is not a compulsory licence, as it is not issued to a specific applicant. It comes close to a statutory licence.

133 S. Anderman, "Does the Microsoft Case Offer a New Paradigm for the 'Exceptional Circumstances' Test and Compulsory Licenses under EC Competition Law?" (2004) 1:2 Competition Law Review 7 at 16.

134 Killick (2004), above note 129 at 30.

3) Canada

The *Competition Act*[135] gives the Competition Tribunal broad remedial powers to address conduct that lessens competition. Section 79(2) of the Act empowers the tribunal to make an order directing the person who has abused a dominant position to take actions as are reasonable and as are necessary to overcome the effects of their anti-competitive act, if the prohibition of the abusive practice is insufficient to restore competition. Thus, compulsory licensing is a possible remedy to abuse of dominance.

However, section 79(5) of the *Competition Act* limits that power, providing that no order can be made when the anti-competitive effect has resulted from an act pursuant *only* to the exercise of an intellectual property or industrial property right. The Competition Bureau takes the position that the exemption under section 79(5) does not extend beyond unilateral acts of exclusion and rights holders' decisions to use or not to use their own intellectual property.

In fact, the immunity may extend somewhat beyond mere exclusion. In *Tele-Direct*[136] the director of investigation and research had argued that the refusal by the dominant publisher of telephone directories to license the use of terms like "Yellow Pages" to some competing suppliers constituted an abuse under section 79. The tribunal rejected that claim. It held that the discriminatory licensing of its trade-mark by the publisher of telephone directories was not anti-competitive. It reasoned that "selectivity in licensing is fundamental to the rationale behind protecting trade-marks which are valuable assets and represent considerable goodwill in the marketplace. The decision to license a trade-mark — essentially, to share the goodwill vesting in the asset — was held to be a right that rests entirely with the owner of the mark."[137] The tribunal argued that a refusal to license a trade-mark is distinguishable from a situation where anti-competitive provisions are attached to a trade-mark licence.[138]

---

135 R.S.C. 1985, c. C-34.

136 *Director of Investigation and Research v. Tele-Direct Publications* (1997), 73 C.P.R. (3d) 1, [1997] C.C.T.D. No. 8 [*Tele-Direct*].

137 *Ibid.* at para. 66.

138 The tribunal did not say whether it applies equally to patents and copyrights.

The apparent implication is that mere selective licensing of a trade-mark cannot trigger remedial action under section 79, even when it serves as a tool to exclude competition.

In regard to the matters addressed in Part VIII of the *Competition Act*, the tribunal has broad powers to remedy anti-competitive effects of exclusive dealing, tied-selling, and market restrictions.[139] It may take measures that contain any requirement that, in its opinion, is necessary to overcome the effects of the anti-competitive act, or to restore or stimulate competition.[140]

The same does not apply to refusals to deal. Under section 75(1), the tribunal may order a supplier of a product to accept a person as a customer where

a) the person is substantially affected in its business or precluded from carrying on in its business due to an inability to obtain adequate supplies of that product in the market;
b) the person is unable to obtain adequate supplies because of insufficient competition for the product;
c) the person is willing to meet the usual trade term for the supply of the product;
d) the product is in ample supply; and
e) the refusal to deal is having or is likely to have an adverse effect on competition in a market.[141]

In the *Warner* case,[142] which involved the refusal by the copyright holder to license the right to make copies from a master recording that would have allowed an entrant to manufacture records that it intended to sell in Canada via mail-order, the tribunal held that section 75 of the *Competition Act* did not apply. It reasoned that the condition of "ample supply" was non-applicable because legal rights to intellectual property are, by their nature, exclusive, and because the expression "usual terms of trade" has no meaning for "legal rights over intellectual property, which are exclusive by their very nature and there

139 See s. 77 of the *Competition Act*, above note 135.
140 See s. 77(2), *ibid.*
141 *Ibid.*, s. 75(1). Before June 2002, s. 75(1) required only conditions (a) through (d).
142 *Director of Investigation and Research v. Warner Music Canada Ltd.* (1997), 78 C.P.R. (3d) 321 (Comp. Trib.) [*Warner*].

cannot be usual trade terms when licences may be withheld."[143] The tribunal reasoned that "[t]he right granted by Parliament to exclude others is fundamental to intellectual property rights and cannot be considered to be anti-competitive, and there is nothing in the legislative history of section 75 of the Act which would reveal an intention to have section 75 operate as a compulsory licensing provision for intellectual property."[144] Still, section 75 clearly applies to physical goods protected by patents and/or copyrights.[145]

In order to maintain competition when threatened by a merger, the tribunal is empowered to choose within a broad class of remedies. Under section 92(1) of the *Competition Act* it may order *any* action with the consent of the commissioner of competition and the party against whom the order is directed. Compulsory licensing, which is a less drastic remedy than divestiture of patents, is therefore a possible remedy.

Also, section 86(4) of the *Competition Act* stipulates that the tribunal may condition the issue of an order to register a specialization agreement on more extensive licensing of patents or registered integrated circuits topographies.[146]

Section 32(1) of the *Competition Act* is a specialized provision. It targets the uses of intellectual property rights that

a) limit unduly the facilities for transporting, producing, manufacturing, storing or dealing in any article or commodity that may be a subject of trade or commerce;

---

143 *Ibid.* at para. 30.

144 *Ibid.*

145 See *Director of Investigation and Research v. Chrysler Canada Ltd.* (1989), 27 C.P.R. (3d) 1 (Comp. Trib.); *Director of Investigation and Research v. Xerox Canada Ltd.* (1990), 33 C.P.R. (3d) 83 (Comp. Trib.).

146 Section 85 of the *Competition Act*, above note 135, defines a specialization agreement as an

> agreement under which each party thereto agrees to discontinue producing an article or service that he is engaged in producing at the time the agreement is entered into on the condition that the other party to the agreement agrees to discontinue an article or service that he is engaged in producing at the time the agreement is entered into, and includes any such agreement under which the parties also agree to buy exclusively from each other the articles or services that are subject of the agreement.

b) restrain or injure, unduly, trade or commerce in relation to any such article or commodity;
c) prevent, limit or lessen, unduly, the manufacture or production of any such article or commodity or unreasonably enhance the price thereof; or
d) prevent or lessen, unduly, competition in the production, manufacture, barter, sale, transportation or supply of any such article or commodity.

Whereas dominance of a market is not a requirement under section 32(1), "undueness" of anti-competitive effect is unlikely in the absence of significant market power.[147]

Upon a showing of undueness, the Federal Court may issue orders that include declaring licence agreements void in whole or in part, restraining any person from carrying out terms of the agreement, and compulsory licensing.[148]

There has never been a court decision involving section 32. Two cases that involved accusations of leveraging a patented product in a market for an unpatented product were settled out of court.[149] Both cases involved Union Carbide. In the first case the government claimed that a licensing arrangement violated section 32 because it contained a provision that prohibited the licensee from applying the patented technology to the extraction of plastic film from imported resin. Union Carbide was one of two Canadian suppliers of the resin. In the second case the government claimed that Union Carbide had discriminated against small users and had acted anti-competitively by requiring licensees not to dispute patents.

The Competition Bureau has stated that it will seek a remedy under section 32 only when conduct involves more than the mere exercise of

---

147 While the focus of s. 32 is the competitive process, it also targets "undue" pricing by the rights holder.

148 Note that s. 32 of the *Competition Act*, above note 135, applies only if the conduct affects a market for *articles* whereas s. 65 of the *Patent Act*, above note 12, also applies when the affected trade concerns *services*. Also, s. 32 of the *Competition Act* focuses on the conduct of the rights holder and its effects on a market, whereas s. 65 of the *Patent Act* gives attention to effects on the well-being of a person or class of persons.

149 *R. v. Union Carbide Ltd.*, Minutes of Settlement in the Exchequer Court of Canada, 9 December 1969 and 19 June 1971.

an intellectual property right, if the circumstances specified in that section are met, and if the alleged competitive harm stems directly from the refusal to license and nothing else. A further requirement is that the anti-competitive threshold be met in "a relevant market that is different or significantly larger than the subject matter of the IP or the products or services which result directly from the exercise of the IP."[150] In the opinion of the Bureau, this threshold could only be met when the holder of the intellectual property is dominant in the relevant market, and when the intellectual property is an *essential* input for firms participating in the relevant market. The Bureau states further that, even then, it will recommend a remedy under section 32 only if the refusal stifles innovation.[151]

Thus it appears that the Bureau's position is that section 32 may constrain the mere exercise of an exclusive right if the market in which competition is lessened extends *beyond the perimeter* of some "core market" that is *somehow directly linked* to the subject matter of the intellectual property. Because the intellectual property must be an input, the market in which competition is lessened must logically be located downstream from the "core market."[152] Application of these conditions seems to call for a two-step procedure: (i) carrying out a mapping from a "subject matter" space into a "core market" space; and (ii) drawing a boundary between the "core market" and other relevant antitrust markets where the patented technology, or the products made with the technology, serve as inputs. The principles that should guide such mapping are unclear. The reason lies in the absence of a one-to-one correspondence between the scope of patent protection and relevant product markets.

The issues raised by the Bureau's approach are evocative of the difficulties encountered by US and European competition authorities in regard to the application of the essential facilities doctrine to refusal to license. And, the reference to research and development, which

---

150 Competition Bureau Canada, *Intellectual Property Enforcement Guidelines* (Ottawa: Queen's Printer, 2000) at 14, online: www.competitionbureau.gc.ca/epic/site/cb-bc.nsf/en/01286e.html [IPEGs].

151 *Ibid.*

152 And the dominance of the intellectual property holder in the relevant market must result from the absence of alternatives in that market.

does not appear in section 32, is also reminiscent of the new product criterion invoked by the EC in the *Magill* and *IMS* cases.

Finally, one must make mention of section 61(1) of the *Competition Act*, which declares that

> no person engaged in business who is engaged in the business of producing a product . . . or who has the exclusive rights and privileges conferred by a patent, trade-mark, copyright, registered industrial design or registered integrated circuit topography shall directly or indirectly . . . refuse to supply a product to or otherwise discriminate against any other person engaged in business in Canada because of the low price policy of that person.

The fact that section 61 refers to a product implies that mere refusal to license can be an offence under the *Competition Act* — a *per se* offence in fact — when it is intended to deter or punish someone else's low pricing policy. Section 61 does not require that the person targeted by the refusal operate in a distinct market.

4) Concluding Remarks

The essential facilities doctrine can be seen as an attempt to ground a monopolist's duty to supply in antitrust principles commonly associated with regulation.[153] The question of under what circumstances, if any, the doctrine could be justifiably invoked, has been the subject of an ongoing debate.[154] A less controversial question — among economists at least — has been whether competition law should make a distinction between anti-competitive acts that derive from the exploitation of market power that rests on intellectual assets and those that derive

---

153 The analogy with regulation is most evident in the European Union, where the arguments invoked by the ECJ to justify unbundling of the IMS brick structure from the sale of reports presented in brick form are the same as those that underlie unbundling issues argued before a regulator like the Canadian Radio-television and Telecommunications Commission (CRTC). For more on the "brick structure," see above notes 115 and 116 and accompanying text.

154 For example, A.B. Lipsky and J.G. Sidak, "Essential Facilities" (1999) 51:5 Stan. L. Rev. 1188 at 1220, maintain that mandatory access under the essential facilities doctrine should be limited to cases of natural monopoly [Lipsky and Sidak (1999)].

from control over physical property. The majority consensus appears to be that it should not.[155]

The problem courts have confronted with respect to mere refusals to license intellectual property is of a legal nature. From an economic perspective, it hardly matters whether or not the impugned conduct extends beyond a mere refusal.[156] After all, the customary argument that curtailing a patentee's or a copyright holder's rights via competition law lowers the expected returns to innovation can apply equally when the conduct under attack extends beyond mere refusal.[157] And, from an economic perspective, there is hardly a reason why one should have less regard with respect to incentives to create and invest in the case of physical property.[158] In addition, conduct that extends beyond mere refusal (for example, some forms of bundling) may for all intents and purposes be indistinguishable from mere refusal in terms of its anti-competitive effects.

---

155 The point is argued convincingly by P. Régibeau and K. Rockett, "The Relationship between Intellectual Property Law and Competition Law: An Economic Approach," Discussion paper, University of Essex and CEPR (2004), online: www.essex.ac.uk/economics/discussion-papers/papers-text/dp581.pdf. They also maintain that antitrust litigation should not be used by competition authorities to revisit the compromise between incentives to create/invent and incentives to disseminate. An additional consideration is that differential treatment under competition law creates incentives to dress up in IP clothes run-of-the-mill refusals to supply material inputs or provide access to facilities.

156 More pointedly, the relevant question is whether mere refusal to supply should be a concern for antitrust, regardless of whether it concerns physical or intellectual property.

157 In this regard, Lipsky and Sidak (1999), above note 154, argue that "application of the essential facilities doctrine to intellectual property is antithetical to the policies of patent, copyright and other kindred legal systems" among others because "under the essential facilities doctrine, the more an invention is unique, valuable and difficult to duplicate, the greater the obligation to share it." The latter statement is of course true, although it fails to account for the fact that payment for access would presumably also be higher for a unique invention. Another, perhaps more convincing point, is that where technology changes rapidly, the determination of "essentiality" hinges on an assessment of the cost of developing non-infringing substitutable technologies. Such assessment is likely to be speculative at best.

158 For example, by building a bridge where one expects that it will likely become a natural monopoly.

To resolve the conflict with intellectual property law that mandatory access entails, competition authorities appear to have struggled with the task of defining modes of exploitation that fall outside the range of uses immunized from competition law by virtue of being protected as intellectual property law. This is a tricky exercise because the notion of scope of protection under intellectual property laws does not always translate into a coverage of antitrust markets.[159] Scope may spread across a variety of product markets or be limited to a portion of a product market.[160]

The notion of a primary and a secondary market would be familiar to antitrust practitioners only if it overlapped with the idea that there exists one market in which the firm already is dominant (the primary market), and another market in which it tries to acquire or increase power (the secondary market). From an antitrust perspective, market delineation is a function of product characteristics and geographical location. This is not the distinction that the courts, in particular the European Court of Justice, have been struggling to establish. The line it has drawn seems intended to separate the collection of markets, where a mere refusal to license is immune from competition law because it clashes with rights explicitly granted by intellectual property law, from the markets (uses) where antitrust can curtail the right to exclude.

The fact that the ECJ drew this line on the basis of a criterion of "newness" — a concept that lacks a clear definition in economics and whose relationship to the notion of a different product market is uncertain — suggests a reliance on intellectual property law concepts such as novelty or creative contribution on the part of the applicant licensee. As of yet, the ECJ has not given a clear definition as to what makes a product new. Also, the relevance of "newness" in terms of efficiency is unclear. The criterion has not been invoked in cases where the essential facility was not protected as intellectual property.

---

159 This is not the case for pharmaceuticals where the scope of patents "tends to be coextensive with the products actually sold": D.L. Burk and M.A. Lemley, "Policy Levers in Patent Law" (2003) 89 Va. L. Rev. 1575 [Burk and Lemley (2003)].

160 And, the opportunity to exploit an intellectual asset in a specific market may appear years after the grant of protection.

Additionally, there appears to be an increasing trend among patentees towards trading in disembodied knowledge as opposed to the physical selling of products that embody the knowledge.[161] While this allows rights holders to capture the returns from their inventions in a larger variety of antitrust markets, it may blur the line between markets considered primary and secondary from the patentee's perspective.[162]

The caselaw in regard to applications of the essential facilities doctrine appears to be in a state of flux in the US and the EU The positions taken by US courts with respect to unilateral refusals to license are at odds with each other. European competition authorities seem to develop new criteria on a case-by-case basis.

In Canada, one examines the effects of conduct that involves intellectual property in two markets: (i) the market in which the intellectual property itself may be transacted; and (ii) the market for products that embody the intellectual property. This makes for a narrower analysis than in the United States, where authorities also consider how the conduct affects the so-called "innovation market."[163] One consequence is that litigation in Canada is less likely than in the US to become an opportunity to revisit the basic compromise that intellectual property law establishes between static and dynamic efficiency. Using section 32 of the *Competition Act* as a port of entry for essential facility principles would draw Canadian competition policy into the murky analyses of market power, rivalry, and their effects on innovation.

For all these reasons, adoption of an essential facilities doctrine, either explicitly or via a section 32 backdoor, does not make the circumstances clearer as to when compulsory licences on intellectual property should be issued. It would not clarify when intellectual property should be made the subject of a compulsory licence and it would not resolve the issue of how conducts and/or areas of activity immune from competition law should be separated from areas that are not. In fact, additional confusion may be created as to the respective roles of sections 32 and 75, and the essential facilities doctrine.

---

161 See H. Ullrich, "Expansionist Intellectual Property Protection and Reductionist Competition Rules: A TRIPS Perspective" (2004) 7:2 J. Int'l Econ. L. 401.

162 For example, would all product markets be considered primary if the patentee always licenses the techonology and never uses it herself?

163 The term "innovation market" is a label that captures incentives to develop new products and processes.

D. COMPULSORY LICENSING AND INNOVATION

The option of compulsory licensing weakens exclusive rights. It is therefore useful to start by briefly reviewing how the strength of protection affects innovation.

More recent literature points out that the reality of this relationship hinges on an inaccurate view of innovation as an isolated event. Recent writings see innovation as a process of accumulation where inventions build on earlier creations and serve as building blocks for subsequent inventions.[164] The latter viewpoint entails a radical change in perception about the effects of stronger protection on innovation. Stronger patent protection may still increase the expected rewards from one's innovation, but only if it does not markedly increase the cost of obtaining the consent of others necessary to produce that innovation, or exploit it.[165] Because widening the scope of protection increases the cost of consent, it has an *a priori* ambiguous effect on innovation.

Stronger protection may buttress incentives to innovate in some industries while weakening them in others. For a given industry, the relationship may be non-monotonic.[166] And, the relationship might well differ across firms within an industry, depending on the extent to which their research and development targets inventions that depart significantly from current technologies.

Furthermore, patenting is just one instrument of appropriation of the returns from innovation. The increment of appropriability obtained via patenting is not the same across industries.

Compulsory licensing is a particular form of scope reduction. It is triggered by specific conditions that may not happen, and whose oc-

---

164 See S. Scotchmer, "Standing on the Shoulders of Giants: Cumulative Research and the Patent Law" (1991) 5:1 Journal of Economic Perspectives 19.

165 Obtaining consent is necessary when the new patent infringes an earlier patent. The cost of consent rises when the number of patentees from whom consent is required increases and when their bargaining power *vis-à-vis* the party needing consent increases.

166 Some authors have argued that the relationship between the rate of innovation and the strength of protection has the form of an inverted U. See for example, A.W. Horwitz and E.L. Lai, "Patent Length and the Rate of Innovation" (1996) 37:4 International Economic Review 785; and J. Lerner, "150 Years of Patent Protection," NBER Working Paper Series No. 7478 (Stanford, CA: National Bureau of Economic Research, 2001).

currence is not disconnected from the patentee's conduct. Therefore, the likely effects on research and development and innovation depend on how past practices in regard to compulsory licensing affect firms' expectations that future orders to license will be issued in their technology spheres. The impact of innovations also depends on how an order to license, when issued, affects expected profitability.

A final consideration is that the vast majority of processes used in Canada and products made or imported into Canada were invented elsewhere. Because Canada represents but a small share of the world market, a weakening of protection — through compulsory licensing *inter alia* — should not attenuate incentives to innovate by foreign firms. This also applies to Canadian innovators, albeit to a lesser extent. As far as Canadian firms are concerned, it is likely to matter in areas where successful exploitation in the home market is necessary before entering foreign markets.[167]

1) Perceptions

An order to license given today could immediately affect research and development conducted by the party to whom the order is given, and by the party that benefits from it. But, in order to affect the research and development of others — whether or not they operate in the same technology sphere — the order must influence their perceptions of the likelihood that future orders will be issued in areas of concern to them.

It is reasonable to assume that when orders to license are issued sparingly, as they have been in Canada since the abandonment of pharmaceutical licensing, the mere existence of the option to make such orders does not affect the protection patentees expect to enjoy. In this regard it is interesting to note that among respondents in Scherer's sample of firms, those that had already been ordered to grant compul-

---

167 The author of this report cannot provide a ranking of industries according to the importance of initial success in the home market. While weakening Canadian patent protection in general may discourage some innovators to set up manufacturing facilities in Canada for fear that local competitors would have less to fear if they copied, the latter appears an unlikely response to an expansion of the range of circumstances under which one grants compulsory licences, provided that production and sales in Canada make it less likely that licences will be granted.

sory licences in the past were less concerned by such a possibility in the future than the firms that were never subject of such order.[168]

2) The Terms of the Licence

There is no clear answer to the question of how a change in the amount of royalties paid for compulsory licences affects innovation. The reason is that royalties on compulsory licences, if they influence research and development at all, do so in opposite directions for licensors and licensees.

Some commentators have remarked that royalties on compulsory licences are on the low side compared to market rates, especially when they are issued to governments in emergency situations. Even so, there is no reason to expect an effect on innovation as long as the emergency is likely to be short-lived and non-recurrent.[169]

Another issue is what instruments the licensing authority can use to insure that the patentee's technology is usable by another person. In some industries, non-codified knowledge about manufacturing techniques is an indispensable complementary input. If the authority that orders the licence does not have the power to order the supply of such non-patentable inputs, compulsory licence is ineffective. If so, it cannot reduce the scope of protection.[170]

3) Empirical Findings

Empirical research on the relationship between compulsory licensing and innovation is just about non-existent. However, some inferences about the likely effects of compulsory licensing can be drawn from studies that focus on the impact of patentability in general.

---

168 F.M. Scherer, *The Economic Effects of Compulsory Patent Licensing* (New York: NYU Center for the Study of Financial Institutions, 1977) at 555 [Scherer (1977)].

169 In emergency situations patentees whose technologies are subject to compulsory licences may in fact enjoy a windfall because they are applied to an unexpectedly large quantity of production.

170 In this regard, one may consider that the option of compulsory licensing is more effective when placed in the hands of a competition authority, endowed with a great deal of discretionary remedial power, than in the hands of a patent agency, whose powers to make orders do not extend beyond the exclusive rights conferred by patents.

In an early study Scherer calculates the ratio of research and development expenditures to sales for a cross-section of 700 US companies, forty-two of which have been subject to compulsory licensing as an antitrust remedy. He finds a positive, albeit very small correlation between research and development intensity and compulsory licensing across all industries. However, he is unable to compare the research and development efforts of individual firms before and after the issuance of the compulsory licence because he does not have time series for research and development (all his data pertain to the year 1975).[171] Because the observed correlation may be due to an industry effect, it is difficult to conclude that there exists a causal effect of licensing on research effort.

Chien avoids this problem by looking at the rate of innovation of six pharmaceutical companies in the same therapeutic area, before and after they were ordered to issue a compulsory licence. All licences in her sample except one were issued by the US Justice Department to counter an increase in market power resulting from a merger. She detects no effect at all for five companies, and a minor adverse effect for one company. Where there is no effect at all, the patentee was ordered to license his current technology but did not have to license improvements.[172] Such obligation existed in the single instance where Chien discerned a very slight effect.[173] Although her evidence is largely anecdotal, she concludes that the "blanket assertion that licensing categorically harms innovation is probably wrong."[174]

Both the Scherer (1977) and the Chien (2003) studies only look at the research and development responses of patentees. They do not attempt to capture the effect on research and development conducted by licensees and by others.[175]

---

171 Scherer (1977), above note 168.

172 C. Chien, "Cheap Drugs at What Price to Innovation: Does the Compulsory Licensing of Pharmaceuticals Hurt Innovation?" (2003) 18:1 Berkeley Tech. L.J. 3 [Chien (2003)].

173 As a matter of fact, the effect is hardly observable from Chien's graphical representation of the research and development time series.

174 Chien (2003), above note 172 at 5.

175 Because there are many such "others" the impact on economy-wide R&D may dwarf the impact on R&D investment by firms subject to licensing orders.

The Harbridge House Study examines the impact of licensing clauses on the use of technologies developed on contract for the US government.[176] The study asks whether the technologies are more likely to be commercialized in the private sector when the government takes a licence than when it takes title. When the government takes a licence, the inventor has exclusivity over the civilian sector. The inventor does not have this exclusivity when the government takes title. The inventor is then exposed to the risk of competition by the government, or the government's licensees. Taking title signals to contractors an intention on the part of government to exploit the patent in the future.

The study, based on a sample of 1,720 inventions, finds that exclusivity in the civilian sector counts, although prior commercial experience is more important as a determinant of the decision to commercialize in the civilian sector.[177] Interviews with contractors reveal that exclusivity is most important to small firms, new entrants, and firms that face substantial development and technological risk.

In regard to the pharmaceutical sector, the Eastman Report notes that compulsory licensing was key to the emergence of the generic industry in Canada, suggesting that profits from generics may have been a factor influencing their own research effort.[178] However, Scherer and Weisburt find no such positive effect from the adoption of patent protection for pharmaceuticals in Italy. They claim that pharmaceutical innovation was not stimulated, largely because the Italian industry

---

176 US, Committee on Government Patent Policy and Harbridge House, Inc., *Government Patent Policy Study Final Report*, looseleaf (Washington: Federal Council for Science and Technology, 1968). The summary report is reproduced in US House of Representatives, Committee on Science and Technology, *Background Materials on Government Patent Policies*, vol. II (August 1976) at 69–140 [Harbridge House Study].

177 Specifically, it finds that contractors with prior experience commercialized 23.8 percent of their inventions in the civilian markets when they held exclusive rights to these markets, but only 13.3 percent when they did not hold such rights. Among contractors without commercial experience, 6.6 percent of inventions were commercialized when the civilian market was reserved for the inventor, whereas only 2.2 percent were commercialized when it was not.

178 Canada, Commission of Inquiry on the Pharmaceutical Industry, *Report of the Commission of Inquiry on the Pharmaceutical Industry* by Harry Eastman (Toronto: Commission, 1985) [Eastman Report].

was specialized in the exploitation of off-brand versions of drugs patented elsewhere.[179]

Taylor and Silberston use the survey method to assess the roles of patenting and licensing in British industry.[180] Their aim is to determine how firms would react to the implementation of a hypothetical compulsory licensing regime in which the grant of licences would be more or less automatic, but licensees would not be entitled to information beyond the specifications published in the patent. Respondents (forty-four firms allocated to five broad industry classes)[181] were asked to evaluate the importance of patent protection on their decision to undertake research. They were also invited to compare their actual patenting and licensing practices with the practices they would adopt under the hypothetical compulsory licensing regime.

Taylor and Silberston found that 60 percent of pharmaceutical research and development, 15 percent of chemical research and development, and about 5 percent of mechanical engineering research and development depends on patent protection.[182] Even so, 75 percent of respondents indicated that prospective patent protection has no effect or very little effect on their decision to undertake research. The proportion of respondents that state that they would not undertake some research and development without patenting is very small.

Taylor and Silberston report that respondents often make the point that although "the size and direction of their R&D programs would probably not be much different in a world of compulsory licensing, their policy with regard both to patenting and to publication

---

179 F.M. Scherer and S. Weisburt, "Economic Effects of Strengthening Pharmaceutical Patent Protection in Italy" (1995) 26:6 Int'l Rev. Ind. Prop. & C'right Law 1009.

180 C.T. Taylor and Z.A. Silberston, *The Economic Impact of the Patent System; A Study of the British Experience* (Cambridge: Cambridge University Press, 1973) [Taylor and Silberston (1973)].

181 The five were chemicals including pharmaceuticals and petrochemicals; oil refining; electrical engineering including electronics; mechanical engineering; and man-made fibers.

182 The percentage is negligible for research and development in electronics.

of their R&D results would probably be more selective."[183] Only a few respondents suggested that they would refrain from patenting.[184]

All respondents who declared that patent protection plays a significant role belong to the following industries: pharmaceuticals, crop chemicals, special industrial chemicals, heavy industrial plant components, and automotive components.[185] Each and every pharmaceutical firm declared that it would not have embarked on research and development on its newer prescription medicines "in an environment of 'thoroughgoing' compulsory licensing."[186] Grabowski explains that patents are important for pharmaceuticals because of the great disparity between the cost of imitation and the innovator's cost of discovering, developing, and gaining regulatory approval for a new medicine.[187]

Mansfield, Schwartz, and Wagner confirm the importance of patents to the pharmaceutical industry.[188] They find that 90 percent of research projects for pharmaceutical innovations and about 20 percent of innovations in chemicals, electronics, and machinery would not have been undertaken in the absence of patent protection.[189]

Levin *et al.* take a different approach.[190] They invited a sample of US firms representing 130 lines of business to score six mechanisms

---

183 See Taylor and Silberston (1973), above note 180 at 210. The type of compulsory licensing that Taylor and Silberston are concerned with is systematic licensing of all patents. Their finding of little effects in most industries would apply there all the more for sporadic compulsory licensing.

184 Some suggested that the period during which know-how could be kept secret would likely be shortened if attention were drawn to an invention by patenting it.

185 In the pharmaceutical industry, approximately two-thirds of research and development is dependent on patent protection, and in "other finished chemicals" it is a quarter, Taylor and Silberston (1973) at 198.

186 *Ibid.* at 206.

187 H. Grabowski, "Patents, Innovation and Access to New Pharmaceuticals" (2002) 5:4 J. Int'l Econ. L. 849.

188 E. Mansfield, M. Schwartz, and S. Wagner, "Imitation Costs and Patents: An Empirical Study" (1981) 91 Economic Journal 907.

189 Interestingly, a later study found that even the industries that do not regard the prospect of patent protection as necessary apply for patents for most of their patentable inventions. See E. Mansfield, "Patents and Innovation: An Emprical Study" (1986) 32 Management Science 173.

190 R.C. Levin *et al.*, "Appropriating the Returns from Industrial Research and Development" [1987] 3 Brookings Papers on Economic Activity 783 [Levin *et al.* (1987)].

for appropriating the advantages of new or improved processes and products. Alternative or complementary mechanisms to patenting are lead time, moving quickly down the learning curve, and sales or service effort. The 650 responses to their questionnaire reveal that patents for new processes are seen as least effective on average among appropriability mechanisms. Although patents for products typically get a better score, they are still considered less effective than lead time, learning curves, and sales and service efforts.

Interestingly, respondents viewed patents to be more important in preventing duplication than securing royalty income.[191] Only in the drug industry did a majority of respondents view patents as more effective than other means of appropriation. In three other industries (organic chemicals, plastic materials, and steel mill products) most respondents rated patents as not less effective (as the best) than alternative means of appropriation.[192]

Levin and his co-investigators reason that "the most probable explanation for the robust finding that patents are particularly effective in chemical industries is that a comparatively clear standard can be applied to assess a patent's validity, and defend it against infringement."[193]

To further elucidate the weakness of patent protection as an appropriability mechanism, the investigators asked respondents to rate the following factors which, on an *a priori* basis, limit patent effectiveness: (i) lack of patentability; (ii) patents unlikely to be valid if challenged; (iii) firms do not enforce patents; (iv) competitors legally invent around patents; (v) technology is moving so fast that patents are irrelevant; (vi) patent documents disclose too much information; (vii) licensing required by court decisions; (viii) firms participate in cross-licensing agreements with competitors.[194]

---

191 The authors point out that this may not be true for small technologically oriented firms for whom the patent could be the most marketable asset.

192 Levin *et al.* (1987), above note 190 at 799–801.

193 *Ibid.* at 798. The uniqueness of a specific molecule is more easily demonstrated than the novelty of, for example, a new component of a complex system.

194 *Ibid.* at 803.

The factor that ranked highest was the ability of competitors to "invent around" both product and process patents.[195] Interestingly, licensing required by law receives the lowest ranking, possibly because it is a rare occurrence.

Roughly a decade later, Cohen, Nelson, and Walsh revisit the appropriability question,[196] drawing on the responses of 1,478 research and development laboratories to a 1994 survey.[197] They focus on the effectiveness of patent protection compared to other appropriability mechanisms.

Most of the thirty-four industries in the sample assign a high effectiveness rating to two or more protection mechanisms. However, they declare patents to be the least central of the major mechanisms overall.[198] Although some report significant effectiveness for patent protection (e.g., more than 50 percent for product innovations in drugs, and 40–50 percent for special purpose machinery, computers, and auto-parts), no industry identifies patents as the most effective appropriability mechanism.[199]

Because sample bias could be a factor explaining the lower reported effectiveness of patents than in Levin *et al.* (1987), the investigators recalculate the scores for a sub-sample that leaves out firms with sales below half a billion dollars per annum. Removing the smaller firms increases the perceived effectiveness of patents in some industries. Among the larger firms, patents obtain the highest scores for

---

195 *Ibid.* That factor was ranked higher than five on a seven-point scale by a substantial majority of respondents.

196 W.M. Cohen, R.R. Nelson, and J.P. Walsh, "Protecting Their Intellectual Assets: Appropriability Conditions and Why U.S. Manufacturing Firms Patent (or Not)," NBER Working Paper Series No. 7552 (Stanford, CA: National Bureau of Economic Research, 2000) [Cohen, Nelson, and Walsh (2000)].

197 Wesley M. Cohen, *Carnegie Mellon Survey on Industrial R&D in the US Manufacturing Sector* (Pittsburgh, PA: Carnegie Mellon University, 1994).

198 Cohen, Nelson, and Walsh (2000), above note 196. This is somewhat surprising as the survey was taken at a time when US courts had already started to enforce patent rights more aggressively.

199 *Ibid.* at 6. Secrecy and lead time were ranked highest overall with a score at just over 50 percent each. The authors explain that because processes are more difficult to observe, a greater effectiveness for secrecy is expected than in the case of product innovations.

drugs, toilet preparations, gum and wood chemicals, pipes/valves, oil field machinery, switchgear, and auto-parts.[200]

Respondents reported that the motivation for their latest decision to apply for the patent was the prevention of copying (95 percent of the cases) and the blocking of rival patents on related innovations (82 percent of cases). Ease of inventing around the patent is the most frequently cited reason for not filing a patent.[201]

Cohen, Nelson, and Walsh conclude that although "patents are still not the dominant mechanism in most industries for protecting product innovations, it now appears that they can be counted among the major mechanisms of appropriation in a more sizeable minority of industries."[202] The disparity in patent effectiveness is confirmed by Arora, Ceccaggnoli, and Cohen.[203] Using the same data, they determined that the extra payoff from patented as opposed to unpatented inventions varies a lot across industries and is positive in only a few manufacturing sectors.[204]

These surveys are interesting because they generate a ranking of appropriation mechanisms' perceived effectiveness. They cannot, however, provide a quantitative measure of the contribution patent protection makes to appropriability. To infer the latter, a number of studies rely on patent renewal data.

Some jurisdictions require the payment of periodic renewal fees to maintain patent protection for the full term. The decision to pay the fees therefore reveals information about the private value of extending protection. Because patentees also use other protection mechanisms, renewal decisions cast a light on the value of the extra appropriability imparted by patents.[205]

---

200 *Ibid.* at 12. The score was at least 50 percent for organic chemicals, fibers, turbines/generators, motors/industrial controls, and medical equipment.

201 *Ibid.* at 15. Information disclosure and lack of novelty rank second in terms of frequency.

202 *Ibid.* at 13.

203 A. Arora, M. Ceccaggnoli, and W.C. Cohen, "R&D and the Patent Premium," NBER Working Paper Series No. 9431 (Stanford: National Bureau of Economic Research, 2003).

204 *Ibid.* at 6. Specifically, pharmaceuticals, biotechnology, medical instruments, machinery computers, and industrial chemicals.

205 A first component of the increment is the additional protection during the year of renewal; a second component is the option value of renewal in the future.

In an early study, Pakes finds that patent protection is valued at \$6,000 on average in France, \$7,000 in the United Kingdom, and \$16,200 in Germany. These numbers imply an annual return from patent protection in each country of 15.6 percent, 11.0 percent, and 13.8 percent, respectively.[206] A subsequent study by Schankerman examines the value of patent protection in four French industries: pharmaceuticals, chemicals, mechanical, and electronics.[207] He found that, averaged over these four technology fields, the subsidy needed to induce French patentees to spend the same amount on research and development in the absence of patent protection amounts to 15.6 percent of their total research and development, and 24.2 percent of company-funded research and development.[208] A similar study by Lanjouw reveals that patent protection gives German patentees an implicit subsidy of 10–15 percent to research and develop across technology groups.[209]

The renewal studies indicate that in most industries patent protection plays a significant, if not decisive role in allowing innovators to appropriate the advantages of their inventions. However, because the counterfactual in these studies is the absence of any patent protection, the estimates of patent value do not rate the probable impact of *changes* in patent protection.

A very small number of studies have examined whether stronger patent protection produces an increase in research and development; they do not find such a result. Jaffe[210] as well as and Kortum and Lerner[211] conclude that the observed increase in research and development

---

206 A. Pakes, "Patents as Options: Some Estimates of the Value of Holding European Patent Stocks" (1986) 54 Econometrica 755 at 779 [Pakes (1986)].

207 M. Schankerman, "How Valuable Is Patent Protection? Estimates by Technology Field" (1998) 29:1 RAND Journal of Economics 77.

208 *Ibid.* at 95–98. The range extends from 4 percent for pharmaceuticals to 21.4 percent for electronics. Shankerman attributes the surprisingly low figure for pharmaceuticals to the tight price controls on drugs in France.

209 J.O. Lanjouw, "Patent Protection in the Shadow of Infringment: Simulation Estimations of Patent Value" (1998) 65:4 Review of Economic Studies 671 at 699. Patent holders in textiles receive an implicit subsidy of 40–75 percent.

210 A.B. Jaffe, "The U.S. Patent System in Transition: Policy Innovation and the Innovation Process" (2000) 29: 4–5 Research Policy 531.

211 S. Kortum and J. Lerner, "Stronger Protection or Technological Revolution: What Is Behind the Recent Upsurge in Patenting?" (1998) 48 Carnegie Rochester Conference Series on Public Policy 247.

spending and patenting in the US is unlikely to have been a response to stronger protection.[212] Similarly, Sakakibara and Branstetter[213] find no evidence of a significant increase in research and development spending or innovative output in Japan that can be attributed to the 1988 patent reform.[214]

4) Conclusion

Patent protection contributes to appropriability, but its role in that regard is secondary for the majority of industries. It is a major mechanism in a small number of industries — above all, pharmaceuticals.[215]

Both the theoretical considerations and the empirical findings suggest that compulsory licensing, if applied sparingly in an industry, cannot be expected to lower research and development or affect innovation by firms that rely on the industry's technologies or products.

E. CIRCUMSTANCES THAT JUSTIFY COMPULSORY LICENSING UNDER THE *PATENT ACT*

A departure from the general rule that rights holders are free to determine whether to license and how to license must be contingent on a circumstance where the exercise of this right thwarts the objectives of patent law, or possibly another public policy objective. For example, that exercise of the right seriously hampers innovation, precludes the exploitation of inventions, or puts a stop to the disclosure of new technologies.

---

212 US patent protection was strengthened by creation of the Court of Appeals for the Federal Circuit, which led to more aggressive enforcement through the enactment of the *Bayh-Dole Act*, above note 53, and by expanding the realm of patentability.

213 M. Sakakibara and L. Branstetter, "Do Stronger Patents Induce More Innovation? Evidence from the 1988 Japanese Patent Law Reforms" (2001) 32:1 RAND Journal of Economics 77.

214 The Japanese reform expanded the number of claims one could make in a single patent and increased the period of protection for pharmaceuticals.

215 One should recognize, however, that the aforementioned studies do not capture the contribution of patents to innovation via the dissemination of knowledge to third parties supported by the disclosure obligation.

The preservation of the interests of individual firms, classes of firms, or industries is not a goal of patent protection. Therefore, the issuance of compulsory licences should not depend on injury to would-be licensees or actual licensees. The public policy issue that the injury conditions of sections 65(2)(d) and 65(2)(e) of the *Patent Act* address is unclear.[216] In the absence of an anti-competitive effect, economic theory does not support a recalibration of patent protection to correct the prejudice to a party caused by a denial of access or the terms of access.[217]

Also, the rationale for making the public interest part of the definition of abuse, as under section 65(2)(d), is not apparent. After all, section 66(1)(e) of the *Patent Act* already instructs the commissioner to refuse the application when he is satisfied that doing so best serves the objects of section 65. One must presume that the objectives referred to in section 66(1)(e) are the public interests served by curbing exclusive rights in the specific circumstances listed in section 65. Furthermore, if curbing one's right not to license is in the public interest, why is it necessary to require abusive conduct?[218]

Section 65(2)(e) of the *Patent Act* makes the issuance of a compulsory licence contingent on prejudice to an industry or part thereof. However, it remains silent on the nature of the attached conditions that would make the prejudice unfair. Because the conduct targeted by this section extends beyond a "mere exercise" of an exclusive right, it can be addressed by competition authorities if it produces an anti-competitive outcome.[219] It is conceivable, however, that some condition attached to the licence frustrates the objectives of the *Patent Act* with-

---

216 Unless it is meant to shift rent from mainly foreign patentees to mainly Canadian licensees.

217 Note, however, that the causation of prejudice requires some market power on the part of the patentee. If the technology or product being denied has close substitutes, prejudice cannot result from a unilateral refusal. This means that in order to establish whether a refusal to license is a cause of prejudice, one must proceed along lines similar to the delineation of an antitrust market.

218 A possible answer is that the *Paris Convention*, above note 3, requires abuse as a condition for compulsory licensing.

219 Doing so allows a wider range of remedies, in particular a simple prohibition to attach the abusive conditions. This avoids entanglement in the regulatory task of setting a "reasonable" royalty.

out rising to the level of anti-competitive conduct, possibly because its effects, although small in individual markets, are felt in a great many markets.

As indicated, Article 31 of the TRIPS Agreement stipulates that compulsory licences cannot be issued until attempts to obtain a voluntary licence on reasonable terms have failed. The breakdown of negotiations indicates that the parties could not establish licensing terms that would make both of them better off than not licensing.[220] In the overwhelming majority of cases, such failure does not, and should not trigger any action on the part of authorities. To justify intervention on efficiency grounds requires clear and significant advantages to third parties (such as consumers).

The circumstances that allow issuance of a mandatory licence to a private person should be limited to the following:

1) Making use of an exclusive right to foreclose access in Canada to products or processes;
2) Making use of an exclusive right conferred by a patent to close-off exploitation in Canada of another patent where such exploitation is of substantial economic significance.

The commissioner should grant a mandatory licence in these circumstances, if doing so is in the public interest. The latter would encompass the objectives of innovation, the dissemination of new technologies, and competition.

An order under condition 1 (above) would only be contemplated if the foreclosed product or process has no substitutes to which Canadian producers or consumers have access via local production or imports. This means that where patentees refrain from working a patent, or where the product made with the patented technology is imported, it would not be considered for licensing in most situations.

Indeed, innovating firms may patent a number of substitutable technologies that could serve to manufacture a product. They may

---

220 The prospective licensee may have rejected the patentee's demands in the hope of getting a more favourable deal for a substitute technology, or in expectation of obtaining a compulsory licence on better terms. The patentee may have rebuffed the applicant's offers, trusting that a better proposal would be made by another applicant.

then determine to use one of these technologies at the exclusion of all others.[221] One would not consider that this provides a ground for issuing a compulsory licence for any of the substitute patented technologies that are not used.

To completely foreclose a market or class of product, the patentee would have to be endowed with exceptional market power.[222] It is easier to imagine a situation where a rights holder sets a price that makes the patented product accessible to no more than a small minority of Canadians. This could happen when the objective is to curtail parallel exports that threaten to undermine a high price in a foreign market.[223]

Another possibility is that the owner of a patent — a private person or a foreign government — relies on exclusive rights to close-off the Canadian market in order to wrest advantages from Canadian authorities in other areas.

The second condition where compulsory licensing could be considered is to address problems flowing from anti-commons situations, patent dependency, patent thickets, and patent sharking.

---

221 Possibly because the technology used is more cost-effective than the other technologies. Another reason could be the patentee's inability to iron out technical hitches that stand in the way of exploitation on an industrial scale. This is more likely when the inventor rushes to the patent office to pre-empt the grant of a patent to another party. Still another reason for not exploiting a patent is the difficulty of coming to an agreement with holders of complementary patents.

222 If the foreclosure of a technology has an anti-competitive effect, one might seek a remedy under the *Competition Act*, above note 135. K.M. Saunders, "Patent Nonuse and the Role of Public Interest as a Deterrent to Technology Suppression" (2002) 15:2 Harv. J.L. & Tech. 389, provides a list of examples. The foreclosure of access by Canadian consumers that does not lessen competition in a market — possibly because entry is highly unlikely — would normally not violate the *Competition Act*. While s. 32 authorizes compulsory licences in cases of unreasonable price enhancement, it does so only in the case of articles. And, as indicated earlier, the conditions under which the Bureau would invoke s. 32 are highly restrictive.

223 The effectiveness of such action depends on the type of exhaustion regime applicable to all categories of intellectual property that cover the product. When the patentee also sells into other foreign markets and does so at a lower price than in Canada, adoption of an international exhaustion regime with respect to the patented product could be an alternative to compulsory licensing.

An anti-commons problem arises when use of a technology requires the aggregation of many patents with dispersed ownership.[224] Aggregation entails search and negotiation cost. These costs increase when dispersion of patent ownership increases. Furthermore, when patents are complementary, rights holders are tempted to play "hold-out" in the hope of getting a larger share of the pie. When they do not hold out, they are likely to set fees that result in a higher product price than if all patents were under common control.[225]

Transaction costs and the decentralization of pricing of complementary inputs give rise to higher product prices and lower manufacturers' profits. They may also preclude production. Research and development may be held back if innovators expect an anti-commons problem.

Patent dependency denotes a particular form of complementarity. A typical situation is where patentee A owns a technology that is improved on by another person, B, who patents the improvement. Although the original technology can be used by patentee A without the consent of patentee B, the converse does not apply. The implications of dependency are similar to those of bilateral complementarity, described above.

A thicket problem arises when patents owned by two or more parties lay claim to the same technology or part thereof. The area of overlapping claims is greater when patents are broader. To eliminate the risk of infringement, a manufacturer must obtain the consent of all persons who hold patents in the thicket. In exchange for that consent the manufacturer will have to share rents with the other patent holders, even though she holds patents to all the technologies she intends to use. The effect is the same as in an anti-commons situation but, unlike

---

224 The term "tragedy of the anti-commons" was coined by Heller, see M.A. Heller, "The Tragedy of the Anticommons Property in the Transition from Marx to Markets" (1998) 111:3 Harv. L. Rev. 621. It refers to a situation where a resource is underused because too many people hold rights of exclusion to that resource. It applies to patents when the manufacture of a product requires the use of a combination of technologies to which a great many individuals hold rights.

225 This is an application to licensing of a pricing problem that is already discussed by Cournot; see A.A. Cournot, *Recherches sur les principes mathématiques de la théorie des richesses* (Paris: Hachette, 1938).

the anti-commons problem, the thicket problem may also arise when the number of technologies required to make a product is small. The effect of a thicket is to reduce, possibly prevent, or delay production.

The opportunity to share in the benefits from new technologies without actually using or licensing them gives rise to a particular type of entrepreneurial activity. The entrepreneurs assemble portfolios of patents that overlap with other patents and cover technologies they do not intend to use. The objective is to wring payments from persons who exploit the same or closely related technologies.[226]

Patent sharking refers to the timing of the shakedown. The shark owns a complementary or overlapping patent and delays the allegations of infringement until the other party has committed resources, preferably by undertaking production. Because an injunction to cease production is more costly to a manufacturer than an order not to undertake it, the shark is in a stronger bargaining position than the rights holder who reveals his patent at an early stage.[227]

A number of commentators have stressed that the anti-commons and thickets problems have become more frequent because innovation is increasingly concentrated in industries such as software, telecommunications, and consumer electronics, where production requires consent from many patentees and there is more overlap in subject matter.[228]

Because such uses of patents hamper the exploitation of patented inventions by others, and because they indirectly discourage innovation and disclosure, they can be seen as conduct that undermines the objectives of patent law. It is true, of course, that the grant of patent to one person has always affected the cost of innovating by others.

---

226 See C. Shapiro, "Navigating the Patent Thicket: Cross Licenses, Patent Pools, and Standard Setting" (2001), online: http://faculty.haas.berkeley.edu/shapiro/thicket.pdf.

227 M. Reitzig, J. Henkel, and C. Heath show why courts' decisions to award lost profits as a remedy for infringement encourage sharking, see M. Reitzig, J. Henkel, and C. Heath, "On Sharks, Trolls, and Other Patent Animals —'Being Infringed' as a Normatively Induced Innovation Exploitation Strategy," online: http://papers.ssrn.com/sol3/papers.cfm?abstract_id=885914.

228 *Ibid.* at 9. The escalation of thicket problems in the US has been attributed to a certain laxity in patent evaluation due to a rapid growth in applications, which has not been matched by a commensurate growth in resources at the Patent Office.

However, the literature suggests an increase in the prevalence of thickets, partly attributed to lack of resources available to patent granting agencies, and in the strategic use of doubtful exclusive rights to wring monies from innovators or their licensees. This development raises the question of whether the compromise between the objective of protecting innovation and of ensuring the use and disclosure of new technologies as reflected in patent law has been significantly perturbed.

As indicated, European jurisdictions have recognized the problem stemming from patent complementarity and have given themselves the option of ordering unidirectional licensing or cross-licensing to address them.[229] In the US, where the law makes no general provision for compulsory licensing, the search for solutions focuses on the use of technology-specific approaches to patent policy. Burk and Lemley provide a very enlightening discussion of policy options. They explore the possibility that courts could use a differential application across industries of the uniform legal criteria in regard to presumptions of validity of patents, the scope of protection, and characterization of misuse. They also suggest that "injunctive relief may be inappropriate where patent rights are asserted primarily as hold-ups rather than as part of an effort to protect a legitimate invention," stressing that "[a]lternatively, injunctive relief may be problematic in industries characterized by anticommons problems, because individual patentees may have an incentive to hold out for a disproportionately high royalty, making it impossible to clear the rights necessary to sell products downstream. Such an industry may benefit from compulsory licensing."[230]

The requirement that exploitation of the closed-off patents be of substantial economic significance means that the demand for the product whose manufacture is prevented by the holdout be important. When the order to license is made to allow the exploitation of a dependent patent, the scope of the compulsory licence should not extend beyond what is necessary to allow the working of the dependent patent.

---

229 These countries, unlike Canada, are not constrained by the *NAFTA* provision, above note 10, that limits compulsory licensing for patent dependency to situations where the licence is a remedy to an adjudicated violation of an anti-competitive act.

230 Burk and Lemley (2003), above note 160 at 1667. A possible alternative route would be to explore ways in which competition authorities could clear the path for agreements between firms that would limit the profitability of holdouts.

Finally, there is no apparent reason to limit authorizations granted under section 19 of the *Patent Act* to government use. Private firms should be allowed to exploit compulsory licences on behalf of governments because the latter may not have the capacity to exploit a licence issued under section 19. These should be issued on the basis of public interest objectives.

F. SETTING ROYALTIES

The terms of a compulsory licence ought to reflect the objectives pursued by the decision to grant it. For example, when an order is made in application of section 79 of the *Competition Act*, the royalty is *reasonable* when it is just low enough to restore competition to the state it would have been in had the patentee not abused its dominant position. And, when the licence is issued to address a failure to meet demand in Canada to an adequate extent under section 65 of the *Patent Act*, its terms — royalty rates in particular — cannot be *reasonable* unless they encourage the licensee(s) to satisfy a significant segment of potential consumers and earn a return on that activity that does not deviate significantly from industry norms.[231]

Section 66(4) of the *Patent Act* directs that, in setting the terms of the licence, the commissioner of patents shall be guided as far as possible by the following considerations:

> (a) He shall endeavour to secure the widest possible use of the invention in Canada consistent with the patentee deriving a reasonable advantage from his patent rights;
> (b) He shall endeavour to secure to the patentee the maximum advantage consistent with the invention being worked by the licensee at a reasonable profit in Canada; and
> (c) He shall endeavour to secure equality of advantage among the several licensees, and for this purpose may, on due cause being shown reduce the royalties or other payments accruing to the patentee under any licence previously granted.

231 Reasonable terms in a context of compulsory licensing could also mean that the royalty paid by the licensee should be less than the amount she would be ordered to pay if she infringed.

Strictly speaking, no single royalty can meet each and every requirement of section 66(4). A particular royalty will not at the same time maximize the use of the patent subject to a minimum profit for the patentee *and* maximize the patentee's profits subject to a minimum profit for the licensee. One may therefore presume that a sensible reading of section 66 is that the commissioner, in setting the terms of the licence, must have regard for the interests of users, patentees, and licensees.[232]

One approach is to ask what licensing terms the "market" would have set. After all, when two people are free to transact they will only exchange when doing so provides a benefit to both. And user's interests are also served by licensees' bargaining for lower royalties.[233] The problem is that negotiations must already have failed before compulsory licensing procedures are initiated. What's more, the situations of extreme urgency and anti-competitive behaviour that do not call for prior negotiations are precisely those where one may shy away from reliance on market processes.

Therefore, the logical approach is to start with the question: what terms, which differ from the conditions that prevailed when actual bargaining broke down, would the parties have negotiated under hypo-

232 The requirement that the terms ensure that the licensee earn a *reasonable* profit is superfluous. After all, the order only applies to the patentee; the applicant would presumably refrain from taking the licence if its terms did not yield him a reasonable return. There is no restriction in the *Patent Act*, above note 12, with respect to the type of compulsory licence the commissioner may order. The TRIPS Agreement, above note 11, and *NAFTA*, above note 10, prohibit exclusive compulsory licences.

233 In reference to the question of how courts should set compensation to be paid by infringers, Lemley and Shapiro point out that relying on negotiated royalty rates involves an element of circularity as the negotiated rates themselves depend on parties' expectations about the damages courts will award if the patents are infringed; see Lemley and Shapiro, "Patent Holdup and Royalty Stacking" (2007) 85 Texas Law Rev. 1991 [Lemley and Shapiro (2007)]. The same point can be made here. Specifically, the negotiated licensing terms would presumably reflect expectations about the likelihood that a compulsory licence would be granted if the negotiation fails and the expectations about the terms of the compulsory licence. In the case of licensing, however, one can presume that the terms of compulsory licences do not have much influence, as long as orders to license remain rare.

thetical circumstances? For example, one could begin by asking: what royalty would the parties have agreed to if the urgency that justifies the order had not occurred? Or, what bargain would they have struck if it were known well in advance that the situation would occur?

Where the licence is issued to address a failure to meet Canadian demand because imports are blocked, one could ask what the Canadian price would have been if the patentee had not been in position to invoke an exclusive right to have imports stopped at the border. One could subtract from that hypothetical product price an amount that represents any cost incurred to manufacture the product in order to determine an upper bound for the royalty that will induce the beneficiary of the compulsory licence to sell at the hypothetical price.[234]

The "hypothetical circumstance approach" was adopted by the European Commission when it ordered Microsoft to issue licences in exchange for a *reasonable* remuneration that could not reflect the strategic value of its intellectual property rights. The bargaining situation the EC ostensibly had in mind was one where the defendant would not, or could not, use its intellectual property to strengthen its dominant position by exclusionary means. Microsoft was allowed to charge a royalty for its intellectual property, but the amount could not account for the contribution the property made to the value of the firm by being used to raise barriers to entry.[235]

Negotiated licensing terms for identical or similar technologies can serve as indicators of market rates, but only if they have been set in an environment that approximates the hypothetical circumstance.[236]

---

234 Because the patentee's product may also enjoy copyright protection and be trade-marked, the ability to have imports blocked also depends on the exhaustion regime applicable to these types of property.

235 See *Microsoft*, above note 125.

236 A US judge has drawn up a list of fifteen factors to assist in the emulation of the bargain that parties would have entered into had they negotiated; see *Georgia Pacific v. United States Plywoood*, 318 F. Supp. 1116 at 1120 (S.D.N.Y. 1970). The factors are (1) The royalties received by the patentee for the licensing of the patent in suit, proving or tending to prove an established royalty; (2) the rates paid by the licensee for the use of other patents comparable to the patent in suit; (3) the nature and scope of the licence, as exclusive or non-exclusive; or as restricted or non-restricted in terms of territory or with respect to whom the manufactured product may be sold; (4) the licensor's established policy and marketing program to maintain his patent monopoly by not licensing others to

It is clear, however, that such terms do not exist when licences are issued in exceptional circumstances such as health crises. Habitual fees are unlikely to be found when the hypothetical environments in which negotiations are imagined have unique features. Also, reliance on market-based licensing terms is problematic when licensors discriminate according to the type of licensee.

When it is impossible to establish what the parties would have negotiated under hypothetical circumstances, one might start by focusing directly on the objective pursued by the order and calculate what licensing terms are most likely to achieve the objective and still meet the requirements of section 66 of the *Patent Act.*

---

use the invention or by granting licences under special conditions designed to preserve that monopoly; (5) the commercial relationship between the licensor and licensee, such as, whether they are competitors in the same territory in the same line of business; or whether they are inventor and promoter; (6) the effect of selling the patented specialty in promoting sales of other products of the licensee, the existing value of the invention to the licensor as a generator of sales of his non-patented items, and the extent of such derivative or convoyed sales; (7) the duration of the patent and the term of the licence; (8) the established profitability of the product made under the patent, its commercial success, and its current popularity; (9) the utility and advantages of the patent property over the old modes or devices, if any, that had been used for working out similar results; (10) the nature of the patented invention; the character of the commercial embodiment of it as owned and produced by the licensor; and the benefits to those who have used the invention; (11) the extent to which the infringer has made use of the invention; and any evidence probative of the value of that use; (12) the portion of the profit or of the selling price that may be customary in the particular business or in comparable businesses to allow for the use of the invention or analogous inventions; (13) the portion of the realizable profit that should be credited to the invention as distinguished from non-patented elements, the manufacturing process, business risks, or significant features or improvements added by the infringer; (14) the opinion testimony of qualified experts; (15) the amount that a licensor (such as the patentee) and a licensee (such as the infringer) would have agreed upon (at the time the infringement began) if both had been reasonably and voluntarily trying to reach an agreement; that is, the amount that a prudent licensee — who desired, as a business proposition, to obtain a license to manufacture and sell a particular article embodying the patented invention — would have been willing to pay as a royalty and yet be able to make a reasonable profit and which amount would have been acceptable by a prudent patentee who was willing to grant a licence.

For example, one could start by defining a range of prices and corresponding quantities that would satisfy Canadian demand adequately. One would then determine a range of provisional royalty rates that would likely result in the production of these quantities. This would be followed by an assessment of whether these rates meet the requirements of sections 66(1)(a) and (b) of the *Patent Act*. If they do not adequately protect the reasonable interests of patentee and licensee(s), the amount payable to the patentee could be adjusted. If the latter prevents attainment of the objective under a uniform royalty rate, one may consider fixed fees or payment schemes for which the royalty rate applicable to the first batch of output is higher or lower than the rate for the following batches.

To establish provisional royalties and/or assess whether royalties meet the requirements of section 66, one could follow an approach used by courts to account for the profits of infringers.[237] The factors assessed include (i) the revenue from sales of the patented and convoyed products; (ii) the cost of other tangible and intangible inputs used in production; (iii) the contribution of the infringed technology to the profits earned by the infringer.[238]

When making that assessment, it is best to have regard to a small number of factors that are relevant in the majority of cases. A simpler formula has the advantage of transparency and predictability. For that reason, it increases the likelihood that the parties will agree to a voluntary licence. The likelihood of arriving at a negotiated royalty would probably increase if, following a determination that the necessary conditions required for compulsory licensing are met, the next decision

237 The maximum amount payable to the patentee can never exceed the incremental amount of profit the user of the patented technology would earn under a zero royalty (or undetected infringement). If it did, the applicant would refuse to take the compulsory licence. In this regard, a determination of terms of a licence is different from the calculation of compensation for infringement. The damages may be larger than the infringer's profit attributable to breach.

238 If a substitute technology in the public domain was available, the contribution would be small. Stack, Davidson, and Cole provide an overview of the procedures adopted by Canadian courts; see A.J. Stack, A.S. Davidson, and S.R. Cole, "Accounting of Profits Calculations in Intellectual Property Cases in Canada" (2001) 18 C.I.P.R. 405–51.

of whether or not to make the order is delayed to give the parties an opportunity to renew bargaining.[239]

Royalties should not be set with the objective of ensuring an acceptable return on research and development. This is probably impossible because there rarely is a one-to-one correspondence between a particular research and development investment and a specific patented technology. Also, one cannot know at the time a compulsory licence is issued how a patented technology will be used in the future, and how future uses will contribute to the patentee's profits.[240]

The determination of licensing terms involves an additional step when the production is contingent on the authorization from several patent holders. The approach is not conceptually different, but it is more complicated.

The starting point is to consider the hypothetical scenario where all technologies required to engage in production are owned by a single entity. The first step would involve the determination of an aggregate royalty for the entire bundle of patents using the same method as for a single patent. The next step should be to determine the contribution of each patent to the value of the bundle, taking into account the licensee's projected uses of the technology. In principle, the royalty on the compulsory licences should reflect their contribution to the value of the bundle. In practice, it is extremely difficult to make such a determination.

There may, however, be special situations that make it possible to set bounds (lower or upper) on the royalty. For example, when the use of a technology is prevented by the holdout of a single patentee, and when data are available on the unit costs of all other inputs — in-

239 One could also imagine a renewed negotiation following the determination of licensing terms. The purpose would be to amend the commissioner's terms in ways that benefit the licensor and the licensee. If the parties arrive at an agreement, they should be given the opportunity to apply to the commissioner for acceptance of the revised terms. Acceptance would be contingent upon meeting all of the goals of the initial terms.

240 Lemley and Shapiro (2007), above note 233, argue that courts should adjust the damages payable by infringers downward when research and development conducted by the patentee has benefited from public support. One can conjecture that in a like situation they would favour a downward correction on royalties for a compulsory licence.

cluding per unit royalties on all other technologies used in proposed production — one could derive an upper bound for the royalty on the holdout technology by subtracting the cost of all other inputs from the projected (or maximum) price, minus a profit margin. Also, it might be possible to proceed by analogy with the terms of the licences in the bundle that were voluntarily granted. And, when the latter terms are not the same for all patents, one might be able to proceed by asking which of the voluntary licences' technologies has the most in common with the holdout technology. Arrangements among patentees who have formed patent pools in related areas may provide another potential source of useful information.[241]

To the extent possible, terms should be set to ensure that they remain reasonable under changing circumstances. When there is considerable uncertainty about future demand, the payments by the licensee should track sales by the licensee. Where technology changes rapidly, provisions should be made for adjustment of the terms in response to improvements of the technology by the licensor or by the licensee.

Finally, it would be worthwhile to reconsider the question of whether the licence should automatically be issued to the person who took the initiative of applying to the commissioner. Under the current regime the licensee is the applicant. However, the applicant is not necessarily the party that can use the patented technology most effectively. A possible way around this problem is to give other firms — at arm's length from the patentee — the option to better the terms set by the commissioner, in a way that respects the objectives pursued by the commissioner, by granting the licence. Because the applicant initiated the process leading to the issue of a compulsory licence and incurred a cost by doing so, she should be granted a first refusal right.

G. RESPONSIBILITY FOR ISSUING LICENCES AND SETTING TERMS

Currently, the responsibility for granting compulsory licences under the *Patent Act* rests with the commissioner of patents.[242] The commis-

---

241 Although, pools will often opt for cross-licensing that bypasses the thorny problem of rate-setting.

242 Under s. 4(3) of the *Patent Act*, above note 12, "the Commissioner may, after consultation with the Minister, delegate to any person he deems qualified any

sioner of competition initiates the process, which may result in the issuance of a compulsory licence under the *Competition Act* by the Federal Court or the Competition Tribunal.

Should this arrangement be revised? A first alternative under consideration is delegation of compulsory licensing to a special regulator. A second alternative is to hand over the issuance of mandatory licences entirely to the courts and litigants. A third option is to have a "formalized board" assist the commissioner on the decision of whether to grant a licence. A different issue is whether that body should also be in charge of setting the terms of the license.

These options are considered below from the following perspectives: (i) openness and fairness of the process, (ii) timeliness and cost, and (iii) matching of required expertise with available expertise.

1) Expertise

Because compulsory licences may be issued in just about any sector of economic activity, sector-specific knowledge is not a particularly valuable asset. General knowledge of the patent issues and the effectiveness of compulsory licensing are more relevant.

When compulsory licensing is considered as a remedy against anti-competitive conduct, the required expertise pertains to evaluation of the effectiveness of compulsory licensing in comparison to alternative remedies or as a complement to other remedies.[243] The required expertise lies primarily in the area of competition. Clearly, the commissioner of competition and the Competition Tribunal are better equipped in this regard than a regulator or ordinary courts. Besides, the commissioner of competition is assisted by an expert staff, which at the stage of remedy selection will have become acquainted with the workings of the industry for which it designs a remedy.

In cases that do not involve competition, expert opinion is potentially helpful in regard to (i) whether the conditions that allow com-

---

of his powers, duties and functions under this Act, except the power to delegate under this subsection." In practice, the power the commissioner delegates is the power to order mandatory licences.

243 Other considerations are the harm alternative remedies cause to the parties on whom they are imposed and the cost and difficulty of administering each remedy.

pulsory licensing have occurred; and (ii) whether compulsory licensing can help attain the desired objective and, if so, how to structure the terms of the licence.

There is no reason to believe that a sector-specific regulatory board would possess qualifications in this regard, which is not already present in the Patent Office.

Senior patent examiners have accumulated knowledge across industries that a sector-specific regulator does not possess. And, there is nothing to prevent the commissioner of patents from seeking expert opinion from his staff or others on matters related to compulsory licensing.

The same applies to a formalized board. In order to endow such a board with the required expertise, one would probably have to draw on people with the qualifications of senior patent examiners. But if so, why not expand the advisory role of the Patent Appeals Board to include the evaluation of applications for compulsory licences?[244]

Also, courts are probably ill-suited to undertake the regulatory role that compulsory licensing entails.[245] The very fact that they rarely specify terms when they order the grant of a licence suggests that they are reluctant or ill-equipped to take on that regulatory role.[246]

---

244 The Patent Appeals Board is not the instance before which decisions of the commissioner in regard to compulsory licences are appealed. As indicated, the commissioner's decisions in regard to compulsory licences are appealed before the Federal Court. The role of the Patent Appeals Board, which is an administrative tribunal, is to provide recommendations to the commissioner on whether a patent should be granted in contentious cases.

245 Courts in Canada have not ordered the grant of compulsory licences (information provided by staff member of the Canadian Intellectual Property Office (CIPO)).

246 Antitrust courts would typically steer clear of meaningful guidelines in regard to royalties on mandatory licences. For example, in *IMS*, above note 114, the commission stated that royalties should be set by mutual agreement between the parties and, failing that, by the commission itself on the recommendation of independent experts: see *Commission Decision on IMS*, above note 117 at para. 215. In *Microsoft*, above note 125, it offered the nebulous guiding principle that royalties should be reasonable, non-discriminatory, and not reflect the strategic value of the information: see *Commission Decision of 24 May 2004 Relating to a Proceeding Pursuant to Article 82 of the EC Treaty and Article 54 of the EEA against the Microsoft Corporation* (Case COMP/C-3/37.792 Microsoft) at para. 274.

Good regulation requires the skills of a business person, which judges, accustomed to deciding by interpreting legal texts, may not possess or be reluctant to exercise. As pointed out by Baldwin and Cave, "trial-type processes (also) involve choices between the arguments of competing parties rather than continuing and rational approaches to the development of strategies for sectors and industries."[247] Furthermore, because judges tend to see problems and solutions in legalistic terms, they focus on the parties involved in court, possibly at the expense of other persons affected by their decision.

All regulation, including compulsory licensing, requires that attention be given to a variety of interests that ought to be weighed in the light of policy objectives. However, in practice, regulatory decisions tend to involve some ill-defined and hard to explain trade-offs. Abstract objectives must

> be broken down into components through the use of criteria that are then applied to alternatives and selections are made. Decisions are not comfortably made through formal administrative or legal decision-making processes. Rather, they are typically reached through the exercise of intuitive, highly subjective judgment, and they are more often the subject of business than of legal decision making.[248]

Also, the courts' perspective is essentially backward-looking. In infringement cases, courts calculate compensation on the basis of the quantities already produced by the infringer, the costs already incurred, and the prices observed during the period of infringement. The licensing authority must look forward. This means that decisions must be made with far less information. Decision making on the basis of partial and often conflicting information is a business skill. Furthermore, the task of a court is primarily to determine compensation. This task is accomplished by setting a lump sum. The regulatory task,

---

247 R. Baldwin and M. Cave, *Understanding Regulation* (Oxford: Oxford University Press, 1999) [Baldwin and Cave (1999)].

248 S. Breyer, *Regulation and Its Reform* (Cambridge, MA: Harvard University Press, 1982) at 81. Section C, above, has already alluded to the lack of enthusiasm on part of the highest courts in the US and the EU towards regulatory-type decision making.

on the other hand, is to assess the pros and cons of alternative royalty structures.[249]

2) Openness and Fairness of Process

Cases decided under the *Competition Act* follow the adversarial procedures of courts of justice. Therefore, involving another court whenever compulsory licensing is considered offers no advantage in terms of openness and fairness.

One may surmise that compulsory licensing would be removed from the list of remedies sought by the commissioner of competition under the general provisions of the *Competition Act* if an order to license could not be made by the Competition Tribunal.[250]

Section 66 of the *Patent Act* provides that if the commissioner of patents is satisfied that the applicant has a *bona fide* interest, and a case for relief has been made, the patentee or any other person opposing the granting of any relief may deliver a counterstatement. The commissioner may then dismiss the case if he is satisfied that the allegations in the application have been adequately answered, unless *any* of the parties demands a hearing, or unless the commissioner himself appoints a hearing.[251] When the commissioner does not dismiss an application, he may, with the approval of the minister, "order the whole proceedings or any issue of fact arising thereunder to be referred to the Federal Court which has jurisdiction in the premises"[252] *if* the parties interested consent or *if* "the proceedings require any prolonged examination of documents or any scientific or local investigation that cannot in the opinion of the Commissioner conveniently be made before him."[253] Experience shows that the parties rarely request that their

---

249 While judges often determine whether a particular contract meets a standard, they do not typically engage in an evaluation of alternative arrangements.

250 This is understood to include all provisions of the *Competition Act* under which compulsory licensing is a possible remedy, except s. 32.

251 The commissioner may in any case require the attendance before him of any of the declarants to be cross-examined or further examined on matters relevant to the issues raised in the application and the counter statement; see s. 69(2) of the *Patent Act*, above note 12. Experience shows that hearings are rarely held.

252 *Patent Act*, *ibid.* at s. 69(3).

253 *Ibid.* at s. 69(3)(b).

case be referred to the Federal Court. It also shows that the commissioner does not refer cases that require prolonged examination.[254]

All of the commissioner's orders and decisions are subject to appeal to the Federal Court. In practice though, appeals are limited to the commissioner's ruling that conduct has been abusive — they do not deal with the terms of a compulsory licence.

The assignment of the responsibility for compulsory licensing to courts presumably means that the whole process, starting with the application and eventually leading to the issue of a licence, would be carried out before a judge and would follow standard adversarial procedures.

The extent to which such assignment would contribute to openness and fairness is unclear. The very fact that the commissioner's decision can be appealed under the current regime already provides a guarantee against arbitrariness.[255] And, further assurance can be provided by an obligation to enunciate in detail the reasons for the decision whether or not to dismiss, and the decision made where the case is not dismissed.

Consistency is a component of fairness. A court of justice may well display greater consistency if it decides primarily on the basis of precedents. However, this would come at the expense of the required flexibility to interpret and reconcile different objectives of the *Patent Act* under varying circumstances.

It is also questionable whether one would achieve greater consistency by having decisions made by a larger group — as would be the case under the option of a formalized board or a regulatory body. A keen observer of the regulatory scene has noted that having more commissioners sit on a regulatory board is in fact more likely to lead

---

254 The person we interviewed at the Patent Office could not recollect such a reference to the Federal Court under s. 69(3), *ibid.*, in the last thirty years.

255 Judicial review may also carry a risk. Baldwin and Cave (1999), above note 247 at 302, point to the danger that judicial review would distort "regulatory processes by inducing a bias toward less reviewable modes of operations. This may be manifest in a movement towards the use of informal pressures and negotiations and may involve a drift towards less transparent and accessible regulatory procedures."

to inconsistency in approach.[256] The primary reason is fuzziness about the goals pursued by regulation and the impossibility of foreseeing outcomes with precision. The observer also argues that there is no basis to support a claim that a panel of regulators will have the inner, if inexpressible, consistency of a single decision maker.

3) Timeliness and Cost

The adversarial process is costly and slow. Assigning the responsibility for compulsory licensing to courts may discourage all applicants, with the exception of large firms, from seeking compulsory licences, especially when patents are owned by large corporations.

In view of the rarity of applications for compulsory licences, the cost of a specialized collegial body — a formalized board or regulator — is difficult to justify.[257] And, one could hardly expect prompter decision making by a collegiate body.

4) Who Should Set the Terms of the Licence?

It should be the person who decides whether or not to grant it. Indeed, the question of whether the licence achieves the desired policy objective and should for that reason be granted depends on the amount of royalty. For that reason it is not sensible to have one person make a determination on whether to make an order and then rely on another person — who may interpret the reason for the order differently than the person issuing the order — to establish the royalty.[258]

---

256 C.D. Foster, *Privitization, Public Ownership and the Regulation of Natural Monopoly* (Cambridge, MA: Blackwell, 1992).

257 Since the abandonment of the special regime for patented medicines and the elimination of non-working as abuse, applications in the pharmaceutical area have been made about once every two years. In other areas, applications have been made at a rate closer to once every five years. In the last six to seven years, not a single compulsory licence has been granted for a pharmaceutical product. Compulsory licensing outside the antitrust area has been equally rare in other countries.

258 The reason for having two separate entities in an anti-dumping case, one to determine if there is dumping and another to set the anti-dumping tariff — whatever these reasons are — is unlikely to be relevant for compulsory licensing. An anti-dumping procedure is much more mechanical, in theory at least.

5) Division of Responsibility between the Commissioners

To date, there has been no case that has received inputs from the commissioner of competition and the commissioner of patents on the question of whether or not to grant a compulsory licence.[259]

All sectors of the economy fall within the ambit of both commissioners, and each is required to determine a course of action according to criteria with little overlap. The "regulated industry defence" under the *Competition Act* presumably applies to the extent that conduct mandated by the commissioner of patents cannot be acted upon as if it violated the *Competition Act*.[260]

One can easily imagine situations where a patentee grants a licence on terms that contravene the *Competition Act* and abuse the *Patent Act*. Under the current regime, it is primarily the party whose application for a licence has been rejected or granted on objectionable terms that selects the forum before which it seeks remedial action. That choice clearly involves a consideration of the chances of success under the *Patent Act* relative to the *Competition Act*.

It is not obvious that such strict partition of responsibilities is optimal. An alternative arrangement that addresses some issues raised in earlier sections is to have an application made under the *Patent Act* transferred to the commissioner of competition and examined under the *Competition Act*, upon a determination by the commissioner of patents that the primary concern raised by the patentee's conduct is competition in the marketplace. Such concern could arise in conduct related to patent dependency.[261]

---

259 Information provided by a senior CIPO staff member.

260 The interface between competition law and "regulation" by the commissioner of patents is different from the delineation of the boundary between regulation by competition and sector-specific regulation. There is no activity of patentees that the commissioner of patents directly regulates and that she could forbear. Some issues revolving around regulation by competition law and direct regulation in Canada are discussed in Anderson *et al.*, "Competition Policy and Regulatory Reform, 1986–1997" (1998) 13:1/2 Review of Industrial Organization 177 at 204.

261 See Section E. For example, the conduct may prevent the production of a product A that would compete with a product B that in the absence of A would not face any competition.

Such transfer would achieve the following in terms of available remedies: [262]

1) it would provide tools besides compulsory licensing to address the competition issues. For example, it would allow making an order that the patentee provide access to complementary assets — physical as well as informational — indispensable to exploit the technology for which a compulsory licence is granted;[263]
2) it could ensure a follow-up that the conditions of the order are met.[264]

H. CONCLUSION

The drawbacks of having a formalized board or a court grant compulsory licences are more apparent than the advantages. It appears preferable to leave the responsibility for granting compulsory licences under the *Patent Act* to the commissioner of patents. However, because of the difficulty of setting royalties, and because orders to license may be ineffective in the absence of complementary orders, it seems useful to explore ways to expand the range of remedies available to the commissioner of patents and explore ways to have applications initially filed under the *Patent Act* also reviewed under the *Competition Act.*

---

262 It is not clear to the author whether such transfer would be necessary to meet the requirement of art. 1709(10) of *NAFTA*, above note 10, which conditions the grant of a mandatory licence to address patent dependency only "for an adjudicated violation of domestic laws regarding anti-competitive practices."

263 Under the current law, the commissioner of patents cannot order access to such complementary inputs.

264 There is no follow-up by the commissioner of patents to ensure that patentee's carry out the terms of his orders.

Commentary on "Compulsory Licensing"

Donald McFetridge[1]

Professor Hollander's paper is thoughtful and thorough. It introduced me to some important literature with which I was not familiar. I am in general agreement with Professor Hollander's methodological approach and with his major conclusions.

Professor Hollander adopts what I would call a global-efficiency approach in his analysis. This is in marked contrast to the historic Canadian approach to patent and patent licensing policy, which viewed Canadians essentially as users of patented technology owned by foreigners. This approach, as exemplified by the report of the Economic Council of Canada on intellectual property and the report of the Working Party on Patent Law Reform, regarded compulsory licensing as a tool of industrial policy along with the tariff and ownership restrictions. It viewed compulsory licensing or the threat of it as a means of increasing the bargaining power of Canadian licensees. It was also hostile to a variety of licensing practices (such as tying and bundling), which it regarded as potentially restrictive of the rights of licensees.

The contemporary approach recognizes that Canadians may be either licensors or licensees and that importing foreign technology

1 Professor, Department of Economics, Carleton University.

requires considerable domestic technological expertise. In essence, international free-riding is not free. The contemporary approach takes the view that the objective of patent licensing policy and jurisprudence should be to maximize the combined benefits of a licensing transaction to both the licensor and licensee.

Professor Hollander also appears to accept the patent right as given for purposes of evaluating alternate approaches to compulsory licensing. He does not embrace compulsory licensing either as a means of fine-tuning patent characteristics (breadth, term, novelty requirements) to suit the circumstances or as a means of correcting past mistakes of the Canadian Patent Office.

The major conclusion of Professor Hollander's paper is that compulsory licensing should be confined to a restricted set of circumstances, making it a relatively rare occurrence. These are (i) making use of an exclusive right to foreclose access in Canada to products or processes and (ii) making use of a patent to foreclose exploitation in Canada of another patent where such exploitation is of substantial economic significance.

Foreclosure of access to a product or process would be defined to have occurred when (i) the product involved is either not available or available in very limited quantities either from domestic or foreign sources; (ii) there are no good substitutes; and (iii) the product is available elsewhere. This definition of foreclosure does not challenge the patentee's right to choose where the patent is worked and how much of the patented product is produced. What it would challenge is a disproportionately small allocation of whatever output is produced to the Canadian market. This might occur, for example, if the patentee were attempting to avoid arbitrage from Canada to a higher priced market.

Making use of a patent to foreclose exploitation of another patent in Canada is defined to occur when (i) a patentee engages in an opportunistic holdout that prevents further development of one or more other patented technologies (the anti-commons) or; (ii) a patent is being used to make opportunistic allegations of infringement (patent sharking, patent trolling, and patent thickets). Notwithstanding the pejorative terms that are being used (shark, troll, holdout), these cases appear to involve commercial disputes that require the adjudication of overlapping claims. This would appear to be a matter for the courts.

Professor Hollander also devotes some attention to other arguments that have been made for compulsory licensing, in particular, the view that an intellectual property right should be treated as an essential facility. In his view, this is not a helpful approach. In the transportation, utilities, and communications industries, regulations requiring access to essential facilities have been used as an alternative to traditional regulation. In these industries, both the market and the essential facilities are relatively well-defined (although disputes over the terms and nature of access remain common). Patents are different. The subject matter of a patent generally does not coincide with an economic market. Whether there are means of competing in the market without access to the patent would likely also be difficult to determine.

The term "patent monopoly" may also be somewhat misleading. The patent right is an exclusive right to use the patented technology. If the exclusive right granted by the patent is to mean anything, a patentee cannot be obliged to provide competitors the wherewithal to compete with him. This is why the Competition Bureau's *Intellectual Property Enforcement Guidelines*[2] interpret section 32 of the *Competition Act*[3] very narrowly. Section 32 provides for the issue of a compulsory licence in cases in which an intellectual property right has been used to lessen competition unduly. According to its *Intellectual Property Enforcement Guidelines*, the Bureau would require that the lessening of competition involved be directly related to the subject matter of the patent, but go much beyond it (and also that the issue of a compulsory licence not discourage research and development). It seems clear that the Bureau would not use section 32 to force a patentee to accommodate a direct competitor as the essential facilities doctrine does. Whether a meaningful distinction can be made between effects that are close to the subject matter of the patent and those that are well beyond or removed from it remains to be seen.

Having determined the grounds on which compulsory licences should be granted, Professor Hollander turns to a number of other issues including royalty determination and who should have the re-

---

2 Competition Bureau Canada, *Intellectual Property Enforcement Guidelines* (Ottawa: Queen's Printer, 2000).

3 R.S.C. 1985, c. C-34.

sponsibility for granting compulsory licences. He concludes, correctly in my view, that in competition matters, the Competition Tribunal has compulsory licensing available as a possible remedy for conduct that substantially prevents or lessens competition. The other instances in which Professor Hollander sees compulsory licences being issued, especially technology foreclosure, appear to involve commercial disputes. One side alleges infringement while the other alleges sharking. Similarly, allegation by one patentee that the holder of a complementary patent is a holdout is also in the nature of a commercial dispute. Adjudicating competing claims of this nature is what the courts do and perhaps it is they, rather than the commissioner of patents, that should have responsibility for it.

To conclude, although I take issue with him in some minor respects, I think Professor Hollander's paper is a very good one and I commend it to anyone with an interest in compulsory licensing.

Commentary: Mending the Gap — Intellectual Property, Competition Law, and Compulsory Licensing

E. Richard Gold[1]

In my comments I wish to speak not so much to Professor Hollander's excellent presentation on the use of compulsory licences as a remedy for anti-competitive conduct, but on the role that compulsory licences play in managing the uncertainties inherent in intellectual property rights. My central argument is that intellectual property rights are inherently incomplete and require a variety of tools, including compulsory licence provisions, to ensure that they best meet our economic and social goals. To make this argument, I will first lay out some general propositions concerning intellectual property before turning to the role of competition law — using compulsory licences as an example — in shaping it.

Intellectual property rights are inherently vague. There are two reasons for this. First, the legal boundaries around knowledge assets are inherently fuzzy. This is because, unlike a table, there is no objective method to identify the edges of a knowledge asset.[2] Legal arguments over where lines should be drawn add to the vagueness of an

---

1 Professor and Director, Centre for Intellectual Property Policy, McGill University.

2 P. Drahos, *A Theory of Intellectual Property Rights* (Aldershot: Dartmouth, 1996).

asset since, at the time an intellectual property right is awarded, we do not—and cannot—know its edges. This problem is exacerbated by the fact that technology changes so quickly: by the time we start to map out the general outlines of a knowledge asset, it has been replaced by another. Second, the technology that mediates the uses of technology—the Internet, nanotechnology, biotechnology breakthroughs, and so on—is rapidly changing. Once again, at the time we award an intellectual property right, we can only guess to which uses a knowledge asset will be put. More importantly, we cannot fully imagine the economic and social uses that will come, at some point in the future, to attach to that knowledge asset.

Intellectual property rights are only partially about economics. While we increasingly speak about the economic incentives brought about by intellectual property rights, this is a rather modern and, if one examines the actual functioning of the system, limited view of what these rights do. The history of intellectual property rights stretch back centuries in the case of patents, several centuries for copyright, and over a century in the case of trade-marks. When one examines this history, one sees that intellectual property rights have been more often shaped by political battles or bureaucratic dictate than economic sense. This is especially so in the arts, where we justify intellectual property rights more on their recognition of artistic contribution than on economic necessity. To be sure, economics has increasingly become important in intellectual property. Nevertheless, it is far less than the whole story.

Intellectual property rights have contradictory effects.[3] We really have very little empirical evidence of how intellectual property rights actually function within an economy. While anecdotal and opinion evidence abounds, most of it is of limited value. This is because it only captures the stories of those who succeeded. The stories of projects never started, groups never formed, and science that did not go anywhere do not exist. As to hard econometric data, little exist. We do know that at certain places and at certain times with certain technologies, technology—for example, the semiconductor industry in the

---

3 E.R. Gold *et al.*, "The Unexamined Assumptions of Intellectual Property: Adopting an Evaluative Approach to Patenting Biotechnological Innovation" (2004) 18 Public Affairs Quarterly 273.

1970s[4] — has advanced rapidly in the absence of intellectual property rights. The opposite is also true. As a consequence of our lack of knowledge, how much (or little) intellectual property rights for what type of knowledge assets lead to the greatest productivity and wealth is simply unknown.

These three points — that intellectual property rights are vague, are as much about social as they are about economic outcomes, and that we have little empirical knowledge about how intellectual property rights actually function — make any notion of an independent and internally coherent intellectual property system absurd. It is within this context that one must address the intersection of competition law with intellectual property law generally, and the role that compulsory licences play in mediating that intersection more specifically.

Added to this fuzziness is how intellectual property law and competition law actually operate. The former is an *a priori* system of awarding rights while the latter is an *ex post* evaluation of conduct. I turn to this next.

Intellectual property rights represent *a priori* decisions by the state to allow an individual to exploit a certain knowledge asset. As noted above, what is included as part of that asset, the social and economic value of the asset, and how that asset will come to be of use in the future are all unknown at the time of grant. The very structure of intellectual property law recognizes this: it employs standard rules that apply regardless of the knowledge asset, its social context, and social value. So, for instance, we do not award patent rights for a period determined as a function of the real value of the underlying knowledge asset; we award rights that last twenty years regardless of the social and economic contribution of the invention. Similarly, we award copyright for the life of the author plus fifty years regardless of its contribution and value. Intellectual property rights are, in sum, simply launched by the state in the hopes that trade winds push them along in the right direction. Sometimes, the wrong wind comes along. It is here that competition law comes into play.

4 B.H. Hall and R.H. Ziedonis, "The Patent Paradox Revisited: An Empirical Study of Patenting in the US Semiconductor Industry, 1979–95" (2001) 32(1) RAND Journal of Economics 101.

Competition law represents *ex post* decisions about the use of knowledge assets. The state can make real time decisions about how to adjust the course of economic activity based on a set of accepted principles. Competition law tends to the flexible, adapted response to a particular situation rather than the one-size-fits-all approach of intellectual property. It can correct against the effect of the wrong wind pushing a knowledge asset in an unwanted direction.

One way to see the intersection between intellectual property and competition law is that the latter completes the former: competition law provides the opportunity for an *ex post* correction of an *a priori* decision to award an intellectual property right. Since at the time of award, the intellectual property right itself is embryonic — in the sense that its contours and social interactions are unknown — competition law can help guide the development of the right into a mature and well-functioning asset.

Competition law completes intellectual property rights in a second way. Intellectual property rights are not simply little bundles of rights to keep others from using knowledge assets; they are just as much about providing others with rights to use the knowledge asset despite the intellectual property right. For example, copyright's fair dealing exception is, according to the Supreme Court of Canada, just as integral to copyright as the right of the copyright holder to prevent others from reproducing a work.[5] Other limits similarly mark out the contours of intellectual property rights. That is, these limits do not take away anything from the rights holder; rather, they trace out the boundaries of what the state has awarded to the rights holder. Competition law constitutes one such boundary.

Given this, it is hard to understand the continued reluctance, expressed in the IPEGs,[6] for competition authorities to fully exercise their role as boundary keeper. As intellectual property rights are half-formed when granted, competition law provides an appropriate, technologically-unbiased way to ensure that knowledge assets do not block innovation and price competition. Unlike the US, Canada even has the clear statutory authority to do so: section 32 of the *Competi-*

---

5 *CCH Canadian Ltd. v. Law Society of Upper Canada*, [2004] 1 S.C.R. 339.

6 Competition Bureau Canada, *Intellectual Property Enforcement Guidelines* (Ottawa: Queen's Printer, 2000) [IPEGs].

tion Act[7] makes clear that "where use has been made" of the exclusive rights offered by intellectual property rights in an unwanted manner, the Bureau may intervene. Nevertheless, the Bureau unduly restrains itself by inserting the words "mere exercise" to its exercise of powers under section 32 without, as Professor Hollander ably points out, any economic or other justification. If the reasoning behind the introduction of the phrase "mere exercise" is to show deference to intellectual property law, that deference is misplaced given the incomplete nature of intellectual property law.

I can now turn to my specific comments about compulsory licences. Compulsory licensing constitutes one of the inherent limits on intellectual property rights. They involve enforcement of the intellectual property right through a liability rule rather than through a property rule. It would be hard to conceive, in fact, of an intellectual property system that did not contain some sort of liability rule. The US, for example, relies heavily on such rights for government use of intellectual property. While some branches of industry, namely the pharmaceutical sector, have tried to argue that compulsory licences are illegitimate, there is no basis in intellectual property law or theory to support that claim.

One of the most important things to recognize is that compulsory licences are designed *not* to be used. That is, compulsory licences work best when an actor has a reasonable expectation that the state will issue a compulsory licence if that actor does not change behaviour. In such a case, the actor will change behaviour rather than suffer the consequence of a (usually) more confining compulsory licence. The fact, therefore, that Germany has not issued a compulsory licence since the 1950s and France has not since the 1970s does not indicate that compulsory licences do not work. In fact, France expanded its compulsory licensing regime to cover diagnostic tests in 2004. This indicates that, despite the fact that France has not issued a compulsory licence in many years, it finds the threat of compulsory licences to be an effective policy tool.

One of the main drivers for invoking a compulsory licence is the threat that intellectual property rights block further development. Governments have invoked the possibility of a compulsory licence to

---

7 R.S.C. 1985, c. C-34.

unblock patents that hampered the development of both the airplane and the radio industries. This concentration on compulsory licensing in the innovation market should tell us something: that it is regrettable that the IPEGs do not take seriously the need to monitor the anti-competitive use of intellectual property rights in that market.

My overall message is the following: it is unreasonable for competition law to wait for intellectual property law to sort out its affairs and define "clear" rights. As I have argued, intellectual property law provides rights that are inherently incomplete given uncertainties as to scope and use. This intellectual property law, as an *a priori* system of rights, will never be able to clear up. Competition law offers us that opportunity. The IPEGs should recognize this.

CHAPTER 5

An Evaluation of Collective Copyright Management in Canada

Jacques Robert[1]

A. INTRODUCTION

1) Objectives of Copyright Management

The general policy objectives of the copyright policy are to encourage the creation and dissemination of original works. The policy should reflect the fairness values of Canadians while promoting economic efficiency. The copyright policy should accomplish two main objectives:

1) Promote the creation of quality and diverse original works. Allow creators to earn revenues from their creations in order to provide strong incentives for the creation of original works.
2) Promote access to quality and diverse original work. The market for original work should be open, without barriers to entry for new creators. Independent creators should be able to compete with creators backed by large corporations.

The first challenge for copyright policy is to find a reasonable way to balance the two conflicting objectives: providing access to original works and rewarding creators. On the one hand, one will wish for

---

1 Professor in the Department of Information Technologies at HEC Montreal and a Fellow at CIRANO.

open and free access to all original works, and on the other hand one must recognize the rights of creators to gain rewards for their original efforts. If we seek to minimize royalties and enhance competition among creators, they will share less revenue and there will be fewer incentives to create. The role of the copyright policy is to balance these opposite objectives and provide a fair and efficient solution. Hence, the fees on the licences should be fair and not so high that they become a barrier to the dissemination of original works.

Original works such as music, literature, multimedia, digital pictures, and drawings enter in the category of what could be called information goods. While the initial cost of production is large, the marginal cost is virtually zero. The essence of what is created can be stored as bytes on a disc, distributed, and reproduced at virtually no cost. Without the copyright protection, information goods would be similar to pure public goods and creators would not be able to earn revenues from their work. Hence, the issue is to find a way to fund the creation of original works while maintaining their access as cheap and open as possible. Granting the creators copyright provides them with the legal right to exclude, and hence provides some form of *de facto* monopoly on the commercialization of their works.

The second challenge associated with copyright protection is enforceability. It could be very costly for a creator to monitor the use of his original works by end-users. In practice, creators must rely on the support of the law and on specialized third parties or technology to monitor and enforce their copyrights. With the advent of Internet technologies, notably the P2P technologies, the enforceability problem becomes even more acute.

The worst-case scenario would be to have creators limiting access to their work by imposing large access fees and complex clearance systems while a large majority of users choose to access these works illegally using new download technologies. In such a scenario, law-abiding citizens would find access costly and complex and the creators would find the number of paying customers progressively shrinking. This could be the future that lies ahead of us. In this context, the copyright collectives could play a major role in responding to these challenges. Copyright collectives should help end-users obtain legal access to copyright-protected work, while helping creators extract more revenues from their work.

The general objective of this study is to provide an assessment of the Canadian copyright management system based on a micro-economic rationale. Does the current Canadian system of copyright collectives achieve its general goals? Should alternative designs and mechanisms be proposed? Eventually, what would be a more appropriate model and what challenges would Canada face in moving to another system? What is the logic of the current system and is it consistent with the general interest?

2) Structure of the Paper

This study is structured as follows. In Section B, the study draws from the economic literature in order to better understand the fundamental market failures (if any) that would justify the need for regulation in the original-work markets. One proposed argument in favour of regulation is the fact that collectives save on transactional costs: a collective can more efficiently negotiate, enforce, and collect fees on behalf of creators than creators themselves. While this argument explains the existence of firms that specialize in copyright management, it does not justify *per se* the existence of a regulated monopoly. While the rationale for a regulated monopoly cannot be based on a transactional cost argument alone, we believe that welfare can be improved by bundling copyrights. Setting a blanket licence that bundles all the rights is often the best practical mechanism to market copyrights. There are many examples of bundled information goods: licences for academic journals (JSTOR), news service subscriptions, cable television subscriptions, etc. Fang and Norman study the optimal provision mechanism for multiple excludable, non-rival public goods. They show that the optimal mechanism involves a fixed fee and bundling.[2] Bakos and Brynjolfsson[3] show that bundling information goods increases both revenue (incentive for creation) and efficiency (reduces dead weight losses). In these cases, there is an economic rationale for the creation of a (regulated) collective: it makes it possible to bundle rights on all creation works.

2 H. Fang and P. Norman, "An Efficiency Rationale for Bundling of Public Goods" (2004) Micro Theory Working Papers online: microeconomics.ca.

3 Y. Bakos and E. Brynjolfsson, "Bundling Information Goods: Pricing, Profits and Efficiency" (1999) 45:12 Management Science 1613 [Bakos and Brynjolfsson (1999)].

In Section C, the main characteristics of the Canadian copyright management system are reviewed. In Canada, there are thirty-six specialized collectives that grant some, or all, of the rights related to the use of literary, musical, or television works. This section describes the role of these various collectives and presents a typology of existing collectives. The objective is to understand the different realities of the different copyright markets (music, literary work, multimedia, and film, etc.) and see whether the different copyright regimes are justified and can be rationalized. International comparison becomes important in doing so. With the exception of the US, the copyright collective structure seems rather similar across countries (the UK, France, Nordic countries, Canada). Section C ends with an assessment of the structure and efficiency of the current copyright collective system in Canada.

Section D is devoted to the impact and role of the technology, notably file sharing, digital copy, and Digital Rights Management (DRM) technologies. Information and Internet technologies have had major impacts over the last decade. They offer new challenges for the regulator and they require that the scope of copyright collective management be extended.

Section E concludes with a list of recommendations.

B. PRICING, BUNDLING, MONOPOLIES, AND OTHER COMPETITIVE ISSUES

Copyrights grant *de jure* monopoly rights to the creator on her works. While monopoly rights tend to create economic efficiencies, they allow creators to extract some economic rents from their original works. Copyrights and intellectual property legislation can be seen as necessary evils — a necessary price to pay to generate incentives for the creation of new original works and ideas. The design of the copyright management system should seek to maximize the incentives to create, while reducing market inefficiencies (dead weight losses) generated by monopolistic behaviour. In light of these objectives, one may ask whether there is some rationale for copyright collectives. In the name of competition, economic efficiency, and antitrust, is the existence of copyright still justifiable or should we recommend change in the current copyright management regime in which copyright collectives play a crucial role? Could and should the system be altered to enhance competition, while promoting creation and dissemination of original works?

1) The Demise of Natural Monopolies

Monopolies are generally unfair and lead to inefficiency. They lead to inefficiencies because monopolies typically charge above marginal cost prices and buyers purchase less than is socially optimal. They are unfair because monopolies are in a position to extract economic rents from their dominant market position to the detriment of the consumers. Monopolies also tend to introduce artificial barriers to entry, in order to protect their dominant market position and hence have the tendency to limit innovation from possible entrants. In simple terms, monopolies are bad and competition (free entry and price equal to marginal costs) should be encouraged. This is, at least, the conventional wisdom. However, in some cases it does not apply.

Natural monopolies arise when there are large economies of scale: one firm can always produce more efficiently than two or more firms. Forcing many firms will lead to unnecessary duplication and will be inefficient. It is better then to regulate one firm than to promote competition among many. Historically, this has been the argument used for the existence of regulated monopolies in utilities and in railway and air transportation. However, natural monopolies are disappearing: flexible manufacturing, large and open markets, and global interconnectivity standards have contributed to reduce the number of truly natural monopolies. Over the last few decades, regulators have revisited old paradigms and competition has been increased in previously heavily regulated industries (telecom, utilities, air travel, etc.).

Another case where the legislator admits and encourages the formation of monopolies is the case of unions. Trade and labour unions are collective entities that act as bargaining agents for all employees in a bargaining unit. The legislator recognizes that groups of workers are entitled to be represented by a single "wage-earners association for the purpose of maintaining or improving the conditions of their employment."[4]

In a series of two papers, Katz revisited the relevance of copyright collectives.[5] He states at the beginning of his first paper that "the

---

4 S. Weeb and B. Weeb, *History of Trade Unionism* (London: Wargmans and Co., 1920).

5 See A. Katz, "The Potential Demise of another Monopoly: Rethinking the Collective Administration of Performing Rights" (2005) 1 Journal of Competition

common explanation behind the proliferation of collective administration is that some aspects of copyright administrations are natural monopolies."[6] He then argues that because of technological innovations this natural monopoly argument does not hold.

The core of the arguments by Katz is the following: a collective is in a better position to monitor and collect fees than individual creators, hence it yields some efficiencies and benefits by reducing transactional costs. These benefits must be weighed against the cost of monopoly pricing. If transactional costs could be reduced with the help of information technologies, then, argues Katz, there would be no need for copyright collectives and we could seek to implement a competitive market.

I agree with Katz that the presence of transactional costs was and still is one of the arguments in favour of copyright collectives. I agree that information technologies can drastically reduce transactional costs and that, in theory, transitional costs can become sufficiently small so that a fully competitive marketplace for copyrights becomes a viable alternative to collective management. I disagree however with the premise that the presence of transactional costs is the only rationale for the existence of copyright collectives. In the next section, another rationale is discussed.

2) The Problem of Pricing Information Goods

Original works such as music, literary works, multimedia, digital pictures, and drawings enter in the category of what could be called information goods. With the rise of the Internet, there is a growing concern about the problem of pricing for information goods.[7] The fundamental problem of pricing information goods is that, by nature, information goods have the characteristics of pure public goods — they are by nature non-rival and non-exclusive. While the initial cost of production is large, the marginal cost is virtually zero. The fact that a person

---

Law and Economics 541 [Katz (2005)]; and A. Katz, "The Potential Demise of Another Monopoly: New Technologies and the Administration of Performing Rights" (2006) 2 Journal of Competition Law and Economics 245 [Katz (2006)].

6 A. Katz (2005), *ibid.* at 541.

7 H. Varian, "Pricing Information Goods" (Paper presented to the Proceedings in Scholarship in the New Information Environment Symposium, Harvard Law School, 2–3 May 1995) at 1.

enjoys a piece of music does not generate extra social cost. Without the copyright protection, information goods can be reproduced and used freely. The copyright protection has been created to prevent this. Under a copyright regime, a creator can charge a price above the marginal cost and earn revenues from its creation. The direct effect is market inefficiencies. When prices are above marginal cost, there are people who do not get the good although they are willing to pay the social cost to acquire it (exclusion).

One way of looking at the information-good pricing problem is to determine how much market inefficiency we are willing to bear in order to allow creators to extract rents from their work. This approach begins with the premise that rent extraction by producers can only be achieved at the expense of social and economic efficiency (marginal price above marginal costs). But what if it was not the case? What if we could reduce the market inefficiency while increasing the rent extracted by creators? By doing so, we would be able to pursue our (seemingly conflicting) objectives. We believe that copyright management can and must use all the available tricks necessary to both help increase the welfare of creators and reduce market inefficiencies.

There is an important microeconomic literature in mechanism design that considers the best way to market and price goods in environments with information asymmetries. This literature may become handy for solving the information-good pricing problem. If the rights holder could perfectly price discriminate, he could both increase his rents and reduce the market efficiency. Price discrimination consists of charging a high price to those that are willing to pay high prices and charging lower prices to those who are not. By doing so, the monopolists can sell to everyone (no exclusion) and make as much revenue as the market can bear. Perfect price discrimination would be ideal, but it is not practical. In order to perfectly discriminate, one would need to know exactly what each individual consumer is willing to pay for the good and prevent arbitrage, which is not the case. The theory of mechanism design considers how a monopolist can best sell and price products when she remains uninformed about the customers' willingness to pay for her products. Non-linear pricing schemes[8] are ways that

---

8 R. Wilson, "Nonlinear Pricing and Mechanism Design" in H. Amman, D. Kendrick, and J. Rust, eds., *Handbook of Computational Economics*, vol. 1 (Amster-

monopolists can use to price discriminate in order to extract more rents and mitigate the social efficiencies, despite information asymmetries.

In the context of information goods, there are various non-linear pricing schemes that have been proposed such as versioning (price discrimination using quality) or bundling (pricing multiple products jointly). These schemes are examined in the next subsection.

3) The Bundling and Versioning of Information Goods

The strategy of bundling consists of selling many products together for a unique price. The practice is quite common in the case of information goods. A single newspaper, for instance, is a bundle of many articles. One individual customer may not read all the articles, but presumably all the articles are read by some customers and all customers read some of the articles. A subscription to a newspaper is obviously also a bundle. JSTOR[9] offers a blanket licence to a large set of articles.

It is argued here that bundling is a way one can use to both reduce market efficiency and increase monopoly rents. This is illustrated with the following (simplistic) example.

Example A

Consider a simple, numerical pricing problem with two consumers, A and B, and two products, X and Y. Suppose that consumer A is willing to pay up to $8 for good X and up to $21 for good Y, while consumer B is willing to pay up to $17 for good X and $10 for good Y. Further, suppose that the marginal cost of each good is zero.

Willingness to Pay

	A	B
X	8	17
Y	21	10
X & Y	29	27

---

dam: Elsevier, 1996); R. Wilson, *Non-Linear Pricing* (Oxford, Oxford University Press, 1993).

9 JSTOR, short for "journal storage," is an online database that offers access to scholarly journals. When a university subscribes to JSTOR, its faculties and students can freely download published and copyrighted articles. See online: www.jstor.org.

The firm selling good X will sell two units if it charges a price of $8 or less and will sell one unit if it charges a price between $8 and $17. Hence, the maximum profit it will make is $17 and it will then sell only one unit. The firm selling good Y will sell two units if it charges a price of $10 or less and will sell one unit if it charges a price between $10 and $21. Hence, the maximum profit it will make is $21 and it will sell only one unit. In both cases, monopoly pricing leads to market inefficiency: only one unit is sold although the production cost of the second unit is zero. Together the monopolists will earn revenues of $38 ($21 + $17).

Now suppose that goods X and Y can be sold together as a bundle. Consumer A is willing to pay $29 for the bundle while consumer B is willing to pay $27. Two units of the bundle X & Y will be sold if its price is $27 or less, and one bundle will be sold if its price is $29. Hence, the maximum profit is $54 (2 × $27) if both consumers buy the bundle.

Notice that, in this example, efficiency is increased (all consumers get all the available goods) and the joint profits of the producers of X and Y have increased (from $38 to $54). This example illustrates how bundling can improve both social inefficiency and seller's profits. If firms split the joint profit equally, the new arrangement is Pareto improving: both firms get more profit and no consumer is worse off. This illustrates a paradox: when bundling is allowed, a monopoly that is allowed to bundle all products can lead to more efficiency than two independent firms for which bundling is not possible.

One can devise alternative examples.

Example B

Willingness to Pay

	A	B
X	8	17
Y	21	10
X & Y	21	17

In this example, the willingness to pay for both goods is not the sum of what one would like to pay for both goods but the maximum one would like to pay for either good. If goods X and Y are sold separately, the competitive prices will be, as before, $17 and $21, respectively, with total profits of $38. Now, if goods X and Y could only be sold in a bundle, then the optimal price for the bundle would be $17, generating profits of $34. In this example, bundling does not change total welfare because consumers have no use for two different goods. However, it decreases the firms' total profit, but it advantages at least one consumer.

Example C

In the following example, the bundle will be sold at a price of $20. This generates total profits of $40, higher than the total profit earned when goods are sold separately. Bundling is welfare-improving since consumers benefit from having two rather than one unit.

Willingness to Pay

	A	B
X	8	17
Y	21	10
X & Y	23	20

However, if revenues from sales are divided equally between the two firms, the firm that produces good Y ends up with less profit than before ($20 rather than $21). In this example, if we allow the firm that produces good Y to withdraw its product from the bundle, it will want to do so and welfare and total profits will decrease.

The above examples generate striking and paradoxical conclusions. Forcing two firms to market their products jointly could be welfare-improving, but not necessarily profitable for the firms themselves.

Example D

In this last example, goods X and Y are perfect substitutes: consumers value the two goods the same and the value of having the two goods is no better than having only one. If goods X and Y are sold together by a monopolist, the bundle will be sold at a price of $11. Only one consumer will buy the bundle and the generated total profit will be $11. However, if goods X and Y are sold by two independent firms, then the fact that the two products are perfect substitutes will drive the price down to zero.

Willingness to Pay

	A	B
X	5	11
Y	5	11
X & Y	5	11

This example illustrates the ill effects of a monopoly. The allocation is inefficient (one consumer does not buy) and the monopoly captures the entire consumer surplus. Two elements contribute to this result: (i) the goods are perfect substitutes and (ii) the willingness to pay is sufficiently different so that it is advantageous to set the price high. On the other hand, without a monopoly the two firms would compete until profits were nil. This, in regards to the objective of generating rents for creators, is not a viable alternative.[10] A regulated monopoly that is forced to set a price of $5 could generate rents for creators while limiting market inefficiencies.

As the above examples demonstrate, bundling can be welfare-improving if (i) consumers typically desire more than one item, (ii) the willingness to pay for one item varies from one consumer to another, and (iii) the willingness to pay for all items averages out to some amount more or less the same for all customers. The above argument has been generalized in Bakos and Brynjolfsson (1999).[11] They consider an economy with many consumers and many goods. The amount that each consumer is willing to pay for each good is independently distributed. By the law of large numbers, what one is willing to pay for a large bundle of products tends to average out and is more or less the same across buyers. They show that profits increase and welfare losses decrease when the number of products bundled increases.[12]

The argument presented above is not merely saying that having four firms can be better than having eight firms, but rather that one firm can be better than two. Provided that the conditions are right, having a unique entity marketing all available products as a bundle can improve social welfare (decrease exclusion) and help extract more rents for producers.

It is not the objective of this paper to survey the bundling literature; however, what this section has argued is that the bundling of information goods and other forms of non-linear pricing schemes can

10 One could imagine two collectives that administer the same set of rights. These collectives could in principle each grant blanket licences for the same repertoire. Clearly, competition is not incompatible with blanket licensing. However, both collectives will be acting as Bertrand competitors. Competition will force the price down leaving little to the creators the collectives were supposed to help.

11 Above note 3. See 1615–19 for a mathematical description of their model.

12 *Ibid.*

offer the best way to extract revenues while limiting the dead weight losses. In these cases, the creation of a monopoly (or an alternative institution) capable of bundling all available pieces of work or offering non-linear pricing schemes not feasible in a competitive environment could be welfare-improving.

4) The Economic Rationale for Copyright Collectives

One of the *raisons d'être* of a collective is that it can market all relevant original works under one blanket licence. No individual creator or organization can do so without having access to all the rights on all relevant original works. A collective, however, can play this role if the legislation supports rights acquisition (i.e., it facilitates the collective effort to include all relevant work in its blanket licences). According to Gervais, in a majority of countries there is only one collective per field of activity.[13] Further, the legislation in these countries tends to facilitate rights acquisition and the formation of blanket licences.[14]

In Canada, the system is largely voluntary. However, the system has been built in such a way as to discourage creators from not joining the collective. This will be discussed later.

Koskinen-Olson attributes the relative success of Collective Management Organizations (CMOs) in the Nordic countries to the "extend repertoire system."[15] The system looks quite similar to the conditions applying to collective labour agreements. Once a CMO-deemed representative of a group of rights holders concludes an agreement with an end-user, the agreement covers also the non-represented rights holders. A non-represented rights holder can always opt out and negotiate an alternative agreement, but he is presumed to accept the umbrella agreement until he explicitly opts out. This system protects the end-users from lawsuits from non-represented rights holders and limits the costs for them of acquiring rights for a substantially large repertoire.

---

13 Daniel Gervais, "Collective Management of Copyright and Neighbouring Rights in Canada: An International Perspective" (2002) 1:2 C.J.L.T. 21–50 [Gervais (2002)].

14 *Ibid.*

15 TarjaKoskinen-Olson, "Collective Management in the Nordic Countries" [Koskinen-Olson (2006)] in D. Gervais, ed., *Collective Management of Copyright and Related Rights* (Alphen aan den Rijn, The Netherlands: Kluwer Law International, 2006) [Gervais (2006)] at 281–82.

Because it is relatively easy to compute what broadcasters are willing to pay for a blanket broadcasting licence, but it is rather difficult to estimate what each broadcaster is are willing to pay for each specific piece of work, we are in a situation much similar to the one illustrated in Example A, above in section A(3). Offering a blanket licence not only decreases transactional costs but it can also increase both the creator's profit and social efficiency.

At the beginning of this section, it was asked whether the system of copyright collectives could or should be altered to enhance competition. We also asked whether in the name of competition, economic efficiency, and antitrust the existence of copyright collectives were still justifiable or whether a change to the current copyright management regime, in which copyright collectives play a crucial role, should be recommended. The short answer to both questions is no.

The general sentiment of this author is that an environment in which creators negotiate their tariff directly with the users and in which they must compete directly against each other is not the best way to manage copyright. Such a solution will certainly involve some major transactional costs, but even if we had the technology to reduce transactional costs to the minimum, there would still be a more fundamental issue to resolve. The issue is that linear pricing, which comes with pure price competition, cannot achieve the two general objectives of the copyright system simultaneously; namely (i) efficient dissemination of the created work (price equals marginal cost) and (ii) revenue generation for creators. Further, a blanket licence provides a better way to fulfill both these objectives. For these reasons, a system of collective management is justified in order to market blanket licences for extended repertoires. It should be well-understood that the rationale defended here is not one based only on transactional costs. Hence, the argument still stands under a new technological environment that would drastically reduce or eliminate these transactional costs.

C. THE COPYRIGHT COLLECTIVES IN CANADA AND SELECTED COUNTRIES

In Canada, there are thirty-six specialized collectives that grant some, or all, of the rights related to the use of literary, musical, or televised works. There is no amalgamated body ("super-collective") with the authority to grant permission to use all works for all purposes. Each of those collectives represents a different group of artists, operates in a different industry, or has a different mission and mandate. In this section, we try to understand the role of each of the existing collectives. The objective is to try to understand whether there is a rationale for having so many organizations. I wish to understand whether the differences between the various art forms (music, multimedia, literary works, or the visual arts) justify the existence of different collectives and/or copyright management regimes, and if so why. Accordingly, I intend to examine whether changes in the number and role of copyright collectives are necessary.

Do the existing collectives behave in the best interests of rights holders and/or end-users? Can the interests of creators and the particular rights holders be better protected by one "super-collective" or by specialized collectives? Does the creation of many collectives create or eliminate barriers to entry for small creators? Can the interests of end-users be better protected by one "super-collective" or by specialized collectives? For example, a Canadian radio broadcaster may be forced to deal with several copyright collectives, each one granting some subset of all the rights needed to legally broadcast music, while a Norwegian radio broadcaster has only to deal with one large collective that can grant all required rights; the transaction costs in each case are likely quite different.

1) A Typology of the Existing Collectives and Markets

Gervais classifies the Canadian collectives using the legal regimes (music performing rights, general regime, retransmissions and educational institutions, and private copying).[16] Collectives can also be classified using alternative criteria:

i) The medium in which they operate (music, literary, multimedia, visual arts, etc.);
ii) Their roles (fee collectors, monitoring, union association for creators);
iii) The type of licensing they use (blanket licences, case-by-case licensing, or both);

---

16 Gervais (2002), above note 13 at 23.

iv) The type of users (educational or commercial transmitters, etc.).

The objective of this section is to understand the differences among the various collectives and to see whether the existence of a large number of collectives and the current legal regimes are justified.

Copyright collectives typically perform three fundamentally different duties. First, they may act as a union, defending the interests of thier members and negotiating on their behalf the fee for their services. As such they act similarly to lobby groups pressuring for new legislations. They also work at raising public awareness of copyright and its virtues. Second, copyright collectives sometimes act like fee collectors under a regulatory mandate. They collect proceeds from the rights users and redistribute the proceeds to the creator, either directly or through another collective. Finally, they may act as agents or brokers. In the last case, they are not necessarily the one setting the rate-of-usage condition, but they simply administer the rights.

Some collectives assume only one of these roles, others assume two or more.

In most countries, professional associations play a key role in the copyright management system. The different trade groups have created their own collectives. Antitrust is not the main issue. These "professional association" CMOs are perceived much like unions. Based on the principle that each group of professionals is entitled to be represented by an association, the legislators have not actively limited the number of active professional association CMOs. The main condition for a CMO to claim some legitimacy is that it represents a large portion of the sector for which it seeks to advocate.

In most cases, the professional association CMOs set the conditions for licences under the supervision of the regulators. This is referred to as collective licensing.[17] Most of the small rights (i.e., rights on a relatively small piece of work such as songs, photocopies of a small number of pages, small documentary segments, etc.) are managed collectively and blanket licences are the rule rather than the exception. The large rights (i.e., rights on a substantial piece of work such as a play, an opera, and a feature movie) are typically managed

---

17 P. Torremans, "Collective Management in the United Kingdom (and Ireland)" in Gervais (2006), above note 15 at 227.

privately. The CMO is then responsible for monitoring and collecting (either directly or indirectly through a collecting society) the fees for the rights holders.

The membership of the professional association CMOs varies according to the population represented. We can distinguish three main categories of members: (i) individual creators or performers, (ii) producing or publishing companies, and (iii) other CMOs.

Next to the professional association CMOs, we find what we can call the collecting societies. The main role of the collecting societies is to actively collect money and levies. Often, these societies are granted an exclusive mandate to do so by the regulator.[18] The Private Copy Collective in Canada is a collecting society. Its only role is to collect levies on reproduction support and to distribute the money to other CMOs responsible for distribution of the proceeds to individual members. For the purpose of this analysis, these are the important collectives because they typically act under a regulatory mandate.

Finally, we find collectives that act simply as agents or brokers. Although they propose a menu of standard tariffs and licences to creators, rights holders can set their own tariffs. These societies are less important for the following analysis as they do not behave differently than other businesses.

2) The Canadian Case: An Overview

As in most other countries, different collectives are responsible for collecting royalties for different activities. These are explored below.

a) Music

Under the copyright law, a song is protected until fifty years after the death of the last surviving author (in this case the composer of the

---

18 In Canada, the Copyright Board plays an important role as a regulatory body. According to its website, "The Board is an economic regulatory body empowered to establish, either mandatorily or at the request of an interested party, the royalties to be paid for the use of works protected by copyright, when the administration of these rights is entrusted to a collective-administration society. The Board also supervises agreements signed between users and collective societies and can issue licences when the copyright owners cannot be located." See online: www.cb-cda.gc.ca/aboutus/mandate-e.html.

music or the lyricist). Any copying of a song or public performance of it must receive the consent of the copyright holders. The role of the music publishers and the copyright collectives is to maximize revenue generated by the exercise of these rights. Theoretically, a song author can ask for payment from anyone who wishes to reproduce, copy, and perform her musical work. For practicality, it is impossible for an individual author to monitor users and collect payment for use of her works. The role of collecting societies is to do this more efficiently. Revenue collected can come from three sources: (i) users who wish to reproduce the song on a mechanical support (CD, tapes, DVD) for commercialization; (ii) users who wish to perform the song in public (broadcasting and public performance); and (iii) copying by an individual for private use.

There are a total of five collecting societies in the field of music: two for the reproduction rights, two for the public performance rights, and one for private copying rights.

Two collectives are responsible for collecting royalties for the reproduction rights of music. The Canadian Musical Reproduction Rights Agency Ltd. (CMRRA)[19] was founded by Canadian music publishers in 1975. According to its website, CMRRA represents more than 30,000 music publishers serving more than 15,000 music users (record and label companies and community users).[20] Licensing is typically done on a per-use basis, with an 8.1 cent fee per song, per copy for a five-minute or less recording.[21]

The Société de reproduction des auteurs, compositeurs et éditeurs au Canada (SODRAC) represents 5,000 mostly French-Canadian authors corresponding to the vast majority of rights holders in Quebec.[22] In 2004–05, SODRAC collected $20.95 million and distributed $16.6 million ($5.5 million to authors and $8.1 million to music publishers). SODRAC has negotiated a per-use charge of 8.9 cents in 2007 for songs of 5 minutes or less.

---

19 For information on CMRRA, see CMRRA "Pay-as-you-press," online: www.cmrra.ca/cmrradocs/mlbe06.pdf.

20 *Ibid.* at 2.

21 *Ibid.* at 3.

22 M. Bouchard, "Collective Management in Commonwealth Jurisdictions: Comparing Canada with Australia" in Gervais (2006), above note 15 at 288 [Bouchard (2006)].

Two collectives administer the public performance rights. The Society of Composers, Authors and Music Publishers of Canada (SOCAN) is responsible for the collection of rights to perform musical work (broadcasting, public performers in restaurants, hotels and motels, ringtones, background music, concerts, etc.). According to Bouchard, SOCAN has 70,000 members and it covers an extensive repertoire.[23] In 2006, SOCAN collected $208 million in revenues and has distributed $164 million.[24] Tariffs imposed by SOCAN must be approved by the Copyright Board of Canada. There is a large set of tariffs depending on the nature of the user.[25] There is a tariff for skating rinks, ringtones, bars and restaurants, karaoke bars, fitness classes, dance clubs, passenger ships, and airplanes among others. The large diversity of the existing tariffs is a clear illustration that the regulator wishes to provide SOCAN with the ability to price discriminate. Most of the fees are blanket fees for general use of the songs in the repertoire rather than per-use fees.

The Neighbouring Rights Collective of Canada (NRCC) has the exclusive mandate to collect royalties for "equitable remuneration of performers and makers for the performance and communication of sound recordings."[26] The NRCC has no individual members. It has five members that are professional association collectives: the Société de gestion collective des droits des producteurs de phogrammes et videogrammes du Québec (SOPROQ), ACTRA Performers' Rights Society (ACTRA PRS), Audio-Video Licensing Agency (AVLA), Union des artistes du Québec (ArtistI), and the American Federation of Musician of the United States and Canada (AFM).[27] According to Bouchard, the NRCC collected some $12 million in 2004 and distributed $10.2 million.[28]

Finally, the Canadian Private Copying Collective (CPCC) has the exclusive mandate to collect levies on sound recording support of the use of private copy.[29] The proposed 2006 tariff recommends special

---

23 *Ibid.* at 287.

24 See SOCAN's 2006 Financial Report, online: www.socan.ca/pdf/en/2006FinancialReport.pdf.

25 See online: www.socan.ca/jsp/en/resources/tariffs.jsp.

26 Bouchard (2006), above note 22 at 287.

27 See NRCC website, online: www.nrdv.ca/english/index.htm.

28 Bouchard (2006), above note 21 at 287.

29 See s. VIII of the *Copyright Act*, R.S.C. 1985, c. C-42.

taxes on cassettes (29 cents), CD-R and CR-RW (21 cents), CD-R-Audio, CD-RW Audio, and MiniDiscs (77 cents).[30] In February 2007, it proposed "rates ranging from $2 to $10 for memory cards and $5 to $75 for digital audio recorders."[31] According to the *Copyright Act*, the revenues collected by the CPCC are distributed to SOCAN, CMRRA, and SODRAC — on account of eligible authors (66 percent), and to the NRCC — on account of eligible performers (18.9 percent) and the eligible creators (15.1 percent).[32] In 2006, the CPCC collected $37.2 million and distributed $33.6 million.[33]

b) Reprography

Two collecting societies act in the field of reprography: Access Copyright and Copibec. It is an infringement of copyright law, *inter alia*, to photocopy or make digital copies of published copyrighted work without the copyright owner's consent or as otherwise permitted under the *Copyright Act*. The role of these collectives is to protect the rights of creators (writers, journalists, playwrights, photographers, and illustrators) and their publishers. The collectives propose a system of licences that make it convenient for school, non-profit and for-profit organizations, and governments to comply with the copyright law.

Copibec is responsible for the territory of Quebec and Access Copyright for the rest of Canada. According to its website, Access Copyright licences works from over 8,000 Canadian creators and 600 publishers.[34] Copibec represents four author associations and four publisher associations from Quebec, including 850 Quebec publishers of books, newspapers, and periodicals and 16,500 authors.[35] It manages a repertoire of 85,000 works from Quebec authors and publishers. Both

---

30 "Statement of Proposed Levies to Be Collected by CPCC on the Sale, in Canada, of Blank Audio Recording Media for the Year 2007," *Canada Gazette*, Supplement, Part I (25 February 2006) at 4 ["Statement of Proposed Levies"].

31 CPCC press release, "Proposed Update of Private Copying Levies Is Supported by Environics Survey" (9 February 2007).

32 "Statement of Proposed Levies," above note 30 at art. 3.

33 See CPCC Financial Highlights, online: http://cpcc.ca/english/finHighlights.htm.

34 See Access Copyright, "2007 Annual Report" at 5 [2007 Annual Report], online: www.accesscopyright.ca/docs/AnnualReports/2007AnnualReport.pdf.

35 See Copibec, online: www.copibec.qc.ca/?action=pr_apropos.

Access Copyright and Copibec have reciprocal arrangements with international associations. As of November 2008, Access Copyright claims a repertoire including approximately 20 million copyrighted works worldwide.[36] The collectives offer both per-use and blanket licences to schools, governments and municipalities, and non-profit and for-profit organizations. The membership is open to every publisher. For the year 2006–7, Copibec collected close to $11.6 million and distributed $10.8 million.[37] Access copyright collected $27.9 million and distributed $20.5 million in 2004.[38]

c) Reproduction Rights—Visual Arts

According to the Copyright Board of Canada, there are two collectives working in the field of visuals arts.[39] The Canadian Artists' Representation Copyright Collective (CARCC) used to negotiate terms for the use of visual and media work (exhibition, reproduction, and reprography). The Société des droits d'auteurs en arts visuels (SODART) negotiates on behalf of 360 members from Quebec. As of 20 May 2008, SODART has ended its activites and has invited its members to entrust their rights to SODRAC.[40]

d) Broadcasting

According to Bouchard, eight collectives act in the field of radio and television program retransmissions.[41] They receive part of the royalties set in the Television Retransmission Tariffs set by the Copyright Board of Canada.[42] These include the collectives representing "broadcasters

---

36 See Access Copyright website, online: www.accesscopyright.ca/Default.aspx?id=35.

37 See "Rapport annuel de Copibec, 2006–2007, " at 6–7, online: www.copibec.qc.ca/pdf/Rapport%20annuel%20de%20Copibec.pdf.

38 Reported in Copibec 2005–2006 annual report (note : no longer available online as of the publication date).

39 See the Copyright Board website for a list of the copyright collectives in Canada, online:www.cb-cda.gc.ca/societies/index-e.html.

40 See "Creators of Artistic Works Represented by SODART Are Invited to Join SODRAC" *SkyNewsWire* (23 May 2008), online: www.skynewswire.com/modules/news/article.php?storyid=3422.

41 Bouchard (2006), above note 22 at 289.

42 The tariffs are published periodically in the *Canada Gazette*. See online: http://canadagazette.gc.ca/partI/2004/20040424/html/suppl1-e.html.

(CBRA, CRRA, and CRC), film and program producers (CCC, CRC), sport teams (FWS, MLB) and music composers (SOCAN)."[43]

e) Other Copyright Collectives[44]

Two distributors (Audio Ciné Film and Criterion Picture) offer blanket licences for non-theatrical film representations. Société québécoise des auteurs dramatiques (SOQAD) is a small society that collects royalties of $90,000 for the performance rights of plays in the Quebec school system.

There are many other copyright collectives in Canada. Their role is to administer rights on behalf of their members. These societies act as professional associations and redistribute royalties collected by other sources.

The Directors Rights Collective of Canada (DRCC) acts on behalf of television and movie directors. The Canadian Screenwriters Collection Society (CSCS) collects royalties for screenwriters. The Société civile des auteurs multimedia (SCAM) acts for francophone authors in the fields of multimedia, television, and films. The Société des auteurs et compositeurs dramatiques (SACD) is a French collective that acts on behalf of creators in the fields of dramatic and audiovisual works. It is unclear whether these societies collect their revenues directly from end-users, or whether they receive royalties from film and television program producers at the rate negotiated by the collectives.

In the field of music, SOPROQ, ACTRA PRS, AVLA, ArtistI, and the AFM are all societies that are members of NRCC and redistribute royalties received from NRCC to their members.

3) Some International Perspective

Gervais provides a rather extensive overview of the copyright collective regime in various countries.[45] The objective of this paper is not to replicate what has been done in this excellent book. The objective is to identify, by looking at various international experiences, the dif-

---

43 Bouchard (2006), above note 22 at 289.

44 See the Copyright Bureau website for a list of other collectives, online: www.cb-cda.gc.ca/societies/index-e.html.

45 Gervais (2006), above note 15.

ferent copyright-collective regime approaches and examine how the Canadian regime compares.

A large variety of CMOs exist. Across countries and media, each individual CMO has different objectives and responsibilities. It is interesting to observe both the difference across countries and within countries. Nevertheless, the structure of CMOs is broadly similar across country, with one exemption — the US.

a) France[46]

Copyright collectives have existed in France since the mid-nineteenth century and the structure of copyright collective management seems to be characterized by a net separation between the professional association collectives and the collecting organizations. Piaskowski identifies eleven professional association CMOs and six collecting CMOs.[47] Table 1, below, presents a list of the various CMOs in France.

Four out of the six collecting organizations have the exclusive mandate to collect levies from reprography and/or private copy. They have no individual or corporate members. Their members are the professional association CMOs for which they have the responsibility of collecting money under the regulatory rules. The other CMOs act as professional associations. Their role is to promote the work of their professionals and represent them in the collective negotiation of their rights. They receive money from the collecting CMO and redistribute it to their members and most are not-for-profit organizations.

The Société pour l'administration du droit de reproduction mécanique (SDRM) acts as a collecting society for the mechanical reproduction rights of composers, lyric authors, and music publishers. It was founded in 1933. The royalties collected by SDRM for the reproduction of sound recordings are distributed among its members. These include professional association collectives: Société des auteurs, compositeurs et éditeurs de musique (SACEM)—108,000 authors of musical works, documentary related to music, poems, and sketches; Société des auteurs et compositeurs dramatiques (SACD)—authors and composers of dramatic works; Société Civile des Auteurs Multimédias

46 Information from this section can, in large part, be found in N. Piaskowski, "Collective Management in France" in Gervais (2006), *ibid.* at 153–92 [Piaskowski (2006)].

47 *Ibid.* at 158–65.

(SCAM)—authors of multimedia works; and Société des auteurs dans les arts pastiques et graphiques (ADAGP)—visual arts.

SESAM managed rights related to the production of multimedia work. It groups together SACEM, SACD, SCAM, and ADAGP. Société pour la rémunération de la copie privée audiovisuelle (Copie France) and Société pour la rémunération de la copie privée sonore (SORECOP) have an exclusive mandate to collect and distribute royalties from private copying of sound recordings and video recordings, respectively. Société civile pour l'Administration des Droits des Artistes et Musiciens Interprètes (ADAMI), Société de Perception Et de Distribution des Droits des Artistes-interprètes de la Musique et de la danse (SPEDIDAM), Société civile des Producteurs de Cinéma et Télévision (PROCIREP), Société Civile des Producteurs Associés (SCPA) are members of one or both of these societies.

The Centre français d'exploitation du droit de copie (CFC) collects levies from reprography rights. Its members are authors, and newspaper and book publishers. Finally, the Société civile pour la perception de la rémunération équitable (SPRE) has the exclusive mandate of collecting remuneration for the public performance of sound recordings. Its members include ADAMI, SPEDIDAM, and SCPA

b) The UK[48]

Much like in Canada or France, collecting societies in the UK are divided into the fields of reprographic rights societies, mechanical rights societies, licensing bodies for off-air recording, performing rights societies, and multi-purpose collecting societies. The UK has some specific particularities.[49] Notably, UK citizens do not have the right to copy their own content for their own personal use—there is no equivalent in the UK to the Canadian Private Copying Collective or Copie France. The absence of private copy provisions is heavily debated.[50]

48 Information from this section can, in large part, be found in P. Torremans, "Collective Management in the United Kingdom (and Ireland)" in Gervais (2006), *ibid.* at 227–56 [Torremans (2006)].

49 A commentator has mentioned that the UK has a typographical arrangement right that gives newspapers a copyright in the layout of their newspapers, separate from any compilation copyright or individual copyright in the articles. Canada lacks such a right.

50 See "Copying Own CDs 'Should Be Legal'" *BBC News* (26 October 2006), online: http://news.bbc.co.uk/2/hi/uk_news/6095612.stm [BBC Report]: "The

Table 1 lists the different collecting societies in France, Canada, and the UK. The table was compiled by the author from the description provided in Torremans (2006) and Piaskowski (2006). Table 1 shows some of the similarities between France, Canada, and the UK In the field of reproduction rights in the visual arts, there is one collecting collective in the UK, one in France, one in Quebec, and one in the rest of Canada. It is the same in the field of reproduction rights for music and reprography. In the field of public performance and broadcasting of music, there are minor differences. In Canada and the UK, performers and makers are represented by different collectives than authors and publishers. Both France and the UK have separate collectives for video and music. There is one collective in Canada responsible for private copy, two in France (music and video), and none in the UK.

The UK collectives include the Copyright Licensing Agency, Ltd. (CLA), the Publishing Licensing Society (PLS), the Author's Licensing and Collecting Society (ALCS), the Design and Artists Copyright Society (DACS), the Music Publishers' Association (MPA), the Mechanical Copyright Protection Society Ltd. (MCPS), the Newspaper Licensing Agency (NLA), the Phonographic Performance Ltd. (PPL), the Performing Right Society (PRS), the Video Performance Ltd. (VPL), the Performing Artisit Media Rights Association (PAMRA), and the Educational Recording Agency (ERA).

c) The Nordic Countries[51]

Koskinen-Olson, in her overview of the copyright collectives in the Nordic countries, highlights the importance and role of the extended

---

Institute for Public Policy Research (IPPR) is calling for a 'private right to copy.' It would decriminalise millions of Britons who break the law each year by copying their CDs onto music players." See also "Private Copy System under Scrutiny," European Digital Rights (7 June 2006), online: www.edri.org/edrigram/number4.11/privatecopy: "The issue of the private copy remuneration system is becoming a subject of debate for interest groups from all over the world. L'AEPO-ARTIS grouping 27 associations of artists of Europe, the International Federation of Musicians and the International Federation of Actors took a stand in the support of the present private copy levy system."

51 Information from this section can, in large part, be found in Koskinen-Olson (2006), above note 15 at 257–356.

Table 1: Collecting Societies

	France	**Canada**	**UK**
Reproduction rights — visual arts	SESAM	CARCC, SODART (Quebec)	DACS
Reproduction (mechanical) rights — music	SDRM	CMRRA, SODRAC	MCPS
Private copies — music or music video	Copie France (Audiovisual) SORECOP (sound)	CPCC	No private copying the UK
Photocopy	CFC	Access Copyright (out of Quebec), Copibec (Quebec)	CLA, NLA (newspapers)
Public performance and broadcasting	SPRE (music), SESAM (multi-media)	SOCAN (music), NRCC (performers), SOQAD (plays Quebec schools)	PRS, PPL, PAMRA (performing artists), VPL (music video)
Retransmission radio and television	No information found	CBRA, CRRA, CRC (broadcasters) CCC, CRC (film and program producers), FWS, MLB (sports teams), SOCAN	No information found
Off-air program recording	No information found	ERCC (educational use), CBRA	ERA (education)
Non-theatrical film representations	No information found	2 Non-theatrical film distributors	No information found

collective licences (ECLs). ECLs have allowed users to have access to a large repertoire.

What a broadcaster desires is to obtain a fully covered licence, one that will protect it from infringement lawsuits. An ECL provides this. It works as follows: (i) a copyright collective representative in a given field negotiates with a user; (ii) the agreement is legally binding for all non-represented copyright holders; (iii) the user obtains a fully covered licence allowing it to legally use all available materials without fear of legal suit from outsiders; (iv) outsiders retain the right to negotiate individual fees or prohibit use of their work.

The system benefits users because it gives them access to a blanket licence that covers all original works. Users can exploit these works without the threat of legal claims from rights holders. The system protects rights holders because, contrary to a compulsory licensing system, it protects their rights to individual bargaining and prohibits use of their work. The ECL approach works under the presumption that original works have been created in order to be broadcast and that, unless the creator explicitly says otherwise, the works are covered by the blanket licensing. Eventually, because users receive a broader licence under the ECL system, they are presumably prepared to pay more for it.

Koskinen-Olson concludes her review of collective management in the Nordic countries with a positive evaluation:

> In the Nordic countries, collective management plays an essential role. Collective management can be measured by different ways, collection of revenue being one indicator. In 2004, the total revenue collected by CMOs in the Nordic market was some EUR 450 million. This represents more than 5 per cent of estimated total revenue in the world. For a market with 25 million inhabitants this is a fair share.[52]

It is difficult to judge from this statement whether the overall system is efficient. The magnitude of total revenue may be simply explained by higher tariffs, and administrative costs of the system can remain very high. One thing is certain, collective management in the Nordic countries is not one where there are very few collectives. Koskinen-Olson lists the main Nordic CMOs. The table is reproduced below.

---

52 *Ibid.* at 281.

Table 2: Collecting Societies in the Nordic Countries

Scope	**Denmark**	**Finland**	**Iceland**	**Norway**	**Sweden**
Music performing rights	KODA	TEOSTO	STEF	TONO	STIM
Music mechanical rights	NCB	NCB	NCB	NCB	NCB
Music-related rights	GRAMEX	GRAMEX	SFH	GRAMO	SAMI (performers) IFPI (producers)
Visual authors	Copy-Dan Pictorial Art	KUVASTO	Myndstef	BONO	BUS
Literary authors		SANASTO		LINO	ALIS
Reprography and certain digital uses	Copy-Dan Writing	KOPIOSTO	FJÖLIS	KOPINOR	BONUS-PRESSKOPIA
Secondary use of audiovisual works	Copy-Dan Cable TV	KOPIOSTO	IHM	NORWACO	COPYSWEDE
Producers of audiovisual works		TUOTOS			FRF

Source: Koskinen-Olson (2006) at 263–64.

d) The American Experience[53]

The case of the US stands out. Copyright collectives seem to be contrary to the American way. Lunney identifies only four US collectives, far less than other countries. The Broadcasting Music Industry (BMI), American Society of Composers, Authors, and Publishers (ASCAP), and SESAC (used to be called the Society of European Stage Authors & Composers) were created in response to unauthorized public performances of musical works. All three have obtained rights for a large proportion of music production and they offer blanket licences to radio stations, restaurants, and others who wish to broadcast music. Founded in 1914, ASCAP is a non-profit organization owned by its 200,000 members. In 1939, members of the broadcasting industry created BMI in order to create an alternative to ASCAP. Both organizations have now developed impressive catalogues, and a public broadcaster must typically obtain blanket licences from both CMOs. SESAC has a limited catalogue and hence is not an important CMO.

The main debate around BMI and ASCAP is whether these organizations violate the antitrust legislation. Numerous litigations have been issued against them on antitrust grounds. Lunney states that the general view is that these CMOs are a "necessary evil," and while the practice of the CMOs goes against the antitrust legislation, they are tolerated because they contributed to reducing the substantial transaction costs associated with the protection of copyrights. In 1950, a decree was set to eliminate some antitrust practices of ASCAP; mainly to assure that some alternatives to the ASCAP blanket licence exist.

The fourth copyright collective is actually a collecting society. The Copyright Clearance Center (CCC) was created in reaction to the growing use of photocopying machines. It is a non-profit corporation that collects fees for authors and publishers for the photocopying of their work and acts as a central hub for businesses, academics, and content providers who wish to obtain licences. The CCC offers two types of licences: (i) an annual blanket licence; and (ii) per-copy licences. The CCC sets the fee for the latter and the individual rights holders set the fee for the former. Glynn Lunney, an American copy-

53 Information from this section can, in large part, be found in G. Lunney, "Copyright Collectives and Collecting Societies: The United States Experience" in Gervais (2006), above note 15 at 311–46 [Lunney (2006)].

right expert, cites the CCC as the example to follow: "the CCC demonstrates that it is practical to offer both individual licences at prices set by the individual rights holders and blanket licences at a price set by a CMO."[54] The author also points out that the CCC has never been subject to antitrust litigation.

4) Membership

As stated above, the collective management system in Canada is largely voluntary. Moreover, the system has been built in such a way that it discourages creators from not joining the collective.

Membership rules are divided into three categories: (i) umbrella organizations (such as, CPCC, Copibec, and NRCC) that have no individuals as members and act on behalf of other collectives or unions; (ii) organizations that open their membership to individuals who are active in the industry, so long as each is willing to pay some minimal membership fee and has produced some original work that can be included in the organization's licensing agreement; (iii) organizations that limit access to full membership and may require prospective members to work first as apprentices before becoming full members.

SOCAN encourages all those "qualifying" as a music creator or as a music publisher to join SOCAN. To qualify as a music creator one must have created a musical work or part of a musical work that has been published by a music publisher, recorded, or has been or will be performed in a public forum play subject to SOCAN licensing. All authors or editors of a creation may become a member of SODRAC; it suffices to sign a contract with SODRAC.

ACTRA PRS and ArtistI have an apprentice program. According to its site, "membership in ACTRA is open to any performer who has enrolled in the Apprentice Membership Program and has attained six professional engagements under ACTRA jurisdiction."[55] In order to become a member of ArtistI, one needs to have a contract from a producer with an agreement with the union, and in order to become a full member one needs to acquire a sufficient amount of credits.

---

54 *Ibid.* at 344.

55 See categories of membership on the ACTRA website, online: www.actra.ca/actra/control/insideActra_become?menu_id=903.

The difference between Copibec and Access Copyright is interesting. Both administer reprographic rights for their respective territory (Quebec and the rest of Canada, respectively). Although Access Copyright has institutional members, it states on its website that any writer, illustrator, or photographer who is a Canadian citizen or a permanent resident can become an affiliate of Access Copyright.[56] This is not the case for Copibec. Members of Copibec include author associations (Association des journalistes indépendants du Québec, or AJIQ; Fédération professionnelle des journalistes du Québec, or FPJQ; Regroupement des artistes en arts visuels, or RAAV; and Union des écrivaines et écrivains québécois, or UNEQ) and publishing associations (Association nationale des éditeurs de livres, or ANEL; Société de développement des périodiques culturels québécois, or SODEP; Les Hebdos du Québec; and Les Quotidiens du Québec). A writer, illustrator, or photographer that desires to be represented by Copibec needs to be represented by one of its institutional members; but becoming a member of one of these organizations is not difficult. Why the two membership structures differ is unclear. Presumably, it has arisen for historical reasons.

It is important to note that an open membership rule is not a guarantee of greater administrative efficiency. Copibec imposes a 13 percent administrative fee for all members.[57] In 2006, Access Copyright had a 16.3 percent operating expenses over revenues ratio.[58] Copibec's membership structure implicitly forces writers, photographers, and journalists to become members of their respective union or association. If one believes in the theory of collective action, namely that a collective can better organize itself and defend collective interests than individual members can, then this is not a bad thing. It may, in the end, help creators get a better deal out of Copibec.

In summary, although the membership rules differ from one organization to the other, it is not hard for a creator to become a member of a copyright collective, either directly or indirectly (i.e., through a collective that is a member). What is striking is the extent of unioniza-

56 See registration page on the Access Copyright website, online: www.accesscopyright.ca/Default.aspx?id=11.

57 See "Lucky 13" *Info@Copibec Newsletter* (May 2003), online: www.copibec.qc.ca/pdf/Newsletter%20may%202003.pdf.

58 See 2007 Annual Report, above note 34 at 10.

tion of the creative professions. Whether you are a journalist, a writer, an actor or director, a music composer or performer, it seems difficult not to become a member of some sort of union.

5) Should the Structure and Number of Copyright Collectives in Canada Be Changed?

One of the objectives of this paper is to try to answer some questions regarding the number of collectives in Canada. There are many collective organizations in Canada; it is hence natural to ask: are there too many collectives in Canada? Would the creation of a "super-collective" be in the interest of users? Of creators?

The current system of copyright collectives in Canada has not been imposed as a grand and comprehensive top-down plan. It is a system that has evolved and adapted through time. It is the belief of this author that adaptive systems evolve as a best response to the environment unless there are major obstacles to efficient amalgamation or disintegration of existing institutions.

In the UK, France, Canada, and the Nordic countries the number and role of the copyright collectives has evolved over time in order to respond to new challenges in the creative industry. As photocopiers made it easier to photocopy protected works, new collectives were created to help end-users secure reproduction rights more easily. Private copying became an issue when tape recorders where created and specific collectives were created for this purpose. In Canada, our system is characterized by our national bilingualism. There are collectives for Quebec and the francophone creators and similar collectives for English Canada. Some francophone collectives are tied to collectives from France. Other Canadian collectives are closely related to American associations. This is evidence that collectives have evolved in a way that reflect our diversity. Published writers, photographers, video producers, music composers, and performers can all find institutions that will help them defend their interest and copyrights.

The structure of copyright collectives in Canada is not drastically different from that of other similar countries (the UK, France, and the Nordic countries), with just a few exceptions.[59] In practice, one

59 The number of collectives in Canada is influenced by the presence of Quebec and two official languages. When the norm is one collective in a given field,

should ask whether there is a natural balance between (i) the need for different communities with different interests and different clienteles to be served with their own collectives, pursuing and defending their own specific agenda, and (ii) the need to exploit economies of scale in administrative costs and to set comprehensive blanket licences for extended repertoires. Accordingly, we must ask two more questions. Is there any reason to believe different communities with different interests cannot exercise their right of association in order to pursue their specific agenda? Is there any reason to believe that comprehensive blanket licences for extended repertoires cannot be obtained or that the transactional costs to secure them are prohibitive for the end-users? The short answer, to each of these questions, is no.

Before I begin to provide the longer answer, I must distinguish between the collective associations and the collecting collectives. France's system is a clear example of a dual system; one where a small number of collectives gather fees and levies on behalf of a larger number of professional association collectives. End-users deal with the collectives that are able to grant a blanket licence for protected rights covering entire repertoires and to collect fees. The creators deal with the professional association collectives. These directly represent creators and protect their rights.

Users may wish to have a limited number of collecting collectives to deal with. Transactional costs may be higher if one has to deal with many different rights holders, each one imposing complex conditions of compliance. Further, as argued above, the existence of a comprehensive blanket licence for extended repertoires may allow the users more choice and improve allocation efficiency. There is no evidence that major obstacles to efficient amalgamation of existing institutions exist in Canada. Users can acquire blanket licences for extended repertoires for all sorts of creative works. The number of different collectives that a user needs to deal with in order to acquire such licences is limited. Of course there is the linguistic barrier that leads to the duplication of collectives (Copibec and Access Copyright, ACTRA and Art-

---

it is not exceptional in Canada to have two collectives, one for Quebec or the French-speaking community and one for the rest of Canada. Further, in the field of broadcasting rights, there are many CMOs in Canada. Otherwise, the number and missions of the collectives are quite similar.

istI, CMRRA and SODRAC, etc.). But the linguistic barrier is a reality that cannot be abstracted from and the collectives on both sides of the divide serve a purpose. For the users, however, it does not necessarily matter; a Quebec institution needs only to deal with Copibec for its reproduction rights because Copibec also represents Canadian and foreign rights holders for the province of Quebec.

There is no indication that there are too many collecting societies in Canada. In the Nordic countries, there are a limited number of collecting societies, but various rights are still managed by different collectives. In Demark, Finland, Iceland, Norway, and Sweden, music performing rights, music mechanical rights, music-related rights, reprography and certain digital uses, and secondary use of audiovisual works are all managed by different collective societies. The absence of a super-collective is reasoned. It is generally agreed that bureaucracies that are too large have a tendency to become inefficient and, since these rights are sufficiently diverse, it does not matter much for end-users that these are managed by different collecting societies. This explains why, across the world, there is no example of such a super-collective, and the creation of a super-collective does not seem to be necessary.

There is no evidence that too few collectives exist in Canada or that there are major obstacles to efficient disintegration of existing institutions. In practice, different communities with different interests and different clienteles do have their own specific associations pursuing and defending their specific agenda. Independent journalists, professional journalists, visual artists, and writers all have their specific associations. In Quebec, their respective associations are all members of Copibec. Therefore, when these multiple associations have common interests, there is nothing that prevents them from agreeing on specific mutual agreements and being represented by a common collecting collective. This is being done across our frontier. The NRCC represents five professional association members and the NRCC is a member, with four other groups, of the CPCC. Hence, although singers from Quebec have an association distinct from the American Federation of Musicians, they are entitled to the same access to collecting societies. This is possible because collectives exist that act on behalf of all professional association collectives in the field. This arrangement makes it possible for creators to exercise their right of association, while limiting the number of collecting societies.

Overall, there does not seem to be a need for a major transformation in the structure of copyright collectives in Canada. The existing system has evolved to respond to the demand of the environment. Many professional association collectives exist to respond to the diverse needs of the creative communities, and a limited number of the fee-collecting collectives offer comprehensive blanket licences to users. There is no indication that there are major obstacles to efficient integration or disintegration of existing institutions. Certainly, as information technology will evolve, the collectives will also have to evolve.

6) Efficiency of the System

Should we conclude from the previous section that the current system is efficient, or as efficient as it could be? The answer is no and it is unlikely ever to be otherwise. An industry is almost never fully efficient. The paper and mill industry in Canada, for instance, is certainly not. In order for an industry to be fully efficient given the current state of the technology, it must have the very best and latest technology and that is not possible. Industries have legacy systems that are far from the edge. It is costly to replace those legacy systems and personnel must adapt to them. Hence, firms cannot afford to have always the latest technology. Some industries have learned to be more flexible and more on edge than others. These are highly competitive industries where technological progresses provide important competitive advantages. But the industry of "copyright collecting" is not one of them.

Copibec states in its 2006 annual report that 40 percent of the 22,800 copyright declarations processed were done manually. The main operational responsibility of Copibec is to process declarations, and still it is not fully automated. Copibec is committed to do better, and it will — but it is not there yet.

In 2004, SOCAN distributed $151 million of the $212 million collected;[60] NRCC distributed $10.2 million of the $12 million collected.[61] One can suspect that their processes could be improved. Yet, the administrative responsibilities of these organizations are not negligible. They must collect fees, acquire information on the usage of creative work in order to redistribute it fairly, and distribute the money

60 Bouchard (2006), above note 22 at 287.

61 *Ibid.*

to a (sometimes) large number of members. The company Apple keeps $0.29 out of every $0.99 paid per song download on iTunes.[62] In comparison, many copyright collectives perform fairly well.

Information technologies offer huge opportunities to transform and improve the business processes of the fee-gathering collectives and consequently reduce the operational fees. Here is a list of possible technologies: self-service websites for creators and users, webservice technologies to help process exchange of services between multiple entities, and online monitoring and data mining to quantify the use of each original work, among many others. It is quite unlikely that all collectives have managed to exploit all of these opportunities.

Section B(3) arrived at a counterintuitive conclusion: a monopoly can increase economic efficiency. We generally believe in the virtue of competition. Competition forces individual agents to be more innovative and motivates them to find new ways to be more cost-efficient. The argument in Section B(3) is only based on observations about pricing strategies and their impact on welfare and rents. How the existence of a monopoly (or of a unique collective that has the mandate to market the extended repertoire of creative work) would limit future innovations is not addressed. The copyright collectives are facing little or no market-based competition and therefore are obliged by market forces to innovate. However, they are responding to the logic of collective governance. Managers of those organizations are facing the demands of the members and are accountable to them.

Collectives are not-for-profit organizations controlled by creators and their representatives. Creators are ultimately the ones who are paying for a collective's lack of efficiency. Creators and their representatives are the ones that control such institutions and hence they theoretically have the means and incentives to make sure that their collectives are as efficient as they can be. There is nothing that prevents collectives from exploiting the new technological advances in order to become more efficient, except for a lack of expertise or a lack

62 See Jody Mitoma, "Apple Wins; iTunes Not Shutting Down; Royalty Rates Staying at 9 cents per song" *Touch Podium* (3 October 2008), online: www.touchpodium.com/2008/10/03/apple-wins-itunes-not-shutting-down-royalty-rates-staying-at-9-cents-per-song/. This article covers the debate between Apple Inc. and the National Music Publishers Association on the royalties to be paid per tune.

of will to invest in new technologies. As time permits, efficiency gains will be made. There is no need for the legislature to intervene.

From a policy perspective, what can be done to increase the efficiency of the collecting collectives? Governments can hardly regulate innovation — they are themselves not very good at innovating. However, one mechanism that may facilitate the development of more technologically savvy copyright management is the adoption of open industry standards. We need open standards to process and automate copyright management.

D. INFORMATION TECHNOLOGIES: CHALLENGES AND OPPORTUNITIES

Over the last ten years, we have experienced a true revolution in information technology. The arrival of the Internet and the digitization of sound recordings have transformed the music industry profoundly. For the management of copyrights, the technological change offers both new opportunities and challenges.

Katz asserts that technology can make the copyright collectives unnecessary. He states that "by lowering many of the transaction costs which previously purported to justify the practice, new digital technologies further undermine the justification for collective administration."[63]

Two technologies may be useful here: (i) the technologies of Digital Rights Management (DRM),[64] and (ii) micropayment technologies.[65] The first provides the means to track down usage of digital data, while

---

63 Katz (2006), above note 5 at 245.

64 See online: http://en.wikipedia.org/wiki/Digital_rights_management. According to *Wikipedia*, "Digital Rights Management (generally abbreviated to DRM) is any of several technologies used by publishers (or copyright owners) to control access to and usage of digital data (such as software, music, movies) and hardware, handling usage restrictions associated with a specific instance of a digital work."

65 See online: http://en.wikipedia.org/wiki/Micropayment. According to *Wikipedia*, "Micropayments are means for transferring very small amounts of money, in situations where collecting such small amounts of money with the usual payment systems is impractical, or very expensive, in terms of the amount of money being collected. 'Micropayment' originally meant 1/1000th of a US dollar."

the latter allows extracting a fee (potentially very small) for each usage. In a digital world, this can provide the means to set up a fully automated and decentralized payment system for pay-per-use of digital work. Each creator could set its own price and fee system, hence creating a truly competitive market.

From an economic perspective, investing massively in DRM technology in order to prevent dissemination of original work (in particular private copy) is not socially efficient. It is costly and it reduces consumers' welfare. Using DRM technology to monitor the private usage of digital work in order to set and levy a per-use tariff generates two problems. First, it raises serious privacy issues. To what extent are we willing to allow corporations to monitor our private use of musical work? Many believe that privacy is a fundamental right that has precedence over music publishers' economic concerns. Second, imposing a per-usage fee on individual songs creates the inefficiencies mentioned in Section B of this paper. Charging a positive marginal price on a product with a zero marginal cost creates suboptimal usage. Even if the new technology could be rendered economically feasible for users of original works to negotiate directly with rights holders, rather than through collective intermediaries, it would be neither socially efficient nor desirable to do so.

Therefore, from an economic perspective the only benefit of using DRM technology with micropayments is to help rights holders extract more rents and protect the incentives to create. But there are better ways to do so. The copyright collectives should play a major role in the solution.

The argument is made here that technologies make collective copyright management even more relevant. Earlier on, when Napster appeared, there was a massive reaction from Internet users. Within a few months, millions of users were sharing music files on the Internet. It was an incredible deal: users could acquire music for free. The music industry reacted strongly, and with good reasons. It quickly sued Napster in order to force it to close its sharing servers and it sued individual users. But Pandora's box was open.

Alternative peer-to-peer technologies that did not use central servers were developed. File sharing could not be stopped. The legal and protectionist positions of the music rights holders were not very popular among music lovers who now wanted to have access to a larger selection of digital songs at a lower cost than the conventional CD. The music industry had to adapt. The creation of digital music stores like iTunes proved to be the best response. It proved that the general public was ready to pay for the right to download quality music. The days when music was sold and kept on discs manufactured by the publisher are all but gone.

With the appearance of iPods and other digital recording devices, a larger and larger share of the music is now copied in personal recording devices. The music has become more accessible for the greater benefit of consumers. In some countries, where there is no "private right to copy," many users act illegally by copying their CDs onto digital music players. The music industry is seeking more aggressive law enforcement. Others, such as the Institute for Public Policy Research (IPPR) from the UK, are calling for a private right to copy. According to the BBC, the IPPR stated in its 30 October 2006 report that "it would decriminalise millions of Britons" and have little impact on the revenues of the music industry.[66] All agree that a change is required.

In the past, the reaction to technological advances, such as the tape recorder or the photocopier, was to create new ways to levy revenues for copyright holders, while providing the means for law-abiding citizens to have efficient access to copyrighted work. The objective of copyright collectives is to make it possible for users to use legally copyrighted work, while also generating revenues for creators. When photocopying machines made it easy to make copies of published work, a large number of users made illegal copies. Photocopying machines could have been banned, but an alternative solution was developed by collecting societies instead. Almost everywhere, there are societies that offer blanket licences for reprography of copyrighted work. It is now possible for users to photocopy or scan copyrighted work legally. A similar attitude should be taken for the challenge posed by file sharing and digital copying.

So far, the Internet has increased the bargaining power of music lovers to the detriment of music publishers. It is not clear whether this fact has threatened the creation of musical work. Nevertheless, music creators are entitled to the gains associated with their work and file sharing causes them great prejudice, and the regulator should try to protect the incentive to create.

---

66 BBC Report, above note 50.

In the context of growing threats from file sharing and digital copying, the role of copyright collectives must be extended to account for these new challenges. The "private copying" rights should be clarified in order to account for activities that cannot be criminalized in a large scale and for which legal rules cannot be enforced. Hence, the levies for private copying should be extended to account for these new activities and to help generate more revenue for creators. The CPCC has already proposed to levy taxes on digital recording players. This is perceived as fair by the general public. It also provides for an economically efficient way to generate revenues for music creators.

E. RECOMMENDATIONS AND OBSERVATIONS

This study ends with a short list of general recommendations and observations.

1) The general sentiment of this author is that pure competition among creators is not the best way to manage copyright. The problem is not whether competition can or cannot be achieved, the issue is that the linear pricing that comes with pure competition cannot achieve the two general objectives of the copyright system simultaneously; namely, (i) efficient dissemination of the creation work and (ii) revenue generation for creators. Efficient dissemination of creative work implies that price equals marginal cost, but that prevents revenue generation for creators. Further, a blanket licence provides a better way to fulfill both of these objectives. For these reasons, a system of collective management is justified in order to market blanket licences for extended repertoires. It should be well-understood that the rationale defended here is not only based on transactional costs: the argument still stands under a new technological environment that would drastically reduce or eliminate transaction costs.
2) The structure of copyright collectives in Canada is not drastically different from that of other, similar countries (the UK, France, and the Nordic countries). The number of fee-gathering collectives is rather similar to the ones seen elsewhere. There is no evidence that there are obstacles to the efficient amalgamation or disintegration of collectives in Canada.

3) The system of copyright collectives has evolved to incorporate two main types of CMOs: professional association collectives and fee-gathering or "collecting" collectives. There are a large number of professional association collectives, with each community of creators having its own association to represent its interests. Conversely, users can acquire blanket licences for extended repertoires for almost all sorts of creative works. The number of different collecting collectives that a user needs to deal with in order to acquire such licences is limited.
4) The creation of a super-collective does not seem to be necessary. Across the world, there is no example of such a super-collective. The number of collecting collectives remains rather limited and each deals with different types of rights.
5) Casual observations indicate that the collecting collectives have not yet exploited the potential of the information technology. But there is little that the regulator can do to accelerate the adoption rate of new information technologies.
6) The Internet has facilitated access to copyright-protected works. File sharing and digital copying have extended the use of private copy and the entrenchment of copyright laws. Nevertheless, this author feels that the extensive use of DRM technology will not drastically limit file sharing and copying activities. Moreover, it will create economic inefficiencies.
7) The objectives of copyright collectives are to make it possible for users to legally use copyrighted work, while generating revenues for creators. In the context of growing threats from file sharing and digital copying, the role of copyright collectives must be extended to account for these new challenges. The "private copy" rights should be clarified in order to account for activities that cannot be criminalized and legal rules that cannot be enforced. The levies for private copy should be extended to account for these new activities and help generate more revenues for creators.

Commentary on "An Evaluation of Collective Copyright Management in Canada"

Paul Audley[1]

I have worked for thirty years as a policy analyst dealing with broadcasting, film, publishing, the music industry, and new media. Since 1983 I have offered a course at the Schulich School of Business in public policy and its impact on the cultural industries. For the past ten years, I have been dealing with copyright policy and, in particular, the value of copyright.

My clients over the past decade include the Neighbouring Rights Collective of Canada (NRCC), the Canadian Private Copying Collective (CPCC), Access Copyright, the Canadian Musical Reproduction Rights Agency (CMRRA) and SODRAC (which is the French language equivalent), and also CSI, which is their combined collective. I do not think it will surprise anyone that I am not going to offer any comments on the econometric models dealt with by Professor Robert. However, I certainly share his view that creators should be able to get the benefits from their creative activity through exercising control of its exploitation, or, at the very least, receiving remuneration. It is not just desirable, but in fact, it is also socially, culturally, and economically both necessary and produc-

1 Adjunct Professor at the Schulich School of Business, York University and President of Paul Audley & Associates Ltd.

tive. I do not lose sleep over the fact that the price charged may be more than the marginal cost, and that the *Copyright Act*[2] permits that.

I want to say a couple of things about enforceability. Early in his paper, Professor Robert raises the issue of enforcement of copyright. This is obviously an increasingly crucial issue. More and more consumers not only can, but also do access protected works without permission and without payment. As a result, the ability to exclude has eroded, and with it the incentive to create is eroding.

If you want to take just one example in an area that I have been involved in, there were approximately one billion tracks of recorded music, the equivalent of about 70 million albums, copied for private use last year. Either that activity happens entirely without payment to songwriters, composers, music publishers, recording artists, and makers of sound recordings, or as at present, the *Copyright Act* permits such activity in certain cases, but subject to payment. There are advocates of what they like to call "fair use" who want the payments to stop, with all the copies to be made for nothing. Professor Robert does not agree and I do not agree. I also share Professor Robert's view that we are going to have to innovate in order to sustain, or perhaps more accurately, to revitalize the incentive to create.

Professor Robert correctly notes that a worst case situation would have creators limiting access to their work by imposing large access fees and complex clearance systems, while on the other hand the majority of consumers have access to the works illegally and pay nothing. This could be the future and it is obviously not just a potential threat. Certainly in the music industry, and increasingly in other industries as well, that is what is happening. Such a situation is probably impractical and, in the long term, unsustainable. If, in fact, protected copyright material is made available for free, it is very difficult to exact a payment. You get into the kind of situation we are in now with the pricing of digital downloads of recorded music, where authorized suppliers such as iTunes are competing with free goods. So this situation has a deleterious effect on the ability of any supplier to effectively impose a market price, or anything resembling the price required to sustain a diverse and substantial volume of creative production.

---

2 R.S.C. 1985, c. C-42.

Why do we need copyright collectives? Are there competitive alternatives? I looked at Professor Robert's description of studies that examine the possibility of using Digital Rights Management and micro transactions to get rid of the collectives and engage in work-by-work payment. I am going to come back to that. Professor Robert also looks at transactional efficiencies and the fact that such efficiencies provide a strong incentive for bundling copyrights through the mechanism of copyright collectives.

There is an interesting situation beginning to develop where we may, and are, in fact, beginning to see a small number of companies gaining control over a sufficient number of copyrights that they have the capacity, in some circumstances, to license those rights directly rather than using a collective society. They can then withdraw from the collective society, or perhaps just not assign their rights for that specific use to one, and they at least will be able to obtain a royalty payment. An interesting example in the US is the agreement between Universal Records and Microsoft under which Microsoft is paying Universal a royalty on the sale of each Zune, which is Microsoft's competitor to the iPod. While the Zune is not doing very well in the market, this negotiated royalty arrangement raises interesting questions. In effect, the payment being made looks like a private copying levy. The difference is that not everybody with a copyright interest in music recordings will receive royalty revenue. To what extent the record label will pass money onto the recording artist, I do not know. Whether independent record labels, or even the other major multinational companies, will have the leverage to exact that kind of payment, from Microsoft, or anybody else, is difficult to guess. Whether music publishers and songwriters have the ability to do that, who knows? At the same time, from the perspective of consumers, such an individual agreement is of little help in settling the issue of the legality of private copying in the US, even with respect to copying onto a Zune player.

I think that we are a lot better off in Canada with the private copying system that we have. The requirement that royalties be paid is not subject to the negotiating strength of an individual rights holder but applies equally to any medium that is subject to a levy. Further, there is a single point of payment for royalties, and all rights holders who qualify under the legislation receive payment based upon a rationally justified allocation of royalties among the different categories of rights holders. For the public, Canada's *Copyright Act* sets out the circumstances in which the making of private copies by individuals does not infringe copyright.

What are the protections against the collectives abusing their rights? First, within the context of Canada's copyright law, the concern about the potential abuse of rights is greatly exaggerated. In fact, to the extent that rights are exercised individually, rather than collectively, for creators this is a highly competitive activity. You cannot just attach any price you feel like to your product because there are other products.

More important for the present purpose, where the focus is on collective licensing under the *Copyright Act*, the role the Copyright Board plays is in fact to prevent the abuse of that power. Generally speaking, the collectives do not decide what they will collect. Either they negotiate a voluntary agreement with users, or the Board sets the rate, after reviewing evidence and argument from both the collectives and the users. Where attempts to negotiate an agreement are unsuccessful, users (or the collectives themselves) can go to the Board and seek arbitration. In such circumstances, the Board will also consider evidence and argument from both parties, before arriving at what it considers an equitable agreement.

What do copyright collectives get out of going to the Copyright Board and how does that relate to the issue of fairness? Going to the Board can address two important problems that copyright collectives typically face: (i) the asymmetry of negotiating power, and (ii) the asymmetry of information.

Let me provide an example of the former. In the recently completed Copyright Board hearing on online music, the parties included CMRRA/SODRAC Inc. (CSI), versus, at the beginning of the exercise, Bell Canada, the Canadian Association of Broadcasters (CAB), the Canadian Broadcasting Corporation (CBC), the Canadian Cable Telecommunications Association (CCTA), the Canadian Recording Industry Association (CRIA), CHUM Ltd., Archambault Group Inc. (Quebecor), Moontaxi Media Inc., MusicNet Inc., Apple Canada Inc., RealNetworks Inc., Yahoo! Canada, and TELUS.[3] While most parties directly affected by the proposed tariff participated fully in the pro-

3 For information concerning this hearing see *Statement of Royalties to Be Collected by CMRRA/SODRAC Inc. for the Reproduction of Musical Works, in*

ceeding, some of those who filed objections subsequently withdrew. The most important reasons for withdrawal can be readily explained.

Information is key to participants engaged in a negotiation. There is a fundamental asymmetry here as well. The users in a negotiation know best what they are able to pay and what the value of the rights is to them; the collectives do not. Before the Copyright Board, this asymmetry can be mitigated or it disappears.

In proceedings before the Copyright Board, information has to be exchanged between the parties. The result is a reasonably level playing field. The Copyright Board, the collective, and the users all have the same information. The resulting exchange of information is often essential to permitting the collective to present an informed case to the Copyright Board. Users also have a full opportunity to use their own information, and any information obtained from the collective, in presenting their case. Most important, the Copyright Board is able to arrive at an informed decision, having the benefit of relevant information, rather than being forced to simply arbitrate between and among competing opinions and arguments.

The result is a fairer conclusion and one that better reflects the actual value of the rights that are being delivered. That is certainly a benefit of the existing system, with its important reliance on collective licensing. I have often not liked the decisions that the Board comes to after looking at all of the evidence and the arguments, but I accept the fact that it is an enormously valuable process, one that deserves support because, on the whole, it functions well.

It is not surprising that some participants want to be able to take part in a board proceeding without having to provide important relevant information. In the Copyright Board proceeding, referred to above, concerning CSI's online music tariff, Archambault went to the Federal Court of Appeal because it did not like the fact that the collectives and the Board were going to obtain information about its business activities and its cost structure and so on. It made no difference to Archambault that other participants in this and in many earlier Copyright Board proceedings had agreed to provide comparable information, on the basis that it would be considered confidential, and

---

Canada, by Music Services in 2005, 2006 and 2007 (2007), 55 C.P.R. (4th) 89 (Copyright Bd.).

in certain circumstances would be considered sensitive confidential information to be shared only with external counsel and external experts in a proceeding.[4]

In his paper, Professor Robert expresses support for the proposal to expand the existing private copying regime to apply, for example, to MP3 players such as the iPod. Since I have done all of the previous valuation reports for the private copying collective in its various hearings, it will not be surprising that this is a position I support. There is also strong support for private copying in the music industry generally, albeit with some exceptions.

As you may be aware, and Professor Robert mentions it, there is a request from the CPCC to have a levy on iPods and other digital audio recorders. While I believe this is a very sound and important initiative, it may be equally interesting to ask what should be the limits of such collective licensing. How far is it reasonable to go in concluding that a specific activity does not infringe copyright but that, as in the case of private copying, there should instead be a right to remuneration, but no right to prevent the activity? What if the industry does not agree?

To take just one example, should the government unilaterally decide that it will proceed to make peer-to-peer file trading of music legal, defining the uploading and sharing of music files as an activity that no longer infringes copyright, subject to the imposition of a levy? In considering this question, one should keep in mind the fact that the existing private copying regime was established precisely because the rights holders in recorded music had no capacity to prevent private copying and no ability to obtain payment. While this is an interesting subject for discussion and debate, unlike the current state of opinion in the music industry with respect to the existing private copying regime, this is an idea that is not supported. In my view, given the strong opposition of the people who would be affected by that decision, as well as its doubtful consequences, it should not be implemented.

---

4 *Groupe Archambault v. CMRRA/SODRAC Inc.*, 2005 FCA 330.

Commentary: Is Collective Administration of Copyrights Justified by the Economic Literature?[1]

Ariel Katz[2]

A. INTRODUCTION

A good starting point for any reasoned policy-oriented discussion of the merits of collective administration of copyright are that the following premises, in a liberal market-based economy, market competition is the rule, and, as a corollary, monopoly is the exception. Prices and other terms of trade are best determined by market players, not by government agencies. While accepting such premises does not preclude the possibility that in some situations fully competitive conditions will not function as well as expected — and intellectual property rights, properly designed, are an example of a solution to such situations — these premises imply two questions that need to be answered: First, what justifies replacing a system of competition between copyright owners with

1 Professor Jacques Robert presented a paper in which he argued that the economic literature on bundling of information goods provides a novel justification for the collective administration of copyrights and made a few other recommendations relating to collective administration of copyright. This comment critically examines this bundling argument as well as the other recommendations.

2 Assistant Professor and Innovation Chair in Electronic Commerce, Faculty of Law, University of Toronto.

a system under which no such competition exists? Or in other words, what justifies augmenting the market power of copyright holders beyond the level conferred upon them in a competitive market by virtue of their exclusive rights? Second, do markets for copyrighted works actually fail such that society is better off by shifting from a paradigm of competition to a paradigm of regulated monopolies?

In recent work I have questioned the various justifications (most of which pertain to some form or another of transaction costs) for the paradigmatic form of collective copyright management: performing rights organizations (PROs). In one article, I argued that the case for PROs is not as straightforward as it is assumed to be. I showed that many of the underlying cost efficiencies that are attributed to PROs are usually simply assumed and, in many cases, could be equally achieved under less restrictive arrangements.[3] In a companion article, I studied the effect of new technologies on the case for collective administration and demonstrated how, by lowering many of the transaction costs that previously purported to justify the practice, new digital technologies further undermine the justification for collective administration.[4] In his current paper, Professor Robert, while not in total disagreement with my views, maintains nonetheless that the economics of bundling provide the requisite justification for the practice. He also doubt that technological advances would improve the competition landscape in this area and generally foresees a much greater role for collective administration. He comments on the optimal number of collectives and on their operational efficiency. My comment will focus primarily on Professor Robert's bundling justification, and to a lesser extent on the other points and recommendations that he makes. Structurally, I will follow Professor Robert's order of recommendations.

---

3 A. Katz, "The Potential Demise of Another Natural Monopoly: Rethinking the Collective Administration of Performing Rights" (2005) 1 Journal of Competition Law and Economics 541 ["The Potential Demise I"].

4 A. Katz, "The Potential Demise of another Natural Monopoly: New Technologies and the Administration of Performing Rights" (2006) 2 Journal of Competition Law and Economics 245 ["The Potential Demise II"].

B. COLLECTIVES AND BUNDLING

The essence of Professor Robert's argument is as follows. Notwithstanding other flaws that might be found in the transaction costs rationales for collective management and the even greater feasibility of individual licensing that new technologies allow, collective management remains an efficient mode to administer copyrights because what collectives do is bundle large repertoires of works under a single blanket licence. Such bundles are attractive, according to Robert, because they allow rights holders to extract revenues while limiting the deadweight losses otherwise associated with the pricing of copyrighted works on a per-work basis.[5] Essentially, bundling allows the seller to price discriminate without needing to know how different consumers value different works. Bundling achieves this result because, under the law of large numbers, consumers' willingness to pay for a bundle tends to average out. Therefore, bundling makes it easier for the seller to predict how consumers will valuate a collection of works, without needing to know how they value any individual work.[6]

I have no quarrel with the argument that bundling of information goods can be efficient (as can other forms of non-linear pricing). I doubt, however, that the economic literature on bundling of information goods can adequately explain, let alone justify, collective administration. While on its face attractive, closer examination reveals that the bundling argument shares the same flaws with many other efficiency-based justifications for collective administration. Like them, the bundling argument simultaneously proves too much and explains too little.

1) Proves Too Much

The bundling argument proves too much because it fails to notice a subtle, yet critical, distinction between acknowledging that bundling

---

5 It should be noted that although that is the common practice, collective administration does not necessarily imply blanket licensing of the collective's repertoire. There is nothing that prevents collectives from licensing on a per-unit basis, while setting the prices collectively. For convenience however I will proceed on the assumption that whenever a collective exists, a blanket licence covering the collective's entire repertoire will be offered.

6 J. Robert, "An Evaluation of Collective Copyright Management in Canada." See Chapter 5 of this book.

can be efficient and concluding that bundling everything is efficient. The bundling argument, as presented, is based on a false assumption that only two options are available: management by the individual authors on a per-work basis or management by a collective using a "mega-bundle" — a blanket licence covering all works. But accepting that management by individual authors on a per-work basis may be inefficient only implies that management will be done by different sorts of intermediaries and aggregators; it explains why we have different kinds of publishers, producers, and agents — it does not explain the need for a single managing entity.

In other words, noting that micro-management may be inefficient does not imply that economies of scale, scope, or aggregation[7] can only be achieved through mega-management by copyright collectives. It may prove the desirability of intermediaries. It may explain why those intermediaries may occasionally sell bundles. But the perceived inefficiency of management at the author/work level does not prove the desirability of a single, ultimate intermediary, offering a mega-bundle. As I have noted previously, the bundling argument fails to distinguish between a situation in which an *individual* copyright holder (or an *individual* intermediary) sells bundles on a blanket basis and a situation in which *all* copyright holders pool their rights and sell only a single bundle.[8] In the first case, bundles compete with each other, with the likely result of a greater quantity and variety of bundles, offered at different sizes and shapes and sold at lower prices, whereas in the second, only a mega-bundle is offered, presumably at a higher price and lower quantity (and by definition no variety).

The question is then why should we not assume that beyond some point, any bundle is subject to diminishing returns to size and scope, and that given the heterogeneity in consumers' preferences, these sizes and scopes vary substantially across different users of different works. We may also assume that competitive markets are quite capable of providing incentives for efficient bundle formation and pricing. The alleged superiority of the all-encompassing mega-bundle that faces no

---

7 The term "economies of aggregation" comes from Y. Bakos and E. Brynjolfsson, "Bundling and Competition on the Internet" (2000) 19 Marketing Science 63 ["Bundling and Competition on the Internet"].

8 "The Potential Demise I," above note 3 at 553–59.

competition must, on the other hand, assume that the marginal utility from adding an extra work to the bundle never diminishes and always outweighs the inefficiencies caused by lack of competition. It must also assume, under the prevailing regulated-monopoly paradigm, that the regulator — the Copyright Board — can successfully mimic the prices and terms under which competitive bundles would be licensed. Despite the best intentions of the Board, the parties that litigate before it, their lawyers, and their experts, I doubt that we can safely make such an assumption.

In fact, closer reading of the bundling literature reveals the shortcomings of applying it to justify collective administration. Professor Robert relies on Bakos and Brynjolfsson (BB) who demonstrated that the optimal pricing for information goods by a monopolist is a single, all-inclusive bundle.[9] However, the BB model relies on the following specific assumptions: first, that the marginal cost of adding works to the bundle is zero; second, that consumers' valuations of the works in the bundle are independent and identically distributed (i.i.d.); and third, that consumers do not have budget constraints. These assumptions might not be applicable to the current context, or at least suggest that the model applies less frequently than suggested by Robert.[10]

More importantly, the BB model *assumes* a monopolist who owns all content and only has to determine whether to sell this content as a bundle or on a per-work basis. The model shows that, when such a monopolist exists, bundling may increase profits while reducing deadweight loss through *de facto* price discrimination. But the model does not address the question of whether having such a monopoly is desirable in the first place, or whether it is possible and preferable to have several bundlers competing against each other. Nonetheless, in a subsequent paper the same authors analyze the consequence of moving from a marketplace with two rival bundlers, each offering its own large bundle, to a monopolist who offers a mega-bundle.[11] In that ex-

9 Y. Bakos & E. Brynjolfsson, "Bundling Information Goods: Pricing, Profits, and Efficiency" (1999) 45 Management Science 1613 ["Bundling Information Goods"].

10 See S. Viswanathan and G. Anandalingam, "Pricing Strategies for Information Goods" (2005) 30 Sadhana 257 (discussing some of the limitations of the BB model).

11 "Bundling and Competition on the Internet," above note 7 at 73–74.

tended model they show that since the bundles are not overlapping consumers purchase both of them (while they are not interested in all the works in both bundles, they are sufficiently interested in some of the works in each). In the two-bundler marketplace, the deadweight loss converges to zero, while consumers retain a third of the consumer surplus. However, a merger between the two bundlers allows the resulting monopolist to capture the entire consumer surplus and double its gross profits.[12] This is undeniably good for the bundlers but comes directly at the expense of consumers.

This situation is analogous to the question of copyright collectives. Consider the paradigmatic case of performing rights. Over 80 percent of all popular music is controlled by the four big multinational labels.[13] Each of them may offer its own large bundle in the form of a blanket licence. Thus, users who are interested in access to very large repertoires may purchase all such bundles. Deadweight loss may be minimized while consumers retain part of the consumer surplus. As the number of bundles increases, the value of any particular bundle decreases, which reduces each bundlers' market power and corresponding prices. If, however, there is only a single bundler (i.e., a copyright collective), this competition disappears and the collective can capture the entire consumer surplus at the expense of consumers, without any marked improvement in efficiency. In sum, instead of providing a novel efficiency-justification for collective administration, the bundling literature actually highlights another ground for objection.

Moreover, even if under some conditions the "economics of aggregation" may confer competitive advantage on one bundler who is then able to out-compete any other competitor (thus in essence creating a new type of natural monopoly),[14] there is a critical difference between such a situation and collective administration. While in both cases all works are ultimately provided as part of a single bundle, in the first case market competition determines the identity of the successful bundler, and the threat of being overtaken by another bundler through periodical competition-for-the-field disciplines its behaviour

12 *Ibid.*

13 See "The Potential Demise I," above note 3 at 575.

14 See "Bundling and Competition on the Internet," above note 7 at 68–70 (showing that when bundlers compete for content on exclusive basis, a larger bundler may out-compete smaller ones).

(at least as long as creators are free to license through other bundlers as well).[15] In the case of collective administration, however, at least in its current form in Canada, no such competitive discipline exists. This is because in some cases the collective model is dictated by the law, while in others the monopolistic position of the collective is cemented with exclusive relations between the collective and the copyright holders that it represents.[16]

Lastly, Robert's examples of bundles actually weaken the case for collective administration, instead of supporting it. Indeed, bundling information goods is ubiquitous, with various bundles often competing with each other. Newspapers are bundles because every issue contains various sections and articles and readers may have different valuations for different articles. But newspapers compete with each other (as well as with other products or services), and absent evidence to the contrary, we have no reason to believe that bundling them all together provides any social value. A more reasonable assumption would be that the benefits of competition among newspapers dwarfs any marginal value created by a super-newspaper. Even JSTOR, the electronic archive for scholarly journals mentioned as an example of a mega-bundle, is markedly distinct from the collective model. JSTOR is a non-profit organization, serving academic and other scholarly institutions. It could be seen, in the words of Bakos and Brynjolfsson as "a consortium or club of consumers [that] purchase access to a variety of information goods and make them available to all members for a fixed fee."[17] Although it is licensed by publishers, it is not owned or governed by them; nor is it run for their benefit.[18] JSTOR has a "dual mission to create and maintain a trusted archive of important scholarly journals,

---

15 If this requirement is met, the scenario described by Bakos and Brynjolfsson may not materialize.

16 See "The Potential Demise I," above note 3 at 578–82 (discussing the contestability of PROs), and "The Potential Demise II," above note 4 at 264–73 (discussing the Canadian model).

17 "Bundling Information Goods," above note 9 at 1625.

18 Under s. 2 of the *Copyright Act*, R.S.C. 1985, c. C-42, a "collective society" is defined as

> a society, association or corporation that carries on the business of collective administration of copyright or of the remuneration right conferred by section 19 or 81 for the benefit of those who, by assignment, grant of

and to provide access to these journals as widely as possible."[19] Its collection is no doubt impressive, but does not cover all scholarly journals. In particular, consistent with its archival mission, its "moving wall" policy excludes the more recent issues of participating journals. Thus cutting-edge scholarship (where competition between articles and journals is presumably fiercer) is licensed by publishers directly, or through other intermediaries. Moreover, as it is only a non-exclusive licensee, JSTOR is just one among many other gateways to the works available through its collection.

In sum, the economics of bundling sheds very faint positive light on the question of collective copyright management. The ability to bundle can explain the existence of publishers and other forms of market intermediaries, but the economics of bundling does not teach us that the most efficient bundle is the mega-bundle, offered by a copyright collective. What the economics of bundling can teach us when applied to copyright collectives is that once a model of collective management is chosen (for whatever reason) the fact that the collective issues a blanket licence is not in itself necessarily objectionable. But that is all. Beyond that, the bundling argument simply proves too much.

2) Explains Too Little

In addition to proving too much, the bundling argument, as presented, explains too little by failing to take into account how collective administration is actually practised in Canada (and elsewhere). A closer look reveals that the argument does not attempt to explain realities that are inconsistent with the argument but are nonetheless pervasive. I will

---

licence, appointment of it as their agent or otherwise, authorize it to act on their behalf in relation to that collective administration, and

(a) operates a licensing scheme, applicable in relation to a repertoire of works, performer's performances, sound recordings or communication signals of more than one author, performer, sound recording maker or broadcaster, pursuant to which the society, association or corporation sets out classes of uses that it agrees to authorize under this Act, and the royalties and terms and conditions on which it agrees to authorize those classes of uses, or

(b) carries on the business of collecting and distributing royalties or levies payable pursuant to this Act.

19 See online: www.jstor.org/about/desc.html.

demonstrate this point through the recent decision of the Copyright Board, approving the tariff proposed by CMRRA/SODRAC for online music services.[20]

Online music services, such as Apple's iTunes, allow their customers to purchase and download songs. These songs are reproductions of sound recordings as well as of the underlying musical and often literary works. When the record labels producing these songs sell them as CDs they have acquired from the copyright holders all the necessary rights to reproduce works and create the copies. But when the same songs are sold online as digital files, further reproduction of the works is done by the online sellers, who authorize their customers to download the files and often to make some copies thereof. Technically, these reproductions and authorizations require a licence as well. In the US, record labels generally secure all the necessary rights and provide them to online services for one fee.[21] In Canada, however, record labels can only grant online services the right to reproduce the sound recording, but the right to reproduce the musical work must be licensed separately and can be obtained from two copyright collectives, CMRRA and SODRAC through their jointly owned corporation CSI. But that is not enough, because the Copyright Board had previously held that the online distribution of the songs also constitutes "communication to the public by telecommunication," which is a separate right requiring a separate licence.[22] In Canada, such a licence can only be secured from a collective, yet a different collective: SOCAN.[23] But if

---

20 *Statement of Royalties to be Collected by CMRRA/SODRAC Inc. for the Reproduction of Musical Works, in Canada, by Music Services in 2005, 2006 and 2007* (2007), 55 C.P.R. (4th) 89 (Copyright Bd.).

21 *Ibid.* at para. 58 (testimony of Mr. Effy Cue, Vice-President of Apple's iTunes).

22 *Statement of Royalties to Be Collected by SOCAN for the Communication to the Public by Telecommunication, in Canada, of Musical or Dramatico-Musical Works* (2006), 52 C.P.R. (4th) 375 (Copyright Bd.), aff'd *Canadian Wireless Telecommunications Association v. Society of Composers, Authors and Music Publishers of Canada*, 2008 FCA 6.

23 A tariff covering these rights has been recently approved by the Copyright Board, see *Statement of Royalties to Be Collected by SOCAN for the Communication to the Public by Telecommunication, in Canada, of Musical or Dramatico-Musical Works*, [2007] C.B.D. No. 7 [Tariff No. 22.A (Internet — Online Music Services) 1996–2006], online: www.cb-cda.gc.ca/decisions/i16032007-b.pdf.

online distribution of songs is indeed "communication to the public by telecommunication," then under section 19 of the *Copyright Act* online sellers are liable to pay an additional fee, "equitable remuneration," to the NRCC,[24] another collective, which will divide such royalties between the performers of the recorded songs and the producers of the sound recordings — the same record labels with which the online sellers have already negotiated.[25]

The bundling argument may explain why record labels might find it beneficial to bundle works and offer their respective repertoires on a blanket basis, and it may also explain why online music services might want to offer bundles to their customers, but it contributes very little to our understanding of the structure of the online music market in Canada. First, the bundling argument does not explain why in the US all the rights that are necessary to run a business such as iTunes can be secured and provided by the producer — the record label — while in Canada some rights may be licensed by the label in a free-market environment whereas others can only be secured from two (or perhaps three) separate regulated collectives. Second, it does not explain why excluding certain rights from what seems like a functioning market is advantageous, not only from the collectives' (and perhaps their members') perspective but also from a general welfare point of view. Third, it raises the question why, despite the claimed efficiencies of the mega-bundle, at least in the case of music downloads and at least so far, the business model that seems to be more successful is iTunes' per-track model and not some of its competitors' one-fee-unlimited-access model.[26] In fact, a possible explanation is that whereas the bundling literature has focused on how bundling maximizes sellers' profits, competition between online music services forces them to design their services in a manner that maximizes consumers' welfare.

Lastly, according to Professor Robert one of the advantages of collective administration is that collectives allow access to every work in their repertoire, thus avoiding the deadweight loss caused when copyrighted works are sold separately. But the online music example reveals

---

24 The Neighbouring Rights Collective of Canada.

25 So far, no such tariff has been proposed to the Copyright Board.

26 See for example, Napster to Go, online: http://napster.ca/more_about_napster_ntg.html.

that this benefit of the mega-bundle must be exaggerated. While the blanket licence issued by a collective generally does cover all the work in the collective's repertoire, under current practices the distribution of copies is typically separate from the licensing of various uses authorized by collectives. Thus, whatever access benefits the mega-bundle confers upon the user are limited to the copies that she actually bought. The inevitable inefficiencies resulting from the grant of intellectual property rights are not fully solved by the bundles currently offered by copyright collectives. The library is bound to the collection of books that it bought; the discotheque to its collection of CDs. Even if they get a licence from Access Copyright or SOCAN, entitling them to photocopy every work or play every song, they can only photocopy or play works that they actually bought, separately. For these reasons, the bundling argument explains too little.

C. NOTE ON INCENTIVES

Professor Robert finds the collective model attractive because in his view it allows maximizing rewards to creators without impeding access. But as noted before, licensing under competitive conditions does not prevent the realization of whatever economies of scale, scope, or aggregation that might exist and therefore would be (at least) just as good. Nonetheless, one may argue (and I think Professor Robert implies this argument) that collective management is still superior because maximizing the reward to creators increases the incentives to create, thus furthering the aims of copyright law. My response is twofold. First, if accepted, such an argument will have much wider consequences because it does not stop at collective administration. Essentially it will permit any kind of collusion between IP owners because allowing IP holders to collude when they find it worthwhile necessarily increases their profit, thereby increasing the *ex ante* expected return on the investment and the incentive to invest. In the same vein, a right to collude may decrease the risk of competition from non-infringing works or technologies, which again may increase the expected return and incentive to invest. But this is definitely not the law. Collusion between IP holders is illegal and the competition laws do not make any dynamic efficiency defense of this kind available to IP holders — nor should they. Maximizing reward has never been the aim of intellectual property law, and overcompensating creators may itself be distortionary.[27] Second, even if increasing reward equals increasing the incentives to create, it does not necessarily mean that it increases the incentives to create socially valuable works. In fact, it may well create incentives to create more works, but mediocre ones.

While copyright law allows the copyright owner to exclude others, this right does not guarantee any reward. Reward in a market where works compete with each other will only be available if two conditions are met. First, the work must be valuable to users (otherwise they will not pay), and second, the work must offer something unique relative to other works that makes it preferable to those existing works. If the work is nothing but a mere or very close substitute to other works, competition between such works will drive their price towards marginal cost (i.e., towards zero). Moreover, the value derived from every work may be comprised of a generic value of playing *a* song, and the unique value of playing *the* song: the marginal value of the particular song. Under competition, an individual creator cannot capture the entire value of the work, only the marginal value of his work relative to other imperfectly fungible works. Assume there are three types of works: masterpieces, generic, and bad. Under competition the bad will not be rewarded (nobody buys them) and the generic will face fierce competition from other generic works providing the same value and therefore will get zero or very little at best. Only the masterpieces will be rewarded but will get only a reward reflecting their marginal value. This creates an incentive to create works of higher quality or variety because only those will be rewarded.

Under collective administration the incentives may be different. The collective's all-or-nothing policy allows it to capture the entire surplus from users — for example the value of all music, not only the sum of the marginal values of works in its repertoire. The pie available for distribution is larger than before. Now I assume that the collective distributes the monies collected according to the number of uses by users, not on a merit basis. I further assume that users such as radio stations require a variety of songs and therefore may be expected to play some generic songs, not only masterpieces. These two assump-

---

27 See for example, Mark A. Lemley, "Property, Intellectual Property, and Free Riding" (2005) 83 Tex. L. Rev. 1031 at 1058.

tions imply that even the randomly selected generic work will get a share of the monopolistic pie, which is bigger than zero. Therefore, from an *ex ante* perspective, while under competition, the expected return from creating a mediocre, generic work is zero, the expected return for the same work in a collective setting is greater than zero. Therefore, under collective administration, even works whose creation has added no social value get rewarded. This may entail a higher incentive to create, but higher incentive to create mediocre works.

This is of course not the only possible outcome. It is possible that the elimination of price competition among creators will lead them to compete on non-price dimensions. Such competition may be on quality (which may be a good thing, but not necessarily so, i.e., merely bells and whistles), but it may also encourage indirect price competition in the form of payola.[28] While anticipating the exact type of impact generated by the additional rents available through collective administration is beyond the scope of this comment, the general point is that we have no guarantee that the additional rents will necessarily create the desirable type of incentives.

D. THE NUMBER OF COLLECTIVES

To the questions of whether the number of collectives operating in Canada is too large, and whether there is a role for mandating the creation of a "super-collective," Professor Robert answers in the negative. He maintains that no apparent obstacles exist preventing the efficient amalgamation or disintegration of existing structures, should it become efficient to do so. I agree that the number of collectives does not necessarily imply any inefficiency and that creating a super-collective is not *a priori* beneficial, but I think that a more nuanced analysis is required here. Regardless of whether a collective model of rights management is desirable or not, once such a model exists the number of collectives that a user has to deal with can matter. Note that the question is not how many collectives exist generally, but how many collectives have to be dealt with to allow a single activity. When a single economic activity implicates more than one type of right and

28 See R.H. Coase, "Payola in Radio and Television Broadcasting" (1979) 22 J.L. & Econ. 269; "The Potential Demise I," above note 3 at 582–90.

each type is administered by a separate collective, the multiplicity of licences required can lead to inefficiency. This can happen, for example, in the case of broadcasts when, as the Copyright Board noted, "[a] sound recording cannot be communicated [to the public] without communicating the underlying work and performances at the same time."[29] This inefficiency stems from the problems of double marginalization, existing whenever complementary inputs are each sold by a separate monopolist. Each monopolist, attempting to increase its profit, sets a monopoly price while ignoring the fact that her higher price negatively affects the demand for the complementary good. The result is that the total price the user has to pay for all complements is too high, leading to underuse or, in the extreme case, to non-use of the resource. The phenomenon has been recently coined "the tragedy of the anticommons,"[30] or the problem of "fragmented management."[31]

Thus, the fact that users often have to deal with only a small number of monopolist-collectives with regard to the same use does not imply that the inefficiency described above does not exist or that it is insignificant. It may—and probably does—exist whenever overlapping licences must be secured from separate collectives. Arguably, the problem has been partially addressed by Parliament when it enacted section 19 of the *Copyright Act*, which provides that payments for public performance of sound recordings will be made in a single payment, later divided between the makers of the sound recording and the performing artists. The problem has been further addressed by the Copyright Board, which has adopted a policy of consolidating tariff hearings when these deal with overlapping rights.[32] It seems to me that

---

29 *Re NRCC Tariff 1.C (CBC-Radio), 1998 to 2002* (2000), 9 C.P.R. (4th) 504 (Copyright Bd.) [*Re NRCC Tariff 1.c*].

30 M.A. Heller, "The Tragedy of the Anticommons: Property in the Transition from Marx to Markets" (1998) 111 Harv. L. Rev. 621.

31 D.J. Gervais and A. Maurushat, "Fragmented Copyright, Fragmented Management: Proposals to Defrag Copyright Management" (2003) 2 C.J.L.T. 15.

32 See *Re NRCC Tariff 1.c*, above note 29; see also "Bill C-32—Ten Years Later," Speech given by the Honourable Justice William J. Vancise Chairman of the Copyright Board of Canada (Seminar jointly sponsored by the Intellectual Property Institute of Canada and McGill University, Toronto, 23 August 2006), online: www.webcitation.org/5OskIM9RR. According to Justice Vancise, though, the policy does not provide a perfect solution. It is not clear whether it can prevent all attempts of individual collectives to act strategically.

more thought should be given to whether a more systematic solution is required.

Given that the fragmentation of licences required for single activities among several monopolist-collectives generates inefficiencies, from which copyright owners as a whole also suffer, one may wonder what prevents the collectives themselves from integrating, either completely or only with regard to their licensing activities. While this is a question worth exploring, Professor Robert's discussion of the productive inefficiencies that characterize many Canadian collectives may suggest that collectives do not face the best set of incentives for improving their own efficiency, as discussed below.

E. COLLECTIVES' PRODUCTIVE INEFFICIENCIES

Professor Robert raises some concerns about Canadian collectives' productive inefficiencies. He notes that they are slow in adopting new technologies that could streamline their operations and probably distribute too little from what they collect.

I believe that these problems are more systemic and it is not simply a matter of time until productive efficiency will make inroads into Canadian collectives' operations. In fact, the inefficiencies that Professor Robert describes reflect an inherently poor governance structure. While he mentions that collectives rarely face competition and its attendant market discipline, Professor Robert believes that, as member-owned organizations, collectives do face incentives assuring their efficiency because the member-owners are those who benefit from greater efficiency and pay the price for its absence. I think that this belief is naïve. In fact, in many cases copyright collectives may demonstrate some of the worst forms of corporate governance. If copyright owners are indeed numerous and dispersed, then we may assume that Canadian collectives will exhibit the classic problems associated with the separation of ownership and control. Collective action problems would prevent the individual members from exercising their right of control to the benefit of insiders (either members with greater representation or influence or managers). While such problems associated with dispersed ownership are pervasive in the corporate world (and have generated a voluminous corporate governance literature), the Canadian collectives' situation is quite unique among Canadian corporations because not only do they not face market discipline, they also do not have to respond to other disciplinary threats: the threat of exit by their members, or the threat of takeover.

Under such conditions, productive inefficiency seems almost inevitable. Whether or not the government can or should do anything about it is another question, but at least this provides yet another reason to prefer a competitive structure when possible, or at least abolish restrictive membership terms (such as SOCAN's requirement that members fully assign their rights to the organization), which unnecessarily constrain the limited ability of members to exit.[33]

F. INFORMATION TECHNOLOGIES: CHALLENGES AND OPPORTUNITIES

Professor Robert raises several objections to my argument that advancements in information technology can render collective administration (even more) unnecessary. He maintains that the use of Digital Right Management (DRM) technologies is not desirable because: (i) it is costly and reduces consumers' welfare; (ii) it raises serious privacy issues; and (iii) it is inefficient because, as the bundling argument implies, per-work licensing is inefficient.

While I am far from being a proponent of DRM technologies and have no stake in their success, as far as I know the government has not seriously considered any proposal to outlaw them.[34] Therefore, I take it as a given that such technologies exist, that they will be further developed and occasionally implemented. And like any technology, it may be used for more or less beneficial purposes, and at times abused. My comment will proceed on these assumptions.

It seems to me that arguing that DRM technologies unambiguously reduce consumers' welfare is a problematic proposition. In theory, they may reduce some consumers' welfare (e.g., a person who buys a copy and wishes to make copies for his friends, or for backup purposes, or for copying extracts for a classroom presentation), but at the same

---

33 See "The Potential Demise I," above note 3 at 578–82 (discussing the limited contestability of performing-rights organizations).

34 This is of course an understatement. The only realistic policy discussions apply to the scope of legal protection that will be afforded to such technologies.

time increase other consumers' welfare (e.g., enable restricted access at lower prices for users who otherwise would not be willing to pay the price for a copy with broader privileges). In the absence of restraints on competition, I would think that the market could determine the menus of option available to consumers and price them accordingly, and that the law may occasionally have to intervene when this assumption turns out to be untrue.[35] The simple point is that we cannot make *a priori* general cost-benefit analyses of such technologies.

Privacy concerns are essentially a subset of the previous point. Consumers may vary in their price-adjusted preferences towards privacy and we can assume that the market can respond according to such preferences (while acknowledging that some market imperfections, such as information asymmetry, or perhaps behavioural biases, may justify occasional intervention). But more importantly, I am afraid that the privacy issue and the question "To what extent are we willing to allow corporations to monitor our private use of musical work(s)?"[36] are a red herring. For the most part, collectives administer rights that are relevant to commercial users, not to individuals.

Moreover, since DRM and other technologies may be highly relevant to the mandate of collectives (either because they may prevent non-licensed uses, facilitate more finely tuned pricing schemes, and improve monitoring to assist in the major challenge of fairly dividing the collected royalties), Robert's implied suggestion that extended collective management will spare us the ills of DRM is false. As I have previously noted, collectives, too, may implement these technologies, in a way that will only increase the concerns about DRM.[37]

---

35 France has recently established a Regulatory Authority for Technical Measures, whose mandate is to assure that DRM systems do not prevent interoperability and do not prevent users from benefiting from exceptions available to them under the copyright law; see N. Jondet, "DRM Watchdog Established in France," French-Law.net (11 April 2007), online: www.webcitation.org/5PAylQJkN.

36 Jacques Robert, "An Evaluation of Collective Copyright Management in Canada," chapter 5 of this book at 439.

37 "The Potential Demise II," above note 4 at 277–79. In fact, collectives may even have stronger motivation than individual rights holders to monitor use because collectives face the challenge of how to distribute the royalties they collect. An individual licensor can grant access to all the works in his repertoire on a blanket basis without worrying much about distribution.

Lastly, since I have already commented extensively on the bundling argument, I will only repeat the point that if it is efficient to bundle, we may expect that in competitive markets copyright owners, either alone or through intermediaries, will offer bundles of varying sizes and shapes. Nothing prevents them from doing so. In fact, casual observation of the online music markets reveals that two models are currently available: a per-song model *à la* iTunes, and a subscription-based unlimited-access model *à la* (the new) Napster. While industry experts and executives argue which model is preferable (currently the per-song model has the upper hand), Professor Robert seems to be so confident that an even more expansive bundling model is preferable that he would like to have it extended. I am less ambitious and make no predictions. If it were up to me I would only make sure that market conditions remain such that industry executives can experiment with different models and let us, consumers, choose at any time the option that suits us best.

G. EXTENDING THE USE OF PRIVATE COPYING LEVIES

Professor Robert lastly recommends extending the use of private copy levies to address the problems created by other advances in information technologies, such as peer-to-peer networks. He correctly maintains that new technologies enable new forms of copying and that outlawing such activities when enforcement is too costly (or intrusive, I would add) is not a good policy prescription. He therefore suggests that the law should clarify and exempt some types of copying, while imposing levies, administered by collectives, to compensate rights holders. While this is a topic that deserves its own symposium, I will only make two short comments.

I agree with Professor Robert that prohibition rules that cannot be enforced do not make good policy. But the alternative to prohibition is not necessarily taxation (which is what private copying levies essentially are). Exemption is also a solution. In fact, copyright's traditional response to prohibitively high costs of maintaining a system of exclusive rights has been exempting such uses.[38] While I would not

38 W.J. Gordon, "Fair-use as Market Failure — A Structural and Economic-analysis of the *Betamax* Case and Its Predecessors" (1982) 82 Colum. L. Rev. 1600.

rule out the possibility of using levies to address the problems arising out of peer-to-peer technologies and other forms of copying, a system of levies does not come without its own flaws, inefficiencies, and distortions. Therefore, before adopting and extending such solutions, I would first like to be convinced that these types of copying are indeed problematic, in the sense that they cause real harm translated into real diminishment of the incentives to create,[39] that levies can actually address this problem, and that the costs associated with such system are smaller than the benefits it creates. I doubt whether the current private copying regime passes this test and would like to know more before I would recommend extending it.

H. CONCLUSION

Professor Robert's main conclusion is that "a system of collective management is justified in order to market blanket licences for extended repertoires."[40] He so concludes on the basis of the perceived efficiencies of the mega-bundle, the blanket licence typically issued by copyright collectives. But the efficiencies of large scale bundling can only explain why micro-management by individual authors on a per-work basis may not always be efficient, and why intermediaries may create bundles. The theory falls short of explaining why the benefits of bundling necessarily imply the formation of the ultimate mega-bundle. Therefore, the bundling argument shares the same flaws of all other

39 The few empirical studies attempting to evaluate the impact of file sharing on sales of music have reached inconsistent conclusions. While S. Leibowitz, "File-sharing: Creative Destruction or Just Plain Destruction?" (2006) 49 J.L. & Econ. 1 at 24 finds a close link between changes in record sales and changes in file sharing, F. Oberholzer and K. Strumpf, "The Effect of File Sharing on Record Sales: An Empirical Analysis" (2007) 115 Journal of Political Economy 1 at 38–40 conclude that downloading has no significant impact on album sales. In the case of DVDs, M.D. Smith and R. Telang, "Piracy or Promotion? The Impact of Broadband Internet Penetration on DVD Sales" (June 2006), online: http://ssrn.com/abstract=918240, find that increased broadband Internet penetration leads to a significant increase in DVD sales. Even if file sharing has harmed the recording and film industries, the translation of such harms to reduced incentives to create is even less clear.

40 Jacques Robert, above note 36 at 441.

efficiency-based justifications for collective administration: they all explain the need of intermediaries, but not the need for a single one.

Canada's existing system of copyright collectives has grown out of legislative reforms based on the government's view that "[i]n many cases, it is impractical, if not impossible, for negotiations and transactions involving copyright to occur without the presence of an organized 'society' representing the interests of creators and copyright owners."[41] It was also believed that legislative reform was necessary because new collectives could not be formed because of concern with prosecution under Canada's competition laws.[42] This rationale for collective administration no longer holds. Therefore, to the extent that these reforms indeed made collective administration immune from Canada's competition laws, my only recommendation is to repeal this wholesale immunity. Collective administration of copyright should not be treated differently from any other horizontal arrangement between competitors. It should be allowed when its efficiencies outweigh its costs and outlawed when they do not. More often than not they do not.

41 J. Erola and F. Fox, *From Gutenberg to Telidon: A Guide to Canada's Copyright Revision Proposals* (Ottawa: Government of Canada, Consumer and Corporate Affairs Canada, 1984) at 6.

42 *Ibid.*

Contributors

Paul Audley is an adjunct professor at the Schulich School of Business, York University, Toronto, where he began teaching in 1983. Since 1977, he has also been president of Paul Audley & Associates Ltd., a company that specializes in providing research and policy analysis concerning the communications and cultural industries.

Marcel Boyer is Bell Canada Professor of Industrial Economics at the Université de Montréal and Vice-President and Chief Economist at the Montreal Economic Institute. He is presently fellow of the C.D. Howe Institute, CIRANO, CIREQ, and the World Academy of Productivity Science, Academic Affiliate of The Analysis Group, member of the executive board of the Canadian Law and Economics Association, member of the board of the Agency for Public-Private Partnerships of Québec, member of the Industry Canada advisory committee on business strategies and innovation, and member of the governance committee of the "Sustainable Development and Socially Responsible Investment Chair" (École polytechnique de Paris and Université de Toulouse). Professor Boyer currently conducts research in the areas of investment valuation (risk, flexibility, and real options); efficient organizations, innovation, and competition (competitive social democracy); incentives, incomplete information, and uncertainty; and law and economics (environmental issues, copyrights, IPR). Professor Boyer has acted as expert economist on behalf of several national and international corporations and government organizations.

Timothy Brennan is a professor of Public Policy and Economics at the University of Maryland Baltimore County (UMBC) and a senior fellow with Resources for the Future (RFF) in Washington, DC. From 1978–86, he was a staff economist with the Antitrust Division of the U.S. Department of Justice, with a continuing affiliation through 1998. During 1996–97, he was the senior economist for industrial organization and regulatory policy on the staff of the White House Council of Economic Advisers. From 2003–05, he served as a staff consultant to the Bureau of Economics of the US Federal Trade Commission, advising on the economics of monopolization law and vertical restraints. During 2006, he held the T. D. MacDonald Chair in Industrial Economics at the Canadian Competition Bureau. He has also worked with competition authorities in Mexico, New Zealand, Sweden, and Uzbekistan. Professor Brennan's research has covered topics in antitrust, regulatory economics, intellectual property, environmental economics, and the methodology and ethics of public policy. His recent antitrust work has focused on single-firm conduct, in particular characterizing exclusion as acquiring horizontal control over complement markets, with recent applications to bundled rebates and resale price maintenance. His work on intellectual property has examined conditions for "copyrightability," similarities and differences with tangible property, and implications of different policy goals for the design of fair use.

Richard Corley is co-head of Blakes national Information Technology Group. He has more than twenty-five years of experience working closely with technology companies in Canada. He has acted as lead counsel to major corporations in complex outsourcing transactions, joint ventures, technology acquisitions and licensing, technology-related competition law retainers, and in a variety of other commercial and corporate law matters. Richard was an instructor in the Osgoode Hall Law School intellectual property LL.M. program and was involved in the development of the Osgoode LL.M. program specializing in e-business law. He has also been actively involved in the development, by the federal Competition Bureau, of guidelines relating to the application of competition law to intellectual property and the Internet. In 1989, Richard graduated as the silver medallist from Osgoode Hall Law School. Upon graduation, he clerked for Chief Justice Beverley McLachlin at the Supreme Court of Canada and, after clerking, attended Yale Law School where he obtained his LL.M. Before attending law school, Richard studied mechanical engineering, mathematics, and computer science and worked for a number of years in the communications industry in computer graphics and the development of international television and multi-image standards.

Paul Grootendorst is Director of the Division of Clinical, Social, and Administrative Pharmacy in the Faculty of Pharmacy at the University of Toronto. He is associate professor in the Faculty of Pharmacy and the School of Public Policy and Governance at the University of Toronto, and is adjunct associate professor in the Department of Economics, McMaster University in Hamilton, Canada. Professor Grootendorst is a collaborator in the Research Program on the Social and Economic Dimensions of an Aging Population, which is a major collaborative research program funded by the Social Sciences and Humanities Research Council of Canada, and he is associate editor of Health Economics and serves on the editorial board of Canadian Public Policy.

Richard Gold is an associate professor and the founding director of the Centre for Intellectual Property Policy. He teaches in the area of intellectual property and common law property at McGill University's Faculty of Law. His research centres on understanding the links between innovation, intellectual property, and development. He led the International Expert Group on Biotechnology, Innovation and Intellectual Property, a transdisciplinary research team that issued a ground-breaking report on the policies and law of innovation and intellectual property. He has published widely in legal and scientific journals on this topic. Professor Gold has been a senior advisor on intellectual property to the Canadian Biotechnology Advisory Committee; legal policy consultant to the Ontario Ministry of Health and Long-Term Care; and a consultant to the Organisation for Economic Cooperation and Development on biotechnology intellectual property issues. He has prepared studies for the World Health Organization and the World Intellectual Property Organization. A former law clerk to Mr. Justice Peter Cory of the Supreme Court of Canada, Professor

Gold is a research associate at the Health Law Institute at the University of Alberta. He received his LL.B. from the University of Toronto and his LL.M. and S.J.D. from the University of Michigan.

Abraham Hollander is a professor of Economics at the Université de Montréal. His areas of specialization are competition policy, trade policy, and intellectual property, mainly copyright. He has published scientific papers in these areas and is the co-author of a graduate textbook in international trade. He has held a position with the World Bank and was T.D. MacDonald Chair at the Competition Bureau in 1994–95. He consults regularly for governments and the private sector in Canada and abroad.

Aidan Hollis is a professor of Economics at the University of Calgary, where he has held an appointment since 1996. He has degrees from Cambridge University and the University of Toronto and has worked in international banking in London and Seoul. He was appointed T.D. MacDonald Chair in Industrial Economics at the Competition Bureau in 2003–04. His research focuses principally on competition and innovation in pharmaceutical markets, though he has also published in other areas of economics. He is a Director of Incentives for Global Health, a non-profit formed to advance the Health Impact Fund proposal. Dr. Hollis has consulted widely on pharmaceutical issues, including for generic companies and industry associations, governments, and consumer groups.

Edward Iacobucci received his B.A. from Queen's University in 1991, his M.Phil. from Oxford University in 1993; and his LL.B. from the University of Toronto in 1996. He joined the Faculty of Law as an assistant professor in 1998, and is now a professor of law. He was a John M. Olin Visiting Fellow at Columbia University Law School in 2002. Prior to joining the Faculty of Law, he was the John M. Olin Visiting Lecturer at the University of Virginia in 1997–98 and served as Law Clerk at the Supreme Court of Canada for Mr. Justice John Sopinka in 1996–97. Professor Iacobucci is co-director of the Law and Economics program and the Osler Chair of Business Law at the University of Toronto. His areas of interest include corporate law, competition law, and law and economics more generally.

Navin Joneja is a partner in the Competition, Antitrust & Foreign Investment Group at Blakes where his practice encompasses a wide range of competition issues. He regularly advises clients engaged in mergers, joint ventures, and other types of strategic alliances concerning the notification and clearance provisions of the *Competition Act* and the *Investment Canada Act*. Mr. Joneja also counsels clients concerning potentially anticompetitive business practices, such as an abuse of dominant position, refusal to deal or exclusive dealing, as well as the conspiracy and related provisions of the *Competition Act*. In addition, his practice entails the provision of advice concerning corporate competition law compliance programs and developments in international antitrust/competition law matters. He has also advised a wide range of businesses and government and non-government agencies on international trade and business regulation issues. Mr. Joneja received his LL.B. from the University of Toronto in 1996 and his LL.M. from New York University Law School in 1999. He is a member of the bars of Ontario and New York.

Ariel Katz is an assistant professor at the Faculty of Law, University of Toronto, and holds the Innovation Chair in Electronic Commerce. Professor Katz received his LL.B. and LL.M from the Hebrew University of Jerusalem and his S.J.D. from the University of Toronto. His general area of research involves economic analysis of competition law and intellectual property law, with allied interests in electronic commerce, pharmaceutical regulation, the regulation of international trade, and particularly the intersection of these fields. Prior to joining the University of Toronto Professor Katz was a staff attorney at the Israeli Antitrust Authority. While there, he litigated several merger appeals and restrictive arrangements cases before the Antitrust Tribunal and negotiated regulatory settlements. Professor Katz currently teaches courses on intellectual property, cyberlaw, and the intersection of competition law and intellectual property.

Ejan Mackaay was a professor of Law at the Université de Montréal from 1972 until his retirement at the end of 2008, and has been an associate professor since then. From 1999 until 2003 he was the Director of the Public Law Research Centre, the largest legal research institution in Canada, and from 2005 until 2008, he was Director of the Centre for the Law of Business and International Trade, both at the Université de Montréal. From 1 January 2001 until 30 September 2001, he was the interim holder of the Jean Monnet Chair in European Integration. Since 1986 he has been the correspondent of the Royal Netherlands Academy of Sciences. He has taught special contracts, intellectual property law, the law of new technologies, patent and trade-marks, and law and economics at the undergraduate as well as graduate level. Since 2000 he has been invited to lecture every year at the Comparative Law Institute of the University of Paris 1 and at the yearly International and Comparative Intellectual Property Law Programme in Oxford and Victoria, BC.

Donald McFetridge is a professor in the Department of Economics at Carleton University in Ottawa, Canada. Professor McFetridge has been teaching and writing in the fields of industrial economics, regulatory economics, and competition policy for thirty-five years. He has advised the Competition Bureau, the Competition Tribunal, and various federal and provincial regulatory agencies, as well as numerous Canadian and international companies, on a variety of competition matters including horizontal restraints, predatory pricing, abuse of dominance, refusals to deal, and mergers.

Michael Meurer is the Michaels Faculty Scholar and a professor of Law at Boston University. His research and teaching concerns patent law, law and economics, antitrust law, copyright law, contract law, and regulation. Before joining Boston University Law he was an economics professor at Duke University and later a law professor at the University at Buffalo. He also taught short courses in American Intellectual Property Law at the law faculties of the University of Victoria and the National University of Singapore. He has a Ph.D. in economics and a J.D. from the University of Minnesota. Professor Meurer has received numerous grants and fellowships, including, the David Saul Smith Award from Boston University Law, a grant from the Kauffman Foundation, two grants from the Pew Charitable Trust, a Ford Foundation grant, an Olin Faculty Fellowship at Yale Law School, and a postdoctoral fellowship at AT&T Bell Labs.

Jacques Robert is an associate professor in the Department of Information Technologies at HEC Montreal and fellow at CIRANO. Professor Robert has a Ph.D. in economics from the University of Western

Ontario. His research interests are applied game theory, mechanism design, and experimental economics. He has published in economics, operational research, and neural computing.

Teresa Scassa holds undergraduate law degrees in civil and common law from McGill University, as well as an LL.M. and an S.J.D. from the University of Michigan. She taught at Dalhousie Law School for fifteen years before joining the faculty of law at the University of Ottawa as a full professor in July 2007. She currently holds a Canada Research Chair in Information Law at the University of Ottawa. She has taught a range of subjects including Intellectual Property, Law and Technology, Public Law, Administrative Law, and Professional Responsibility. She is a member of the Nova Scotia Barristers' Society. She is a former editor of the *Canadian Journal of Law and Technology*, and co-author of the book *Electronic Commerce and Internet Law in Canada* (CCH Canadian Ltd.). Her research and scholarship is primarily in the areas of intellectual property law, law and technology, and privacy. She has written articles on a range of topics in theses areas.

Michael Trebilcock is University Professor and Professor of Law and Economics at the University of Toronto. In 1999, Professor Trebilcock received an Honorary Doctorate in Laws from McGill University and was awarded the Canada Council Molson Prize in the Humanities and Social Sciences. In the same year he was elected an Honorary Foreign Fellow of the American Academy of Arts and Sciences. In 2003, he received an Honorary Doctorate in Law from the Law Society of Upper Canada and in 2007 he was the recipient of the Ontario Attorney General's Mundell Medal for contributions to Law and Letters.

David Vaver obtained his B.A. and LL.B. from the University of Auckland, his M.A. from the University of Oxford, and his J.D. from the University of Chicago. He is the Emeritus Reuters Professor of Intellectual Property and Information Technology Law at the University of Oxford, an Emeritus Fellow of St. Peter's College, Oxford, and former Director of the Oxford Intellectual Property Research Centre, having retired in 2007. He has published and spoken extensively on domestic and international intellectual property law reform and policy. Before going to Oxford in 1998, Professor Vaver taught in New Zealand (University of Auckland, 1972–78), in Canada (University of British Columbia, 1971–72, 1978–85, Osgoode Hall Law School, Toronto, 1985–98), and elsewhere as a visiting professor. He has been a consultant to the Canadian government on intellectual property reform (1989–98), served the UK government's IP Advisory Committee, (2001–05) and participated in the Royal Society working group that produced the report *Keeping Science Open: The Effects of Intellectual Property Policy on the Conduct of Science* (April 2003). As of July 2009, Professor Vaver is Professor of Intellectual Property Law at Osgoode Hall Law School of York University, Toronto.

Ralph Winter is a professor in the Strategy and Business Economics Division at the Sauder School of Business, University of British Columbia and is a Canada Research Chair in Business Economics and Public Policy. His research interests include competition policy related to mergers and business practices, insurance markets, and corporate finance. He received his B.Sc. from the University of British Columbia, and his M.A. and Ph.D. from the University of California, Berkeley.

Kolibri 360 GmbH
Ferdinand-Jühlke-Straße 7
99095 Erfurt, Deutschland
produktsicherheit@kolibri360.de